Hindi

INDIA

Cadogan Books plc
London House, Parkgate Road,
London SW11 4NQ, UK

Distributed in North America by
The Globe Pequot Press
6 Business Park Road, PO Box 833,
Old Saybrook, Connecticut 06475–0833

Copyright © Frank Kusy 1996
Illustrations © Polly Loxton 1996

Book and cover design by Animage
Maps © Cadogan Guides, drawn by Map Creation Ltd

Series Editors: Rachel Fielding and Vicki Ingle

Editors: Vicki Ingle and Dominique Shead
Copy-editing: Dominique Shead and Fiona Clarkson Webb
Proof-reading and glossary: Philip Ward
Indexing: Valerie Elliston
Production: Book Production Services

**A catalogue record for this book is available from the
British Library**

ISBN 1–86011–022–3

Printed and bound in the UK by Redwood Books Ltd.

*The author and publishers have made every effort to ensure
the accuracy of the information in the book at the time of
going to press. However, they cannot accept any
responsibility for any loss, injury or inconvenience resulting
from the use of information contained in this guide.*

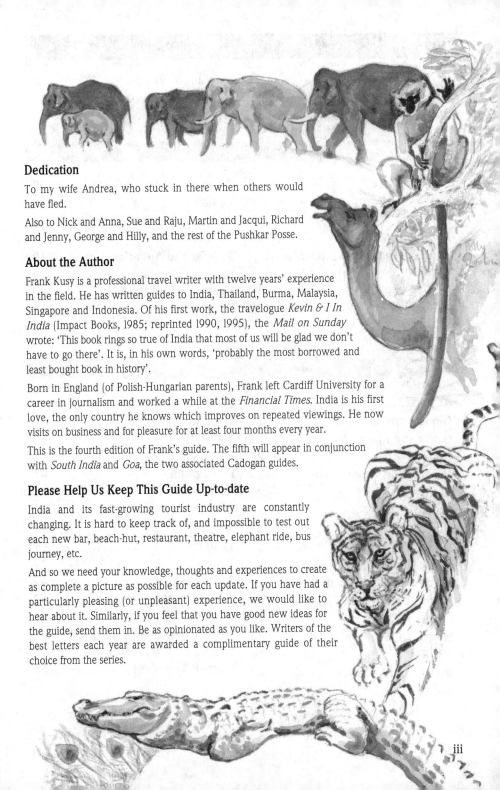

Dedication

To my wife Andrea, who stuck in there when others would
have fled.

Also to Nick and Anna, Sue and Raju, Martin and Jacqui, Richard
and Jenny, George and Hilly, and the rest of the Pushkar Posse.

About the Author

Frank Kusy is a professional travel writer with twelve years' experience
in the field. He has written guides to India, Thailand, Burma, Malaysia,
Singapore and Indonesia. Of his first work, the travelogue *Kevin & I In
India* (Impact Books, 1985; reprinted 1990, 1995), the *Mail on Sunday*
wrote: 'This book rings so true of India that most of us will be glad we don't
have to go there'. It is, in his own words, 'probably the most borrowed and
least bought book in history'.

Born in England (of Polish-Hungarian parents), Frank left Cardiff University for a
career in journalism and worked a while at the *Financial Times*. India is his first
love, the only country he knows which improves on repeated viewings. He now
visits on business and for pleasure for at least four months every year.

This is the fourth edition of Frank's guide. The fifth will appear in conjunction
with *South India* and *Goa*, the two associated Cadogan guides.

Please Help Us Keep This Guide Up-to-date

India and its fast-growing tourist industry are constantly
changing. It is hard to keep track of, and impossible to test out
each new bar, beach-hut, restaurant, theatre, elephant ride, bus
journey, etc.

And so we need your knowledge, thoughts and experiences to create
as complete a picture as possible for each update. If you have had a
particularly pleasing (or unpleasant) experience, we would like to
hear about it. Similarly, if you feel that you have good new ideas for
the guide, send them in. Be as opinionated as you like. Writers of the
best letters each year are awarded a complimentary guide of their
choice from the series.

Contents

Culture

North India

West India

Maps

Acknkowledgements

The list is endless, but special thanks go to Vicki Ingle at Cadogan (truly one of life's great saints), and to Fiona, Dominique and Simon for all the slog behind the scenes that so often goes unappreciated.

We must have been doing something right with this edition, because lots of things went wrong—including a lost disc with all the names of travellers who wrote in letters. To these, I can only say a big thanks for all your helpful suggestions and an even bigger 'sorry' for not mentioning you by name. Your true reward will be the silent appreciation of those travellers who come after you.

There are many without whom this guide would not have been possible (or as much fun to research), including the following long-time friends: Steve Pettitt and Nigel Berry (Pettitt's India), Maggi Nixon (Oberoi Hotels), Matthew d'Costa (Taj Group of Hotels), Martin Palmer and Jo Harris (Portsmouth), Richard O'Toole and Jenny Dodd (London), Col Fateh and Indu Singh (Hotel Megh Niwas, Jaipur), Mr Ajit Bansal (Hotel Bissau Palace, Jaipur), Mr Bhati (Hotel Jagat Niwas, Udaipur), and Mr Singh at the Pushkar Palace Hotel. Not forgetting the staff at the Oberoi Maidens Hotel in Delhi—Mr Bhatia, Anil Kumar, Alam, Ved, Sanjesh, and Kuldeep Singh. Whenever I arrive, guys, you always make me feel at home.

India is a big, big country for a solo writer to take on. Some places you come into, you think 'God, I've only got 6 hours—where do I start?' Then, as if by some divine chance, someone turns up to show you the way. As Goethe once wrote: 'The moment one definitely commits oneself, a whole stream of events issues from the decision, raising in one's favour all manner of unforeseen meetings and material assistance which no man could have dreamed would come his way.' The result, in my case, were guardian angels like the following: Cyberjack and Sweetie (alias Jack Bzoza and Susan Warsh, Canada), Rajat and Halla Chhabra (Bhubaneshwar), Mrs Ameeta Munshi (Bombay), Ms Roma Nath (Bangalore), Mr Strikwerda (Madras), Mr Tondare (Delhi), Mr Upendra Gupta (Varanasi), Mr Nagendra Singh Hada (Sasan Gir), and Mrs Jayanti Doshi in Calcutta. To all of the above, I can only say 'If you're ever in town....'

This edition's award for the best tourist officer in India goes to Mr Udaipal Singh at the Jaipur railway information counter. I asked him 57 questions, got 57 clear answers, and was in and out of his office in 20 minutes flat. This man should be on Mastermind.

Three other information centres deserve a special mention: the Government of India tourist offices in Bombay and Calcutta, and the TTDC office in Madras. If all other branches in India were as good, you wouldn't need this book.

The publishers would like to thank Philip Ward for proof-reading and compiling the glossary, Valerie Elliston for the index, Map Creation for the maps, and Animage for the design.

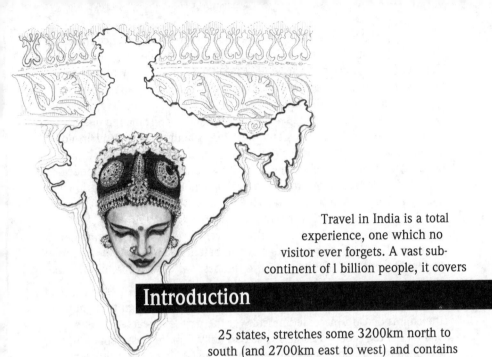

Travel in India is a total experience, one which no visitor ever forgets. A vast sub-continent of 1 billion people, it covers

Introduction

25 states, stretches some 3200km north to south (and 2700km east to west) and contains more different languages, religions, races and cultures than any other country in the world. It is also one of the oldest civilizations known, dating back about 5000 years, and was in its heyday one of the richest, known as the Golden Bird of the East.

Whatever you want from a holiday, it's here in India—royal palaces, desert fortresses, beach resorts, hill stations, temples, mountains, lakes, and lots more besides. Outside of the expensive capitals, you can still live like a maharajah for as little as US$60 a day, and there's all sorts of tempting shopping bargains to be had—silks and brocades, paintings and furnishings, carvings and carpets, gems and jewellery. If your taste runs to sports and recreation, many cities have facilities for swimming and golf, tennis and squash, fishing and horse-riding, while in outlying areas you can explore wildlife parks on elephant-back or cross the desert on camel safari. Finally, don't forget India's rich cultural heritage. Here you can enjoy some of the best music, dance and theatre in Asia.

But this is only one side of India. It has great natural beauty and enchantment, yes, but is also a place of unbelievable noise, squalor and destitution—a large country with large problems. Everything here is on a grand scale, both good and bad. The powerful contrasts this produces—a constant alternation between luxury and poverty, beauty and ugliness, efficiency and chaos—is the key to understanding India and the main reason why so many travellers develop a love-hate relationship with it.

In India, you don't have to find the experience. The experience finds you. You just stand there in the street and things happen all around you. Somebody shoves something in your face, and you decide whether to look at it or not look at it. A cow nudges you into traffic, and you miss death-by-rickshaw by the thickness of a Rizla paper. Mixed fragrances of jasmine, urine and temple incense drift by, and then someone offers you a lift on an elephant. If you stand there long enough, a whole swarm of beggars, pedlars and drug dealers descend upon you at once—and that's when you break and run. India, it must be stated, is not for the indecisive. Before long, you've stopped dawdling and have begun walking with purpose. You go deaf when anybody tries to sell you something, you smirk cynically at taxi drivers who say their meters are 'broken', and your vocabulary shrinks to stern perogatives like yes, no, how much, and go away. Then, just as you've decided to hate the country, everything suddenly turns around and you have the best day of your life. India is like that—one extreme to the other and all of the time.

Despite figures released by the Indian tourist board, foreign tourism to the country hasn't increased much over the past few years—and when you take into account various crises like Rajiv Gandhi's assassination, the Ayodhya temple riots and (most recently) the Gujarat plague problem, this is hardly surprising. Less than 60 people died as a result of the 1994 'plague', but the Indian media made such a meal of it that tourists stayed away in droves. They also put the boycott on Kashmir, in the wake of recent terrorist activity.

Only in the business sector has travel to India increased dramatically—and this has created its own problems. With India fast becoming the convention centre of Asia, planeloads of corporate staff are coming in from Japan, Hong Kong, Thailand and Singapore—filling up every decent hotel in Delhi and Bombay, and forcing up tariffs to London or Frankfurt levels. The implications for the leisure traveller are obvious—in high season, all the best hotels are booked up and even if you're lucky enough to get a room, you can often only hold it for a night or two. The business boom can't last forever—in fact, it has probably already peaked—but for the time being at least I would recommend anyone landing in Bombay, Delhi or Calcutta, and wanting a comfortable stay there, to book their accommodation as far ahead as possible.

A lot of travellers will tell you how much better India was ten years ago. This is not true. Yes, it may have been cheaper and less crowded, but the infrastructure wasn't there and you had to queue up for hours for a train ticket. At street level, India will *never* really change (it's too big and too set in its ways for that) and any time you go will be the right time for you. A long time ago, I met a freak on the beach in Goa. He was standing on his head, in some strange yogic posture, and when I asked him what he thought of the sunset, he said. 'It's all right man, but you should have seen it *ten years* ago!' These people are very boring.

Planning your Trip

This is not a guide to the whole of India—if it were, it would be twice as long and half as comprehensive. What you have here is a route-planner to 60 or so of the country's main highlights, along with a number of off-the-beaten-track excursions for the adventurous traveller. And in a country this big (nearly the size of Europe) that's more than enough to be going along with.

For practical reasons, the book is divided into 13 recommended routes. Each route is self-contained, has a separate travel itinerary, and can take anything between 1 and 3 weeks to cover at leisure. For travellers with more time to spare, there are additional options suggested on each itinerary, connecting each route with its neighbours. Every route starts from one of the four capital cities—Delhi, Bombay, Calcutta and Madras—and includes a number of half or full-day sightseeing tours (at least one for each place mentioned), enabling you to cover all the main points of interest in the minimum amount of time.

Route-planning is a serious business. I once met four young hikers who wanted to go to Goa, Calcutta, Manali and Kathmandu in six weeks—they never made it. Just as pie-in-the-sky was the lady who came to India to see the Taj Mahal and who (because she got on the wrong bus) ended up seeing everything else *but* the Taj Mahal. There are two lessons here: first, if you're on a short break as opposed to an extended stay, select a small area of India and see it properly; second, once you've decided on a route, *stick* to it.

Nothing of course is certain. Planes get cancelled, taxis get lost, and whole towns close down for unannounced festivals. If you do miss something along the way, don't panic—just put it down to experience and push on to the next place. At other times, unexpected good things happen—a colourful street party or an invitation to an Indian wedding perhaps—and you'll be glad you didn't lose your cool. Experienced travellers are right about one thing—you can only 'plan' India up to a point. Past that, you just have to go with the flow.

To select your route, just decide what your priority is—deserts, beaches, hill-stations etc—and then see the 'Itinerary' at the start of each chapter to receive directions. Currently, the bulk of tourist traffic is headed for Goa, Kerala, Varanasi, and (of course) the Golden Triangle of Delhi, Jaipur and Agra. But you don't have to follow the crowd. Less-visited areas like Gujarat, Tamil Nadu or the Eastern Triangle of Bhubaneshwar, Puri and Konark are just as interesting—and a lot less hassle too.

How long you go for is up to you, but you'll need at least three weeks. Anything less, and you'll only just have begun to enjoy yourself when you have to go home again. The first week, you'll be busy getting used to the climate and to the intensity of the place; the second, learning to let go and have fun with the people; the third, feeling like you never want to leave. The ideal introduction to India is, however, two to three months—this gives you time to really get to grips with the country. Anything more than three months is not recommended—sensory overload is a common problem, and people start feeling jaded.

Distance Chart (km)

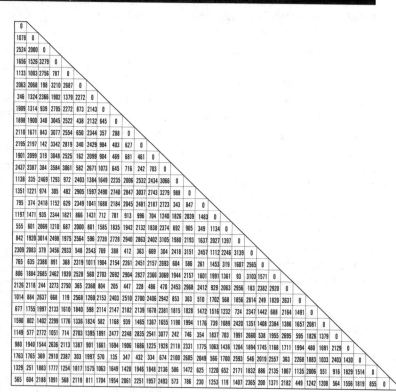

	Varanasi	Udaipur	Trivandrum	Srinagar	Shimla	Pondicherry	Patna	Panjim	Mysore	Mangalore	Madurai	Madras	Kanyakumari	Jodhpur	Jammu	Jaipur	Hyderabad	Gwalior	Gangtok	Cochin	Delhi	Darjeeling	Coimbatore	Chandigarh	Calcutta	Bombay	Bikaner	Bhubaneshwar	Bangalore	Ahmedabad	Agra
Varanasi	0
Udaipur	1078	0
Trivandrum	2524	2000	0
Srinagar	1656	1526	3279	0
Shimla	1133	1003	2756	787	0
Pondicherry	2063	2068	198	3210	2687	0
Patna	246	1324	2366	1902	1379	2272	0
Panjim	1909	1314	939	2795	2272	873	2143	0
Mysore	1898	1900	340	3045	2522	438	2132	645	0
Mangalore	2110	1671	843	3077	2554	650	2344	357	288	0
Madurai	2195	2197	142	3342	2819	340	2429	984	403	627	0
Madras	1901	2099	319	3048	2525	162	2099	904	469	681	461	0
Kanyakumari	2437	2387	384	3584	3061	582	2671	1073	645	716	242	703	0
Jodhpur	1138	335	2469	1293	972	2403	1384	1649	2235	2006	2532	2434	3066	0
Jammu	1351	1221	974	305	482	2905	1597	2490	2740	2847	3037	2743	3279	988	0
Jaipur	795	374	2418	1152	629	2349	1041	1688	2045	2481	2187		2723	343	847	0
Hyderabad	1197	1471	935	2344	1821	866	1431	712	701	913	996	704	1240	1826	2039	1483	0
Gwalior	555	601	2069	1210	687	2000	801	1585	1835	1942	2132	1838	2374	692	905	349	1134	0
Gangtok	842	1920	3014	2498	1975	2564	596	2739	2728	2940	2863	2402	3105	1980	2193	1637	2027	1397	0
Cochin	2309	2083	379	3456	2933	548	2543	769	388	412	363	669	304	2418	3151	2457	1112	2246	3139	0
Delhi	765	635	2388	891	368	2319	1011	1904	2154	2261	2451	2157	2693	604	586	261	1453	319	1607	2565	0
Darjeeling	806	1884	2685	2462	1939	2528	560	2703	2692	2904	2827	2366	3069	1944	2157	1601	1991	1361	93	3103	1571	0
Coimbatore	2126	2118	244	3273	2750	365	2360	804	205	447	228	486	470	2453	2968	2412	929	2063	2956	183	2382	2920	0
Chandigarh	1014	884	2637	668	119	2568	1260	2153	2403	2510	2700	2406	2942	853	363	510	1702	568	1856	2814	249	1820	2631	0
Calcutta	677	1755	1997	2133	1610	1840	598	2114	2147	2182	2139	1678	2381	1815	1828	1472	1516	1232	724	2347	1442	688	2164	1491	0
Bombay	1590	802	1402	2299	1776	1336	1824	582	1168	939	1465	1367	1655	1190	1994	1176	739	1089	2420	1351	1408	2384	1386	1657	2081	0
Bikaner	1149	577	2772	1051	714	2703	1395	1891	2477	2248	2835	2541	3077	242	746	354	1837	703	1991	2660	538	1955	2695	595	1826	1379	0
Bhubaneshwar	980	1940	1544	2636	2113	1387	901	1661	1694	1906	1686	1225	1928	2118	2331	1775	1063	1436	1204	1894	1745	1168	1711	1994	480	1691	2129	0
Bangalore	1763	1765	369	2910	2387	303	1997	570	135	347	432	334	674	2100	2605	2049	566	1700	2593	546	2019	2557	363	2268	1883	1033	2403	1430	0
Ahmedabad	1329	251	1883	1777	1254	1817	1575	1063	1649	1420	1946	1848	2136	586	1472	625	1220	652	2171	1832	886	2135	1867	1135	2006	551	916	1829	1514	0
Agra	565	604	2188	1091	568	2119	811	1704	1954	2061	2251	1957	2493	573	786	230	1253	119	1407	2365	200	1371	2182	449	1242	1208	564	1556	1819	855	0

Travel

Getting There

By Air

Try to book your flight to India three months or so before departure, so that you can take advantage of any cheap flights and get a firm reservation with the airline of your choice.

The price of air tickets to India varies according to three major factors: whether you pay a full fare or a discount fare, when you go, and how long you're planning to stay. If you contact an airline direct they will usually give you *full* fare prices, which tend to be much the same no matter what the airline. Standard fares are cheapest when you book an *excursion fare*, which requires that you to stay in India for a minimum of 2 weeks and no more than 3–4 months.

Ticket prices for excursion fares vary according to season. For Air India, the low season is from 16 February–31 May and 1 September–31 October; the shoulder season from 1–15 February, 1–30 June and 1–31 August; and the high season from 1–31 July and 1 December–31 January. Other airlines' seasonal dates may vary (*see* below). If you want to stay in India for longer than a few months, you can get what is known as a **one-year open-ended return**, which allows you to stay in India up to one year and to be flexible about what date you want to return (fares usually do not vary according to season). These tickets can be surprisingly cheap if you ring around the 'bucket shops' or discount airline specialists.

Discounted fares of up to 50% are often available from bucket shops. Major airlines sell these travel agencies a certain number of tickets at greatly reduced rates, so it is always worthwhile taking the time to find the best deal (*see* below). Discounted fares often have restrictions on cancelling or changing your ticket, so make sure you know all the relevant details before you commit yourself.

From the UK

scheduled carriers

If you buy *direct* from an airline, the standard round-trip excursion fare from London (low season, economy class, minimum stay 14 days, maximum 4 months) is £742 to Delhi or Bombay and £825 to Calcutta or Madras. In shoulder season the fares are £779 and £866, and in high season £816 and £907 respectively. A one-year open-ended return costs £995 to Delhi or Bombay and £1190 to Madras.

Airlines providing good, regular and reliable services from the UK to one or more cities in India include **Air India, British Airways, Air Canada, Air France, Alitalia, Emirates, Gulf Air, KLM, Lufthansa, Singapore Airlines, Swissair** and **United Airlines**. Air India and Singapore Airlines offer departures from Manchester as well as London, while KLM has flights from over 16 UK airports via Amsterdam.

discount air travel

Many cheap discounted fares are advertised in magazines like *Time Out, LAM, TNT* and *Australasian Express*, and there are many cut-price travel agencies around Earls Court,

London (see below). If you're flying to Delhi, you have plenty of choice. For Bombay, Calcutta, Madras and other cities, you may have fewer options, but fares on Air India to other cities are often common-rated, depending on the season and on the agency from which you buy your ticket.

Basically, the more popular the airline you choose, the more you'll pay. Non-stop flights from London to Delhi on carriers like British Airways and United Airlines are from around £500 return in low season, whereas indirect flights (long stopovers) on carriers like Aeroflot or Uzbekistan Airlines can be obtained for as little as £330. Other airlines pitch their fares between these extremes. Shoulder and high season fares are higher, the level depending on demand. 'Special offers' are nearly always available at short notice, even on popular airlines.

A word about seasons: although Air India officially divides the year into three seasons, most discount fares are quoted only as low season or high season. What complicates matters is that the exact seasonal dates vary with each airline, reflecting that carrier's perception of demand, so you should shop around.

The minimum stay is usually either one or two weeks, the maximum anything between one month and one year, depending on the season and the airline. Single fares are usually only about 25% lower than return fares, so it pays to commit yourself to a return date when you book. We found one agency, however, quoting a 'special offer' single fare to Bombay on a European airline for only £204, so again it's a good idea to shop around. If you want to continue on to the Far East or Australasia, enquire about discounted round-the-world (RTW) fares.

The following agencies are good for discount fares to India and have a range of deals with various airlines—though Greaves Travel only deals with British Airways, and Welcome Travel only handles Air India.

Bridge The World, 47 Chalk Farm Road, London NW1, ✆ (0171) 911 0900

Flamingo Travel, 24 Wardour Street, London WC1, ✆ (0171) 287 0402

Flightbookers, 178 Tottenham Court Road, London W1, ✆ (0171) 757 2000

Greaves Travel, 34 Marylebone High Street, London W1, ✆ (0171) 487 5687, and 46 Brazenose Street, Manchester M2, ✆ (0161) 835 2564

Hindustan Travel, 30 Poland Street, London W1, ✆ (0171) 439 9801

STA Travel, 6 Wrights Lane, London W8, ✆ (0171) 361 6262

Trailfinders, 42–50 Earls Court Road, London W8, ✆ (0171) 938 3366

Unijet Travel, Sandrocks, Rocky Lane, Haywards Heath, West Sussex RH16 1RH, ✆ (0990) 114114

Welcome Travel, 55–57 Wells Street, London W1, ✆ (0171) 439 3627

charter flights

Several UK tour operators offer charter flights and package holidays in winter (October–April) to Goa. There are departures direct from Manchester as well as London

Gatwick. Prices start as low as £375 for 7 nights including accommodation and from £369 flight-only.

Most operators offer add-on tours to other parts of India, but avoid people like Inspirations and Cosmos who deliberately sell places like Kovalam Beach (a poor man's Goa with minimal nightlife) as an alternative Torremolinos. Without being disrespectful, it's absolutely misleading. As for Goa, if you must go by package (*see* Hayes & Jarvis or Unijet, p.8), at least check the introduction to the beaches (*see* p.313) before booking yourself into somewhere horrid like Calangute or Colva.

From Mainland Europe

Full fare from **Paris** to Bombay on Air France (3-month maximum stay, no high or low season) is FFr10,595. A one-year ticket is FFr16,000. Going direct to Air France, you can also get a non-refundable reduced fare ticket for FFr8270 (3-month maximum stay, no high or low season).

Full fare from **Frankfurt** to Bombay on Lufthansa (3-month maximum stay) costs DM1572 in low season, DM1722 in high season and DM4773 for a one-year ticket. Frankfurt to Madras is DM1772 in low season, DM1922 in high season and DM5368 for a one-year ticket.

Full fare from **Amsterdam** to Bombay on KLM (economy class, 2-month maximum stay) is DFL2175 for low season and DFL2440 for high season. One-year tickets cost DFL5752. Your local travel agent should have more details on discounted fares.

From North America

Full fare from **New York** to Bombay on Air India (4-month maximum stay) costs US$1433 in low season, US$1601 in high season, and US$2722 for a one-year ticket. New York to Madras is US$1540 in low season, US$1712 in high season, and US$2882 for a one-year ticket.

For discounted tickets, try calling STA Travel in New York, ✆ (212) 477 7348, or **San Francisco**, ✆ (415) 391 8407, or look in the Sunday travel section of your nearest big city newspaper. To save money and to get the best flight availability, many American travellers fly into New York on cheap internal flights from various other parts of the country. Those flying from the west coast may also cut costs by flying west via Bangkok, as certain airlines—Singapore, United, Korean and Northwest Orient—offer discounted rates in this direction.

While discounts can be found in the US if you're prepared to shop around, many Americans travel to India via London, where cheap flight deals are readily available—pre-booking the connecting flight from the UK to India via UK travel agents (*see* pp.8–9).

Air Canada has a one-stop service to Delhi from **Vancouver** via London. Connections to London are available from Calgary, Edmonton, Montreal, Ottawa and Toronto. Discounted fares may be obtained from local agents.

From Australia and New Zealand

Full fare from **Sydney** to Bombay on Cathay Pacific (3-month maximum stay) costs A$1868 in low season, A$2322 in high season and A$4956 for a one-year ticket.

Full fare from **Auckland** to Bombay on Cathay Pacific (3-month maximum stay) costs NZ$2150 in low season, NZ$2350 in high season and NZ$5596 for a one-year ticket, with an overnight stay in Hong Kong.

Many Australians and New Zealanders go to Singapore or Bangkok and fly on to India from there. **Jetset**, 99 Walker Street, North Sydney, NSW, ✆ (02) 956 9333, offers attractive flight discounts, or try the **STA Travel** chain in both Australia and New Zealand. From both countries, the cheapest option of all is a flight hop to Bali, followed by an overland trek up through Southeast Asia to India.

Flight Reconfirmation

The first thing to do, once you've got over jet lag, is to reconfirm your flight back home. This may sound boring, but you'd be amazed how many travellers leave it to the last moment, only to find their seat long gone. Ticket reconfirmation may be done in person, or you can pay a travel agent Rs50/100 to handle it for you. Some of the better hotels will do it for you by telephone, from reception. If for any reason you forget to reconfirm, don't panic. They'll just put you on a different plane the next day, or the one after.

Instead of buying a round-trip ticket to India, you can buy a one-way ticket and purchase the return flight once there. Full one-way fares originating from India are, however, more expensive than from abroad, so ask a travel agent if he can suggest a discounted ticket. Flights out of Delhi or Bombay are cheaper than from Madras or Calcutta, and you can also book through travel agents in Bangalore, Madras, or Trivandrum. Be persistent in tracking down cheap tickets. Some agents will tell you that no reduced fares exist and that you must pay the full published fares. Don't believe them. Discount fares from Bombay to major cities in Europe cost from Rs10,000 to 15,000, and Bombay to the US from Rs15,000 to 20,000. Carriers like Kuwait Airways or Tarom (Romanian Airlines) offer good deals and are definitely worth investigating.

Note: anyone staying in India for more than 180 days is supposed to obtain an income tax clearance certificate (*see* p.7) Most airlines mark their discounted tickets 'subject to income tax clearance', though in practice airport officials very rarely ask for this certificate.

Overland

Both **Encounter Overland**, 267 Old Brompton Road, London SW5 9JA, ✆ (0171) 370 6951, ✆ (0171) 244 9737, and **Dragoman**, 63 Camp Green, Debenham, Stowmarket, IP14 6LA, ✆ (01728) 861133 or ✆ (0171) 370 1930, ✆ (01728) 861127, offer overland trips from London to India.

Passports and Visas

All foreign visitors to India must obtain a **visa** in advance from the Indian embassy or consulate of their home country. Make sure you have a full, up-to-date passport. Visa fees and requirements change frequently, so use the following information as a general guide only and check with your nearest Indian tourist office or consulate for current information.

The **standard tourist visa** is valid for either 90 or 180 days, and entitles the holder to multiple entries into India within that period. Visas can be applied for from any Indian consular office or High Commission. In the UK, a multiple entry visa costs £13.00 for 90 days, or £26.00 for 180 days (rather less in other countries). Once in India, visa extensions can be obtained from various Foreigners' Registration Offices. Though it's getting more and more difficult, you used to be able to get a six-month visa to India and extend it umpteen times while you were there. Recently, however, India has decided that it doesn't want long-stay travellers ('hippies') any more. So it has changed the rules. Now, you have to get out of the country for a year after each six-month visit before you can come back again. Another blow to the freak brigade are the new rules governing repatriation. Time was, they could go to India, do all their drugs and run out of money, and then go to the British Embassy and ask to be flown home for free. But several countries, including the UK, won't do that any more.

Special long-term visas are available for business, education, the study of yoga, dance, traditional medicine, or other specific projects. Applications for these visas must be submitted well in advance.

In the **UK**, visas can be applied for at the High Commission of India, Consular Dept., India House, Aldwych, London WC2B 4NA, ✆ (0171) 836 8484/0990 (open 9.30am–5.30pm). Application forms are available from here and from the Government of India Tourist Office, 7 Cork Street, London W1X 2LN, ✆ (0171) 437 3677, ✆ (0171) 494 1048. You can apply either by post, which can take up to four weeks to process, or in person, which takes two days. Arrive with your passport, three passport-size photos and an application form at the High Commission building, 9am latest, to avoid the queues. It's open 9.30am to 1.00pm weekdays, and you'll have to return the next working day to collect your passport and visa between 4.30 and 5.30pm.

Trailfinders, Thomas Cook and American Express have **quick visa services** for travellers, and for a small charge will do all the waiting and queueing for you.

Travellers from other nations should apply to the nearest Indian embassy, consulate or high commission.

Australia: 3–5 Moonah Place, Yarralumla, ACT 2600, ✆ (06) 273 3999

Canada: 10 Springfield Road, Ottawa, K1M 1C9, ✆ (613) 744 3751

France: 15 Rue Alfred Dehodencq, 75016 Paris, ✆ (1) 40 50 70 70

Germany: Adenauerallee 262, 53113 Bonn, ✆ (0228) 540 50

Ireland: 6 Leeson Park, Dublin 6, ✆ (1) 497 0843

New Zealand: 180 Molesworth St, Princess Towers, Wellington, ✆ (04) 473 6390

UK: India House, Aldwych, London WC2B 4NA, ✆ (0171) 836 8484; 8219 Augusta Street, Birmingham B18 6DS, ✆ (0121) 212 2782

USA: 2107 Massachusetts Avenue NW, Washington, DC 20008, ✆ (202) 939 7000; 3 East 64th Street, New York, NY 10021, ✆ (212) 879 7888; 540 Arguello Boulevard, San Francisco, CA 94118, ✆ (415) 668 0662

baggage and customs

Your normal baggage allowance is 23kg in economy class and 66lbs in 1st and club class—*plus* hand luggage of up to 5kg. Coming out of India (weighed down with presents/ souvenirs), you can usually get away with a few kilos extra (i.e. without paying the current £10 per kg excess luggage charge) but don't push it. The maximum I've ever got out of Delhi was 70kg main-hold and 28kg by hand—but only by inventing a girl-friend, stuck in a Delhi hotel with malaria, whose luggage 'had' to go home ahead of her. Do *not* follow my example; big fines are likely. Leaving India, anything over 27/28kg should be stuffed into a largeish soft bag—one that fits into an overhead plane locker—and carried through as though it doesn't weigh much. If you're discreet, a small shoulder bag (for in-flight essentials) may also get through, though more and more airlines are catching onto this one.

Indian customs can be very thorough. Visitors over 18 years of age can bring in up to 1 litre of spirits and 200 cigarettes (or 50 cigars/250gm of tobacco) as a personal allowance. Delhi airport has a much cheaper (though limited) duty-free shop than UK or US airports—buy your fags or booze here while waiting for your baggage to crawl through. Expensive items like video cameras, personal radios and fax machines may be entered into your passport on arrival; this is to ensure you take them out of the country again, and don't sell them in India. Batteries, electronic items and penknives should be packed in your main baggage—they may be confiscated as part of your hand luggage. Leaving India, export of antiques, art objects, animal skins, ivory and rhino horns are strictly prohibited.

airport departure tax

On exit from India, you'll be required to pay Rs300 foreign travel tax (Rs150 if travelling on to Thailand, Burma, Nepal or Sri Lanka). This is paid at special desks inside the airports (Delhi, Bombay, Calcutta or Madras) *before* joining the check-in queues. Don't worry if you've spent all your rupees; foreign currency is usually accepted.

Main Agents and Special-interest Holidays

With so many different cultures, languages and customs, the variety of things to do and see in India is endless. For general tours or private itineraries, look under the main agents section below. If you are after something more specific, go straight to the special-interest holidays section further down.

individual packages

If you're a couple wishing to travel on your own, rather than with families or groups, contact a company like **Pettitts India**, 14 Lonsdale Gardens, Tunbridge Wells, Kent, TN1 1NV, ✆ (01892) 515966, ✆ (01892) 515951. They're not cheap, but they tailor their holidays to your individual requirements and provide cars in India with English-speaking guide-drivers. They discuss the whole itinerary with you, only book you into hotels that have been thoroughly checked, and make sure that you spend only as long as you need to in any one place. To take full advantage of this service, you want to start planning with them at least 6 weeks before departure. Itineraries may be fixed, but there's still some degree of flexibility with them once in India. You can for example ask their drivers to make detours to unscheduled places (time allowing) or change your hotels if desired. You can even extend your stay in the country, by contacting their Delhi office. Tours can be organized throughout India, and are particularly recommended for Kerala and Rajasthan.

Two other tour operators who do the same kind of thing—both well-established and very reliable—are **Cox and Kings**, Gordon House, 10 Greencoat Place, London SW1P 1PH, ✆ (0171) 873 5000, ✆ (0171) 630 6038, and **Abercrombie and Kent**, Sloane Square House, Holbein Place, London SW1W 8NS, ✆ (0171) 730 9600, ✆ (0171) 730 9376. They are also extremely good (if expensive) for group packages.

group packages

Also recommended for group holidays in India (at less cost than Cox & Kings or Abercrombie and Kent), are the following travel companies:

In the UK: Coromandel, 54 High Street East, Uppingham, Rutland, LE15 9BZ, (01572) 821 330, ✆ (01572) 821 072; **Global Link Ltd**, Colette House, 52–55 Piccadilly, London W1V 9AA, ✆ (0171) 409 7766, ✆ (0171) 409 0545; **Bales Tours**, Bales House, Junction Road, Dorking, Surrey RH4 3EJ, ✆ (01306) 885 991, ✆ (01306) 740 048; **Explore Worldwide**, 1 Frederick Street, Aldershot, Hants GU11 1LQ, ✆ (01252) 319448, ✆ (01252) 343170; **Inspirations Holidays**, Victoria House, Victoria Road, Horley Road, Surrey RH6 7AD, ✆ (01293) 822244, ✆ 821732; **Jasmin Tours Ltd**, High Street, Cookham, Maidenhead, Berks SL6 6SQ, ✆ (01628) 531121, ✆ (01628) 529444; **Kuoni Travel Ltd**, Kuoni House, Dorking, Surrey RH5 4AZ, ✆ (01306) 740500, ✆ (01306) 740719; **Lunn Poly Ltd**, Clarendon Ave, Leamington Spa, Warwicksire CV32 5PS, ✆ (01926) 452245; **Manos Holidays** (Kerala only), 168–172 Old Street, London EC1V 9BP, ✆ (0171) 216 8000, ✆ (0171) 216 8099; **Hayes & Jarvis**, 152 King Street, London W6 0QU, ✆ (0181) 748 0088, ✆ (0181) 741 0299; **Unijet**, 'Sandrocks', Rocky Lane, Haywards Heath, RH16 4RH, ✆ (01444) 458611 (especially Goa); **NADFAS Tours**, Hermes House, 80–98 Beckenham Road, Beckenham, Kent BR3 4RH, ✆ (0181) 658 2308, ✆ (0181) 658 4478; and **Somak Holidays**, Somak House, Wembley Hill Road, Wembley, Middlesex HA9 8BU, ✆ (0181) 903 8166, ✆ (0181) 903 9464.

In the US: Abercrombie & Kent, 1520 Kensington Road, Oak Brook, IL 60521–2141, ✆ (708) 954 2944, ✆ (708) 954 3324; **Cox & Kings**, 511 Lexington Avenue, New York,

NY 10017, ☎ (212) 935 3935, 🖷 (212) 935 3863; **Sita World Travel Inc.**, G.M. Plaza, 767 Fifth Avenue, New York, NY 10153, ☎ (212) 759 8979, 🖷 (212) 759 0814; **World Wide Travel**, 1815 H. Street NW, Suite 10001, Washington DC 20006, ☎ (202) 659 6430, 🖷 (202) 659 1111; **Absolute Asia**, 155 W. 68th Street, Suite 525, New York, NY 10023, ☎ (800) 736 8187; **Asia Pacific Travel Ltd**, P.O. Box 350, Kenilworth, IL 60043, ☎ (800) 262 6420; **India Tours**, 230 N. Michigan Avenue, Chicago, IL 60601, ☎ (312) 726 6091, 🖷 (312) 726 6121. As in the UK, the first two are expensive but give top service.

Specialist Holidays
in India

These are best booked direct through a good Indian agent. The most reliable in the south is **Clipper Holidays**, Suite 406, Regency Enclave, 4 Magrath Road, Bangalore 560 025, ☎/🖷 (080) 5599032/34/5599833, who handle trekking, riding, wildlife viewing and cultural activities. In the north, **Distant Frontiers**, B2/1, Safdarjung Enclave, New Delhi 110029, ☎ (011) 685 8857, 🖷 687 5553, offers a wide range of special-interest breaks. On the downside, booking to India from abroad can be both slow and costly—especially when you have to phone or fax.

in the UK

For convenience, specialist holidays can be pre-booked from the following companies: **Explorasia Ltd**, 13 Chapter Street, London SW1P 4NY, ☎ (0171) 630 7102, 🖷 (0171) 630 0355 (sports); **Encounter Overland**, 267 Old Brompton Road, London SW5 9JA, ☎ (0171) 370 6951, 🖷 (0171) 244 9737 (trekking); **Abercrombie and Kent**, Sloane Square House, Holbein Place, London SW1W 8NS, ☎ (0171) 730 9600, 🖷 (0171) 730 9376 (riding and fishing); **Butterfield's**, Burton Fleming, Driffield, East Yorkshire, YO25 0PQ, ☎ (01262) 470 230 (rail tours); **World Expeditions**, 7 North Road, Maidenhead, Berkshire, SL6 1PE, ☎ (01628) 74174, 🖷 (01628) 74312 (cycling); **Discover India Tours**, 29 Fairview Crescent, Rayners Lane, Harrow, Middlesex, HA2 9UB, ☎ (0181) 429 3300, 🖷 (0181) 248 4249 (temples); **Swan Hellenic**, 77 New Oxford Street, London WC1A 1PP, ☎ (0171) 831 1515, 🖷 (0171) 831 1280 (historic towns); **Holt's Tours**, 15 Market Street, Sandwich, Kent CT13 9DA, ☎ (01304) 612 248, 🖷 (01304) 614 930 (battlefields); **Indian Encounters**, Creech Barrow, East Creech, Dorset BH20 5AP, ☎/🖷 (01929) 480 548 (crafts/painting); and **Maxwell Scott Agency**, Foss House, Sutton Road, Strensall, York YO3 5TU, ☎ (01347) 878 566, 🖷 878 493 (dance festivals).

in the US

Similar specialists operating out of the USA include **Abercrombie and Kent**, 1520 Kensington Road, Oak Brook, Illinois 60521–2141, ☎ (708) 954 2944, 🖷 (708) 954 3324 (wildlife, fishing, riding, temples and culture); **American Museum of Natural History Museum Discovery Tours**, Central Park West, 79th Street, New York, NY 10024, ☎ (800) 462 8687 (wildlife); **Wonderbird Tours**, P.O. Box 2015, New York, NY 14851, ☎ (800) BIRDTUR (bird-watching); and **Craft World Tours**, 6776 Warboys Road, Byron, NY 14422, ☎ (716) 574 2667 (crafts/dance festivals).

Unless you are flying, and thus missing all the scenery between your destinations, travel in India is slow. For overland travel, whether by bus or train, you should reckon on an average of 20–25 miles per hour in flat country and 12–18 miles per hour in mountains. Even major highways are only two lanes wide, and are always clogged with bullock carts, trucks, cyclists, walkers or people sitting inexplicably in the middle of the road. Trains are more comfortable but not necessarily faster. This naturally limits the amount of ground you can cover during your trip and will often reduce people in a hurry to quivering wrecks of frustration.

Allow yourself more time in a few places, rather than trying to rush between a score of different ones, and you will come home with good memories, rather than ones of sweaty, overcrowded bus and train rides.

To ease matters, you should always book your onward bus or train ticket as soon as you arrive; if you decide to stay longer, then losing your reservation doesn't matter, but leaving your departure to the last minute always seems to coincide with a miraculous drying-up of available tickets.

By Air

Domestic flights are much more reliable than they used to be, possibly because of the competition from private airlines which has spurred Indian Airlines, the main domestic carrier, to previously undreamt of heights of efficiency. The number of airlines has increased dramatically in recent years and the domestic network now includes all major towns. On the downside, ticket costs have soared—you're now looking to pay US$200 one-way to Goa from Delhi, and US$280 to Trivandrum, for Kovalam beach.

If you have a choice, always fly **Indian Airlines** for domestic sectors. Unlike the other private airlines, they take care of your meals and lodging in case of cancellation. Of the new private airlines, **NEPC Skyline**, **East-West**, **Modiluft** and **Jet** are coming up fast. They're very flexible too—if one airline cancels a flight due to insufficient passengers, another one will often put you on their half-empty plane. Some of these airlines are better established and more reliable than others, particularly Modiluft and NEPC, who don't cancel so much.

Fares are changing and new routes being added all the time, so get an update from a travel agent (or any airline office) on arrival.

Indian Airlines Offices

Agra: Hotel Clark's Shiraz, 54 Taj Road, ✆ 360948, airport ✆ 263982
Bangalore: Housing Board Building, Kempe Gowda Road, ✆ 2214784, airport ✆ 5266233.
Bombay: Air India Building, Ist Floor, Madam Cama Road, Nariman Point, ✆ 2876161, airport ✆ 140—you can call the airport line 24 hours a day.
Calcutta: 39 Chittaranjan Avenue, ✆ 263390, airport ✆ 5529721

Cochin: Durbar Hall Road, Ernakulam, ✆ 353901, airport ✆ 2204433.

Delhi: Malhotra Building, Connaught Place, ✆ 3310517, airport ✆140.

Goa (Dabolim): Dempo House, Cample, Panjim, ✆ 224067, airport ✆ 512788.

Gwalior: ✆ 326872, airport ✆ 368124.

Hyderabad: Saifabad, near Legislative Assembly Building, ✆ 243333, airport,✆ 844433.

Jaipur: Tonk Road, ✆ 514407, airport ✆ 550222.

Jodhpur: Airport Road, ✆ 36757, airport ✆ 30616.

Madras: 19 Marshalls Road, ✆ 8251677, airport ✆ 141.

Trivandrum: near Mascot Hotel, Museum Road, ✆ 436870, airport ✆ 451869.

Udaipur: LIC Building, Delhi Gate, ✆ 410999, airport ✆ 527711.

Varanasi: Mint House Motel, ✆ 43746, airport ✆ 43742.

Other Domestic Airlines (Head Offices)

East-West Airlines, 18 New Kantwadi Road, Bandra, Bombay 400050, ✆ (22) 642 8388, ✉ (22) 643 3178.

Jagson Airlines, Vandana Building, Tolstoy Marg, New Delhi 110011, ✆ (11) 372 1593.

Jet Airways India, S M Center, Andheri-Kurla Road, Bombay 400059, ✆ (22) 821 5080, ✉ (22) 821 5079.

Modiluft, 2 Commercial Complex, Masjid Moth, Greater Kailash, New Delhi 110048, ✆ (11) 643 1128, ✉ (11) 643 0929.

NEPC Airlines, G R Complex, Anna Salai, Nandaman, Madras 600035, ✆ (44) 434 5538, ✉ (44) 434 4370.

Sahara India Airlines, Ambadeep 14, Kasturba Gandhi Marg, New Delhi 110011, ✆ (11) 322 6851.

Skyline NEPC, 17 Nehru Road, Vokola-Santa Cruz East, Bombay 400055, ✆ (22) 610 3536, ✉ (22) 610 2544. Skyline NEPC is as yet the only 1st-class domestic airline in operation.

booking

Book internal air flights well in advance, as demand normally exceeds availability. Go to a travel agent to buy your ticket, as they will find you the best price and not charge any commission.

discounts

Domestic flights are surprisingly good value. If you have booked your flights from home, you'll need to reconfirm your entire itinerary as soon as you arrive in India to be sure of keeping your reservations.

Indian Airlines offers a 25% youth discount for those between 12 and 30 years of age. Children between 2 and 12 get a 50% discount, and infants under 2 travel at 10% of the adult fare. Students between 12 and 26 years of age get a 50% student discount, though certain formalities prior to booking student tickets are required. Check with your travel agent for details. If you are under 30 years of age, you qualify for cheap 'Youth Fares', which are 25% less than normal tariffs, e.g. US$100 Delhi to Bombay as opposed to the usual US$125.

Indian Airlines (and Skyline NEPC) also offer cheap air deals. They're not bad value if you've got a lot of India to see in a short time. The 'Discover India' package buys 21 days of unlimited economy class air travel anywhere in India for US$400. You have to buy it in conjunction with your international flight ticket, though a lot of travel agents/airlines won't touch it as it takes a lot of phoning and faxing to set up. The 'India Wonderfares' package buys you 7 days unlimited economy class travel within one region of India (north, south, east or west) for US$200.

Indian Airlines tickets are refundable up to one hour before scheduled flight departure, minus a Rs100 fee. No refunds are applicable for lost tickets. If your flight is delayed for over one hour, a full refund is also allowed.

airport–city transport

Once you've arrived at an airport, you normally have three options for getting into town: taxi, auto-rickshaw and bus (though luxury hotels often lay on free transfers). Auto-rickshaws are cheaper than taxis but not as comfortable. Buses into town cost next to nothing, but often stop running by 10pm—no use if your flight has arrived in the early hours (as international flights often do). If arriving late at night, your best bet is a pre-paid taxi into town (look for the pre-paid taxi counters inside the airport).

A word of warning: The jet-lagged traveller arriving in India for the first time is a perfect target for crooks. One common scam actually operates in collusion with airport pre-paid taxis. As one woman reported:

'I arrived in India at 3am, after an exhausting 30-hour plane flight and hired a pre-paid taxi to my hotel, where I had a reservation. Somewhere en route I was asked to get out of the taxi and into an auto-rickshaw, on the pretence that the rickshaw driver knew the directions and the taxi driver did not. I was then driven to my hotel, but the night guard there—no doubt working with the others—stated that he did not have my reservation and refused to let me into the hotel. He then told me that rioting had broken out in the city and the streets were unsafe. I asked the rickshaw driver to take me to another hotel quickly, and he started telling me that all the hotels in town cost between US$200–300. I knew these prices were grossly inflated, and was extremely frightened, especially as someone on the street had tried to grab my bag out of the open-sided rickshaw (this stunt perhaps being part of the scam). I was taken to a small dreary hotel and told it would cost US$70 for a room. Tired, scared, and alone, I felt I had little choice but to pay what was demanded. I went straight to the room, locked the door, and stayed there until dawn broke.' To avoid stunts like these, don't travel from the airport into town in the middle of the night (especially if a woman on your own)—wait inside the terminal until light. If you must get to your hotel, call ahead from the airport to confirm your reservation. If you do get into trouble, make a scene and demand to be taken to the nearest police station. Indians often respond to forcefulness, even from women (*see* 'Women Travellers', p.55).

By Boat

The most famous south Indian boat journeys are: firstly, the catamaran trip from Bombay to Goa and, secondly, the many small-boat trips through the backwaters of Kerala. The first takes 8 hours and costs US$35 for foreigners, but you get wonderful views of the mountainous Malabar Coast (*see* p.297). The second journey is like slow buses moving through a watery paradise, and is very relaxing (*see* p.493).

By Rail

Since the days when it was developed to link the commercial and military centres of the Indian Empire, the Indian Railways system has expanded considerably. By the close of the 19th century, there were 40,000 miles of track, stretching to the remotest parts of the country. Today, Indian Railways is the largest system in Asia, and the second largest in the world. Each day, over 11 million people travel to and from a total of 7021 railway stations.

Rail travel is a leisurely way of taking in the varied scenery—mountains, lakes, rivers, fields, forests, dense jungles and hill terrains. It also offers the opportunity to meet a great many people who are eager to share food and conversation with you. Whenever the train pulls into a station, platforms are an explosion of noise and colour: cries of '*chai-ya!*' and '*samo-sa!*' float invitingly over the general hubbub. Here you can buy fresh(ish) fruit and vegetables, *idlis* or *pakoras* for next to nothing. Or you can wait until the daily shipment of *thali* suppers is loaded onto the train and dine in a more civilized fashion later on. Train food is cheap (around Rs20–30), though rather bland. If on a marathon journey, it's a good idea to bring along supplies of your own water, chocolate, biscuits and oranges. Hot drinks are never a problem. At the larger stations, a boy with an aluminium teapot will invariably be beetling up and down the aisles doling out tea or coffee.

India's rail network is extremely extensive, always a madhouse and yet amazingly efficient (though few trains leave on time). If you're going to be doing a lot of train travel, buy a copy of **Trains at a Glance**. Sold cheaply at most large rail stations, this booklet provides a complete timetable of the rail services in India.

There are six basic classes of passenger rail travel: 1st class air-conditioned sleeper (operates on certain trains and routes only); 1st class non air-conditioned sleeper; 2nd class air-conditioned sleeper; 2nd class express sleeper, air-conditioned chair-car; 2nd class express seat only and 2nd class ordinary. For overnight journeys, the nicest way to travel is 2nd class a/c sleeper (costing half of the overrated 1st class a/c sleeper, far more private and comfortable). However, if the weather's not too hot, a 2nd class non a/c sleeper is relatively clean and cheap. For day trips, a/c chair-cars are cool, spacious, and relaxed, whereas 2nd class is often hectic and crowded. The latter does, however, allow you to meet and interact with a broad and interesting range of local people.

Always choose the quicker mail, express or superfast trains, as local passenger trains take ages. A sleeper berth on an overnight train is a smart way to travel since you don't have to pay for a night's hotel accommodation and time passes more quickly while you're unconscious! Better yet, a berth offers privacy and room to stretch out during the daytime portion of your trip.

You should always travel with a reservation for long train journeys, this being absolutely essential for air-conditioned and sleeper classes. Popular routes often fill up weeks in advance so the sooner you book your ticket the better. For short hops you can usually buy your ticket the same day. Just make sure you get to the platform 30 to 60 minutes early to buy your ticket, and push your way on to the train when it arrives to ensure you get a seat. If all the seats are taken, just stand or sit in the aisle-way until one becomes vacant.

Train reservations are made at a separate reservation office, which is normally adjacent to the station itself. Sometimes, you'll get a doleful shake of the head from the reservation clerk and the apologetic words, 'So sorry, all full'. This means you'll have to apply for the **tourist quota** of tickets. Most popular trains have a tourist quota, which must be paid for in foreign currency, and which are usually issued by the District Commercial Superintendent of the railway department. His office is sometimes miles away from the station, but you'll be surprised how easily he'll supply you with a ticket. Other 'quotas' are hidden away in all sorts of subterranean places in and out of the station complex. If you are really stuck, ask the nearest tourist office if there's a quota on the train you want. Or approach the stationmaster and try and break into his **VIP quota**. If nothing works, it's worth paying a few rupees baksheesh to a station porter to get a seat in an unreserved compartment.

Once you have your tickets sorted out and are ready to get on the train, it's sometimes difficult to find the right platform. At the larger stations there will usually be an electronic board that lists the relevant out-going train information. If not, there should be an inquiry desk which can help you (or a passing porter), but avoid spurious 'guides' who will see you to the train and then try to extort as much money as possible out of you. Your train ticket will have your carriage and seat number printed on it and there will also be a 'reservation sheet' posted on the sides of each carriage with your name and berth number (assuming you've bought a reserved ticket).

Hiring a porter to carry your bags is a luxury that is easily affordable in India. The going rate is about 5 or 10 rupees per bag (depending on how far the bags need to be carried), although the porter will start out asking for something five times as high. Just hold firm to your price and he'll (sometimes grumpily) relent.

Indian railway stations often have good waiting-rooms and a decent restaurant. Tourists can use both 1st and 2nd class waiting-rooms, and can even sleep free in them, provided they have a valid train ticket. Most stations also have a **left-luggage** room where you can leave your bags for just a few rupees per day—very useful if you're only spending a few hours in a town and don't want to book into a hotel.

Indian rail fares (Rs)

Note that railway tickets can be cancelled and your money fully refunded (minus a Rs10–30 cancellation fee) if you cancel more than one day in advance. You pay a 25% cancellation charge if your ticket is cancelled one day in advance up to 6 hours before scheduled departure and 50% if cancelled within 6 hours before scheduled departure and up to 3 hours after the actual departure of the train.

The following table lists railway fares on routes according to distance. For a complete listing of routes and fares in India, buy a *Trains at a Glance* booklet, or inquire about your desired journey at any Indian railway station reservation office.

Distance (km)	1st a/c (a/c)	1st class	A/c chair	2nd class express, sleeper	2nd class express, seat	2nd class ordinary
50	Rs186	Rs83	Rs65	Rs62	Rs17	Rs9
100	Rs299	Rs126	Rs77	Rs62	Rs27	Rs14
200	Rs450	Rs202	Rs124	Rs62	Rs49	Rs26
300	Rs630	Rs281	Rs173	Rs85	Rs68	Rs36
500	Rs952	Rs421	Rs250	Rs128	Rs102	Rs50
1000	Rs1557	Rs687	Rs381	Rs208	Rs166	Rs72

To work out the approximate cost of your journey, use the table of fares above. For example, the overnight sleeper from Delhi to Shimla, a journey of 350km, would cost Rs68 in 2nd class (plus Rs17 for sleeper reservation) and Rs281 in 1st class non a/c. Fares do increase from time to time, but not by much.

Indrail passes

Indrail passes are valid for one year from purchase date, and give you unlimited travel on Indian trains for specified lengths of time (from 7 to 60 days). They're supposed to save you lots of queueing up for tickets, but you still have to confirm when you get to India, and confirming is the same as booking; worse, bookings made before departure have been found to have dropped off the computer on arrival in India, which means starting all over again. If you have foreign currency, you might just as well go to New Delhi railway station and book your whole train itinerary at the computerized tourist desk there. Also, the passes are save no money at all, unless you plan on doing a lot of train travel within the country. I personally wouldn't touch them with a barge-pole! In India, Indrail passes are sold by many travel agents or central reservations offices at major railway stations.

Outside India, Indrail passes can only be bought through authorized agents. In the **UK**, you can buy the Indrail pass from S D Enterprises Limited, 103 Wembley Park Drive, Wembley, Middlesex HA9 8HG, ✆ (0181) 903 3411; in **France**, from Carrefour, 15 Rue des Ecoles, Paris; in the **USA**, from Hari World Travels, 30 Rockefeller Plaza, Shop No.21, Mezzanine North, New York; and in **Australia**, from Penthouse Travel, Suite 5, Level 13, Commercial Union House, 109 Pitt Street, Sydney. Contact your local Government of India Tourist Office to find out the agent in countries not listed.

Indrail passes are sold only to foreign nationals and Indians residing abroad holding valid passports. Payment is accepted only in US dollars and pounds sterling. A tourist travelling on the Indrail pass is exempt from paying reservation fees, sleeper charges and other supplementary charges levied in the case of ordinary tickets. Children aged between 5 and 12 years are charged half the adult Indrail pass fare.

Indrail Pass Costs (£ sterling)

Validity	1st class a/c	2nd a/c (not sold in India)
7 days	200	100
14 days	248	124
21 days	294	147
30 days	368	184
60 days	534	267
90 days	706	353

By Bus and Luxury Coach

You can get just about anywhere by bus, and it's cheap. India has a very extensive and comprehensive bus system. Each state offers its own service—usually a combination of local, deluxe, super-deluxe and video buses—and tickets are usually purchased direct from the bus stands. Buses are often cheaper and more exciting than the trains, and go to several places not linked by rail. They can also be a lot quicker. Most buses in India, whether local, state, or privately run, roar to their destinations with reckless verve and daring. Their drivers seem to have a particular grudge against 'public carrier' trucks, which often carry provocative slogans like 'Owner is God—God is Grate'. All bus drivers have a little box containing their personal gods above their seat. From time to time, generally when stopped by the police for not paying a speeding fine, they will pray to these. At other times, they will pull up at a roadside Hindu shrine and pay a priest to ring a bell to summon the major deities; this is often to give thanks for avoiding a major collision.

Every bus journey is an experience in itself, especially the ones which wind round an escalating series of hairpin bends on their way up to remote hill stations. And when the interior is full your only option is to wait for the next bus or sit on the roof. But there are always entertaining road-signs to keep your mind off the perilous drive. These signs are the creation of Public Works Department (PWD) poets, who are notoriously sexist. 'When you approach a corner, get horny', is one of their classics. 'Don't gossip—let him drive' is another. 'Family awaits—please oblige', is a direct appeal to the paternal instinct, and is the only thing likely to make manic fathers slow down at tight corners.

Buses sometimes stop at spots of great natural beauty, which makes a pleasant change from the hurly-burly of railway platforms. They also leave at frequent intervals (every hour or half-hour) and are much less trouble to book and board than trains. The more popular buses are best booked two or three days in advance. If you have to charge onto the bus, it helps to have two of you—one to get a seat, the other to mind the bags.

Local bus drivers have a secret language all of their own. They communicate with each other by means of their horns, which they toot at every opportunity, accompanied by a complicated series of hand gestures out of the window. The more frantic the horn and gestures, the more likely it is that you will go home in a box. Sometimes a cow or goat will get on board, only to be gently ushered off again. More often, would-be passengers will run alongside the bus and try to board it while it is racing along at 30km per hour. In the meantime, the conductor moodily distributes his tickets without ever having the right change. He has a whistle, which he peeps to stop or start the bus. When he is in a good mood, this whistle echoes in strange harmony with the Indian video playing up front. When not, it emits a piercing shriek which stabs you in the eyes and gives you a headache.

Local buses are incredibly cheap and will often run you from one end of a state to another for less than Rs50. They are however crowded, dirty and uncomfortable; a/c or non a/c 'deluxe' buses are slightly less so. Video bus journeys are a nightmare: constant disco music and blaring video shows can grind you down, especially when sharing a two-seater built for one. It's almost impossible to hear yourself think, let alone read, but the more distorted the sound, the more some of the Indian passengers seem to like it.

Whenever leaving a bus to go to the toilet or to eat, leave a book or newspaper or something on your seat. This will reserve it. Take any other hand luggage off the bus with you. Backpacks and large cases are usually strapped under tarpaulin on the bus roof, or stored in the hold-all. If they're stored under your seat, make sure they are securely zipped and locked (padlocking to a bolted seat is best) before vacating the bus.

Bus stops can be either very short or very long (driver wanders off to visit his family). Passengers have been known to be left holding full cups of tea or squatting in ditches while the bus roars off without them. The only way of tracking its movements is to keep one eye constantly on the driver. As soon as he's back in his seat, you've got approximately 20 seconds to get back in yours. Don't panic; just wave at the driver and smile.

Bus travel is best over short distances—for long journeys take the train. Indian roads are badly surfaced, full of yawning potholes, and always liable to collapse. So are the back axles of the overloaded buses. The hard, cramped seating, the draughty, rattling windows, the screaming children, the infrequent toilet stops and the constant blare of the air-horn as the bus ploughs inexorably towards its destination, may leave you blinded, shell-shocked and with your nerves (and your backside) shot to pieces. But the network is extensive, and you can always reduce your discomfort by inserting earplugs and bringing a neck-rest air pillow and a pillow to sit on.

prices

Deluxe buses cost approximately double ordinary buses—a little more than the corresponding 2nd class rail ticket. The longer the journey, the lower the rate per mile.

Sample deluxe bus fares are:

Delhi to Shimla (350km) Rs140
Jaipur to Delhi (260km) Rs105.
Bombay to Goa (600km) Rs250.

by sightseeing tour bus

Costing around Rs45 for a half-day, Rs80 for a full day, sightseeing coach tours from tourist offices are a cheap, quick introduction to the larger Indian centres. There are rather too many stops at obscure holy places for most Western passengers, and the deluxe buses themselves are sometimes draughty and dilapidated but you'll cover an incredible amount of ground in a short time and other forms of in-town transport can be even less comfortable. Sightseeing buses can also be a great way of meeting people because you'll often be the only foreigner on board and will commonly be fed large quantities of picnic lunches by friendly Indian families. When booking your tour, ask for a seat at the front of the bus—it's far less bumpy, quicker to get to the toilets, and you'll hear more of the guide's talk. Make friends with both guide and driver, so they will remember if you are missing.

By Car

Most hotels and travel agents in India can arrange car hire. They usually provide a white Hindustan Ambassador (an unashamed replica of a 1950s Morris Oxford), with plush seating but no windscreen wipers. Car hire is incredibly cheap by Western standards, between US$30 and $40 per day. This usually covers you for up to 300km travel (around 8hrs on a good road). The car should come with an English-speaking driver, preferably one who knows where he's going.

Whether you get one or not is down to luck. I booked a car in Udaipur once, for a 6-day tour of Gujarat, and requested a good English-speaking driver with a thorough knowledge of the region. In due course, my *non*-English-speaking with a total ignorance of the area turned up. Not only had he never been to Gujarat, he didn't even know where it was. Several hand signals and mimed grunts later, we shot off—with me urgently studying a road map and him anxiously asking 'Where?' (his only English word) every five minutes. Halfway to Ahmedabad, darkness fell and he switched on his headlamps, only to find them dead. As I busily set about sellotaping the full-beam indicator to the steering wheel, hoping to produce enough light to proceed, he squatted at my side and began happily committing all my English curses to memory. This done, he indicated that we should do *darshan* (worship) at a local temple and when I said no, he got quite sulky. I think he wanted to apologize to dairy-god Krishna for the cow he had nudged into a ditch earlier. We eventually rolled into Ahmedabad six hours late, with me leaning over his lap to hold the sellotape together, and him braying 'Bastard car!' (his favourite English curse) out the window. Strangely enough, the next five days were a breeze.

By Taxi and Auto-rickshaw

These are the two most common forms of in-town transport, mainly useful for short hops to and from bus and rail stations (when loaded down with luggage), or for solo sightseeing in smaller towns where tour buses aren't such good value. Taxis are usually black, with yellow tops, and are quite comfortable. Auto-rickshaws are three-wheeler scooters (with two-seater canopy strapped behind them), which are noisy but nippy. They cost around half as much as taxis.

Taxis and rickshaws are supposed to be metered, but the meters often don't work. As soon as you walk off in search of another taxi, they suddenly begin working again. If they don't and you're in a hurry, bargain the cost of your journey before setting off. A succession of fuel price increases has left taxi and rickshaw meter-readings way out of date. You'll often be handed a fare adjustment card indicating a far higher fare than that shown on the meter. In Bombay, where taxi meters haven't been recalibrated in ages, surcharges of 400–500% can come as a real shock to the penny-wise traveller.

If overcharged, don't get angry. Just write down the taxi number and announce in a calm, determined voice that you're going to the police. There are stiff fines for extorting money from tourists and your driver will usually 'remember' the correct fare instantly.

Another popular scam used by taxis and auto-rickshaws alike is to drive you miles out of your way, in order to collect a decent fare. Take a good city map with you and as soon as it's apparent that you're being taken miles out of the way, tell the driver firmly 'wrong way!' But don't be too hasty to jump to conclusions—sometimes he will genuinely lose his way, or won't be able to understand where you want to go. Again, a city map is useful because you'll be able to point out your exact destination. In case you're totally lost in a big city, and need to get back to your hotel, always keep a hotel card handy. Drivers will usually take one look at the card, and take you straight home.

Some major airports, including Bombay, Bangalore and Madras, have introduced a system of 'pre-paid taxis'. Look for the booth either just inside or outside the terminal and buy a ticket to where you want to go. This service ensures that new arrivals don't get over-charged and reach their destination without detours (*see also* p.12 for airport taxi scam).

By Cycle-rickshaw

Unless you love an argument, it is best to avoid this mode of transport. These rather anti-quated vehicles can be found only in certain places, usually in smaller towns. Cycle-rickshaws are cheap—usually just Rs2/3 per km (again, try and fix a rate in advance), but their drivers are notorious for trying to overcharge, often very forcefully. This is because they are usually unable to afford their own vehicles and are just hiring them out for a few rupees a day from someone else. Cycle-rickshaws are commonly ridden by loquacious old pirates who haven't the slightest idea of where they're going. It's accepted custom to get off and give them a push up steep hills. You'll probably also have to give them lots of directions and prompts—especially when they want to stop for tea or for a chat with their mates halfway through your journey.

By Bicycle and On Foot

by bike

In the quieter towns, such as Goa's resorts, Hampi, Mysore, Pondicherry and the hill stations, cycle hire is a good option for getting around. The usual daily tariff is Rs15–30 (bargain hard). You should *always* test the brakes, wheels, tyres and seats before paying. Most places will let you take a trial run around the block. If they refuse, try somewhere else. Don't bother with bikes in big cities unless you have some experience with Indian traffic—it simply isn't worth the risk. The one thing your bike *must* have is a bell. In dense traffic you'll be ringing this continually (like everybody else) to avoid being mown down. If you get a puncture, you'll have no difficulty finding a repair man (they're all over the place), but you may well be hanging around for an hour while he slowly fixes it. You can usually speed him up by offering him extra. Women in India travel side-saddle on cycles, so there is a great shortage of ladies' bikes. To snap up the few going, be at the hire shop first thing in the morning.

In places like Goa and the hill stations, you can often hire **motorbikes** (Rs200–300 a day), which are a nippy way of getting around.

on foot

Wandering off on foot down small, narrow backstreets can turn up all sorts of delights—tiny local temples, quaint pavement shrines, colourful markets and bazaars, and out-of-the-way curio shops. Off the beaten track is usually where you'll find the real India—small yet lively communities of local people working, eating, resting, playing and praying, mostly happy to meet and talk to foreign tourists.

Practical A–Z

Airports

The most important thing to remember about Indian airports (especially Delhi) is that once you go outside them, you often can't get back in: security is very tight. Arriving from abroad in the middle of the night, the last thing you must do is absentmindedly wander out of the terminal to see the night sky. Unless you've changed money inside and have booked a pre-paid taxi (and more and more airports have these), you're immediately at the mercy of tourist-hungry taxi touts who want to take you places that you don't want to go. There are exceptions of course, but single people (especially women) are advised not to travel into town at night—pay out for a pre-paid taxi or wait inside the airport until dawn.

When **leaving** India by air, note that certain airports (notably Delhi) won't allow anyone inside without an out-bound flight ticket for that day. If you've got family/friends seeing you off, they'll have to make their farewells at the entrance. Anyone meeting people off international flights from Delhi are advised that this airport has *two* exits. With two of you, you can guard an exit each. If you're on your own, all you can do is sprint back and forth between the two exits until your guest turns up!

Baksheesh

Unlike tipping, baksheesh is something you pay to get things done, not to reward things done already. Discerning use of baksheesh, often just a few rupees, can save you hours of pointless waiting and queueing. You can use this subtle form of bribery for just about anything: to hire a boy to wait in an endless rail-ticket queue while you go sightseeing; to send a station porter in search of a seat on a train which is apparently fully booked; even to get a berth on the roof of the Keralan backwater boat from Quilon to Alleppey.

The trouble about baksheesh is that once you start paying it out to speed up room service in hotels, for example, it's very difficult to stop. It also makes it twice as expensive for the next person. In general, you can achieve far more with a big smile than having to pay for it.

One English couple tried to board a packed train without tickets. They were carrying heavy packs, including unwieldy fishing-rods and full tackle. Instead of asking the ticket collector for a private chat to negotiate berths on the train, they loudly offered him baksheesh within earshot of the whole platform. The ticket collector began dancing up and down in a frenzy of affected affront, and even called the station police. The point is, baksheesh is strictly against the law. If you're trying it on with public servants, be extra discreet.

Beggars

You'll see lots of beggars, mainly around temples, railway stations and tourist spots. The Indian people themselves respect their beggars and usually go into temples with a handful of small change to give to the less fortunate. To donate to the poor is considered the duty of anyone with personal good fortune.

This unofficial form of social security ensures that at least some beggars are better off than they appear. In the big cities they are often experienced professionals who shed their grime and rags for new, clean clothes when 'off duty'. Unfortunately for the foreign tourist, faced by armies of young girls toting dirty babies and old men wearing identical doleful expressions, there is no way of knowing who really needs help and who doesn't.

Giving money to beggars is a very personal matter. The usual policy among Indians is to give nothing to a man who is able-bodied because he can make more money from begging than from working, and to give nothing to children because it will encourage them to leave school and to take up begging as a full-time occupation. Many however give to the elderly, sick or disabled, either small change or food. Giving food or sweets instead of money can be a good alternative, but often they just want money.

If you feel strongly about this issue, there are of course many charities in India which will always be grateful for anything you are able to give.

Books and Maps

The best general preparation for a trip to India is to read as much about her history, society, culture and religion as possible. There are a few bookshops which specialize in Indian literature:

in the UK

Books from India, 45 Museum Street, London WC1A 1LR, ✆ (0171) 405 7226.

The Travel Bookshop Ltd, 13 Blenheim Crescent, London W11 2EE, ✆ (0171) 229 5260. It also has an excellent programme of talks, events, and a useful noticeboard.

Trailfinders, 194 Kensington High Street, London W8 7RG, ✆ (0171) 938 3939. For people booking flights through them, it has access to a very good library.

Daunt Books, 83 Marylebone High Street, London W1M 4AL, ✆ (0171) 224 2295. Here, a wide range of fiction and non-fiction titles are grouped according to their country or place of association.

Stanford's Map and Travel Bookshop, 12–14 Long Acre, London WC2E 9LP, ✆ (0171) 836 1321. The biggest specialist store for maps and guides in London.

The best general **map** of the Indian subcontinent is still Bartholomew's one-page *Travel Map* (No.15 in the series)—if nothing else, it gives you an idea of the sheer size of the country. Good maps of major Indian cities are sold by **Stanford's**. **Books from India** stocks a useful compendium of India city maps called *The Metro Atlas of India* (TPP, 1992) and the more comprehensive *An Atlas of India* (OUP, New Delhi, 1991).

in the US

Most major bookstores in the US have extensive travel sections.

Pilot Books, 347 Fifth Avenue, New York, NY 10016, produce their own list of travel books.

Unless you're going on a beach holiday (the only chance you'll get to do a lot of reading), only take a couple of books. You can always buy more in India, where they're cheaper, or swap the ones you have with other traveller's books.

Popular **novels** on the India circuit are M M Kaye's *The Far Pavilions*, Salman Rushdie's *Midnight's Children*, Vikram Seth's *A Suitable Boy* and Ruth Prawer Jhabwala's *Heat and Dust*. JG Farrell's *The Siege of Krishnapur* is a rumbustious account of the Indian Mutiny, while (in a more serious vein) Dominique Lapierre's *City of Joy*, recently bastardized by the film (starring Patrick Swayze), is still the definitive account of life on the streets in Calcutta, depicting the triumph of simple values over desperate poverty. If you're going to read one book on India, make it this.

Two good titles for anyone interested in the role of women in Indian society, past and present, are *Raj* by Gita Mehta and *May You Be the Mother of a Hundred Sons* by Elisabeth Bumiller. Gita Mehta has also written *Karma Cola*, an entertaining commentary, on the clash between eastern and western cultures.

Worthwhile **historical** reads include *Plain Tales from the Raj*, edited by Charles Allen, and *Freedom at Midnight* by Larry Collins and Dominique Lapierre. KM Sen's *Hinduism* (Penguin) is a succinct introduction to the Hindu religion.

Travelogues on India are an individual thing. You either love them or hate them. Three we like are John Keay's *Into India* (John Murray, 1973), Trevor Fishlock's *India File* (Rupa, 1984) and Paul Theroux's *The Great Railway Bazaar* (Penguin, 1977).

Cinema

More films are made in India than in Hollywood—mostly in Madras or Bombay ('Bollywood')—and top matinée idols can command a salary of over Rs5 million a film, placing them among the highest earners in the country. Male movie stars still owe a lot of their dress sense to John Travolta in *Saturday Night Fever* or to early Engelbert Humperdinck. Female stars are sexy, extravagant, heavily made up and ultra-glamorous. Both leads burst into (dubbed) song at every opportunity, and the villain is so villainous as to be laughable. The huge success of the Indian film industry owes something to the low taxation levied on its profits, but is due mainly to the mass popularity of the colourful, fantastic, escapist entertainment provided on the celluloid screen. The première of a major new film is the cue for massed crowds and blockaded ticket offices. Many cinemas are air-conditioned and comfortable, and seats go for as little as 10p/15 cents. The films themselves are often very long, 3 hours or more, but there's a break in the middle for refreshments. The cinema that travellers like best is the beautiful Raj Mandir in Jaipur. If you come here it's worth paying a little extra for a box—it makes it a very special experience.

Climate and When to Go

Whatever the time of year, there is always somewhere in India where you can enjoy a relaxing and memorable vacation. But the climate varies, depending on season and location, and you need to consider this when planning your holiday. The country has four seasons—spring, autumn and two monsoons. The southwest monsoon starts in June on the west coast and slowly wends its way northwards; the northeast monsoon takes place between October and December. This can actually be

T = Temperature in °C, R = Rainfall in mm

City	Jan	Feb	Mar	Apr	May	Jun	Jul	Aug	Sep	Oct	Nov	Dec
Ahmedabad												
T max.	29	31	36	40	41	38	33	32	33	36	33	30
min.	12	15	19	23	26	27	26	25	24	21	16	13
R avg.	4	0	1	2	5	100	316	213	163	13	5	1
Bombay												
T max.	31	32	33	33	33	32	30	29	30	32	33	32
min.	16	17	20	24	26	26	25	24	24	23	20	18
R avg.	0	1	0	0	20	647	945	660	309	117	7	1
Calcutta												
T max.	26	29	34	36	36	34	32	32	32	31	29	27
min.	12	15	20	24	26	26	26	26	26	24	18	13
R avg.	13	22	30	50	135	263	320	318	253	134	29	4
Cochin												
T max.	31	31	31	31	31	29	28	28	28	29	30	30
min.	23	24	26	26	26	24	24	24	24	24	24	23
R avg.	9	34	50	139	364	756	572	386	235	333	184	37
Darjeeling												
T max.	9	11	15	18	19	19	20	20	20	19	15	12
min.	3	4	8	11	13	15	15	15	15	11	7	4
R avg.	22	27	52	109	187	522	713	573	419	116	14	5
Delhi												
T max.	21	24	30	36	41	40	35	34	34	35	29	23
min.	7	10	15	21	27	29	27	26	25	19	12	8
R avg.	25	22	17	7	8	65	211	173	150	31	1	5
Hyderabad												
T max.	29	31	35	37	39	34	30	29	30	30	29	28
min.	15	17	20	24	26	24	22	22	22	20	16	13
R avg.	2	11	13	24	30	107	165	147	163	71	25	5
Madras												
T max.	29	31	33	35	38	37	35	35	34	32	29	28
min.	20	21	23	26	28	28	26	26	25	24	23	21
R avg.	24	7	15	25	52	53	83	124	118	267	309	139
Panjim (Goa)												
T max.	31	32	32	33	33	31	29	29	29	31	33	33
min.	19	20	23	25	27	25	24	24	24	23	22	21
R avg.	2	0	4	17	18	580	892	341	277	122	20	37
Puri												
T max.	27	28	30	31	32	31	31	31	31	31	29	27
min.	18	21	25	27	27	27	27	27	27	25	21	18
R avg.	9	20	14	12	63	187	296	256	258	242	75	8
Shimla												
T max.	9	10	14	19	23	24	21	20	20	18	15	11
min.	2	3	7	11	15	16	16	15	14	10	7	4
R avg.	65	48	58	38	54	147	415	385	195	45	7	24
Varanasi												
T max.	23	27	33	39	41	39	33	32	32	32	29	25
min.	9	11	17	22	27	28	26	26	25	21	13	9

a most pleasant time to go. In between the sudden, short downpours of rain are periods of clear, brilliant sunshine, and all the foliage and flowers suddenly burst into colour. It's a photographer's dream, and the heat at such times is rarely unbearable.

The movements of foreign tourists tend to follow a set pattern. From November to January, you'll find many travellers in the south. It's always hot in the south, but this is the 'coolest season'. By February, the annual migration northwards has begun. Travellers move slowly up the western coast, settling briefly in Kovalam and Goa between February and early March, before arriving in Bombay, Calcutta or Delhi by mid/late March. These are the three main jump-off centres for (respectively) Kashmir, Darjeeling and Nepal. At the time of writing, continuing political unrest makes Kashmir an unsafe destination, but the cool mountain resorts of the north are where the bulk of travellers relax between April and June. Then come the monsoons, and it's only in the autumn, from October onwards, that tourists re-appear in any force, usually to take in the clear mountain views and the beautiful plants and foliage that blossom in the wake of the rains.

As a general guide, **Delhi** and **Rajasthan** (along with the cities of the northern plains) are most pleasant from late September until late March, very hot during April and May, and very wet from mid-June. **Bombay** and **Goa** are best from November to February, thereafter hot and humid until the monsoons break in early June. **South India** is coolest from November to April, and receive the rains as early as late May.

Most foreign tourists visit India in season, to enjoy the best weather and facilities. A cunning minority go off season—usually a week or two before everybody else—to take advantage of the 30–50% accommodation discounts offered by many hotels. Travelling off season also means fewer crowds, more seats on buses, and no long queues for train tickets.

Don't travel north during May and June. In early May, Indian schools break up. This is the cue for a mass exodus of home tourists to Darjeeling and Shimla—and practically everywhere else that qualifies as a holiday or honeymoon resort. Secondly, try to avoid Bombay, Calcutta, or Delhi during March. All three centres are packed with travellers then, and accommodation can be very difficult.

Communications

Post offices provide a good, reliable service, and are generally open from 10am to 5pm on weekdays; until noon on Saturday. The cost of postage for letters sent within India is currently Rs1, and for international mail the cost is Rs12 for a letter, Rs6.50 for an aerogramme, and Rs6 for a postcard. Mail sent to Europe, North America, Australia or New Zealand usually takes 10 to 14 days to reach its destination. Most of the larger post offices now offer a Speed Post service which links over 60 towns in India and delivers to most countries worldwide. For sending documents, this service is a bit slower than a private courier company, but costs about half as much. For example, a speed posted letter sent from India will reach the UK in 4 to 5 days and cost Rs400. Private courier companies such as Blue Dart (the Indian company linked up with Federal Express) can deliver a letter in 2 to 3 days, but it will cost you Rs900.

A word of warning: one or two postal staff have been known to remove unfranked (uncancelled) stamps from letters and postcards, which then go precisely nowhere. Either have your mail franked before your eyes in a post office, or (better) buy a stack of pre-stamped aerogrammes, which can't be interfered with.

Postes restantes are usually located in main post offices. These provide a good service, and your expected mail is nearly always waiting for you when you call. If it isn't, check not only under the initial of your surname, but under that of your christian name (misfiling is common). When collecting mail from a *poste restante*, you'll need some proof of identity (e.g. a passport) to claim it. If you don't claim it within a month, it's often returned to the sender. Have all letters and cards addressed to you in the following manner: Bloggs, J, *Poste Restante*, Bangalore 560001, India.

If you want your mail from home to be redirected to a different *poste restante* than the one you originally specified, visit the old post office and fill out an instruction slip forwarding the mail to the new location. This procedure takes just a minute and will save your having to write home to tell people you've moved.

Posting parcels home can be difficult. If possible, get someone to do it for you at a postal packing service. Otherwise, allow a whole morning to: a) take the parcel to a local tailor, and ask him to stitch a linen bag for it, with the seams sealed with wax. This service is sometimes also available from people sitting outside major post offices in big cities, and will cost around Rs50; b) fill out two customs declarations forms at a post office, stick one to the parcel with glue, write your passport number and 'bona fide tourist' somewhere on the forms, describe the parcel contents as a 'gift', and its value as not more than Rs1000 (to avoid more paperwork hassle); c) have the parcel weighed, and establish the cost (air mail is a lot more expensive than sea mail, but gets home in a few weeks as opposed to a few months); d) buy the appropriate stamps, and glue them on; e) give the package in to the parcel counter and ask for a receipt.

Books or printed matter can be sent by bookpost at greatly reduced rates. These packages can't be sealed because their contents need to be inspected later on, so simply wrap the package in brown paper and tie it with some string.

Don't count on any parcels sent from home making it to you, especially if they have interesting contents like cassette tapes.

Telephones tend to be rather unreliable; the quality of the line often depends on the weather. The system is improving but many exchanges are overloaded and this leads to numerous problems. With local calls, you'll either get through immediately or not at all. If you don't get straight through to someone it may be quicker to hail a rickshaw and visit them personally. Luckily, long-distance calls are less of a problem.

For **long-distance/local calls** you can use any number of STD/ISD offices. These are private concerns that offer international or interstate calls at government authorized rates. International calls cost around Rs80 per minute peak-time, with interstate rates varying depending on distance and the time of day (rates are cheap at night). Some STDs are high-tech communications centres, complete with fax machines, whereas others consist merely of a booth in a xerox shop, or perhaps a phone on a shelf at a roadside food stall. It's easy to spot these centres by their large posted signs reading STD/ISD. Making calls at STDs is easy and efficient; a digital readout let's you know how much cash you owe the shop-keeper. One drawback of the service is that you often have to make your call in the midst of a room full of people, which makes for lots of noise and little privacy. If you look around, however, you can often find a quieter shop with a private calling booth.

Fax services are available in most of the larger cities. You can usually send a fax at a luxury hotel, though their rates are often exorbitant, or at the better STDs for about Rs150 per page. Faxes can also be sent at the government's local Central Telegraph Offices. With private companies, you have to pay for faxes that don't transmit properly. At the government offices, rates are cheaper to begin with (about Rs100), and the clerk will often try several times to get your fax through, without recharging you each time.

Telex messages can be sent from luxury hotels (again subject to a hefty service charge) or from main post offices, which are relatively cheap. The advantage of the telex is that it gives you a record of any hotel bookings or airline confirmations made—a wise precaution in a country notorious for double-booking suites and seats.

A few 24-hour communications centres with both phone and fax services, are run by VSN Ltd. In Bombay the centre is located at Mahatma Gandhi Road, ☎ 204 2728; in Madras at Swami Sivananda Salai, ☎ 56 6740.

Cows

In this country cows get a very good deal. They are sacred to Hindus, who paint their fore-heads with *bindi* spots, adorn their horns with sweet-smelling jasmine, tie little bells around their feet and let them wander wherever they please.

These animals are the unofficial rubbish collectors of India. They eat anything from news-papers to oil-soaked doormats. They are particularly fond of cardboard boxes. Because they are so numerous, and because they like wandering the streets, they constitute a major traffic hazard. Drivers have been known to plunge a whole busload of people off a cliff rather than hit a cow. One driver who did hit a cow was stoned to death by his passengers.

Indian myths and legends abound with cows. The cow draws its mythical and religious sanctity from the multitude of nourishing products that can be drawn from its body. Being largely a vegetarian country, India relies on the cow for the proteins in its milk, on its dung for fuel or fertilizer, and on its strength for ploughing the farmers' fields. Cows extend their influence to every aspect of Indian life, and very few of them end up as steaks.

Dhobi

India doesn't have launderettes, but it does have dhobi. These magicians spirit away your dirty clothes first thing in the morning and return them, sparklingly clean and immacu-lately pressed, the very next day. The cost is rarely more than a few rupees per item and, because every hotel has one, or can send out to one, you could get away with just one change of clothing throughout your whole stay in India—if you had to.

Your dhobi will take your clothes down to a dhobi ghat, a public washing area, where he will pound them mercilessly with a big stick, or flog them viciously against a washing stone. Not a speck of dirt survives this kind of treatment. In time, neither do your buttons, so bring some extras. Once washed, the clothes are hung out to dry in the sun, along with miles of other wet togs. Then they go to the ironing sheds to receive knife-edge creases from conscientious ironers. Finally, and this is the miracle, they are picked out from thousands of other garments and returned to your room, looking as good as new.

Disabled Travellers

India is not a country which is easy to travel around if you have limited mobility, although (or more probably because) so many of her own population are disabled. Airlines and some major hotels are often helpful, but you can never rely on special facilities being available. For example, wheelchair ramps do not exist and access to bathrooms, restaurants and even hotel bedrooms is often impossible for those who cannot use stairs or pass through narrow doorways and passages. It may be possible to overcome these problems with the help of a companion.

The following organizations will be able to help you:

in the UK

RADAR (The Royal Association for Disability and Rehabilitation), 12 City Forum, 250 City Road, London EC1V 8AF, ✆ (0171) 250 3222, has a wide range of travel information.

in the USA

SATH (Society for the Advancement of Travel for the Handicapped), 347 5th Avenue, New York, NY10016, ✆ (212) 447 7284, offers advice on all aspects of travel for the disabled.

Electricity

The electric current used in India is 220 volts AC, 50Hz. Sockets have two large round-pin holes, so bring an adaptor. Current failures and power cuts are common all over the continent, so it's a good idea to bring candles or a torch in case of blackouts.

Embassies and Consulates

If you find yourself in serious trouble, contact the Consular Section of your embassy or high commission in New Delhi. Many countries also have consulates or deputy high commissions in Bombay, Calcutta and Madras. These are listed in the respective city sections.

For visa applications in your home country, *see* 'Entry Formalities', p.6.

Festivals and Public Holidays

The Indian calendar is an ongoing procession of thousands of annual festivals. Nearly everywhere you go, some sort of temple celebration, religious pageant or colourful arts festival will have just started or ended. They are always worth going out of your way for, being highly spectacular and great fun. All Indian festivals have a strong cultural, artistic and religious flavour, and the major ones attract some of the best exponents of music, dance and theatre in the country.

There are no fixed dates for many of these festivals. Their timing is determined by the Indian lunar calendar, and is calculable only during the previous year. Around October, your nearest Government of India tourist office should have the full list of festivals and dates for the forthcoming year. There are, however, a few national holidays when shops, banks and government offices are closed, notably **Republic Day** on 26 January, **Independence Day** on 15 August and **Mahatma Gandhi's birthday** on 2 October.

Some major religious rites and rituals, like **Dussehra** and **Diwali**, are celebrated in differing regional forms all over India. Other celebrations, like the popular **International Film Festival**, are held in different locations (best in Delhi) in alternate years (1993, 1995, etc.).

A new series of festivals has been started by the state government tourist departments to promote tourism. They are organized at well-known historical sites (Konarak, Khajuraho, Elephanta near Bombay, and Mahabalipuram near Madras) and usually consists of evening dance recitals over a few consecutive days. Eminent exponents of the many indigenous dance forms are invited to perform, among others, *Bharatnatyam* from south India, *Kathak* from northern India, *Odissi* from Orissa, *Kuchipudi* from Andhra Pradesh and *Kathakali* from Kerala. These festivals provide an excellent opportunity to see a major historical site and high-quality dance performances at the same time.

The more interesting and worthwhile festivals and fairs are listed below. You'll find more details in the relevant route sections in this book.

mid-Jan	**Pongal (Sankranti)**. A 3-day harvest festival, best seen in Tamil Nadu and Karnataka (south India). Lively processions, bullfights, and much decorating of sacred cows. *Pongal* is a sweet rice preparation prepared from freshly harvested rice.
17–20 Jan	**The Great Elephant March**, Kerala. Elephant rides, dances and boat races celebrate Kerala's rich heritage.
26 Jan	**Republic Day**. Important national festival celebrated all over the country, notably in New Delhi. On 27 and 28 January, a big folk-dance festival takes place in Delhi. On 29 January, the famous 'Beating the Retreat' ceremony takes place below the magnificent Secretariat buildings.
Jan/Feb	**Vasant Panchami**. All across India, especially in the north (marks first day of spring), and in West Bengal, where the celebrations are public and include colourful kite-flying. This Hindu festival is held in honour of Saraswati, goddess of learning.
Jan/Feb	**Desert Festival**. With the magnificent Jaisalmer Fort as the background, this festival gives an opportunity to listen to the music of the desert, to see local craftsmen at work and to watch dance performances.
Jan/Feb	**Float Festival**, Madurai. Commemorates the birth of Tirumalai Nayak, the city's 17th-century ruler.

Feb	**Carnival.** Held in Goa, this non-religious celebration is similar to Mardi Gras, complete with feasting, drinking and costumed revellers dancing in the street.
Feb/March	**Shivratri.** All over India, especially at important Shiva sites like Khajuraho and Varanasi. Devotees perform 11 nights of vigil and fasting, then enjoy a 'break fast' of fruits, nuts, sweet potatoes and rice.
Feb/March	**Holi.** This is the big one. Throughout northern India (best in Mathura and Rajasthan), everybody pelts everyone else with coloured water and powder. It's their way of celebrating the advent of spring.
early March	**Khajuraho Dance Festival.** An unmissable display of performing arts at Khajuraho in authentic temple surroundings.
mid-March	**Id-ul-Fitr.** The end of Ramadan, the Muslim month of fasting, is marked by much feasting and rejoicing.
March/April	**Gangaur.** In Rajasthan (especially Udaipur and Jaipur), West Bengal and Orissa. The festival honours Parvati and is named after a mythical embodiment of wifely devotion called Gangaur. Therefore, it is the culmination of marriage ceremonies (very colourful) in these parts.
mid-April	**Ramnavami.** Lord Rama's birthday is commemorated by the reciting of the epic *Ramayana* in homes and temples throughout India.
April/May	**Spring Festival and Baisakhi.** Two celebrations with a horticultural theme, best seen in Punjab. The latter marks the Hindu solar New Year.
April/May	**Meenakshi Kalyanam**, Madurai. Spectacular annual solemnization of Meenakshi's marriage to Shiva, held at the end of a 10-day non-stop festival in and around the famous Meenakshi temple. Excellent music.
May/June	**Buddha Purnima.** Commemorates the date of Buddha's birth, death and enlightenment. Best at Sarnath and Bodhgaya.
June/July	**Rath Yatra.** Held at Puri, this is the temple festival to beat them all. Three gigantic temple chariots, containing the deities Jagannath, Balabhadra (his brother) and Subhadra (his sister), are dragged in awesome procession through a living sea of pilgrims. Unbelievable atmosphere.
mid-July	**Teej.** To welcome the monsoon, and particularly colourful in Rajasthan.
15 Aug	**Independence Day.** The anniversary of India's independence from Britain is observed all over India.
mid-Aug	**Onam.** The harvest festival of Kerala is marked by various cultural programmes and the decoration of homes with flowers and swings. Snake-boat races, featuring the 100-oared boats once used by warring princes, are a big attraction.
Aug/Sept	**Ganesh (Ganpati) Chaturthi.** The elephant-headed god of good luck, Ganesh, is fêted in many areas, but especially in Bombay where huge processions take clay images of the deity into the sea.

Sept/Oct	**Dussehra**. A 10-day festival of national importance, most colourful and entertaining in Mysore, Kulu and West Bengal (also in Delhi). At Ramnagar, across the river Ganges from Varanasi, a many-night-long theatrical performance called *Ram Lila* draws many visitors.
2 Oct	**Gandhi Jayanti**. A national holiday marking the birth of Mahatma Gandhi.
Oct/Nov	**Diwali**. The liveliest and noisiest of all Indian festivals, a night-long revel of firecrackers, illuminations and general pageantry. In some parts of the country, Diwali marks the start of the Hindu New Year. It's best seen in Delhi and the north.
Nov/Dec	**Pushkar Fair**. Annual cattle fair, held on the very edge of the desert. A real tourist favourite.
25 Dec	**Christmas Day**. Celebrated all over India with music and dance festivals, but best in Goa, Delhi and Bombay.
mid-Dec– early Jan	**Madras Dance and Arts Festival**. Held in Madras, and getting better every year.

Apart from official public holidays, there are a number of unofficial ones. The unofficial ones—which are never advertised and which always seem to coincide with your planned shopping trip or visit to the bank—take place for a variety of obscure reasons, ranging from the opening of an important temple to the death of a prominent politician. When I last visited, the whole of Goa shut down for a day to watch a cricket match between India and New Zealand.

Be warned: Indian festivals may be wonderful, exciting occasions most of the time, but some do go way over the top, and you would be well advised to check the festival diary before you travel. A common culprit is Holi, during which foreign tourists are a favourite target not only for the usual coloured powders, but also on occasion less pleasant things like paint, ink, axle grease and even car battery-acid. The place not to be when things go out of control is on the open streets, or in trains. Excited crowds are common, and can be frightening. At such times, police find it difficult to keep public order.

Food and Drink

Food in Indian restaurants tends to be fairly basic, though a number of excellent speciality restaurants have sprung up in the major cities over the past few years. As a rule, it's far better to eat Indian rather than western food—it's cheaper, tastier and more interesting. Go ahead and get your burger or pizza fix once in a while, but expect to pay for it and to be generally disappointed—-the quality is rarely as good as you'd get back home.

If you like your meat, the bowls of spicy vegetarian mush served up in roadside restaurants (*dhabas* or *bhojanalyas*) will hardly pass muster for food at all. Carnivores will find some relief in the north, where there is a wide variety of meat dishes (mainly in Muslim restaurants serving non-veg 'Mughlai' cuisine), but will shed pounds in the south, which is almost exclusively vegetarian.

Meat dishes can be good, but are often pricey. Recommended main courses are *biriani* (usually chicken/mutton cooked in spices, mixed in with saffron rice), meat-based curries like lamb *roganjosh* with tomatoes, *do-piaza* with onions, *vindaloo* (Goan pork speciality) with hotly spiced meat marinated in vinegar, and *korma* which contains only mild spices; also (in the north) *tandoori*, usually chicken deliciously marinated in herbs and spices, baked in a clay oven. *Biriani* and *tandoori* make a pleasant change from curries, as they are generally much milder. If you're a meat-eater on budget, you may have to make do with stringy mutton or emaciated chicken.

Indian vegetarian food is often safer and tastier than meat dishes. In fact, many travellers become dedicated vegetarian.s

Vegetarian dishes usually appear on a *thali*, a steel tray with a number of small *katori* bowls. These contain an assortment of vegetable or *dhal* (lentil) preparations—commonly potatoes, carrots, beans and cauliflower, plus a chutney of chillies, onions, tamarind, coconut and mint. Every tray should include a dish of *raita* or curd (yoghourt). Most people eat *thali* with their fingers, and use *papad* or *chapati* to mop up the drippy mush and carry it to their mouths. These breads come with the *thali*, and again, you get as much as you want.

Soups are very erratic in quality—you're generally safe with *sambhar*, a filling soup of vegetables and lentils spiced with tamarind; or with the very hot and savoury *rasam*, a popular southern consommé with a lentil base. But beware of ordering 'veg soup' in backwoods places; it can be nothing more than a bowl of green water, with a single cabbage leaf floating in it.

Seafood can be excellent, notably at Goa, in Kerala, near Mangalore and other coastal resorts, where lobster, prawn, crayfish, crab and shark are often served fresh off the beach.

Desserts or sweetmeats in India are very sweet. But nobody makes ice cream like they do in India. Major brands like Vadilal, Milkfood, Cadbury's and Gaylord do a wide, mouthwatering range of flavours—as good as anything you will find in the West. Worth trying are traditional Indian desserts like *gulub jamun*, a fried doughnut in syrup; *barfi*, a sweet coconut mixure; *jalebi*, small snail-shaped pancakes, dripping with syrup; and milk/curd-based sweetmeats like *rasgulla* and *sandesh*. If you're hard up for a sweet, you can always buy a chocolate bar, though the quality of the chocolate leaves much to be desired. The wonderful-looking cakes sold at every bakery are usually disappointingly dry and bland, with the notable exception of honey cake. The most popular Indian sweet is *chikki*. Similar to peanut brittle, but with a higher peanut-to-brittle ratio, this wonderful sweet can keep you going for days. *Chikki* varies, but it should be crisp and not stick to your teeth.

Fresh fruit is one of the best things about India. Mangos, pineapples, bananas (five or six different varieties), melons, coconuts and tangerines are widely available from markets and street vendors at very little cost. It's often a bad idea to buy fruit/veg cut into segments since they attract flies. Always buy complete fruits, and peel them yourself, or have the vendor cut open a new fruit for you. You'll soon get used to the luxury of never having to go more than a few paces to buy a piece of fruit. And the more fruit you eat the better (within reason), as your body seems to crave the vitamins after the strain of constantly moving about.

Breakfast, interestingly, is the main meal westerners have problems with in India. Unless you stay in big hotels where they serve continental, you'll often have to make do with greasy chilli-pepper omelettes, horribly sweet toast and jam, and even sweeter tea and coffee. Even if you are in a big hotel, one can only live so long on under-fried eggs, fatty bacon and soggy chips. Fortunately, a lot of luxury hotels are now offering good buffet breakfasts, which give you a wide choice of dishes, but my advice to anyone who likes to start their day with something savoury on their palate is to bring along some Vegemite, peanut butter or cheese—*anything* to jazz up your breakfast.

regional cuisine

The South

The base of almost every traditional southern meal is rice, rice, and then more rice. When you order food in a south Indian restaurant, you'll usually be given a huge portion of rice with various things to put on it—*sambhar*, mild, vegetable and lentil soup spiced with tamarind; *rasam*, a hot and savoury thin soup; a vegetable mixture of some sort, for instance green beans with coconut; and curd. You'll also be served *poori*, a small fried bread to help scoop up your rice. Most such 'meals' (thali) include unlimited portions, and you may have to put your hand firmly over your plate to refuse second or third helpings. You can also get a variety of prepared rice dishes such as *pulao*, made with tamarind and ground nuts, or chopped vegetables.

A bread that is particularly associated with the south is *dosa*, a thin, fried pancake made from rice and lentils. Filled with spicy potato and vegetable curry, it is called a *masala dosa*. When prepared with onions and hot chillies, it is called an *onion dosa*. Prepared as a thicker and chewier pancake, it is a *set dosa*. Made with fermented dough it becomes a *rava dosa*. A *dosa* will normally be served with a delicious coconut-based chutney and sometimes a spicy vegetable mixture as well. Try the different varieties to see which you like best. *Dosa* is incredibly cheap, around Rs10, and very filling.

Also famous in the south are *idli*, delicate and subtle-tasting mounds of sticky rice flour, served with *sambhar*. *Chaat* is the name given to a variety of spicy and savoury snacks served in the south which can be combined to make a wonderful meal. Look for *bhel puri*, a spicy, sweet and sour puffed rice mixture, *masala puri*, a green spicy sauce with peas, yoghourt, and bits of fried pastry, *pani puri*, fried round pastry shells filled with onions, tomatoes and coriander, or *sev dahi potato puri*, which is fried round pastry shells filled with potato and topped with a savoury sauce. Most *chaat* items only cost between Rs5 and Rs10, so just try anything on the menu that looks intriguing and see what appears! Most south Indian restaurants are vegetarian unless stated otherwise.

South Indian fare may be very simple, but is cheap and fast. It has been said that the Indians invented the concept of fast food. Their ability to feed a whole busload of people at a roadside stall in under 10 minutes is quite remarkable.

The North

North Indian food is more familiar to Westerners. Here you'll find the usual *nan* and *chapati* breads, curry dishes like *palak paneer* (cheese cubes in a spinach sauce), and *aloo gobi* (potatoes and cauliflower). There's also no shortage of burger, pizza and fried chicken places.

Northern Indian cuisine is characterized by a greater use of dried spices, which are not as violent on the palate as the green spices of the South. Combining green and dried spices for any particular dish, you have a *masala*. The hottest northern Indian variety (apart from *vindaloo*) is called *garam masala*, a mixture of cardamom, cinnamon, black pepper, cumin, cloves and coriander seeds, all freshly ground into a powder with a mortar and pestle. Indian curries (actually a British term, covering the full range of spiced Indian foods) are prepared from any combination of about 25 spices. The most widely used are cardamom (used a lot in Kashmiri tea, Indian sweets, and to flavour meat dishes); coriander (a cooling agent), garlic and ginger (digestive aids); and sometimes chillies, cinnamon, fenugreek, mace and cloves.

drinks

The most popular beverage by far in India is *chai* or tea. Brewed up on every street corner, for Rs1/2 a shot, it usually appears as a glass of strong, filmy, dark brown liquid. *Chai* is commonly made with boiled buffalo milk, and is loaded with sugar. You come to crave the stuff after a while, even if you take your tea black at home, because it gives you an undeniable energy boost. You can however order black tea (*kali chai*) at restaurants if desired. Some travellers give up on tea completely and switch to coffee. This is often very good in the south and is available from Indian coffee-houses in most towns and cities.

One of the best drinks to have when you're hot and thirsty is a tender coconut, widely available and full of cool, delicately flavoured milk. It costs about Rs5, and the flesh on the inside can also be eaten (the vendor will usually split it in half for you, and give you a sliver of the husk with which to scoop out the flesh). Indian doctors swear by coconuts as a general health aid, especially for stomach problems.

Excellent fruit juices and curd-based *lassi* are widely available in India, as are a vast selection of carbonated bottled drinks. These go under names like Gold Spot (sickly-sweet orange), Citra, Limca, 7-Up or Teem (lemon), Campa Cola and Thums Up (cola). Pepsi and Coca Cola are also popular. To replace all the fluids you sweat out in the heat, however, your best bet is bottled mineral water, sold at many street kiosks and restaurants (Rs10–15). Just make sure the seal on the bottle is intact.

Alcoholic drinks can be relatively expensive, and imported liquor is only available at luxury hotels for outrageous prices. Indian brands are generally of a low quality, but are acceptable. Beer is widely available, a large bottle of chilled, gassy, lager selling for around Rs30, though in Goa and a few other states the price is lower. Popular brand names include Golden Eagle, Black Label and Kingfisher. In centres like Delhi, Bangalore and Bombay, you can enjoy a glass of draught beer.

Indians are very much into whisky, which sells in 'wine' shops (a real misnomer since few of them sell wine). It's very raw and hasn't got much of a bouquet, but at around Rs80 per half-bottle it's very cheap. Only a few places (Goa, Bangalore, Delhi, Bombay) actually sell wine, and it can be expensive. Indian rum is generally good, as is locally made gin and vodka. In Goa you can find coconut or cashew nut *feni,* which at Rs5–10 a shot is laughably cheap. For best results, try mixing coconut *feni* with Teem or Limca.

At present, the only two 'dry' states are Gujarat (except Daman and Diu) and Andhra Pradesh. Here, you can drink at big hotels only, and buy an alcohol licence at reception.

Eating Out

At a high-class restaurant, especially in the big international hotels, you can expect to pay anything between Rs250 and Rs800 for a meal—including a beer or glass of wine. Smart hotel restaurants also levy a 10% sales tax, but the food is rarely worth it. Most towns/cities now have mid-priced restaurants aimed at tourists and middle-class Indians which are far better value.

Etiquette in basic eating houses, especially in the south, requires that you eat with your fingers. This looks strange at first, especially since soupy rice forms the base of most meals, but Indians swear that the food tastes better this way and that spices can't be mixed properly into rice with a utensil. Waiters will usually give you a spoon if you insist, but try eating with your hands a few times. Where else will you get the opportunity to do so in public? Most Indians eat with their right hand only (the left is used for something else), though most foreigners are forgiven for eating ambidextrously! Learning how to tear a *poori* (a fried bread) with one hand is a major step forward.

Indian menus are famous for murdering the English language. Items like 'Sour and Acrid', 'Scream Bled Eggs' and 'Lemon Sod' will keep you entertained while you are waiting for your food.

Restaurant bills normally come on a dish of caraway seeds, or a wad of *pan* (a mixture of spices, lime paste, and mildly addictive areca nut wrapped in a betel leaf), both popular aids to digestion.

Health and Insurance

Not essential, but certainly advisable, are a course of vaccinations and a supply of malaria tablets for India. While sanitation and hygiene in India remain at their current levels, it's wise to take every possible precaution against ill health.

See also 'Packing', p.45.

Jabs and Tabs

You'll need jabs for typhoid, tetanus, polio and hepatitis, and meningitis.

In the UK, either see your GP (cheapest) or contact a local vaccinating centre. London has several quick and efficient drop-in centres: **West London Vaccinating Centre** at 53 Great Cumberland Place, W1H 7LH, © (0171) 262 6456, open 9am–4.45pm; the **London Hospital for Tropical Diseases**, 4 St Pancras Way, NW1 0PE, © (0171) 530 3429, open 9am–5pm, appointments only; **Trailfinders**, 194 Kensington High Street, W8 7RG, © (0171) 938 3999, open weekdays 9am–5pm, Thursday 9am–6pm, Saturday 9.30am–4pm; **British Airways Travel Clinic**, 178 Tottenham Court Road, © (0171)

637 9899, open daily 10am–5pm, Saturday 10am–2pm. Expect to pay up to £60 for a full course of injections at a commercial travel clinic.

Vaccinations are best administered two weeks before departure. This gives them time to take full effect (typhoid immunity takes ten days to settle in properly), and allows you to get over any unpleasant side-effects before you travel. The commonly used vaccine against hepatitis A, gamma globulin, remains at peak strength for only a few weeks, so take it as close to departure as possible. If you are intending to stay in India for six months or longer, you might want to consider the newer, more expensive vaccine, which affords protection for up to a year. For frequent travellers, there is now a course which immunizes you for life. You can also get a rabies vaccination, although this must be done 3 months before you travel.

Start taking malaria tablets ten days before you leave for India. This gives you a chance to change them if the ones prescribed don't agree with you; it also allows your body to start building up some immunity before you arrive. It's important to keep taking them for six weeks after returning home. Equip yourself with a mosquito net for extra protection, and buy a good local repellent (like Odomos). This is available from most high street chemists, and is especially useful when the malarial strain of mosquitoes wake up around dusk.

Keeping Healthy

Eating sensibly, drinking bottled water, and getting enough sleep/rest are the keys to good health in India. All too many cases of illness and theft reported by travellers come back to exhaustion caused by living too cheaply for too long. And it's easy to do—the tendency to save money is infectious (even compulsive) in a country where poverty is the general rule.

If you get past the first few days, you've got a fair chance of avoiding India's most common bug—the common cold. Two best preventatives are a daily intake of Vitamin C tablets and a headscarf/hat to protect your head/neck from taxi draughts, breezy room fans, and constant to-ing and fro-ing between chilly a/c hotels/restrooms and hot, humid streets.

Other common ailments are diarrhoea, amoebic dysentery, giardiasis (drastic stomach upset) and hepatitis. The best prescription for **diarrhoea** and any stomach complaint is fasting, followed by a strict diet of black tea, boiled water, plain boiled rice, curd and bananas. This is a lot more effective than taking tablets, which simply block up the infection in your stomach. Oral rehydration salts are readily available from street chemists in many tourist centres:-they quickly replace lost minerals and salts.

If you have **giardiasis** ('fart-burps'), the best remedy is a course of the antibiotic Tinidazole. Your GP can give you a prescription for this, but don't use the tablets for anything else—you could end up with another infection.

Amoebic dysentery is probably the worst thing you can expect. It's the same as diarrhoea, with the added attractions of fever plus blood/pus in the stool. Indian doctors may be able to provide temporary relief by prescribing a course of Flagyl, but you're best going straight home and getting proper treatment. The longer you leave hepatitis and amoebic dysentery, the more difficult they are to cure. The same is true of **malaria**, which can lie dormant for a long time.

Rabies, caused by bites or scratches from 'friendly' stray dogs and temple monkeys, should be dealt with on the spot. If the animal draws blood, go straight to the nearest Indian hospital (better than a doctor) and take a full course of rabies injections. You'll have to stay in one place for 14 days to have them administered, however. The only alternative is to buy the whole course of vaccine (about Rs50) plus sterilized needles from a street chemist, and to administer them yourself. If travelling about, this raises one big problem: the vaccine must be kept at a constant temperature of between 2° and 10°C (35° to 50°F), so you'll need fresh ice daily to keep it in. A new vaccine is available in the major cities, which involves a course of just three injections, but it is expensive. In the final analysis, the best preventive against rabies is to be aware (not paranoid) of animals, and to be especially careful in places like Pushkar, Jaisalmer and Kovalam beach.

Since most diseases are water-borne, never drink any water (even in restaurants) that has not been filtered, sterilised with water-purification tablets, or boiled for at least 10 minutes. Bottled water, such as 'Bisleri', is widely available at little cost—though you should always check that the wrapping on the cap is intact (there's a widespread racket in re-filling used bottles with tap water). If no fresh water is available, stick to hot tea or buy some oranges. When brushing your teeth, always use boiled or bottled water—and don't swallow water in showers. Strictly avoid ice cubes and always ask for a straw with aerated drinks or fruit juices—don't drink from the bottle. As for food, always peel your own fruit and vegetables and steer clear of raw vegetable salads, raw sugar-cane or iced cane-juice (a major cause of amoebic dysentery). Adjust slowly to Indian food. At the start of your journey, when the stomach is likely to be ultra-sensitive, stick to mild foods, such as boiled rice, yoghourt (*raita*), breads and boiled eggs. And try to eat three square meals a day. In hot, dry climates, like Rajasthan, the best way of quenching thirst is to drink deeply and seldom, not little and often. Yet many travellers go right off solid foods and live on a watery diet of fruit salads, curd, and loads of bottled drinks. The inevitable result is diarrhoea. To soak up all that excess liquid, eat some bread, cake, bananas or biscuits immediately.

When eating with your fingers, clean them first—most restaurants have a wash-hand basin. Better still, use moistened medicated tissues or orange-skin peelings. It is very difficult to keep clean in India, though the Indian people themselves are among the cleanest in the world.

If you do become ill, bear in mind that Indian doctors are generally excellent. The better hotels have their own doctor on call, while others can suggest a good local GP. Most main cities also have good hospitals and superior nursing facilities. This said, medical treatment abroad is expensive for those used to the European welfare state, and many hospitals are both overcrowded and understaffed.

Before leaving home, it's worth seeing a **dentist**. Ask for spare caps, plus glue kit, for any teeth presently capped. While dental treatment in the major cities is of a high standard and not expensive, facilities outside the major cities are often basic.

Contact-lens wearers should consider switching to specs for India, because of dust, heat and intense glare. **Spectacle wearers** should note down their prescription. Opticians in India are very cheap, lenses and frames costing only a fraction of their UK equivalent.

AIDS in India is much more prevalent than officially accepted. The problem is now wide-spread, not just confined to the 'red-light' areas of the major cities. Anyone seeking a working or student visa for more than one year must now take an AIDS test and submit a copy of the certificate verifying a negative result along with the visa application.

Travel and Medical Insurance

You don't have to believe everything you hear about theft and illness in India, but you can't afford to ignore it either. Good travel insurance is essential for your peace of mind, and has saved many travellers heartache. Take great care when choosing your policy, and always read the small print. A good travel insurance should give full cover for your posses-sions and health. In case of illness, it should provide for all medical costs, hospital benefits, permanent disabilities and the flight home. In case of theft or loss, it should recompense you for lost luggage, money and valuables, also for travel delay and personal liability. Most important (and this could be a life-saver), it should provide you with a 24-hour contact number in the event of medical emergency.

If your own bank or insurance company can't help you (they usually can), then try the comprehensive schemes offered by **Trailfinders**, ✆ (0171) 938 3939, **Jardine's**, ✆ (0161) 228 3742, or **American Express**, ✆ (01444) 239900. Travel companies often include insurance in the cost of a luxury tour but this is not always adequate. Once you've got a policy, take a copy of it to India with you. Most important, have a separate note of the 24-hour emergency number and keep it on you at all times.

Should anything be stolen, keep a copy of the police report or FIR (First Information Report). You may need this to put in a claim.

Hippies

They used to be called hippies; now they're called new-age travellers. You'll find them at the beach resorts of Goa and Kovalam, the hill stations of Kodai and Dharamsala, the pilgrimage centres of Varanasi and Pushkar, and the mountain valley resort of Manali. In these places, Bob Dylan, the Doors, Hendrix, Jefferson Airplane and Cream rise eerily from the grave and sing once again. Bright, patterned clothes, headbands and joss sticks, baubles, bangles and beads are all back in style. Beach parties, skinny dipping, living in trees, and mystic encounters with gurus and sadhus are still the rage. It's a tremendous nostalgia trip if you've done it before, and a real buzz if you missed it the first time around.

It was the hippies who first opened up India to foreign tourism in the '60s. They found all the best beaches, settled in the most atmospheric holy spots and established communities in remote hill and desert areas. Indians nowadays regard them with some distaste, and the government, in a serious attempt to attract a more respectable class of foreign tourist, is now enforcing two laws. The first requires all hotels in India to register their guests, making it very difficult for foreigners to remain anonymous and to outstay their welcome in the country. The second enforces stringent penalties against the smoking of, or posses-sion of, dope. If anyone is caught, they go straight to jail. In the main tourist areas, it is not uncommon to be spot-searched by police if you look the part. Apart from places like Goa, where the police are allegedly open to bribery, the penalty for being caught with drugs is long-term imprisonment, plus a hefty fine.

Insects and Crawlies

If you don't like insects, don't go to India during the monsoons. From June to September, the rains bring to the surface all manner of creatures in search of moisture. The problem is worse in the damp, humid south than in the dry, dusty north.

Vermin and rodents proliferate in the big cities, where they have abundant litter and refuse to feed on. Flies are an intrinsic part of India, buzzing round your face, going up your nose and sitting hopefully on restaurant tables. In the evenings, there are fewer flies and more mosquitoes. Local repellents keep mozzies at bay for a while, but they always get you in the end.

Basic budget lodgings are notorious for ants, bedbugs, cockroaches, rats and practically anything else that buzzes or scurries around in the dead of night. If you don't want to be a sleeping lunch for these creatures, *never* leave food and drinks (especially sweet stuff) lying around. It brings them all running.

Another species of persistent room-guest, found mainly in the south, is the small lizard called the gecko. These are quite harmless and spend most of their time plastered to walls and ceilings, sound asleep. The only time they wake up is to eat flies and mosquitoes, which is a good thing. If they disturb you, guide them out of the window with a bright torch-beam.

To prevent too many insects coming into your room, make sure all windows are closed from half an hour before sunset until an hour after sunset. Mosquitoes are also very active at first light, so if you haven't got a net to protect you, keep your room fan on overnight.

Loos

Old habits die hard, and many Indians still prefer squatting in the street to sitting on a bowl. Public urinals are only for men and are often overflowing due to lack of maintenance. Signs announcing 'Please do not commit Urine!' are largely ignored, and while western-style loos are fairly common at the better hotels and restaurants, squat toilets are still the norm in budget lodges and cafés. Toilet paper is a rare find in public toilets but is generally available at local stores.

On the open road, there are conveniences at most bus and rail stations, but to say they are basic would be a compliment. Women travellers certainly can't use them, and it is a common complaint that, outside the big cities, toilet facilities for women just don't exist. The problem is always worst on long bus journeys, where the one or two stops made are at ill-equipped *chai* places with no toilet at all, just a public urinal wall for the men. Women use an open field, behind a ditch.

The Indian rupee (Rs) divides into 100 paise (p). There are coins of 5, 10, 20, 25 and 50 paise, Rs1, 2 and 5. Notes are Rs2, 5, 10, 20, 50, 100 and 500. The approximate exchange rates at the time of writing are:

A$1 = Rs23
C$1 = Rs23
DM1 = Rs22.50
FFr1 = Rs6.40
Jap ¥100 = Rs37
NZ$1 = Rs21
UK£1 = Rs54
US1 = Rs34

Visitors are normally asked to declare the amount of foreign currency in their possession upon arrival in India. Those having more than US$10,000 in the form of travellers' cheques or bank-notes are required to obtain a **Currency Declaration Form** before leaving Customs. This will ensure that you can reconvert any excess rupees upon departure. You will also need **encashment certificates** for the reconversion (*see* below).

Since you can't bring Indian currency into the country (or take it out again) you'll have to buy your rupees after arrival, ostensibly at **banks** or official money-changers. Indian banks can however be exceedingly slow. There is a **black market** for foreign currency, and you are likely to be approached by various unofficial money-changers during your trip. However, since the rupee is now a fully convertible currency, there's only about 5% difference between the black rate offered and the official bank rate. Changing money on the streets may be far quicker than banks, but is still illegal and risky.

Whatever you do, don't get stuck with worn or torn notes—the only place you'll get rid of them are banks: Indians always refuse them, too.. Whoever changes your money (even hotels) should give you an **encashment certificate**—you'll need these if you want to re-exchange excess rupees for home currency when you leave the country.

If you stay in India for 180 days or more, you're supposed to obtain an **income tax clearance certificate**, for which encashment certificates are also required. This clearance is needed to show that you have been living off your own money (i.e. not working illegally) during your stay in India. The Foreign Section of the Income Tax Offices in Delhi, Calcutta, Bombay and Madras issue these certificates on sight of passport, airline ticket, visa and encashment certificates. You are then supposed to show this document to officials at the airport when you leave the country. Hardly anyone asks for it though.

Transferring money is best done through a foreign bank or Thomas Cook/American Express in one of the main cities—Indian banks can be slow and unreliable.

Travellers' cheques and **currency** should be ordered from your bank or travel agency at least 7 days before departure. Trailfinders (*see* p.3), and Thomas Cook can process them in a couple of days, but they take only cash, not cheques. When ordering your currency for

India, aim for a 50/50 split between cash and travellers' cheques. This kind of balance is best, because some Indian banks only change cash, and travellers' cheques can be refunded if lost or stolen. Visa travellers' cheques are the best bet—many Indian centres are now suspicious of American Express (too many travellers reporting them lost, getting a new set, and fobbing them off on Indian shops/hotels). It is a common misconception, that if you have travellers' cheques and lose them, they will be refunded immediately—some banks only refund them when you return home (useless), while others don't offer any refunding facilities at all. **Thomas Cook** is the best option, with solid refunding agents in most major tourist spots. If you order cheques from a bank, choose one whose insurer gives you (in writing) the addresses of the refunding agents in India. Sign your travellers' cheques immediately on receipt. Then take a separate note of the cheque numbers, to facilitate their refund in the event of theft.

Budgeting Your Trip

Though prices have risen in India, your money is still worth the same as it was 25 years ago. In 1970, the exchange rate was 7.5 rupees to the US dollar—now, it's 34 rupees. So while hotels may charge 4 times as many rupees as they did then, you still pay the same amount of dollars. And, as a general rule of thumb, your foreign cash buys around ten times as much here as it would in England or the States.

How much money you take with you is up to you, but don't leave yourself short. To be on the safe side, bring all your credit cards. Most large hotels, restaurants, shops (and Indian Airlines) accept them, and the bills don't get home to you for ages. Some of the grander Indian hotels seem almost disappointed when you decide to pay cash.

A month spent in India can cost anything between Rs12,000 (on a shoestring) and Rs150,000 (all the luxury trimmings), exclusive of any shopping purchases. Travelling in mid-range comfort, budget for around Rs30,000 a month. This includes eating and sleeping at good, moderate restaurants and hotels, travelling 2nd class by rail and bus, and all in-town taxi/rickshaw/bus transport. Make extra allowances for the inevitable shopping expeditions. For 'irresistible' bargains, carry a couple of personal credit cards. In India the American Express card justifies its additional expense by enabling you to raise cash readily from Amex offices, getting you into hotels if you've just lost all your money, and letting you use their mail-receiving facilities.

Running Out of Money

This is another good reason to bring credit cards, as getting money wired over through the banks is slow and painful. It's not completely unknown for banks to keep the money in their system for up to three weeks before admitting that it has arrived. A good travel agent may advance you money if you put up your passport as security—but only if they know you. Always keep US$100 cash stashed away somewhere safe in the event of losing the bulk of your money. If you find yourself really destitute, head for the nearest *gurdwara* or Sikh temple. These have a law of hospitality similar to some Christian monasteries, and you will be fed and sheltered until rescue arrives.

Opening Hours and Admission Times

Most **government organizations** and **private businesses** are open weekdays, from 9.30 am to 5.30pm. Some state government offices are open on Saturdays, but often take the second Saturday of the month as a holiday. All offices are closed on Sundays.

Most **airline offices** are open daily except Sundays, also from 9.30am to 5.30pm; the four major international airports are open 24 hours. **Banking hours** are generally 10am–2pm weekdays, until noon only on Saturdays.

Opening hours at **post offices** are uually 10am–4pm, Monday to Saturday; in the major cities one branch will stay open 24 hours. **Shops** are normally open 10am–8pm (except Sundays), though some shopkeepers (especially in places like Pune or Goa) take a siesta.

Packing

Clothes

Cool, clean cotton garments which cover the chest, back and legs are the most acceptable wear in India. They are also extremely comfortable, and very cheap to buy inside the country. The few clothes you'll need to bring with you should be durable, comfortable and above all practical. A lightweight zipper **jacket**, with large, deep front pockets to accommodate passport and documents while in transit, is indispensable. Take a couple of cotton **shirts**, again with large breast pockets if possible. These are practical wear when it gets too warm to wear the jacket. Two pairs of light, loose-fitting cotton **trousers** will be sufficient. They should have pockets secured by zips or velcro, and loops for a belt: you'll be amazed at how many inches drop off the waist and buttocks travelling in India). Jeans are bulky, hot (too tight-fitting) and not always practical.

A few **T-shirts** are a must. They take up little room, make a quick change of shirt, and can double as substitute pillow-cases in grubby backpacker lodges or on overnight trains or buses.

Take a pair of light casual **shoes** or trainers—sandals and flip-flops you can buy out there. Women need a pair of decent shoes for evening wear. Feet tend to swell in hot climates, so choose a pair with wide fittings.

On beaches, men can usually get away with a pair of **trunks** or shorts; women should wear a one-piece suit, or be prepared to attract attention.

Some **warm clothing** may be necessary—a single medium-thickness sweater covers most occasions, including draughty train journeys, cool desert evenings, chilly hill stations, or (a big consideration) padding for bone-hard bus and train seats.

Consider taking a **hat** to protect the head, neck and face from the sun. The wide-brimmed floppy cotton variety, with a string cord, is most suitable. In the south, a practical alternative is a ladies' **umbrella**, though you can buy these just as easily out there. A decent pair of **sunglasses** is a good idea.

Indians go a lot by appearances, and it's very much a case of you are what you wear. This does not mean you have to dress ultra-chic or smart, simply that you should wear sensible, comfortable clothes and dress with a view to what is acceptable and appropriate in the circumstances.

Indian people do not smile upon hippy clothes (ragged old jeans, dirty old shirts, beads and headbands) and consider short skirts, sleeveless/backless shirts (from the male perspective) a big come-on. Long hair and drug-taking aren't likely to win you any medals either. You may get away with skimpy Western-style dress in tourist centres and some of the big cities, but in most of the country, old customs die hard and you may cause a lot of offence if you're not properly covered. When visiting a temple, or mosque, it is important to be sensitive to the feelings of worshippers and dress accordingly. Women should avoid baring their shoulders and arms, or wearing skirts that are too short. In Sikh *gurdwaras*, it is important for both men and women to cover their head—a clean handkerchief will usually do.

Equipment

If you're heading out to desert regions, a large 2-litre water-bottle is a good investment. The 'thermal' model is the best because it keeps water fresh and cool, even in the most torrid external temperatures.

For personal security, you'll need either a **money-belt** or a zipped document-holder. A body-belt can be bulky, uncomfortable to wear, and surprisingly vulnerable to theft. You're better off with a cotton neck-purse (from a camping shop), or buy a transparent document holder with zip (from stationery shops), and then sew an elasticated armband onto it. The pouch should be large enough to hold your passport, plane tickets, credit cards, currency and travellers' cheques, and should fit snugly out of sight round the upper arm. Nobody should underestimate the skill and enterprise of pickpockets. For your own peace of mind, carry your vital documents on your person at all times. If staying in budget lodges, get into the habit of sleeping with your security pouch nestling in the safe embrace of your armpit.

A strong **combination padlock** is another essential. Its mere presence deflects potential thieves from your luggage, and you can use it to bolt bags or rucksacks to train bunks, to bus seats or to hotel-room furniture. Padlocks also give added security when fixed to the doors of cheaper lodges which either have poor locks, or no locks at all. If taking small ordinary locks for securing rucksack pockets, take two sets of keys.

A small powerful **flashlight**, together with spare bulb and a stock of batteries, is a worthwhile investment. In desert or village areas, there is often no electricity at night. And few places in India are exempt from power-cuts. A useful back-up to a flashlight is one of the squat 'everlasting' candles sold in many camping shops. Voltage in India is 220 (occasionally 230), and if you take a **travelling iron**, an **electric shaver**, or **hairdryer**, you'll need the appropriate **adaptor**.

Other useful inclusions are a **universal plug** for baths/basins in basic lodges, a small **penknife** for peeling fruit, a small **alarm watch** (for catching elusive early-morning trains and buses), a box of waxed **earplugs** (to double the chance of a good night's sleep), some **writing materials** (many travellers become prolific diarists), and a **sewing kit**, with scissors, buttons, thread, zips and needles.

If you're off to the beaches, a **face-mask** and a **snorkel** could come in handy. Don't take your heavy hiking boots for hiking/trekking—India manufactures excellent light canvas **jungle boots** with firm rubber grips and ankle support. These are called 'duckbacks' and sell for about Rs150–250 in the hill stations (you might not find them in lowland cities).

Medical Kit

Apart from regular toiletries, this should include **sterile gauze pads** (better than band-aids), a good **moisturizing cream**, a high-potency **sunblock**, some flat packs of **men's tissues** (toilet rolls are too bulky) and a good supply of **multi-vitamin tablets** (important in a country where one's diet tends to suffer). Medical wipes are useful for keeping hands and equipment clean when washing facilities are not available.

Other useful inclusions are **water-purification tablets** (to sterilize drinking water); a small bottle of **antiseptic liquid** (for throat or mouth infections), and zinc-based ointment for fungal infections, including below-the-belt 'dhobi' itch.

There is no medical cure for diarrhoea, though your doctor should be able to prescribe something for short-term relief. Sunstroke, vomiting and dysentery are all common causes of dehydration and loss of body salts. The best antidote is **Dioralyte rehydrate powder**, which is readily available in India.

Take a good **mosquito repellent** such as Jungle Formula for protection in the daytime; the Indian-brand Odomos is, however, better. Treat bites with a soothing **antihistamine cream**, sold by most UK/US chemists. A **mosquito net** is a definite consideration—it folds up small and guarantees an undisturbed night's sleep. Shake out well before retiring each night—mosquitoes have an uncanny knack of climbing into bed with you, either buried in the net or in trouser cuffs.

Finally, take an additional supply of **contraceptive** and **malaria tablets**. It's easy to run short after bouts of sickness and vomiting.

Personal Luxuries

A small pocket **cassette recorder** plus a selection of your five favourite tapes can help break the monotony of long bus/train journeys; a light-weight shortwave radio can provide a respite from Indian music, which is often loud, insistent and omnipresent. Most tourist centres now sell cheap bootleg tapes (and sometimes CDs) of Western music, even jazz and classical.

A pair of strong **binoculars** is recommended for those who enjoy wildlife or bird-spotting. Others, who fret in long queues (lots of these in India) or who like something to do on long, dull evenings (very few of these), take along a couple of **pocket-games** like chess, backgammon, pocket-scrabble or playing cards.

If heading up to cool damp areas like the hill stations, a **sleeping bag** may be a necessity. There are excellent lightweight (1kg) pure down bags available, which take up surprisingly little space. The place to sell them at a profit later on, if headed that way, is Nepal. Regular budget travellers to India opt instead for a sheet sleeping bag. This is a sewn double sheet, similar to those found in youth hostels, which you can either make yourself or buy in

Bombay or other main centres. It is useful for basic lodges with dirty bedding or for overnight train journeys. It is also much cooler than a regular sleeping bag, and takes up even less room in your luggage.

One luxury you should allow yourself is a small **inflatable pillow**. You can sleep anywhere with this, even on bumpy buses and trains. Seasoned travellers prefer a down-and-feather pillow, and spend the bulk of their stay in India sitting on it—bus, train, cinema and restaurant seats in this country being notoriously hard.

Photography

In India, every glance is a photograph, and you can count on using your camera a lot more than anticipated. Intense glare, hazy atmosphere, powerful light and deep shade however, all present the serious photographer with problems. Inevitably, the more sophisticated the camera you bring, the more difficult it is to line up a shot and to get a sharp result. Polarized filters improve your chances, but not by as much as you might expect. You should always take special care with photos taken in mountain or hill station regions—over-exposure is very common.

A light, fully-automatic 35mm camera has three distinct advantages over a big, expensive model—it's easier to carry, it's less prone to theft, and it catches 'instant' shots which would otherwise be missed. Photography at airports, military bases, railway stations, even of public notices, can cause problems and is in many cases prohibited. Most other things, with the exception of funeral pyres, inner temple sanctums and Muslim women in black purdah, are fair game. Indeed, most Indians love being photographed and are often disappointed when you run out of film.

Film is readily available everywhere, though do check the date. Most of it is surplus stock bought from returning tourists and resold to the incoming lot at inflated prices. Slide film is less easy to find, so bring a good stock from home.

Recreation

Indians are keen followers of sport (especially cricket), and many towns have facilities for tennis, squash, golf, riding and swimming. Elsewhere, there's an inexhaustible range of recreations: trekking, camel safaris, white-water rafting and game viewing, to name just a few. Discos and nightclubs are normally restricted to the 5-star hotels (big cities only), and only guests and invited members are allowed in. To become an 'invited guest', you'll need to make friends in high places.

Security

This is a very personal matter. Some travellers go completely overboard and clank their way into India loaded down with more padlocks, chains, zips and clips than Marley's ghost. Others take the opposite line, and lounge about in crowded bazaars with wads of money sticking out of every pocket. Both approaches attract the attention of every beggar and thief in town. Very few Indians are villains, but if you make a show of wealth, it's an invitation to trouble. Westerners can be rather insensitive to the poverty around them; whipping out a ripple of 100-rupee notes in search of small change for a rickshaw man will not only magnetize a whole street, but is an appalling demonstration of bad taste. It's far safer and kinder to keep a small amount of money sufficient for the day's needs in a small neck-purse separate from your main stash.

India is actually a very safe country indeed, and the local people will often go out of their way to help foreigners. This said, it is tempting providence to stroll off down dark back-streets at night or to sleep out alone on lonely beaches or in empty fields.

general security points

- On the streets, wear shoulder-bags across the body (impossible to snatch), and keep all money and valuables out of sight (never in unzipped pockets). Beware of being frisked by beggars pretending a friendly hug. Never give anyone your camera, radio or Walkman to 'look at'—you might not get it back again.

- On Indian trains, where robbery is rife, use your rucksack or bag as a pillow, or stash it under your knees, when you are sleeping. If going to the bathroom, bolt your bag to a fixed compartment attachment or to a window bar.

- On crowded local buses, keep a constant eye on your luggage. You may be asked to put your bags under a seat to make room for other passengers. Don't do it: one woman who did lost a £300 camera lens.

- In cheap lodges, double-lock the door with a combination padlock, and secure all windows before retiring for the night. Thieves are adept at creeping into unsecured hotel rooms.

- If leaving your luggage anywhere, for any reason, padlock it to a pipe, a bedstead, or anything that can't be moved. Some hotels will mind it for you (and have safety-deposit boxes for valuables), but always get a receipt, and always check nothing's missing on your return.

Your best security is yourself. Fear, anger or carelessness all attract theft; calmness, confidence and alertness deter it. If you become a victim, report your loss to the police by all means (you'll need their report for any insurance claim), but don't expect any sympathy. India is for the self-reliant—a quality that some travellers have to learn the hard way.

Shopping

India is one of the great markets of the world. Here you can find a remarkable range of fabulous produce—silk, cotton, leather, jewellery, carving and handicrafts—at low, low prices—provided you bargain. The quality of craftsmanship is often excellent, and even if what you want is not in stock, it can invariably be made up for you—either on the spot or sent on later. Tailors can run up clothes overnight, and since they can copy any design you provide to perfection, it's worth bringing along a favourite piece of clothing to duplicate. Bulky purchases, such as carpets and large ornaments, can be shipped home by the vendor. Expensive jewellery buys can be verified (if you're in Rajasthan) at the gem-testing laboratory in Jaipur. Large hotels have their own shopping emporia, packed with a wide variety of goods, where you can browse in air-conditioned comfort.

Always try to start your shopping tour with a visit to a government or state emporium. These stock the full range of local produce and handicrafts; also some goods from neighbouring states. All prices are fixed, so you can get a rough idea of what's available, and how much it should cost. This knowledge can be invaluable when it comes to buying things at less scrupulous places.

A good place to start is the huge Central Cottage Industries Emporia in Delhi, Bombay, Calcutta, Jaipur and Bangalore. Here you can do all your shopping in one place—great for people making last-minute purchases before flying back home. The best of the smaller state emporia are at Gujarat and Rajasthan, offering a wide choice of colourful and attractive handmade goods.

On the streets, you'll have to bargain hard for everything. There's an 'Indian' price and a 'tourist' price for everything, so never accept the first price given—it will always be too high. You can try the 'walk away' technique to reduce it, but many Indians have got wise to this, and you may end up walking away from something you really want, and never being called back. It is often far more effective to pretend interest in something you don't want, haggle over it a bit, pretend to lose interest, then pick up the article you *do* want as an afterthought. To make some sort of sale, the vendor will often give a half-decent price immediately. If he doesn't, some well-chosen Hindi phrases will always improve your chances of getting the local price *(see* 'Language'). It is also helps to ask someone the 'Indian' price before entering the shop.

Bargaining can be great fun. Once you've got the hang of it, it's possible to buy things in markets and bazaars cheaper than in fixed-price emporia. But beware: travellers do get carried away by success, and it's not uncommon to meet someone stuck with $3000-worth of useless carpets, the result of being talked into some street-tout's 'uncle's shop' or 'brother's silk emporium'. With big buys, you really do have to know what you're talking about. Don't let anyone take you anywhere you can't afford to go. In any shopping situation, as soon as you've lost the initiative, you're halfway to buying something you don't even want. Even worse, you may have to lug it halfway round India until you find some way of sending it home.

The better shops and emporia ship stuff home for you, and give you a certificate of origin with major purchases plus a receipt (for when the article hits customs; very expensive otherwise). It's a good idea to photograph or mark freighted items at the time of buying it, just in case a completely different article turns up at your front door.

Unless you have to, don't buy everything in one place. Different areas of India are famous for different things. Go to Agra for sublime marble inlay work, to Jaipur for gems and jewellery, to Mysore for incense and sandalwood, to Varanasi for silks and brasswork, to Hyderabad for silver inlay/pearls, to Udaipur for miniature paintings/wall hangings, and to Rajasthan in general for chunky folk-art jewellery, colourful mirror-embroidery and ethnic furnishings.

There is no obligation to buy anywhere in India—just a lot of friendly pressure.

Temples

Most temples are open to foreigners, though you are expected to observe a few restrictions. These include taking off your shoes when visiting Jain, Hindu or Muslim shrines, and covering your head when entering a Sikh one. It is also customary to have a bath before entering a temple, but this is not expected of tourists. Women should be appropriately dressed, and leather articles like handbags and camera bags may have to be left at the entrance. In certain temples, notably Jain ones, women having their period are considered unclean and are denied entrance. If you think you can slip past undetected, think again. Priests claim to be able to tell exactly where you are in your cycle by looking at your eyes.

Time

There are no time differences within India. Time differences between India and some major international cities are: Auckland +06.30; Berlin −04.30; London −04.30; Los Angeles −13.30; New York −10.30; Paris −04.30; Sydney +02.30; Toronto −09.00.

Tourist Information

There are national and state tourist offices in most Indian centres, which vary considerably in their degree of efficiency. Many state tourist offices run tourist bungalows which offer cheap (if bland) accommodation. Tourist office tel nos/addresses are given throughout this book. Tourist information is also available from any self-respecting hotel.

guides

Licensed **guides** are available at all important tourist centres. They are supposed to offer fixed rates, but often ask for more. Before hiring one, make sure that he/she speaks English well and has a personality you can live with. Some guides are very knowledgeable and enthusiastic, others annoying and totally unintelligible.

international tourist offices

For general literature (brochures, maps, hotel and festival lists etc.), visit your nearest Government of India Tourist Office. The main ones are:

Australia: Level 1, 17 Castlereagh Street, Sydney, NSW 2000, ✆ (02) 232 1600.

Canada: 60 Bloor Street (West), Suite No.1003, Ontario M4W 3B8, ✆ (416) 962 3787.

France: 8 Boulevard de la Madeleine, 75009 Paris 9, ✆ (42) 65 83 86/77 06.

Japan: Pearl Building, 9–18 Ginza, 7 Chome, Chuo-Ku, Tokyo 104, ✆ (03) 571 5062/63.

UK: 7 Cork Street, London W1 2AB, ✆ (0171) 437 3677/8.

USA: 30 Rockefeller Plaza, Room 15, North Mezzanine, New York, NY 10020, ✆ (212) 586 4901; 3550 Wilshire Boulevard, Suite 204, Los Angeles, CA 90010, ✆ (213) 380 8855.

Travelling Alone

Even if you've agreed to tour in company, do spend a few days travelling on your own. India is very much a country for the individualist, quickly bringing out all your hidden resources. On your own, there is no room for doubt, indecision or complacency. Without the insulation of a boon companion (a permanent reminder of home) you'll feel compelled to attune to the country, its people and its customs, at top speed. It's also an excellent spur to making new friends. You don't have to worry about feeling alone. In India, nobody's alone for very long. With no-one holding you back, you can go exactly when and where you please, with a growing sense of freedom and confidence. The perfect place for a modern-day walkabout, India rewards the solo traveller with a rich variety of intense experiences—some good, some bad, none dull—and brings him or her to a deeper understanding of the country. The reason so much more happens on your own is simple: you have to *make* it happen.

Where to Stay

Until quite recently, Indian accommodation fell into two general categories—luxury hotels for the rich and soulless hovels for the poor. There was rarely anything in the middle. Happily, that situation is now changing. India has finally realized that most westerners are coming here for a holiday, not for a 'survival' experience. Not only are mid-range hotels in the ascendancy, but many of them are making a genuine effort to look and feel ethnic. As one traveller wrote: 'I'm not into survival. I'm here to *enjoy* India, not endure it. I don't want to stay in any hotel where, when I walk out of my room, I don't know what city I'm in. So I stay in places which have that dash of local colour and character—and I'm prepared to pay for it too, because hey, I'm supposed to be having the holiday of a lifetime!'

In India, more than anywhere else in the world, you can live like a maharaja if you have money and on the surface of insanity if you haven't. There's a whole world of difference between spending say, US$50 a day on accommodation and spending just US$5. Even if you are on a budget, it is generally a good idea to treat yourself to a decent hotel once in a while. It does wonders for the morale. By the same token, it's important for well-heeled travellers to go down to street level once in a while to stay in the odd backpacker lodge: it's a far better way of experiencing the 'real India' than living like a prince in exile in international hotels.

For comfort, expect to pay between US$15 and US$30 a day on lodgings—this gives you the freedom to stay at cheap places for half your stay and to live it up the other half. You can live for just US$2/3 a day, but you soon get to feel like a piece of dirty laundry. Times to treat yourself to a good hotel are the first night or two in the country, the night before you fly home, and any night in India when you arrive exhausted after a 10-hour bus or train journey. A nice hot bath, a candle-lit meal, a couple of chilled beers and a large soft bed with freshly-starched sheets is all it takes to feel human again, and ready to dodge those curved balls that India throws at people when they're tired and rundown.

air-conditioning

Be very careful when asking for air-conditioned rooms. Lots of Indian hotels advertising 'air-con' or 'a/c' only have air-cooling (a noisy box blowing cool air, dust and the remains of birds' nests into your room) or what they call 'natural air-conditioning', which is just a breeze wafting in through your window. What you have to ask for is *central* air-conditioning, and whether it is adjustable or not. If not, be prepared for extreme room temperatures—Indians like their air-con very cold in the summer and very warm and stuffy in the winter.

room service

Most hotels in India have room service, which is normally summoned by pressing a button on your room telephone. Don't assume that what you are brought will bear any resemblance to what you order.

television

Ten years ago, the corner of every room was occupied by a picture of baby Krishna or an indianized Jesus; now there is the new god TV, mounted on a pedestal and sometimes framed with plastic flowers and greenery. The roomboy no longer asks you if the bed is comfortable or whether the air-conditioning is to your satisfaction. Instead, he rushes over to the telly and sets the volume to maximum. He proudly informs you how many channels there are and then he flicks through them to show you what to expect. Sometimes, he sits down and starts watching one of them, and it will be up to you to usher him firmly out the door before he gets too interested in the plot.

There's not much danger of *your* getting interested in the plot, however. Of the twenty of so channels on offer, ten or so are invariably blank and the rest are a combination of western sitcoms which no other country would buy, and jolly Hindi epics with heroes rolling down mountains or singing to trees. There's the odd nugget like *Star Trek* or *The X Files* of course, but these are often terminated by a power-cut. If your television isn't working, just be grateful. Remember, you're in India to see India, not *Santa Barbara* or *Aerobics Oz-Style*.

Price Categories

This book lists price categories for accommodation per room, per night. All prices were valid at the time of publication; expect them to increase by 10/20% each year thereafter. Cheap lodges rarely put their tariffs up by much—there's too much competition!

As a general rule the further south you go in India, the less expensive accommodation becomes. In Goa, Kovalam and Ooty, prices rise by 25% in the high season (from November to February), and go down by 40/50% outside these months if you bargain. The same kind of discounts apply in the north, most commonly during the monsoon months of June to September. In the mountain resorts of the far north (Shimla, Dharamsala etc.), it's the snowbound months of December to February when hotels are cheapest—if they're open!

Most mid-range and all luxury hotels charge an additional 10% 'luxury tax' on top of their published tariffs. At the cheaper mid-range places, this tax can be only 5%. Another hidden charge is a 10% 'service tax' which usually refers to just food, room service and use of telephones, but sometimes may be applied to accommodation also. To save money, go easy on the phone and pay for meals/drinks delivered to your room on the spot: don't sign them over to your room bill. In major international-style hotels, scan the tariff sheet for a possible 15% 'sales tax'—if you have to pay this too, you may be looking at 35% taxes on top of the advertised room rate!

Hotels listed in this book are divided into five categories—luxury, expensive, moderate, inexpensive and budget—according to the facilities provided. Room prices described as 'Rs250/350 to Rs500/700 with a/c' mean: '250 rupees for a single room without air-conditioning, 350 for a double room with no air-conditioning, 500 for a single room with air-conditioning and 700 for a double room with air-conditioning.'

Though a dollar rate is officially applied to foreign guests in all Indian hotels, most below the luxury category only have a rupee tariff. Even in 5-star hotels, you can usually pay in rupees against an encashment certificate—faced with no choice, the hotel staff are not going to refuse your money in whatever form it comes.

luxury

In big cities like Bombay and Delhi, a night in a top hotel can cost as much as Rs5000 (about £100 or US$160). This buys you a smart air-conditioned double suite (probably with private balcony and view), access to a good swimming pool, and a number of useful facilities like a shopping arcade, travel agency, bank, restaurants, in-house entertainments, car park, beauty parlour and health club. Car hire and sightseeing tours can also be arranged, along with a range of sports and activities. Out of the main cities and resort beaches, the standard of luxury hotels varies markedly, but the prices are far lower—around US$50/60 per room per night in 1996/7.

expensive

Hotels in this category vary tremendously—the price is seldom an indication of quality. Often a town's best hotel will fall into a lower price bracket than this, and you should choose your accommodation according to the comments in each 'Where to Stay' section of the guide (or ask other travellers), rather than expect automatic value for money.

moderate

A double room in a decent hotel in this category will often buy the same facilities as an expensive one—air-conditioning, attached restaurant, some sort of room service and (occasionally) a lift and room telephone.

budget

Before you take a room in a budget hotel, give it a thorough once-over for cleanliness and for facilities. In economy places, you can perhaps overlook the chipped basins, the peeling plaster and the old coffee stains on walls. What is *not* acceptable is: dirty bed linen, bedbugs under mattresses, cockroaches in bathrooms and waste bins, overhead fans that don't work (or which have only two speeds: turbo or snail), dead electric lights, no hot water (or no water at all) in showers, no lock on the door (or latches on windows) and broken toilets.

In practice, a lot of travellers put up with basic, even unfriendly, accommodation and rarely give rooms a proper check. This is because they often arrive in towns too tired to really care, or too late to have much choice in the matter. Others put up with really awful dives on the basis that they're going to be out and about all day, and will only need a room to sleep in. A good way to make any room habitable is to buy a lightweight tropical mosquito-net before you go to India (see 'Packing', p.45). These excellent cocoons will protect you from all creeping, biting things, but will also allow the airflow to pass freely over you, so that you can lie naked and unbitten in the most bug-infested hole.

As a general rule, if you're just staying in a town for one or two nights, you're not going to have time or energy to traipse around looking for a decent hotel. If the recommended ones are full or unsatisfactory, you may have to take the first adequate place that comes along. This often means hiring a local hotel tout. There is no problem finding them—they find you. Bear in mind that they get a tidy commission for placing you, so don't pay them more than a few rupees.

Hotel Scams

A common scam worked by hotel touts, taxi-drivers and rickshaw drivers is to deny that the hotel you want has any vacancies. 'Oh no, sahib', they will say, 'all full up'. But they're not full up at all. And even if they are, you can probably find something else much better without their help (and without paying the big commissions they earn for placing you there). If the popular places have no room, take the time to wander round a few streets directly adjoining them. Remember, a lot of new hotels are opening all the time, and they're often just off the main tourist drag.

Having booked into a cheap hotel, you'll often be approached for tips, in return for no service at all. Rs5 is ample for genuine service (Rs15/20 in big hotels), nothing at all for anything less.

Wildlife Sanctuaries, National Parks and Reserved Forests

As elsewhere in the world, India has an ambivalent relationship with its wealth of animals and plants—torn between admiration and respect on the one hand, and the relentless demands of its burgeoning human population on the other. Sadly, while there are at present 443 protected areas in the country, many of them are protected in name rather than in reality. And while almost all hunting has been banned, poaching of both plants and animals does unfortunately continue in some areas.

The forests and plains of India are home to 2094 species and sub-species of birds, of which about 1750 are resident and the balance migratory. The country sustains over 350 species of mammal and 353 species of reptile. The diversity of amphibians, insects, plants and trees is equally impressive. Only about eight per cent of the country's forest cover has survived, however, and as the human population continues to grow by leaps and bounds, the needs of villagers for grazing land and fuel has put enormous pressure on the country's forests and begun to threaten the protected areas. The axe and the chainsaw have accelerated the destruction of wilderness areas and pessimists feel that much of what is left is doomed. This said, successes like Project Tiger—which in 20 short years brought the number of tigers in India up from an alarmingly low 1800 in 1972 to a healthy 5000 in 1992—demonstrate what can be done (though recent poaching has precipitated another decline). The country has a range of overlapping conservation plans, many of which have been triumphant, and there is no real reason, apart from human ignorance and greed, why India's national parks and reserves should not remain as rich, if not richer than they are today.

Wildlife Sanctuaries & National Parks

The Indian Tourist Board has traditionally promoted its northern wildlife sanctuaries/national parks to foreign agents. A few tour operators have an understanding of the needs of a tour of wilderness areas and can help make arrangements. Try **Clipper Holidays** with offices in Madras and at Suite 406, Regency Enclave, 4 Magrath Road, Bangalore 560 025, ✆/✇ (080) 5599032/ 34/5599833, tlx 0845-3095; or **Mountain Travel India**, 1/1 Ranj Jhansi Road, New Delhi, ✆ 7533483, ✇ 777483; or **Abercrombie & Kent**, Chiranjiv Tower, 43 Nehru Place, New Delhi, ✆ 6436207,✇ 6444966. Going through an agent often makes a tour more expensive but is of great help if your time is limited. Larger sanctuaries provide vehicles, boats and sometimes elephants for tourists to view wildlife. These go out for an hour, morning and evening, from the main reception office at the park entrance. Unfortunately, a tour in one of these vehicles is often spoiled by noisy Indian tourists who tend to scare the game off with their excited clamour.

In the north at the foothills of the Himalaya, a 7-hour drive from Delhi, is an important Project Tiger reserve and Indian's oldest park, **Corbett Park**, founded in 1935. The region is very beautiful and apart from the occasional glimpse of a tiger, or the more elusive leopard, there are numerous prey species to be seen, and herds of elephant migrate through the area. Corbett also has an extraordinary range of birds.

Also in the north, 2 hours drive from Jaipur is **Sariska** (antelope, deer, extensive bird life); **Bharatpur** (a host of endangered birds); and **Sasan Gir** (Asiatic lions). In central India, try **Kanha** (swamp deer) or **Bandhavgarh** (probably the best place in the country for seeing tiger). In the south, **Nagarhole** is known for big cats; **Periyar** and **Anamalai** for large elephant herds; the **Moyar River** area for bear and leopard; and **Rajamalai** for the Nilgiri ibex (or *tahr*).

This guide includes the major sanctuaries on or near the recommended routes.

accommodation

Most sanctuaries have accommodation in Forest or Wildlife Department resthouses, at an average tariff of Rs100 per person per night. You supply your own food. Resthouses usually have to be booked in advance through the Wildlife Department Office in the town nearest to the sanctuary.

Most private camps and lodges are located on the borders of national parks and provide board and lodging. Some include visits into the park by jeep or on elephant back within their charges; others can provide this but charge separately for it. Almost all projected areas close during the monsoon and only reopen in October or occasionally November.

trekking

This is the most rewarding way to see both the forests and their wildlife. Trekking with a trained guide can be arranged at most of India's sanctuaries, whether by the day, staying in the same resthouse by night, or over several days with accommodation in caves.

Officially, treks have to be arranged in advance at Wildlife Department offices in town, usually close to sanctuaries. In practice, you can often arrange them by turning up and chatting to the sanctuary's chief conservator. This is not a foolproof method, however. To be absolutely safe, your best bet is to put your arrangements into the hands of a competent local travel agent used to dealing with trekkers.

Reserved Forests

Serious wildlifers should avoid the big parks and sanctuaries and try reserved forest areas instead. These offer quieter wildlife viewing., but (like national parks) can be difficult for foreigners to enter. Often backing onto wildlife sanctuaries, reserved forests act as buffer-zones between the sanctuaries and settled countryside. They also often protect tribal peoples and wildlife that wanders freely from reserved forest to wildlife sanctuary with no regard for the bureaucratic boundaries between them.

Trekking in reserved forest area is very rewarding if you can organize it: you can find tribal guides who will lead between forest settlements, staying overnight in their guest huts, and your chances of seeing wildlife are just as good as in a wildlife sanctuary.

As with trekking in many of the wildlife sanctuaries, the amount of paperwork you have to wade through before you get permission can be daunting. Get one of the recommended operators or agents to help you out (for addresses, *see* above).

Women Travellers

India is one of the world's safest countries to travel in, and few women experience any serious danger here, unless out on their own after dark, when Indian men become drunker and bolder. However, 'eve-teasing', as the Indians call sexual harassment of women, can be a common sport among groups of Indian men. This is almost always confined to stares and rude remarks, but women may find themselves groped in crowds. If this happens, don't be afraid to make a scene, or even strike your molester—public opinion will certainly be on your side.

There are strong advantages and drawbacks to travelling in India as a woman. On the plus side, women are rarely required to queue for anything—they can generally walk straight to the front of train, bus or cinema queues to buy their ticket. There are often special ladies' carriages in trains and sometimes seats reserved for women on buses. Many other places, including some cinemas, have special ladies' facilities. Finally, being young, single and even remotely attractive is the passport to all sorts of freebies (*see* **Calcutta**, 'Leisure', p.375).

On the downside, Indian society is decidedly non-liberated. Western women travelling on their own (i.e. without a husband or male relative) can attract a lot of unwelcome attention—often simply by being too open and friendly. Many Indian men, unused to such interest from females, can interpret such openness as a big come-on, with predictably embarrassing results. To avoid unwanted attention, don't smoke in public (this is a sign of a 'loose woman'), don't wear short shorts or leave the whole arm uncovered when out in public and don't respond to persistent questioning—learn to be rude (everyone else in India has to). Do not go topless.

You can avoid a lot of hassle by wearing a wedding ring, but you're still not immune. As one woman remarked: 'You still have to deal with the following problems: first, finding a place to pee; second, Indian men 'accidentally' brushing past your breasts; third, learning to walk without swinging your arms—swing them forward, no problem; swing them *back* and one guy is cupping your breast while another's genitals have somehow found their way into your hand. Nobody ever asks my husband if I am his wife; they only ask if I am his girlfriend. If you're a 'girlfriend', you're a loose slut and a whore. If you're a wife, you're okay!'

Culture

India is a wide-ranging amalgam of races, religions and cultures. There are Tibetans up in Ladakh, Kashmiris of central Asian stock in the far north, Bengalis in the east, negroid aboriginals in the Nicobar Islands, dark-skinned Dravidians in the south, and all manner of Aryan, European, Arab, Semite and Mongol permutations throughout the north and down the western coast. They are dissimilar in hundreds of ways, but have succeeded in becoming a single nation.

This unity has been achieved (even more impressively) in the face of a dramatic population explosion. The current figure of around 900 million increases at a rate of 18 million a year—that's the size of the population of Australia, and the size of the workforce on Indian Railways. Following the unfortunate experiment in enforced sterilization in the mid-'70s, subsequent Indian governments have adopted a very low profile on population control. It is probable that, by the end of the century, there will be one billion Indians.

The unexpected (to Western prophets of doom) national unity of India following Independence was largely due to the age-old moral and spiritual unity of the people. The essential beliefs and social institutions which marked Indians as a self-contained people originated long before the time of Buddha; their domestic rituals and ceremonials were inscribed three centuries or more before Christ; and their legal system was codified two millennia ago. Little wonder, therefore, that Indian society, morals and laws resisted and often absorbed the civilizations of numerous foreign invaders, or that they formed the strong, solid basis on which to unite modern, free India.

Hindu society, from the earliest times, was distinguished by three characteristics: the caste system, the joint family, and the codified system of law.

Caste

The caste system is highly complex, dividing the whole of society (in theory at least) into four castes—**Brahmins** (priests, men of learning, and general arbiters of morals); **Kshatriyas** (soldiers and administrators); **Vaisyas** (traders, men of commerce); and **Shudras** (farmers, peasants and the great mass of the working people). In practice, with social evolution these basic four divisions have fragmented into hundreds of sub-castes, and the original definitions have lost their meaning. Only the Brahmin class, by virtue of its exclusiveness, can be said to have clung, more or less, to its original function. This is perhaps appropriate, since it was the Brahmins—doubtless to preserve their privileged rights and position in society—who have developed the caste system in the first place. The legendary explanation is that the four castes sprang from the mouth (Brahmins), arms (Kshatriyas), thighs (Vaisyas) and feet (Shudras) of the creator, Brahma.

Joint Family

The joint family was a system by which property was held in common, and brothers and sons lived together under one roof: lacking in privacy, yes, but also productive of great community spirit and strength, as can be seen in many of the village areas of India today. A less satisfactory consequence of the joint family arrangement, however, was that all property was inherited not by succession to the eldest son, but divided equally between all sons. In the long term, this led to wide and disparate fragmentation of the land, each successive generation inheriting less property than the last.

Law

The system of law was a complicated batch of rights and obligations based on ancient texts and local customs. Eventually associated with Hindu religion, it was archaic in the extreme, particularly where women were concerned. An independent life for women had never been contemplated under Hindu law, and their economic dependence on men (including only limited right to property) was at all times heavily emphasized.

Then came the social revolution. At Independence, the new constitution set itself the task of bringing India up-to-date with the rest of the modern world. It abolished untouchability, redesignating the *harijans* as a 'scheduled caste' with full democratic and human rights; it offered a secular law for all Indian citizens to opt for while allowing all communities to retain their own traditions; it broke down the joint family system with new inheritance laws, giving daughters equal rights to inherit with sons; it offered a unified marriage law all over India, not only permitting marriages between different castes and religions, but allowing women the right of remarriage and divorce.

In theory, modern India is no longer a socially backward country, dominated by caste and anachronistic customs, denying millions of people social rights. It has promised itself a major revolution, and would like to think of itself as moving rapidly towards it. In practice, however, India has always been slow to change. To understand why this is so, one has to appreciate the great social emphasis of the country. Far more than in the West, Indian life is governed at all levels by the extended family, a system of favours and obligations, of communal identity and sharing, by age-old social ethics and morality.

Marriage Act

The 1952 Marriage Act, for instance, gave women the right of remarriage, but very few young widows, even today, take advantage of it. The customs of thousands of years that have proved for some reason beneficial to society are very difficult to break, and even if these women were to declare themselves available, few Indian men would have them. Arranged marriages are still the general rule, and 'love matches' the notable exception. Marriage in India always was, and still is, a social phenomenon first, and a matter of personal preference second. In most cases, parents and relatives continue to select the bride from a similar background with some political, financial and social benefit; in some states (notably Rajasthan) child marriages still go on, despite being strictly illegal; and it is still rare today for the bridegroom to be left alone with his betrothed before the marriage

ceremony. The pertinent traditional argument in favour of arranged marriages (and a major stumbling block to social liberation in the Western sense) is that the bride and groom have to make the alliance work. Both parties are responsible not so much to each other, but to society, for a successful married life. To fail in marriage is to fail in society, and the divorce rate is consequently low. Because Indians can't think simply of their own needs, but must also take into account their wider responsibility to society, they generally make far greater efforts than Westerners to make marriages work. But when they do break down, it can be very tough on women. To leave a marriage is, effectively, to step right out of society. Disownment by the family, loss of caste and social identity, and, in the absence of any social security arrangement, financial deprivation, are all problems faced by women seeking divorce in India today. And modern Indian marriages are by no means as stable as before. The tradition of dowries—whereby the prospective bride's father practically gives the shirt off his back—persists despite being against the law. Today, the average dowry demanded by middle-class parents for their often overpriced boys can be anything from Rs10,000 to Rs1,000,000, which often puts the bride's family into debt for the rest of their lives. The scale peaks for boys living and working abroad, with those holding US green cards fetching the best price. IAS officers (the senior cadre of civil servants), doctors and lawyers receive higher bids than idealistic teachers or publishers. Worse, 'kitchen accidents' still occur: young wives who disappoint greedy in-laws are doused in kerosene and incinerated in locked kitchens. This leaves the husband free to remarry and collect another handsome dowry. Such practices reflect the temptations generated by an increasingly consumer-oriented society.

Distribution of Wealth

Another thorn in the side of social progress is the unequal distribution of wealth in the country. As one young Brahmin remarked: 'For many ages past, the rich have been lazy and the higher castes spoilt, leaving the lower castes to work all day long for practically nothing.' At present, about 2% of India's population are rich, with some 25% salaried; the remainder are the homeless, jobless and often landless poor, who live mainly in the villages. Indians of education and vision point out that the same state of affairs existed in England and the USA a century ago, when similar socio-economic inequalities existed, yet were quickly harmonized after the triumph of democracy. The more optimistic of them predict the same rapid improvements in India. But others, more realistically, fear that India will make the same mistakes as the West and that society will lose its cohesiveness.

Society still tends to determine every facet of an Indian's life: the kind of work he can do, the woman he will marry, the people he will (and won't) mix with, and the type of religious observances he will perform. This gives him a strong social identity, a certain sense of 'belonging', and a definite rôle in life. All these things contribute to the great openness, lack of social inhibition and personal confidence of the Indian people. Yet caste, despite its great social value, can be construed as a severe restriction on individual growth and national progress. Many well-qualified and professional Indians, for example, find caste a real block to incentive, and prefer to work abroad. It is still possible that a man might wait 10 years for promotion, working in the same low-paid job, and then when his superior leaves or dies finds that someone of a higher caste but less experience has been promoted above his head. On a wider level, the lack of social mobility created by caste is 'free' India's most complex challenge. Whether or not it is conducive to widespread apathy among the people is open to debate, but it is certainly no spur to individual incentive.

Cracks in the armour of caste have started to appear. Curiously, these are less the result of legislation than of the powerful stimulus of the West. The new Indian middle class which arose in the 19th century was formed as a result of Western education and industrialization with its attendant economic changes. The powerful Indian business class that had gained power over centuries became concentrated in the big capitals of Bombay, Calcutta and Delhi during the rapid industrial growth after Independence. The critical factor, though, was the legacy of the British Raj. When the British moved out in 1947, they left behind the elitist and influential traditions of the armed services, the civil service, the judiciary, the universities, the press and the political structures. This new Indian elite was brought up with alien concepts of Western clothes, ideas, food and social customs. For the previous century at least, this created a market and a dumping ground for all sorts of Western produce. Even India's street lamps were imported from Britain.

But it is in the continuing tradition of British education that the Raj continues to influence every level of Indian life. Those who can afford a British education for their children are the 'haves', while those who can't are the 'have nots'. All sorts of doors—social, political and economic—open to people with the right (British) education, especially in the British heritage of clubs and societies. This breed of snobbishness, a direct hangover from the Raj, is Britain's own contribution to the Indian heritage of class and caste. In effect, the Raj created a completely new caste, one that was particularly relevant to modern industrial India—of the privileged, British-educated ruling elite.

Small wonder, then, that Indians are so keen to communicate with English-speaking visitors. For English is the chosen *lingua franca* of India's upper classes. It has status value, it is a passport to senior jobs, it is the language of central government, of the higher law courts, of business and of the professional classes. Most important of all, it is a language of opportunity, unfettered by traditional caste and social restrictions, to which anyone with enough enterprise and money can aspire. Not that this is a desirable situation. Advancement, restricted to the urban middle classes on which the Raj pinned their hopes, is still denied to the great mass of the poorer people who flock to the great towns and cities of British India—notably Bombay and Calcutta—in search of food and work.

History

As late as 1920, it was believed that civilization in India dated back only to the time of Alexander's invasion in the 4th century BC. The problem was that the Hindu people, unlike the Greeks, the Europeans, the Chinese and the Arabs, never developed the art of historical writing. India did have a considerable historical tradition, embodied in both its literature and its semi-religious works known as the *Puranas*, but until the early 1800s little was known of the history of the Hindu people before the Muslim invasions of the 11th century AD.

Ancient India

Then came the discovery of the ancient Indus civilization. Some time in the mid-19th century, British engineers laying a rail track between Karachi and the Punjab stumbled across a vast quantity of ancient sun-baked bricks, which were being used by locals to provide solid foundations for the track. It was later found that these bricks were over 5000 years old. Intrigued, archaeologists visited the area in the 1920s and presently came up with two buried cities—Mohenjodaro (mound of the dead) along the Indus, and Harappa on the Ravi. A rapid series of other discoveries, in the Punjab and in Gujarat, confirmed that an ancient civilization with well-planned cities, large-scale commerce, skilled craftsmen, knowledge of mathematics and script, and sophisticated social structure existed in India as long ago as 3000 BC. This was a timely discovery. To know that they belonged to one of the earliest areas of civilization in the world, contemporary with ancient Egypt and Sumer, provided the modern Indian people with just the kind of national pride and feeling they needed to achieve unity, and with it Independence.

The Indus civilization was created by the 'original' Indians whose descendants still inhabit the south of the country today. This civilization then spread to northern and western India while the original cities fell into disuse. Around 1500 BC the Aryans came from the north, mounted on horses and riding in chariots. They were a Caucasian people who brought a rich linguistic and literary tradition to India, later to result in the Sanskrit literary classics of the *Vedas*. Around 800 BC they learned how to make iron tools and weapons, and then pushed further east and southwards to the Gangetic plain where they founded villages, tribal republics and well-governed powerful states. These communities developed agricultural and mercantile wealth.

Under Cyrus, then Darius (521–485 BC), the Persians conquered the Indus Valley regions of the Punjab and Sind. Theirs was a passing visit, but they left some interesting influences on religion, art and administration. The Greeks, under Alexander the Great, spent even less time in India—Alexander overthrew Darius III in 331 BC, advanced as far as the Beas River in 326 BC, conquered King Porus and his elephants, and was then compelled by his troops to return home, leaving behind a series of garrisons and administrative systems to keep the trade links open with west Asia and the consequent exchange of ideas and art.

The powerful Maurya dynasty of Magadha (present-day Bihar) which rose in the 4th century BC under the monarch Chandragupta, cut out an extensive swathe of territory across the Indo-Gangetic plain, from Bengal in the east into the heart of Afghanistan in the northwest. By this time the religious legacy of the first Aryans, Brahmanical Hinduism, had laid down firm roots, and the early 5th-century BC protest movements of Buddhism and Jainism were also well-established. The caste system, interestingly, was starting to splinter—by Chandragupta's time, the original four castes had given way to at least seven definite classes of Indian society: philosophers, peasants, herdsmen, craftsmen and traders, soldiers, government officials, and councillors.

The Mauryan empire reached its zenith under Ashoka (268–31 BC), who consolidated the north, conquered as far south as Mysore, and then drove east to Orissa. His fateful battle here, at Kalinga, caused him to renounce warfare forever (so appalled was he by the carnage that he had wrought) and to espouse Buddhism. He had messages of peace inscribed on rocks and pillars all over his domain, notably in Orissa, in Gujarat, at Sarnath and Sanchi, and in Delhi. He also sent his son Mahendra over to Sri Lanka (armed with a sapling of the bodhi tree) to spread the message of Buddhism.

The Mauryan power collapsed within a century of Ashoka's death. In its heyday though, this empire probably ruled over more of India than any other until the time of the British. In its wake, came a number of different dynasties: Brahmin rulers in the Indo-Gangetic plains, Telugus in the Deccan plain, and Cholas (round Madras), Cheras (Kerala) and Pandyas (Tamil Nadu) in the south. While the Tamils busied themselves in exporting Hinduism, Buddhism, Jainism and Indian philosophy, art and medicine to Ceylon, Cambodia, Java, Rome and the Far East (either by invasion or trade), the Telugus—self-styled 'Lords of the Deccan'—were mainly engaged in building Buddhist stupas (burial mounds). During their rule Hinayana Buddhism, in which the Buddha was represented by stupas, footprints, elephants and trees, flourished. This form of Buddhism continued to around AD 400, but had been effectively supplanted by the Mahayana form at least a couple of centuries earlier. The Buddhist influence at this time was so strong that when the Greeks revisited, occupying the Punjab and invading the Mauryan capital of Pataliputra (Patna) in 150 BC, their king (Menander) promptly converted to Buddhism. But what was happening in the north of India was invariably a very different story to what was happening in the south. In the north, Hinduism continued to flourish more or less unaffected.

Invasions

As foreign invasions became more and more frequent, India became a virtual melting pot of different cultures. The northernmost zone of the country—the soaring Himalayan range of mountains—gave Indians the illusion of being guarded by an impassable wall. But there was always a series of accessible passes—the Khyber, the Bolan and the Khurram in the northwest, and others linking India to Tibet—and these were the routes which for three millennia at least brought invader and trader across the Afghan-Punjab saddle. They came in the main to loot the vast Indo-Gangetic plains, an apparently inexhaustible granary. They were marauders from the north, who crossed over the passes in the autumn before snowfall, descended to the Indian plains just as the crops began to ripen, fought the traditional big battle in the Punjab, spent the winter methodically looting the rich cities and raiding winter crops, and then—unless they decided to found an empire—disappeared back across the mountains before the hot season arrived.

As such invaders continued to make their inroads through the northwestern passes, India received visits from western China, from the Scythians (around 130 BC), from the Parthians, and from the Kushans of central Asia. Then came a century-long free-for-all, followed by the rise of India's greatest Hindu dynasty—the Imperial Guptas. This empire was founded by Chandragupta II in AD 319, and for the ensuing three centuries (ending in AD 647) ruled an extending domain which eventually included the whole Indo-Gangetic plain down to the northern boundaries of the Deccan. During this period of peace and stability, art and literature flourished (polished Sanskrit replacing Pali script) and extremely fine painting and sculpture were executed at Buddhist centres like Ajanta, Sarnath and Sanchi. By the end of the Gupta period, however, the popularity of Buddhism had begun to wane, and the star of Hinduism rose once again. The break-up of the Gupta Empire meant the general splintering of north India into a number of separate Hindu kingdoms. Prominent amongst these were the Prathiharas of central India, Gangas of eastern India, the western and eastern Chalukyas and further south the Cholas, Cheras and Pandyas. By the 10th–11th centuries these powerful dynasties had created vast kingdoms, built impressive capitals and magnificent temples. In eastern India the temples of Bhubaneshwar and the Sun Temple of Konarak are a reminder of the splendid Ganga kingdoms. The temples of Khajuraho, which draw thousands of tourists to their erotic sculptures, are the best surviving examples of central Indian temples. While many thought that India was in a state of decadence, thus paving the way for the advent of Islam it appears that this was not the case. It was during the 9th–13th centuries, and in some case the late 15th century, that the greatest achievements of Hindu art, music, literature and philosophy were made.

The Muslims

The Muslim conquest of India had far-reaching effects on the political, social and cultural life of the country. Between AD 1001 and 1027, the infamous Mahmud of Ghazni mounted 17 separate attacks, eliminating Hindu armies, ransacking temples, and sacking cities on each occasion. His most notable victory was the capture of the holy city of Somnath—the wealth and booty he found here were so great that even he couldn't carry it all away. Mahmud also picked up the nasty habit of collecting severed Hindu fingers, one for each chieftain vanquished. But he was never anything more than a glorified bandit, who returned home to Ghazni in Afghanistan after each individual raid. The real conqueror-founder of Islam in India was Muhammad of Ghor, who mounted the first wholesale invasion of the country in 1192, and brought Muslim power to stay. The Hindu kingdoms of the Gangetic Valley fell without effective resistance to his attacks within a single decade. One of his generals, Muhammad Khilji, swept through Bihar in 1193 and effectively destroyed Buddhism overnight—razing all the monasteries and massacring all the monks. Another general, Qutb-ud-din, became Muhammad of Ghor's direct successor, and after the latter's death in 1206 became the first Sultan of Delhi. But it was left to the Khilji monarchs, notably Ala-ud-din Khilji, to consolidate the Muslim conquest. He ruled for 20 years (1296–1316).

The next Turkish dynasty, the Tughlaqs, ruled from 1320–97. It had two great kings: the first, Muhammad Tughlaq was very eccentric; the second, Muhammad Firuz, was a great patron of the arts and architecture. His successor, Nasir-ud-din, fell victim to the encroaching Mongol hordes. In 1397 Timur (known as Tamerlane to Europeans) swept over the Indus, massacred 100,000 Hindu prisoners captured in the Punjab, and toppled the Delhi Sultans. The direct result of his invasion, which nobody could withstand, was to sever India into two parts. Parts of northern India returned to the Turks and the Afghan princes; the south regained independent status under Hindu kings. The latter development was significant. Even while the Muslim Sultans of Delhi were in control of parts of the north, in south India the mighty Vijayanagar Empire was founded in 1336 with its capital at Hampi.

The Mughal Emperors

Of all the invading dynasties, the Mughals were the most influential. A succession of six Mughal emperors left behind a powerful legacy of magnificent buildings, including the Taj Mahal. Their rise was quick and dramatic. The first Mughal monarch, Babur, ruled from 1527 to 1530. He believed it his duty to conquer India and release it from the rule of the Turks. But he started with the Afghan Lodhi rulers of Delhi, employing superior tactics to defeat an army 10 times stronger than his own. Then he advanced, with some trepidation, against the Hindus. The reason for his nerves was that, for once, the Hindu forces had buried their differences and managed to form a united confederacy under the Rajput monarch, Rana Sanga, ruler of Mewar. This redoubtable individual was a living tapestry of warlike wounds—he had lost an eye and an arm, and had 80 battle scars on his body. But Babur won the day, and raised himself to the status of 'Ghazi', slayer of infidels.

He had intended to stay, but then found he didn't much care for India after all. He liked its countryside, its monsoon and its gold, but he was plagued by its heat, winds and dust. He died, still dreaming of a return to the cool, fragrant air of Kabul, and India passed to his even more hesitant son, Humayun. This young man was a natural recluse, more interested in scholarly pursuits than in administering an empire. Seizing on this weakness, the brilliant chieftain Sher Shah attacked and retook parts of the empire for the Afghans (1540). He was an enlightened ruler, who ruled only five years but achieved more in them—far-reaching administrative, financial and transport improvements—than did his three weak successors (1545–56) put together. Then, after 15 years of exile, Humayun finally recaptured Delhi and Agra for the Mughals (1556). His honour vindicated, he enjoyed a few weeks of power, then tripped down some steps hurrying to prayer, and fractured his skull.

Humayun's son, Akbar (1556–1605) was only 14 when he came to the throne. It took him six years to remove power-hungry guardians (one was flung off the ramparts of a Delhi fort) and to become the real ruler. He then revealed himself to be the greatest of the Mughal emperors. A man of culture, intelligence, wisdom and equity, he was also a military genius with a practical motto: 'A monarch should be ever intent on conquest, otherwise his neighbours will rise in arms against him.' Instead of trying to subjugate the Hindus (an impossible task, in view of their numbers) he went far to integrating them into his empire with a policy of effective administration. To start the ball rolling, he married a Hindu and raised her Rajput kinsmen to high rank. Then he recruited several Hindu advisers, generals and administrators, abolished a number of taxes on Hindus, and evolved his concept of a secular state with an eclectic faith combining the best of Islam, Hinduism, Jainism, Christianity, Zoroastrianism and Buddhism. This enlightened experiment failed (with Akbar himself as the supreme god-head, it could only be short-lived), but the memory of it still lives on in Akbar's greatest monument, the ghost city of Fatehpur Sikri.

On Akbar's death, his son Jahangir (1605–27) took over. He was an excellent builder, who left fine marble tombs and mosques in and around Agra (and in his beloved Kashmir), but his achievements were obscured by two things: his craving for alcohol and women, and his sadism. Gifted with none of his father's vision for a united people, he put down the Hindu Rajputs and the Deccani Muslims with calculated ruthlessness.

The fifth Mughal, Shah Jahan (1627–58), spent half his reign campaigning against the Rajputs and the Deccan kingdoms. Merciless in his dealings, he gave his Hindu subjects very short shrift (even destroying their places of worship), but in his case military shortcomings were obscured by architectural triumphs. Shah Jahan created the greatest Mughal monuments, including the Taj Mahal, the famous Pearl Mosque in Agra Fort, the Royal Mosque (Jama Masjid, then the biggest mosque in the world) and the Red Fort in Delhi. But this passion for building eventually led to his downfall, and his son Aurangzeb had him imprisoned for the last seven years of his life—partly to stop him spending any more money.

Aurangzeb (1658–1707) was the last and the dullest of the great Mughal emperors. He was a pious ascetic, who dressed simply, lived frugally and died having given strict orders for a modest tomb. Aurangzeb was also a single-minded religious zealot, who systematically murdered his brothers and their sons, extended the empire's boundaries even further in order to replace as many Hindu temples with Muslim mosques as possible, and reduced his non-Muslim subjects to second-class citizens. In later years, after much spilling of blood, he realized that he had sown the seeds of the Mughal Empire's destruction.

After Aurangzeb, came a long line of insignificant, wastrel and weak kings. The dynasty degenerated, and finally came to an end under the profligate Muhammad Shah, nicknamed the 'Merry Monarch', who was still drinking, fornicating and generally having a ball in Delhi's Red Fort when the Persian invader, Nadir Shah, suddenly dropped in. He arrived in 1739, stripping Delhi clean of its wealth, massacring 150,000 of its civilian population and, in five short months' stay, wrecking her system of administration. To load all the booty he had collected and take it back home to Persia, he employed 1000 elephants, 7000 horses and 10,000 camels.

The Mughal king he left behind now ruled just the four walls of Delhi's Red Fort, but the bell had tolled for the Mughals a lot earlier. When the blood-thirsty Aurangzeb began to assert his Islamic stamp on the Mughal Empire he provoked the Hindu revival, under the Maratha monarch Shivaji, which was to lead to its downfall. By the middle of the 18th century, authority over practically the whole of Hindustan outside the Punjab had passed to the Marathas. It was only when Arthur Wellesley (later Duke of Wellington) broke their power at Assaye (1803) that the British finally became the leading power in India, and only when the Maratha Empire was finally extinguished (1818) that the East India Company became the effective sovereign of the country.

The Mughals, in a sad postscript, had come to blows with the British some time earlier, in 1757, at the battle of Plassey. Their defeat here signalled the birth of a new (and final) imperial power in India—the British Raj.

The Raj

The British were not the first Europeans to arrive in India—that privilege went to the Portuguese. In 1498 Vasco da Gama landed at modern-day Kerala, commencing a century-long trade monopoly for the Portuguese, and establishing the base for their later conquest of Goa (1510), then Daman and Diu. The British first appeared in 1612, establishing a trading-post at Surat in Gujarat. For the next 240 years Britain's interest in India was administered not by the crown or the government, but by the London-based East India Company. This founded bases at Madras (1640), Bombay (1668) and Calcutta (1690). To consolidate them, and to establish its trade dominance in India generally, the British had to deal with the Dutch and the French, both of whom had similar trading-posts in the country. The French took Madras in 1746, but lost it back to the British in 1749. Their power in India ended with the surrender of Pondicherry in 1761. The Nawab of Bengal took Calcutta in 1756, but lost it back to Robert Clive in the following year. In the south, the 'Tiger of Mysore' Tipu Sultan (and his father Hyder Ali) inflicted a series of defeats on the British, then were overcome in 1799. With the defeat of the Marathas in 1803, it only remained for the Company to fight the two Sikh Wars and gain control of the Punjab (1849) to put the final seal on empire. The British had come to trade but the need to seek more markets and protect sources of supply led to an imposition of an alien administration supported by an ever-expanding army.

The success of the British was partly the result of Mughal collapse and subsequent Hindu disunity, but owed more to their policy of toleration towards the conquered. Following Akbar's lead, they made little attempt to interfere in Hindu religion, customs or culture; rather, they made it quite clear that they had come just for trade. Many Indian princes no doubt threatened by the disciplined British army, decided to take a

Tipu's tiger: a carved and painted wooden effigy which simulates the growls of a tiger and the cries of his victim. Presented to the Sultan of Mysore in the 1790s and seized by the British after his death at the siege of Sriringapatnam in 1799. It is now on display in the Victoria and Albert Museum, London.

break from in-fighting and to accept British suzerainty. They included most of the Rajput princes, the relics of the Mughal Empire like the Nizam of Hyderabad (at that time, and for a long time to come, among the richest individuals in the world) and various survivors of the defeated Maratha confederacy.

The British achieved the closest thing to an Indian empire yet (even the most powerful of prior civilizations had not encompassed all of present-day India), but the country remained just a motley of separate states, each one ruled in name by a Prince, Nawab or Maharaja, but in actuality by the residing British Viceroy or Governor-General. The first of these crown-appointed officials, who replaced the old Company Governor-Generals, which had begun with Warren Hastings in 1774, was Lord Canning in 1859; the last was Mountbatten in 1947. With their rule established, the British went into large-scale iron and coal mining, tea production, coffee and cotton growing, and generally exploited India's vast, largely untapped natural resources. In order to facilitate this exploitation they developed an extensive system of railways, massive irrigation and agricultural programmes, and (some say most importantly) a code of civil law. Actually, it was far from democratic since the conquerors always held the privileged position, but it did ensure an element of equality among the Indians themselves. And this was in a country where Hindu law had previously differentiated strictly between Brahmin and non-Brahmin, where Islamic law had one set of codes for Muslims and quite another for 'kafirs' or infidels. The British also instituted the bureaucracy of the civil service and, while keeping the Indians at a comfortable distance from any real power within it, set about creating an Indian middle class with an increasing responsibility for it. Ultimately, knowledge of ideas and institutions brought an intense desire for self-government.

But the first sign of Indian disaffection against British rule probably had little to do with Independence. The Indian Mutiny of 1857–8 had, in fact, no real discernible cause apart from greased bullets. Somehow, a rumour spread among Muslim and Hindu troops serving with British forces that new bullets being issued were greased with pig (unclean to Muslims) and cow (sacred to Hindus) fat. Too slow to deny this rumour, the British soon had 47 mutinying Indian battalions on their hands. The Mutiny erupted at Meerut, near Delhi, and spread rapidly across north India. The sepoys, actively assisted by disaffected Sikh forces, visited Delhi, dug up the phantom Mughal emperor there (Bahadur Shah) and appointed him reluctant Emperor of Hindustan. His rule lasted just six months. There were repeated massacres and sieges on both sides before the Mutiny ran out of steam. In January 1858 Bahadur Shah was sentenced by a British military tribunal to life imprisonment, and with his departure into exile the great Mughal dynasty came to an ignominious end.

The Mutiny was the cause of the transfer of India from the rule of the East India Company to sovereignty of the British Crown. It had been an unexpected blow to British confidence, and it was one which both sides never forgot. The Indian Mutiny had been crushed, but the spirit of rebellion remained alive and slowly began to grow. Resistance was centralized in a sudden, wholesale reform of Hinduism itself. Previous attempts to rally Indians round the banner of the Hindu religion had always foundered on the rocks of caste—the exclusiveness of the Brahmins gave them no feel for the mass popular pulse. But a few determined visionaries—Ram Mohun Roy, Ramakrishna, Swami Vivekananda, Dayananda and even the European Mrs Annie Besant—led a series of important reforms designed to revive Hinduism as a truly modern religion, and thus to reorganize (and standardize) Hindu society totally. The movement for social reform ran alongside a parallel movement for national identity and freedom. The latter was fed by a number of timely developments, including the discovery of India's antiquity (excavation of Indus Valley civilization); the revival of Sanskrit and renewed appreciation of its classics like the *Bhagavad Gita*; and the repatriation of Buddhism, with the coming to light of its long-lost literary, artistic and philosophical achievements. Hindu history and heritage was refound, largely through the researches (ironically) of Western scholars, and this contributed significantly to the evolving national self-image of India as a whole. Other groups, such as the Muslims, also began to develop a sense of national pride and seek self-determination.

The Indian National Congress, founded in 1885, was destined to give the British their most prolonged opposition. It began by trying to unite all the communities in India under one banner, but this was not always possible. The Muslims, in particular, still regarded themselves as a race apart, with their traditions rooted outside India, and were alarmed by the growth of Indian nationalism and its demands for political freedom. Faced by the prospect of a Hindu-dominated free India, they founded the Muslim League in 1906 and began making demands for a separate communal electorate for themselves. The Anglo-Muslim alliance of 1906 was a decisive development: it split India into two nations, and Hindus and Muslims were embarked on two entirely different courses. In 1909, perhaps the greatest mistake the British ever made, the Morley-Minto reforms initiated the creation of separate Muslim electorates which directly paved the way for the partition of the Indian Empire.

Gandhi and Independence

The cry for independence, which had become nationwide by the turn of the century, was muted by the arrival of the First World War. Then it burst forth again—this time as an insistent roar—under the charismatic leadership of Mohandas Karamchand Gandhi. Soon to be styled the Mahatma (Great Soul) of the nation, Gandhi arrived in India in 1915, following a long period of fighting on behalf of human rights in South Africa. Gandhi fervently believed in Hindu-Muslim unity: at no time did he contemplate India as an exclusively Hindu state. His life and thoughts were a direct reflection of the 'Karma Yogin' (saint in action). His campaign for the abolition of untouchability, his famous fasts compelling Hindus and Muslims to live together in harmony, his ideals of *ahimsa* (non-violence) and *satyagraha* (passive resistance), and his own life of extreme austerity were all in strict accordance with Hindu traditions. He focused on the movement for independence after the disgraceful massacre of peaceful protesters by armed British troops at Amritsar in 1919, and turned the movement from an ineffective middle-class one to a village-based one of irresistible power.

As the clamour for independence reached its peak, Gandhi was forced to fight a rearguard action against the revived Muslim League under Muhammad Ali Jinnah. After 1936 a demand began for the creation of an independent homeland for Islam, and the fight was on for a partitioned India. The Second World War brought matters to a head. When in 1942 the Mahatma launched his last great struggle, two things became clear: first, that independence was the only settlement possible with Indian nationalism after the war; second, that partition was inevitable. Jinnah out-manoeuvred both the British and the Indian Congress. When, on 9 August 1942, Gandhi uttered the words in every Hindu's heart and told the British to 'Quit India', Jinnah followed with the demand to 'Divide and Quit'. Against their better judgement, the British were forced to do just this. It was a simple case of partition or civil war. As bloody clashes between Muslims and Hindus mounted in frequency and intensity, even the Congress—after a few months' experience of coalition government (1946–47)—realized that partition was inevitable. As the new British Viceroy, Lord Louis Mountbatten, issued the date for Independence—14 August 1947—the old Indian spokesman, Mahatma Gandhi, left the political scene, darkly predicting chaos.

It was worse than chaos. In 1947, the Indian subcontinent had its eastern and western extremes sliced off to form West and East Pakistan, present-day Pakistan and Bangladesh. But at the time of partition, the new India contained over 35 million Muslims, while the new Pakistan housed vast numbers of Hindus. The problem was worst in the new border states of Bengal and the Punjab, which had very mixed populations and a long history of intercommunal antagonism, and which were both neatly chopped in two by partition. The situation became explosive, and when, during the weeks following Independence, the mass exodus of Hindus and Muslims, uprooting homes in now 'alien' states and travelling to their new homelands, began, it was the signal for bloody and prolonged carnage on an unimaginable scale. Trainloads of Hindu and Sikh emigrants going east were stopped and butchered by Muslims, while parties of Muslims fighting their way west suffered the same fate from Hindus and Sikhs. Around 10 million people were 'exchanged' following Independence; some 500,000 perished en route.

Such was the extent of the holocaust that Jawarhalal Nehru, Gandhi's political disciple and the first Prime Minister of India, made an unexpected plea for help to the ex-British Viceroy, Mountbatten. 'Ours is the politics of agitation, not of government!' he declared. 'Please come back and help us out till we find our feet!'. Mountbatten returned and the crisis was soon overcome. Only in Kashmir was a satisfactory long-term solution not found. The region was claimed by both Pakistan and India, and since neither would give way over it, the UN was forced to step in and divide it with a demarcation line. And Kashmir continues to be a strong bone of contention, neither side having ever agreed to an official state border.

On 30 January 1948, the last act in the bitter-sweet drama of Independence, Gandhi was assassinated. Shot three times by a Hindu fanatic, he died a disappointed man, his dream of an undivided, free India never realized.

Since Independence

Fortunately for India, Nehru was a capable successor. Following Independence, he steered the country on a balanced course which made the initial transition to self-government both quick and painless. His favourite word may have been 'dynamic', but his political, economic and social outlook was basically conservative (some say, even static). 'The developing countries need peace for their development,' he stated. 'They need at least two decades of uninterrupted peace.' To ensure this, he adopted a strict policy of non-alignment with other world powers. For the first nine years of his premiership, it worked. But at heart Nehru was a convinced socialist, more than somewhat influenced by Marxism, and he tended to lean markedly towards the communist world rather than to the democracies. For a non-aligned country to align itself heavily on one side put India at a disadvantage, and lost her both friends and influence over the years. Then in 1956 Russia invaded Hungary. Nehru was forced to show his hand (India was the only non-aligned country to support the USSR's move), and henceforth nobody took his non-alignment seriously. The final humiliation took place in 1962, when Sino-Indian border clashes led to the threat of a Chinese invasion. Nehru made pleas for military aid to both East and West, but while Britain and the US promised immediate help, the USSR stood on the fence of 'non-alignment' and simply advised restraint.

Domestically, Nehru's record was far better. He used a charismatic persona and an unchallenged majority to build up a strong, cohesive central government and thus to consolidate the nascent unity of India. He also made important, progressive social changes, especially with regard to the liberalization of policies for women. Despite criticism, he also retained good relations with the British ex-colonisers, and encouraged both a free press and an independent judiciary.

He was succeeded by Lal Bahadur Shastri (for just 20 months), a meek but (when the occasion called for it) surprisingly strong-willed leader. His premiership was overshadowed by Pakistan's twin attack on India—in the Rann of Kutch and in Kashmir—in 1965.

Shastri, who had never felt that Nehru was militant enough, abandoned India's long-standing policy of peaceful neutrality and retaliated with force. But he was essentially a man of moderate views, and his untimely death, shortly after the Pakistan armies had withdrawn, spelt the advance of extremism in the country.

A feature of Indian politics is its emphasis on 'personality' leaders. A second has been the failure of these leaders to surround themselves with strong, capable lieutenants. Mahatma Gandhi was an exception. He had begun grooming Nehru for power as early as 1929, realizing perhaps the truth of the old Buddhist precept, that a master's prime duty is to create a disciple even stronger than himself. But Nehru himself failed to groom a successor and the vacuum of younger generation leaders in the Congress following his death left it seriously out of touch with the masses. Inevitably, the old and the new had to fall out, and Congress was doomed to split.

Into the political breach created by Shastri's death, stepped Indira Gandhi, Nehru's only daughter. She was elected Prime Minister in 1966. Her landslide victory at the polls was partly due to her extravagant promises of bread for the masses, but doubtless owed more to the magic of the name 'Gandhi' (though no relation to the Mahatma), coupled with the right amount of forceful 'personality'. Subsequent re-election in 1971, swept in on a tidal wave of war-fever created by Pakistan's treatment of East Pakistan and the subsequent creation of an independent Bangladesh, confirmed her in a dangerous situation of unchallenged power. By 1975, as attempts to suppress the free press and to muzzle the judiciary gave way to more openly dictatorial policies, serious opposition to her rule surfaced. She retaliated with the so-called state of emergency, freeing herself of regular parliamentary restraints and functioning virtually as an unchallenged ruler. This enabled her to push through a number of positive economic reforms and generally improve efficiency. On the other hand, the imprisonment of protesting elements and the disastrous sterilization and 'people's car' programmes initiated by her son, Sanjay, set the nation against her. (The idea behind this was to produce a car made in India costing Rs10,000, but the programme failed and the enterprise was nationalized in 1978: Suzuki now own 50% of the factory.) Under the illusion that the people would support her whatever she did, she unwisely went to the polls in 1977 and lost.

In the place of Indira and Congress came the conservative Morarji Desai and his uncohesive Janata 'People's Party'. Inadequate to the task of government, unable to stop inflation spiralling, Janata broke apart in 1979, and Indira Gandhi returned triumphant in 1980. She tried and failed to deal with escalating social problems including rife corruption, police brutality, persecution of untouchables and Hindu/Muslim/Sikh intercommunal unrest. And her drastic solution to Sikh unrest in the Punjab, culminating in the armed occupation of the Golden Temple in Amritsar, eventually cost her her life. She was shot by an assassin's bullet in October 1984.

The circumstances of her death ensured her son, Rajiv Gandhi, an unprecedented victory at the polls in December 1984. In early 1985, everyone was confidently predicting great things of the young Rajiv. 'If the man is not assassinated first,' joked one prominent official, 'he will challenge caste, remove poverty and rid us of corruption.' Within three years

Rajiv Gandhi was under attack in his own country. People were sceptical of his promise to usher India into the 21st century by means of a technological revolution. Many Indians see technology as a threat to jobs, and it was almost with glee that Delhi newspapers announced, in 1987, that two defence scandals had surfaced: the Swedish Bofors company admitted paying millions of pounds in 'commission', and a 7% 'agent's fee' had been involved on a German submarine deal. Members of Rajiv Gandhi's own family were implicated, and his own image as 'Mr Clean' was tarnished beyond repair. To make things worse, he embroiled himself in several regional conflicts, starting with Tamil Nadu (where his peacekeeping force sent to Sri Lanka, was nicknamed 'Indian people-killing force' by resentful Tamils), and later with Pakistan, West Bengal, Kashmir and the Punjab, where his soft approach brought forth a growing voice of disapproval. Rajiv Gandhi lost the next general election in 1990.

For the second time since Independence the Congress Party found themselves in opposition. A coalition government lead by V.P. Singh, who had earlier been Finance Minister and Defence Minister under Rajiv Gandhi, tried to form a united government and weather the storm created by Congress rule. Failing miserably in its task, the National Front government was replaced by an interim minority government under Chandra Shekhar. This led to fresh elections in May 1991. Congress under Rajiv Gandhi were confident of winning because the National Front government had been unable to govern, and many of its policies were thought to have divided the country. Congress saw themselves as a party of unification. What the result would have been under normal circumstances will never be known, for Rajiv Gandhi was assassinated on 21 May 1991. Congress was returned to power as the largest party in Parliament but was without a majority. P.V. Narasimha Rao, an elderly, experienced Congress politician became the next Prime Minister and has had to face the effects of years of misrule. The new government instituted major economic reforms to stabilize and open the Indian economy to the world market.

The last five years have seen various internal conflicts: the Hindu/Muslim riots over Ayodhya Temple in central Uttar Pradesh (both religions claim it); the ongoing Kashmir problem, now escalated to include armed kidnap and summary execution of foreign tourists; the so-called 'plague' of 1994, which began in Gujarat and fizzled out in Delhi (total fatalities: 56). Despite all these things, combined with regional explosions of violence like the recent Bombay riots (a blockbuster film on the same subject appeared in Bombay three months later), Rao has, to the surprise of many, remained firmly in control, and has shown himself to be possibly the strongest national leader since Nehru.

Today India is still struggling towards a clear, solid identity—with unity as its prime objective. No amount of self-criticism, however, can disguise some truly remarkable achievements since Independence in 1947. India is presently one of the top industrial powers in the world. Her government and her legal, educational, and military institutions are strong. She is agriculturally self-sufficient, and making rapid strides in space-age technology (in Delhi, computer technology now helps the railways make 60,000 seat reservations a day).

Westerners have difficulty understanding the importance of religion to the average Indian. It governs his every thought, regulates his every action, and gives him his strong sense of identity—his 'dharma', or personal course in life. Religion is everything in India, and there are just as many different faiths to be found here—Hinduism and Buddhism, Jainism and Sikhism, Christianity, Zoroastrianism and Islam—as there are different peoples, tongues and cultures.

Some 80% of Indians are Hindus; another 10% follow Islam; Sikhs and Christians, combined, make up a further 5%. All the others—Jains, Parsis, Buddhists, Bahai, etc.—comprise the remainder. Social traditions differ among the Muslim, tribal, Christian, Sikh, Parsi and other communities that constitute around 20% of India's population today. Each of these communities is governed by its own social mores and traditions.

Hinduism

An ancient repository of Indian spiritual consciousness, Hinduism is the oldest surviving religion in the world, and has more adherents than any other religion in Asia. Hinduism went through various periods of prosperity and decline, but demonstrated the most amazing capacity for absorbing and assimilating all competing faiths, and was never down for long. One of its earliest scriptures, the *Upanishads* (400–200 BC), stated 'The Great God is One, and the learned call Him by different names'—and it was this aphorism which encapsulated the unique talent for Hindu religious toleration. It never destroyed other beliefs, just synthesized them into its own philosophical system.

Although all forms of worship are acceptable to Hinduism, there are a few basic beliefs which tie the various creeds together. The main three are Samsara, Karma and Dharma. **Samsara** is the eternity of life in which the soul is believed to pass through a cycle of births and deaths on its way to perfection, and to union with the Supreme Being (Brahma). **Karma**, or the law of cause and effect, is where every thought, word and deed produces a reaction (good or bad) in this or in a subsequent incarnation. **Dharma**, the code of living, decrees that every person has a specific role or set of moral duties to perform in life, through which he or she can break the cycle of rebirth and attain *nirvana* (heaven).

There are many thousands of gods in the Hindu pantheon. The Aryans were a nomadic people, worshippers of the natural elements. They had a Supreme Being, a central figure who controlled everything in life, but they also had gods to represent all forms of natural energy (sun, moon, wind, water, etc.) and all facets of human life and endeavour (courage, faith, luck, beauty, etc.). The total number of gods was calculated from the estimated population of the known world round the time of the epic poem, *Mahabharata*, which describes the war between good and evil in which five good brothers, aided by the god Krishna, defeat 100 wicked cousins. It was written down between 200 BC and AD 500, and Indian literature is full of references to it.

Over the centuries, many stories and legends grew up round the various gods and goddesses. The main group—the Puranas (AD 500–1500)—became the base of all art in India. Most sculptures and paintings told a 'purana' story, and through such legends and parables, Hindu morals, customs, manners and traditions slowly became crystallized. It was the only way in which the common people received any social education, for the Brahmin priest caste had exclusive access to the ancient Vedic scriptures and holy books, and never transferred this knowledge to the masses, except in such symbolic form.

The one supreme God of Hinduism, **Parabrahma**, has three physical manifestations— **Brahma** the Creator, **Vishnu** the Preserver, and **Shiva** the Destroyer. Representing the three basic processes in human life (birth, life and death), this main trinity rules over all the lesser gods. All three deities are normally depicted with four arms, but Brahma also has four heads to show his omniscient wisdom. Unlike the other two, however, he has had very few temples built for him. Each god has a 'carrier', an animal or bird who transports him about.

Vishnu is often seen sitting on an eagle with human features called a *Garuda*. He has visited earth in nine incarnations (avatars), and is due to pay one last visit, as the horse-headed Kalki. He has already appeared as a fish, a tortoise, a boar, a half-man, a beggar-dwarf, and in human form carrying an axe. On his seventh call, he came as **Rama** with an impossible mission to destroy the demon king Ravana of Lanka (Ceylon). The dramatic story of his success, aided and abetted by the faithful monkey-god **Hanuman**, became one of the world's greatest epics, the *Ramayana* (350 BC–AD 250). Vishnu made his eighth appearance as **Krishna**, the dark-skinned boy of the Mathura milkmaids, whom he married 'en masse' after releasing them from the demon king Naraka. The ninth incarnation of Vishnu, an imaginative ploy to reabsorb Buddhism back into the Hindu religion, is supposed to have been the **Buddha** himself.

Shiva's main symbol is the cobra, the virulent snake of death and destruction, though he generally rides out on the bull *Nandi*. His creative/sexual function is symbolized by the stone lingam. He is often shown with a third eye (sometimes used as a death-ray), and is believed to spend a lot of time in his Himalayan mountain home smoking the holy weed (*ganja*). When roused, Shiva has a very nasty temper. First he chopped off Brahma's fifth head, and had to wander round as a beggar until the severed skull unstuck itself from his palm. Then he lopped off the head of his younger son, **Ganesh**, for refusing to let him visit his wife **Parvati** while she was having a bath. Repenting of his error, Shiva looked round for a new head for his offspring, and came up with one of an elephant. Thus, 'lucky' Ganesh, god of good fortune (and divine remover of obstacles) was born. His animal vehicle is the bandicoot, or rat.

Each of the Hindu trinity has a consort, representing the feminine side of their energy. Brahma is married to **Saraswati**, the goddess of learning, and her vehicle is the swan. Vishnu's consort is the beautiful **Lakshmi** (Laxmi), goddess of wealth and prosperity.

Shiva started out with **Sati** (who burnt herself to death—the original 'sati' victim), then acquired **Parvati**, symbol of cosmic energy in the form of **Shakti**, the World Mother. She is also symbol (in her dark aspect) of destruction in the form of either **Kali**, wearing a wreath of skulls, or **Durga** the terrible, riding a tiger and waving weapons from 10 hands. In addition to Ganesh, Parvati had one other son by Shiva, the six-headed God of War, **Kartikkeya** (Murugan in south India or Subramanhya).

The good-humoured, indulgent, even playful attitude of many Hindus to their gods is something that mystifies many Westerners, used to religion as rather a solemn business. But while Hinduism is a strict faith, with many rituals, ceremonies and practices geared towards keeping the individual on the general strait and narrow, it has a great inbuilt sense of fun and spectacle. This is especially true on a social level, where births, marriages and even deaths are all an occasion for colourful, noisy bands and processions, complete with caparisoned elephants, performing monkeys, lots of firecrackers and entertainments, and (of course) plentiful free food. It's all a perfect reflection of, and a tribute to, a pantheon of gods who may be gaudy, boisterous, flamboyant but never dull.

Jainism

Jainism was the first major sect to break away from Hinduism, and was founded around 500 BC by Vardhamana Mahavira. He was the last of the 24 Jain saints or **Tirthankars**, and was an older contemporary of the Buddha. The schism from Hinduism came from his belief that there was no Supreme Creator of the universe, but that it was infinite and eternal. The Jains did believe in reincarnation (like the Hindus), but their method of achieving salvation was much more extreme. Mahavira preached the total subjugation of the senses as the most direct path to the world of the spirit, and Jain monks became noted for their great asceticism. They wandered about in a loincloth, with just an alms bowl and a stave as possessions. In this, they resembled the Shaivite Hindu ascetics called *sadhus*, but their strict doctrine of *ahimsa* (non-violence to any living creature) caused them to go even further—thus, they also carried a broom to sweep the ground before them clear of any insects, and wore a muslin mask to prevent them swallowing any flying parasites. The Jains found little problem finding a sanctuary in India—for the simple reason that the Hindus considered them even better Hindus than they were.

Around the 1st century AD, the Jains split into two sects: the white-clad **Shvetambaras** and the sky-clad **Digambaras**. The latter were literally 'sky-clad', being so contemptuous of material possessions that they wore no clothing at all. Jain temples are often quite beautiful, with highly ornate carvings on columns and ceilings. The best of these can be seen in Rajasthan (Mt Abu and Ranakpur), Gujarat (Palitana and Junagadh) and Bombay, the main Jain centres. Jainism is particularly strong in Rajasthan, for it is believed that the tirthankars were also Rajput princes. The Jains themselves are today few in number, but have great commercial and business influence. Many of them are successful traders, bankers and philanthropists.

Buddhism

The Buddhist religion was the second reformist offshoot of Hinduism, and presented it with a far greater threat. Founded by **Siddhartha** (Shakyamuni) **Gautama** (during the 5th century BC) in northern India, it was a dynamic force which thrived for 1700 years before slowly being won back to the Hindu fold by the revivalist movement started by Shankara in the 8th century AD.

Buddha was a Kshatriya prince who, preoccupied by the human problems of old age, sickness and death, forsook riches to embark on a long quest for the Truth. After several years of rigorous ascetic practice, he attained his enlightenment at Bodhgaya and spent the final 45 years of his life teaching his new philosophy. This incorporated Hindu elements, like the doctrines of *karma* and reincarnation, but reinterpreted them in a far more dynamic form. As far as Buddha was concerned, *karma* had nothing to do with fate or predestination. It was a strict causal law of dynamic action. He taught that every living being (not just priests or ascetics) could aspire to enlightenment in this lifetime, without passively awaiting better circumstances in a future incarnation. His central doctrine, whereby enlightenment could be achieved and the cycle of rebirth extinguished, was the eightfold path of the 'middle way'. This put the case for moderation in all things, and rejected as harmful the rules, regulations and general extremism of Hinduism and Jainism (Buddha had tried ascetic starvation, but found it more likely to lead to death than enlightenment). It was a simple, optimistic message, but the Hindus rejected Buddhism as a religion of compromise. With the 'middle way' discarded, India became progressively a land of extremes and stark contrasts.

Buddhism took its big leap forward in India when adopted by the great emperor Ashoka (3rd century BC). It was carried outwards to every part of his extensive empire, and spread in time to Burma, Thailand, Sri Lanka, Korea, China, Vietnam, Nepal, Tibet, Central Asia and Japan. But in India, it quickly experienced a schism, leading to two main schools. The **Hinayana** or 'lesser vehicle' held that enlightenment was an individual pursuit; the **Mahayana** or 'greater vehicle' held that it was a collective one, with the ultimate aim of bringing all humanity to salvation. After Buddhism's collapse in India, the centre of Mahayana transferred to Japan, where the essence of Gautama's final teaching (the *Lotus Sutra*, or *Myoho Renge Kyo*) was revealed by the 13th-century monk Nichiren. Unlike the Hinayana sect, who always referred to the Buddha in terms of external symbols (the lotus for his birth, the tree for his enlightenment, the wheel of law for his first sermon, and the stupa for his final *nirvana* or salvation), the growing realization of the Mahayana sect was to seek Buddha nowhere else but in themselves, and in every living thing.

Islam

There are more Muslims (around 100 million) than any other religious minority group in India. The most recent and successful Asian religion, it was founded by the prophet **Muhammad** in the early 7th century AD. The Muslim canon, the **Koran**, is a collection of apocalyptic messages delivered to Mohammed by Allah (God). A keynote of the faith was its militancy, its evangelical zeal to spread the good word—by the sword, if necessary. Starting in Arabia, Islam extended its influence east for several centuries, and was eventually firmly established in three continents.

Conversion was easy—to become a Muslim required only saying the words, 'There is no God but Allah and Muhammad is his prophet'. It was especially easy in India, where the Muslims came in the 11th century AD, for a great many low-caste Hindus sought to escape from the discriminations of Brahmanical Hinduism. They could no longer turn to Buddhism (there were no Buddhists left), so their only recourse was Islam. But in the long term Hinduism was too strong to be dislodged.

There are two types of Muslim, resulting from an early schism. These are the **Sunnis** (the majority), whose allegiance is to the succession from Muhammad's direct successor, the Caliph; and the **Shias** or Shi'ites who follow the descendants of the prophet's son-in-law, Ali. For both, the big objective is to make the pilgrimage to Mecca (Muhammad's birthplace in AD 570) and become a *hajji*. The Muslims may have come to north India first as ruthless, iconoclastic conquerors, but their contribution to Indian civilization is still prevalent in art, architecture and culture.

Sikhism

The Sikh religion is comparatively new, having broken away from Hinduism as late as the 15th century. It was born of the frictions between Hindus and Muslims in the Punjab, and was founded by **Guru Nanak** (1494–1538). Originally a pacifist movement, aimed at synthesizing the best of the Hindu and Islamic religions, it turned into a militant brotherhood under the tenth Guru of the line, Guru Gobind Singh, in the 17th century. This was a reaction to the extreme persecution which the Sikhs of those times were suffering, and all of them thereafter bore the surname Singh or 'Lion'.

The Sikh Bible is called **Granth Sahib**. It is opposed to several Hindu tenets, including the caste system and the dominance of the Brahmins. It differs from other Hindu-based faiths in its rejection of non-violence, and it condones the killing of animals for food. The Sikhs believe in one god, have temples known as *gurdwaras*, and have had a total of 10 Gurus whose collected writings (plus various Hindu and Muslim scriptures) form the Granth Sahib.

Sikhs are instantly distinguishable by their five symbols or *kakka*, introduced by Guru Gobind Singh: *kesa* or unshorn hair (normally wrapped under a turban); *kachcha* or short trousers; the steel bracelet or *kara*; the wooden or ivory comb called *kangha*; and the *kirpan* or sword.

Although just 2% of the Indian population follows the Sikh religion, Sikhs dominate the army, and the transport and light engineering industries. They have a well-earned reputation for a no-nonsense attitude, a capacity for hard work, and skill in mechanical matters—they are said to be the best car mechanics in the world.

In the early 1980s a section of Sikh extremists took up the call for a separate country, called Khalistan. This led to the political and economic decline of the Punjab, the most prosperous state in India. The terrorists converted the Golden Temple, the most venerated Sikh shrine, into their headquarters, and this led to army action in 1984. This further alienated Sikhs from the rest of the country, and ultimately resulted in the assassination of Indira Gandhi by one of her Sikh bodyguards. The subsequent riots, during which several thousand innocent Sikhs were massacred, led to an even greater rift.

At the time of writing, the political situation has yet to be resolved, but personal relationships between Sikhs and other members of the Indian community remain relatively unscathed.

Zoroastrianism

The tiny community of Zoroastrians, commonly known as **Parsis**, are concentrated mainly in Bombay. Theirs is one of the oldest religions known, founded by the prophet **Zoroaster** (Zarathustra) in Persia, around 800 BC. Forced to flee their native country by a Muslim invasion of Persia, they were given sanctuary in India.

Their scripture, the **Zend-Avesta**, describes the ongoing battle between good and evil, and their god is **Ahura Mazda** who is symbolized by fire. Parsis revere the elements of nature, but are not fire-worshippers: they keep the sacred flame burning in all their temples only as a symbol of their god. To preserve the purity of the elements they do not defile fire, earth, water or air by burying or cremating their dead. Instead, they leave the bodies atop 'Towers of Silence' to be devoured by vultures.

As a community, the Parsis are distinctive, enterprising and have contributed much to modern India. They have an extraordinary talent for commerce, and the Tatas, a highly respected Parsi business group, have wide-ranging and extremely profitable interests in the oil, steel, automobile, computing and tea industries, amongst others. The Taj Group of Hotels is run by Tatas, and Air India was a Tata enterprise which was later nationalized. Parsis are also renowned for their philanthropy, and run a range of trusts to look after the interests of their own community.

Only if the father is Parsi can the children be Parsi, and you cannot join Parsi ranks through conversion. This, combined perhaps with the apparent reluctance of well-educated and increasingly independent Parsi women to settle down, has resulted in a marked decline in numbers of the Parsi community.

Christianity and Judaism

There have been Christians in India since St Thomas, one of Christ's Disciples, arrived in Kerala in AD 54. The Syrian Church he founded here is the second oldest Christian Church in the world, after that in ancient Palestine. During the mid-4th and 8th centuries, two waves of Christian immigrants arrived from the Middle East, and a substantial community of 'Syrian Christians' grew up in Kerala.

Later still, in the 16th century, Catholic and Protestant missionaries made a number of converts from various Portuguese, Dutch, French and English settlements. In the Indian community, they concentrated mainly on areas where large numbers of labourers were gathered, such as tea gardens and oil fields, and on the tribal areas of Bihar and northeast India, where they experienced considerable success. The lower castes were naturally more susceptible to conversion, as a means of escape from their unchangeably low status in the Hindu caste system.

However, only in Goa, where the Portuguese left a sizeable Christian community of relatively influential men, were the efforts of the missionaries longlasting; though the Syrian Orthodox Church in Kerala is still fairly strong. Amongst the disaffected Hindus of the lower castes, the religion could not find the power it needed to become widespread. Nevertheless, Christians in India have made their mark in social, medical, educational and philanthropic fields.

In Kerala once more, the Jews of Cochin deserve a special mention; their ancestry goes back to the 6th century BC. They were a highly influential community in their time and the Cochin synagogue is the oldest in the Commonwealth, but at present there are only about 28 Cochin Jews remaining, most of whom are in their seventies.

A more ancient, larger and more significant Jewish community called the Bene Israel exists in and around Bombay. It is estimated that there are about 4000 Jews in the whole country but, like the Parsis, their community is declining.

North India

Hawa Mahal, Jaipur

India has always been invaded from the north—first by foreign invaders and most recently by tourism. It remains the most popular area of the country, not least because because of its cooler climate, its imposing Mughal architecture and its wide range of attractions—the fairytale desert forts of Rajasthan, the hill stations of Himachal Pradesh, the pilgrimage sites of Bihar and Uttar Pradesh, Varanasi and Bodhgaya, the seat of government—and, most famously, the unforgettable Taj Mahal.

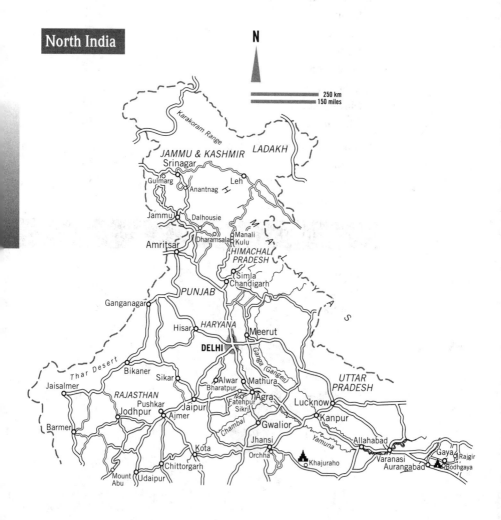

Capital of India, Delhi is two cities in one—first the Old Delhi of the Mughals, created by Shah Jahan and still a medieval place of forts, mosques and bazaars; second, the New Delhi built by the British, an elegant metropolis of broad avenues, stately homes and landscaped gardens. The co-existence of the old and the new, a common feature of modern Indian cities, is nowhere more obvious than in Delhi; with the poor inner city leading a life of its own, the rich and the political élite retire to the sophisticated diplomatic enclaves and debate the encroaching poverty from behind closed doors. Delhi is the seat of Indian government, and what visitors see here is a reflection of what is happening in the country as a whole.

History

When the great coastal cities of India were still mud-flats, Delhi was already a thriving capital of an ancient empire. Legend has it that the Pandavas, heroes of the *Mahabharata* epic, founded a city on this site, called Indraprastha, around 1200 BC. Certainly, it has for many centuries exerted a powerful influence on the history of the country. Its strategic situation between the Aravali hills and the river Yamuna was one that no prospective Hindu ruler or northern invader could afford to ignore. Consequently, it was built, fought over, defended, destroyed, deserted and rebuilt on several occasions over the ages. In the process, it absorbed many different cultures and became uniquely cosmopolitan in its outlook.

No fewer than 15 different cities are said to have risen and fallen in and around Delhi since the 11th century. The first four 'Dillis' were Rajput structures, erected in the southern hills near the present situation of the Qutb Minar. The first historically recorded citadel was Lal Kot, built by the Tomar Rajputs (founders of 8th-century Dillika) in AD 1060. Taken by the Chauhan Rajputs in the 12th century, it was enlarged and renamed Qila Rai Pithora. Then came the Turk slave-king Qutb-ud-Din Aibak, the first Sultan of Delhi (1206), who built India's first mosque (Quwwat-ul-Islam) and her symbolic tower of victory, Qutb Minar. Under the Khilji dynasty, Islam's influence spread and the prosperous city of Siri sprang up (Delhi II, 1290–1320) near to present-day Hauz Khas. Next came the Tughlaqs, a bulldog breed who built no fewer than three new cities here in the 14th century—first Tughlaqabad, a massive 13-gate fort 10km (6.3 miles) southeast of Qutb Minar (used for only five years), then Jahanapanah (rapidly abandoned by the mad Sultan Mohammed, who marched the whole population off to distant Daulatabad, near Aurangabad, and then marched them all back again 17 years later), and finally Ferozabad (creation of Mohammed's more stable successor, Feroz Shah), in its day the richest city in the world. This fifth version of Delhi marked the critical move north to the river settlement along the river Yamuna. It lasted a remarkably long time (Delhi's turbulent history considered), the Tughlaq's successors (Sayyids and Lodhis) being too busy building tombs to construct new cities. Emperor Sher Shah, the

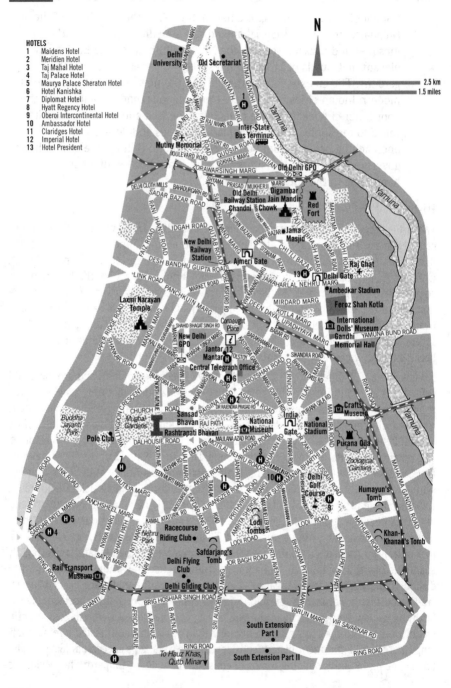

Delhi

HOTELS
1 Maidens Hotel
2 Meridien Hotel
3 Taj Mahal Hotel
4 Taj Palace Hotel
5 Maurya Palace Sheraton Hotel
6 Hotel Kanishka
7 Diplomat Hotel
8 Hyatt Regency Hotel
9 Oberoi Intercontinental Hotel
10 Ambassador Hotel
11 Claridges Hotel
12 Imperial Hotel
13 Hotel President

N

2.5 km
1.5 miles

Afghan usurper, displaced the Mughals just long enough to build a sixth Delhi, Shergarh, before they won it back again (1555).

But it wasn't for another century that the seat of Mughal power transferred back to Delhi from Agra. The move took place under Emperor Shah Jahan, who built Shahjahanabad (the present Old Delhi) between 1638 and 1648, obliterating most of old Ferozabad and Shergarh to provide building materials. His son, Aurangzeb, made some improvements to the new capital, but the succession of weak Mughal rulers who came afterwards only paved the way for the infamous invasion of Nadir Shah (1739), when 30,000 Delhi inhabitants lost their lives overnight. After this, the Mughal emperor could only sit sadly in his sacked Red Fort (Lal Qila) and utter the epitaph of his conquered dynasty: 'My kingdom extends no further than these four walls.' Delhi then fell to the British, returning only briefly to Mughal rule during the Indian Mutiny. The last Mughal emperor, Bahadur Shah, was reluctantly persuaded out of retirement for this, and suffered for his decision by being marched off into exile in Rangoon. It was the end of the great Mughal Empire in India.

Under British rule, Delhi remained in the backwaters until 1911, when the King-Emperor announced the creation of a new city, New Delhi, and the transfer of the government from Calcutta, and Delhi became a capital once more. To mark its new status as a brand-new city, the eighth (New) Delhi was constructed. The creation of two British architects—Edwin Lutyens and Herbert Baker—it was designed in magnificent style to reflect the might of the British Empire in India and to accommodate 70,000 people. The new, modern city sprang up from out of a bare wilderness previously inhabited only by wild animals, a mirage of planned gardens, noble monuments and enormous avenues. Completed in 1931, on the very eve of Independence, it is today considered either the blindest folly of the British Raj or (being generous) its finest gift to modern, free India.

Today, New Delhi remains distinctly British. The old imperiousness of the Viceroys has become the political élitism of the Indian ruling-class, and many of the parliamentary, legislative and educational procedures of the Raj remain not only intact, but reinforced by the Indian love of red tape. In Connaught Place, while young gum-chewing Delhiites queue with foreign tourists in fast-food Wimpy bars, politicians and place-hunters jostle with film stars and media types in swanky upmarket hotels and restaurants, and at private dinners.

Delhi elicits strong likes and dislikes amongst foreign travellers. On the plus side, it's an easy introduction to India, with some of the best hotels, restaurants and facilities in the country. It's also a very convenient base for sightseeing: from here you can jump off to Rajasthan, Varanasi, Kashmir (if the political situation allows) and the ever-popular Golden Triangle. But many find it lacking in colour, character and expression—a city without a face, not like real India at all. In an important sense, what started out being considered the Raj's greatest contribution to free India could well become a long-term hindrance, a continuous reminder of a past best forgotten.

When to Go

Delhi is at its most pleasant in October/November and February/March. It suddenly turns cold round mid-December and stays like that till late January, so bring your woolies. By April, the heat is getting up and from mid-May to early June temperatures peak at around 46°C. After this, the rains come and it's not until early September that Delhi becomes bearable once more.

The city's biggest party is **Republic Day** (26 January), celebrated here as nowhere else in the country. The day itself is marked by a military parade along the length of Rajpath and on to Connaught Place and the Red Fort. There follows a whole week of festivals, dance performances, massed bands and ceremonial displays. In September/ October, the emphasis shifts from a military to a cultural show of strength, the 10-day **Dussehra** festival coinciding with plays, classical dance, music recitals and readings of epic poems. The festival to *avoid* is **Holi** (February/March) when unwary travellers, along with everyone else, are pelted with coloured water, powder or paint. *Not* a good day to go out in your best bib and tucker.

International Arrivals and Departures

Indira Gandhi International Airport has two separate terminals—Terminal 1 at Palam, 17km from Connaught Place, for domestic flights (1A for Indian Airlines,1B for private airlines) and Terminal 2, 22km from Connaught Place, for international flights. A shuttle bus service connects the two terminals after every flight. The international airport is about a 50-minute drive from the city centre, and the domestic airport around 40 minutes.

Arriving from overseas, expect to spend a good hour between landing and finally clearing the airport building. Do *not* leave the airport building without changing at least some money (for your taxi/bus trip into town) at Thomas Cook or State Bank of India inside the arrivals hall. Once you're outside, they won't let you back in again.

Note: Leaving Delhi for home, make sure that your flight ticket has been reconfirmed (do this the first day after arrival, to save forgetting later) and that you still have enough rupees for both your transport to the airport and the Rs300 departure tax levied on all international flights out of the capital.

Airport to city: there are pre-paid taxi booths inside both terminals, charging Rs100–140 from domestic, Rs160–200 from international, into the city. Both airports also operate two cheap bus services which stop off at various hotels before reaching the centre. The EATS bus (Rs25) terminates at Malhotra Building, Connaught Place, next to Indian Airlines, and the Delhi Transport Corporation bus (Rs20) at Air India office in Janpath. The latter makes useful drops at New Delhi railway station for Paharganj and at ISBT bus station for Hotel Oberoi Maidens.

If this is your first time in India and you're landing at night, consider stay-ing inside the airport until dawn. If you must go into the city in the wee small hours, don't let taxi drivers from the airport 'recommend' a place to stay. They know that most cheap guest houses are bolted shut between midnight and 6am, and they are very skilled at duping exhausted travellers arriving in the middle of the night into over-priced hotels where they get lots of commission. Whatever they say—whether it's that your hotel has been closed for weeks, burnt down yesterday or raided by the police today—insist on going to the hotel of *your* choice and not theirs.

City to airport: taxis (Rs150–170) and auto-rickshaws (Rs70–80) to the international airport should be pre-booked, especially if you're travelling by night. The cheapest if not the fastest way to the airport is the EATS bus service from Janpath (opposite Palika Bazaar) which leaves every hour or so from 4am to 11.30pm. Or the DTC bus service, which leaves every 45 minutes (24hrs) from ISBT bus station and New Delhi railway station. Before leaving your hotel, it's a good idea to ring the airport and check that your flight is not delayed. It's also a good idea to avoid the 5 to 8pm rush hour when travelling to the airport.

Getting Around

Delhi may be a sprawling giant of a city but at least (unlike Bombay or Calcutta) it has a definite centre, which greatly eases orientation. Travellers collect in three major 'pockets'—in and around the central-city hub of Connaught Circus (for airline offices, tourist offices, banks, travel agents, cheaper hotels and better restaurants); in the Paharganj area 2km north of Connaught Place (for New Delhi rail station and more budget accommodation); and occasionally in hotels like Oberoi Maidens in the old city (for Old Delhi rail station, Red Fort and the bazaars). A fourth pocket, reserved for the rich and influential, is round Lutyens' imperial complex and the new post-Independence colonies of south Delhi. This is where you'll find most of the five-star hotels and the smarter residential and shopping areas.

No matter how you get around, there's no escape from Delhi diesel. Dense clouds of fumes from countless buses, trucks and auto-rickshaws clog the highways all day long and are especially noxious during the rush hour. Street touts do a roaring trade in Rs35 anti-smog masks, but apart from making you look like Darth Vader they're not much use. Despite the constant build-up of pollution however, Delhi continues to fascinate and most travellers love it.

By auto-rickshaw and taxi: Auto-rickshaws in Delhi hate using their meters—even the most streetwise traveller has to bargain hard for every ride. If you can get one from say Paharganj down to Connaught Place (a short 5-minute hop) for Rs15, you're doing well. Taxis do use their meters, but often only when you tell them to. Unlike Bombay or Calcutta, they can be hired off the street (Rs3.50 per km) as well as from big hotels (expensive). Taxi drivers are adept at telling who is new to the country and who is not. If they peg you in the former category, expect to be offered all manner of things you don't want. When you've had enough, feign deafness over the noise of the traffic.

Note: Don't go anywhere until you've either agreed a fair price, or (better) have persuaded your driver to flag down his meter. Theoretically, you can report him to the police for overcharging, but hardly any travellers have time for that. The threat is usually sufficient. The minimum fare for a taxi is Rs7 and for an auto-rickshaw Rs4.40. This covers you for the first 2km of your journey. The meters, being old, will only read Rs5 and Rs3 respectively. At the end of your journey, add 50% to whatever is on the meter to arrive at the correct fare.

By bicycle-rickshaw: Cycle-rickshaws are useful for negotiating crowded thoroughfares like Paharganj or Chandni Chowk, where motorized transport is restricted or not allowed. They're slow but inexpensive—rarely more than Rs10/15 anywhere. It's still important to agree a price first though. Don't be fobbed off with the old 'as you like' gag when you ask the fare—unless you pin them down to a specific amount before climbing aboard, the final fare will invariably be what *they* like.

Delhi ✆ (011–)   ***Tourist Information***

Delhi is *the* place to gather information. Wherever you're heading for next, gather all relevant maps, brochures and books here. Also use Delhi to do as much advance travel-planning as possible, in particular rail and domestic flight bookings.

The Government Of India **tourist office** at 88 Janpath, ✆ 3320005, is open 9am to 6pm weekdays, 9am to 2pm Saturdays, closed Sundays and holidays. It tries hard but is generally too inundated with enquiries to be of more than superficial help. Come armed with specific questions and make it clear that you need only a minute of their time—it's the best way of grabbing their attention. Other information desks are at the domestic (✆ 3295296) and international (✆ 3291171) airports.

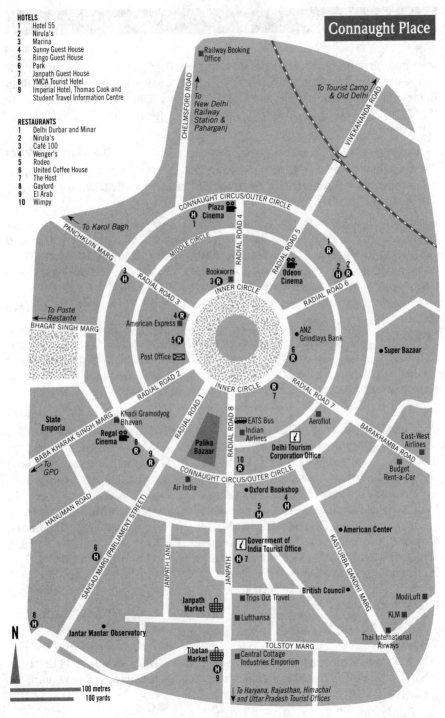

Connaught Place

HOTELS
1. Hotel 55
2. Nirula's
3. Marina
4. Sunny Guest House
5. Ringo Guest House
6. Park
7. Janpath Guest House
8. YMCA Tourist Hotel
9. Imperial Hotel, Thomas Cook and Student Travel Information Centre

RESTAURANTS
1. Delhi Durbar and Minar
2. Nirula's
3. Café 100
4. Wenger's
5. Rodeo
6. United Coffee House
7. The Host
8. Gaylord
9. El Arab
10. Wimpy

Railway Booking Office

To New Delhi Railway Station & Paharganj

CHELMSFORD ROAD

To Tourist Camp & Old Delhi

VIVEKANANDA ROAD

CONNAUGHT CIRCUS/OUTER CIRCLE

Plaza Cinema

To Karol Bagh

PANCHKUIN MARG

MIDDLE CIRCLE

RADIAL ROAD 4

RADIAL ROAD 5

RADIAL ROAD 3

Bookworm

INNER CIRCLE

Odeon Cinema

RADIAL ROAD 6

To Poste Restante

BHAGAT SINGH MARG

American Express

ANZ Grindlays Bank

Super Bazaar

Post Office

RADIAL ROAD 2

INNER CIRCLE

RADIAL ROAD 7

BARAKHAMBA ROAD

State Emporia

BABA KHARAK SINGH MARG

Khadi Gramodyog Bhavan

RADIAL ROAD 1

RADIAL ROAD 8

EATS Bus
Indian Airlines

Aeroflot

East-West Airlines

Regal Cinema

Palika Bazaar

Delhi Tourism Corporation Office

Budget Rent-a-Car

To GPO

CONNAUGHT CIRCUS/OUTER CIRCLE

Air India

Oxford Bookshop

American Center

HANUMAN ROAD

SANSAD MARG (PARLIAMENT STREET)

Government of India Tourist Office

KASTURBA GANDHI MARG

JANPATH LANE

JANPATH

British Council

ModiLuft

KLM

Janpath Market

Trips Out Travel

Lufthansa

Thai International Airways

N

Jantar Mantar Observatory

Tibetan Market

TOLSTOY MARG

Central Cottage Industries Emporium

To Haryana, Rajasthan, Himachal and Uttar Pradesh Tourist Offices

100 metres
100 yards

banks

Most major international banks have offices in New Delhi, but most are slow and few change travellers' cheques. For fast service use **Thomas Cook** at Imperial Hotel, **American Express** in A Block, Connaught Place, or **DTDC Tourist Office** at N Block, Connaught Place. The latter is open till 9pm daily. If you need money fter this, there's a 24-hour branch of the **Central Bank** at the Ashok Hotel in Chanakyapuri.

books and libraries

Two libraries to spend a civilized afternoon in, reading newspapers and catching up on home news, are the **American Centre** and the **British Council Library** at 24 and 17 Kasturba Gandhi Marg.

Bookshops are dotted all around Connaught Place. Three good ones are **Empire Book Depot**, 74 Janpath Market, **Mehta Bandhu** next to the tourist office, and **New Bookland** opposite the tourist office. They all sell *Delhi Diary*, *Here Delhi* and *Perfect Media*, full of cultural, culinary and travel information; also maps, foreign newspapers and big novels to while away long bus or train journeys.

embassies

Most **foreign embassies** are at Shantipath, Chanakyapuri, and include the UK ($\mathcal{C}$ 6872161), USA ($\mathcal{C}$ 600651), Australia ($\mathcal{C}$ 6888223), Canada ($\mathcal{C}$ 6876500), France ($\mathcal{C}$ 6118790), Germany ($\mathcal{C}$ 604861) and Japan ($\mathcal{C}$ 6876581). Nepal is at Barakhamba Road ($\mathcal{C}$ 3328191), and Thailand ($\mathcal{C}$ 605679) and New Zealand ($\mathcal{C}$ 6883170) are both at Nyaya Marg, Chanakyapuri.

international airline offices

International airlines flying to Delhi include: **Aeroflot**, BMC House, N 1 Connaught Place ($\mathcal{C}$ 3312843); **Air France**, Scindia House, Janpath ($\mathcal{C}$ 3310407); **Air India**, Jeevan Bharati Building ($\mathcal{C}$ 3310407); **Alitalia**, 2nd floor, DCM Building, 16 Barakhamba Road ($\mathcal{C}$ 3313777); **British Airways**, DLF Building, Sansad Marg ($\mathcal{C}$ 3323332); **Gulf Air**, G-12 Connaught Circus ($\mathcal{C}$ 3327814); **Iran Air**, Ashok Hotel, Chanakyapuri ($\mathcal{C}$ 606471); **Iraqi Airways**, Ansal Bhawan, KG Marg ($\mathcal{C}$ 3318742); **Japan Airlines**, Chanderlok Building, 36 Janpath ($\mathcal{C}$ 3324922); **KLM**, Tolstoy Marg ($\mathcal{C}$ 3326822); **Lufthansa**, 56 Janpath ($\mathcal{C}$ 3323310); **Pakistan International (PIA)**; 201 New Delhi House, Barakhamba Road ($\mathcal{C}$ 3711396); **Royal Nepal Airlines**, 44 Janpath ($\mathcal{C}$ 3321164); **SAS**, 1st floor, Amba Deep Building, 14 KG Marg ($\mathcal{C}$ 3352299); **Singapore Airlines**, G-11 Connaught Place ($\mathcal{C}$ 3326373); **Syrian Arab Airlines**, 66 Janpath ($\mathcal{C}$ 3713366); **Thai International**, Amba Deep Building, 14 KG Marg ($\mathcal{C}$ 3323608); **United Airlines**, Amba Deep Building, 14 KG Marg ($\mathcal{C}$ 3715550).

medical services

In case of **medical emergency**, contact the **East West Medical Centre** at 38 Golf Links Road, $\mathcal{C}$ 699229. This place has been recommended by many travellers, and though not cheap gives the best care available.near Kashmiri Gate.

The main **GPO** is on Sansad Marg, ✆ 344111, open 10am to 8pm weekdays, to 5pm only on Sundays. Most travellers use the more convenient post office at A Block, Connaught Place, ✆ 3364214, which has a parcel-packing service. The Foreign Post Office for **poste restante** mail is on Bhai Vir Singh Marg, about 1km from Connaught Place. It's open 9am to 5pm weekdays only. Tell your family and friends to write to you at NEW Delhi—mountains of mail marked simply 'Delhi' are still sitting unclaimed in the Old Delhi post office

The **parcel packing service** at T298 General Market, Main Bazar, Paharganj, is very useful for sending home bulky presents and various stuff that you thought you'd need in India but don't. Air-mailing a 10kg gift parcel (£60) may cost much more than seamail (£25), but it'll get home a lot quicker and usually in one piece. For larger exports, *see* p.27.

Cheap **overseas calls** can be made from the several STD booths dotted around Janpath and Paharganj. The Saina Hotel in Main Bazar, for example, has a 24-hour service with off-peak rates as low as Rs55/minute (11pm to 7am) to London. Normal rates are Rs66/minute.

travel agents

Useful travel agents for flight bookings and upmarket travel arrangements are **Cox & Kings** (✆ 3320067), **TCI** (✆ 3312570) and **Sita World Travels** (✆ 3311133), all located in Connaught Place. The **Student Travel Information Centre** (✆ 3327582) in the Imperial Hotel is a good place to renew or obtain student cards.

Cheap flights abroad can be purchased from **Tripsout Travel** at 72 Janpath, ✆ 3322654, **Hans Travel** at Hotel Vishal, Paharganj, ✆ 733927, and **Rajiv Travels** at Saina Hotel, Paharganj, ✆ 529144. At the time of writing, all three are offering one-way tickets as low as US$140 to Kathmandu, US$170 to Bangkok, US$220 to Singapore, US$650 to Sydney, US$530 to New York and US$250 to London. Round-trip tickets are cheaper and make sense if you're coming back soon, since they often have a 3–4 month validity. Currently, you can buy a return flight to London for just US$440, while two-way tickets for New York and Sydney can cost as little as US$700 and US$800. All fares can be paid for in rupees or foreign currency, though a 5% surcharge is applied if you're paying by credit card. Most travel agents, worth noting, need at least 24 hours notice to arrange ticketing.

Note: Youth fares for under-30s can be up to 25 per cent less than the above-quoted rates. Visas for Thailand can be arranged by all the above agencies for around Rs500. Deluxe buses to Kathmandu (Rs550, 36hrs) are also on offer, but you'll thank me for suggesting the plane.

visa extensions

The **Foreigners' Registration Office** on the 1st floor, Hans Bhavan, near Tilak Bridge rail station, ✆ 3319489, is where to come for 3-month visa extensions if you need extra time in the country. For quick service turn up at 9.30am sharp (any weekday) with your passport and four photos. A photographer outside the building takes photos for a small charge.

Delhi Tourism Development Corporation at N Block, Middle Circle, Connaught Place, ℃ 4697250, is open 7am to 9pm daily. Come here to book **city sight-seeing tours** (New Delhi, morning; Old Delhi, afternoon; Delhi by Evening, night), and/or the popular Agra day-tour by bus. DTDC also has counters at New Delhi (℃ 3732374) and Old Delhi (℃ 2511083) rail stations, at ISBT bus stand (℃ 2962181), and at the domestic (℃ 3295609) and international (℃ 3291213) airports.

State tourist offices, for collecting specialized information on particular areas you're likely to visit, are at three separate locations: Bihar, Gujarat, Karnataka, Maharashtra, Orissa, Tamil Nadu, Uttar Pradesh and West Bengal are on Baba Kharak Singh Marg; Haryana, Himachal Pradesh and Rajasthan are at Chanderlok Building, 36 Janpath; Jammu and Kashmir, Kerala and Madhya Pradesh are at Kanishka Shopping Plaza, near Kanishka Hotel.

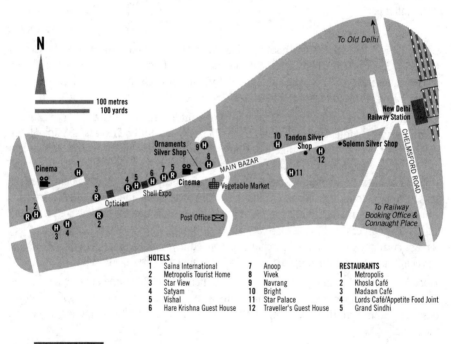

HOTELS

1	Saina International	7	Anoop	**RESTAURANTS**
2	Metropolis Tourist Home	8	Vivek	1 Metropolis
3	Star View	9	Navrang	2 Khosla Café
4	Satyam	10	Bright	3 Madaan Café
5	Vishal	11	Star Palace	4 Lords Café/Appetite Food Joint
6	Hare Krishna Guest House	12	Traveller's Guest House	5 Grand Sindhi

Paharganj

Delhi has more sights than any other Indian city, so you'll need to be selective. As a new arrival, you're probably best off taking a conducted tour. Delhi's tours aren't the best—far too much time is wasted on picking up passengers before hitting the sights—but you do cover a lot of out-of-the-way spots which would otherwise cost a fortune by rickshaw or taxi.

One tip: before taking on a tour, give yourself a day or two to get over jet-lag. Like all major Indian cities, Delhi can be pretty overpowering and during the summer incredibly hot.

Tour 1: City and Surrounds

By conducted sightseeing coach, 4 hours. Jantar Mantar–
Laxmi Narayan Temple–Rashtrapati Bhavan–India Gate–Safdarjang Tomb–
Qutb Minar–Quwwat-ul-Islam–Humayun's Tomb.

Leaving Connaught Place down Parliament Street, you'll first see the salmon-pink astronomical observatory of **Jantar Mantar**. Built in AD 1724, this was the first of five brick-and-mortar observatories created by the starstruck Maharajah Jai Singh II of Jaipur. It consists of four differing masonry instruments designed to predict eclipses and to plot the course of the planets, stars and sun. The big feature is the huge 'Prince of Dials' sundial. But Delhi city-dwellers come here mainly for picnics on the pleasant garden lawns.

The next stop is **Laxmi Narayan Temple** on Mandir Marg, 2km west of Connaught Place. This colourful pink and gold 'modern' Hindu temple, erected by the philanthropist G.D. Birla (1938) and commonly referred to as **Birla Temple**, is interesting because it's so different from normal Indian temples: first, it's composed of several different-coloured stone materials (instead of the traditional red sandstone); second, it's open to all Hindus, including the *harijans* (ex-'untouchables'); third, it's a mixture of various Hindu architectural styles instead of just one; finally, it's dedicated to a number of other gods (notably Ganesh, Hanuman and Durga) in addition to the focal deities of Vishnu, god of preservation, and his consort Laxmi, goddess of wealth. The ecumenism of the temple even extends to other religions, and inside you'll find not only some fine Buddhist and Sikh wall-frescoes, but also a huge bronze bell and a huge marble globe presented by Chinese Buddhists. But it's Krishna's shrine which visitors come to see—an ingenious mirror-chamber where, everywhere you look, Krishna's reflection is staring back at you. In the courtyard, you'll see the fine equestrian statue of Arjuna and the other Pandava brothers who helped Krishna defeat the forces of evil in olden times.

Rashtrapati Bhavan, the former Viceregal Lodge, now the official residence of India's President, is the best example of Lutyens' expansive, imperialist vision, built, like the massive complex of government buildings and offices it overlooks, of red sandstone in the Indo-Saracenic (eastern baroque) style. Once irreverently described as 'a British matron in fancy dress', it covers 330 acres of Raisina Hill. Since the tour bus only speeds past, you may want to see it properly another day; you won't be allowed into Rashtrapati Bhavan, but you can visit the beautiful 10 acres of Mughal gardens behind it (*open Feb–Mar*) on production of a pass obtained from the tourist office. There are two new museums at Rashtrapati Bhavan—one at 1 Willingdon Crescent, containing a documentary and photographic history of the building, and a second in the Marble Hall within the building, which is more of a portrait gallery and open only on certain days. You may also, with an introduction from your Embassy, visit nearby **Sansad Bhavan** (Parliament House), the vast, circular, colonnade-rimmed building designed by Baker on the south end of Sansad Marg.

A scenic drive down stately, tree-lined **Rajpath** brings you to **India Gate**, the symbol of modern Delhi. A 42m-high white-sandstone monolith, it was built by the British to salute the 90,000 Indian soldiers who lost their lives in the First World War. The small eternal flame, or *Amer Jawan Jyoti*, beneath it was added later by Indira Gandhi, in memory of Indian casualties of the 1971 war with Pakistan. Modelled on the Menin Gate in Belgium, India Gate is today a favourite tourist attraction—another place where Delhiites come to wind down after work.

A long drive south (8km from the city centre) is **Safdarjang Tomb**, built between 1753 and 1774 for Mohammed Shah's prime minister, Safdar Jang, the second Nawab of Oudh. The mausoleum is set on a raised terrace in fountain-sprinkled gardens, and comprises a 12m-high central hall supporting a bulbous dome, with marble minarets. It is notable for being the 'last great flicker in the lamp of Mughal architecture at Delhi'.

Towering over the ancient monuments of Lal Kot is Delhi's most famous landmark, the **Qutb Minar**. Situated some 15km south of New Delhi, it is the highlight of the tour: a soaring tower of victory, commenced in AD 1199 to mark the Muslim defeat of the last Hindu king, and once used as a minaret by the muezzins. It has five storeys, three of red sandstone and two of marble and sandstone, and tapers up to a height of 72.5m. Despite earthquakes, lightning, and the general ravages of time, it remains in

India Gate Delhi

remarkably good condition. A masterpiece of perfect proportion, with exquisite embellishments adorning the walls (intricate carvings of quotations from the *Koran* growing ever-larger the higher up the tower you look, so that the words are easy to read at both the top and the bottom), it has been called one of the wonders of the ancient world. Visitors used to be allowed up the tower stairway to enjoy views from the top balconies, but a series of suicide attempts caused the stairway to be closed.

Below the Qutb Minar stands the earliest extant mosque built in India, the **Quwwat-ul-Islam** ('Might of Islam') Mosque. Commenced in AD 1193 on the site of an old Hindu temple, it was plastered and richly ornamented with floral designs and text from the *Koran*, to cover over the old Hindu decorations. But time has eroded the plaster and you can now see some of the original carving, and the places where the faces of the Hindu gods have been hacked away. Within the mosque is the famous Iron Pillar. Probably cast in the 4th century AD, nobody knows where it came from, what it's doing there and why it hasn't gone rusty. A popular myth is that if you can clasp your hands standing with your back to the pillar, you'll get your wish. This pillar is so strong that someone once fired a cannon at it, and it wasn't even dented.

Leaving the mosque, you'll come across the enormous base of the **Alai Minar**, an attempt by the Afghan Sultan Ala-ud-Din to build another tower of victory twice the size of Qutb Minar. The surviving 27m base was as far as he got, because after his death (1315) nobody had the courage to continue the work. He did, however, complete the **Alai Darwaza** (1310), a richly ornamented gateway of red sandstone, with two huge marble-latticed window screens. It has been described as the most beautiful specimen of external polychromatic decoration in the world.

Tour buses sometimes slot in **Humayun's Tomb** on the way back north. This first substantial example of Mughal architecture lies on the edge of the new city, on the Delhi–Mathura road. It was built in AD 1556–69 by Bega Begum, the widow of the second Mughal emperor Humayun, and employs various prototype features of Mughal architecture—octagonal plan, lofty arches, pillared kiosks, bulbous dome and gardens with fountains—which were later to culminate in Agra's Taj Mahal and Itmud-ud-Daulah's Tomb. Bega Begum is buried here, along with Humayun and a few unlucky (murdered) princes. This was also the place where Bahadur Shah II, last of the Mughal emperors, hid out in the wake of the Indian Mutiny, until captured by a British officer.

After the tour, take a walk round **Connaught Circus**, built by Robert Tor Russell and opened in 1931. A double concentric circle of colonial-style buildings with colonnaded verandahs centred round a park, it is New Delhi's original shopping and entertainment centre. A series of broad 'radial roads' run out from it like spokes on a cartwheel, and getting lost here is a foregone conclusion. Even taxi drivers who have been working for 20 years haven't got the hang of it, and to do a full circuit you'll need a lot of stamina and a good map. Head for the inner circle for lunch at one of the Western-style restaurants, then head off down Radial Road 8 for a relaxing afternoon's swim in one of Janpath's luxury hotel pools.

Tour 2: Old Delhi

By rickshaw/taxi, 4–5 hours. International Dolls Museum–Feroz Shah Kotla–Raj Ghat–Jama Masjid–Chandni Chowk–Red Fort.

Start after lunch with a cab or rickshaw to the **International Dolls Museum** in Nehru House, Bahadur Shah Zafar Marg. It's 2km east of Connaught Circus, and is easy to find, being practically the only non-newspaper building in Delhi's 'Fleet Street'. Open 10am to 5.30pm daily except Monday, it features a beautiful collection of 6000 dolls from 85 countries plus 500 more in traditional Indian costumes.

Further up the same road, you'll find **Feroz Shah Kotla**, the historic fifth city of Delhi, just outside Delhi Gate on the Mathura Road. Built in AD 1354 by Feroz Shah Tughlaq, most of the structure, including much of the original 9m-high wall, was knocked down to provide materials for the later city of Shahjahanabad, but what remains is nevertheless impressive. Worth seeing are the ruins of the old mosque, the Baoli (well) and the Wazir's house near the northern wall. Best of all, there's the striking monolithic **Ashoka Pillar**, a 13m-high sandstone column inscribed with Ashokan edicts. This dates back to the 3rd century BC and was brought here from Ambala by Feroz Shah. When the traveller William Finch visited Delhi in 1601, the pillar was surmounted by a glittering globe and gilded crescent, but these were destroyed by lightning in 1715–19.

Leave Feroz Shah Kotla at the eastern end for Mahatma Gandhi Road. Turning left, a 10-minute walk brings you to **Raj Ghat**, the simple, black marble platform commemorating the place of Mahatma Gandhi's cremation. Set in green, tranquil gardens, it is a popular pilgrimage spot—especially on Friday evenings, when (in commemoration of Gandhi's assassination on a Friday, 30 January 1948) a special ceremony is held. Opposite and to the left is the small but interesting **Gandhi Memorial Museum** (*closed Mon*), where a film on Gandhi is shown every Sunday at 5pm.

From the museum, it's a short stroll left to **Delhi Gate**, then a fascinating 30-minute walk up Netaji Subhash Road (site of a remarkable pavement bazaar) to the **Jama Masjid**. This is India's largest mosque, approached via a grassy maidan. The massive red sandstone structure—rivalled only by the similar mosque at Fatehpur Sikri—was initiated by Shah Jahan (his final extravagance) in 1644 and completed by Aurangzeb in 1658. The Jama Masjid has three great gateways, entrance usually being via the grand flight of stairs at the Eastern Gate. Women not accompanied by a 'responsible male relative' are instantly ejected. Once inside the massive cloistered courtyard (capacity 25,000 worshippers!), buy a Rs5 'Meenar Ticket' from the booth just left of the entrance. This gains you access to the 46m-high southern minaret, which provides superlative views of the Red Fort and old city. This is one of two such minarets, both built of strips of red sandstone and white marble, which flank the imposing 61m-high central dome. On your way up the narrow 122-step staircase to the top, firmly discourage bogus guides—they'll go up there with you, follow you back down and demand money for doing precisely nothing. The best day to visit the Jama Masjid is Friday (Muslim holy day), or during the annual festival of Ramadan. Non-Muslims can enter only at the following times: half an hour after sunrise until noon, then

1.45pm to twenty minutes before sunset. There's a Rs15 charge for bringing a camera into the mosque, and another Rs15 for taking it up the minaret.

Leaving the mosque by the Northern Gate, you'll soon enter the crowded 'moonlit cross-roads' of **Chandni Chowk**. Constructed in 1648, this 21m-wide road was once the richest street of India and the most famous bazaar in the East. Today it is a frantic, heaving shopping-centre full of covered arcades, tiny roadside temples, pavement vendors and novelty stores, with a quite electric atmosphere. For minimal shell-shock, take a short rickshaw-ride up and down before getting swallowed up in the crowds. Ask to be put off near the excellent gold and silver jewellery market at the red-sandstone fountain (the big landmark), then take a wander through the labyrinthine backstreets, full of little curio shops, before returning to the top of the street for the **Digambar Jain Mandir** (1656), an elegant Jain temple with a charming marble courtyard and a profusion of interior paintings and gilded carvings. It is best known as a hospital for sick birds.

Across the road is the mighty red-sandstone **Red Fort** (Lal Qila), overlooking the river Yamuna (*adm Rs0.50, free on Fri*). This was built by Shah Jahan (1638–48) as his personal royal residence within his new capital of Shahjahanabad. Deposed by his son Aurangzeb, he hardly ever used it, but left behind one of the most magnificent of all Indian royal palaces. The battlements alone are 2.4km long and, at certain points, 18.5m high. There are two massive gates: **Delhi Gate** to the south, **Lahore Gate** to the west. The visitors' entrance is via the Lahore Gate, which leads directly into the vaulted shopping arcade of **Chhatta Chowk**. Once the province of quality court jewellers and weavers, it is now full of tourist shops. Run this gauntlet to emerge at the 2-storeyed palace entrance gate, the **Naubat Khana**. It opens out into pleasant gardens—look out for bullocks mowing the lawn—and the public audience hall of **Diwan-i-Am**, where the Emperor heard commoners' complaints from a 3m-high marble recess, fronted by a huge *shamiana* decorated with pearls, jewels and golden embroidered work. All this finery, together with the beautiful bird, flower and fruit mosaics of the Emperor's Seat itself, was picked out and looted in the aftermath of the 1857 Mutiny.

Beyond is an open courtyard with serene, green gardens and six palace *mahals*. To the far right is **Mumtaz Mahal**, now a small museum (*open 9am–5pm, except Fri*), and next to it the **Rang Mahal** (Painted Palace), which once had a rich silver ceiling ornamented with golden flowers, later melted down to augment the royal coffers. Its lotus-shaped marble tank was the starting-point of the 'Stream of Paradise' (Nahr-i-Bashisht) which ran through the centre of the *mahals* and kept them cool. Moving left, there is the **Khas Mahal**—three connecting marble apartments, where the Emperor used to pray, sleep and live. The centrepiece of the complex however, was the adjoining **Diwan-i-Khas** or private audience hall. A magnificent marble pavilion supported by 32 richly carved pillars, inlaid with precious gems, it was stripped of its magnificence (including the solid-silver ceiling) by Jat looters in 1779. Forty years earlier, it had lost its greatest treasure, the priceless **Peacock Throne**, to the Persian invader Nadir Shah. A fabulous work of art, the throne was made of solid gold and constructed in the shape of two dancing fantailed peacocks. Their eyes were studded with rubies and diamonds, and between their tailspreads stood a parakeet carved

Acrobats
Red Fort
Delhi

from a single huge emerald. Clusters of diamonds were set into the throne's legs, and on either side of it were two human figures made of gold, pearls and precious stones. The Diwan-i-Khas has just one 'treasure' left—the famous (though as it turned out, premature) sentiment of Shah Jahan: 'If on earth there be a paradise of bliss, it is this, it is this, it is this.' You'll find it inscribed in gold Persian lettering, over an arch in the central hall.

Next door are the three **hammams** or royal baths, where the emperor and favoured guests took hot saunas round perfumed fountains fed by the marble 'stream of paradise'. Pause here to look over the fort wall towards the Yamuna. There's normally some sort of entertainment taking place for the benefit of tourists—rope-climbers, magicians, fakirs or contortionists.

From the *mahals*, cross over to the charming **Moti Masjid** (Pearl Mosque), constructed by Aurangzeb in 1659 for private worship. It's a little gem. The original gilded copper domes vanished during the Mutiny, but the present marble ones are a good substitute and it's a small-scale masterpiece throughout, right down to the small, handsome entrance gate of worked brass.

By now, if you've timed things right, it should be early evening and time for the excellent **Sound and Light show** at the Red Fort. The English version starts at 7.30pm Nov–Jan, at 8.30pm Feb–Apr and Sept–Oct, and at 9pm May–Aug. Admission is Rs20, the show runs for one hour, and it's a good idea to slap on some mosquito repellent before arrival.

Tour 3: Other Sights

*By rickshaw/taxi, 5 hours. National Museum–Zoological Gardens–
Purana Qila–Crafts Museum–Rail Transport Museum–Hauz Khas Village.*

Delhi's lesser-known sights don't get seen often enough, partly because there are so many of them, but also because 2 days' sightseeing is more than enough for most people. But some places are well worth a third day's outing. To find them all open, go any day except a Monday or a Friday.

Start with a ride down Janpath to the **National Museum**, just below the Rajpath crossing (*open 10am–5pm except Mon*). This is a relatively new museum (1950), with one of the most comprehensive collections of Indian art and artefacts in the country. The ground floor has magnificent miniature paintings on silk and paper, copies of murals, stucco figures dating back to the 7th and 8th centuries, exhibits from the Prehistoric and Indus Valley civilizations, and bronzes/sculptures from the Maurya, Gandhara and Gupta periods. On the first floor is an excellent Central Asian gallery and a fine collection of tribal costumes and musical instruments. The museum has film shows most days of the week and the occasional lecture programme.

A 3km drive east brings you to the **Zoological Gardens** on Mathura Road (*open 9am–5pm, except Fri*). Founded in 1959, this is one of the largest zoos in Asia, and the most important in India. A vast array of species, including descendants of the rare white tiger of Rewa, live here in acceptable surroundings, and you can wander round the large, open area for hours watching not only the many representative species of India's extensive fauna but also many species from other parts of the world, including a magnificent pair of jaguars. If you're here in the autumn, you will witness large flocks of migratory birds. Above the zoo, to the north, there soars the old fort or **Purana Qila**, the broken shell of Sher Shah's ex-capital (*open daily 8am–6.30pm*). It is believed to have been erected on the site of the first Delhi, Indraprastha, and is worth a visit. Enter the fort by the south gate to find the Sher Mandal, a small, red-sandstone octagonal tower probably built by Sher Shah. It is chiefly remembered today as the place where Emperor Humayun, who had converted it into a library, tripped down the stairs on his way to prayer and sustained mortal injuries. Just north of the tower, see **Qal'a-i-Kunha Mosque**, a fine Indo-Afghan structure of red sandstone incorporating marble, slate and coloured stonework. The fort has a small **Field Museum**, housing a good collection of archaeological site recoveries.

Set within the main exhibition grounds, Pragati Maidan, slightly to the north of Purana Qila, is the **Crafts Museum** (*open daily 9.30am–4.30pm*)—an interesting complex made up of replicas of village houses from the various regions of India, with a central building used for both permanent and special exhibitions. From September to April craftspeople from throughout the country work at the museum displaying and selling their products which may vary from a clay pot to a sari that has taken a full month to weave. The museum has a small shop where you can buy a book describing its collection.

A 5km ride west to Shantipath, Chanakyapuri, brings you to Delhi's popular **Rail Transport Museum** (*open 9.30am–5pm except Mon*). This is a superb collection of old trains and rolling stock dotted around a pleasant garden compound. The exhibits include the charming 1908 Memorial Engine with its single steamroller wheel, the mammoth 1923 Bombay Mail with a fog-lamp the size of a dinner table, and the elegant 1908 Viceregal dining-coach with gilded wood-panelled interior and baize-covered card tables. At the back of the compound, there's the showpiece Beyer-Garratt locomotive: 35 yards of gleaming green majesty, with silver-rimmed wheels and vermilion piston shafts. Climb the hump-back bridge at the rear of the compound for the obligatory photograph. Then visit the museum, full of interesting brass engine-plates from all over the world, lots of exotic silver and ivory dinner cutlery, and photographs illustrating the development of India's historic rail network (some of the mountains cut through to lay track claimed the lives of 30 per cent of the workforce). There are some lovely model locomotives, including one of the Rocket itself, and don't miss the prize exhibit—the skull of a wild elephant which charged a Calcutta-bound train in 1894 and lost. The train-driver kept one of the tusks; the other is in the British Museum. Keen gricers can choose from a selection of original builders' plates sold at the entrance.

Delhi's newest and most interesting shopping-centre is at **Hauz Khas**, 10km south of Connaught Place. Site of a great 13th-century tank built by Ala-ud-din Khilji, this old village has been absorbed by the southward spread of New Delhi and many of its buildings have been converted into chic and glitzy shops for the élite and fashion-conscious. One of the first shops you see on entering is Dastkar, a sort of mini-Cottage Industries emporium with traditional village crafts from all over India on sale. Other shops are 'high fashion' outlets with expensive designer items. Some good restaurants have been opened (*see* 'Eating Out', p.107), including Delhi's only jazz club. Walk through the village and explore the ruins of the old religious college (1352) and nearby, Feroz Shah's tomb (1398).

Shopping

Most of Delhi's shops are open 9am to 7pm daily except Sundays. The only shopping area not closed on a Sunday is Paharganj. It's supposed to be closed on a Monday instead, but isn't. Common belief holds that the shops of Main Bazaar would still be trading after World War III—probably during it too.

Delhi is without doubt the premier shopping centre in the country. It hasn't got much of its own to offer (even its silver comes from Jaipur), but it *does* have everything from everywhere else in India, and often for less cost than at its point of origin. Smart leather shoes for example, will sell for 20–30 per cent less in Delhi than in Agra, where most of them are produced. One tip though: don't go mad buying stuff at the start of your trip. If you're coming back to Delhi again, do all your shopping then—it won't go away!

The **Central Cottage Industries Emporium** is a huge building in Janpath where you can see produce from all over India and check how much it should cost before hitting the bazaars and shops. As in the various **State Government Emporia** along Baba Kharak Singh Marg (*also open 10am–5pm daily except Sun*), all prices are fixed and you won't get ripped off too badly.

The **Tibetan Market** on Janpath, near the Hotel Imperial, is full of interesting crafts, curios, jewellery and (often new) antiques. A safe shop to start looking is **Tibetan Arts** (No. 17), which is friendly, honest and no-hassle. Walking further up Janpath, you'll quickly come to **Janpath Market**, good for quality leather bags and accessories, fashion clothing (including brand-name copies) and silk scarves. Beware of pickpockets in this area, and remember to bargain hard.

At the top of Janpath, cross over to the underground **Palika Bazaar** in Connaught Circus. This is another good place for a browse, with lots of leather, clothes, books, giftware and electronics. Audio and video cassettes are a popular buy—they're compatible with Western systems and cost much less than in London.

Up at Main Bazaar, Paharganj, reliable silver shops include **The Ornaments** next to Hotel Vivek and **Solemn International** at the top of the market (railway station end). For incense, perfumes and glassware, as well as wood, bone and brass items, there's **Shell Expo** just above Hotel Vishal and **B D Handicrafts** opposite Hotel Anoop. The latter is used to export and can send stuff home for you—not just what you buy there, but any excess luggage you've accumulated too. Naturally, the more you send, the cheaper it gets per item. As a general guide, anything less than 30/40kg should be sent home as 10kg gift parcels (*see* p.26) via the post office. Air freight is only worth doing if you send 100kg or more, in which case it costs around Rs80 per kg. Sea freight is charged not by weight, but by the amount of space it occupies in a ship's hold. Currently, it costs US$120 per cubic metre. Sea freight is around three times cheaper than air freight but takes about three times longer (2/3 months) to get home.

Hauz Khas Village in south Delhi is one of the newer shopping areas with a good range of craft shops, fashion clothes and leather goods. There are also good restaurants here (*see* 'Eating Out', p.107) and two decent art galleries with regular shows.

Leisure

The regular Dances Of India programme is a popular introduction to **Indian classical dance**. It starts at 7pm daily at Parsi Anjuman Hall on Bahadur Zafar Marg, opposite Ambedkar Stadium. Tickets are sold at the door, but can be pre-booked from a travel agent or via your hotel. More professional and less touristy are the dance performances at the India International Centre, 40 Max Mueller Marg, ✆ 4619431. Details of other cultural entertainments can be found in the weekly *Delhi Diary*, available from most bookstalls.

If you can afford it, you can go **swimming** at the pools of the Imperial and

Kanishka hotels. The stiff non-resident fees of Rs550 and Rs300 per day are aimed at keeping out 'undesirable elements' (read budget travellers).

There are numerous **cinemas** in Delhi (programmes listed in *Times of India*) but only one to write home about. This is the Priya in Modern Bazaar, Vasant Vihar, which has full stereo-sound and shows all the latest Western releases. (Modern Bazaar is also the biggest and best department store in the city, and well worth a visit.) High-brow foreign films are regularly shown by the British Council, on Kasturba Gandhi Marg, © 3710111.

Delhi's top **disco** is the Oasis at the Hyatt Regency hotel (© 6881234), followed by the Ghungroo at the Maurya Sheraton (© 3010101) and My Kind of Place at the Taj Palace Intercontinental (© 3010404). The best crowd is at the weekends, but you won't get in unless you're a hotel guest or are 'recommended' by another prestige hotel. A friend of mine rang the Oberoi hotel, got the name of the front desk manager, and used this name over the phone to 'recommend' himself to the Maurya Sheraton. He got in, no problem.

Delhi © (011–)   **Where to Stay**

Prices in Delhi have gone through the roof recently, putting most luxury hotels out of the reach of the average traveller. The growing housing shortage in the capital has forced a lot of big companies to put up their executives in the star hotels, resulting in high prices and few vacancies. Most of the city's principal hotels are in fact *dis*couraging leisure travellers, and even tour groups, from staying. 'It's not just that few ordinary tourists want to pay US$280 a night,' I was informed by the **Taj Mahal Hotel** (© 3016162) at 1 Mansingh Road, 'But we are now geared exclusively to very high-profile business clients. They use the hotel facilities more, and spend more money with us.' This kind of attitude, which you will find at other 5-star properties like **Le Meridien** (© 3710101), the **Maurya Sheraton** (© 3010101), and the **Oberoi** (© 4363030), reflects Delhi's new image as a business capital where the 5-star hotels are just too busy with VIPs and multi-national convention delegates to give individual travellers much in the way of personalized service. In addition, most of these sterile properties are miles south of Connaught Place, cut off from the city's vital pulse and heartbeat. My advice, unless you *are* here on business, is to save your pennies and stay at less prestigious places where you don't feel isolated from real India and where the staff have more time for you.

luxury (from US$130)

If you are going to spend US$250+ anywhere in Delhi, make it the **New Delhi Hilton** in Barakhamba Avenue, © 3320101, 🖷 3325335. This is the closest 5-star property to Connaught Place and the friendliest too. It has a pool, good restaurants, every conceivable facility, and people who really look after you.

The same level of personal care can be found at the cheaper **Park Hotel**, 15

Parliament Street, ✆ 3733737, ✉ 3732025. This has a central location too, as well as a pool, 24-hour restaurant, pub-cum-nightclub, beauty salon and business centre. Standard rooms are large and comfortable, but it's the suites that are the best deal—US$200 buys you a fully self-contained flat with complimentary breakfast and evening tea/snacks thrown in. Sometimes, if you loiter outside the entrance, touts come up and offer 20 per cent discounts—ironic really, since this is one of very few high-class hotels actually worth the full tariff.

The **Imperial Hotel** on Janpath, ✆ 3325332, ✉ 3324542, is an oasis of calm away from the noise and hype of the city. A favourite with Westerners, this stately colonial-style hotel has a nice pool, a big garden and bags of old-world character. If you have a choice, plump for one of the older rooms. The new-wing ones lack charm and are definitely overpriced. **Claridge's** at 12 Aurangzeb Road, ✆ 3010211, ✉ 3010625, is another old property with pre-war ambience and Elizabethan restaurants, but it hasn't got the same style and isn't as well located.

expensive (from US$60)

Top marks in this category go to the **Oberoi Maidens**, 7 Sham Nath Marg, Old Delhi, ✆ 2525464, ✉ 2915134. This is a jewel of colonial architecture set amidst eight acres of emerald-green lawns, with tennis courts, a quaint 'peppermint' pool and fine Indian/Continental food in its famous Curzon Room restaurant. Despite its remote situation (10km from the city centre) it has marvellous Raj-style grandeur, ever-friendly and courteous staff, and the biggest rooms (they're actually suites) I've seen in India.

The quiet and very central **Marina**, G-59 Connaught Circus, ✆ 3324658, ✉ 3328609, is another renovated old hotel with well-appointed rooms, well-priced suites and a superior restaurant. No pool here, but the travel desk, 24-hour room service and 24-hour coffee shop compensate. Also, breakfast is complimentary. The well-run **Hotel Kanishka**, 19 Ashok Road, ✆ 3324422, ✉ 3324242, is very affordable and centrally located. The staff are friendly, it has a pool, and the rooms, though bland, are a great deal if you're here on your own; the single rooms are often bigger and brighter than the doubles! **Nirula's Hotel**, L-Block Connaught Place, ✆ 3322419, ✉ 3353957, doesn't look much from the outside but is very professionally managed. The rooms are rather small (ask for a quiet one at the back) but you don't have to go far for a snack—the famous restaurants are just downstairs. Like all the above hotels, it is centrally air-conditioned throughout.

moderate (from Rs300)

If you're new to the country, the best inexpensive base is the **New Delhi YMCA** on Jai Singh Road, opposite the Jantar Mantar, ✆ 3361915, ✉ 3746035. Open 24 hours, it's only a short walk from Connaught Place, and has all sorts of useful facilities—money exchange, travel agency, pool, gym, tennis courts, left-luggage room, restaurant, international phone/fax facility, and free airport–city transfer.

Rooms are quiet and cheerful, and the tariff includes breakfast. Ring ahead to book this one, or be at the desk 12 noon sharp to snap up any vacancies.

The funky **Janpath Guest House**, 2nd floor, 82–84 Janpath, ✆ 3321935, ✉ 3321937, is another old favourite with a TV lounge, roof-terrace restaurant and useful travel service. There's a wide choice of rooms here, from small scruffy ones with cracked loos up to spanking new a/c ones with TVs and immaculately tiled bathrooms.

Hotel Fifty-Five at H-55 Connaught Circus, ✆ 3321244, ✉ 3320769, is a quiet and personal place with good service, friendly management, free baggage service and 15 centrally a/c rooms (sterile but quiet) around the £20 mark. The open rooftop terrace offers sweeping views of central Delhi traffic.

Up in Paharganj, there's **Hotel Saina International** behind the Imperial Cinema in Main Bazaar, ✆ 529144, ✉ 7520879. It can be noisy, but the management is hands-on, the staff wacky, and the travel agency efficient. All rooms have TV and attached bath and are generally good value. If that is full, the nearby **Metropolis Tourist Home**, ✆ 7531794, ✉ 7525600, has a few a/c rooms and suites, and the food downstairs is superb. Across the road, **Hotel Star View**, ✆ 3556300, has nice rooms with satellite TV and a range of 'suites' from around £10. The latter are Paharganj's only real claim to luxury.

A couple of paying guest houses get good reports. One is **Yatri House** at 3/4 Punchkuin Road, off Radial Road 3, Connaught Place, ✆/✉ 7525563. This is run by the urbane Mr Puri, who has created a real 'home away from home', with a cosy garden sit-out, snacks on call, and provision for car hire and airline ticketing. Rooms are all well-furnished doubles with attached bath and air-cooling. They're often full, however, so phone ahead to book. The **Master Guest House** at R-500 New Rajendra Nagar, ✆ 5741089, is a cheaper fallback but the rooms are all common bath and it's 3km further out of the centre.

budget

The centre for budget accommodation in Delhi is the Main Bazaar area of Paharganj, north of Connaught Place. It's not the cleanest part of town, but is very convenient for the railway station and is a great introduction to real India. Paharganj is full of tourist 'friends', holy men, lost cows, unemployed rickshaw men, people aimlessly digging up the road, and limbless beggars rolling around in the dust trying to collect money. This is Delhi at street-level, and if you turn up on market day (Monday) you'll see it at its most vital and colourful. Actually, Main Bazaar is just one long market street, lined on both sides with cheap cafés, shops, restaurants and guest houses. There are dozens of places to stay, most of them charging Rs100 to 200 for a basic room with common bath, Rs150 to Rs250 for a bigger room (usually air-cooled) with attached bath/hot shower. If they're all full—and they often are when you turn up (as I did) from Shimla at 5am in the morning—all you can do is sit around in 24-hour restaurants like the Grand

Sindhi and swap horror bus stories with other droopy-eyed travellers until rooms come vacant again around dawn.

Most of the better places are located in the *lower* half of Main Bazaar, a 10-minute walk from New Delhi railway station. At the bottom of the market, there's **Metropolis Tourist Home**, ✆ 7531794, with air-cooled dorm beds at Rs150. Behind this, opposite the Saina International, the quiet and homely **Hotel Major's Den**, ✆ 7529599, has a few rooms from Rs200 to 400, some of them with balconies.

Then, moving up the bazaar from the Metropolis, you'll find **Hotel Satyam**, ✆ 525200, with nice quiet rooms at the back, **Hare Rama**, ✆ 7518972, opposite Khanna Talkies, **Hotel Vishal**, ✆ 527629, with a rooftop restaurant, storage/left luggage service, fax/STD phone facility, doctor on call, and two premium rooms at the top for Rs250 (Nos. 27 and 34); then the friendly **Hare Krishna**, ✆ 529188, with great veggie snacks (but slow service) in its rooftop canteen, the lethargic but ever-popular **Anoop Hotel**, ✆ 526256, with a travel desk and a rooftop restaurant, the newly-renovated **Hotel Vivek**, ✆ 7777062, with smart a/c rooms at Rs375/450, a useful travel desk and 24-hour STD facility; lastly **Hotel Navrang**, ✆ 521965, down a lane opposite the veggie market, with rooms (bath attached) for just Rs70/80.

Two decent places at the *top* of Main Bazaar (railway station end) are **Traveller's Guest House**, ✆ 3544849, with spotless rooms, bath and TV included, for Rs160/180 and, below this, down a lane opposite Hotel Bright, **Hotel Star Palace**, ✆ 7528584, has big a/c rooms from Rs400/450, a rooftop restaurant and an owner who loves foreigners to bits.

The second centre for cheap digs, quieter and more sedate than Paharganj, is in and around Connaught Place. Two guest houses which have become institutions over the years are **Ringo's** (✆ 3310605), and **Sunny's** (✆ 3312909), both located down a small alley behind the Janpath tourist office. Run by the same people, they both have rooftop restaurants, useful facilities (left-luggage, bus/rail bookings, city-sightseeing tours etc.) and are always buzzing with busy travellers. They are also good places to meet people and make friends. Dorm beds go for Rs60 and rooms from Rs90/160 common bath to Rs210/260 private bath. If full, they'll give you a Rs50 *charpoy* (Indian rope bed) to sleep on until a bed comes free.

If you're really counting the rupees, you can find a Rs25 shared dorm bed at several dives across the road from New Delhi railway station. These places are rough though. Padlock your pack to the bed, or even better sleep on it.

Delhi ✆ *(011–)*   ***Eating Out***

Delhi may be a fiesta of good food, but it's not as cheap as it once was. Inevitably, the quality cuisine is in the big hotels, where prices are now not far off what you would pay in London or New York.

For that special meal out, sample top-class Indian fare at Maurya Sheraton's **Bukhara** (✆ 3010101), Hyatt Regency's **Aangan** (✆ 6881234), Taj Mahal's **Haveli** (✆ 3016162), or Oberoi's **Kandahar** (✆ 4363030). The first and last of these specialize in Northwest Frontier food, which is largely meat dishes marinated in yoghourt and lime, cooked to perfection in 'tandoor' clay ovens. The average cost is £20 per head (inclusive of drinks), and it's a good idea to pre-book by phone.

Easily the best Chinese restaurant in town is the **House of Ming** (✆ 3016162) at the Taj Mahal hotel. It's Szechwan, so pretty spicy, but the experience is unmissable and—at around £15 a head (excluding drinks)—not bad value. Over at the Oberoi, the **Tai Pan** (✆ 4363030) is also good for Chinese, while the **Baan Thai** (same ✆) has allegedly the best Thai food in Asia. The 'tom yam' soup, according to local gourmets, is even better than at the Oriental Hotel in Bangkok!

To experience Continental food at its finest, there's the **Captain's Cabin** at the Taj or **La Rochelle** at the Oberoi. Also at the Taj is the exclusive **Oriental Express** which offers a top-drawer 4-course lunch and dinner (including champagne) for £25 per head. Less expensive is Ambassador Hotel's **Dasa Prakash** (✆ 4698300), which apparently has the best south Indian food in the capital. Also mid-priced is Park Hotel's **Someplace Else**, which is a cosy 'English' pub during the day (with Thai/Italian snacks and steak 'n' kidney pie!) and a residents-only laser disco at night.

The Hyatt Regency has recently opened two excellent new restaurants, the beautiful **La Piazza** with a pricey but popular Italian-style buffet at Sunday lunchtime, and **T K's Grill** where all the high-ups go for Japanese food. The latter is probably Delhi's most expensive restaurant at the moment.

Outside the hotels, Indian cuisine is far cheaper and just as wholesome at **Gaylord**, **Standard** and **Host** restaurants, all on Connaught Place. Gaylord has particularly good food and the service is quick. **Delhi Darbar**, a few doors down from Nirula hotel, is another popular Indian restaurant, though it's sometimes hard to get a table. **Rodeo**, at 12A Connaught Place, is a fun place with a great Mexican menu and waiters dressed like cowboys. In the same Rs100-per-main-dish bracket, **El Arab** at the top of Sansad Marg has a fine Middle Eastern menu as well as a good-value buffet.

Nirula's, the original fast-food joint on Connaught Place, has now developed into a massive concern. It now comprises an excellent Chinese restaurant-cum-bar (**Chinese Room**) with great veggie dishes, an American-style diner (**Potpourri**) with 'lamburgers', pizzas and popular salad bar, a busy ice-cream parlour (open 10am to midnight), a bakery and a snack bar. All of this in one building! Minutes after opening at 7.30am, Nirula's is often packed out and the excess drifts over to **Café 100** on B Block, which has similar stuff only cheaper; or to **Wimpy** on Janpath at N Block, which does (100 per cent lamb) burgers, chips and shakes in a familiar anaesthetic setting. During 1995, **Kentucky Fried Chicken** opened in

New Friends Colony Market, closed when a customer found a cockroach in the batter, and then reopened in exactly the same spot.

Down at South Extension there's an amazing building called **Food Court**. This has four floorfuls of Indian, Chinese, Continental and fast food, each cuisine on a separate level. In the same neck of the woods is Hauz Khas Village, where the young trendy crowd hang out. Places like the popular **Bistro** (multi-cuisine), the **Sukhothai** (the only decent Thai restaurant outside a 5-star hotel) and the new **Café Pedro** (Mexican) are the nearest Delhi gets to café society, and at around Rs200 per head they are very affordable.

Paharganj is the place to go for cheap travellers' food. It's often pretty basic stuff, but you can live for a week here on what a big dinner at any star hotel would cost. For a quick overview, start at the bottom of Main Bazaar and walk up. First, there's the **Metropolis** with possibly the longest menu (Indian, Continental and Chinese) in India and certainly some of the best sizzlers and steaks. The next-door **Malhotra** is fine for seafood and the **Khosla** and **Madaan** cafés, a few doors up, are where shoestringers eat as many omelettes, chips and rice pudding as they can for less than £1 a day. Above these are Hotel Vishal's twin eateries, **Lord's Café** and **Appetite Food Joint**, both air-conditioned and different only in that Appetite does *thalis* and Lord's attempts some Chinese. Finally, a little further up, there's the **Grand Sindhi** with an extensive Indian-Chinese menu and a sit-out section for watching India, the non-stop video, go by.

There's a similar clutch of travellers' restaurants near Ringo's guest house in Janpath. The **Don't Pass Me By** is good for Chinese, the **Kalpana** for *thalis* and south Indian food, and the **Vikram** for a bit of everything else. They're all cheap and, by Indian standards, relatively safe. Also in this area is the **Anand** with reportedly the best naan bread and mushroom *paneer* in north India. I've heard that before somewhere…

Bars are few and far between in the city, owing to the strict licensing laws. There is however nothing to stop you buying a beer, or even a bottle of wine or champagne, from Delhi's many 'wine' shops which stay open till 8pm daily. Two of the cheapest are next to DTC tourist office and a few doors down from Nirula hotel.

Moving On
by air

Indian Airlines, F block, Malhotra Building, Janpath, ✆ 3310517 (open daily except Sunday 10–7; ✆ 140 for general enquiries or ✆ 142 for 24hr pre-recorded flight information) flies daily to Agra, Ahmedabad, Bagdogra (for Darjeeling), Bangalore, Bombay, Calcutta, Cochin, Goa, Hyderabad, Kathmandu, Khajuraho, Madras, Patna (for Bodhgaya), Pune, Trivandrum and Varanasi. On a less regular basis, it has flights to Jaipur (6 days a week), Jammu and Udaipur (5), Jodhpur, Gwalior and Aurangabad (4) and Bhubaneshwar (3).

Modiluft, Vandana Bldg, Tolstoy Marg, ✆ 6430514, flies daily to Bangalore, Bombay, Goa, Jaipur, Khajuraho, Madras, Udaipur and Varanasi. It also has six flights a week to Ahmedabad and Cochin, and four to Jammu.

Jet Airways, 2E Hansalaya Bldg, Barakhamba Road, ✆ 3724727, flies daily to Ahmedabad, Bagdogra, Bangalore, Bombay and Goa.

Sahara India, Amba Deep Bldg, 14 K G Marg, ✆ 3326851, flies Bagdogra and Bombay daily, and Ahmedabad six days a week.

East-West Airlines, DCM Bldg, Barakhamba Road, ✆ 3755167, flies daily to Bombay and Madras, and to Calcutta six times a week.

Skyline NEPC, G39 4th floor, Pawan House, Connaught Circus, ✆ 3322525, has daily flights to Bombay, Aurangabad and Madras, and three flights a week to Jaipur, Calcutta, Patna and Varanasi.

Jagson, Vandana Bldg, Tolstoy Marg, ✆ 3711069, has three flights a week to Shimla, Bhuntar (for Kulu), Gagal (for Dharamsala), Jodhpur and Jaisalmer.

Archana Airways, 41A Friends Colony East, Mathura Road, ✆ 6842001, flies to Shimla and Kulu three days a week, but services are often suspended.

UP Air, A2 Defence Colony, is a new airline which has just commenced flights to Jaipur, Udaipur, Bombay, Aurangabad, Kulu and 'Buddhist sectors'.

All the above airlines have offices at the domestic airport, and are constantly adding new sectors to their routes. It's worth ringing around before finalising your domestic flight itinerary. Check-in for domestic flights is 75 minutes before departure. Flying time is anything between 40 minutes (Agra/Jaipur) and 2 hours (Udaipur/Khajuraho) in the north, and between 2 hours (Bombay/Goa) and 2½ hours (Madras/Bangalore) going south. The longest domestic flight out of Delhi is to Trivandrum (5hrs). It's worth noting that in December/January there's a big risk of not going anywhere by air, owing to fog, snowfalls and general bad weather. If your hotel room has a TV, check the forecast before booking.

by rail

Trains run from Delhi to all major tourist destinations and can sometimes (e.g. the Shatabdi Express to Agra and Jaipur) be quicker than travel by air. The city has two main stations: **New Delhi** railway station at Paharganj, close to Connaught Place, and **Old Delhi** railway station above Chandni Chowk in the old city. The latter is a long 40/60-minute haul through heavy traffic from Connaught Place. A third station, **Nizamuddin**, is a 20–30-minute rickshaw ride from New Delhi and is a useful place to disembark if you're coming into Delhi by train and want the airport or the bigger hotels south of Connaught Place.

Useful trains from New Delhi railway station include the **Shatabdi Express** (a/c only; fare includes meals and drinks) to Agra (dep 6.15am, 2hrs) and to Jaipur (dep 5.50am, 4½hrs, not Thurs), the **Karnataka Express** to Bangalore (dep 9.15pm, 4lhrs), the **Frontier Mail** (dep 8am, 22hrs) and the **Rajdhani Express** to Bombay (dep 4.05pm, 27hrs), the **Shalimar Express** to Jammu Tawi (dep 4.10pm,

The crack-of-dawn Shatabdi Express and Taj Express trains are really only for those who must see Agra in a day. If you have the time, you're much better off getting a later train—at 11.30am, 2.30pm or 5.50pm (2½hrs, no advance reservation required)—from New Delhi station, staying overnight in a room with a view of the Taj, enjoying it by moonlight over a cocktail or two, and being one of the first to see it when it opens at 7am in the morning, before the hordes of Delhi day-trippers swarm over it around 10am.

14/15hrs), the **Tamil Nadu Express** to Madras (dep 110.30pm, 33–34hrs), the **Kerala Express** to Trivandrum (dep 11.30am, 53–55hrs) and the **Poorva Express** to Varanasi (dep 4.30pm, 12½hrs, Mon/Tues/Fri only). For Shimla, the **Himalayan Queen** leaves at 6am daily, arriving in Kalka at 11.15am; switching onto narrow-gauge track, it leaves Kalka at 11.45am, passes through 102 tunnels and arrives in Shimla at 4.50pm. For Dharamsala, take the **Jhelum Express** to Pathankot (dep 9.50pm, arr 8.25am).

From Old Delhi railway station, the fast **Ahmedabad Mail** goes to Ahmedabad (dep 9.10pm, 25hrs), calling in at Ajmer (12hrs) on the way; the **Jammu Tawi Mail** is useful for Dharamsala (dep 9.10pm, arr Pathankot 7.20am). Popular trains from Nizamuddin railway station include the **Taj Express** to Agra (dep 7.10am, 2½hrs), the **Rajdhani Express** (a/c only; fare includes meals and drinks) to Bangalore (dep 9.30am, 35hrs) and the **M G Goa Express** to Miraj/Vasco da Gama, for Goa (dep 3pm, 36/38hrs). The latter is a long haul, but at US$13 for a second-class berth or US$30 for a/c chair car, it's a lot cheaper than a US$200 flight ticket.

All the above trains are daily, except when otherwise stated. Train services to Rajasthan are slow at present, due to conversion of the track to broad gauge from metre gauge. Popular fast trains like the Pink City Express to Jaipur and Udaipur may well be back on line by the time you read this. Ring railway enquiries on ✆ 131 to find out.

Rail **ticket bookings** should be a lot easier than they actually are. The main ticket office on Chelmsford Road, on the way to New Delhi railway station from Connaught Place, is fully computerized but still overworked. As you enter, collect a numbered ticket from the counter and sit down at the window allocated. If you don't want to wait long, arrive just as it opens at 7.45am or when it reopens at 2pm after lunch. The office closes at 9pm daily, except for Sundays when it closes at 1.50pm.

There is also a special booking office for foreign tourists on the 1st floor of New Delhi railway station, open daily except Sunday from 7.30am to 5pm. This is where to come to buy/use Indrail Passes or to apply for tourist quota tickets on busy trains like the Shatabdi Express to Agra and Jaipur. You can in fact advance-book any train(s) here, though you must pay in foreign currency.

Delhi's main bus station is ISBT (Interstate Bus Terminal) above Old Delhi railway station, but few travellers go there to buy tickets. It's far more convenient to book through cheap hotels in Paharganj and Janpath area, many of whom have travel agents. They sell the daily deluxe a/c buses to Shimla (Rs300), Manali (Rs400), Jaipur (Rs175), Ajmer (Rs225), Jodhpur/Udaipur (Rs260), Bombay/Kathmandu (Rs600), Jammu (Rs250) and Pathankot (Rs230).

Buses requiring no prior reservation include the hourly deluxe service to Jaipur (6am to 8pm, 5–6hrs) from Bikaner House, near India Gate, and the hourly express/deluxe bus service to Agra (4–5hrs) from the new Sarai Kale Khan bus terminal, near Nizamuddin railway station. Buses to Agra however, like taxis (Rs1800), take a lot longer than the train.

The best day tour by bus to Agra (Rs300) is sold by Delhi Tourism Corporation (DTDC) at N Block, Middle Circle, Connaught Place. It runs from 7am to 9pm daily, except Monday, and takes in Sikandra, the Taj, and Agra Fort.

Corbett National Park

India's earliest park, founded in 1935, Corbett is a large and important tiger reserve. Situated in the foothills of the Himalaya, it's a 7-hour drive from Delhi or a train journey via Moradabad and Ramnagar. **UP Tourism**, © 3322251 (*see* p.92) runs regular buses to the park from November through to April or May. The reserve is set in an extraordinarily beautiful region, through which run the Ramganga river and several ridges of the Shivalik foothills. Apart from the occasional glimpse of a tiger, or the more elusive leopard, there are numerous prey species and herds of elephant which migrate through the area. Because of the varied topography and habitat and the large intrusion of the Ramganga reservoir, Corbett has an extraordinary range of birds—quite possibly more species than any other park in the subcontinent. **Forest rest houses** and a small 'tourist complex' at Dhikala, within Corbett, can be booked through UP Tourism offices in Lucknow or New Delhi. Outside the park boundary, overlooking the Kosi river, are two lodges. The better of the two, with trained naturalists and a high level of service, is the **Tiger Tops Corbett Lodge**. Rooms, food and game-viewing cost US$120 per person per night, and can be booked through Tiger Tops India, 1/1 Rani Jhansi Road, New Delhi, © 7771055/7525357, ✉ 7777483. The second lodge has a better location slightly beyond the park entrance, but the lodge is not of the calibre of Tiger Tops. The **Quality Inn Corbett Jungle Resort**, with rooms from Rs500, is booked through Quality Inns, 51 Vasant Marg, Vasant Vihar, New Delhi, © 675347.

Route 1: From the Taj to the Ganges

Situated close to historic Delhi, cradle of numerous civilizations and cultures, the corner-stones of this route—Agra, Khajuraho and Varanasi—witnessed astonishing bursts of creative energy from various dynasties. The finest accomplishments of medieval and Mughal art and architecture, they today represent many of the popular images with which India is associated. If Agra's Taj Mahal, the most extravagant monument to love ever built, can be said to define the romance of India, then the erotic temples of Khajuraho must describe its sensuality and the holy city of Varanasi its divine mystery. Certainly, no other three places in the country have been turned into so many postcards.

Also at Agra is an imposing fort and—at nearby Fatehpur Sikri—a ghost city of poignant grandeur. South of Agra is the Maratha city of Gwalior, dominated by one of the finest forts in India, and, just off the road to Khajuraho, the Rajput township of Orchha, site of a well-preserved complex of palaces and temples. Then 50km to the west of Agra lies Bharatpur, which has one of the world's most important wetland bird sanctuaries.

From the Hindu centre of Varanasi, the pilgrim's trail continues in the footsteps of the Buddha—to nearby Sarnath, a peaceful centre of stupas, shrines and monasteries, where the Buddha came to preach his first sermon. And finally, if time allows, to Bodhgaya where—over 2500 years ago—the Buddha achieved his enlightenment under the Bodhi Tree.

Itinerary

If this is your first time in India, it goes without saying that you'll want to see the Taj Mahal. The efficient express trains draw into Agra station from Delhi each morning, full of travellers who have come to see Agra in a day, many of whom will return on the same train in the evening. But a day is simply not enough. Not only does the Taj itself require repeated viewings (under different lights) to be appreciated fully, but it is the showpiece of Mughal grandeur and artistry and is not to be rushed. Allow two days for sights and possibly one more for shopping.

At Agra, it's decision time. Do you go west to Rajasthan (*see* p.161) or east to Varanasi? Agra is perfectly positioned for both routes, and, unless you've got a month or more in the country, you can do only one of them. The only compromise, if money allows, is to fly.

Fortunately, Indian Airlines links Delhi–Agra–Khajuraho–Varanasi with a daily flight in both directions. That means you can do most points on this route in ten days—Delhi (2 nights) to Agra (2) to Khajuraho (2) to Varanasi (3) back to Agra (1)—and then hop on a bus to Jaipur for a week or two in Rajasthan.

To cover all points on the route described below, you'll need at least two weeks. My suggestion would be Delhi (2 nights) to Agra (2/3) by surface transport, then fly to Khajuraho (1), by road to Gwalior/Orchha (3) and back to Khajuraho (1), then fly to Varanasi (3). From here, you can either jump on a plane back to Delhi (1) or continue on by road to Bodhgaya, thence to Calcutta and the Eastern Triangle (route 7).

The best time to do this route is between October and March, avoiding the mid-June to September monsoons. The temperature ranges from 11° to 48°C in summer and 2° to 32°C in winter.

Agra

Little is known about the city's early history, but a small settlement was possibly first established some 5000 years ago. Agra's strategic situation on the right bank of the Yamuna made it an ancient frontier defence of the Aryans. At one time it may have been known as *Agrabana* ('Paradise' in Sanskrit), a possible corruption of the name of its founder, Maharajah Ugersen. But the city achieved fame and wealth as the capital of the Mughals. Today, it is famous as the home of the Taj Mahal, the most popular tourist attraction in India.

History

Agra came to prominence in the early 16th century, when the Mughals seized it from the Hindu Lodhi dynasty. In 1566 the modern city of Agra was established by the Emperor Akbar, and was made capital of the Mughal empire. Fabulously wealthy, it soon rose to great importance. The commentator Abul Fazal reported:

> *A great city having esteemed healthy air. Pleasant houses and gardens inhabited by people of all nations and exhibited with the production of every climate are built on both banks of the river [Yamuna]. A castle of red sandstone, the like of which no traveller has ever seen, has been created by the Emperor. The fort alone contains five hundred wonderful stone buildings in the Bengal, Gujarat and other styles. Formerly Agra was only a village depending upon Bayana, where Sikander Lodhi [founder of Sikandra, 8km out of present Agra] held his courts. At the same spot His Majesty has laid the foundations of a most magnificent city.*

Under Akbar's son, the talented drunkard Jehangir, Agra became a major industrial and commercial city. But it was Shah Jahan, Jehangir's successor, who left Agra her most enduring legacy—the Taj Mahal. This most beautiful (and most costly) monument to love remains today the finest wonder of the modern world. Having created it, Shah Jahan moved his capital from Agra to Delhi, and the city—together with the fortunes of the Mughals in general—fell into slow decline. In 1803, after a long period of being ransacked and pillaged by local Maratha and Jat forces, it came under British rule and was until 1877 the capital of present-day Uttar Pradesh. It never however regained its former glory, but remained trapped in time, a bitter-sweet reminder of the peak of Mughal power and glory.

Agra today is a city of over a million people, a busy centre of education and commerce. Its main industry, by virtue of its many well-preserved Mughal monuments, is tourism. The

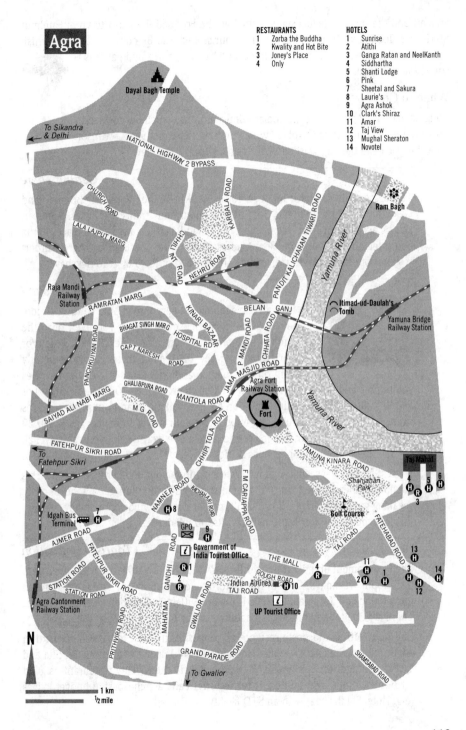

RESTAURANTS
1 Zorba the Buddha
2 Kwality and Hot Bite
3 Joney's Place
4 Only

HOTELS
1 Sunrise
2 Atithi
3 Ganga Ratan and NeelKanth
4 Siddhartha
5 Shanti Lodge
6 Pink
7 Sheetal and Sakura
8 Laurie's
9 Agra Ashok
10 Clark's Shiraz
11 Amar
12 Taj View
13 Mughal Sheraton
14 Novotel

area around the three principal sights—the Taj, the Fort and the ghost town of Fatehpur Sikri—are flooded with touts, beggars and tourist emporia. By contrast, the old British cantonment with its wide, spacious streets and peaceful parks and gardens is surprisingly relaxed.

When to Go

Most people visit Agra during the cooler winter months of October to March. Possibly the best month is October, when the town is wreathed in crimson bougainvillaea and the Taj, washed by the rains, gleams like a new pin.

Getting There

There are daily flights from Agra to Delhi, Khajuraho, Varanasi, Bombay and Calcutta.There are no flights from nearby Jaipur, only trains and buses. Agra can also be accessed by road/rail by most centres in Rajasthan andd some places in the South (eg direct trains from Goa, Madras, Trivandrum and Bombay. Agra's airport is 7km from the town centre, about Rs100 by taxi or Rs20 by auto-rickshaw.

Getting Around

Agra isn't a big place, but it's very spread out. Touring on foot can be a hassle—cycle-rickshaws follow you even onto the pavement—so many travellers hire a bicycle (Rs15/day) or rent a rickshaw for the day. What these charge is greatly dependent on how many handicraft shops and carpet factories you're prepared to visit. If none, you'll be asked around Rs100 (cycle-rickshaw) or Rs250 (auto-rickshaw). But if you don't mind walking in and out of these shops every so often (pausing just long enough for your driver to collect his Rs10/20 'appearance' commission and for you to have a free fizzy drink), you can travel all day for little or nothing. Short hops by rickshaw should never cost more than Rs10.

A stress-free way of seeing Agra is to hire a car from your hotel or travel agent. This cuts out endless diversions to tiresome shops and you often get a good English-speaking guide as a driver. If you don't, proper licensed guides can be hired (again, through your hotel) for Rs200 half-day, Rs300 full-day.

Agra ℂ (0562–)   ***Tourist Information***

The Government of India **tourist office**, ℂ 363377, is at 191 The Mall, open 9am to 5.30pm weekdays, 9am to 1pm Saturday, closed Sunday. The Uttar Pradesh tourist office 64 Taj Road, ℂ 360517, is open 10am to 5pm daily except Sundays. There are also tourist information counters at the rail station and at the airport.

The **post office** and poste restante are opposite the Mall tourist office. **Indian Airlines** is at the Clark's Shiraz Hotel, ℂ 360940, along with Mercury, Sita and TCI **travel agents**. Modern Book Depot, close to the Kwality restaurant, is good for **books, maps and guides. International calls** are cheapest at budget lodges (e.g. Hotel Siddhartha) with an STD facility.

Tour 1: Major Sites

By tour bus, full day. Fatehpur Sikri–Agra Fort–Taj Mahal.

Tour buses pick up Delhi day-trippers from Agra Cantonment station at 8.30am and 10am daily, following the arrival of the Shatabdi Express and Taj Express trains. Tickets cost Rs100 and Rs125 respectively, and are sold on board the bus. The charge includes an English-speaking guide. If you're staying overnight, you can keep your luggage on the bus and use the tour as an introduction to the city. If already in Agra, you can pick up either bus from the tourist office in The Mall.

Fatehpur Sikri

Open from sunrise to sunset; adm Rs0.50.

The first place you'll be taken is the legendary ghost city of the Mughals, **Fatehpur Sikri**, 40km southwest of Agra. This well-preserved 'City of Victory' was commenced in 1569 by Emperor Akbar as a grateful tribute to the celebrated saint, Shaikh Salim Chishti, who successfully predicted the birth of three sons to his childless wives. It is said that the first

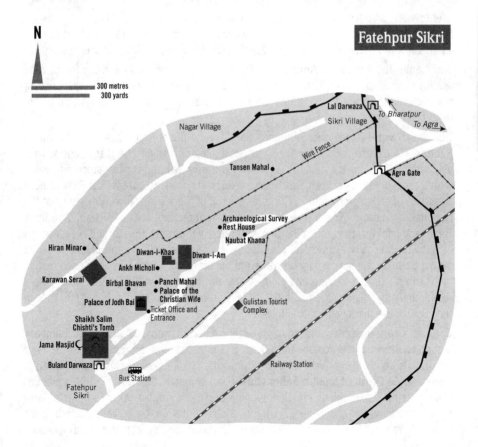

son, Salim, later to become Emperor Jehangir, was born here. Upon the site of the Shaikh's humble homestead, in the small village of stonecutters called Sikri, there arose a vast imperial capital. Akbar was convinced that this place would continue to bring him good fortune but his confidence was misplaced. Having used 10,000 artisans to create a Hindu-Persian masterpiece of red sandstone architecture, with 500 beautiful palaces and buildings spread over a circumference of 14.4km, he was forced to abandon it, probably due to severe water shortage, just 14 years later.

Fatehpur Sikri

Today, his achievement remains remarkably intact. Fatehpur Sikri's isolated situation spared it from the wholesale destruction inflicted by later invaders on other Mughal cities. Indeed, so untouched by time is this finest of India's ghost towns, that you require only the slightest bit of imagination to visualize how it must have been 400 years ago, a refined and elegant Mughal court capital.

You'll enter the fort by the **Agra Gate**. There's a fork in the road here, the left turning leading to the modern town where (if staying the day) you can visit the workshops and see the traditional art of Sikri stonecutting. The right turning leads straight up to the royal palaces.

Past the **Diwan-i-Am** (Public Audience Hall) beyond the entrance gate, you'll come to **Pachesi Courtyard,** where Akbar played sexist games of *pachesi* (similar to chess) with his harem ladies as pieces. A little further on is **Panch Mahal**, the five-storeyed edifice which probably best encapsulates Fatehpur Sikri. Its design combines the best of both Hindu and Persian architecture. Climb to the top of this elegant tower for views of the surrounding palaces. The interesting blend of architectural styles (Persian, Buddhist, Hindu and Jain) incorporated in Panch Mahal runs right through the city and is a reflection of Akbar's unusually ecumenical philosophy. Having met with Hindu priests, Muslim elders, Catholic fathers and various gurus and monks of other faiths, he concluded that all paths in religion led to the same God. A brave attempt to synthesize all beliefs into a single, unifying religion called 'Din Ilahi' (Religion of God), was sadly short-lived, though the architecture that typified it still lives on.

Through a vast, magnificent maze of pink-sandstone courtyards, palaces, royal chambers, meeting-halls, balconies, colonnades, baths and minarets, one comes at last to the huge quadrangle south of the fort. Here you'll find the city's finest treasure—the glittering white marble **Tomb of Shaikh Salim Chishti**, an important Sufi shrine. Visiting pilgrims from all faiths—particularly childless women hoping to emulate Akbar's miracle—seal their prayers by binding pieces of string to the beautiful marble screens encircling the cenotaph, returning to remove the threads when their wish has been granted. The canopy of *shishma* wood above the inner shrine is exquisitely inlaid with mother of pearl, and the air is sweet with the heavy scent of attar of roses.

To the side of Salim's tomb is the city's largest and grandest structure, the **Jama Masjid**, constructed in 1575 to hold 10,000 worshippers. Facing it is India's 'grandest gateway', the massive 54m-high **Buland Darwaza**, erected in 1602 to commemorate Akbar's victory in Gujarat. Once the highest gate in the world, it bears the Arabic legend, 'The world is a bridge, pass over it but build no house upon it. He who hopes for an hour may hope for eternity.'

This Victory Gate is the normal exit from the fort and provides fine views over the village of Sikri. Originally however, it was designed as an entrance so it's worth looking over your shoulder as you walk away. If visiting in spring, watch out for dead bees on the way out.

There's no fee for cameras but licensed guides at the entrance charge Rs50. They're a lot better than the unofficial 'guides' hovering around inside. The tour bus only gives you an hour or so to look around though, which is not nearly enough. To see the complex properly, visit by local bus (Rs10, from Agra's Idgah bus-stand), by auto-rickshaw (Rs250) or by taxi (Rs400 non a/c, Rs600 a/c). Prices quoted for rickshaws and taxis include the hour's drive there, a couple of hours to sightsee at leisure and the drive back to Agra. Alternatively, you can stay overnight in Fatehpur Sikri (well worth it for the sunset) or continue on to Bharatpur (another bus, 45 minutes) for the evening. In Fatehpur Sikri, the most comfortable lodge is **UPSTDC's Gulistan Tourist Complex**, ✆ 05619-2490, with clean, spacious rooms from Rs300 non a/c, Rs600 a/c, and a good restaurant. If you're on a budget, there's **Maurya Rest House**, ✆ 05619-2348, below the Buland Darwaza. You can dump your bags here if you're just passing through, and use its toilet.

Agra Fort

Open from sunrise to sunset; adm Rs10.50 (free Fri).

From Fatehpur Sikri, the tour moves on to Agra Fort. Built by Akbar between 1565 and 1573 on the site of an earlier Lodhi fort, and much added to by Jehangir and Shah Jahan, this 'Red Fort' is just as interesting as the one in Delhi and is far better preserved. In Mughal days, this massive red-turreted fortress with its 24km circuit contained some 500 stone buildings within its sturdy double wall and was encircled by a wide moat. It served a dual function, housing both residential palaces (for the royal family) and defensive military quarters (for the Mughal, then the British, now the Indian armies). There are guides for hire at the Amar Singh Gate entrance. By the time you read this, Agra Fort may have a *son et lumière* show in the evenings.

The great Mughal emperors ruled India for a century from this fort, and within it you will find their palaces—Akbar's (broken foundations, situated behind a small tree), Jehangir's (to the front, with rich carvings and marble inlay work) and Shah Jahan's (a simpler, white-marble effort). At the great Hall of Public Audience, the Diwan-i-Am, Shah Jahan held court for the common people. When, as was common, proceedings dragged on too long, decorated elephants paraded up and down in front of him to bring matters to a speedy conclusion. Next door is the exquisite little Pearl Mosque, named after the large, priceless pearl which used to hang by a golden chain from the ceiling. It is widely considered the most beautiful mosque in India.

For the perfect preview of the Taj Mahal, pass round the flower-laden garden of the central courtyard and climb the stairs up to the Musamman Burj. It was here, in this small octagonal, turreted room, that Shah Jahan spent the last eight years of his life, a prisoner of his son Aurangzeb, looking over the Yamuna to the shrine of his beloved wife Mumtaz—the Taj Mahal. This 'Jasmine Tower', so-called because of its adornment of jasmine blossoms, is surrounded with marvellous marble filigree screens. The adjoining Diwan-i-Khas is remarkable for its mosaics, their original colours intact, and for its flower-wreathed columns, inlaid with precious stones. Outside, on the palisade, are the two marble thrones of Shah Jahan (white) and Jehangir (black). One feature common to all Mughal gardens was the use of water. The fountain and sunken courtyard opposite the lovely Sheesh Mahal (Mirror Palace) are fine examples of water engineering. The palace itself—composed of two rooms, artificial fountains and a cascade, the walls enriched with badly renovated mirror-work—was once the bath-house of the *zenana* (women's quarters).

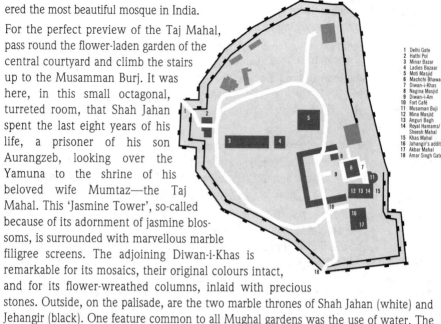

1 Delhi Gate
2 Hathi Pol
3 Minar Bazaar
4 Ladies Bazaar
5 Moti Masjid
6 Machchi Bhawan
7 Diwan-i-Khas
8 Nagina Masjid
9 Diwan-i-Am
10 Fort Café
11 Musaman Buji
12 Mina Masjid
13 Anguri Bagh
14 Royal Hamams/
   Sheesh Mahal
15 Khas Mahal
16 Jahangir's additions
17 Akbar Mahal
18 Amar Singh Gate

Taj Mahal

Open 6am–7pm daily; adm Rs10.50, or Rs100 at sunrise (6–8am) and sunset (4–7pm; 5–7pm 1 Apr–30 Sept); free Fri.

The final stop of the day is the 'Crown of Palaces', the . Many people visit this essential symbol of India fully prepared to be disappointed. But few are. The most photographed, filmed, drawn and described building in the world, it is one of those few rare places in India which consistently meets (even exceeds) expectations. The secret of its success lies largely in its simplicity. True beauty, as its architect Shah Jahan proved, needs no ornament; it is essentially pure and simple.

The Taj is the most accomplished monument to love the world has ever seen. It was the creation of Shah Jahan, built to immortalize the memory of his beloved wife, Mumtaz Mahal, who died tragically in 1631 giving birth to her 14th child. He intended it to be the culminating masterpiece of his many buildings and so used the best artisans to ensure the highest possible quality of design and craftsmanship. An incredible 20,000 workmen laboured day and night for 22 years to bring it to completion. One of the less charming myths surrounding its construction is that many of the principal architects and sculptors lost their hands afterwards lest they should ever build such a masterpiece again.

The main mausoleum went up first: 22 tons of white marble inlaid with semi-precious stones. Then, because no tomb was complete without one, a mosque was added. A 'dummy' mosque, to provide symmetry, appeared on the right side. Then the gardens were laid out and the gigantic red-sandstone entrance gate erected. It was inscribed with Koranic texts in letters that appeared totally uniform in size, whether viewed at the top or the bottom. And on the tomb itself was inscribed Shah Jahan's tragic prayer: 'Help us, O Lord, to bear that which we cannot bear'.

You don't have to be a romantic to fall in love with the Taj; it moves even hardened cynics. The smooth white marble has a supple, sensual quality that has visitors compulsively stroking and touching it or standing back to photograph it. Much of the attraction, as one traveller observed, has to do with coming face-to-face with something which one has always associated with India, ever since reading storybooks as a child, yet somehow never expected to be real. It's one of those few times in life when fantasy and reality perfectly coincide.

The Taj is something to be seen at leisure, not rushed. Instead of bolting down to see it at close quarters, start with a general appreciation from the mammoth entrance gate: first the beautiful canals, fountains and tanks (sometimes with water in, sometimes not); next, the sweeping green lawns (minus the original fruit trees and gardens, but still pretty); then the two red-sandstone side buildings including the mosque; finally, the huge domed mausoleum in the centre. The Taj Mahal stands on a raised marble platform, with a tall, narrow minaret at each corner. The minarets were built to lean very slightly outwards, to save the tomb from damage should they ever topple. The huge bulbous dome atop the main structure is surrounded by four smaller domes. The four sides of the Taj are identical, and the building itself sits against a backdrop of empty sky, a conscious device producing the illusion of a palace seemingly suspended in the air.

Taj Mahal

The approach to the mausoleum is via long paths separated by a long central watercourse, in which (when there is water) it is beautifully reflected. The illusion of perfection is maintained even when viewing the structure at close range. The walls and arches are elegantly engraved with screen and mosaic work, the exquisite tracery and carving more like lace than sculpture. Semiprecious stones have been inlaid into the marble in incredibly precise patterns, a distinctive process of craftsmanship called *pietra dura*. Midway along the western wall of the garden is the small Taj Museum (*closed Fri*) with an interesting collection of Mughal items and 19th-century photographs.

Inside the cool cenotaph chamber, decorated with emeralds, jaspers, sapphires and other precious stones, a plain marble screen runs round the two dummy tombs of Shah Jahan and

Mumtaz (the real ones, to avoid looting, were placed in the dark, humid basement chamber below). The original gem-studded gold screen was replaced by the present plain one in 1642, because Shah Jahan wanted to discourage grave-robbers. But the Taj was a natural target for looters, and the real tombs below were stripped of all their gold and jewels by Jats from Bharatpur in 1754. The chamber itself has fine inlay work—mainly floral designs on red, green, gold or black marble. The Cairene lamp hanging from the dome of the cenotaph was donated by Lord Curzon in 1909.

After exploring the mausoleum, stroll outside to view it at leisure from the cool, shaded gardens. It's all been said before, but the Taj is unique—a rare masterpiece of perfect proportion, symmetrical construction and harmonious form. Blinding-white at noon, the stark Makrana marble mellows by dusk to a sultry orange-cream, only to adopt a deathly blue-white pallor at night. Full-moon nights used to be a popular viewing time, but in 1985 security precautions caused the building to be closed after dark. There are plans to re-open it on moonlit nights but, until that happens, the only way you'll see the Taj at night is to book a room at the Taj View Hotel directly overlooking it.

The main entrance is on the western side. The higher admission prices at sunrise and sunset are 'a nice little earner', as someone observed, 'but clearly not thought through. The result—delightfully calm, quiet and uncrowded for sunrise, but hordes buying tickets just before 4pm, leading to queues at the check-in gate and crowds inside for 2–3 hours.' Fridays are free, but impossibly noisy and congested.

Plans to open the Taj at night, and to give it a *son et lumière* show along the same lines as the Red Fort in Delhi, have been put on hold until it has been decided whether or not the halogen beams used to illuminate the building will damage the marble.

Environmentalists have rather too late come to the rescue of the Taj, which has been enveloped by smog and smoke from nearby industrial factories for over 30 years. The worst culprit is an iron smelting plant owned by the government itself. If this were not enough, armies of tourists troop through the building daily, digging out semi-precious stones, writing ugly graffiti and running dirty hands over the marble. From the ground up, sadly, the Taj is beginning to disintegrate.

Tour 2: Other Sights

By rickshaw, taxi or cycle, half-day. Itmud-ud-Daulah's Tomb–Chini ka Rauza–Ram Bagh Gardens–Sikandra.

For day two, start with Agra's most underrated sight: **Itmud-ud-Daulah's Tomb**, 4km upstream from the Taj and across the Yamuna river (*open from sunrise to sunset; adm Rs5.50, free Fri*). The tomb of a Persian nobleman, Ghiyas Beg, who became Jehangir's chief minister and took the title Itmud-ud-Daulah, was built in just 6 years (1522–8) by his powerful daughter, Empress Nur Jahan (Jehangir's consort). It was the first monument in India to feature Persian mosaic-style inlay work, or *pietra dura*. Greatly resembling the Taj in its use of inlay on white marble, its twin sandstone mosques and its (smaller) ornamental sandstone gate, this elegant tomb in fact directly preceded it. The use of *pietra dura* here was simplified and brought to its most elegant flowering in the construction of the Taj Mahal.

If anything, the quality of precise, delicate workmanship at Itmud-ud-Daulah is far superior to that of its more fêted rival, making its popular pseudonym of the 'Bibi-Taj' (little Taj) rather unfair. Like the main Taj, it is a simple white mausoleum, but its four minarets are far more sturdy and broad, and instead of a dome it has a Chinese palanquin-type top, with two spires. Though beautifully preserved, it receives very few visitors. This is a pity, since the elaborate inlay patterning (mainly floral) on the exterior is quite remarkable. The yellow and white inlay is Indian, the grey and multi-coloured stonework Persian. The ceiling of the edifice was originally decorated with gold and silver paintings, later scraped off or plastered over by looters or defilers of fine art. Lord Curzon achieved a partial restoration in 1905, preceding the Prince of Wales' visit, notably on the floor and ceiling. The four sandstone gates of the tomb are perfectly symmetrical, and the plaster interior has attractive hand-painted floral designs. Within are the tombs of Nur Jahan's parents (brown marble) and of Mumtaz's parents and various relatives. The surrounding gardens are well-kept and tranquil, full of blooms, plants and birds.

From here, it's only 1km north to the once blue-tiled, but now much damaged, **Chini ka Rauza**. This Persian-influenced tomb was built by Afzal Khan (died 1639) for his own use. A further 2km north brings you to Ram Bagh—the rather unkempt prototype of future Mughal gardens, built by Emperor Babur in 1528.

Ten kilometres (6 miles) north of Agra, along the Grand Trunk Road to Delhi, is Akbar's mausoleum at **Sikandra**. Combining architectural themes and motifs from both Islam and Hinduism, it was started by Akbar but finished by his son, Jehangir. This tomb lacks the grace of either Humayun's tomb in Delhi or the Taj Mahal, but is something of a design-prototype to both and is set in peaceful, extensive gardens.

Bharatpur Bird Sanctuary

A worthwhile excursion from Agra (53km) is to Bharatpur Bird Sanctuary at **Keoladeo Ghana National Park**. There are buses from Agra to Bharatpur, but the comfortable option is by taxi, only 1½hrs.

Bharatpur is home to one of the world's most important wetland sanctuaries. About a third of the park's 29 sq km is flooded during the monsoon and is host to tens of thousands of resident breeding birds from August to November. In October, large groups of migratory waterfowl, waders and birds of prey arrive from Siberia, Central Asia, Tibet and the Russian Steppes. The best time to visit is between November and February, when a relaxing day or two can be spent photographing storks, spoonbills, egrets, cranes etc. (at the entrance they give you a checklist of 200 birds to tick off), in butterfly-filled marshes dotted with deer, snakes, hyenas and blue buck (*nilgai*). Rather than walking, you can hire a boat on the lake (Rs80) or a cycle-rickshaw to tour the park. The latter charge Rs25 an hour, and it's helpful to get one with a driver who speaks good English so that you can find out something about the birds you see.

The only place to stay the night within the park is the government-run **Ashok Forest Lodge**, with dirty rooms at a rip-off Rs2200 and mediocre buffet dinners for Rs275. Just outside the park, five minutes away by rickshaw, there's half a dozen better hotels with nicer restaurants, costing only a quarter as much. Try **Falcon Guest House** near the (awful) Saras Tourist Bungalow; it's very quiet and peaceful. Wherever you stay, remember to bring lots of mosquito repellent.

Shopping

Agra is a positive mecca of handicraft shops and emporia, selling a wide range of goods from marble curios, brassware and embroidery to wood carvings, leather shoes, carpets and jewellery. Every taxi and auto-rickshaw driver will try to punctuate an afternoon's tour of monuments with one or more visits to an emporium. The best general shopping area is Sadar Bazaar, below the tourist office, where you can pick up good marble, leather and clothes bargains. A reliable place to start is **Dawoor Footwear** for leather shoes, bags, accessories and readymade garments.

Agra is not nicknamed 'Agro' for nothing. Agra-vation comes at you from all sides and it's all aimed at getting you into shops selling imitation or inferior produce at inflated prices. Many travellers shut down completely and buy nothing, which is something they often regret later.

Three tips: first, don't go into any shop with touts, 'students' or rickshaw men. They get up to 40 per cent commission on anything you buy; second, if you must pay by credit card, always keep copies of the bill and voucher copy. Shopowners are very skilled at adding a couple of zeros to the price shown on receipts; third, don't believe anyone who tells you that you can recoup the entire cost of your trip by buying a few precious stones from them and selling them at a huge profit in your own country. They'll even give you addresses to sell them to, but both the addresses and the stones will be fake.

Agra has a particularly fine handicrafts pedigree. When Humayun returned here from his exile in Persia, he brought with him a retinue of captive artisans and weavers. His son Akbar gave these craftsmen, painters, jewellers a royal commission. At this point, Agra became the handicrafts centre of north India, and the country's very first carpets came into being. Inevitably, these were of Persian design. There are many carpet wholesalers in Agra today, but only one—**Harish Carpet Co** in Vibhav Nagar Road—which is fair-price. Guarantees are supplied with all purchases and shipping home is no problem.

Agra is especially famous for its high-quality marblework, the presence of the Taj having encouraged the local people to develop a real expertise in it. There are presently hundreds of factories in Agra working on marble, most of them in the Balu Ganj area, just up from the Mall. Every one of the workers seems to have had an ancestor who worked on the Taj Mahal itself. The hard, durable, non-staining marble used comes not from Agra, but from Makrana, southwest of Jaipur. The process of working it has remained more or less unchanged since the days of the Taj. An easy way of telling marble from inferior soapstone, by the way, is to scratch the item being sold against a piece of wood. Soapstone marks, marble doesn't.

Typically, in a place that really needs it, Agra has no government-authorized emporium to check prices at. There are lots of government-*approved* shops but they are definitely not the same thing. Currently, shopping for marble products is best done at fair-deal places like **Akbar International** opposite the Taj View Hotel, **Subhash Emporium** opposite the Central Telegraph Office on Gwalior Road, and **Oswal Emporium** at Nanulakha, off Mall Road. At the latter, you can see workers doing *pietra dura* inlay work, with no obligation to buy.

Leisure

You can go **swimming** at the Clark's, Taj and Sheraton hotels, though the non-resident fees are quite high—up to US$10 per day. If you're on a budget, there are cheaper pools at the Amar (Rs100) and Sakura (Rs50) hotels. The Clark's Hotel has folk dance/puppet programmes in the evenings and live sitar/tabla music at its nightly poolside barbecues. The Soor Sadan cultural centre, opposite Anjuna cinema, lays on regular **dramatics and dance shows**. Programmes are listed in *Amar Ujala Danik Jakran*, along with local **cinema** details, but this is a Hindi newspaper so you'll need a translator!

The annual **cultural festival** of Taj-Mahotsav takes place between 18 and 27 February at Shilpgram, near the eastern gate of the Taj Mahal. Daily programmes of events are posted at all the better hotels and tickets can be booked through the tourist office in The Mall.

Agra © *(0562–)*   ### Where to Stay

For a major tourist centre, Agra has remarkably few high-class hotels and restaurants. This is because so many travellers day-trip from Delhi and don't stay overnight. The introduction of charter flights (Jan 1996) was the first step towards promoting Agra as a week-long holiday base, and has indeed generated a cluster of new hotels in the mid-bracket, but the overall infrastructure is not expected to improve until the city gets its international airport, probably around the end of the century.

luxury (from US$125)

For service and style, you can't beat the **Hotel Taj View** at Taj Ganj, Fatehabad Road, © 361172, ● 361179. Personal and cosy throughout, this is the most agreeable of the chain, with the nicest pool (completely marbled), the most courteous staff, and the classiest rooms. Ask for one with a 'telescopic' view of the Taj—it's worth the extra US$20.

The other two prestige hotels in Agra are the **Mughal Sheraton** on Fatehabad Road and the **Clark's Shiraz Hotel** on Taj Road, but I can't recommend them.

expensive (from US$38)

The new **Novotel Agra** on Fatehabad Road, 1.5km from the Taj, © 368282, ● 360217, is a very friendly place offering 4-star facilities at incredibly low tariffs. Everyone can afford US$38 for a luxury single room, so the place is nearly always full. It's a bit far out of town, but has a pool (5ft deep, surrounded by lovely gardens), a decent restaurant and the poshest bar in town. Book ahead or be disappointed.

moderate (from Rs600)

Until the much-advertised **Howard Palace** (with its Taj-view rooftop revolving restaurant) opens on Mall Road, the best buy in this bracket is the new **Atithi** on Fatehabad Road, ✆ 3611474, ✆ 360077. No pool yet, but the restaurant is good and the a/c rooms very spacious. The nearby **Hotel Amar**, ✆ 360695, ✆ 366999, has a pool and a health club, but the rooms don't compare to the Atithi's and the service has slipped. Behind the Amar, on Vibhav Nagar, there's the very neat and clean **Sunrise**, ✆ 360315, ✆ 360126, with well-appointed rooms and suites, hospitable staff and a rooftop restaurant. On Bansal Nagar, off Fatehabad Road, a trio of new hotels are the **Ganga Ratan**, ✆ 266529, ✆ 266693, the **Savoy**, ✆ 269749, ✆ 381439, and the **Neelkanth**, ✆ 362039. They're all good, especially the Ganga Ratan. Finally, a special mention for **Laurie's Hotel** on M G Road, ✆ 364536, not far from the GPO. It's a bit dilapidated, but is run by a lovely old couple who really look after their guests. The garden and pool are relaxing, and there are large, airy rooms at the back.

budget

Every second hotel in this class claims to have the 'only' view of the Taj, and if challenged they'll say they have the *best* view of the Taj. In actual fact, only two have a *complete* close-up view, unrestricted by other buildings, and they're both cheap guest houses in the Taj Ganj area, just south of the Taj Mahal.

The first is **Shanti Lodge**, ✆ 361644, near the South Gate with its rooftop restaurant, ten Taj-view rooms (ask for 70 or 108) at Rs200 and several no-view rooms from Rs100. Second, there's the cheaper **Hotel Kamal**, ✆ 360926, where the dinginess of the rooms is offset by unparalleled views from the roof. Other good places along South Gate are **India Guest House** with one viewpoint room on the roof for Rs70, and the spotless new **Hotel Raj** with no views at all but really nice rooms with TV and air conditioning from Rs300. Near the western gate, the friendly Sikh-run **Hotel Siddhartha**, ✆ 360238, has clean rooms from Rs100 and a relaxing sit-out garden restaurant. **Hotel Host**, ✆ 361010, a few doors down, is even cheaper and has bike hire for Rs10/day. Finally, by the East Gate, there's **Hotel Pink**, ✆ 360677, with a range of rooms from Rs40 to Rs150 and Taj views from the terrace.

A brand-new hotel has just opened opposite the Shanti Lodge. No name available, but it has a Taj view and a very nice cafeteria with delicious honey pancakes. Rooms are said to be better than Shanti Lodge, from Rs150 with bath and running hot water. Sounds like a good deal.

If you've got an early bus to catch, the adjoining **Sakura**, ✆ 369793, and **Sheetal** hotels near Idgah bus terminal have cheap rooms from Rs150 to 350. Ashu, the

Sakura's friendly proprietor, is going all-out to attract foreigners—he's just built a pool and is now planning a terrace restaurant-cum-disco with 'fast' music and a salad bar.

Agra ℂ (0562–)   ***Eating Out***

The Clark's Shiraz Hotel has a popular lunchtime buffet at Rs300, evening poolside barbecues with live traditional music at US$20, and the only rooftop restaurant in town, with live 'ghazals' every night from 7.30 to 11pm. If you prefer a specific cuisine, the Ashok Hotel on the Mall does the best Chinese (all their restaurant/kitchen staff are from Sikkim and Manipal) while the Maurya Sheraton offers top-notch Indian and Continental fare. Over at the Taj View, the **Nazara** specializes in Mughlai cuisine and the coffee shop is good for buffets. The Novotel lays on a superb breakfast buffet for under £5.

Outside the hotels, there are surprisingly few decent restaurants. Your best bet is a rickshaw to the bottom of Sadar Bazaar , where you'll find **Hot Bite** and **Kwality** serving popular mid-priced food in air-conditioned comfort. Kwality is the cheaper of the two and has a delicious bakery. For cheaper fare, try **Zorba the Buddha** below the tourist office. This is a Rajneesh place, much-loved by travellers, with pure veg food at unbeatable prices. Pity it's so small though. Over the road, the **Prakash** is still famous for South Indian dishes but is rather rundown nowadays. The multi-cuisine only restaurant on Taj Road (close to Clark's Hotel) specializes in Mughlai cuisine and has a pleasant sit-out lawn.

There are several cheap travellers' restaurants in Taj Ganj area, south of the Taj Mahal. Most of them require a government health warning, so check for clean glasses and cutlery. The new **Saroj**, opposite Shanti Lodge, is very clean and well-patronized. **Shankara Vegis** is a popular 'pure veg' hangout with books/mags, Western sounds and an airy sit-out section on the roof. **Joney's Place** is a good place to meet people (it's so small, you don't have much choice), though its 'yum yum' food is not what it once was. Over at Western Gate, near Hotel Host, there's **Lucky** restaurant, serving simple but tasty food at rock-bottom prices.

Moving On

By air: Indian Airlines offers daily flights between Agra and Delhi/Khajuraho/Varanasi. Modiluft and U P Airways offer the same route daily but sometimes cancel due to insufficient bookings.

By rail: Until the line between Agra and stations in Rajasthan have been converted from narrow to broad gauge, there is only one slow train daily to Jaipur, leaving Agra Cantonment at 8pm and arriving 6am the next day. For Khajuraho, catch the daily a/c Shatabdi Express to Jhansi (2hrs) and then a local bus (6hrs). For Delhi, it's the Shatabdi Express again (dep 8.15pm, 2hrs) or the slower Taj Express (dep

6.35pm, 3hrs) which also runs daily. Slow trains go to Varanasi (16–18hrs) from Tundla station, 25km out of Agra. By 1997, there should be one direct train to Goa, taking 36hrs. At present, your best bet is the 3pm train to Pune (24hrs), then a bus to Goa (9hrs).

By road: Buses to Delhi (5hrs) leave every hour or so from Idgah bus terminal, but most people go by train. For Jaipur, there are hourly buses (5hrs) from outside Hotel Sakura, just up from Idgah bus terminal. There are no convenient buses to Khajuraho. It's a good idea to go by taxi, stopping midway to appreciate the temples and palaces of Orchha. There are two local buses daily to Ajmer, via Jaipur (9hrs), leaving at 8am and 10pm, and a couple of early morning buses direct to Pushkar. Private companies run buses to Udaipur and Jodhpur (not recommended)

Gwalior population 800,000

Sutter Widows hands
Gwalior

The ancient city of Gwalior is dominated by its strategically important fort, which for centuries controlled one of the major routes between north and south India. Its history goes back 2000 years, with rock inscriptions from the 5th century AD still extant. The first Muslim ruler to hold it was Qutb-ud-din-Aibak during the 12th century. After that, control of the fort and the surrounding area passed through a succession of Muslim, Tomar Rajput, Afghan, Mughal, Maratha and finally British rulers. The greatest of the Tomars was Man Singh, who came to power in 1486. It was during his reign that many of the great battlements and interior palaces were built. After a short period of control by the Lodhis (Afghans), the first Mughal Emperor Babur took the fort and described it as 'the pearl among the fortresses of Hind'. During the slow collapse of the Mughal empire the Scindia line of Marathas conquered the area in 1754. The British took control of the fort at various points during the Maratha wars, and then—having captured the Rani of Jhansi within its walls in 1858 and ending the Indian Mutiny—held it for 30 years.

Once one of the largest and richest of the Indian princely states, Gwalior is today a large, sprawling city with rich agriculture and an expanding industrial base. The new town, Lashkar, is south of the fort and the railway station to the southeast.

Getting There

Gwalior can be accessed by air from Delhi and Bombay. There are taxis and auto-rickshaws from the airport to the town centre for Rs140 and Rs80. the quickest trains are the *Shatabdi Express* from New Delhi (dep 6.15am, arr 9.30am) and the *Taj Express* from Delhi, Hazrat Nizammudin (dep 7.15am, arr 11.55am. Both stop at Agra along the way, departing at 8.15am and 9.50am respectively. Slower buses run to Gwalior daily from Delhi's ISBT bus-stand (8hrs), Agra's Idgah bus-stand (3hrs), Khajuraho (9hrs) and Jhansi (3hrs). *See* 'Moving On' for the above places.

Gwalior ✆ (0751–)   **Tourist Information**

The **tourist office** is at the Tansen Hotel, ✆ 342606. It has cars for local excursions and trips to Orchha, as does the Usha Kiran Palace hotel.

Touring Gwalior

Start at the fort. This is an immense structure about 3km in length and up to 2km wide. On a clear day, it commands a fantastic view of the city and its environs; the old city lies to the north and northeast. There are two ways of entering the fort: by car via the Urwahi Gate, passing *en route* 21 Jain sculptures carved out of the rock between the 8th and 15th centuries (mutilated by the first Mughal armies on Babur's orders and only partially restored). On foot, the easiest access is via Alamgir Gate, but many travellers take a taxi or auto-rickshaw to the top (it's a stiff climb) and save their energies for walking back down. There are no refreshments in the fort, so bring a water-bottle and supplies.

The fort walls and the buildings within were constructed by various generations of rulers. The **Suraj Kund**, inside the outer walls, is an ancient tank at the site of the original pond where Suraj Pal was supposedly cured of leprosy by Saint Gwalipa in AD 8. The **Teli-ka Mandir**, dedicated to Vishnu and built by the Pratiharas (8th–11th centuries) is one of the oldest buildings in the fort. Intricate stone carvings decorate the doorway. Two 11th-century temples known as the **Sas-Bahu ka Mandir** are also dedicated to Vishnu. Their open design contrasts with the Teli-ka Mandir. The 15th-century **Gujri Mahal Palace** near the **Hindola Gate** now houses a small **Archaeological Museum** (*open 10am–5pm, closed Mon*). One of the finest buildings in the fort is the four-storey **Man Mandir Palace** built in the late 15th century by Raja Man Singh. A blue and patterned tile decoration dominates one side of the fort's exterior wall. Other

Peacock Fort Gwalior

buildings of interest are the interconnected **Vikramaditya** and **Karan Palaces** on the western side of the fort. There may be a *son et lumière* show in operation by the time you read this—check at the entrance.

In the 'new' town is the huge 19th-century **Jai Vilas Palace** (*open 10am–5pm, closed Mon; adm Rs30; photography is not allowed*), housing what are supposedly a pair of the world's heaviest chandeliers in the **Darbar Hall** and a crystal staircase. The dining table has an electric train made of silver with which the Maharajah delivered cigars, port, brandy and other items in crystal wagons to favoured guests. Thirty-five rooms have now been converted to a museum filled with the family's memorabilia.

There are two notable tombs in the old town, about 15 minutes' walk from the north-eastern gate of the fort. The early Mughal **tomb of Muhammed Gaus** is built as a hexagonal tower with a dome, once covered in blue ceramic tiles. The nearby **tomb of Tansen** commemorates the great musician who played at Akbar's court. The **Royal Chhatris** or cenotaphs are near Jayaji Chowk market.

Leisure

There's a sporadic **son et lumière** show at the Man Mandir Palace in the fort. Timings vary, so check locally. Non-residents can use the **pool** at the Hotel Gwalior Regency for Rs30 and its **health club/jacuzzi** for Rs100.

Gwalior ✆ (0751–) ### Where to Stay

Gwalior's most expensive hotel is the bland **Usha Kiran Palace** behind Jai Vilas Palace, ✆ 323993, ✉ 321103. Originally the Maharajah's guest-house, it has an attractive garden, an underground pool and many recreational facilities. Rooms start at US$35/70. M P Tourism's **Hotel Tansen** is 1km from the railway station at 6A Gandhi Road, ✆ 340370. It has an a/c restaurant-bar and adequate rooms at Rs250/320 non a/c, Rs450/550 a/c. Close by is the a/c **Hotel Gwalior Regency**, ✆ 340670, ✉ 343520, which is probably the best deal of the lot, with smart a/c rooms around US$20/30 and more facilities (including a pool) than there are letters in a Welsh train station name. If you want something cheaper, there's **Hotel Vivek** near Bada Chowk, ✆ 27016, or **Hotel India**, ✆ 341983, near the rail station. Both places have non a/c rooms from Rs100 and a/c ones from Rs300.

Gwalior ✆ (0751–) ### Eating Out

Indian food is good but pricey at the **Usha Kiran Palace**. The nearby **Volga Restaurant** has similar fare at rather less cost. Cheap and best for veggie snacks (*dosas*, *idlis*, etc.) is Hotel India's **Indian Coffee House**. The canteen at the railway station does a good cheap *thali*.

Moving On

Indian Airlines offers 4 flights a week from Gwalior to Delhi and Bombay. The daily *Shatabdi Express* and *Taj Express* trains return to Agra and Delhi at 7pm and 5pm respectively. Buses from Delhi, Agra, Jhansi and (mornings only) Khajuraho leave from Gwalior's government bus-stand near the railway station.

From its founding in 1531 right through to 1783, Orchha was the capital of a locally powerful Rajput kingdom. Built on a large rocky island in the Betwa river by Rudra Pratap, it was consistently added to by subsequent Rajput chieftains until they took a new capital (1783) at nearby Tikamgadh. From this point on, its fortunes declined. Today, Orchha is a small village with a population of only a couple of thousand. Rarely visited, but in fact fairly easy to reach from Delhi, Agra or Khajuraho, it is one of India's many surprises. The ruins are located in the middle of a primaeval forest, with extinct volcanoes on the horizon. 'It belongs in a Boy's Own adventure story,' wrote one traveller, 'the lost jungle city of Orchha.'

Getting There

Jhansi, 19km to the west, receives buses from Khajuraho and is the most convenient railhead. The *Shatabdi Express* links it with Delhi, Agra and Gwalior (*see* 'Moving On' sections) and arrives at 10.40am daily. Buses and tempos leave Jhansi's bus-stand at regular intervals for Orchha (40mins away). There are also taxis from the railway station. The road from Gwalior passes **Datia Palace** (1620), described by Edwin Lutyens as the finest building in India. Don't stop, you can't go in.

The **fort** occupies much of a low-lying rock island and is reached by an arched bridge. Inside, you'll find three palaces set in an open courtyard. The tiered **Jehangir Mahal** was built to commemorate the visit of Emperor Jehangir in 1606 and has good views from the top. To fully appreciate it, rent a Walkman commentary from Hotel Sheesh Mahal (Rs25 plus Rs500 deposit). The arrows and numbers on the palace floor show you which way to go. The **Raj Mahal**, to the right of the courtyard, was built by Madhukar Shah. Its plain exterior gives no indication of the bold and colourful murals inside. The third palace, **Rai Praveen Mahal**, is a two-storey brick structure set in the gardens of Anand Mahal, with the royal baths and camel stables nearby.

Of the many temples within the fort, three are of special interest. The **Ram Raja Mandir** was originally a palace and became a temple by accident rather than by design. An image of Rama was temporarily installed here while the Chaturbhuj temple intended for it was under construction. Then the image could not be moved and the palace despite its spires and ornate decoration became a shrine. Curiously, the image has since migrated back to its rightful home in **Chaturbhuj Temple**, but is hidden behind silver doors. A short walk away, there's the **Lakshmi Narayan Temple**, the interiors of which have some of the best-preserved murals and wall paintings in Orchha.

Much of the fort area is in ruins and you'll need sturdy shoes and trousers to pick your way through the thorns and rubble. One traveller suggests care when exploring. 'Certain palaces have cobra nests in the deeper cellars, and once we had to sprint downstairs at speed to avoid a monkey with an over-developed sense of territory.'

From across the river, there's a marvellous view of the royal *chhatris* (burial domes). On winter evenings, these are beautifully silhouetted against the setting sun.

Where to Stay and Eating Out

The budget **Hotel Mansarovar** is in the village, the mid-range **Betwa Cottage** (nice) a few hundred yards away near the river, and the charming **Hotel Sheesh Mahal**, © 224, tucked away at one corner of the Jehangir Mahal. This has only eight rooms, ranging from a Rs100 single through to an air-conditioned suite for Rs600. Staff are friendly, the views are great (even from the loos) and vultures fly amazingly close overhead before clustering on the palace roofs.

Not many travellers stay overnight in Orchha, but they do eat at the Sheesh Mahal's restaurant (the only one in town) to break their journey between Khajuraho and Agra.

Moving On

There's nowhere to go from Orchha, except back to Gwalior/Agra by *Shatabdi Express* (dep 5.50pm daily) or on to Jhansi, for buses to Khajuraho (departures 6am to 1pm only).

Khajuraho

The famous temples of Khajuraho are a major tourist draw for three reasons—they have the most sublime, sensuous and erotic sculptures in India, they are romantically situated miles from anywhere in the dry, hot plains of Madhya Pradesh, and they are remarkably intact, their remote location having spared them the customary desecrations inflicted by Muslim invaders on other north Indian temples.

Over 80 temples, of which 22 survive, were built by the mighty Chandela dynasty, which claimed descent from the legendary moon god Chandra. The bulk of them appeared in a single, sudden burst of creative and religious energy between the mid-10th and mid-11th centuries. Just as suddenly, after 500 years of supremacy, the Chandelas fell to the might of Islam (AD 1203) and the ancient religious centre of Khajuraho was deserted. But the sculptures live on—a vital, exuberant depiction of life in a society which recognized no restriction on sex and which held that full enjoyment with all the senses was the natural, obvious path to 'nirvana'. Though the 'dirty postcard' touts at Delhi would have you believe otherwise, Khajuraho is not a place for the thrill-seeking voyeur. It is rather a frank expression of joy in life, a remarkable symphony in stone erected in praise of love and women. And while the purpose of the sculptures has been debated ever since the temples were rediscovered in 1838, it seems likely that they were at least partially educational—aimed at enlightening young couples and newly-weds to the (largely physical) joys of marriage. The skill and the vivacity of the carvings themselves have rarely been equalled.

Khajuraho today is a small semi-modern village in a surprisingly green and pastoral setting. Remote and inaccessible, it has spent a long time on the back-burner of tourism but is now beginning to attract the attention of the package-tours. You know that from the rash of big hotels which have sprung up on the outskirts of town, and from the sudden increase in flights being offered by domestic airlines. But despite efforts by the tourism department to push surrounding natural attractions (like the Panna National Park) the infrastructure really isn't there yet and it will take a lot more work to dissuade the general traveller from viewing Khajuraho as a 'one-day temple stop' between Agra and Varanasi.

Most visitors fly in from Delhi or Agra in the morning and continue to Varanasi the next day. But although Khajuraho is small enough to see in a day, a few short hours simply aren't enough. You'll need at least two days to see the temples at leisure and to appreciate the glorious sunrises and sunsets; if you have extra time on your hands, you can also spend a profitable day or two exploring the local waterfalls, crocodile sanctuary, forts and museums by bicycle or jeep. The lack of infrastructure may make it hard going at times, but at least you're 'off the beaten track'.

When to Go

Khajuraho has an extreme climate—very hot in summer, very cold in winter. The most comfortable months are November to February. The special **Dance Festival**, which takes place over 10 days in March, is a marvellous opportunity to see some of India's top dancers and musicians performing in an original setting (the floodlit temple grounds) for only a nominal cost.

Getting There

You can fly into Khajuraho from Delhi, Agra, Varanasi, Bombay and Calcutta. The airport is 3km from the larger hotels and 5km from the town centre—an expensive Rs70/80 by taxi. Going back to the airport, it's possible to get a cycle-rickshaw for Rs30.

There's talk of moving the airport 20km further out of town, to protect the temples from flight vibration damage, but this is not likely to happen in the near future.

The nearest railheads to Khajuraho are Satna, 120km to the east and Jhansi, 145km to the west. The former receives fast daily trains from Varanasi/Calcutta, the latter from Delhi/Agra/Gwalior. *See* also 'Moving On' for these places.

Getting Around

Flat and uncrowded, Khajuraho is an ideal place to explore by bicycle. There are several hire places (Rs15/20 per day) in the new village. Cycle-rickshaws charge too much for short hops—you're best negotiating a daily rate. Taxis cost Rs180/280 for a half/full-day, and can be booked from the better hotels and travel agents.

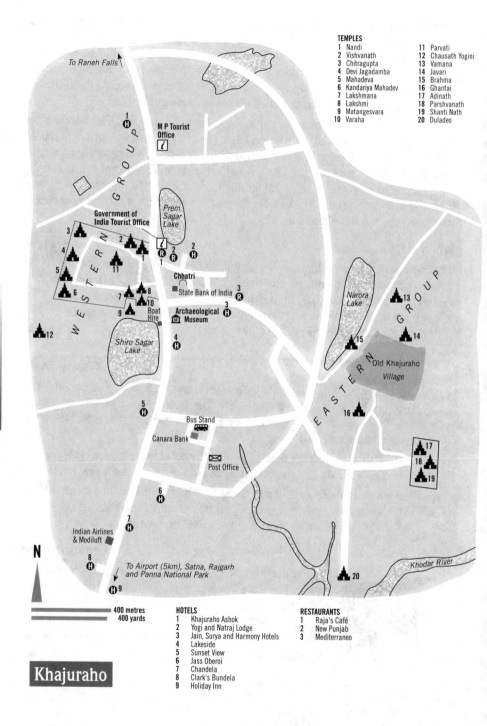

TEMPLES

1 Nandi	11 Parvati
2 Vishvanath	12 Chausath Yogini
3 Chitragupta	13 Vamana
4 Devi Jagadamba	14 Javari
5 Mahadeva	15 Brahma
6 Kandariya Mahadev	16 Ghantai
7 Lakshmana	17 Adinath
8 Lakshmi	18 Parshvanath
9 Matangesvara	19 Shanti Nath
10 Varaha	20 Duladeo

M P Tourist Office

Government of India Tourist Office

Prem Sagar Lake

Chhatri

State Bank of India

Archaeological Museum

Boat Hire

Shiro Sagar Lake

WESTERN GROUP

Narora Lake

EASTERN GROUP

Old Khajuraho Village

Bus Stand

Canara Bank

Post Office

Indian Airlines & Moduluft

N

To Raneh Falls

To Airport (5km), Satna, Rajgarh and Panna National Park

Khodar River

400 metres
400 yards

HOTELS
1 Khajuraho Ashok
2 Yogi and Natraj Lodge
3 Jain, Surya and Harmony Hotels
4 Lakeside
5 Sunset View
6 Jass Oberoi
7 Chandela
8 Clark's Bundela
9 Holiday Inn

RESTAURANTS
1 Raja's Café
2 New Punjab
3 Mediterraneo

Khajuraho

The Government of India **tourist office** is near the Western Group of temples, open 9am to 5.30pm weekdays, to 1pm Sat, closed Sunday. Information is good, but only if you have specific questions. English-speaking guides can be booked here (Rs300/day, up to 4 persons) or from Raja Café, a few doors up. The Madhya Pradesh tourist office, ✆ 2051, near the Circuit House is only useful for booking accommodation in Panna National Park.

Indian Airlines, ✆ 2035, and **Moduluft**, ✆ 2158, are next door to the Clark's Hotel. A good **bookshop** is Shilpa inside the Taj Hotel. Two reliable **travel agents** are Khajuraho Tours, ✆ 2207, opposite the entrance to the western group of temples, and Chandela Tours, ✆ 2340, opposite the Hotel Jain. The **State Bank of India** is open for longer hours than is usual (up to 5pm weekdays, up to 3.30pm Saturdays) and is a short walk south of the main tourist office. **International calls** can be made from various STD booths in town, notably opposite Hotel Jain and opposite the State Bank of India. The **post office** is just in front of the new bus stand.

Temple Tour

On foot or cycle/rickshaw, full-day.

There are three groups of temples. The larger Western Group is conveniently near the modern part of town, with its hotels, restaurants, shops and bus-station. The unkempt but interesting Eastern Group is a mile away in the old village. The Southern Group is some distance south of the new town.

The temples are open from sunrise to sunset and you cover the lot in 5–6 hours. To make best use of your time, hire a proper badge-carrying guide from the tourist office. Touts and unofficial guides are prohibited inside the Western Group of temples, which is a good thing. Every temple however has a guard with a large store of anecdotal information to impart. If you happen to miss any of the sex scenes, he'll eagerly point these out to you. He'll be even happier if you tip him for his unsolicited services.

Khajuraho has been declared a World Heritage Monument, under the UNESCO scheme. The temples are maintained by the Archaeological Survey of India and are kept in very good condition. The erotic carvings are well distributed, but not exclusive. As one archaeologist observed: 'Khajuraho's temples belong to that stage of development of the religious art of India when sculpture and architecture were perfectly integrated'.

The Western Group

Most tours start at the Western Group of temples. The Rs1 admission (shortly to increase to US$1 for foreigners) covers entry to the Archaeological Museum across the road, which you can visit later when the day becomes hotter. Open 10am to 5pm (*closed Fri*), it houses a beautiful collection of sculpture from the temples and takes just 20 minutes to walk through.

The Western Group of temples make particularly easy viewing. They are all contained in a

large garden enclosure and take around 2 hours to see at leisure. Photography is allowed everywhere except in the museum outside.

As a general introduction, the architecture of the main temples follows a five-part pattern. Each of them has an *ardhamandapa* or entrance porch, leading into a pillared *mandapa* hall, then an *antarala* or vestibule, and finally an enclosed corridor or *pradakshina* which runs around the inner sanctum or *garbha griha*. In addition, they each stand on a high masonry platform, the primary exterior features being the distinctive spires or *shikharas*, which move vertically upwards in rhythmic stages. The total effect is one of grace and lightness, reminiscent of an ascending series of Himalayan peaks.

Left of the entrance is the first group of four temples. The largest is the Lakshmana, a very early example (*c*. AD 930–50) and the only Khajuraho temple to have remained completely intact. The decorative sculpture includes fine figures of *apsaras* (heavenly nymphs), erotic scenes and an orgiastic frieze running right round the base. The two small shrines opposite the Lakshmana are the Devi and Varah temples, the latter dedicated to Vishnu in his incarnation as a boar. Outside the enclosure is Matangesvara, the fourth of the group, which is still used for worship. Each evening between 6.30pm and 7.30pm, depending on the time of year, you can see the evening ceremony of *arti* or prayer.

At the back of the Western enclosure, you'll find the biggest and best temple of them all, **Kandariya Mahadev,** built between 1025 and 1050. The zenith of Chandela art, its main spire soars to a height of 31 metres and every inch of its surface is covered in intricate carvings, each one a masterpiece. Among the 872 statues inside and out can be found some of the most frenetically erotic (and athletic!) images in the entire complex. Kandariya is the showpiece temple of Khajuraho—its carvings turn up on all the naughty postcards touted round India. Two other temples share the same extended platform—the small **Mahadeva** with its famous sculpture of a lion being fondled by an androgynous figure, and the **Devi Jagadamba** with images of Vishnu on the lower levels, and yet more erotics from band three upwards.

At the northeastern corner of the enclosure, you'll find **Chitragupta Temple,** dedicated to Surya, the sun god. It's in generally poor condition, but some fine processional, dancing and hunting sculpture reliefs remain. So does an 11-headed statue of Vishnu (10 incarnations, plus Vishnu himself) and a lintel relief of Surya being pulled along in his chariot by seven spirited steeds. Completing your circuit of the compound at the southeast end, there's the Parvati and Vishvanath temples—the latter being dedicated to Shiva (with a large Nandi bull) and having particularly fine sculptures of women engaged in various types of daily activity.

The Eastern Group

After a pause for lunch, head out to the Eastern Group of temples. These fall into two parts—three Hindu temples to the north of old Khajuraho village, and three Jain shrines within a walled enclosure. The largest and finest of the Jain temples is the **Parsvanath**, unique in that it lacks a platform base and the sculptures are mainly at eye level. The famous figures of a woman applying make-up and of another removing a thorn from her foot can be seen here. The two other Jain temples are the old Adinath and the relatively new Shanti Nath, both housing ancient images of Lord Adinath. Walking over to old Khajuraho village, the first Hindu shrine you'll come to is the **Javari Temple** (c. 1075–1100, dedicated to Vishnu and notable for its fine small-scale architecture. A short distance north is the Vamana, commemorating Vishnu's incarnation as a dwarf and adorned on the outside with a profusion of 'celestial maidens'. Last, on the way back to the modern village, there's the very old Brahma Temple originally dedicated to Vishnu but containing a four-faced Shivalinga. If you've timed things right, wisely visiting the Eastern temples in the relative cool of the mid-afternoon, you'll just be strolling back into town when the sun sets over the western temples, their range of soaring *shikhara*-spires haloed by the bright crimson sky.

The Southern Group

Save this last group of temples for another day, or skip them altogether. There are only two of them—the well-preserved Duladeo temple a few hundred metres south of the Jain enclosure, and the Chaturbhuj some miles south of the river. The former has yet more erotics and the latter an impressive statue of Vishnu.

Excursions from Khajuraho

By now, you should be well and truly templed-out. Reward yourself, if you've the time and money, with a day excursion to various out-of-town attractions. This is best done by car or jeep, hired from one of the travel agencies in town (*see* p.133). Be warned however—these attractions are very spread out and unless you're here from July to September (when the local waterfalls are in their full glory) you're best just visiting the two primary sights—the national park and the Rajgarh Fort—in a single day. Bicycling out to these places is not really practical (the roads are hard going) though you can cycle out to a Nature Trail laid out by the tourism department and see some interesting ancient buildings and gorges. The 'budget' way to see some wildlife, by the way, is to get a window seat on a bus leaving Khajuraho to Satna—it passes right through the national park!

The big drawback to visiting **Panna National Park** is the lack of infrastructure. It's a beautiful place—546km of splendid scenery, densely forested hills, dramatic rocky gorges and waterfalls—but if you want to see big cats like tiger and panther you've got to be here at sunrise. That means either a *very* early start from Khajuraho (an hour's drive away, 40km) or staying overnight at one of the treehouses near the Gate One entrance. You can book rooms (Rs250 to 500) at **Ken River Lodge** from the M P tourist office or enquire direct at the nearby **Gilles Lodge**. Otherwise, be content to see the park in the daytime. Enjoy the mixed forest fauna (dominated by teak forestry) and look out for the occasional bear, wild boar, blue bull, Indian gazelle and blackbuck.

Rajgarh Fort, 24km out of Khajuraho, is a beautiful hilltop fortress commanding panoramic views of the surrounding mountains, lakes and countryside. Built by the Maharajah of Chhatarpur over 700 years ago and rebuilt in the early 19th century as a hunting palace, it retains a poignant sense of grandeur and is full of interesting features— subterranean horse stables, an underground passage leading all the way to Khajuraho and lapis-blue terracotta-topped turrets and towers. Often used as a film location (most notably in Merchant Ivory's *The Deceivers* and the German-Indian production of the *Kama Sutra*) it is shortly due for conversion to a government heritage hotel, so see it while you can!

Bandhavgarh and Kanha National Parks

Some of the country's largest tracts of forest are in the central state of Madhya Pradesh. Large areas are sparsely populated and it is these jungles that formed the backdrop to Kipling's Jungle Book. There are many protected areas in the state but two national parks are among the best in the country.

Bandhavgarh National Park 220 km (138 miles) southeast of Khajuraho, is probably the best place in the country to see tiger. The original park area was relatively small and had a high density of tigers—22 in 105 sq km. Apart from tiger the park has a good mix of prey species and a large number of bird species. A private, deluxe camp, run on the line of the luxury camps in East Africa, operates near the park entrance. **Bandhavgarh Jungle Camp** has inclusive rates of US$105 per person and includes accommodation, food, game-viewing, elephant rides into the park and all fees (book through a travel agent or directly: B-21 Greater Kailash Enclave II, New Delhi 110048, ✆ 6411619/ 6412501, ✉ 6428311.

Kanha National Park, 220 km (138 miles) south of Bandhavgarh, has long been considered one of the best in Asia. It was one of the first parks to come under Project Tiger management and flourished. Among the park's success stories is the reestablishment of a viable breeding population of the Central Indian race of swamp deer. Near Kisli on the western edge of the park are various private camps including **Kipling Camp**, with accommodation and all services from Rs1500. Book through Kipling Camp, c/o Tollygunge Club, 120 D P Sasmal Road, Calcutta.

Shopping

Khajuraho is not a good place to shop. Nothing is locally produced and though there are dozens of shops that will tell you otherwise, everything is brought in from Agra and Jaipur. Be especially wary of 'antiques'; none of them are.

Leisure

Unless you're in town for Khajuraho's annual **dance festival** in March, cultural programmes happen as and when they do. Contact the M P tourist office for information; or stroll up to the luxury hotels in the early evening. All the top places—Taj, Oberoi, Clark's and Holiday Inn—are close to each other and by wandering back and forth you'll generally find something—a poolside puppet show, a cocktail party, a garden barbecue or a classical dance programme—to drop in on. If nothing else, they all have temple musicians playing in their lobbies.

Non-guests can use the luxury **pools** of the Ashok (Rs75) and Holiday Inn (Rs100) hotels—though to swim at the latter you have to either stay at the Sunset View lodge (same management) or be recommended by its owner. **Paddle-boat** hire (Rs20/hr) is available from the artificial lake just down from the western group of temples.

Khajuraho ✆ (076861–)

Where to Stay
luxury (from US$40)

The four best hotels are clustered together on the road between the airport and town, 1.5km from the western group of temples. They all look much the same—low-level whitewashed buildings with pleasant pools and landscaped gardens—and they all charge the same. Nowhere else in India, apart from Bhubaneshwar, can you get so much luxury for so little cost. And during the rainy season of mid-April to mid-July, rates drop even further.

Until Clark's open their new 5-star super-deluxe property in 1997/8, all the top hotels are around the same standard. The **Clark's Bundela**, ✆ 2360, ✉ 2359, has the best-value rooms, **Holiday Inn**, ✆ 2178, the nicest suites, Taj's **Hotel Chandela**, ✆ 2101, ✉ 2095, the most beautiful gardens, and Oberoi's **Jass**

Oberoi, ✆ 2085, ✆ 2088, the best food and service. Otherwise, there's little to choose between them. They all have nice restaurants and pools.

moderate/budget

The **Hotel Payal,** ✆ 2076, 1km behind the Western Group of temples, offers homely accommodation with lovely bright rooms with private balconies for £5 non a/c or £10 with a/c. It's a peaceful place with friendly staff, a good restaurant and nice gardens. **Hotel Lakeside,** ✆ 2120, overlooking the artificial lake, gets a lot of business—it's very clean and has a range of rooms from Rs200 to 700.

Arriving by bus, there's the usual horde of rickshaw touts offering cheap rides to hotels. To avoid paying commission, let them take you to a hotel *near* the one you want and walk the rest of the way.

Three adjoining favourites, just up from the old bus stand, are **Hotel Harmony,** ✆ 2135, with clean, comfy rooms from Rs250, **Hotel Surya** with a pleasant sit-out garden and rooms from Rs250 to Rs550 with a/c, and **Hotel Jain,** ✆ 2052, with singles/doubles from Rs80/120. Also popular is **Hotel Sunset View,** ✆ 2077, with rooms from Rs50 to Rs250 with a/c and fine temple/sunset views from the rooftop terrace. It also has dorm beds for Rs25. Shoestringers favour **Yogi** and **Natraj** lodges behind the Government of India tourist office.

Khajuraho ✆ *(076861–)*   ***Eating Out***

Oberoi's **Apsara** restaurant is excellent for Continental dishes and tandoori snacks. It has a very relaxed, sophisticated ambience, enhanced by live classical music drifting in from the lobby. Arrive around 7.30pm to grab a pool-facing table, and enjoy after-dinner cocktails at the cosy bar-cum-coffee shop. There are many cheap restaurants in town, including the **Agarwal** for veg-Western, the **New Punjab** for non-veg, **Raja's Café** for Swiss *röstis*, **Jati Shankar** for veg *thalis* and (opposite Hotel Jain) the **Mediterraneo** for salads, crêpes, pizzas (bad) and pasta (good).

Moving On

By air: Indian Airlines flies daily to Delhi, Agra, Varanasi and Kathmandu. Modiluft offers daily services to Delhi, Bombay, Varanasi and Calcutta.

By rail: Early morning buses run to Satna (4hrs) from the new bus stand and connect with the fast Howrah Mail to Varanasi (dep 4.15pm, 8hrs) and Calcutta (21hrs). There are also morning buses to Jhansi (5½hrs) for the Shatabdi Express (dep 5.55pm) to Gwalior (arr 6.30pm), Agra (arr 9.10pm) and Delhi (arr 10.20pm).

By road: All buses, including ones to Agra (12hrs) and Delhi (16hrs), leave from the new bus stand near the post office.

Ancient capital of Hindu faith and learning, Varanasi is one of the oldest cities in the world. In many ways this is India in a nutshell—an inextricable maze of narrow, winding streets and alleys, domes and minarets, pinnacles and towers, derelict 18th-century palaces and hundreds of temples, the whole a continuous riot of noise, colour and clanging temple gongs. A haunting vision of dignified buildings, many crumbling and sliding inexorably into the holy Ganges, the old 'eternal' city retains a very special vitality.

Varanasi's early history is lost in antiquity. Ancient accounts like the *Mahabharata* and *Skanda Purana* mention its existence at least 3000 years ago, though traditionally it was founded around 1200 BC. The Chinese pilgrims Fa-Hsien and Hieun Tsiang, writing in the 5th and 7th centuries AD respectively, give the first historical accounts of its many Hindu temples and monasteries, but it had long since become a flourishing centre of religion, education and commerce. The Buddha came to Sarnath, just 10km north of the city, to preach his eight-fold path to truth and enlightenment. And along the holy ghats by the Ganges, numerous shrines and temples arose, dedicated to Shiva, the presiding deity. Rich and powerful, Varanasi became an inevitable bone of contention between local rulers, and an irresistible lure to northern invaders. From the 11th century on, it was regularly looted by the Muslims, and later on by Aurangzeb, the Mughal Emperor, who destroyed nearly all the temples and rebuilt the most famous one as a mosque. Few of the present Varanasi shrines, therefore, are older than the 18th century. Only in 1738, with the accession of a strong Hindu monarch, was firm rule re-established. Ceded to the British in 1775, Varanasi finally entered an era of consolidation and rehabilitation. Mark Twain, who visited India in the late 19th century, wrote that 'Benares is older than history, older than tradition, older even than legend, and looks twice as old as all of them put together'.

The present name of Varanasi is a restoration of its ancient title meaning the city between two rivers—the Varuna and the Asi. Its spiritual name is Kashi, meaning the city that shines with *kasha* (divine light). The city's other name of **Benares**, by which it has been known for the last 300 years or so, is probably a corruption of Varanasi. Most visitors are Hindus making the requisite once-in-a-lifetime pilgrimage to clean away all sins; and all will want to return at the end of their life, it being believed that to die here ensures rebirth in the most favourable circumstances possible. They all attempt the 55km walk round the Panchakroshi Road, even the many old, sick and infirm who come here to die. And all visit the Holy Ganges for the requisite purification dip. Here, more than anywhere else in India, religion—with all its rituals, dedications and celebrations—is an intrinsic part of life.

Varanasi is just as popular with tourists as with pilgrims. Yet many Westerners—deterred by the noise, the hassle, the sweet (and not so sweet) smells of sanctity—stay just one or two days. Those who look like easy pickings can't walk five paces down the road without being accosted by a money-changer, a dope dealer or a silk emporium salesman. Others, who stick it out and get beneath the surface annoyances, discover the spiritual depth and beauty of the place. Intense, yet rarely overpowering, it is the amazing street-life that absorbs visitors most—a rapid, continuous slide-show of crazy traffic, clamouring devotees, sacred cows, road-side barbers and flamboyant funeral processions—set against a medieval backdrop of palaces and smouldering cremation pyres along the timeless Ganges.

When to Go

Varanasi is coolest but most crowded from November to February. For a warm but less stressful stay, come in March/April, when most foreign tourists have migrated north to Nepal or Himachal Pradesh. To get the feel of the place, turn up for the magical 10-day **Dussehra** festival in September/October. The party continues with the 4-day **Ganga** 'holi'-day in late October/early November, which is a photographer's delight. All the ghats (stepped embankments) are prettily illuminated with oil lamps and thousands of candle-lit earthen pots are floated down the Ganges. There's a good cultural programme too.

Getting There

There are daily flights from Delhi, Agra, Khajuraho, Kathmandu, Calcutta, Bhubaneshwar, Bombay and Hyderabad. For details of trains/buses to Varanasi from Delhi, Calcutta and Agra, *see* relevant 'Moving On' sections. Babatpur airport is 22km from the city centre—Rs25 by bus (drops and picks up from the Vaibhav hotel), Rs100 by auto-rickshaw and a rip-off Rs250 by taxi. The bus stops at various hotels in the Cantonment area, either going to or from the airport, and it's free if you stay at the Vaibhav.

Getting Around

Taxis are best booked from hotels. These work out a lot cheaper than street taxis, which are not metered and charge exorbitant rates. If you're staying in the Cantonment area, use the taxis outside Clark's Hotel—they have fixed rates (about Rs5/km) and are good for short tours like Sarnath and Ram Nagar Fort. Ask for Soaib-Guddu (car 5110), he's a good man.

Auto-rickshaws aren't metered either, so expect to waste time bargaining. As a rough guide, it shouldn't cost more than Rs30 from the Cantonment down to the ghats—though you can expect the driver to make at least one stop along the way to show you his brother's emporium or uncle's silk shop. Probably your best bet, if you've got a lot to see and do, is to negotiate a daily rate—around Rs550 for taxis, Rs250 for rickshaws. This cuts out a lot of unsolicited shopping 'detours'.

Cycle-rickshaws are a slow but leisurely way of touring the city. They should cost only half what an auto-rickshaw asks, but getting a fair fare out of them is equivalent to beating Boris Spassky at chess. Many travellers enjoy touring Varanasi by bicycle. There are many hire-places (Rs15 per day) around Lanka bus-stop, near Benares Hindu University.

Note: No motorized transport is allowed to approach the main Dasashwamedh Ghat after 8.30am. Either get there early or travel down by cycle-rickshaw.

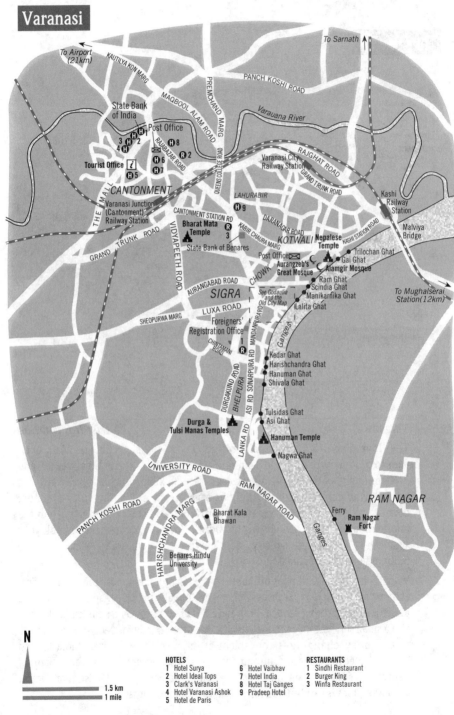

Varanasi

To Airport (21km)

To Sarnath

KAUTILYA KON MARG

MAQBOOL ALAM MARG

PANCH KOSHI ROAD

PREMCHAND MARG

Varauana River

State Bank of India

Post Office

3 **H** 1
2 **H** 2
4 **H** 2

RAJBAZAR ROAD

QUEENS COLLEGE ROAD

H 8
R 2

Tourist Office [i]

H 6
H 7

H 5

Varanasi City Railway Station

RAJGHAT ROAD

GRAND TRUNK ROAD

Kashi Railway Station

CANTONMENT

Varanasi Junction (Cantonment) Railway Station

LAHURABIR

H 9

Malviya Bridge

THE MALL

CANTONMENT STATION RD

DARANAGAR ROAD

KASHI STATION ROAD

VIDYAPEETH ROAD

Bharat Mata Temple

KABIR CHAURA MARG

KOTWAL

Nepalese Temple

Trilochan Ghat

State Bank of Benares

R 3

Post Office

Aurangzeb's Great Mosque

Gai Ghat

Alamgir Mosque

GRAND TRUNK ROAD

AURANGABAD ROAD

SIGRA

CHOWK

Ram Ghat
Scindia Ghat

To Mughalserai Station (12km)

LUXA ROAD

Manikarnika Ghat

SHEOPURWA MARG

See Godaulia and the Old City Map

Lalita Ghat

Foreigners' Registration Office

CHINTAMANI ROAD

MANDANPUR RD

R 1

Ganges

Kedar Ghat
Harishchandra Ghat
Hanuman Ghat
Shivala Ghat

DURGAKUND ROAD

BHELPURA

ASI RD SONARPURA RD

LANKA RD

Tulsidas Ghat
Asi Ghat

Durga & Tulsi Manas Temples

Hanuman Temple

Nagwa Ghat

UNIVERSITY ROAD

RAM NAGAR

PANCH KOSHI ROAD

HARISHCHANDRA MARG

RAM NAGAR ROAD

Bharat Kala Bhawan

Ferry

Ram Nagar Fort

Benares Hindu University

Ganges

N

1.5 km
1 mile

HOTELS
1 Hotel Surya
2 Hotel Ideal Tops
3 Clark's Varanasi
4 Hotel Varanasi Ashok
5 Hotel de Paris
6 Hotel Vaibhav
7 Hotel India
8 Hotel Taj Ganges
9 Pradeep Hotel

RESTAURANTS
1 Sindhi Restaurant
2 Burger King
3 Winfa Restaurant

141

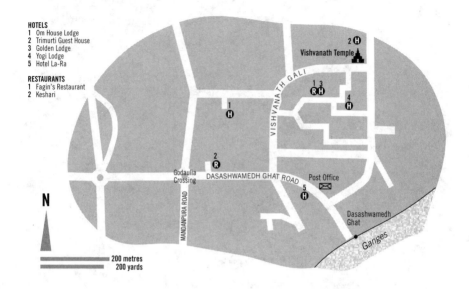

The Old City

HOTELS
1 Om House Lodge
2 Trimurti Guest House
3 Golden Lodge
4 Yogi Lodge
5 Hotel La-Ra

RESTAURANTS
1 Fagin's Restaurant
2 Keshari

Vishvanath Temple

VISHVANATH GALI

Godaulia Crossing
DASASHWAMEDH GHAT ROAD
Post Office

MANDANPURA ROAD

N

Dasashwamedh Ghat

Ganges

200 metres
200 yards

Varanasi ℂ (0542–)   **Tourist Information**

The Government of India **tourist office**, ℂ 43744, is at 15B The Mall, open 9am to 5.30pm weekdays, to 1pm on Saturdays. Don't turn up between 1 and 2.30pm though—the tourist officer has a very 'flexible' lunchbreak. He also has a chum who contradicts everything he says. At the end of my visit, the chum bounced up and said (pointing at the tourist officer) 'This man is giving you the information, but I am giving you the *facts*!' Whatever, come here to book your sightseeing tours (sunrise/city, 6am to 1pm, Sarnath/Ram Nagar, 2pm to 5.30pm) and to hire guides.

Varanasi has two useful **post offices**—one for Cantonment, near the tourist office, and one for the old city, at Bisheswarganj in Kotwali area (*see* map). The latter has a useful parcel-packing service. Both have STD booths for **overseas calls**. There's also a small sub-post office in the old city (*see* map), handy for people staying in the area. **Money changing** is convenient at the new State Bank of India branch behind Hotel Ideal Tops, Cantonment. Or, in the old city, at the State Bank of Benares near Dasashwamedh Ghat (*see* map). The Foreigners' Registration Office, ℂ 153960, for **visa extensions** is in Srinagar Colony, Sigra.

Indian Airlines, ✆ 45959, **Air India**, ✆ 46326, and **Lufthansa**, ✆ 46625, all have offices in The Mall, next to Hotel Ideal Tops. In the same building are **travel agents** like TCI, ✆ 46209, and Mercury Travels, ✆ 43296. Sita Travels, ✆ 348445, is just in front of the tourist office. Discounted air tickets, as well as bus/train bookings, are offered by Golden Travels, ✆ 323832, next to Golden Lodge in the old city.

A good **bookshop** is Nandi in Ashok Hotel. It sells Diana Eck's 'Benares: City of Light', a fine introduction to the city and to Hinduism in general.

Touring Varanasi

Sightseeing is pretty informal in Varanasi. A good proportion of travellers come less for the city's sights (fine though they are) than for its unique atmosphere and for some kind of personal spiritual experience. All the 'action' takes place in the old city, which sprawls out along the west bank of the Ganges and falls back from the riverside ghats in a twisting maze of narrow alleys and medieval ruins—expect to get lost at least once. The new city, centring on the Cantonment area beyond the rail station, is a total contrast of quiet, civilized tree-lined avenues.

You can see all the principal attractions of the city, plus Sarnath, in just two days. But this is one place in India to linger longer if necessary.

Tour 1: The Ganges and Old City

By boat, full day. River Ganges–The Ghats–Nepalese Temple–
Golden Temple–Aurangzeb's Mosque–Durga Temple–Tulsi Manas Temple–
Benares Hindu University–Bharat Kala Bhawan–Bharat Mata Temple.

The essential Varanasi can be found on the river-front at dawn—when Hindu pilgrims flock to the ghats on the bank of the Ganges to perform their ablutions, do their gymnastic exercises, have a ritual bath in the river, and perform *puja* to the rising sun, all rituals evolved and derived from thousands of years of worship and tradition. It's a rich and fascinating sight to see.

Whether or not you've booked a sunrise tour through the tourist office (they were discontinued, but are due for re-introduction), arrange to be woken at least an hour before dawn and take a rickshaw down to the central **Dasashwamedh Ghat**, which offers a splendid view of the river-front—and, if you're lucky, of dolphins at dusk. This is the ghat of the 10 (*das*) horse (*aswa*) sacrifice (*madh*), performed by Brahma, which paved the way for Shiva's return to Varanasi after a brief spell of banishment by the then ruler.

From the ghat steps, watch the huge red orb of the sun creep over the horizon and cast its rosy warm glow over the holy Ganges, then board your boat and coast silently up the river. With the coming of sunrise, the slumbering ghats suddenly burst into lively, colourful activity. The faithful flock down to the riverside, and the Venice-like vista of ruined temples (many sliding into the sea) and bathing ghats is filled with priests invoking the dawn, young men practising yoga exercises, people washing clothes or having the ritual morning bath, and pyres being lit for the first cremations of the day. On a particularly auspicious day, as many as 30,000 pilgrims may show up at Dasashwamedh Ghat to greet the dawn.

Whether you take an organized boat-trip or hire a private boat is up to you. There are always young lads patrolling the river, offering to show tourists the ghats as part of a private boat excursion (Rs50/70, 2hrs). Going solo certainly has its advantages: tour boats attract a lot of unwelcome attention from begging *sadhus* or insistent salesmen. But the conducted tour gives good information, and guides you round the principal old city temples off the river.

Boats generally proceed south from Dasashwamedh Ghat (with its shrine to Sitala, goddess of smallpox) to **Kedar Ghat** (fine lingams and temple), **Harischandra Ghat** (secondary burning ghat, bodies cremated by *chandal* outcasts), **Dandi Ghat** (used by ascetics), the popular **Hanuman Ghat** (used by worshippers of the monkey god), **Shivala** (Kali) **Ghat** (owned by the Maharajah, has a famous lingam), **Tulsidas Ghat** (dedicated to the poet Gosain Tulsi Das; now sliding into the river), and **Asi Ghat**, the furthest ghat upstream and one of the holiest. It marks the confluence of the Asi and Ganges waters, and is the first of the five special ghats pilgrims must bathe in (during a single day) to fulfil the purification ritual. The other four are Dasashwamedh, Barnasangam, Panchganga and Manikarnika.

From Asi Ghat, you'll return back downstream to see the northern ghats. First, next to Dasashwamedh, is **Jai Singh's observatory** built within Mansingh's old palace (1600) at **Man Mandir Ghat**. The observatory, constructed in 1710, is one of only three surviving (*see* Jaipur, p.168). Much of the palace was restored in the 19th century and the fine north-corner stone balcony is original. After this comes **Lalita Ghat**, below the **Nepalese Temple**, and (further back) the **Vishvanath Temple**. At the adjoining **Jalsain** and **Manikarnika Ghats** (main burning ghats), photography is strictly forbidden. Jalsain is named after Vishnu's incarnation as Jalsai, sleeper on the ocean. Manikarnika is most sacred because Shiva dug a tank here, filling it with sweat as he tried to recover an earring Parvati had dropped inside. Between the tank and ghat is the **Chandrapaduka**, a slab of stone with Vishnu's footprints. Further on is **Dattatreya Ghat** (with the footprints of a Brahmin saint in a small temple), the huge **Scindia Ghat**, the **Ram Ghat** built by the Rajah of Jaipur, and above this Aurangzeb's small **Alamgir Mosque**, which incorporates earlier Buddhist columns. Further north, **Gai Ghat** is marked by its stone figure of a cow, and **Trilochan Ghat** by its two turrets (between which pilgrims bathe in the extra-holy water). These last two ghats are also where most of the vultures hang out, waiting for lunch to float by. From here, enjoy close-up views of the stately new **Malviya Bridge**, before returning to Dasashwamedh Ghat.

Off the boat, it's up the steps and to the right for the marvellous little **Nepalese Temple**, recently renovated and full of exotic wood carvings depicting Shiva, Parvati, Hanuman and various other deities. Diving into the tunnel backstreets of the old city, you'll emerge presently at Varanasi's famous **Vishvanath (Golden) Temple**. You can't go in but if you climb the stairs of the old house opposite, you can get reasonable views from the balcony. Don't let the soldiers on guard catch you taking photos though. The solid-gold plating of the

temple towers was donated by Maharajah Ranjit Singh of Lahore in 1835. Dedicated to Shiva as Vishvanath, Lord of the Universe, the present temple was erected by Rani Ahalyabai Holkar of Indore in 1776. Adjacent to it is the site of the original temple, built in 1600, which Aurangzeb destroyed to make way for his **Great Mosque** in the 17th century. The foundations and rear of this mosque still display rare examples of temple design and the columns in front also came from the earlier building. The two minarets rise to a height of 71 metres and dominate the skyline of this part of the city when seen from the river. The **Gyan Vapi** (Covered Well) to the side of the mosque is a favourite resting place of pilgrims.

Though the tour continues on to Benares Hindu University, you may well decide to remain in the old city and do some shopping (*see* 149). Later on, take a short walk south to the red-ochre stained **Durga Temple**, commonly known as the Monkey Temple owing to its resident population of mischievous monkeys. Built by an 18th-century Bengali Maharani, it is dedicated to Parvati's manifestation as the 'terrible' Durga, and goat sacrifices are common. Entrance to the temple is prohibited, but you can look down on it (quite enough for the queasy) from the walkway above. Next door is the modern **Tulsi Manas Temple**, built in 1964 to commemorate the home of the 17th century poet-saint Tulsi Das. The marble walls of this *shikhara*-style temple are inscribed with the entire text of the epic *Ramacharitamanas*—expounding the history and deeds of Rama, one of Vishnu's incarnations—composed by the poet. A short rickshaw ride south down Asik Road brings you to **Benares Hindu University**, some 11km from the city centre. This turn-of-the-century university is a vast complex featuring one of India's finest museums, the **Bharat Kala Bhawan**. This houses a superb collection of Indian miniatures, sculptures and terracottas (*open daily except Sun 11am–4pm and 8am–12.30pm May/June*).

Take a rest, then use the afternoon for a return visit to the old city. If you get lost wandering through the bazaars, shops and stalls, either follow a sacred cow or ask for directions. There are over 100 ghats to explore, so there's no danger of getting bored. Be careful however around the 'burning' ghats—the cremation pyres can be unsettling, and you may have your camera destroyed (or worse) for taking photos of them. The funeral ceremonies themselves, however, are fascinating; here in Varanasi, more than anywhere else in India, life and death are on constant public view.

If you still have time, finish the day off with a rickshaw ride to **Bharat Mata Temple** 1½km south of Cantonment station where, instead of the usual images of gods and goddesses, there is a relief map of 'Mother India' engraved in marble. This temple was inaugurated by Mahatma Gandhi.

Tour 2: Sarnath and Ram Nagar Fort

By tour bus, half-day. Chowkandi Stupa–Archaeological Museum–Ashoka Pillar–Dhamekh Stupa–Mulagandhakuti Vihara–Ram Nagar Fort.

The ancient site of Sarnath, 10km north of Varanasi, is a principal centre of Buddhism. It was here around 530 BC that the Buddha came from Bodhgaya after gaining enlightenment and preached his first sermon in the large garden known as the Deer Park. This initial message of the Middle Way (the path of moderation leading to *nirvana*) became the corner-stone of the Buddhist religion.

Sarnath probably gets its name from Saranganath, Lord of the Deer (one of the Buddha's titles) and was for long known simply as the Deer Park. From the remains of the famous **Dhamekh Stupa** here, it seems probable that the first monastic communities came to the site around the 3rd century BC. Ashoka, the warlord turned man of peace, patronized Sarnath as a centre of the Buddhist religion and erected several magnificent stupas and buildings. Visiting Sarnath in AD 637, the Chinese pilgrim Hieun Tsiang described its structures as:

> *In eight divisions, all enclosed within one wall with tiers of balconies and rows of halls, extremely artistic, inhabited by 1500 monks. Within the great enclosing wall was a temple above 61 metres high, surmounted by an embossed gilt amra (mango); in the brick portion above were more than 100 rows of niches, each containing a gilt image of the Buddha; inside the temple was a bellmetal image of the Buddha in the attitude of preaching, as large as life.*

But as early as the 3rd century AD Buddhism had fallen into decline, the squabbles of the various splinter sects paving the way for its eventual reabsorption into the mainstream of Hindu faith and philosophy. The last of Sarnath's great monasteries, built by the devout Kumara Devi, Queen of Varanasi (1114–54), fell quick victim, along with the rest, to the Muslim invasions of the 12th and 17th centuries. Today, the ruins of Sarnath afford only a glimpse of the magnificent monastery of the Turning of the Wheel of Law described by visiting Chinese pilgrims.

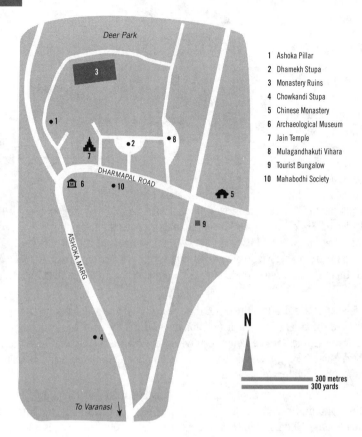

Sarnath

Deer Park

1 Ashoka Pillar
2 Dhamekh Stupa
3 Monastery Ruins
4 Chowkandi Stupa
5 Chinese Monastery
6 Archaeological Museum
7 Jain Temple
8 Mulagandhakuti Vihara
9 Tourist Bungalow
10 Mahabodhi Society

DHARMAPAL ROAD

ASHOKA MARG

N

300 metres
300 yards

To Varanasi

If running, the good conducted tour round Sarnath leaves the tourist office at 2pm daily. It stops just before Sarnath at the modest **Chowkandi Stupa**. Buddhist stupas fall into three main categories: commemorative, relic and votive. This is a commemorative one, marking the place of the Buddha's reunion with his five ascetic friends. They had earlier deserted him when he accepted milk from a cowherd's daughter, breaking his fast. The stupa is a simple redbrick octagonal structure, situated on a small hillock and erected by Akbar in the 16th century to mark an original 5th-century site.

Sarnath itself is a pleasant and peaceful place. A charming **Chinese Monastery** opposite the bus stand points the way to the outstanding **Archaeological Museum** (*open 10am–5pm, except Fri*). This houses several fine recoveries from the Sarnath ruins, notably the **Lion Capital** which originally surmounted the huge Ashoka Pillar. Adopted by free India as her state emblem, this well-preserved capital was carved from a single block of stone. It features four back-to-back lions, beneath which is a four-panel band. The panels have spirited sculptures of a lion (Buddha as 'lion king'), an elephant (Buddha's mother, Maya, dreamt of a white elephant before his birth), a horse (the one he rode away on, abandoning princely comforts to search for truth) and a bull.

The base of the capital is an inverted lotus flower, symbolic of the seven lotus blossoms which sprang from the waters on Buddha's death. It was constructed, along with its ex-pillar, by Ashoka in the 3rd century BC. Most of the museum's exhibits—mainly Buddhas, two life-size Bodhisattvas, flowers and animals in carved sandstone—date from the Mauryan period of the 3rd to 1st centuries BC, though there is also a selection of later Hindu images from the 9th to 12th centuries AD.

Sarnath's ruins are pretty ruined. Of the towering **Ashoka Pillar** only a short jagged shard remains. The inscription on it directs the community of monks to 'act in such a way that the *sangha* cannot be divided by anyone. Verily, that monk or nun who shall break up the *sangha* should be compelled to put on white robes and to reside in what is unfit for the residence of a recluse.'

Of the two magnificent ancient stupas for ceremonial public worship, only the Dhamekh remains standing (the other, the Dharmarajika, was dismantled in the 19th century by fortune-hunters). The **Dhamekh Stupa** dates back to around AD 500, is 338 metres high, and is covered with interesting swastika and floral motifs. It commemorates the spot where Buddha gave his first sermon. He delivered it to his five closest disciples, and in it he preached the doctrine of the four 'noble truths'—namely, that suffering is part of life, there is always a cause for suffering, suffering can be overcome, and there are eight righteous paths by which to achieve this.

Close to the Dhamekh Stupa is a **Jain Temple**, built in the 19th century in honour of the 11th Jain *tirthankar*, Sriyansanath. Also nearby is the elegant **Mulagandhakuti Vihara**, erected by the Mahabodhi Society in 1931. This is a modern temple enshrining ancient relics. The silver casket within is said to house the original relics of the Buddha, as recovered from a 1st-century BC temple during a 19th-century archaeological dig. Consequently, it is a major Buddhist pilgrimage spot, second in importance only to the Bodhi tree at Bodhgaya. The interior has a series of frescoes, depicting scenes in the Buddha's life, painted by Kosetsu Nosi, a famous Japanese artist. The main shrine has a graceful gold replica of the Buddha, modelled on an original 5th-century AD statue.

If not on tour, you can visit Sarnath by auto-rickshaw (20 minutes, Rs80 return) or by taxi (Rs175 return). In either case, vehicles will wait a couple of hours while you look around. To stay overnight in Sarnath, you can book its **Tourist Bungalow** (Rs70 to 160) by ringing Varanasi ✆ 43413, or just turn up at the **Mahabodhi Society** for cheap, clean rooms from Rs30.

The Sarnath tour bus often goes on to **Ram Nagar Fort** on the far bank of the Ganges (*open 9am–noon and 2–5pm; adm Rs3*). This is the residence of the Maharajah of Benares and houses a rather dilapidated museum, containing textiles, ivory coaches, duelling pistols, elephant-foot stools and motheaten tiger-skin rugs.

During the annual Dussehra festival the story of Lord Rama is retold in a traditional play, the *Ramlila*, over a period of 30 days. The version enacted at Ram Nagar is considered an important interpretation of the story and if you're in Varanasi at this time it's worth spending an extra day to see an episode.

Shopping

Varanasi's silks—saris, brocades and cloth—have been famous for centuries. Even the Buddha is known to have valued them when he was a young prince.

Shopping in this city is, however, a nightmare. Everybody tries to sell you stuff you don't want, and even when you do, it's too expensive. In the absence of any decent government emporia, it can be very difficult to determine what's available and how much it should cost. This makes foreigners very vulnerable to the onslaughts of persistent, smooth-talking operators whose 'uncle' always has a silk shop. The only way to get round the problem is to make up your mind exactly what you want, where you're going to look for it, and how much you're prepared to spend. Be quite firm with anybody who tries to change your mind.

A reliable shop for silks and brocades is **Oriental Arts Emporium** in Maqbool Alam Road. For carpets, try **Benares House** next to Clark's Hotel. Both places are 'fixed price' but are still open to bargaining. The Taj and Clark's Hotels have shopping arcades offering the full range of local produce, and though prices are higher than in town at least you have the satisfaction of not being cheated. Elsewhere, apply the 'burning test' to any silk items before purchasing. Take a thread (or a knot, if a carpet) and light a match to it. Cheap cotton-silk has a relatively slow burn, but real silk goes off like a quick fuse, leaving a small knob on the end of the thread. Something else to steer clear of is so-called Moradabad brass, which is fake unless it shows a good pink colour, denoting high copper content.

Far better than shops, since you can compare prices, are the bazaars of the old city. The central Chowk Bazaar, which runs between (and behind) the two main burning ghats, is good for everything—silk scarves, brocade saris, carved walking sticks, cheap cotton clothes, wooden toys, baubles, bangles and beads. At night, the atmosphere is electric. For better-quality silk, try Satti Bazaar, and for ornamental brassware (Varanasi's other speciality) the Thetary Bazaar. For fabulous glass bangles (often lacquered) and other ornamental/novelty items, the city market around the Golden Temple is best.

Leisure

After a long, dusty day's touring, there's nothing to beat a cool dip in a luxury **swimming pool**. You can use the nice pools at the Clark's and Ashok Hotels for Rs125 and 75 respectively—but don't turn up looking like a beach bum, or they won't let you in.

Varanasi may be home to some of India's best musicians, but there's nothing much laid on for tourists. The only place to see classical dance and local folk music in an authentic setting is Hotel Clark's new **Culture Centre** at Raja Ghat (*see* map), overlooking the Ganges. The performing artists come from Benares Hindu University, so the quality is assured. It runs daily (less often, off-season), bookings can be made from travel agents or at the Clark's Hotel, and the US$10 charge includes transport to and from your hotel. Expect to leave at 5.30pm and to head back at 8.30pm—though you can stay on for delicious vegetarian food.

The Clark's and Ashok Hotels lay on live classical music as part of their restaurant dinners (*see* 'Eating Out'). Cinema programmes and other upcoming entertainments are listed in *The Pioneer* newspaper.

Varanasi Ⓒ *(0542–)*   ### Where to Stay

In general, it's much quieter and safer to stay in the Cantonment area. Living in the old city may be cheap and convenient for the ghats, but be warned—a lot of travellers fall prey to street-thieves and clever scams. The two most common cons at present are being fined up to $100 for taking photos of the burning ghats; and being taken by an unlicensed car to an emporium, where a policeman handcuffs the driver and threatens to take him to jail unless you take pity on him and pay his bail!

Currently, tourism is way down in Varanasi, so many hotels are offering heavy discounts. Even if they don't, it's worth asking.

luxury (from US$80)

Varanasi's top hotels are all in the Cantonment area, either on The Mall or close to it (*see* map for locations).

Until the new 5-star **Ideal Tops** Hotel (next to the present Ideal Tops) is completed, the nearest thing to luxury is the **Hotel Taj Ganges**, Ⓒ 345100, ⓐ 322067. This is a posh modern property, surrounded by lush gardens and mango groves, with welcoming staff, a lovely pool and many useful facilities. It's worth paying a few dollars more for a spacious deluxe room—the standard ones are snug but small. Ask to stay on the 2nd or 5th floors, with (respectively) the best decor and views.

Even more personal and friendly is the **Clark's Varanasi**, ☎ 348501, ✉ 348186, which also has a better choice of rooms—either colonial-style ones in the old block, full of period furnishings and charm, or smart modern ones in the new extension. Unlike its associate hotel in Agra, this place is very well managed and has probably the best pool and restaurant/bar in town. There's even a yoga centre.

expensive (from US$30)

Hotel Ideal Tops, ☎ 348091, ✉ 348685, is indeed 'tops' in this category, offering 5-star comforts at 3-star tariffs. No pool unfortunately, but the service is spot-on and the rooms extremely well-priced at US$30/40 single/double.

Hotel Varanasi Ashok, ☎ 46020, ✉ 348089, is a cut above the usual government-run hotel and scores over Ideal Tops in having a pool. The single rooms are well worth their US$38 tariff, but the doubles are not at twice the cost.

moderate (from Rs200)

Just up from the tourist office, the **Hotel de Paris**, ☎ 46601-8, ✉ 348520, will appeal to anyone wanting to relive the 'past glory of British India'. Once an army officers' club, this is a pleasantly rundown building with the ghost of the Raj still clinging to it. There's a homely bar and restaurant, extensive green grounds, and spacious (if gloomy) rooms at Rs550/760.

Also on The Mall is **Hotel Surya**, ☎ 348330, with a nice garden and rooms from Rs110 to 300. Ask for a deluxe one, if you can afford it. Also recommended are two adjoining hotels on Patel Nagar, close to the railway station: the clean and quiet **Hotel Vaibhav**, ☎ 46477, ✉ 348081, with rooms for Rs225/300 non a/c and Rs425/500 a/c, and **Hotel India**, ☎ 43261, with its own restaurant/bar and a few rooms around Rs250. The latter is due for renovation however, so expect rates to rise considerably.

Pradeep Hotel, ☎ 44963, in Lahurabir is a very good two-star property, used a lot by travellers. It has a fine Indian restaurant and a tourist information counter—preferred by many to the government tourist office. Like the nearby **Hotel Siddarth** in Sigra, ☎ 352001, it charges around Rs200/250 for ordinary rooms, Rs350/400 with a/c.

In the old city, the only comfortable option is the new **Hotel La-Ra** in Dasashwamedh Road, ☎ 320323, ✉ 323501. It's right near the river, so you don't have to walk far for the sunrise. Ask for a quietish back room (from Rs150) or one with a fiercely buzzing a/c unit which blocks out the noise of the streets (Rs300 to 500). The downstairs restaurant is air-conditioned and ideal for watching the world go by.

budget

Budget lodges are concentrated in the old city, mostly near the Golden Temple. Rooms go from Rs30 to 100 and are pretty basic. Many head for **Yogi Lodge**,

322588, but few get to it in one hit—rickshaw drivers steer them to inferior copies like Gold Yogi Lodge, Old Yogi Lodge (not bad) or Yogi Guest House, where they get commission. Yogi Lodge is the nerve centre of the old city, and is a great place to meet people and gather information. It has a good travel service, a lively restaurant and popular rooms from Rs25 to 80. Apart from **Trimurti Guest House**, ℯ 323554, round the corner, it's the only lodge with rooftop views of the Golden Temple—albeit only the spire of it and the mosque.

If the Yogi's full, try the nearby **Golden Lodge**. Outside this one, I found a German juggling a set of toilet brushes. 'I *like* my toilet brushes!' he said proudly, 'I lost my clubs on a train from Delhi.' Even cheaper is **Om House Lodge** near the entrance to Chowk area, with a relaxing rooftop terrace, yoga lessons, and clean rooms (with bath and balcony) from just Rs30. **Fagin's** restaurant, next to Golden Lodge, has a few rooms too—often occupied, but worth waiting for. It has lots of facilities (STD phone, rail-bookings etc) and a dog called Blackie. If he thinks you're a monkey, he'll go for you.

Varanasi ℯ (0542–)   ***Eating Out***

Clark's Hotel's **Amrapali** restaurant has a great Continental menu—everything from fish and chips to chicken 'sizzlers'—and lays on a multi-cuisine buffet dinner (the Chinese dishes are good) for US$10 per head. The Taj has two speciality restaurants, both with attached bars. The **Mandap** is for Continental cuisine, with well-priced breakfast/lunch buffets, and the **Varuna** is for North Indian dishes, all cooked to perfection, with live instrumental music from 8pm. The Ashok hotel offers similar entertainment, but the place lacks atmosphere. Better is the **Haveli** at Hotel Ideal Tops, which specializes in Lucknowi and Benares fare. Prices are very reasonable, and it's very popular with locals.

Outside the hotels, the best Indian food (pure veg only) can be found at **Sindhi** restaurant, close to Lalita cinema in Bhelpura. In Lahurabir area, **Winfa** (behind the cinema) and **Poonam** (at Pradeep Hotel) are recommended for Chinese and Indian respectively. Also in this district is **El Parador**, the closest thing to a Kathmandu restaurant you're likely to come across outside Delhi—with all the delicious cakes and crêpes, waffles and pancakes, soups and salads, that go with the tag. Other fast-food joints, like **Burger King** at Mint House, Cantonment, and **Kamesh Hut** near Pradeep Hotel, are okay but don't compare. Two good restaurants near the railway station are **Paradise** and **Hotel Surya**, both offering tasty Chinese/Indian meals for well under Rs100 a head.

In the old city, there are several funky little restaurants—mainly in Golden Temple area—offering travellers' fare along with tinny taped sounds. Current favourites include **Fagin's** ('Weston music ool the time'), **Yogi Lodge** and **Blue Moon**. The ever-popular **Keshari**, just off Dasashwamedh Ghat Road, is tops for cheap vegetarian food. However, a lot of people staying in the old city find that they lose their appetite and can't eat for days. Old Varanasi is like the Paharganj district in Delhi—unforgettable but stomach-turning.

Moving On

By air: The popular Delhi–Agra–Khajuraho circuit is covered daily by Indian Airlines, who also fly every day to Kathmandu and tri-weekly to Bhubaneshwar. Modiluft offer daily flights to Delhi, Calcutta and Bombay. Sahara Airlines fly five times a week to Delhi, Bombay and Hyderabad.

By rail: Fast trains from Varanasi Junction station include the Amritsar–Howrah Mail to Calcutta (dep 4.30pm, 15hrs), the Poorva Express to Delhi (Mon,Tues, Fri only; dep 7.45pm, 12hrs), the Himgiri Express to Pathankot, for Dharamsala/Jammu (Wed, Sat, Sun only, dep 2.40pm, 22hrs), and the Farakka Express to Agra (dep 12.35pm daily, 16hrs). A quicker way to Agra is to hop off the Delhi-bound Poorva Express at Tundhla (arr 4.30am) and do the final 30km to Agra by auto-rickshaw—arriving just in time for sunrise at the Taj.

There is no direct rail-link to Khajuraho. Your best bet is the 11.45pm Kurla Express to Satna (7hrs), then a shared jeep (Rs100, 4hrs) to Khajuraho.

For Darjeeling, take a rickshaw to Mughalserai station, 20km out of Varanasi, and catch the 6.35pm N E Express train to New Jalpaiguri (15hrs). From here, it's 3 hours by minibus/shared jeep to Darjeeling.

Another useful train from Mughalserai is the 2382 Poorva Express to Gaya, for Bodhgaya (dep 6.15am, arr 9am), which continues on to Calcutta (arr 4.15pm).

Arriving by train, don't get off at Varanasi City station; the main station is Varanasi Junction (Cantonment). The booking office there is separate and to the left of the main station building, open 8am to 8pm (to 2pm only on Sundays).

By road: There are buses to Satna, for Khajuraho, but they're slower and less comfortable than the train. Private deluxe buses to Kathmandu/Pokhara (Rs250) can be booked from Yogi Lodge (*see* p.151) or Golden Lodge (*see* p.152) in the old city.

Taxis to Bodhgaya (260km) cost in the region of Rs2500 and to Khajuraho (410km) around Rs4000—it's the same charge one-way or return.

Bodhgaya population 25,000

India, birthplace of two major world religions—Hinduism and Buddhism—is a land of pilgrims. Joining the trail is a unique experience, one which no traveller ever forgets. Birthplace of Buddhism, and home of many aboriginal tribes, the northeastern state of **Bihar** is the poorest state in India, with very limited tourist facilities, but compensates with a spiritual authenticity born of destitution and want. Alongside the modern towns of industry stand the proud ruins of monasteries, temples and universities, reflecting the bygone might of a great world religion. From the major Hindu pilgrimage centre of

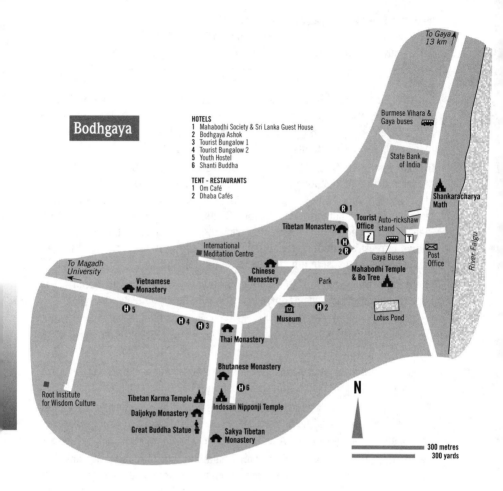

Bodhgaya

HOTELS
1 Mahabodhi Society & Sri Lanka Guest House
2 Bodhgaya Ashok
3 Tourist Bungalow 1
4 Tourist Bungalow 2
5 Youth Hostel
6 Shanti Buddha

TENT - RESTAURANTS
1 Om Café
2 Dhaba Cafés

To Gaya
13 km

Burmese Vihara &
Gaya buses

State Bank
of India

Shankaracharya
Math

River Falgu

Tibetan Monastery

Tourist Auto-rickshaw
Office stand

International
Meditation Centre

Chinese
Monastery

Park

Gaya Buses

Post
Office

Mahabodhi Temple
& Bo Tree

To Magadh
University

Vietnamese
Monastery

Museum

Lotus Pond

Thai Monastery

Bhutanese Monastery

Root Institute
for Wisdom Culture

Tibetan Karma Temple

Daijokyo Monastery

Indosan Nipponji Temple

Great Buddha Statue

Sakya Tibetan
Monastery

N

300 metres
300 yards

Gaya, it's just a short drive down to **Bodhgaya**, where the Buddha achieved his enlightenment beneath the Bodhi Tree. Also close by are **Nalanda**, site of the world's oldest university, and **Rajgir**, capital of the ancient Magadha empire, where the Buddha and Mahavira (founder of the Jain religion) delivered their most important teachings.

Bodhgaya is where Buddhism, one of the great religions of the world, was born. To this small secluded spot on the banks of the Niranjana came Siddhartha, the royal prince of Kapilavastu, after nine long years of searching for the Ultimate Truth. And here, under the holy peepal or bo tree, he became Buddha—the enlightened one—and dedicated himself to the good of humanity.

Since this event, some 2500 years ago, Buddhists all over the world—together with Hindus who regard Buddha as an avatar or incarnation of Vishnu—have considered Bodhgaya a major pilgrimage spot, the most important of the four holy places associated with the Buddha. The others are Lumbini in Nepal, where he was born, Sarnath near Varanasi, where he delivered his first sermon, and Kushinagar near Gorakhpur, where he died.

Bodhgaya attracts just as many Westerners as it does Indian pilgrims. Some of them are here to learn about Buddhism or meditation, others just to find peace and solitude. There's a serene, tranquil atmosphere to the place, especially at dawn or dusk, which draws visitors back time and again.

According to legend, Buddha spent his young life as a prince of the Sakya people, and was even married with a young son. It was however predicted before his birth, that were he ever to see the sickness, old age and death outside his father's (the king's) palace, he would abandon his family and become a spiritual rather than a secular leader. Despite his father's effort, this in time came to pass and he went out into the world to beome a wandering ascetic.

What Buddha came to realize under the bo tree was that a life of extreme privation was no short-cut to enlightenment. On the contrary, because he desired it so intensely, and because any earthly desire stood between him and 'nirvana', he was in fact further away from it than when he had started. After years of sitting on thorn bushes and living on rice (sometimes just one grain a day), he now sat down to a hearty meal and began the meditation that led to the teaching of the Four Noble Truths (see p.xxx) and the Eight-Fold Path. The central tenet of this teaching was that between the two extremes of self-indulgence and self-mortification there existed the 'Middle Way', whereby all mankind could live and find happiness in this world. It was this teaching that he delivered to five former companions at Sarnath, a sermon that began 50 years of wandering and instruction until his death in around 480 BC.

When to Go

Bodhgaya comes into its own during the annual Buddha Jayanti festival, held here each May. It celebrates the anniversary of the day Buddha was born, the day he gained enlightenment, and the day he died, and attracts thousands of devotees from all over the world. Packed to capacity with people sleeping back-to-back on every roof top, the small hamlet generates a quite unbelievable atmosphere. If you can put up with the noise, the crowds and the mosquitoes, this is when to experience the 'spiritual buzz' of Bodhgaya commented on by so many travellers.

Otherwise, the best time to come is from November to mid-February, when the town is enlivened by Tibetan pilgrims visiting from Dharamsala. The Dalai Lama himself usually spends December here.

See 'Moving On' section in **Varanasi**, p.153.

The nearest railway station is at Gaya. Auto-rickshaws meet travellers off the train there, and fleece them for a minimum of Rs80/90 for the short 13km trip to Bodhgaya. A half-hour walk takes you to the Kacheri share-rickshaw stand, where it's only Rs4 plus Rs2 for your pack.

Late arrivals in Gaya should stay overnight—the road to Bodhgaya is not safe after dark. For digs, choose between the budget **Ajatsatu Hotel** opposite the railway station and the upmarket **Hotel Siddhartha International**, ✆ 21254, which has a/c rooms around US$25/30 and a good non-veg restaurant.

Vishnu may have given Gaya the power to absolve all sinners—making it a pilgrimage magnet to Hindus—but he didn't give it much else. Apart from a 1000-step climb to the top of **Brahmajuni Hill** for views over the town, or a 10-minute walk right out of the railway station to the late-18th century **Vishnupad Temple**, there's little to see or do. The temple has a 40cm long 'footprint' of Vishnu embedded in solid rock, but only Hindus can see it.

Getting Around

Bodhgaya is a tiny place with one main street, one main attraction—the Mahabodhi Temple—and several small international temples and monasteries. There are cycle-rickshaws for those short on time, but you can easily cover everything by foot in a day. A second day can be profitably spent meeting with pilgrims, monks and students, a good way of getting the flavour of the place. For peace and quiet, spend at least one sunset on the banks of the river Niranjana, where the Buddha bathed after gaining enlightenment. It flows gently just outside town.

Bodhgaya ✆ *(0631–)*   *Tourist Information*

There's a **tourist office**, ✆ 26, opposite the Mahabodhi Temple, open 10am–5pm daily. It's not very useful, but hires out decent guides.

Walking Tour

4–6 hours; Mahabodhi Temple–Bodhi Tree–Tibetan Monastery–Wheel of Law–Archaeological Museum–Japanese Temple.

Arrive at the large, enclosed **Mahabodhi Temple** around 8am, when it is pleasantly deserted (*adm Rs1, plus Rs10 for a camera, closed between noon and 2pm*). The present brick structure is a relatively modern restoration (1882) of an earlier 11th-century temple, but probably differs little from the 7th-century AD version. It is quite unique among north Indian temples in having a 50m-high pyramidal spire (capped with a stupa) instead of the usual curvilinear summit contours. The four distinctive corner turrets erected round the base of the main temple were 14th-century additions of Burmese Buddhists, aimed at giving the structure balance. The original shrine on this site is believed to have been constructed by Ashoka in the 3rd century BC.

At some point in the 19th century, powerful local Brahmins—backed by the British—assumed control of the Mahabodhi temple. They 'Hinduized' it by giving the images of Buddha the appearance of Brahminical deities. In 1949, after 50 years of agitation from Buddhists to liberate the temple, the state handed over its administration to a council of eight members—four Hindus and four Buddhists—but left the Hindus still in control with an additional 'ex officio' chairperson.

In November 1995, following the conversion of five images of Lord Buddha into likenesses of the five Hindu Pandava brothers, a riot broke out. The temple was stripped of its Hindu trappings, and Buddhist monks threatened self-immolation and fasting unto death. Their demands were two-fold: first, that Hindus be prevented from managing their temple; second, that Hindu rites and rituals (including marriage) should be prohibited inside it. Amongst growing controversy, the main voice of reason (surprisingly) has come from the Chief Minister of Bihar, who has publicly declared: 'If Muslims, Sikhs and Christians can manage the affairs of their religious shrines, why can't Buddhists?'

The Mahabodhi Temple lies within a large walled enclosure dotted with numerous sculptures and ornamented votive stupas, dedicated by pilgrims. The richly carved railings to the south and west of the enclosure are Bodhgaya's oldest remains. They are notable for their lotus, bird and animal motifs, and their *jataka* stories portraying the Buddha's previous incarnations.

Entering the temple complex by the main gate, turn right for the inner shrine. This contains a colossal image of the Buddha, brightly gilded and festooned with flowers, in his 'earth-touching' posture. Buddha had cited the earth as witness to the austerities he had practised on his long journey to enlightenment.

A saffron-robed monk escorts you to the western side of the temple, where you'll find the famous **Bodhi Tree**. This sits on a small, elevated platform within a gated pavilion, and is surveyed by a small gilded Buddha. It is customary to make a donation of money, but not obligatory. The tree itself is gaily adorned with fluttering flags and streamers. It is also alive with chattering birds, which settle and sing on this tree, and no other. This is not the original peepal tree under which the Buddha gained nirvana, but is a direct descendant of it. Ashoka sent saplings of the original to Sri Lanka along with his son Mahinda, both to spread the message of Buddhism and to ensure that when the mother tree perished there would be saplings from grown Lankan trees to bring back and re-plant at Bodhgaya. Under the tree is the red-sandstone slab said to be the *vajrasan* or diamond throne on which the Buddha sat.

Leaving the tree, walk clockwise round the circumference of the temple. Pilgrims follow this circuit three times in succession to complete their ritual. On your round, look out for the beautiful Lotus Pond at the northern wall of the compound. This contains a life-size Buddha, shielded by the cobra which apparently saved him from drowning while he was in deep meditation. Just past the pond is the famous **Jewel Walk**—a raised platform, lined with small pillars, where Buddha paced up and down meditating on whether or not to reveal his knowledge to the world. Further on, you'll see the place of 'Buddha's footprints', often heaped with floral offerings. Elsewhere, sandwiched between numerous tiny stupas and statues in the compound, athletic ascetics engage in excruciating exercises.

Across the road, you'll find the Tibetan **Mahayana Monastery**, built in 1938. The main attraction here, just left inside the entrance, is the massive **Dharma Chakra** or Wheel of Law. This is a 10m-high metal drum, painted in bright reds and golds, within a richly decorated chamber. To be absolved of all your past sins, simply revolve it three times from left to right. At the rear of the chamber, there's a showcase of sculpted Buddhas and near-Buddhas (Bodhisattvas). The largest one is Avalokiteshvara, Bodhisattva of Compassion and patron saint of Tibet.

A 10-minute walk up the hill brings you to the **Chinese Temple** (1945). Turn left here for the **Archaeological Museum** (*open 10am–5pm, closed Fri*) with its fine collection of bronzes and stone sculptures recovered from the local area. Finally, visit the **Japanese Temple**, just beyond the Thai Temple. This houses a beautiful image of the Buddha, brought over from Japan.

Shopping

If you hunt around, you may come across miniature paintings on paper or leaves, a traditional art of the villages round Bodhgaya. They generally depict scenes from the life of Buddha. Nice little souvenirs are small packs of leaves from the Bodhi tree, sold along with the admission to Mahabodhi Temple. Small soft-stone images of the Buddha, carved in the nearby village of Patthalkatti are sold in a number of shops.

Leisure

A number of meditation courses and retreats are offered between November and early February. Some are advertised in the Om Café. Others, like the popular Root Institute for Wisdom Culture, ✆ 81714, and the International Meditation Centre, ✆ 81734, or 01803-813188 in the UK, you're advised to ring ahead and book.

Bodhgaya ✆ *(0631–)*   ### Where to Stay

Hotel Bodhgaya Ashok, ✆ 22708, is nothing special, but at least it's air-conditioned and the food is good. Rooms cost Rs900/1400 or Rs1195/2200 with a/c—less between April to September. The mid-range **Hotel Shanti Buddha**, ✆ 81785, asks too much, Rs350/450 or Rs700/850 with a/c, though the new hotel next door may force it to revise its prices. Budget accommodation is available at the two adjoining Tourist Bungalows—one with dorm beds only for Rs35, the other with dorm beds for Rs45, doubles with bath for Rs200, and a/c rooms for Rs275. The Mahabodhi Society's clean and popular **Sri Lanka Guest House**

charges Rs100 per double and is often full. If you want to know how the Buddha felt before discarding asceticism, stay at one of the monasteries. The most luxurious is the **Bhutanese Monastery**, with common-bath rooms from Rs30 to 50. The most spartan is the **Burmese Monastery**, which asks a Rs10 donation for ultra-basic cells. On my first visit in 1984, I paid Rs2 for a room with no furniture at all—just a marble bed with a marble pillow!

In **Gaya**, the new **Centaur Hotel**, charges around US$30 a night and is the only place to stay in comfort if you want to be close to Bodhgaya.

Bodhgaya ☏ (0631–)   ***Eating Out***

As one would expect of a place of pilgrimage, Bodhgaya has no pretensions to 'haute cuisine'. The **Mahabodhi Canteen** at the Sri Lanka Guest House is okay for Chinese food, the **Siva Hotel** close to the tourist office attempts some Western dishes, and there are popular snacks and taped music at the various tent-restaurants opposite the Burmese Monastery. During the season, a few Tibetan-style restaurants—like the **Om Café**—open up around the Tibetan monastery. If spartan living gets too much, splurge out at the Bodhgaya Ashok.

Moving On

Gaya, the nearest railhead, has fast direct trains to Calcutta (dep 1am, 4hrs; dep 8.50am and 11.15pm, 7–8hrs), to Varanasi (dep 6am and 1.47pm, 3hrs), Puri (dep 1.10pm and 9.10pm, 17–18hrs) and Delhi (dep 1.30am and 147pm, 15–16hrs). There are also trains and buses to/from Patna, 3 hours to the north, but this is a truly abysmal city—to be avoided at all costs.

If you're a keen pilgrim, you can continue on by bus to **Rajgir** (Rs13, 2hrs) from Gaya's Gaurakshini bus stand across the river. It was at Rajgir that the first Buddhist Council, convened shortly after Buddha attained nirvana, was held. Many of his teachings were written down at this point, and he spent the next 12 years in this area, delivering many of his more important sermons. He won round his main opponent, the murderous King Ajatshatru, by curing him of boils.

At the entrance to the site, buy a (useful) local guidebook and hop on the chairlift (Rs8 return, 8am to 5pm) up Ratnagir Hill. While airborne, look down on the ruins of the ancient fortress city and see the Jivakamarvana monastery with large elliptical halls, a favourite retreat of the Buddha. At the top is the Japanese **Shanti Stupa** and its adjoining monastery. Back in the village, hire a horse-drawn tonga or taxi to see the other (very spread out) sites—first, a short climb up **Vaibhara Hill** to **Saptaparni Cave**, site of the first Buddhist Council; then to the pink **Lakshmi Narayan Temple** beside the popular hot springs; finally, to the large **Ajatshatru Fort** (6th century BC), where Buddha cast out the king's boils.

Cheap hotels in Rajgir include the **Anand** near the bus stand and the **Siddharth** near the hot springs. For comfort, there's the 3-star **Centaur Hokke Hotel**, ✆ (06119) 5231, 3km west of the hot springs.

From Rajgir, you can visit the site of the world's earliest known university at **Nalanda**. Get a Rs3 shared jeep to the village (Rs3, 15km), then a Rs2 shared tonga to the extensive ruins. From its foundation in the 5th century BC right up to its sack by Muslims in AD 1199, Nalanda produced some of the most prestigious and learned scholars of the ancient world. Its wholesale destruction sounded the death knell of Buddhism in India. At the site, visit the **museum** (*closed Fri*) with its fine collection of 7th- to 15th-century bronzes and sculptures, together with the Great Seal of the Nalanda University. Pick up a Rs3 guidebook, and make for the **Great Stupa** inside the site. This 31m-high ruin has terraces, steps and a few intact votive stupas. From the top, you have the best view of the university complex, which once housed up to 10,000 monks and students. At the bottom, look for the famous 'elfin' Buddha panel, which is Nalanda's finest surviving treasure.

Street Basket makers

Route 2: Rajasthan

Exotic 'Land of Princes', Rajasthan is a barren desert territory, dotted with battle-scarred forts and palaces. Its harsh climate and rough terrain gave birth to a proud warrior people of legendary courage and valour. Over the centuries, the Rajput chieftains resisted all and any foreign invaders, and whenever faced by certain defeat, invariably preferred glorious death to ignoble surrender. But martial traditions co-existed with love of colour, culture and pageantry, and today Rajasthan is just as famous for its gardens and lakes, festivals and handicrafts as for its fortress theatres of war. It's also one of the few states where one feels compelled to learn some Hindi—the proud Rajputs often won't speak to you in English. Once the ice is broken, however, they are among the friendliest and most hospitable people in India. You'll love them.

The bustling state capital of Jaipur is most often classed as the third city of India's Golden Triangle, but is in fact the entry point to a large and fascinating state. The towering fort of Jodhpur, with the finest palace museum in the country, leads out to the rolling dunes of the Great Thar Desert, where you can take camel safaris from Khuri village. The medieval mystery of Jaisalmer, a desert city of filigree merchants' houses and lively bazaars, gives way to cool, refined elegance at Udaipur, a famous 'lake city' of charming gardens and palaces. The sole hill station of the state, Mount Abu, is famous for its sunsets and for its Dilwara temples—the most exquisite examples of Jain architecture in the country. Nearby Chittorgarh, 'City of Valour', is the fortress site of the Rajputs' most glorious hour. Finally there's Pushkar, a peaceful oasis in the desert, where pilgrims and travellers gather to pray, relax or just hang out.

Itinerary

Of all routes in India, Rajasthan is the most popular. Not only is it easy to get to from Delhi, but it has always had—even before films like 'The Far Pavilions'—the most powerful associations with romance, chivalry and adventure.

You'll need three weeks to do this route at leisure. From Delhi (2 nights), try the following circuit: Jaipur (2), Pushkar (3), Jodhpur (2), Jaisalmer (3) via Pokaran (1), back to Jodhpur (1), Udaipur (3) via Ranakpur (1), Mount Abu (1), back to Udaipur (1), fly to Delhi (1). If you sacrifice Chittorgarh and Ranakpur, you have two days over for an excursion from Delhi to Agra for the Taj Mahal. Cutting out Mount Abu and Pokaran, you'll have more time for special places like Jaisalmer, Udaipur and Pushkar.

If you only have two weeks, you'll have to prioritize. From Delhi (2), travel to Jaipur (2), Pushkar (2), Jaisalmer (3) and Udaipur (2) by surface transport, then fly back to Delhi (1). This leaves a couple of days over for side-trips to Agra and to Bharatpur bird sanctuary.

Long-stay travellers can wind up this route at Udaipur/Abu and continue on to Gujarat, the next route south (*see* p.334). It makes sense to fly home from Bombay not Delhi.

The best time to do this route is between October and March. In summer temperatures are 17°–50°C, and in winter 7°–32°C. Monsoon lasts from late June to early September.

Festivals in Rajasthan

Venue	Festival	1996	1997	1998	1999
Nagaur	Desert Fair		Feb 13–16	Feb 3–6	Jan 24–27
Jaisalmer	Desert Festival		Feb 20–22	Feb 9–11	Jan 29–31
Jaipur	Elephant Festival		Mar 23	Mar 12	Mar 1
Jaipur	Gangaur Fair		Apr 10–11	Mar 30–31	Mar 20–21
Udaipur	Mewar Festival		Apr 10–11	Mar 30–31	Mar 20–21
Jaipur	Teej Fair		Aug 6–7	Jul 26–27	Aug 14–15
Jodhpur	Marwar Festival	Oct 25–26	Oct 15–16	Oct 4–5	Oct 23–24
Pushkar	Camel Fair	Nov 22–25	Nov 11–14	Nov 1–4	Nov 20–23

Jaipur
population 1.8 million

Surrounded on three sides by the rugged Aravali hills, Jaipur is the picturesque capital of Rajasthan. It takes its name from the prince, soldier and astronomer Jai Singh II, who moved his capital here in 1727. The old capital of Amber (or Amer) had long been a stronghold of Rajput power, but had become too cramped at its hillside site. Jai Singh built his new city according to a geometric plan: it was divided into seven rectangular blocks, built on a grid of nine squares as detailed in the Shilpa Shastra, an ancient Hindu architectural treatise. The broad and precise main streets (34m wide) cut the side lanes at right angles. The entire city is encircled by fortified crenellated walls and guarded by seven gates.

Jaipur is notable for its distinctive pink-orange colouring. The whole of the old city, including many fine palaces and buildings, was constructed from solid blocks of sandstone or faced with the same stone. But it was only in 1853 that it gained its famous title, the 'Pink City': it was painted pink in that year for the first time, in honour of a visit from Prince Albert. The soft glow of its buildings and monuments, most magical at sunset, have fascinated visitors for over two centuries.

Though a busy commercial capital, Jaipur is the real gateway to Rajasthan and the underlying Rajput spirit stubbornly lives on. The traditional dress, decoration and colour can be seen everywhere—the station porters in bright red turbans and jackets, the veiled women in loose-flowing robes of red, orange and yellow, the tiny kohl-eyed infants in swaddling clothes of rich, embroidered silk. Inside the old city, the atmosphere is electric—a bustling, jolly round of ringing bicycle bells, teeming traffic, itinerant sacred cows, busy bazaars and tourist-hungry rickshaws.

When to Go

Situated on the plains, Jaipur gets pretty hot. Coolest from October to February, busiest and most popular from January to March, it remains pleasant up to mid-April. Two important dates for your diary (*see* p.162) are the **Elephant Festival** in March and the spring festival of **Gangaur** in March/April when the Goddess Gauri (Parvati) is paraded from the City Palace and through the city streets. The Teej festival of early August, a celebration of the monsoon, is an important one for local women .

Getting There

Jaipur can be reached by air from Ahmedabad, Aurangabad, Bombay, Calcutta, Delhi, Jodphur, Madras and Udaipur; by train/bus from Ahmedabad, Jodphur, Ajmer, Delhi, Agra, Jaisalmer and Udaipur. The airport is 15km from the town centre—around Rs150 by taxi, Rs60 by auto-rickshaw and Rs20 by airport bus. For further information, see 'Moving On' from Jaipur, p.177.

Getting Around

Jaipur is divided into the 'old' city, with its many sights enclosed behind high pink-sandstone walls, and the modern, commercial 'new' city which has grown up to the south. Most visitors stay in the new town—it's much quieter and far less humid. **Cycles** are a good way of getting around (Jaipur has some of India's best paved roads) and can be hired for Rs20 per day from many budget lodges, as well as from the Hotel Arya Niwas. **Auto-rickshaws** don't have meters—you'll have to bargain hard for a fair fare (Rs15–20 for short hops) and as often as not you'll end up at a gem or carpet shop instead of your required destination. You're probably better off renting by the hour (Rs50) or even by the day (Rs300). Taxis have meters, but rarely use them. **Cycle-rickshaws** are cheap and slow, and their drivers talk business constantly. Local buses, if you can handle them, are far less trouble. They are especially useful for visiting Amber Fort. Cars can be hired from most hotels at fixed rates for a half/full day (Rs400/700). Some hotels, such as Megh Niwas and Arya Niwas, can also arrange cars to the airport (Rs180), to the bus/railway stations (Rs30/40) and to out-of-town destinations like Pushkar (Rs1000), Delhi (Rs1800) and Agra via Fatehpur Sikri/Bharatpur (Rs1600).

Jaipur ✆ (0141–)   ### *Tourist Information*

The main **tourist office**, ✆ 315714, is at the railway station (platform 1), open 6am–8pm daily. Come here for good handouts and maps, badge-carrying guides (Rs100 half-day, Rs150 full-day) and city sightseeing tours (half day: 8am–1pm, 11.30am–4.30pm and 1.30–6.30pm; full day: 9am–6pm). The staff here are among the most helpful and informative in the country.

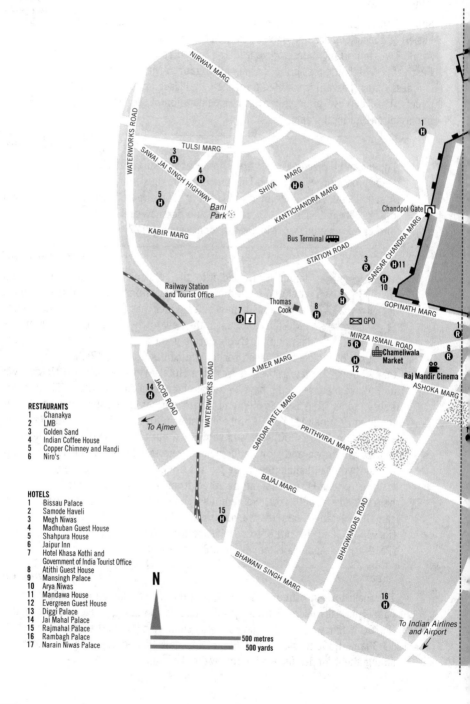

RESTAURANTS
1 Chanakya
2 LMB
3 Golden Sand
4 Indian Coffee House
5 Copper Chimney and Handi
6 Niro's

HOTELS
1 Bissau Palace
2 Samode Haveli
3 Megh Niwas
4 Madhuban Guest House
5 Shahpura House
6 Jaipur Inn
7 Hotel Khasa Kothi and
  Government of India Tourist Office
8 Atithi Guest House
9 Mansingh Palace
10 Arya Niwas
11 Mandawa House
12 Evergreen Guest House
13 Diggi Palace
14 Jai Mahal Palace
15 Rajmahal Palace
16 Rambagh Palace
17 Narain Niwas Palace

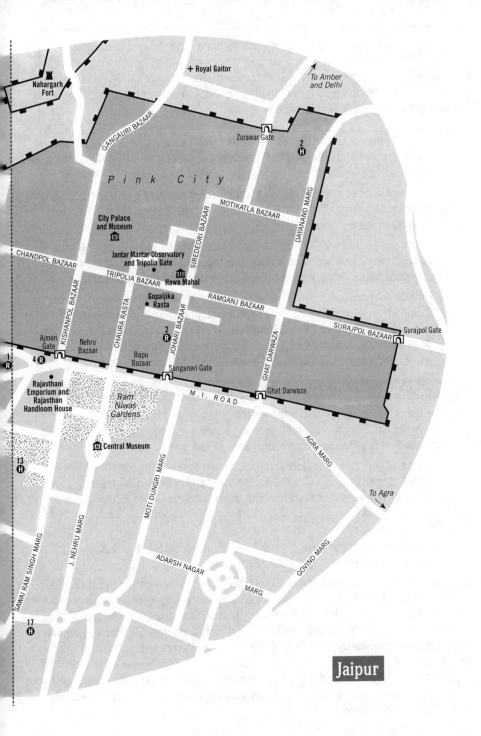

Nahargarh
Fort

+ Royal Gaitor

↗ To Amber
and Delhi

GANGAURI BAZAAR

Zorawar Gate

Pink City

2
Ⓗ

City Palace
and Museum
Ⓜ

MOTIKATLA BAZAAR

SIREDEORI BAZAAR

DAYANAND MARG

CHANDPOL BAZAAR

Jantar Mantar Observatory
and Tripolia Gate

TRIPOLIA BAZAAR

Hawa Mahal

KISHANPOL BAZAAR

CHAURA RASTA

Gopaljika
Rasta

RAMGANJ BAZAAR

JOHARI BAZAAR

2
Ⓡ

Ajmeri
Gate

Nehru
Bazaar

Bapu
Bazaar

Sanganeri Gate

SURAJPOL BAZAAR

Surajpol Gate

GHAT DARWAZA

1
Ⓡ

4 Ⓡ

Rajasthani
Emporium and
Rajasthan
Handloom House

Ram
Niwas
Gardens

M.I. ROAD

Ghat Darwaza

AGRA MARG

Ⓜ Central Museum

13
Ⓗ

MOTI DUNGRI MARG

To Agra

SAWAI RAM SINGH MARG

J. NEHRU MARG

ADARSH NAGAR

MARG

GOVIND MARG

17
Ⓗ

Jaipur

165

Jaipur auto-rickshaws don't just rip you off, they ask you to conspire with them to help rip *yourself* off—by not telling the police that they are ripping you off. So, if a policeman comes up to you and asks 'Is this man using his meter?', you're supposed to say 'Yes' when he's not, knowing full well that if he *was* you'd be saving a lot of money.

The Government of India tourist office is at Hotel Khasa Kothi, ✆ 372200, open 9am–6pm weekdays, 9am–1pm Saturdays. The **GPO** is on M I Road and has a parcel-packing service at the entrance open 10am–4.30pm daily.

Thomas Cook has a very quick counter for **foreign exchange** at its Jaipur Towers office on M I Road, open 10am–6pm daily. So does State Bank of India (closed Sunday) on the first floor of its M I Road branch at Sanganeri Gate.

Books Corner next to Niro's restaurant on M I Road has a good selection of **guides, maps and western books and magazines**. It also sells the monthly periodical *Jaipur Vision*, which is choc-a-bloc with useful city information.

Indian Airlines, ✆ 514407, is at Nehru Place on Tonk Road, **Air India**, ✆ 368569, in Rattan Mansion on M I Road, and most other international airlines in Jaipur Towers on M I Road. **Modiluft**, ✆ 363373, is at Ahinsa Circle, **East-West Airlines**, ✆ 514159, at Vishal Chambers, Tonk Road. Reliable travel agents are Sita Travels, ✆ 364104, Mayur Travels, ✆ 361269, and TCI, ✆ 380050.

Touring Jaipur

To cover the main sights and fit in some shopping, you'll need two full days in Jaipur—possibly even an extra day to recover. Sightseeing is most comfortable by RTDC's morning conducted tour—full-day tours are very tiring and not recommended.

If you can only handle two sights, hire an auto-rickshaw to take you up to the Amber Fort and then back into town to the City Palace. Consider taking along a government-authorized guide (the cheapest and best are from the tourist office inside the railway station).

City Tour

By tour bus, morning. Nawab Sahib ki Haveli–Hawa Mahal–Amber Fort–Gaitor–Jantar Mantar–City Palace and Museum.

This tour usually starts in the heart of the old city, at the 18th-century merchant's house called **Nawab Sahib ki Haveli**. The remarkable panoramic views from its roof-top terraces make it the ideal introduction to Jaipur. First, look down onto bicycle-infested Tripolia Bazaar—the wide central avenue which cuts right through old Jaipur—then over to **Jai Singh's Observatory**, the **Clock Tower**, the **City Palace** and, up on the hill opposite, **Nahargarh** or Tiger Fort, once Jai Singh's treasury. This is also a good place to appreciate the unique city planning of Jaipur: all those symmetrical main streets, neatly intersected by little narrow side-roads. There's a clear guide service at the *haveli*, often followed by a puppet show.

Just down the road, at the junction of Tripolia Bazaar and Siredeori Road, is the high pyramidal façade of **Hawa Mahal** (*open 10am–4.30pm daily except Fridays; adm Rs3, free Monday*). This famous landmark of Jaipur, nicknamed 'Palace of Winds' (the cool westerly winds blow through it), was built by Pratap Singh in 1799. It comprises five storeys of semi-octagonal overhanging windows, with domes and spires. From the windows, the ladies of the court used to view the city below. Entrance is from the rear of the building, and you can climb to the top for some of the best photography in Jaipur—though you have to pay Rs50 to use a camera.

Leaving the pink city by the Zorawar Gate, it's an 11km journey north to the old capital of **Amber**, with its majestic hilltop fortress. Local buses go there every few minutes from the Hawa Mahal (fare Rs3). About halfway to Amber, look out for Pratap Singh's cream-yellow **Jal Mahal** or Water Palace. The vast rainwater reservoirs are now overrun by water hyacinth and visitors aren't allowed in.

A little further on is **Jaigarh Fort** (*open 9am–4.30pm daily*), built by Jai Singh in 1726 on the site of an earlier 11th-century construction. This is an elegantly harmonious affair, most beautiful at dawn and dusk when it glows with a yellow, luminous quality. To reach Jaigarh, take the turning to the left soon after passing the Jal Mahal and follow the road up the hill. The fort offers magnificent views from its elevated watchtower.

Continue to **Amber Fort**, which has a spectacular location overlooking the Moata Lake, surrounded by a wide ring of craggy watchtowers and fortifications. It was built by Rajah Man Singh, the first local ruler to have felt pressure from the Mughals as they headed west from Delhi. Man Singh guaranteed the safety of his kingdom only by giving his sister to the Mughal Emperor Akbar in marriage. In return he was made a general in Akbar's army and gained sufficient wealth and power to start work on the imposing fort-palace of Amber in 1592. Amber was, however, seen by other Rajput rulers as having sold out, a blot on her record which transferred to Jaipur, and which time has not erased.

At Amber, you can either walk up to the fort via the narrow, cobbled path (10–15 minutes), or go up and down by overpriced elephant (Rs250, 1 to 4 people). If you walk it, there's a perfectly adequate elephant-ride round the *chowk* (square) at the top, only Rs25 if you bargain hard. Below the fort, just over the small bridge, there's a place to hire boats on Moata Lake, though it rarely has much water in it.

Up at the fort, pass through the **Suraj Pol** or main gate and enter the small square with its monkey-infested banyan tree, colourful spice stalls and elephant rank. Proceed to the left for the **Kalimata Temple**, often packed with jostling pilgrims. This temple, with its silver doors, beautiful carved pillars and walls, contains an image of Shila Devi brought here by the grateful Man Singh from East Bengal, following his successful defeat of the warlord Kedar in 1604.

If you're here on your own, you can hire a guide from near the elephant rank (Rs30). Otherwise, follow the tour up the stairs and into the palace. The first attraction inside is the Mughal-influenced **Diwan-i-Am**, to the left of the courtyard. At the rear of the courtyard is the ornate **Ganesh Pol** (Elephant Gate), a façade of colourful frescoes constructed by Jai Singh. This leads the way into the private quarters of the palace and the royal apartments, a glittering array of mosaic, marble and mirrors, all grouped around a central ornamental garden. The main attraction is the showpiece **Shish Mahal** or Mirror Palace, again built by Jai Singh. The exterior is a studded jewel-box of polished mirror fragments set in plaster. Within, glass mosaic panels vie for attention with highly ornamented plaster reliefs, inlaid with glass and marble carvings. Pass stained-glass windows to lookout points affording fine views down over the lake and old palaces.

Proceed next to the magical **Chamber of Mirrors**, formerly the Maharajah's bedroom. The whole ceiling is a glitter of tiny mirrors which, when illuminated by the guide's candle, produces a spectacular illusion of a galaxy of stars traversing a night-time sky. Outside is a cool pavilion, the **Jas Mahal**, from which there are good views over Amber town, the lake and the palace.

Across the formal garden is the **Sukh Niwas**, or Hall of Pleasure. The main chamber has decorative relief work in plaster and a marble cascade to the rear. Together with the breeze passing through its perforated marble screen, this water cascade served as a cooling device during the summer. The pavilion doors still retain some of the original ivory and sandalwood inlay work. On the way out, steal a minute or two to appreciate the beautiful gardens.

Amber Palace is open 9am to 4.30pm daily, admission Rs4. It's up to you whether or not you declare your camera/camcorder at the entrance—the Rs50–100 charges are pretty stiff. An evening *son et lumière* show may be in operation by the time you read this. Enquire at your hotel.

From Amber, the tour returns to town via **Gaitor**, the royal cremation ground. This site, located some 8km out of Jaipur, contains a number of elegant chhatris or cenotaphs of various kings and queens. The white marble structure of Jai Singh II is the most striking, with its intricately carved dome and 20 supporting pillars. Members of the royal family, mainly the ladies, are still cremated at Gaitor: a new cenotaph is erected for each sad occasion.

Back in the walled city of Jaipur, you'll enter the precincts of the City Palace (which covers one-seventh of the original city's area) and be taken to Jai Singh's most interesting legacy, the **Jantar Mantar** observatory (*open 9am–4.30pm daily; adm Rs4, free Mondays*). The starstruck young ruler first conceived the idea in 1718, and sent out scholars to study foreign observatories in Britain, Greece, Arabia and Portugal, with a brief to gather all the information they could. An experimental prototype at Delhi (1724) was followed by others at Ujjain, Varanasi and Mathura. Then, in 1728, he realized his dream of India's greatest astronomical observatory here at Jaipur. It is the largest of the series, and has the unique *Rashi Valaya* instrument in which Jai Singh himself used to sit to make his observations.

Renovated in 1901, this is a surreal collection of yellow sandstone sculptures, each with a specific astronomical function—be it to measure the sun's declination, azimuth or altitude, or to determine the declination of fixed stars and planets. The tall sundial, with its 30m-high gnomon, is the most notable instrument. It casts a shadow which moves some 4m each hour, giving the time down to 2-second accuracy—though only of course when the sun is shining!

Peacock Gate City Palace Jaipur.

From the observatory enter the **City Palace**, an imposing blend of traditional Rajasthani and Mughal architecture. The first building you'll see is the two-storey **Mubarak Mahal**, the upper floor of which now houses a costume and textile museum. To the northwest of the court-yard is an arms gallery with a typically inventive array of Rajput weapons. An impressive gateway, the **Singh Pol**, leads through to the Diwan-i-Khas, complete with antique carpets and chandeliers which are unrolled and unbagged for holy festivals. Also here are two huge silver urns built for Sawai Madhu Singh in 1902 to carry water from the Ganges to London for Edward VII's coronation. He wouldn't drink anything else.

Passing through a small portrait gallery to the north of the Diwan-i-Khas, watched over by a Chinese Buddha, you'll come into a spacious courtyard. Here dancing used to take place, watched by the Maharanis in the balconies above. Looking up, you'll see the seven-storey **Chandra Mahal**, where the present Maharajah and his family live today. The ground floor is open to the public (*open 9.30am–4.45pm, closed Sun; adm Rs30, half-price for students and teachers*) and leads onto a lawn with 356 fountains still in working order, perfectly complementing the beautiful gardens. So do the green, violet and red chandeliers and the plain marble doors leading off the mosaic courtyard.

The Art Gallery and **Maharajah Sawai Man Singh II Museum** (*open same hours as palace*) are housed in the Hall of Public Audience to the southeast of the inner courtyard. The gallery has some of India's largest and richest carpets, most of them from Herat (Afghanistan) and Lahore (Pakistan). Several date back to the early 17th century and the largest is 18m long. There's also a fine collection of ivory elephant howdahs, and the second-largest chandelier (Czech) in the country. The art gallery is famous for its Jaipur and Mughal miniature paintings and for its 20,000 handwritten Sanskrit manuscripts (only a few are on show—you'll have to ask if you want to see more). As with Jaipur's other main sights, there's a Rs50/100 fee for still/video cameras.

For most people, this will be quite enough sightseeing for one day. The afternoons are often sticky and hot, and are best spent under a fan or at the pool. Dusk is the time to venture forth again, either for rowing round Moata Lake and enjoying the sunset at Amber Fort, or for climbing the huge sundial at Jantar Mantar for an equally fine sunset over the pink city.

Sariska and Ranthambore National Parks

Sariska National Park near Alwar is only 2 hours from Jaipur (110km; 68 miles). Although not a good area for seeing tiger, the protection given to the area under Project Tiger has benefited the large populations of antelope and deer as well as the extensive bird life. Opposite the park entrance is the **Sariska Palace Hotel**, ✆ Sariska 222, with rooms from Rs600 and organized jeep trips into the park, ✆ Delhi 739712. Also at the park entrance is a **forest rest house** and Rajasthan Tourism's **Tiger Den tourist bungalow** with rooms from Rs250.

Further south is **Ranthambore National Park**, 132km (82 miles) south-east of Jaipur and well connected by train with Delhi and Bombay. Sawai Madhopur station is 13km (8 miles) from the park entrance and most express trains between Delhi and Bombay stop here. Jeeps are available at the station and the Park Director's office is just opposite. Ranthambore is considered by many as one of the best places for seeing tiger, although in the summer of 1992 reports of poaching in the area has probably made this more difficult. One kilometre from the station is the Taj Group's **Sawai Madhopur Lodge**, ✆ 2541/2247, with rooms including food at US$70 single, US$85 double. RTDC **Castle Jhoomar Baori**, ✆ 2495, is midway between the park entrance and Sawai Madhopur and has rooms from Rs400. Two other small **camps** are located toward the park entrance.

Shopping

Jaipur is a shopper's paradise, even for Indian people. They come here from all over the country to buy tie-and-dye *bandhini* bed linen, handwoven blankets, dhurrie rugs, mirror-inlaid bangles, enamelled and blue pottery, gold and silver jewellery. Most of these things can be bought at reasonable prices at the many bazaars south of the old city, or at the several shops in M I Road (*most bazaars and shops closed Sun*). **Bapu Bazaar** and **Nehru Bazaar** are where to buy textiles, local perfumes and camel-skin shoes, and **Johari Bazaar** is the best place to window-shop for jewellery, tie-and-dye saris and textiles—all for less than at the high-street shops. Before hitting the markets though, pay a visit to the fixed-price **Rajasthani Government Emporium** (*open 8am–8pm daily*) on M I Road, opposite Ajmeri Gate. In a place like Jaipur, where scams are more common than mosquitoes, an hour spent here could save you plenty.

Jaipur is famous for gems and jewellery, and attracts dealers from all over the world. Sapphires, emeralds, rubies, diamonds and all other precious and semi-precious stones sell at a fraction of what they fetch when they get to Cartier or Tiffany. Gems are still mined in India, but roughstones are brought here to be processed from several other countries because the craftsmen here can get a better yield. They examine and sort roughstones into three main categories: the clearest and finest, which are cut and polished into gems; the second-grade, which are made into necklaces and bracelets; and the low-quality, which are generally ground down into powder to make durable mineral paints and dyes for textiles and miniature paintings.

Jaipur has hundreds of gem 'factories', most of them located in the Parganj area of the old city (near Suraj Old Gate). These factories are usually small household concerns, run by families who polish and hand-cut the gems, then deliver them to the overseer of each area. The workers are generally children, who start their apprenticeship at about age 8 and are fully skilled by about 20. Watching them at work is a fascinating experience. To produce small gems, they glue the rough stone to the end of a long cane, which enables them to manoeuvre it easily while they use an electric rotating wheel to cut in the facets. To produce the facets on larger stones, they use a manual cutting-machine which resembles a saw.

Nearly every street tout and rickshaw driver in Jaipur will try to steer you to a gem factory. They will tell you that you'll save up to 30% by buying 'at source' rather than at a high-street shop. Be warned, however—if they get in the shop with you, you're likely to pay 30% more, not less.

For the best deal on stones, avoid both the factories and the high-street shops. Check out the small 'gem alley' of Gopalji ka Rasta, opposite LMB restaurant in Johari Bazaar. This is the recognized gem centre of Jaipur, where you can pick up all kinds of loose stones at rock-bottom prices. But you must know what you're looking for. If you're after semi-precious stones of medium quality, the best time to visit is around midday. As soon as you enter the alley, you're assaulted by a scrum of urgent, insistent guys screaming 'Buy my packet!' Their packets contain glittering arrays of random rough-cut stones, offered at low, low prices. Often, the reason why these guys are so urgent to sell (and why the gems are so cheap) is that they are factory workers who have pocketed stones they've been working on and have to get rid of them in their lunch breaks. It's an ideal market for a young jeweller who has some knowledge of gems, but even the average tourist can't go far wrong—provided he or she makes no 'offer' until ready to buy. Once you've made an offer, you've got to pay up. No offer should be made until you've had a good look at several packets, and have compared price and quality. When making your selection, bear in mind that these stones are not sized—you'll have to pay extra later on, to have them made up into rings, necklaces, pendants, cufflinks etc. This is best done at a reputed jeweller like Silver Mines (*see* below) in Chameliwala Market. Gem alley really hots up in the late afternoon, from 4pm on, when the big wholesalers gather to buy high-quality stones. It's a good idea, if you're going to be doing any serious buying, to take a broker along. Goverdhan at Silver Mines will fix one up for you, and the small commission you'll pay for this service (around 8%) will save you a great deal of time and money at purchase point.

Actually, gem buying is not as specialized a business as one might think. Following a few basic rules, you're bound to win. Take emeralds, for instance. Shades vary from dark to light green. The darker and greener the stone is, the more value is placed on it. Next, look at its opaqueness. A transparent stone has more value than an opaque one. But the 'colour' should be primarily clear, giving it 'brilliance'. Next, take out your eyeglass (something which always impresses street-traders) and examine the stone for 'cut'. The cut should be even, and the number of 'carats' not less than 16 to 18. This means the stone will contain 125 facets, giving it a good colour and lustre. A stone with few facets will have little transparency, and this will detract significantly from its value. A lot of 'street-cut' jewellery is of dubious quality: with gems, the facets may be uneven, the colour poor (look out for flecks and impurities), and there may even be unsightly scratches and chips. You're fairly safe with semi-precious stones, like garnets and lapis lazuli, but several so-called emeralds will look more like cheap green malachite. With an eyeglass, you should be able to detect any flecks, flaws and hairline cracks. Sometimes you'll come across a stone which is absolutely perfect—no impurities whatsoever. In 99% of cases, it will be synthetic. Fortunately, however, the human eye is very accurate—given a choice of several rough stones, it will usually select the very best one. If you don't trust your judgement, pop over to the **Gem Testing Laboratory** on M I Road (near New Gate), where for a nominal sum (Rsl00 per stone) you can have your purchases verified and valued. Steer clear of diamonds, by the way—they must be paid for in foreign currency, carry special setting restrictions, and require an export certificate.

Silver is excellent value in Jaipur. The standard retail rate for made-up silver is anything between Rsl4 and 20/gram, depending on the amount of work involved. But if you buy in quantity, you're entitled to ask for the 'wholesale' rate, which can be as low as Rsl0/gram for rings and Rsl2/gram for earrings. All silver is guaranteed sterling with a 925 hallmark, and all stones purchased—precious or semi-precious—are supported by a written guarantee. If buying antique silver, count on paying double the price of 'new' silver. You're allowed to take silver out of the country as hand luggage, as long as you have a bona fide receipt for it, plus foreign encashment certificates (from a bank/hotel) to back up your purchases. Buying goods for export with 'black' money is not a good idea.

Persian-style carpets, stone carvings and miniature paintings are not a good deal here. One look in the government arts emporium is all it takes to convince you that prices are too high. Carpets are cheaper and better in Jaisalmer, and miniature paintings in Udaipur.

To do all your shopping in one place, try the small **Chameliwala Market** opposite the GPO on M I Road. Here you'll find two sister concerns, **Texstyles** and **Silver Mines** (© 360313, ✆ 374211), run by friendly Goverdhan ('Gordon') Agarwal and his son Girish. Both shops offer a great export service abroad and are very tuned into what westerners like and what they are prepared to pay. You can give them any pattern of clothing or design of jewellery and they'll run it up for you in double-quick time. Texstyles offer a wide range of ready-made stuff too—garments, handicrafts and embroidery—at around 40% of prices charged by more fêted shops like **Anokhi**, 2 Tilak Marg, or **Soma**, 5 Jacob Road. Silver Mines has a regular clientele of western buyers choosing from thousands of designs—rings and earrings, bracelets and necklaces—in both Indian and continental styles. The rule here is: the more you buy, the cheaper it gets.

Leisure

If you're going to see only one Hindi **film** in India, it has to be at the Raj Mandir off M I Road. This is one of the biggest cinemas in Asia, with a mind-boggling lobby and urgently flashing lights around the screen whenever the film reaches a crescendo. To be sure of a seat, arrive at least half an hour before the film commences and push any female among you into the fast 'ladies' queue.

You can go **swimming** at the pools of hotels Mansingh Palace, Bissau Palace and Jaipur Ashok for a daily non-guest fee of Rs100. The Evergreen guest house has a small pool which costs only Rs75.

The Jai Mahal Palace hotel offers free **folk dance** programmes every evening from 7.30 to 8.30pm, preceded by a puppet show. This takes place out on the lawns, right by the bar, and is best enjoyed over a beer or cocktail. Another evening, visit the Panghat open-air theatre at the prestigious Rambagh Palace. This puts on an excellent Rajasthani folk song/dance programme from 8pm daily, cost Rs275. You can stay on afterwards for a Rajasthani buffet dinner.

For details of luxury **camel-cart and elephant safaris** to places like Pushkar, contact the rail station tourist office. They're very well priced.

Jaipur ☎ (0141–)

Where to Stay
luxury (from US$70)

Jaipur's premier hotel is Taj Group's sumptuous **Rambagh Palace** on Bhawani Singh Marg to the south of town, ☎ 381919, ✆ 381098. This magnificent old building, formerly the palace of the Maharajah of Jaipur, is a picture postcard of delicate cupolas and fretted screens amid sprawling lawns and landscaped gardens. Fully air-conditioned, it features a fantastic indoor pool, a famous polo bar and a Regency-style dining hall. The standard rooms are overpriced, but the larger, more opulent 'deluxe' rooms are a good deal at US$200.

Taj's second palace property is the smaller **Jai Mahal Palace** on Jacob Road, south of the rail station, ☎ 371616, ✆ 365237. Originally the residence of royal physicians and dewans (ministers), it may lack the character of the Rambagh, but it's newer and more functional. There are 18 acres of landscaped gardens here, as well as a fine restaurant overlooking regal lawns and a quaint *haveli*-style bar.

The third of Taj's properties, south of the city on Sardar Patel Marg, is the small but personal **Rajmahal Palace**, ✆ 381757. This was the British Residency until 1947, and has a pool, extensive gardens, a restaurant and just 13 rooms at US$70/90.

All three Taj hotels listed above give generous discounts, up to 40%, from May to September.

Finally, there's the **Hotel Mansingh Palace** in Sansar Chandra Road, ✆ 378771, ✉ 377582. It's rather run-down now, but the a/c double rooms still cost the same as they did five years ago and there's nothing wrong with the pool, the coffee shop (very cosy) or the upstairs restaurant with its panoramic city views.

moderate (from Rs700)

It's in the moderate category that Jaipur really comes into its own. If you want to live like a maharajah and don't want to pay the earth, Jaipur has four heritage hotels—all former palaces or royal residences—where for less than £20 a night you can easily imagine yourself on the set of *Heat and Dust* or *A Passage to India*.

Of the four, it's the **Hotel Bissau Palace** outside Chandpol Gate, ✆ 304371, ✉ 304628, that gets the best mentions. 'It's a real throwback to the days of the Raj,' wrote one satisfied guest. 'You half-expect Julie Christie or Greta Scacchi to appear out of the woodwork.' This place is the pre-war summer house of the *rawal* (duke) of Bissau, the most warrior-like state of Shekhawati region, and if you're lucky you may get to meet the present incumbent, Mr Sanjai ('Juno') Singh and his lovely wife 'Twinkle'. He just loves telling his foreign guests tales of 'derring do' and showing them around the property, which is choc-a-bloc with historical exhibits and royal paraphernalia, most of which belong in a Sotheby's catalogue. There's a quaint library-cum-museum here, traditional food and service, lawn tennis and badminton courts, and a small but adequate pool. Each room is beautifully done up with period furnishings and romantic lighting, so ask to see a few before accepting one.

Northeast of the old city is the similar **Samode Haveli**, ✆/✉ 42407, which was used as a location for the film *The Far Pavilions*. Originally the town house of the *rawal* of Samode (aka the prime minister of Jaipur), this 200-year-old building has a lovely open terrace area, a beautifully painted dining room and a couple of stunning suites at Rs1300/2000. Many travellers rate this place over the Rambagh Palace for style and service.

South of the city is **Narain Niwas Palace Hotel**, ✆ 562191, ✉ 563448, another wonderful old palace property which was originally the residence of the *rawal* of Kanota, 15km from Jaipur. Popular with ornithologists—it has acres of land favoured by several rare species of bird—it's a very peaceful, relaxing haven with an elegant oriental-style pool, traditional meals service and old-fashioned rooms with air-conditioning.

Another heritage hotel is **Mandawa House**, ✆ 365398, ✉ 371795, a short walk above the Arya Niwas hotel (*see* below) on the same side of Sansar Chandra Road. This is a 100-year-old house, originally the Jaipur residence of Maharajah Bhagwati

Singh of Mandawa (145km away), with a dusty old-colonial lounge, various arms and paintings dotted around the walls and liveried servants silently delivering meals on silver platters. The best rooms (actually suites) are up on the porticoed open terrace, priced from Rs800 a night.

Moving from old-style charm to modern-day personal service, the **Hotel Megh Niwas** at C-9 Sawai Jai Singh Highway, Bani Park, ✆ 322661, 🖷 321420, is a large private house with lawns front and rear, run in ultra-efficient manner by Col Fateh Singh (retired) and his charming wife Indu. The restaurant, which overlooks the relaxing garden pool, serves a wide variety of tasty meals and snacks, together with very drinkable tea. The Singhs handle all your travel arrangements, drive you round town and even help you out with your shopping. If staying here, enquire about car tours round Rajasthan and 'desert camps' at Pushkar's Camel Fair—they're good value too.

Two cheaper alternatives in Bani Park area are **Shahpura House** at D-257 Devi Marg, ✆ 321494, 🖷 367760, and **Madhuban** at D-237 Behari Marg, ✆ 319033, 🖷 322344. Both have a quiet location and nice lawns, and are run by friendly noble families.

Also recommended is the newly renovated **Alsisar Haveli**, located about a block and a half north of the Arya Niwas hotel (*see* below) on the same road. This is a beautiful property with lovely gardens and lawns, monkeys in the trees and a lovely terrace. Double rooms cost Rs1200 and the best one (no. 12) has great views.

Note: The railway tourist office has a list of paying guest houses, charging from Rs100 to Rs1000 a night.

budget

It's in this class that you have to be careful. Most of the hotels below don't pay commission to rickshaw drivers, so if they pick you up from the railway or bus station they'll either try to take you somewhere else (where they get up to 30% commission) or they'll charge you double the usual fare. As in other tourist centres, the only way round this scam is to let them take you to a hotel of their choice *near* to the one you want, and then walk the rest of the way.

The best budget bet is without doubt the spotless **Hotel Arya Niwas** just off Sansar Chandra Road, ✆ 372456, 🖷 364376. Run by a friendly family, it has delicious vegetarian food and offers a complete service to travellers—money exchange, car rental, bicycle hire, doctor-on-call, bus/rail ticketing, reconfirmation of air tickets, free baggage store, bookshop, travel agency, and full city information posted in the lobby. The sit-out verandah and garden are perfect for relaxation and the rooms are excellent value at Rs200/300 standard to Rs400/500 deluxe. Advance-book this one, as it's nearly always full.

So is the long-running **Evergreen Guest House** off M I Road, opposite the GPO, ✆ 363446, which has recently added a new pool and restaurant. Useful services include baggage store, laundry service, bus and rail ticketing, message board, travel desk, crafts shop and 24-hour fax/STD facility. Most rooms overlook the central garden courtyard and run from Rs100/120 non-a/c to Rs400/450 a/c. Dorm beds cost Rs50.

The popular **Atithi Guest House** is located at 1 Park House Scheme, Motilal Atal Road, off Station Road, ☎ 378679. This is another family-run place, offering bright and cheerful rooms, all with air-cooling and attached bath, from Rs300. Delicious meals are served either in the small dining area or up on the new rooftop garden terrace. The better rooms have private balconies. If full, try the nearby **Karni Niwas** at C-5 Motilal Atal Road, ☎ 365433. Travellers recommend it for its good meals service and clean rooms with private bath.

The **Jaipur Inn** at B-17 Shiv Marg, Bani Park, ☎ 316821, is a wonderfully eccentric place, run by a retired wing-commander who wanders around in a tweed jacket looking for new ways to make it more English. Instead of the planned English pub, he now has a pub-style restaurant on the roof with regular activities (bonfires, classical music recitals, theme dinners etc.) aimed at 'involving' his foreign guests. If you agree to cook for the hotel, he'll even give you a free room! Other services include left luggage, book exchange, message board, table games, and all-you-can-eat *thali* suppers for Rs50. Rooms go from Rs80/90 up to Rs300/500, the latter being rooftop specials with private balconies and fine views of the surrounding fort and terrain. Dorm beds cost Rs40 but many lockers are broken so bring your own padlock. For Rs25, you can camp on the lawn (if you have a tent) or in the resident van.

The cheapest of Jaipur's heritage hotels is the charming **Diggi Palace** off Sawai Ram Singh Marg, about 1km south of Ajmeri Gate, ☎ 373091, 🖃 370359. Nobody eyeing its sweeping lawns and palatial courtyard can believe it's a budget place, but rooms go as cheaply as Rs100. 'Yes,' you can tell the people back home, 'We stayed in the guest-palace of the King of Diggi, a village 80km west of Jaipur, for only two quid a night.' You can also play up the resident polo ponies, the peacocks on the lawns, the traditional meals at the terrace restaurant, and the 200-year-old banquet hall with its stunning collection of Raj memorabilia. If you can run to them, the old-colonial suites are a real snip at just under £10 a night.

Jaipur ☎ (0141–)   ***Eating Out***

Visit the **Rambagh Palace**'s magnificent dining-hall for the decor, but be warned—the food is still the hotel's weakest link. If you're going to eat here (buffet dinners are best, with live classical music thrown in) you're well advised to stick to the western dishes. Over at the **Mansingh Palace** hotel, there's an exceptional coffee shop with excellent buffets and a speciality Mughlai restaurant where you can enjoy Indian classical music along with your evening meal.

Outside of hotels, Jaipur's two finest restaurants are both on M I Road. The pure-veg **Chanakya** is always packed with local Indians, which is nice to see, and rarely costs more than £5 a head. Start with delicious tomato soup, and follow with specialities like 'chanakya special', 'veg au gratin' and 'dal makhani'. A bowl of fresh curd on the side will enhance the various flavours and ease digestion. **Niro's**, by contrast, is a real yuppie restaurant, always full of western tourists and offering all sorts of non-veg delights from Continental 'Chicken Strongoff' to Chinese jumbo prawns and Indian tandoor items. Don't worry if you have to wait for a table: it's worth it.

Non-veg food is also good at restaurants like **Golden Sands** opposite Hotel Arya Niwas, **Copper Chimney** just up from Niro's on M I Road, and **Handi** (famous for its kebabs and barbecues) opposite the GPO. The ultra-kitsch **LMB** in Johari Bazaar (old city) has slipped of late, but still fascinates with its weird 50s decor and Indian *nouvelle cuisine*. Have a pure veg meal here just for the experience.

If you're not staying at the hotel Arya Niwas, at least drop in for breakfast. Here you can enjoy a range of tasty vegetarian and western-style snacks out on the lawn, on the open-air verandah, or in the self-service restaurant. People hang out here for ages—reading, writing, playing games or simply taking in the sun—and if you don't know anybody when you arrive, you generally do by the time you leave. It's a particularly good place to come for a pot of tea.

If your taste runs to coffee, try the **Indian Coffee House** on M I Road near to Ajmeri Gate (down an alley next to Snowhite dry cleaners). It also offers cheap south Indian *dosas* and snacks, served by waiters with turbans, cummerbunds and uniformly dour expressions.

Moving On

By air: From Jaipur, **Indian Airlines** flies daily to Delhi/Bombay and four days a week to Aurangabad, Jodhpur and Udaipur. **Modiluft** has daily flights to Delhi, Bombay, Bangalore, Udaipur and Goa, also three flights weekly to Cochin. **Skyline NEPC** flies to Delhi and Bombay three days a week. **East-West Airlines** has five flights weekly to Bombay and Jodhpur.

By rail: For Delhi, there's the fully air-conditioned Shatabdi Express (dep 5.50pm daily except Thursday, 4½hrs) or the cheaper Jammu Tavi Express (dep 4.30pm, 5hrs). There's only one fast train daily to Agra at present (dep 11pm, 6hrs), due to line conversion from metre to broad gauge. Other express trains will be reintroduced shortly. Jodhpur is serviced daily by the **Intercity Express** (dep 5.30pm, 5hrs) and Udaipur by two slow trains (dep 12.20pm and 9.45pm, 12hrs). Arrival times are inconvenient though, so most people go by bus.

Ticket bookings are quick and easy from the computerized rail reservation office at the station entrance, open 8am to 8pm daily except Sundays.

By road: Deluxe buses link Jaipur hourly with Delhi (6hrs) and Agra (5hrs). There are also 6/7 departures daily to Ajmer (2½hrs), Jodhpur (7hrs) and Udaipur (10hrs). Tickets should be booked a day in advance from the new computerized reservation office on platform 1 at the central bus stand on Station Road.

A charming oasis on the very edge of the desert, Pushkar is one of those places where you come for a day or two and end up spending a week. It is a tiny pilgrim town, fronting a holy lake, separated from nearby Ajmer by the 'Snake Mountain' of Nag Pahar.

Pushkar is unique in having (allegedly) the only Brahma temple in India. The legend is that a lotus blossom (*pushpa*) fell from the hand (*kar*) of Brahma while he was searching for a place to perform his *yagna* (sacrifice), and a lake sprang up. He promptly made 'Push-kar' his home, and a temple was built in commemoration. Through the ages, Hindu pilgrims have flocked to this spot. Rama, hero of the Hindu epic *Ramayana* (1500 BC) is said to have paid his respects here, and the journals of Fa Hsien, the 4th-century AD Chinese traveller, confirm it as a major pilgrimage centre. The palaces and temples around the lake were a later addition of the Rajput maharajahs. Man Mahal, the palace built by Rajah Man Singh I of Amber, stands on the bank of the lake, and has been converted into the present Tourist Bungalow. Today, there are over 400 temples in Pushkar, and most of the population still belongs to the community of priests.

For much of the year, Pushkar is a peaceful place with the emphasis on relaxation. It has a reassuring village-style ambience—everybody knows everybody—and travellers come here for a total break from the sightseeing circuit. But at the annual **Cattle and Camel Fair** each November, it's quite a different story: up to 200,000 traders and 50,000 cattle pour into town, along with numerous festooned camels and colourful pilgrims. After 10 hectic days of livestock dealing, camel racing and colourful festivities, everybody goes for a big holy dip in the lake on the night of the full moon (*Kartik Purnima*). Billed as 'an explosion of fun, frolic, games and laughter', the fair provides some wonderful photographic opportunities and is a rare chance to see Rajasthani women decked out in all their traditional jewellery, dress and finery. If this sounds your idea of fun, contact the Rajasthan tourist office, which organizes traditional dance programmes, cultural events and tented accommodation.

Getting There

The nearest railhead is Ajmer, 13km away. There are no flights to Ajmer, only trains and buses from Ahmedabad, Delhi, Hyderabad and Udaipur, and direct buses to Pushkar from all major Rajasthan centres, plus Delhi. *See* also 'Moving On' from Pushar, p.186.

Ajmer–Pushkar transport: If you're coming in by bus or train to Ajmer, it's another 13km over the mountains to Pushkar—Rs60–70 by auto-rickshaw or Rs3 by local bus, from the stand above Ajmer railway station. If you have to stay in Ajmer for any reason, there's inexpensive accommodation available at hotels **Poonam**, ✆ 31711, and **Samrat**, ✆ 31805, both in Kutchery Road, or at RTDC's **Hotel Khadim Tourist Bungalow**, ✆ 52490, a short rickshaw ride from the bus or rail station. The only luxury option is the **Hotel Mansingh**, ✆ 425702, on the road out to Pushkar, with air-conditioned rooms for US$40/60.

Sightseeing is probably the last thing on your mind when you come here. Pushkar is a tiny, sleepy desert town which instantly envelops visitors in a calm embrace of inertia. The little activity there is—shops, restaurants and cafés—centres on the single long street which tracks round the northern end of the lake, parallel to the bathing ghats. There are no taxis or rickshaws, nor any need for them. Cycles can be hired from Moon Bicycle Works at the Ajmer bus stand, but most people prefer to walk. There's a regular parade of travellers trooping up and down the high street—trying on hippy clothing, buying silver bangles, doing *puja* at the ghats, or organizing camel treks. Spend your first day or two winding down—sunbathing, shopping, swimming and making new friends. Then, when you're up to some activity, try the following early morning jaunt.

Pushkar ✆ (0145–)	***Tourist Information***

The nearest **tourist office** is at the Khadim Tourist Bungalow in Ajmer, ✆ 52426, open 10am to 5pm except Sundays. In Pushkar itself, the Palace Hotel gives the best information. The main **GPO** is near the Marwar bus stand, open 10am to 5pm except Sunday. You may find the small sub-post office in the market more convenient. Of the several **STD booths** in the market, the most scenic is at Vahara ghat—turn up around sunset and enjoy breathtaking views while you wait for your call to go through. There is a **bank** in the main street, but hardly anyone uses it. Most people change their money on the black market.

Desert/Town Tour

On foot, 3–4 hours. Savitri Temple–Brahma Temple–Ghats–Old Pushkar.

Set out early, around 8am, to avoid the heat. Walk down to the lakeside, below the Tourist Bungalow, and cross over the narrow whitewashed bridge. At the far side, turn right and proceed up through a series of ghats until you emerge at the edge of the desert. Up ahead, atop a high peaked hill, is the small white **Savitri Temple**, dedicated to Brahma's first wife. The legend goes that after Brahma dropped his lotus flower at Pushkar, he returned to do *yagna* (purification ritual) here. Unfortunately, he didn't wait for his wife Savitri to show up. Instead, he took a substitute bride called Gayatri to help him officiate at the ceremony. Gayatri (who has a temple of her own, above Marwar bus stand) was an untouchable, and in order to make her holy, she was apparently 'put into the mouth of a cow and removed from the anus'. Drastic, but apparently effective. When Savitri finally put in an appearance, she was not amused. In fact, she began cursing people. First she cursed Vishnu with everlasting estrangement from his wife. Then she cursed Shiva with eternal unhappiness. Then she cursed the Brahmins with never-ending poverty. She even cursed Gayatri's cow. At last, having cursed everyone who had approved the marriage, she turned on Brahma himself, saying, 'Take Pushkar, it's yours. But it's going to be the only home you ever have!' With this, she stormed off up the hill and has been sulking there ever since. Brahma tried to cheer her up with the present

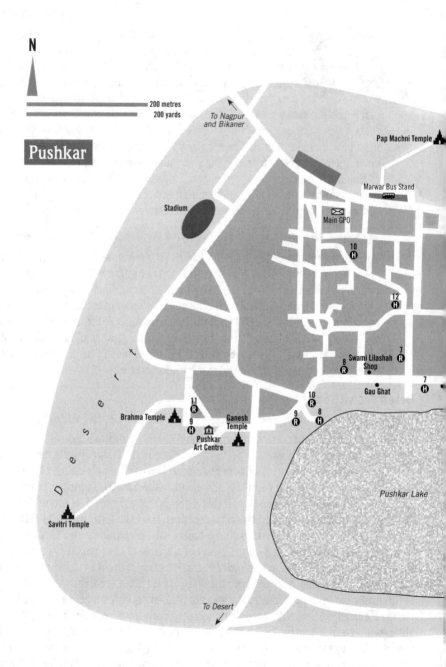

N

200 metres
200 yards

Pushkar

To Nagpur
and Bikaner

Pap Machni Temple

Marwar Bus Stand

Stadium

Main GPO

10
H

12
H

7
R

8
R
Swami Lilashah
Shop

7
H
Gau Ghat

11
R
Brahma Temple

10
R

8
H

9
H
Pushkar
Art Centre

Ganesh
Temple

9
R

D e s e r t

Pushkar Lake

Savitri Temple

To Desert

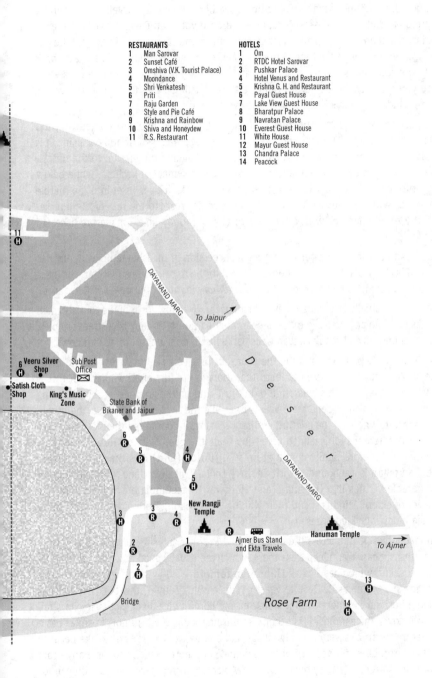

RESTAURANTS
1   Man Sarovar
2   Sunset Café
3   Omshiva (V.K. Tourist Palace)
4   Moondance
5   Shri Venkatesh
6   Priti
7   Raju Garden
8   Style and Pie Café
9   Krishna and Rainbow
10 Shiva and Honeydew
11 R.S. Restaurant

HOTELS
1   Om
2   RTDC Hotel Sarovar
3   Pushkar Palace
4   Hotel Venus and Restaurant
5   Krishna G. H. and Restaurant
6   Payal Guest House
7   Lake View Guest House
8   Bharatpur Palace
9   Navratan Palace
10 Everest Guest House
11 White House
12 Mayur Guest House
13 Chandra Palace
14 Peacock

DAYANAND MARG

To Jaipur

D e s e r t

DAYANAND MARG

Veeru Silver Shop

Sub Post Office

Satish Cloth Shop

King's Music Zone

State Bank of Bikaner and Jaipur

New Rangji Temple

Ajmer Bus Stand and Ekta Travels

Hanuman Temple

To Ajmer

Bridge

Rose Farm

temple, but she's still not happy. Going up to see her involves a marvellous 20-minute stroll across the rolling dunes—a real compensation if you didn't see any at Jaisalmer—followed by a half-hour hike up an ancient, crumbling stone stairway (built around the 4th century AD), with the views getting better the higher you go. The temple itself dates back some 2000 years, and is a small, well-kept affair. At the top, get out your camera—the views down over Pushkar and its surrounds are spectacular, while to the rear the white, undulating sands stretch back for as far as the eye can see.

Walking back across the dunes, re-enter Pushkar to the west for the pink-domed **Brahma Temple**. This is a bright, Disneyish effort—a riot of blue, green, yellow and red paint. It is immaculately clean and sits within a small enclosure backing directly on to the desert. Over the entrance gateway, you'll find the *hans* or goose symbol of Brahma, while below it (facing into the shrine) there is his 'carrier', a silver turtle. This is inset into the marble floor, together with neat serried rows of old silver coins. Walk to the rear of the temple, through the small chamber with a 'Donate to Cows' money box, for picture-postcard views of the desert.

The main road back into town runs alongside a succession of roadside temples (mainly to the left) and lakeside **ghats** (the northern series, all to the right). You can visit any of these ghats, but be warned: you'll be expected to do *Brahma puja* at least once—*see* Recreation.

Pushkar town is actually larger than may at first appear. Walking north of the touristy main street takes you into an extensive maze of charming old houses, sleepy backstreet temples, pilgrims' dharamsalas and shady banyan trees parked with dozy dogs, camels and cows.

Later on in the day, you can continue the tour, but first you need to know a little more mythology. You may be surprised to learn that there is not just one Pushkar, but three. When Brahma let fall his lotus blossom it didn't just land on the ground—it skipped along and touched down at three separate places, rather like the Barnes-Wallis bouncing bomb. **Senior Pushkar**, where all the pilgrims and tourists stay, is considered the most holy spot because this is where the lotus landed first. After that, it hopped over to **Middle Pushkar**, 2km up the road, before finally coming to rest at **Junior (Old) Pushkar**, 3km further north. Indian pilgrims are bound to visit all three spots. This duty done, they move on to other venerable venues like Badrinath and Hardwar to accumulate even more karmic virtue. A lot of elderly Hindus spend their waning years roaring from one holy spot to the next in death-defying video buses.

You can take a bicycle out across the desert to Old Pushkar and surrounding villages, and several outfits run camel and jeep treks there, which are usually good fun. You can stop off at Middle Pushkar, which has a small **Hanuman temple**, a 200-year-old banyan tree, and a natural ground-water well. Despite years of successive drought, this tank has not run dry. Middle Pushkar is where the incurably insane come twice a year, at auspicious full moons, to recover their minds. It is otherwise unremarkable. Old (Junior) Pushkar has a small **Krishna temple**, a very friendly village and a large ex-lake. It's an ex-lake because of successive droughts and because of the pipeline sunk here, which has for many years supplied water to Ajmer railway depot. It is now planted with sugar-cane and you can for the time being forget all about swimming. The legend of Old Pushkar is that the Muslim emperor Aurangzeb came here once, intent on destroying more temples. After washing his face in the lake, however, 'his hair turned grey and he began to look like an old man.' This experience apparently cured Aurangzeb of iconoclasm for life.

Pushkar (Senior) is best at sunset when the dry heat is relieved by a cool breeze, the glare of the sun dies away, and the fading desert lights turn the lake a fiery blood-crimson. As the time approaches for worship, the hundreds of little temples by the lakeside come to life and the air is filled with the clanging of bells, the beating of drums and the hypnotic drone of prayer. If you don't make it to Varanasi for sunrise over the Ganges, this is possibly the next best thing.

Shopping

Pushkar is the 'cheap and best' place to shop in all India. Like Goa and Manali, it has a long history of dealing with foreigners and is used to gearing its produce to western tastes. Here you can pick up a silk dress, a velvet top or a pair of cotton trousers for under £1, and if it doesn't quite fit a tailor will adjust it in minutes. The main street, from the Krishna Guest House all the way up to the Brahma Temple, is just one big shopping arcade left and right. Starting at Sri Venkatesh restaurant (*see* map) and working down, there's **Prem Art Emporium** for leather goods, **Ashok** (opposite Prem) for antiques and keepsakes, **Vijay Art Gallery** for paintings on silk, **Veeru's Silver Shop** ('Vimi is here') for jewellery, **Satish Cloth Shop** for woollen blankets and clothing, **Raj Kumar Jain** (opposite Satish) and nearby **Unique Jewellers** for silver, **Swami Lilashah** for clothes, textiles and embroidery, and finally **Dilip Babu** (near Bharatpur Palace) and **Pushkar Art Centre** (below Brahma temple) for more of the same. Just up from the Krishna restaurant, friendly Krishna specializes in antique silver and curios.

Pushkar is also a great place to stock up on cheap music tapes and secondhand books. There's a good selection opposite the Krishna Guest House. For Indian classical music, try **Azad Music Centre** close to Payal Guest House or **King's Good Music Zone**, nearby, which has CDs as well as cassettes.

Leisure

Swimming is available at the Peacock Hotel, the Tourist Bungalow, the Om Hotel or at JP's Tourist Village, 2km out of town. You can still swim in the lake but few people bother. Not only is it mucky, but it has dried out a lot in recent years. The reason for this drought, say locals, is that Brahma is angry with greedy *puja* boys for extorting money from tourists down at the lakeside. And it's true that no sooner have you arrived than these touts try and coax you down to one of the 52 ghats where a so-called priest is waiting to send your prayer (*puja*) to Brahma onto the lake in a leafboat filled with flowers and incense. At some point in the prayer, he'll ask you how much you intend giving to Brahma (whatever it is, it's never enough) and once you've paid, he'll whap a red string around your wrist. This is called a 'Pushkar passport', and once you've got one, you won't be bothered again.

If you want to avoid this particular scam, make your own 'passport' from a bit of cheap string in the market.

Pushkar barbers are famous. They don't just cut your hair, they give you the full works: **head/body massage** and (on request) **hair-plaits, dreadlocks and body tattoos** with fresh needles. If you want to go the whole hog, there are several self-styled 'masters of nose and ear holes' in town, who will pierce anything you like, including nipples and belly-buttons.

For evening fun, drop in on the **Sunset Café**. In season, there's usually something going on: a party, a bonfire, a music evening or just good old Bob Marley pumping out of the sound system. Be discreet with drugs, though—police informers are all over the place.

Camel treks are a great thing to do, especially around full moon. Actually, the best place to *be* at full moon is on a camel, since the noise of temple bells round the ghats, combined with rave/reggae sounds from the Sunset Café, will, if you're staying anywhere near the lake, keep you awake till dawn. Camel treks from Pushkar are far superior to ones from Jaisalmer—here you hit the dunes within minutes and the desert-scape is far more diverse and interesting. There's no problem finding a camel trek (they generally find you) but you should always ask what is included in the price before booking. The better treks charge around Rs200–250 per night and include meals, a camp fire and some sort of music/dance entertainment. If you want alcohol (not allowed in Pushkar proper) you'll have to pay extra in advance. For many, a short 2/3-hour trek out to the dunes for the sunset will be sufficient. In this case, contact Mr Jagat Singh at the Pushkar Palace Hotel. He also offers 'luxury' treks (Rs750/day) to off-the-beaten-track venues, with overnight stays in comfortable tents.

desert camps

You don't have to wait till the annual Camel Fair for a desert camp experience. Colonel Fateh Singh's **Desert Camp**, located on his farm on the outskirts of Pushkar, now runs from October right through to March. Here you can enjoy a tent-style holiday in the desert from US$50 (shared toilet) to US$100 (own toilet) per night. The price includes bonfire barbecues, traditional music/dance programmes, camel/horse rides and all meals. To book, contact Hotel Megh Niwas in Jaipur, ✆ (0141) 322661. The more upmarket **Royal Desert Camp** offered by Mr Jagat Singh at Pushkar Palace Hotel has deluxe tents for US$85 and 'Swiss cottages' for US$115, but runs only during the Pushkar Fair and at Christmas/New Year. Finally, there's the super-deluxe **Royal Camp** offered by Maharaja Resorts, c/o Umaid Bhavan Palace, Jodhpur, ✆ (0291) 33316 ext. 231. This provides custom-made tents, each with its own verandah, bedroom and bath-room, for US$75/125. The price includes all entertainments as well as camel treks and 'royal' Rajasthani cuisine. It operates at the Pushkar Fair, at Christmas/New Year and at the Nagaur Camel Fair (*see* p.162) in January/February.

The place to stay is **Hotel Pushkar Palace** overlooking the lake, ☎ 72001, ✆ 72226. Originally the summer palace of the Maharajah of Kishangarh, this 400-year-old building is a model of desert-palace architecture, lovingly restored to its former glory by present proprietor Mr Jagat Singh. The staff are friendly, the food good, and the sun roof ideal for sunbathing. Every evening, people gather from all over town to watch the sunset from the palm-laden garden patio, often staying on for simple but tasty buffet dinners in the attached restaurant. There are still a few cheap/mid-range rooms at Rs150/450, but most rooms are now a/c deluxe at Rs950/1050. The best two (nos. 111 and 112) have premier views of the lake and ghats.

Next door is the government-run RTDC **Hotel Sarovar Tourist Bungalow**, ☎ 72040. Formerly the property of the Jaipur maharajahs—they came here at festival time to do *puja* and to buy horses and camels for their cavalry—it's rather run-down nowadays but is quieter than the Palace Hotel and has a pool and a restaurant. Rooms are a lot cheaper too, from Rs100/125 ordinary to Rs275/350 lakeview, and there are dorm beds for Rs50. Take the time to look around before choosing digs—there's a great choice, including a couple of tiny "turret' rooms where you open the door and literally fall onto the bed—it's the only piece of furniture they can squeeze in! During the high season, room rates rise by Rs40 but include a free buffet dinner.

Apart from the big two, there are dozens of cheap guest houses offering basic rooms for around Rs50/100 or Rs100/200 with bath attached. The better ones, starting at the Tourist Bungalow and working up the market, are **Hotel Om**, ☎ 2143, with a dinky pool and friendly management, **Krishna Guest House**, ☎ 72091, with a rooftop restaurant, **Hotel Venus**, ☎ 72323, with a better rooftop restaurant, Suresh's **Payal Guest House**, ☎ 72163, with a relaxing garden courtyard and sun terrace, the **Lake View**, ☎ 72106, with some lake-view rooms and a great viewpoint terrace, **Bharatpur Palace**, behind Krishna restaurant, with more nice views, and **Navratan Palace** below the Brahma temple, with a (leaky) pool.

On the road out of town, above the Ajmer bus stand, there's the popular **Peacock Hotel**, ☎ 2093, with a pool and jacuzzi, a garden restaurant and rooms from Rs150 to Rs550. Dorm beds cost Rs50. The nearby **Chandra Palace** has a quiet rural setting and a few large, airy rooms at Rs100; it's rather like living on a farm.

North of town, on the way to Marwar bus stand, there's a clutch of decent cheapies including **White House**, **Everest**, **Evergreen** and **Mayur**. The first two get the best mentions.

Finally, on the path leading down to the Pushkar Palace Hotel, there's the reliable **V K Tourist Palace**, the proposed **Buddha On The Lake**, and just below the Palace Hotel the much-maligned **Sunset Café**, with surprisingly nice rooms from Rs200.

A lot of travellers get sick in Pushkar, either from eating cheap buffet dinners that have been reheated or left out too long, or from dining off plates that have been washed in scummy lake water. The worst offenders are the rash of rooftop restaurants that have sprung up all over town. Of these, only the **Venus**, the **Krishna**, and the **Om Shiva** at V K Tourist Palace are entirely safe. Take care too with Pushkar's famous 'special' *lassis*. Many restaurants sell these marijuana-based drinks, but they're lethal.

If you do get sick, avoid Pushkar's notorious hospital. Go instead to St Francis's Nursing Home in Ajmer.

For just 50 pence you can score a 'special *thali*' at the Venus or a top breakfast buffet at the Om Shiva. Elsewhere, there are a few decent garden restaurants including **Raju's** opposite Hotel Lake View, **Priti** opposite the bank, and **Moondance** near Om Hotel. The latter has a German bakery, as do the **Pushkar Palace Hotel** and the **Sunset Café**. The latter is where the Goa crowd collect to play rave/techno sounds and to watch the sunset. If you just want a bit of peace and quiet, the **Man Sarovar** below Ajmer bus stand serves up good wholesome food in a laid-back garden setting. The **Sri Venkatesh**, Pushkar's original restaurant, fell into a hole in the road recently but is now back in business, serving good and cheap veggie fare to hungry pilgrims. Last, try **Kashmiri Fruit Juice** next to Payal Guest House for juices, **Lalita Restaurant** at the bottom of the market (where it bends to the left) for top *lassis*, and **Style & Pie Café** near Gau Ghat for yum-yum cheesecake, chocolate cake and brownies.

Carnivores fed up with pure veg living in Pushkar can escape to Hotel Mansingh in Ajmer—only 30 minutes away by auto-rickshaw— where they can enjoy a couple of beers and a plate of chicken tikka masala, accompanied most evenings by live traditional music. While in Ajmer, check out **Heera Pana** wine shop on Prithviraj Road, opposite the Municipal Office. It's one of the few places in India where you can buy imported French champagne—it's only Rs400 a bottle and very acceptable.

Moving On

By rail: From Ajmer, the Shatabdi Express leaves daily for New Delhi (dep 3.10pm, arr 10.15pm) via Jaipur (arr 5.35pm). The fast train to Udaipur is the overnight Chetak Express (dep 12.30am, arr 8.30am).

By road: Pushkar has two bus terminals: Marwar bus stand to the north of town and Ajmer bus stand to the east. The local bus from Ajmer (30mins) terminates at the Ajmer bus stand, and it is from here that buses return to Ajmer (direct to the rail station, Rs4) every half hour or so from 6am to 8.40pm. Deluxe buses to Delhi (9hrs), Jaipur (3hrs), Jodhpur (5hrs), Udaipur (8hrs), Jaisalmer (9/10hrs), Mount Abu and Ahmedabad are sold by **Ekta Travels**, © 72131, with offices at both bus stands. All the above buses start from Marwar bus stand and pick up from Ajmer bus stand 15 minutes later, before proceeding to their destinations. Ekta also handles air and rail ticket bookings and offers taxis at very reasonable rates, e.g. Rs1000 to Jodhpur, Rs2200 to Jaisalmer.

Deluxe buses to Udaipur arrive around 3am in the morning, a bad time to start looking for digs. Unless you're booked into the Rang Niwas Hotel (*see* p.219), you're well advised to take the train or to catch a morning bus from Ajmer which gets you to Udaipur in the early evening.

Jodhpur
population 725,000

Thar Desert

Situated close to the edge of the Thar Desert, Jodhpur is the second city of Rajasthan. It was founded by Rao Jodha in 1459, following the capture of the old capital of Mandore nearby, home of the Rathore Rajputs since the 12th century. Lying on the rich camel caravan routes, it became a very wealthy city, with stately palaces, beautiful buildings and gracious temples. Up until recently, it was capital of the state of Marwar.

Jodhpur's pride is her mighty, 15th-century Meherangarh Fort, which stands on a low range of sandstone hills. It lies within the 10km-long stone wall encircling the old city and has eight immense gates. Facing the fort, on the other side of the city, is the magnificent Umaid Bhawan Palace. A modern creation, completed in 1945, it was the then Maharajah's way of keeping his population busy during a time of severe famine. Today, it is one more of Rajasthan's fantasy hotels.

Jodhpur is one of India's most interesting cities, especially in the narrow, bustling streets and bazaars of the old city, and there is a great deal to see and do. Most travellers, however, use it simply as a jumping-off point to nearby Jaisalmer (west), Udaipur (south) and Jaipur (northeast), and few linger more than a day or two. This is a shame, since few places in India have finer palaces or bazaars, and the fort is perhaps the best-preserved and most attractive in the country.

Of late, Jodhpur has undergone something of a transformation. Lots of modern buildings, mainly in red sandstone, have sprung up south of the city walls, lending it a sophisticated 'new town' feel. The old city remains pretty much unchanged, but if you travel up to the fort by rickshaw you'll be struck by how much cleaner and less congested it is than either Jaipur or Delhi—much easier on the eye too. Looking down from the top of the fort over the neat, serried ranks of brilliant-blue Brahmin houses, you can see why Jodhpur has been termed the 'blue city' of Rajasthan, just as Jaipur and Jaisalmer are called the 'pink' and 'amber' cities respectively. The test of Jodhpur's growing popularity is the rapid acceleration of foreign visitors to its famous fort: over 50,000 in 1995, compared to 4000 in 1980.

Getting There

Jodhpur can be reached by air from Bombay, Delhi, Jaipur, Jaisalmer and Udaipur. There are also buses and trains from these places, and Pushkar, though train services in Rajasthan are presently disrupted. *See* also 'Moving On' from Jodhpur, p.196.

The airport is 5km from the city, about Rs30 by auto-rickshaw or Rs70 by taxi.

Getting Around

 For a large city, Jodhpur is quite easy to negotiate. The central market cuts through the centre of town, with the tourist office, bus stand and railway station to the south, the fort and the old city to the north. For in-town transport, you have auto-rickshaws (real bandits; go for a half-day rate of Rs150 rather than haggling over every fare), tempo minibuses (useful for visiting Mandore) and horse-drawn tongas (from the railway station, Rs5 per km). Bicycles can be rented for Rs10 per day from outside the Kalinga restaurant or from just inside Jalori Gate. Non-metered taxis can be hired from the better hotels and should charge around Rs5 per km. A 4-hour sightseeing programme, taking in all the major points of interest, will cost a fixed Rs500.

For those short on time, the major sights are well covered by RTDC's half-day city sightseeing tours (*see* 'Tourist Information'). Licensed guides can be hired at the fort (Rs80/120 per half/full day). If you want them to join you on the bus, make that clear from the start. Otherwise, they'll only guide you round the fort.

Jodhpur ℃ (0291–)   ### Tourist Information

The new **Tourist Reception Centre**, next to the Tourist Bungalow in High Court Road, ℃ 45083, is open 9am–7pm daily. Staff are helpful and full information on accommodation and transport is posted. The adjoining Tourist Bungalow sells the good half-day city **sightseeing tours**—two daily, starting at 9am and at 2pm.

Jodhpur

HOTELS
1 Adarsh Niwas Hotel & Shanti Bhawan Lodge
2 Ajit Bhawan Palace
3 Fort View Guest House
4 Galaxy
5 Ghoomer Tourist Bungalow
6 City Palace
7 Karni Bhawan
8 Residency
9 Umaid Bhawan Palace

RESTAURANTS
1 Agra Sweet Home

Jaswant Thada
Nagauri Gate
To Balsamand & Mandore
Fatehpole
Meherangarh and Museum
Sardar Market
Clock Tower
State Bank of India
Central Bus Stand
Government Museum
Raika Bagh Railway Station
NAI SARAI
Zoo
Tourist Reception Centre
To Ajmer & Jaipur
High Court Road
Circuit House
Antique Shops
To Chopasni
Siwanchi Gate
Railway Booking Office
GPO
GAVSHALA ROAD
Jalori Gate
Jodhpur Railway Station
AIRPORT ROAD
N
To Udaipur & Mt Abu
RATANADA ROAD
Indian Airlines
500 metres
500 yards
To Airport

The new **GPO** is a short walk north of the railway station. **East-West Airlines**, ✆ 37343, is in front of **Indian Airlines**, ✆ 36757, on Airport Road. For **Jagson Airlines**, ✆ 44010, ext 360, and **Modiluft**, ✆ 48333, enquire at the Tourist Bungalow. You can phone home from the **STD booths** across the road from the railway station, opposite Midtown restaurant. A good **bookshop** is Sarvodaya, above Kalinga restaurant.

City Tour

By tour bus, half day. Umaid Bhawan Palace–Meherangarh Fort and Museum–Jaswant Thada–Mandore Gardens.

The stately **Umaid Bhawan Palace** was commenced in 1929 by Maharajah Umaid Singh—probably as 'famine relief work' for his drought-stricken subjects—and took 13 years, with 3000 labourers working day and night, to complete. Its architect, H.V. Lancaster, was told to build a structure to rival if not surpass that of Lutyens' Delhi, which was then under construction. The result was an exquisite example of the art-deco style of the '30s, covering a built-up area of 3½ acres. Many features, notably the side minarets, are reminiscent of Lutyens' Rashtrapati Bhavan in New Delhi. The palace is a masterpiece of construction, fashioned completely of interlocking sandstone blocks; like a giant Lego set, it can be dismantled anytime and reassembled anywhere. The structure is dominated by a central dome which rises 56 metres high and provides a natural source of light and cross-ventilation. Today, the palace is part hotel, part maharajah's residence and part museum. The sophisticated young Maharajah still lives in, making this the largest private residence in India.

Entry to the palace is restricted; unless you are a hotel guest, you have to pay the stiff Rs330 visiting fee, which is then deducted from any food or drink you have here. The **museum** (*open 9am–5pm, adm Rs45*), features an illuminated model of the palace (prepared in England as a design model for the actual building), beautiful miniature paintings, elegant Grecian-style paintings by the European painter S. Norblin, delicate Japanese/Chinese china and pottery, an exquisite collection of clocks and a 3-D portrait of Maharajah Umaid Singh. Wandering round the palace, you'll find a weird Roman bath and a stuffed bear waiter (with white gloves and wine tray) standing outside the restaurant. The whole thing is one big memory trip for anyone who remembers the Raj, and a real eye-opener for anyone who doesn't.

If not on tour, it's a pleasant auto-rickshaw ride (or 30-minute walk from Jalori Gate) up to **Fatehpol**, the entrance to the fort. The drive north takes you through the old city market, a teeming thoroughfare of narrow, winding lanes crammed with bicycles, carts, cows and camels. If you get stuck in the narrow-lane traffic (and this is common) watch out for young lads playing 'catch that rat' with live examples. It's not unknown for flying rodents to end up in stationary rickshaws.

The **Meherangarh (Majestic) Fort** is Rajasthan's finest. Built on solid rock, towering 400ft above the plains, this massive 15th-century fort was once described by Kipling as 'the work of angels, fairies and giants'. It was never captured, and if you attempt the climb up there—a crippling 30-minute ascent, via huge gates pocked with cannonball scars and daubed with *sati* handprints—you'll know why.

The remarkable **museum** at the top (*open 9am–1pm and 3–5pm in winter; 8am–1pm and 3–6pm in summer*) is worth every paisa of the Rs50 admission. This charge includes a guided tour by smartly uniformed attendants who explain the history and contents of the museum in impeccable English. The Rs50 camera charge is a bit steep, despite excellent photography, but the Rs10 lift ticket saves you a long climb, if you're on foot, and the Rs50 fee for an earphone-cassette set is definitely worth it. All tickets should be purchased together at the main entrance, to save repeated queueing.

The fort-museum houses 18 different sections, full of well-displayed antiquities. Nowhere else in India will you find so much opulence, ostentation and fine craftsmanship in one place. Starting with the chamber full of baby-carriages (home of many fledgling maharajahs), you'll pass through a whole series of palaces and courtyards before coming to the show-stopping royal bedchamber. Festooned with coloured Christmas balls and bedecked with wall-to-wall carpets, mirrors and mosaics, this is an enormous room with a stunning centrepiece: the vast bed where the Maharajah entertained his 35 wives. Below is Maharajah Bhai Singh's 18th-century **Dancing Hall**—the fort's principal attraction—with a ceiling of pure gold, all 80kg of it. The armoury section has a brace of gigantic elephant guns and leads on to a rich assortment of elephant howdahs, folk music instruments, palanquins, furniture and costumes. In the tent room, you'll find a huge Mughal tent made of silk and velvet for the Emperor Shah Jahan.

The museum is in superb condition throughout. Unlike so many of India's palace attractions, the mosaics of jewels and semi-precious stones, painstakingly inlaid into marble walls, ceilings and floors, have not been picked out by invaders or tourists, leaving it in pretty much the same condition as when first built. If you've only got time for one sight in Jodhpur, make it this.

Certain sections of the fort—notably the ladies' quarters inside the museum—provide fine views down over the Brahmin quarter of town, which is painted bright blue in honour of Lord Krishna. To see all this royal blue to best advantage, though, head out of the museum past the Sun Goddess (Chamundi) temple until you reach the fort rampart. This gives the best overall view over Jodhpur city, and has one of the rarest displays of cannon in India.

The exit from the fort is to the left as you leave the museum. Just above the **Hero's Chhatri**, a monument to a brave hero who fell out of a window, there's a sharp bend in the road. The left fork leads down to **Jaswant Thada**, the white-marble cenotaph to Maharajah Jaswant Singh II built in 1899. Also here are the translucent marble tombs and portraits of the 12 rulers of old Mandore, with the royal crematorium nearby. If this doesn't appeal, the right fork takes you down (if you're on foot) to lively **Sadar Market** with its quaint clock tower. From here, it's right again into **Central Market** (*see* 'Shopping') or a short rickshaw ride to colourful **Umaid Gardens** near the Tourist Bungalow with its small and sleepy zoo. At the northeastern end of the gardens, you'll find the **Government Museum** (*open 10am–noon and 3–5pm daily exc Fri; adm Rs2*). This has some nice porcelain and pottery pieces, some boring bits of old rock from Mandore, and some stuffed predators and reptiles restlessly roaming the walls. On entrance you are warned that 'Dogs and Hobnail Boots Are Not Allowed'.

The tour bus proceeds from the fort and Jaswant Thada to **Mandore**, the old capital of Marwar, which lies 10km to the north of Jodhpur city. If visiting independently, minibuses go there every few minutes from outside the Tourist Bungalow, fare Rs5.

From its (probable) founding in the 6th century, Mandore was mostly ruled by the Rajput Rathore clan, but was periodically captured by the Delhi sultans and other invaders. Originally an important centre of architecture and culture, as indicated by the many ancient sculptures found here, Mandore is today a popular local picnic spot with extensive gardens and high rock terraces.

The famous **Mandore Gardens** are most beautiful in March/April, when all the flowers are in full bloom, though the magnificent rose garden comes into its own in February. A riot of bougainvillaea, sunflowers, azaleas, tobacco plants and wall flowers, the general overall effect is that of an English country garden, and the air is heavy with the scent of flowers. As you stroll around, you'll find many unusual species of cacti, a greenhouse with no glass in it, several species of birds and monkeys, and flocks of strutting peacocks. At the top of the gardens are the impressive cenotaphs of the old Jodhpur rulers, most of them in excellent condition. They are raised on high terraces, their soaring spires and exquisite sculptures a tribute to Mandore's high architectural tradition. Mostly constructed of red sandstone, these *devals* or royal cenotaphs were built in the form of temples, to immortalize the memory of Maharajah Jaswant Singh and other rulers.

The nominal entry fee to the gardens includes access to the strange **Government Museum**, *open 9am–1pm and 3–5pm daily exc Fri)*. This houses an elegant display of lacquer, wood and ivory crafts, but is mainly remarkable for its astonishing collection of tat: a giant model ear, an odd montage of human entrails, a boil-ridden child and a ghastly flayed traffic policeman. A dark, dank tunnel, with stuffed bullocks and crocodiles lurking in the gloom, leads down to the **Hall of Heroes**, a collection of 18th-century figures carved out of the rock wall, and the temple of 330 million Hindu gods, full of painted deities, spirits and divinities.

Out of the museum, it's a 15-minute walk up to the hills beyond the lake to the ruins of old Mandore fort and palaces. The **Balsamund Lake Palace**, site of the maharajahs' beautiful fruit orchards, is located 1½km beyond the museum. The reservoir was first created in AD 1159. Mandore's own gardens, prettily illuminated in the evenings (in season), are worth staying back to see.

Returning from Mandore, you can get down from the bus 2km before Jodhpur city for the small walled town of **Mahamandir** (Great Temple). A hundred pillars support the roof of this unique structure, and the interior is richly ornamented with bas-relief designs depicting various postures of yoga.

Shopping

The famous jodhpurs (polo pants) are now out of fashion, and you'll be hard pressed to find a tailor in town who can make them. Try Sohan Singh at **India Tailor** on High Court Road, between Sojati Gate and the Tourist Bungalow. Alternatively, ferret around in the market. One girl came up with a perfect pair of faded antique jodhpurs—complete with silver buttons and royal stains—for only Rs50. They were repaired by **Roopali** tailor, opposite the Fort View Guest House.

A good buy in Jodhpur, at least until recently, was antique furniture. There's a group of handicraft shops below Umaid Bhawan Palace who will, if you show genuine interest, open up their back yards and show you their collections. Be warned, however: most of what you'll see will be clever reproductions of original furniture, not the real thing. Regular western dealers have already creamed off the best pieces, and unless you know your antiques it's generally not a good idea to lash out lots of money, especially in view of the freight costs of sending furniture back home.

Jodhpur is a shopping attraction less for its handicrafts than for its large, vibrant Central or Old Market, now known as the **Ghasmandi Bazaar**. This clean, colourful and friendly market is many people's favourite in India. There is no pressure on you to buy; the atmosphere is relaxing and civilized; and the air is sweet with spices and perfumes. Also, a big plus, the bazaar is divided into sections: starting from the Clock Tower, there is first a general market, then a series of other markets for cloth and textiles, for ivory and bamboo, for jewellery, silks and spices, and finally for fruit, vegetables and sweets. Check out the old stone-carved *havelis* (merchants' houses) above the shop fronts, and look out for the charming **Krishna Temple**, with its ceiling watercolours and 'scientific quartz clock', located halfway down the market through a small gate on the left.

Leisure

Swimming is available at the underground pools of the City Palace and Ratanada Polo hotels for Rs200 per day (Rs100 per day out of season). To get in, look presentable and ask politely.

There are no organized culture shows as such, but the Ajit Bhawan Palace offers a nightly **Rajasthani folk music/dance** programme from 6 to 8pm in its courtyard. For local **cinema** listings, buy a copy of *Rajasthan Patrika* newspaper.

Jodhpur ℂ *(0291–)*

Where to Stay
luxury (from US$125)

Welcomgroup's **Umaid Bhawan Palace**, ℂ 33316, ℊ 35373, has recently been renovated without losing any of its charm or regal ambience. Here, as the brochure says, you really can live like a Maharajah. This place has one of the largest collections of 1930s art-deco in the world, in addition to an underground pool, two dining halls, badminton and tennis courts, and lavish flare-lit buffets on the sweeping lawns. It's a great place to send a postcard home from, if you can afford to stay, and in the low season (when rates are discounted by 40%) this becomes quite possible. On the down side, food and service are not up to scratch, and the ordinary rooms are very ordinary indeed. If you're going to spend a night here, opt for one of the sumptuous suites from US$250.

> The Umaid Bhawan Palace has to be the most luxurious place to spend a penny in India. 'To say the toilets are opulent is an understatement,' wrote one satisfied customer. 'There are two sofas, two armchairs and a tiger-skin hanging from the wall—and that's before you get to the urinals!'

The new **Hotel Ratanada Polo** on Residency Road, ✆ 319102, 📠 33118, may lack the character of the Palace hotel, but is certainly cooler. It is fully air-conditioned, with a nice pool and restaurant, a smart tennis court, and large bright rooms/suites from US$125/170. Again, there are substantial discounts in the off-season.

moderate (from Rs700)

The recently revamped **Ajit Bhawan Palace Hotel** on Airport Road, ✆ 37410, 📠 37774, is now the most sublime piece of high kitsch in Rajasthan. It's a self-contained low-level fortress, complete with turrets and battlements, a fantasy swimming pool (with giant waterwheel and grotto bar), a Flintstones-style 'rocks' restaurant, an antique bullock chariot on the lawn and 20 or so stone cottages dotted around a central desert-village compound. Each of these cottages has a theme and, if you decide to stay, you should see a few (including the 'milkman's' room and the 'room with a tree') before accepting one. Cottages go for around £20 and are generally booked out before the pricier old-colonial suites in the main building. The palace belongs to Maharajah Swaroop Singh, the present Maharajah's uncle, who often joins his foreign guests on organized jeep safari out to nearby villages. These start at 9am daily (subject to demand) and are good value at Rs450 including lunch.

Handy for the airport, **Hotel Karni Bhawan**, ✆ 32220, 📠 33495, is a charming heritage hotel built in the style of a colonial bungalow. Owned by the Maharajah's private secretary, Mr Sunder Singh, this is a peaceful, relaxing retreat from the heat and dust of the city centre. Here you can enjoy Royal Rajasthani campfire suppers in the *dhani* village-hut complex (accompanied by live folk music) or sip exotic local cocktails on the immaculate lawns. The rooms are well-furnished, but it's worth paying extra for one of the beautiful suites with four-poster beds. The new twin pool is a bonus, as is the upcoming bar.

Three swish new hotels, all charging under £20 for a/c rooms, are the **Residency** at H C Colony Road, ✆ 31747, the **Sandu Palace** at 169 Ajit Colony, ✆ 32611, and the **City Palace** at 9 Nai Sarak, near the Clock Tower (off New Road), ✆ 39033. The last two have cheaper non-a/c rooms also.

budget

The convenient **Hotel Adarsh Niwas** opposite the railway station, ✆ 23658, has an air-conditioned bar and clean rooms with TV at Rs400/550 or Rs600/800 with a/c. RTDC's **Ghoomar Tourist Bungalow** on High Court Road, ✆ 44010, has huge double rooms, very quiet and with bath attached, for Rs200. City tour buses and the bus to Jaisalmer leave from here, so it can be a convenient place to stay. There are also a/c rooms from Rs400 and dorm beds for Rs40.

The **Fort View Guest House** inside Jalori Bari, ✆ 39923, is run by a friendly Brahmin ex-teacher, Allen, who really looks after his 'fatigued foreign friends'. Rooms start at Rs40 and are pretty basic, but there's a nice one on the roof for Rs100 and a big 'suite' downstairs for Rs150. Meals are interesting—chocolate tea, rose-water *lassi* and 'different varieties of Rajasthani Royal Food'. The fort view is on the sun roof.

On the circle below the tourist bungalow, there's the clean and good **Hotel Galaxy**, ✆ 25098, with rooms from Rs200. The run-down **Shanti Bhawan Lodge** opposite the station has cheap rooms from Rs50/75. If you're really counting the rupees, the **railway station** has 'retiring rooms' (doubles with attached bath) for Rs90 and dorm beds for Rs50. Bookings are through the International Tourist Bureau inside the station.

The Tourist Reception Centre offers a directory of paying-guest houses from Rs100 to 1000 per night.

Jodhpur ✆ *(0291–)*   ***Eating Out***

For a big night out, choose between the **Umaid Bhawan Palace** and the **Ajit Bhawan Palace**. Both hotels have popular evening buffets—for Rs550 and Rs200 respectively—with live classical music from 7.30pm onwards. Of the two, the Ajit Bhawan's **Rocks** restaurant has by far the better food. If you must eat at the Umaid Bhawan, try its **Risala** coffee shop—far cheaper than the **Marwar Hall**'s buffet and far less spicy too. Meals at both hotels should be advance booked, especially in high season.

The multi-cuisine **Kalinga** restaurant opposite the rail station gets a lot of tourist business. Prices have gone up some, but it's still excellent value. Rs70 buys you a great continental breakfast or, up to 6.30pm, a massive veg/non-veg *thali*. Also on offer are pizzas, sandwiches, *dosas*, shakes and ice creams. The favourite local snack is baked beans on toast.

A few doors down, the **Midtown** restaurant has a similar menu at rather less cost. It's a pure veg place specializing in south Indian cuisine—the Rs40 'super family *dosa*' has to be seen to be believed, and if you're here at the weekend they lay on a special Rajasthani *thali*. This is also a good joint for veggie burgers and *lassis*.

Makhania lassi, Jodhpur's favourite tipple, is best tried at **Agra Sweets** opposite Sojati Gate. Flavoured with saffron and very sweet, you'll either like it or hate it. Whatever, this small shop sells over 1000 glasses a day in the summer heat.

For pure veg food and good coffee, try **Pushpa Dal Bati** just outside Jalori Gate. Near Sojati Gate, you'll find **Jodhpur Coffee House**, full of *thali* aficionados and coffee-slurping locals.

The **Refreshment Room** on the first floor of the railway station is also popular for *thalis* and is a good place to fill up before boarding the train to Jaisalmer.

By air: Indian Airlines flies four days a week to Bombay, Udaipur, Jaipur and Delhi. Jagson Airlines offers three flights a week to Delhi and Jaisalmer. Modiluft flies daily to Delhi, Jaipur and Udaipur. East-West has an erratic flight service to Jaipur and Bombay.

By rail: Until conversion from metre to broad-gauge track is complete, there is only one train from Jodhpur to Jaisalmer daily, leaving 10.15pm and arriving 6.30am. Other useful trains are the Intercity Express to Jaipur (dep 6am, 4½hrs), the 10.30am and 10.30pm expresses to Udaipur (11hrs), and the 6.30pm Mandore Express to Delhi (11hrs).

To grab the tourist quota for busy trains to Jaisalmer, go straight to the railway reservation office on Station Road, next to the GPO. Open till 8pm daily, this office is fully computerized and can block-book tickets for all other places on your itinerary. If you're in Jodhpur only for the day, you can leave your bags (and even have a shower) at the International Tourist Bureau inside the rail station.

By road: Frequent buses to Jaisalmer are sold by private companies opposite the railway station. From the Ghoomar Tourist Bungalow there are half-hourly deluxe buses to Jaipur (7hrs), six buses a day to Udaipur (7hrs), two buses daily to Chittorgarh (dep 11.30am and 10.30pm, 8hrs), to Pushkar (dep 7.30am and 10am, 5hrs) and to Abu Road (7.15am and 6pm, 6hrs); also one bus a day to Delhi (dep 4pm, 12hrs) and to Ahmedabad (dep 6pm, 11hrs). The fast minibus to Jaisalmer leaves 5.30am daily and takes only 5 hours. Unless you're into long train journeys, it's by far the best bet.

For car hire to Jaisalmer/Udaipur, phone **Dial and Travels** on ✆ 33336. Ask for Vivi and enquire about his 'village safaris' by car in the Jodhpur area. They cost Rs250 per person (inclusive of food) and are apparently a good day out.

Ranakpur

The early bus from Jodhpur to Udaipur makes an unmissable stop here, for some of the biggest and best Jain temples in India. You'll arrive around 10am, and even if you're not staying the night you'll have time to explore the temples at leisure before hopping on one of the mid-afternoon buses to Udaipur.

Ranakpur's temples are beautifully preserved, and compare favourably with Mount Abu's Dilwara group. Built in 1439, the main **Chaumukha ('Four-Faced') Temple** is a massive marble structure dedicated to Lord Adinath and containing 29 halls supported by 1444 pillars, no two the same. One of the largest and most important Jain temples in India, it is flanked by two smaller temples to Neminath/Parasnath, and there's also a Sun Temple nearby. Non-Jains can enter from noon to 5pm daily, but must leave their shoes and any leather articles at the entrance. Admission is free, and the Rs20 camera charge permits you to photograph anything except Jain deities.

To stay, there's the bland RTDC **Hotel Shilpi Tourist Bungalow**, ℭ 26, with rooms for Rs125/150, or Rs200/250 with air-cooling.

A more attractive alternative is the **Maharani Bagh**, ℭ 3705, 4km up the road from Ranakpur on the way to Jodhpur, with comfy cottage accommodation for Rs675/975 and a full meals service. It's a family-style place, very hospitable, with (on request) horse safaris, visits to neighbouring villages and a chance to experience the local opium ceremonies. In this neck of the woods, people don't say 'Good morning'—they say 'Have you had your opium yet?' To book this place, contact Maharaja Resorts c/o Umaid Bhawan Palace, ℭ (0291) 33316 ext 231, ℘ 35373.

Jaisalmer   population 45,000

Jaisalmer, the 'Oasis of Jaisal', was founded in 1156 by the Bhati prince Jaisal to replace the old capital of Lodruva, 17km away, which had proved too vulnerable to attacks from neighbouring tribes. Perched on a high hill within the powerful embrace of the Meru mountains and enfolded by solid yellow-sandstone battlements and fortified walls, it was built to last. Best of all, it lay directly on the camel caravan routes leading out to Sind (now in Pakistan), which brought its Jain merchants and bankers great power and wealth between the 14th and 16th centuries. In thanks for their good fortune, and as an external depiction of status, they spent heavily on domestic architecture—leading to the creation of the famous Jaisalmer *havelis* or merchants' houses, with their intricate trellis-work balconies, ornamented windows and domed arches; and the equally distinctive Jain

Jaisalmer. Rajasthan

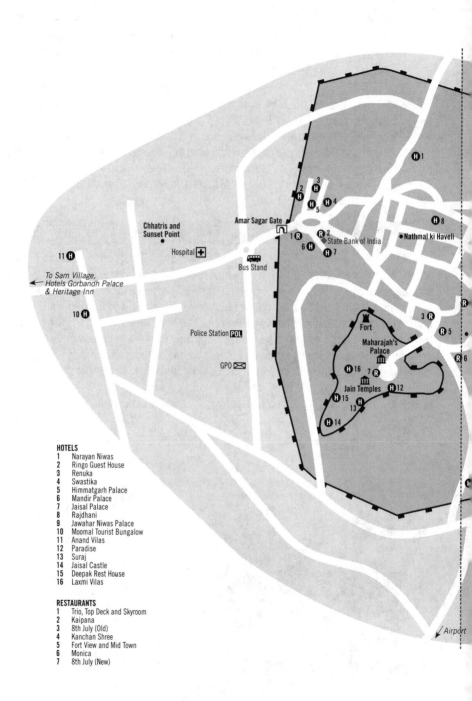

Chhatris and
Sunset Point

Amar Sagar Gate

State Bank of India

Hospital

Nathmal ki Haveli

Bus Stand

To Sam Village,
Hotels Gorbandh Palace
& Heritage Inn

Fort

Maharajah's
Palace

Police Station POL

GPO

Jain Temples

HOTELS
1 Narayan Niwas
2 Ringo Guest House
3 Renuka
4 Swastika
5 Himmatgarh Palace
6 Mandir Palace
7 Jaisal Palace
8 Rajdhani
9 Jawahar Niwas Palace
10 Moomal Tourist Bungalow
11 Anand Vilas
12 Paradise
13 Suraj
14 Jaisal Castle
15 Deepak Rest House
16 Laxmi Vilas

RESTAURANTS
1 Trio, Top Deck and Skyroom
2 Kaipana
3 8th July (Old)
4 Kanchan Shree
5 Fort View and Mid Town
6 Monica
7 8th July (New)

Airport

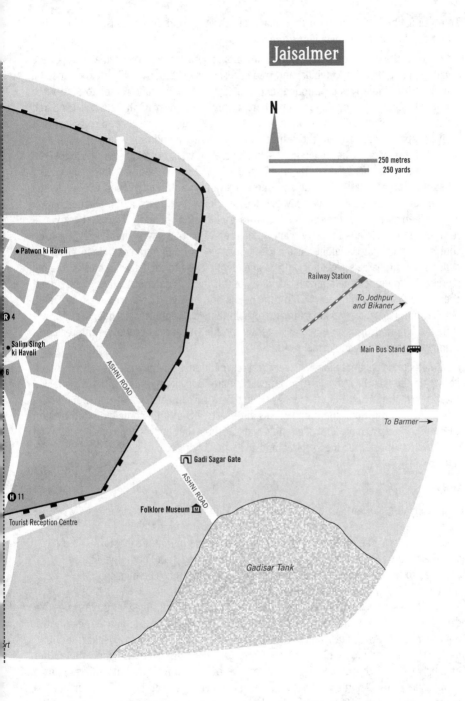

Jaisalmer

N

250 metres
250 yards

Patwon ki Haveli

Railway Station

To Jodhpur
and Bikaner

R 4

Salim Singh
ki Haveli

6

Main Bus Stand

ASHNI ROAD

To Barmer

Gadi Sagar Gate

H 11

ASHNI ROAD

Folklore Museum

Tourist Reception Centre

Gadisar Tank

rt

Temples in the Old Fort, with their elaborate carvings and decorations, together with numerous statues depicting a Jain *tirthankar.*

Throughout the centuries, the 6½km of ramparts at Jaisalmer Fort repelled all prospective invaders, including the Mughals, and trade prospered. Then, in 1947, it experienced a sudden crisis: India was partitioned, and the camel caravan trade routes to Sind were abruptly blocked by a new international border only 55km away. Only between 1965 and 1971, when the Indo-Pakistan wars revealed its strategic importance, did its fortunes revive. Rapidly connected to the rest of Rajasthan by road and rail to support a military base, it was inevitable that this remote, exotic desert township would soon be discovered by tourism. In the hard days of the 1940s and 1950s, the people of Jaisalmer had turned for survival both to cattle farming and (more relevantly) to the production of high-quality woven handicrafts—notably camel-wool rugs, special wool carpets and fine hand-embroidery. When, therefore, the tourists began to trickle in in the early 1970s, there was a ready-made handicrafts industry waiting for them. But times were hard, and Jaisalmer couldn't rely on tourism alone. As a back-up, its age-old trading tradition smoothly channelled itself into large-scale smuggling. Conveniently close to the Pakistan border, the old merchants' town became a modern-day den of thieves. Jaisalmer sent silver, whisky and beedies to Pakistan, and received in return gold and heroin. The heroin went to Delhi, Bombay and Jaipur, and an amazing amount of it ended up in Europe. Though still prevalent, the whole drugs scene is now very low profile. All Jaisalmer will be interested in selling you are carpets and camel treks.

Jaisalmer's principal attraction is its very real feel of antiquity—the majestic sand-coloured fort up on the hill, the atmospheric medieval town of lace-like *havelis* and narrow cobbled backstreets, the proud Rajput men in their bright turbans and patterned slippers, the elegant women in their coloured scarves and skirts, beautifully complemented by slim embroidered waistcoats. Travellers never forget their first impressions of this town, an ethereal ambience of subdued yellow sandstone, mellowing to pale gold by the light of the setting sun.

When to Go

Monsoons don't often get to Jaisalmer. From May to July, the thermometer bursts at temperatures of up to 52°C and many locals retire, bleeding at the nose, to cooler climes. The worst month to visit is June (blinding sandstorms) and the best are December/January, when it is pleasantly cool and airy. The accepted tourist season is from September through to March. The high-spot of the year is the annual **Desert Festival** (20–22 Feb 1997; 9–11 Feb 1998, 29–31 Jan 1999) when the plateau below the Fort is a rich, lively extravaganza of camel caravans, acrobatics and races, traditional music and dance shows, tug-of-war and turban-tying competitions. Like the similar festival in Pushkar, it culminates on the full moon night of *purnima.* Of late, this event has become rather expensive (book through RTDC at Moomal Tourist Bungalow) but still remains a popular favourite. Another good event, if you can bear the heat, is the Gangaur Festival of early April (*see* p.162) when the Jaisalmer ladies take the floor for a colourful, attractive spectacle of dance and song within the fort walls, performing to the god Isht Dev for happy marriages and the happiness of their menfolk.

Getting There

Jaisalmer can be accessed by air (infrequent service only) from Delhi and Jodphur. The popular approach is by bus, train or taxi from Jodphur; less frequently, by express bus from Udaipur and Pushkar. *See* also 'Moving On' from Jaisalmer, p.209.

The airport is close to the fort, only Rs40 by jeep, Rs30 by auto-rickshaw.

Getting Around

 The fort city of Jaisalmer merits a good couple of days' stay—there is not a lot to see, but what there is is top quality. Every building is a masterpiece of fine craftsmanship, and even the new *havelis* (commissioned by those who have grown rich on tourism) have been designed to blend in perfectly with the old, resulting in a total absence of the usual Indian contrast between traditional and modern architecture.

In town, you have a choice of wandering around the narrow streets and bazaars on your own (the town is small enough for it not to matter if you get lost) or hiring a guide from the fort entrance to point out buildings and places of special interest.

Local transport is pretty thin. Cycles can be hired at Rs10–15 a day from just inside Amar Sagar Gate, in Gandhi Chowk, and opposite the State Bank of India. Unmetered taxis and auto-rickshaws charge Rs30 and Rs15 respectively to take you to or from the railway station.

Jaisalmer ☏ *(02992–)*   ***Tourist Information***

The new **tourist reception centre**, ☏ 52406, is close to Gadi Sagar Circle (*open 8am–noon and 3–6pm daily exc Sun*). It sells two tours; 9am–noon, Gadisar Tank, fort, Jain temples and *havelis*, and 3–6pm (sunset from Sam dunes).

The **State Bank of India**, below Skyroom restaurant, changes most foreign currencies and travellers cheques. **Jagson Airlines**, ☏ 52722, is directly opposite. The **post office** is outside the city wall, below the police station (*see* map).

City Tour

On foot, full day. Gadisar Tank–Fort–Jain Temples–Salim Singh Haveli–Patwon ki Haveli–Nathmal ki Haveli.

This tour is best done on foot, and in the cool of the morning. Set out around 7am, taking a 10-minute stroll down Ashni Road (from the fort entrance) to **Gadisar Tank**, just below the city walls to the southwest. This large artificial tank, built by Maharajah Gadi Singh in 1367, was the city's main source of water until the droughts of the early 1960s. It's now supplied with water from an underground pipeline, and you can go paddle-boating round the cenotaphs, a popular recreation, for Rs30 an hour. There's a small **Folklore Museum** near the entrance, (*open 9am–noon, 3–6pm daily except Fri; adm Rs5*), which has recently been expanded and much better lit. It is a private concern, run by the erudite N.K. Sharma, a retired teacher whose popular pamphlet *Jaisalmer: The Golden City* sells here for Rs20 or (in larger form) Rs70. The beautiful arched gateway fronting the lake is said to have been erected by Tilo, a famous prostitute. Her nemesis, the then Maharajah, threatened to knock the structure down because of its immoral connections, until Tilo outwitted him by setting up a Krishna temple right next to it.

From the museum, stroll back via **Gadisar Pol** (Gate) to Jaisalmer proper. The powerful fort within the city, perched on the Tricuta (three-peak) hill of antiquity, is also known as **Sonar Qila** or Golden Fort because all its fortifications and residential buildings are made of yellow sandstone. Built over a period of seven years and much added to in the subsequent seven centuries, its meandering, snake-like wall is buttressed by 99 bastions and corner towers. The unique feature in its construction is that no mortar or cement was used to join the huge blocks of stone, only sand. It was only in the mid-18th century that the fort's inhabitants began to come off the heights and settle on the downslope below. Over a 100 years of flurried building ensued, and it was during this period that the wealthy city merchants formed their *mohallas* or guilds, laid their streets, and erected their imposing town houses (*havelis*). The fort was attacked many times during its long history, notably by the Tughlaqs and the Mughals, and was captured on at least three occasions. Its walls bear the telltale scars of fireball and cannonball attack, and the battlements within are still littered with original cannon and stone balls. Red *sati* handprints daubing each of the gates are the sad legacy of doomed Rajput wives who committed suicide rather than be taken prisoner by invading forces.

Ascend the sloping stone ramp until—many twists and bends later—you come to the large open square in the centre of the old Castle Fort. Soaring above is the magnificent seven-storey **Raj Mahal** or Maharaja's Palace, part of which is open to the public (8am–1pm and 3pm–5pm, adm Rs5). This palace, started in the 14th and enlarged by successive Maharajahs up until the 19th century, is a different experience from all the other palaces you're likely to see in Rajasthan. It's not been prepared for tourists at all and you really do feel as if you're exploring a 'living' palace that someone has just left. You're free to wander round unattended, uncovering beautiful art-nouveau ceramic tiles in the upper courtyards, balconied verandahs for the ladies of the court, and amazingly intricate stone carvings inside and out. The views of the fort and city get more spectacular the higher you go, and the open terrace on the roof affords a glorious panorama of the whole surrounding area. The best time to visit is around 4pm, when the soft light enhances photography. Guides can be hired at the entrance for Rs50, but they aren't much use.

Turning right out of the palace, the **Diwan-i-Am**—a beautiful marble throne, from where the Maharajah held open court with his subjects—points the way up to the **Jain Temples** (*open 7am–noon daily*). This highly decorative group of seven temples, constructed between the 14th and 16th centuries, contain a total of numerous images of the Jain *tirthankars*, mythological figures and gods. The carvings are uniformly magnificent, and you can photograph anything but the deities. Shoes and leather articles must be left outside, and a sign above the entrance denies entrance to women having their monthly cycle. Also here is a small library (*open 10–11am only*) with a rare collection of miniature paintings, books and manuscripts.

A short walk left out of the temple complex brings you to **Dop Khana** ('place of cannon'), affording marvellous views down over Jaisalmer town. To the right of this rampart can be seen the fanciful **Salim Singh ki Haveli** (*open 8am–6pm daily; adm Rs10*). This palatial structure with its peacock-motif arched roof was built by the powerful late 18th-century prime minister Salim Singh. A man of overweening ambition, he earned his notoriety by wiping out two nearby villages (3000 people) in a single night. Then he set about building a house high enough to permit a bridge running across to the Fort itself, to give him private access to the king's ear. But his plans went awry, the other Rajput courtiers persuading the king to fire on Salim Singh's high-rise *haveli*, blowing the top two levels clean away.

To see it at close range (excellent façade, disappointing interior), leave the fort and cross over the central market to the north part of town. It offers spectacular views of the fort from the upper balconies (don't forget your camera) and has a beautiful Rs50 calendar of miniature paintings for sale in its small shop. Near the *haveli* you'll also find the huge 19th-century **Mandir Palace**, with its beautiful silver furnishings. Just north of this is the finest example of Jaisalmer's architecture—the group of five ornate merchants' houses collectively known as **Patwon ki Haveli**. Contracted by the wealthy jeweller Patwon for his five sons, and built between 1800 and 1860, they represent the finest achievement of Jaisalmer's fastidious *silavats* or stone-carvers. Every pillar, bracket, window and balcony is an individual masterpiece. The graceful filigreed windows, in particular, remind one of merchants' houses of Venice. From the top terraces, you have the best views possible of the yellow-gold fort and of its surrounding medieval backstreets. Three of the five *havelis* are now government-owned, only two are open to the public (*10.30am–5pm daily*).

Finish off with a visit to nearby **Nathmal ki Haveli**, built as a prime minister's residence in the late 19th century. The right and left wings of this beautiful house were carved separately by two Muslim brothers, yet exhibit only minimal differences. The front door, guarded by a brace of elegant sandstone elephants, is a *tour de force*. The first floor is magnificently painted. The archway of this five-storey edifice presents the best views. Outside, explore the countless other mansions and houses dotted around town—every bend in the road turns up fresh delights.

After a siesta, you'll be ready for a 'sunset experience' at **Sam Dunes**, 40km west of Jaisalmer. Check out the sunrise/sunset timings at the tourist office, then arrange a jeep ride. Your hotel should handle this, and if you get a group together it should only cost about Rs70–80 per head. On the way to the dunes, stop off at **Mool Sagar**, 7km out of Jaisalmer, to see the Maharajah's 15th-century country house. When not stricken by drought, this is a popular picnic spot with beautiful gardens. The deep, dry well has an interesting camel pulley and there are some nice carvings on the walls. At Sam Sand, take a camel onto the dunes—pick one with no noisy home tourists on it—and pray for a decent sunset.

Jaisalmer produces more wool than any other Indian town. Together with two neighbouring Rajasthan townships—Bikaner and Barmer—it also produces perhaps the best-quality camel and sheep wool in India. The best buys therefore are woollen carpets. The wool is gathered, sorted and spun in Jaisalmer, then sent to Gadera (near Barmer) for weaving. The finished carpets return to Jaisalmer for sale. While the chance of getting an original carpet is pretty slim—patterns are generally copied from traditional designs and the only real variations are those of colour—the quality of workmanship is quite high. At about £120–150 (inclusive of shipping costs) a standard 2.2m x 1.5m carpet (288 knots per sqare inch) is very good value.

Shopping in Jaisalmer can be a hassle. There's a lot of pressure on you to buy, and prices are hiked up depending on how dumb you look. The golden rule still applies: don't accept any recommendations from hotel owners or street touts. They are all helping themselves, not you. If you can face the heat, April–May is the best shopping season—there are few tourists about, and even hardened traders are forced to drop their prices. A good year-round shop is Damoder Handicrafts up in the fort (near fourth gate). Bargain hard here for wall hangings, bedsheets, embroidery, paintings and leather goods at rock-bottom prices. To see the complete range of Jaisalmeri produce—Mughal-design carpets (a mix of Australian and Gadera wool), pastel woollen dhurries, mirrored wall hangings and beautiful cushion-covers—check out **Jaisalmer Rugs 'n' Arts** in Chirriya Haveli, near Patwon ki Haveli. Similar fair play is to be had at **Kamal Handicrafts Emporium**, near the Jain temples in the fort, famous for its embroidery items from Barmer. A lot of the hand-embroidered crafts sold in Pushkar, Jaipur and even Delhi originate from Barmer, where they were traditionally produced as heritage items handed down from father to son, or as marriage gifts.

Jaisalmer has a government-authorized *bhang* shop. It's located just below the fort first gate and sells marijuana-based cookies, cakes, *lassis* and juices.

The menu tells you exactly what to expect from your experience: Do not anticipate or analyse. Just enjoy. You will not sell, drink elephants, jump off all buildings or turn into an orange, and you will remember most of your experience in the morning.' What it doesn't tell you is how to get back to your hotel at night when you're off your head and there's a power cut.

Jaisalmer's sprawling **Bhatia Market** runs all the way down from the fort entrance to the State Bank of India. Here you can buy just about anything—cool kurta-pajamas from **Khadi Gramodyog**, near the old 8th July Restaurant; hand-worked silver from **Krishna Jewellers** near Kalpana restaurant; patterned *mojaris* or desert slippers from Vijay Leatherwork in Ashni Road; bright 14m-long turbans and huge 7m gathered skirts from the local clothes market opposite Vijay's. As elsewhere, remember to bargain hard.

Leisure

The big thing to do in Jaisalmer is a **camel trek**, though the person who first suggested this failed to add that the dunes are a long, hard 2-day trek out of town. This leaves all but the rugged with four choices: 1) a short taster trek round the empty scrubland surrounding the fort; 2) a jeep out to Sam dunes at sunset, followed by a short camel ride in full view of hordes of other day-trippers; 3) a bus out to Khuri, 40km out of Jaisalmer, for a 'real' camel trek from a real desert village; 4) forget the whole thing and do a trek from Pushkar instead.

The best thing about option 1 is the spectacular view coming back into town. Emerging from the empty wilderness, the towering hilltop fort suddenly looms up out of nowhere, a fantastic mirage straight out of the Arabian Nights. You can score a short 3–4 hour trek for Rs150 from just outside Amar Sagar Gate, and an overnight one (inclusive of meals) for Rs250 from just about anywhere. If you want tented accommodation rather than a night under the stars, you're looking to pay around Rs600.

Option 2 is a bit touristy, and it's all over in half an hour, but at least you can walk without a limp next day.

Option 3 gets mixed reports. Since I first promoted **Khuri** ten years ago, it has (inevitably) gone into decline. I still hear from satisfied customers who praise it as the highlight of their entire trip. Sadly, I receive just as many complaints of accelerating prices, fiercely competing guest houses, children begging and women selling photographs. Whatever, it's still your best chance of a decent trek on the dunes in the Jaisalmer area, and the 'desert' food is always fresh and delicious. If you do decide to go, there are two buses daily to Khuri, leaving the local bus stand just outside the city walls at 9am and 2pm. The journey takes about 2 hours, and if you're not met as you board the bus, you almost certainly will be when you get off. Permits for Khuri, by the way, are no longer necessary.

For details of option 4, camel treks from Pushkar, *see* p.184.

Real Jaisalmer is no longer in the small town (which is already becoming plugged into tourism, albeit in a pleasant way), but out in the desert villages. This said, a number of villages covered on camel treks from Jaisalmer are now over-exposed to tourists. The result is a strong accent on money, rather than hospitality. Hassle is the name of the game in the fort area, where every hotel owner and every restaurateur seems to have 'the best camel trek in town'. A few places like Fort View Hotel, New Tourist Hotel and Hotel Paradise offer cheap day treks (inclusive of fairly uninteresting meals) out to the old capital of **Lodruva**, with its impressive ruins and fine Jain temples, to the modern village of **Rupsi**, or to the cenotaph point of **Bara Bagh** for the sunset. Even here though, you need to check exactly what is included in the price before booking.

Traditional Jaisalmeri music employs varying themes of *maand* (Rajasthani chamber music) songs, which are usually melancholy. Street musicians and camel drivers prefer cheery *ghoomals* (dancing melodies) or lung-bursting *bharat* chants, used by warriors of old to summon the terrible power of Durga before each battle. Several hotels lay on traditional **folk-music shows**, performed by the guild of fort musicians. They normally play for marriage ceremonies, but they play even better for foreign dollars.

Jaisalmer ✆ (02992–)   ### Where to Stay

In 1992, all but two of Jaisalmer's hotels were aimed at the budget traveller. With the start of flights from Delhi and Jodhpur, however, the luxury hotels are finally setting up shop and there is now a good selection of accommodation at all levels.

On arrival by bus or train, a mad mob of touts will try and take you to the hotel of their choice, where they get commission, and will insist that the hotel of your choice is closed, full up or the same hotel as the one they like, but with a new name. If you refuse to believe them, they'll take you as far as the main fort gate and no further. To bypass all this nonsense, get an auto-rickshaw the whole way to your destination.

Another annoyance is the trend among Jaisalmer hotels to refuse rooms to travellers who don't want to go on their camel trek, and to kick out anybody who has booked a trek elsewhere. If you are going on someone else's safari, it's probably best to keep quiet about it.

expensive (from US$30)

All hotels in this category are outside the city walls and offer generally fine views of the fort at sunrise and sunset. The furthest out (3km) are the adjoining **Gorbandh Palace**, ✆ 53111, 📠 52749, and **Heritage Inn**, ✆ 52769, 📠 53038, on Sam Road. You could do a lot worse than stay at the first and eat at the second, since the Gorbandh has by far the nicer rooms (and an open-air pool) while the only good thing about the Heritage is its excellent restaurant. Both places are modern properties with concessions to traditional architecture, and are air-conditioned throughout. One tip though: don't go to any shops recommended by either hotel—they get a fat commission on anything you buy.

Just outside the city walls (1km to the west), the delightfully run-down **Jawahar Niwas Palace**, ✆ 2208, dates back to the mid-19th century and simply reeks with character. Originally the guest-palace of the Maharajah of Jaisalmer, it has only 13 rooms—all large and airy, so no need for air-conditioning—and fantastic views of the fort from the parapets. Meals are unsurpassed (authentic Rajasthani cuisine at its finest) and the staff make you feel instantly at home. Advance-book this one, as it's often full.

A little further out, but with first-rate views of the fort and of the royal cenotaphs (a short stroll away), the new **Himmatgarh Palace** on Ramgarh Road, ✆ 52002,

✆ 52005, is a modern structure with a friendly manager, good food and service, a fine sunset point on the open terrace and well-priced 'turret' rooms (kitsch but cosy) with air-conditioning. The new rooms in the main block are no comparison.

The nearest thing to luxury inside the city walls is **Narayan Niwas Palace**, ✆ 52408, ✆ 52101, a converted caravanserai at the foot of town. Once the best place in Jaisalmer, and still possessed of beautiful architecture and an underground pool, it is now sadly let down by scruffy rooms and lethargic staff. Stay here only if you want somewhere central with air-conditioning.

Most of Jaisalmer's better hotels offer discounts of up to 20% from April to September. Haggle for more: you'll often get it.

moderate (from Rs500)

Behind Trio restaurant you'll find the newly converted **Mandir Palace**, ✆ 52788. Formerly the property of the Maharajah of Jaisalmer, this is a beautifully preserved old *haveli* dating back 200 years. The central *chowk* is particularly striking, especially when illuminated at night, and is now often used for dance programmes. The wonderfully antique rooms come in all shapes and sizes, so see a few before deciding.

The **Hotel Jaisal Palace**, down an alley behind the State Bank of India, ✆ 52717, is another good choice. Clean and well-run, it has great fort views from its rooftop restaurant and very comfortable rooms—ask for nos.107–109. Facilities include air, rail and bus bookings and an overseas phone booth. This is a modern building, not a palace, but it has taken a lot of business away from older places like the Narayan Niwas—possibly because it's the only hotel in town with clean carpets.

Hotel Jaisal Castle, ✆ 52362, has a choice location on the fort ramparts, overlooking the desert. This is a restored *haveli* with a wide selection of clean rooms (see several before choosing) and extremely friendly staff. They show their darker side, however, if you book a camel trek with someone else.

budget

Most cheapies are in Gandhi Chowk, opposite Trio restaurant. Best are hotels **Swastika**, ✆ 52483, and **Renuka**, ✆ 52757, both with rooftop views, and **Ringo Guest House**, ✆ 53027, with two especially nice rooms on the roof. Tariffs depend a lot on whether or not you take their camel safaris, but are usually around Rs40/80. The Renuka and Swastika have dorm beds for Rs20/30.

The popular **Hotel Fort-View**, close to fort first gate, ✆ 52214, has a rooftop restaurant, rooms for Rs60–300 (two with fort views), dorm beds for Rs20 and useful facilities like money-exchange and air, rail and bus ticketing. If you can't get in, the adjoining **Hotel Flamingo** has cheap cells for Rs30/40.

Up in the fort, most travellers make a beeline for the **Hotel Paradise**, ✆ 52674, which has an excellent situation right on the ramparts. The rooftop terrace is ideal for chilling out or watching the sunset, and there's a 24-hour chilled beer service.

> The dogs of Jaisalmer are famous for their ferocity. They start barking around 4.30am, when loudspeakers announce the start of Muslim prayers, and they don't generally stop until dawn. The most important things to bring, if you're staying anywhere near the fort, are earplugs.

Chandra, the helpful manager, is well tuned into the needs of his foreign guests. He is one of very few hoteliers in Jaisalmer that doesn't shove a camel trek down your throat the moment you arrive. Rooms go for Rs150–600 (ask for no.105) or you can sleep on the roof for Rs30. Meals and drinks are served on request.

A worthy fallback is **Hotel Suraj**, close to the Jain temples, ✆ 53023. This is another *haveli*-style place, with fine views, good food and friendly people. Of the five beautifully painted suites, ask for the one at the front. In the same vicinity are **Hotel Laxmi Vilas**, ✆ 52758, with a rooftop restaurant, and **Deepak Rest House**, ✆ 52665, with a prime location on the fort wall. Both these places are much cheaper and more basic, but the Deepak has two 'character' rooms for Rs120 and Rs180 (nos.8 and 9) which are worth waiting for.

Southeast of the fort is the small but good **Anand Vilas**, with nice people and just six rooms. **Hotel Rajdhani**, near Patwon ki Haveli, ✆ 52746, has the advantage of a rooftop restaurant with views. Both places charge around Rs150/250 per night.

Jaisalmer ✆ (02992–)   ***Eating Out***

Food is generally cheap but dull. Jaisalmeris are intractably vegetarian, the staple diet being boiled vegetables, fried *roti* and green *milos* or wheat balls. But few travellers are very interested in eating. The air is so dry and hot that most live on a diet of Limcas, *lassis* and lime sodas. Even locals aren't immune—they drink up to 10 litres of liquid a day.

Jaisalmer's best restaurant is the rooftop **Trio** down by Amar Sagar Gate. This has a wonderful menu ('morsels of young bringle, the way deserters like') and live music nightly. It has, however, become rather too popular—especially with meat-eaters—and disappointed diners fed up of waiting for a table have begun to drift over to the nearby **Top Deck** or **Skyroom** rooftop restaurants (both in the same converted *haveli*) where they are pleasantly surprised to find similar food served faster.

Outside the city walls is the **Rawal** restaurant on Hanuman Circle, just in front of the police station. It's a local joint, well-known for Rajasthani cuisine, where you can dine out in an authentic setting without being surrounded by other westerners.

Up in the fort, it's the popular **8th of July** restaurant that steals most of the business, despite the odd report of sickness, though the **Beas Meals Service** is getting a good name for *thalis* and Indian-style snacks.

Near the fort first gate, travellers like the 'old' **8th of July** (only open in-season), and the **Midtown** rooftop restaurant with its fine views of the fort. There are lots of other rooftop restaurants around, notably the **Natraj** (good food, fast service) next to Salim Singh ki Haveli. Behind Hotel Fort View is **Kanchan Shree** restaurant, with 18 varieties of *lassi* and all manner of vegetarian 'snecks'.

Moving On

By air: Jagson Airlines connects Jaisalmer with Delhi via Jodhpur three times a week, but doesn't always fly. Jaisalmer has a defence airport, not a civil one, and it's up to the army whether commercial aircraft can land and take off.

By rail: Until the new broad-gauge line has been tested, there is only one morning train to Jodhpur, leaving 7.30am daily and arriving 9–10 hours later. The popular overnight train may be back on track by the time you read this. Tickets are available from the reservations office at the station—open 8–11am, 2–4pm and just before the train leaves. Also at the station is an International Tourist Bureau where you can relax in comfy armchairs and have a shower before departure.

> Buses to Udaipur arrive around 4am in the morning. Most hotels are closed then, so if you don't want to spend 2 or 3 hours fending off rickshaw drivers, book your accommodation ahead.

By road: Most hotels sell daily deluxe buses to Jodhpur (5hrs), Jaipur (13hrs), Ajmer (11hrs), Udaipur (12hrs), Mount Abu (11hrs) and Delhi (16hrs). All these buses leave from the main bus stand just outside Amar Sagar Gate. The main sales agents, if you want to book direct, are **Sahara Travels** and **Swagat Travels** near the first fort gate.

Pokaran

Pokaran, the largest noble estate of Jodhpur area, is now attracting interest from travellers wishing to see what Jaisalmer was like 20 years ago, before it was overrun by tourism. It's easy to get here—all buses and trains to Jaisalmer stop at Pokaran.

Pokaran's **fort** is a striking sandstone fortress which is slowly and painstakingly being converted into a modern-day luxury hotel. Several of the rooms were originally stables for the royal horses, though you'd never know it. The huge dining hall with its elegant balconies and painted walls was the bedroom of the maharajah. The family collection of antiques (mainly arms and textiles) is displayed in the small museum here, and hotel guests are taken on a free tour. Ask to see the silver-plated temple shoes and the 25kg chain-mail armour suit worn by Maharajah Mangal Singh in the mid-18th century. Elsewhere, there are charming courtyard temples to Lord Ragunnath and a buffalo-sacrifice sword weighing in at 35kg. It was so heavy to lift that it was later used on goats, because they were easier to slaughter.

Nagendra Singh, the present proprietor, was granted the fort by his father (the *thakur* or duke) in 1976, and it was he who opened it as a fully functional hotel in 1993. His family has lived here for the past 350 years. The fort's origin is obscure, but certain portions of it were already there when Rao Naoroji, the ruler of Mandore, conquered the local area in 1532 and began rebuilding and extending it. Prior to this, according to legend, the fort was the province of a local saint but was abandoned for reasons of plague or invasion. Certainly Pokaran was always of strategic importance, since, like Jaisalmer, it lay on the ancient caravan trade route from Karachi to Delhi. In olden days, if a European merchant turned up with 20 Arabian horses, the ruler of Pokaran would take the two best ones as a 'tax' and would pay for the rest in gold coins or with opium from Kabul. At that time, Pokaran was famed for having the best stables in the land.

With the partitioning of India in 1947 and the sudden severance of the lifeblood trade route to present-day Pakistan, Pokaran's prosperity inevitably faded. Due to its proximity to the Pakistan border, it is home to an important military base. Yet the growing presence of the army is unobtrusive. Even when Pokaran was chosen as the site of India's first nuclear blast in 1974, nobody in town was told about it. Most locals thought it was an earthquake!

Pokaran is definitely somewhere to stay *after* you've seen Jaisalmer. Doing it the other way round—i.e. using Pokaran as a base to sightsee Jaisalmer— involves a tedious 2½-hour drive to Jaisalmer every morning (110km) and a similarly dull 2½-hour trip back again every night. The road to Pokaran is so boring that many taxi drivers in Jaisalmer refuse to go there and local dogs queue up on the hard shoulder to fling themselves in front of passing trucks.

Unlike Jaisalmer, which used tourism to rise phoenix-like from the ashes, this sleepy little town remained cut off from the modern world. Even today, most foreigners only stop for lunch at the fort before moving on. They rarely make time to see the market or to explore the town. This is a pity, since Pokaran is totally untouched by tourism and, though of limited interest, has some beautiful old merchant's *havelis* in red sandstone (as opposed to Jaisalmer's yellow) with lovely balconies embellished with carved parrots, peacocks and elephants. The people are not at all used to westerners. They are shy, yet invariably friendly and eager to communicate. The bazaar is a good place to shop for silver articles, fresh spices and terracotta pottery, and you can have fun exchanging goods on the old barter system, which is still as popular as regular money deals. If you're staying up in the fort, the proprietor will send a boy with you to help with shopping. He will also, if you are interested in wild-game photography, show you the best spots to shoot migratory birds like wild grouse and the Great Indian Bustard. Finally, in an effort to patronize the local crafts of the area (dhurries, shawls, bedcovers and pottery), he is offering his foreign guests free half-day camel treks to neighbouring desert villages, as well as to the family cenotaphs.

If your budget can stretch that far, stay at **Fort Pokaran**, © 274 (*see* above). At present, there are only ten rooms and four suites—all priced at Rs750 per night—and it's a good idea to advance-book since groups often visit.

The fort is not the only accommodation option. RTDC have opened their **Motel Midway Pokaran** on the outskirts of town, © 2275, which has light snacks and a few rooms with bath for Rs200/300. In the town itself, there's the **Hotel Monica** near the bus stand, with basic rooms (common bath) for Rs50 a night.

Udaipur   population 350,000

Venice of the East, the lake city of Udaipur is perhaps the most romantic of all Indian centres. A fairytale collection of exotic gardens, mirror-calm lakes and fantasy island palaces, it has long been a firm favourite with travellers.

Udaipur was founded by Maharana Udai Singh, who moved the Mewar capital here following the third and final sack of Chittor in 1567. Udai Singh was ruler of the foremost Rajput clan, the Sisodias, who claimed direct descent from the sun. He was also a keen gardener, and he chose this site not only because of its excellent natural protection—encircled by the rugged Aravali mountains—but because it had a good water supply. Under his auspices, Udaipur quickly gained fame as a place of colourful and scented gardens, island parks, pavilions and fountains.

But the city's history is mainly one of blood and glory. Udai Singh left his son, Maharana Pratap, a difficult legacy: the new city of Udaipur fell under immediate attack from Akbar, the Mughal emperor of Delhi. Pratap was a stubborn yet courageous man. Angry at the capitulation of Jaipur's Man Singh to the Mughals, he made it a matter of personal honour to resist the northern invaders. With only meagre resources at his disposal, he kept the Mughals successfully at bay for 25 years, before finally being overpowered in 1576. Subsequent Maharanas were involved in constant intrigue, warfare and bloodshed, and Udaipur regained its peace only in 1818 when it came under British control, like much of the rest of Rajasthan.

Today, Udaipur is still very much a traditional 16th-century Rajput town, proud of the fact that throughout its turbulent history it never succumbed to foreign cultural influences. Here, most families still cook, wash, pray and eat together as a family unit, and the city's strong heritage of community life remains pretty much intact. Only during the past 20 years or so has the social structure suddenly shifted—a growing number of people have now broken the tradition of centuries and moved out of the old city palace area to settle in the busy commercial centre of the modern new town.

For the visitor, this development is reflected by the sharp contrasts in the way of life here. Down by the lakes, and especially to the east of Lake Pichola, Udaipur is a picture of peace and tranquillity. Outside the old city walls however, and especially round the rail and bus stations to the southeast, it is the familiar story of mad, feverish traffic, dust and smoke. The odd thing is that such semi-rural romanticism and urban chaos can exist in harmony.

When to Go

Situated in the shade of dark green hills, and cooled by its three lakes—the Pichola Sagar, Fateh Sagar and Udai Sagar—Udaipur has a uniquely refreshing climate. Pleasantly dry and cool from September to March, it's a nifty getaway from Rajasthan's heat and dust. By April, though, the heat is rising, and only a hardy few make it for the June/July monsoons when Udaipur is at its most attractive, with all the lakes and gardens a rich, luxuriant burst of colour.

Getting There

There are flights to Udaipur from Aurangabad, Bombay, Delhi, Jaipur and Jodphur. Train services from Jaipur, Ajmer, Jodphur and Jaisalmer are slow and heavily booked—not recommended. Buses from these places are preferable by far. *See* also 'Moving On' from Udaipur, p.221.

Dabok airport is a long 25km from the city centre, around Rs120 by taxi.

Getting Around

Udaipur has many attractive sights, especially around the lakes, which make for a wonderful day's cycling. If your hotel can't supply a bike, several hire places along Lake Palace Road will. Auto-rickshaws have 'broken' meters, love taking you to shops where they get commission, and will say just about anything to get your business. 'Hello James Bond!' one greeted me, 'where is your horse?'

Private cars can be hired from hotels or from travel agencies like **Rajasthan Tours** on Garden Hotel Road, ✆ 525777, and **Parul Tours and Travels** at shop no.5, Lake Palace Road, ✆ 520111; they also have a desk at Jagat Niwas Hotel. The charge is around £20 a day.

Udaipur ✆ (0294–)   ***Tourist Information***

The **tourist reception centre** is at the Tourist Bungalow off Shastri Circle, ✆ 411535, (*open 10am–5pm, closed Sun*). It sells morning tours of the city (8am–1pm) and afternoon tours to Eklingji and Nathdwara temples (2–7pm). Other information booths are at the airport, ✆ 528011, and the railway station, ✆ 131.

Changing money/traveller's cheques is simplest at the small Bank of India above the Bansi Ghat boat jetty. Otherwise, there's the State Bank of India on Hospital Road. The main **GPO** is on Chetak Circle (behind the cinema) but the *poste restante* is in the small sub-office on Shastri Circle, near the tourist office. The airport has a postal counter, open 7am–10am and 4–8pm.

Udaipur

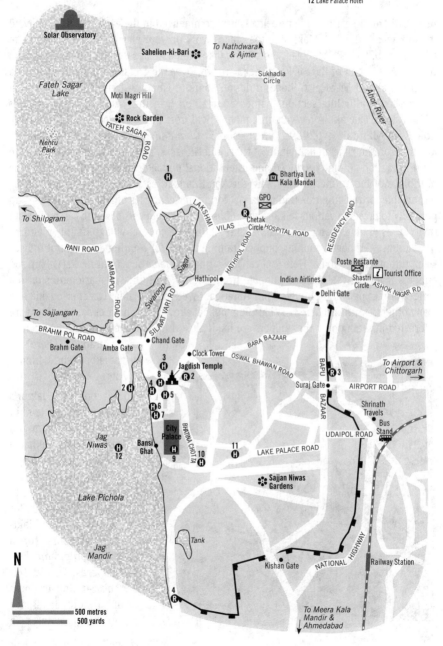

City Tour

By bicycle, full day. Bhartiya Lok Kala Mandal–Sahelion-ki-Bari–Fateh Lake–Nehru Park–Pratap Smarak–Jagdish Temple–City Palace and Museum–Lake Palace.

As elsewhere in Rajasthan, sightseeing is best commenced in the early morning, to avoid the full heat of the day. Make sure the brakes work on your bicycle, then head down to the bottom of Lake Palace Road. From here, take a left and pass through the narrow Bapu Bazaar. At the end of Bazaar Road, head straight over the crossroads and curve left via the hospital and Medical College until you come to Chetak Circle (surely one of the world's few traffic intersections named after a horse, in this case Maharana Pratap's faithful steed, Chetak). A few hundred metres right from the circle, look out for **Bhartiya Lok Kala Mandal**, ✆ 529296 (*open 9am–5.30pm daily; adm Rs7*). This is a famous folk museum housing an exhibition of tribal knick-knacks, musical instruments and—the main attraction—home-produced and international puppets. Rajasthan is said to be the birthplace of Indian marionettes, and the Kala Mandal (established 1952) is the place responsible for reviving this traditional art form after centuries of neglect. It was set up primarily to preserve various folklore traditions, but once puppets began to catch on again (mainly as a children's education aid, though also for village family-planning programmes—it began running puppet training camps for aspiring artistes, not only in Udaipur but all over India. Here you can see string and *lalua* puppets from Rajasthan, rod puppets from Bengal, shadow puppets from Andhra, and Orissan marionettes; also a variety of muppets and puppets from America, Sweden, Romania, Czechoslovakia and many other countries. There is a charming 'puppet show' every hour or so, and if you are interested in seeing how the puppets are made, just drop into the small training centre left of the entrance. There's a special puppet show from 6 to 7pm.

To see one of Udaipur's finest gardens, cycle right out of the museum and then left at Sukhadia Circle. The first major turning right along this road brings you to **Sahelion-ki-Bari** or Garden of the Maids of Honour (*open 9am–5pm; adm Rs2, camera fee Rs10*). This striking example of Hindu landscape gardening features a

Udaipur

picturesque lotus pond (turfed with radiant yellow blossoms in the spring), four magnificent marble elephants and myriad 'rainbow' fountains. The pretty pool pavilion within its small enclosure has been much-photographed, but you should save some shots for the curious **Community Science Centre**. This is to the rear of the pavilion and is unmissable: sea-monsters in milk bottles, neanderthal heads, moulting stuffed bats and a skeleton with a fag in its hand.

After a rest (the gardens are a popular picnic spot, ideal for a packed lunch) head left, then right up a steep rise, until you emerge at **Fateh Lake**. The pretty island garden shimmering in the centre of it is **Nehru Park**, which you can visit by Rs3 tourist boat (8am–6pm daily). The island is visually stunning—a riot of colourful blossoms and landscaped lawns—and there's a small restaurant for snacks. Back on land, proceed a few hundred yards along the lakeside until steps leading up to **Pratap Smarak** appear on the left. Here, atop the Pearl Hill of Moti Magri, stands the ebony-black statue of Maharana Pratap (1540–97), mounted on his 'loyal and faithful mount' Chetak (*open 9am–7pm daily, adm Rs2*). The steep climb up is relieved by pretty gardens, and at the top there's a marvellous view down over the lakes.

Below the entrance, you can hire a boat and laze awhile on the tranquil Fateh Lake (scooped out by Maharana Fateh Singh after the original 1678 construction was destroyed by torrential rains). Back on your bike, head back inland via the **Lake Swaroop Sagar causeway** (just keep to the left) and take directions for Hathipol, where the Rajput princes used to house their elephants in times of war. Past this, near the top of the hill, you'll find **Jagdish Temple** on your right. This is the biggest and best temple in Udaipur, built in the Indo-Aryan style by Maharana Jagat Singh in 1651. The black stone image enshrined within depicts Vishnu as Jagannath, Lord of the Universe, the brass Garuda outside representing his animal-carrier, the man-eagle. The exterior walls are notable for their beautiful elephant-motif carvings. A good time to arrive here is late afternoon, when you may be lucky enough to find local ladies singing prayer-songs and traditional hymns, accompanied by lively temple musicians. The foot of the temple steps is the favourite pitch of Udaipur's best drinks vendor, with a selection of about 20 differently-flavoured fruit cordials—a real treat after all that hot cycling.

Just up the road, you'll find the grandiose **City Palace and Museum**. This largest of all Rajasthani palace complexes stands on the crest of a ridge, poised over the serene Pichola Lake.

You'll enter from the northern end, through the triple **Tripolia Gate** (1725), with its eight exquisitely carved marble arches. This is where the Maharanas used to be weighed in gold or silver on their birthdays, and the copper equivalent was later distributed to the populace. Study the exterior—a breathtaking array of white filigreed balconies and windows, ornate arches and cupola-topped octagonal towers—then purchase the useful guide book at the entrance, and go exploring. The **museum** (*open 9.30am–4.30pm daily; adm Rs15, plus Rs30 charge for cameras; you can hire guides at the entrance for Rs40*) actually takes up most of the sumptuous palace complex, and is full of delights: the glorious peacock mosaics of the **Mor Chowk**, depicting India's national bird at different seasons of the year; the mirror-encrusted **Moti Mahal**; the porcelain and glass of **Manak (Ruby) Mahal**; the fine collection of miniatures in **Zenana Mahal**); and the ornamented Chinese tiles of **Chini Mahal**.

Climbing through a maze-like succession of staircases and small rooms, many of them decorated with mirrors, stained-glass windows, latticed balconies and ostentatious columns, enter a small second museum—with more superb miniatures, toys and royal knick-knacks—via the **Rai Angam** or Royal Courtyard. The views down over the Pichola, with its coronet backdrop of gaunt desert mountains, and of the glittering bone-white **Lake Palace**, framed, perhaps, in an ornamented palace window, are something you'll remember for years to come. Last, cycle down to **Bhansi Ghat**, below City Palace, and look over to **Jag Niwas** island. Built around 1740 as a summer palace for the Maharana, the centrepiece Lake Palace Hotel is a utopian fantasy in dazzling white marble—the place to be at sunset, sipping a cool cocktail or an ice-cold 'deluxe' beer, perhaps, watching the bird-scarers on the top terraces lassooing pigeons (they spoil the paintwork) and waiting for the still waters of the lake to turn first coppery-yellow, then a fiery blood-red. After dusk, flocks of giant fruit bats sweep over the lake, like a scene out of Hitchcock's *The Birds*. On the subject of films, the nearby **Jag Mandir** island—another summer house of the Maharana—was used in James Bond's *Octopussy*. Its other famous guest was the Emperor Shah Jahan, who apparently got the idea of building the Taj Mahal while imprisoned here.

Shopping

To see the full range of attractive handicrafts—wooden folk toys, hand-printed textiles, tie- and-dye saris, wall hangings, miniature paintings and chunky silver jewellery—start at **Rajasthan Government Emporium** in Chetak Circle. Then visit **Hathipol Market**, the best general area for shopping, to make your purchases. This market is especially good for antiques, paintings on silk, and clothing. It's not so good for batiks, *picchwais* and jewellery, which sell for up to 50% less at small local factories. Don't worry about finding these places—their touts will find you.

Udaipur's best buys are batik wall hangings, a traditional art form of the Muslim community. The special dyeing process uses various applications of wax to produce a unique cracked, marbled effect on the cloth. There are many con-artists around producing inferior examples, so play safe and buy from a reputable shop like **Apollo Arts**, near Hathipol, where prices are quite reasonable. Apollo also sell attractive miniature paintings on bone which keep their colour and quality far longer than paintings on cotton, paper and silk. Here and elsewhere, you'll find the framing of pictures extremely cheap—only £3 for a 28in x 14in frame. **Madhu Kant Mundra** at 152 Jagdish Chowk, just up from Mayur Café, does limited-edition etchings on a fixed-price basis (commission-free), which make excellent souvenirs.

Udaipur is also the base for *picchwais*—colourful wall hangings painted with durable mineral colours on cloth or silk. This art form originated in nearby Nathdwara (48km to the north), when a holy image of Krishna was smuggled here from Mathura to save it being destroyed by Aurangzeb, and a series of 'atmosphere' painted backdrops were created to help Krishna play out his half-dozen daily roles. At 9am, for instance, he appeared as a cowherd—and a *picchwai* of cows, meadows and rolling hills would be hung out. In time, these temple wall hangings, depicting Krishna in his varying moods, became popular souvenirs for pilgrims. Today, there are many 'schools' of *picchwai* painters and there is little point recommending any single one—they just move around in the wake of tourist traffic. Prices range from Rs60 all the way up to Rs10,000 and more, and the more reliable shops are in the area of Lake Palace Road.

> Udaipur is many people's favourite destination in India, partly because the people don't treat tourists as objects. You go into a store and they say 'Do you like this?' and you say 'No,' and they say 'Okay, no problem.' They don't try and sell you something you don't want.

The main shopping area, where all the tourist shops are, runs all the way down from the City Palace entrance past Jagdish Temple to the Clock Tower. Here you can find mirror-embroidered skirts, colourful wall hangings, appliquéed bedspreads, silver jewellery and curios—all at tourist prices.

Don't go into any shops recommended by your hotel, no matter how friendly or honest they might seem. The commission system is nowhere worse in India, except for Agra. If you're a woman and want to kit yourself out in a full crepe machine-silk outfit (sari/blouse or jacket/suit), take a rickshaw down to local markets like **Bapu Bazaar** and **Hathipol**, and bargain hard for an all-in rate of around Rs2000. The standard starting price at the touristy handicraft shops is Rs3500/4000—and that's just for the fabric.

Leisure

If you can't get in at the Lake Palace Hotel for dinner, but want a closer look at it, take a **boat trip around Lake Pichola**. There are two types of ride, one lasting an hour (Rs110), the other half an hour (Rs45). The longer version circuits Jag Niwas island (site of the Lake Palace Hotel) and makes a stop for snacks at Jag Mandir island. Boats leave at regular intervals (10am–noon and 2–6pm Oct–Mar, 8am–11am and 3–6pm Apr–Sep) from Bansi Ghat below City Palace. You can also take the popular **sunset cruise** (Rs110) from here, or charter your own boat for around £10 an hour.

The Laxmi Vilas Hotel has a lovely **pool**, open to non-residents for Rs150/day. The Rang Niwas Hotel charges Rs125. You can also go swimming at Shilpi (10am–4pm daily, Rs150) outside the crafts village of Shilpgram, 6km from the City Palace. After your dip, enjoy an Indian/Chinese meal at the attached restaurant, then pay a visit to Shilpgram itself. It's open 9.30am–4.30pm daily, and even if you're not around for the big **music/dance/crafts festival** of 1–10 December, there's nearly always something going on.

Udaipur offers Rajasthan's best cultural entertainments. You can see **traditional folk dancing** performed by professionals at Meera Kala Mandir, ✆ 523976, at Hiran Magari opposite Paras cinema (5km out of town, Rs25 by auto-rickshaw). Shows take place at 7pm daily except Sundays (August to April), and tickets cost Rs25. There's a more touristy evening folk-dance programme nightly at the Lake Palace Hotel, along with a fun **puppet show** in the courtyard. A better 'puppet circus' runs from 6 to 7pm daily at Bhartiya Lok Kala Mandal, ✆ 583176.

Udaipur ✆ (0294–)   **Where to Stay**

Udaipur has some of the most beautiful hotels in Rajasthan, especially at top level. They're expensive, though, even when low season rates are in force (April to September).

luxury (from US$80)

If you can only afford one night of luxury in India, the ultra-romantic **Lake Palace Hotel**, ✆ 527961, ✆ 527974, just has to be it. A poem in white marble, it sits on calm Pichola Lake like an iced wedding cake on a tray of glass, and is for many of its foreign guests the highlight of their entire trip. Some complain of its dinky pool and sugar-cake *Neuschwanstein* ambience, but nothing can detract from its sumptuous decor, excellent facilities and indelible views over Pichola Lake. Food, service and in-house entertainments are all top-drawer, and the rooms and suites are truly palatial. This is one to book well in advance—especially if you want a room with a view of the lake.

The Lake Palace Hotel is presently run by the Taj Group, though as soon as its lease expires it is quite possible that the Maharana of Udaipur may try and run the hotel himself. This is the *younger* son of the old Maharana, who (totally against tradition) was bequeathed the city in preference to his elder brother. The latter has assumed the title also, which is rather confusing, but it is the younger brother who has control over all the palace properties, and it is he who has done so much to convert some of them—such as Shiv Niwas, Shikarbadi and Fateh Prakash below—into modern heritage hotels.

Two other lovely hotels, both part of the City Palace complex, are **Shiv Niwas Palace**, ✆ 528016, ✆ 528006, with 46 rooms and suites crammed with family antiques, and the smaller **Fateh Prakash Palace**, same ✆/✆, with only six rooms and three suites. Both these places are real royal experiences—so breathtaking indeed that even their rooms have been turned into postcards! The Shiv Niwas has the most spectacular pool you're likely to see in India—completely marbled, framed by balustrades and palm trees, and set in a huge ancient courtyard. The

Fateh Prakash has its own pool, lots of recreational facilities and a show-stopping Maharani Suite at US$200.

expensive (from US$35)

Less exotic but with a lovely pool and lake views is the a/c **Laxmi Vilas Palace** on Fateh Sagar Road, ✆ 529711. All rooms and furnishings are perfectly colour-matched, and the whole palace is a model of architectural symmetry. The Maharana was so concerned with perfection that he knocked it down and started again whenever defects in workmanship appeared.

Another royal establishment is the 4-star **Shikarbadi Hotel**, some 5km out of town on Ahmedabad Road, ✆ 583200. Remote, perhaps, but this is the Maharana's personal hunting lodge, with a pool, a lake and extensive grounds. There are horse and elephant rides on offer and a deer park for picnics. Rooms are air-conditioned and generally good value.

If you're looking for a modern rather than a traditional place, the **Hotel Rajdarshan** near Hathipol, ✆ 526601, could be for you. It's cheaper than the rest, around US$25 for an a/c double, and keeps its standards high for western groups. There are only 15 rooms, though, so book ahead.

moderate/budget (from Rs30)

With its prime location on Lake Palace Road, the well-renovated **Rang Niwas Palace Hotel**, ✆ 523891, ✉ 520294, is the Maharani's old guesthouse, with lovely gardens, a 3-in-1 restaurant, attentive staff and cosy home-style atmosphere. Recreations include snooker, ping-pong, swimming in the new pool and (on request) camel safaris. Catering to all types of traveller, it has dorm beds for Rs30, amazing old-style rooms from Rs200/250, and well-furnished a/c suites with sit-out balconies for Rs660/770. It even has a rest room where, if you've just come in on an early-morning bus from Jodhpur or Jaisalmer, you can lie down for free until you check into a room at noon. 'Do not hesitate to bombard us with questions,' is the hotel's proud boast. 'It will be a pleasure to satisfy you with most authentic information!'

A little further down the same road, the **Hotel Mahendra Prakash**, ✆ 529370, says 'Welcome to home-away home' and means it. The double rooms are excellent value at Rs150—bright furnishings, clean bathrooms, running hot water etc.—and guests alternate between snacking in the pleasant garden-courtyard restaurant and relaxing on the viewpoint rooftop terrace. The staff are very helpful and the building itself has exterior features suggestive of a past incarnation as a minor palace. If the planned pool happens, room rates are expected to rise by Rs50.

Up in Lal Ghat area, above Jagdish Temple, the best place to stay is **Jagat Niwas Palace Hotel**, ✆ 529728, ✉ 520023, a well-restored *haveli* right on the banks of the Pichola Lake. Originally the town house of a local Charan (poet-caste) chieftain, it dates back to the mid-18th century and still retains many of its original follies—a medieval courtyard, a cunning series of stairways and terraces, one of which has now been converted into a colonnaded restaurant cum dance area. The food is excellent and so are the views of the lake. The old-style rooms start at Rs200 (common bath), but the one to ask for is No.1 (Rs750), with stained-glass windows, tiled flooring, German chandeliers and a huge Mughal-style double bed. Desk manager Mr Bhati is 'Mr Memory' when it comes to city information, and owners Raja and Raju periodically spirit guests off to their country farm for a day's riding or an evening barbecue. These guys are great fun, but you won't stay sober long.

Close by is the high-rise **Hotel Caravanserai**, ✆ 521252, a new place with a viewpoint rooftop restaurant/bar and clean, cheerful rooms for Rs675/700. It's not been going for long, but is already much in demand. If you have a choice, ask for a lake-facing room on the third floor. The same people have just opened **Kankarwar Haveli**, adjacent to Jagat Niwas hotel, ✆ 411457, which promises similar standards and even better views of the lake.

The **Lake Pichola Hotel** across the lake from the Jagat Niwas, ✆ 529197, is a new building on the site of an old *haveli*. The huge ground-floor hall encompasses a restaurant and bar, and the upper terraces command fantastic views of the Lake Palace Hotel. Some rooms have balconies and are good value at Rs600/800, but others smell musty and could use a lick of paint. On the plus side, the friendly staff are well tuned into the needs of westerners.

Walking down to the ghat from the City Palace entrance, you'll find two newer properties—**Ratan Palace Guest House**, ✆ 527935, and **Sai Niwas**, ✆ 524909. Both have clean, comfortable double rooms around Rs400/600, some of them with lake views. The Ratan Palace is the cheaper option and has better food.

Despite an outrageous Rs75 charge for a dorm bed ('to keep out noisy elements') the **Lalghat Guest House**, ✆ 525301, is still the best budget bet in town, with useful facilities (air and bus bookings, full travel information etc.) and a prime location overlooking the lake. Rooms go for Rs150 or Rs250 with bath or lake views, but they're not well-kept. The only thing which keeps this place on top is its friendly proprietor, Mr Brij, who goes to great lengths to 'involve' his foreign guests. His latest scheme is a self-catering kitchen where, if you can't make your own food, he'll get up and help you.

The nearby **Badi Haveli**, ✆ 523500, is a maze-like old property, full of nooks and crannies and run by a nice family. There are great views from the twin rooftops, clean rooms with shared bath for Rs100/140, and a big room on the top (with bath) for Rs250. The more modern **Anjani Hotel**, ✆ 527670, is only a few steps away.

Eating Out

Subject to availability, the **Lake Palace Hotel** still accepts non-guests for buffet lunches (Rs450) or dinners (Rs550), but you need to ring ahead and book (✆ 527961). If they let you over, take a beer onto the roof terraces for sunset, drop down to the bar-side courtyard for the puppet show/dance programme at 6pm, and make a quick tour of the hotel before the restaurant opens at 7.30pm.

If you can't get in, as is often the case nowadays, do not despair. The plush **Fateh Prakash Palace** is now offering afternoon 'English' cream teas and continental dinners in its elegant gallery restaurant. You don't get the same experience as at the Lake Palace, but you do have fantastic views of it from the gallery alcoves. The cream teas run from 3 to 5pm and cost just Rs100. The *à la carte* dinners are prepared by a top English chef and are served on a full silver service, accompanied by live Indian classical music. It's all very posh, but not too expensive, and the adjacent banquet room with its huge chandeliers is a real eye-popper, so don't forget your camera.

For hotel food, you can't beat the **Jagat Niwas**. Five years ago, you couldn't get scrambled eggs until the 'big cook' arrived by boat at 8am. Nowadays, the breezy Mediterranean-style restaurant offers a fine range of mid-priced dishes to suit all palates. Drop in for afternoon toasties or phone ahead for a table at dinner. Continental specialities include fish *à la Jagat* and chicken *à la king*. For Indian, try the tandoor dishes—they're exceptional.

Most budget restaurants, especially those in the Jagdish Temple area, suffer from poor hygiene. Only the well-run **Mayur Café** has maintained its standards—the slightest suggestion of dirty water or unfresh vegetables and Kalpat Singh, the proprietor, dashes off to berate his kitchen staff. He was the first to screen *Octopussy* in his restaurant and still does so on a regular evening basis. 'When I watch now,' he declares wearily, 'I am getting boring.' This is a small place, often full, with delicious south Indian and western snacks. The nearby **Evergreen Guest House** restaurant is also good, but it's right by the ghats and can be whiffy. Down in Bapu Bazaar, the popular **Natraj** restaurant does the best Gujarati *thalis* in Udaipur. You pay Rs25, and they keep filling up your plate until you say 'no'.

In town, the only two restaurants of note are **Parkview** opposite the Town Hall and **Berry's** near Chetak Circle. Both are multi-cuisine, mid-priced and very popular with Indian families. The Parkview is cheaper and does great tandoori chicken. Berry's is cleaner and has the better service.

Moving On

By air: Indian Airlines, ✆ 410999, flies six days a week to Jaipur, Delhi and Bombay, and four times a week to Jodhpur and Aurangabad. If you're heading south, the Aurangabad flight is particularly good value. Moduluft, ✆ 655281, flies daily to Bombay, Delhi, Jaipur, Bangalore, Cochin and Goa. Moduluft has the better planes, but doesn't fly from May to July. U P Air, ✆ 524388, is due to start flights to Delhi and Bombay.

By rail: Nobody goes anywhere by train from Udaipur. Buses are much quicker and far easier to book.

By road: Private express buses can be booked from the Lalghat Guest House (behind Jagdish Temple) or direct from Shree Nath Travels near the bus stand. They go to Bombay (18hrs), Delhi (16hrs), Jaipur (9hrs), Jodhpur (7hrs), Jaisalmer (12hrs), Ahmedabad (5hrs), Pushkar (7hrs), Mount Abu (5hrs) and Agra (13hrs). Local buses are okay for short-distance trips to Ranakpur (4hrs), Chittorgarh (3hrs), Eklingji and Nathdwara. They leave from the main bus stand and don't require advance booking.

The fast buses to Jaipur and Jodhpur arrive at 5am, a dodgy time to start looking for a hotel. Advance-book your accommodation if possible.

Mount Abu   population 18,000

Rajasthan's only hill station lies on a 1200m-high plateau, in pleasantly green and lush surroundings. Principally a place of pilgrimage, it has recently come up as a summer retreat for honeymooning Indian couples (mainly from nearby Gujarat) and is strongly geared to home tourism.

Abu derives its name from Arbuda, the serpent son of the Himalaya who rescued Shiva's bull Nandi from a watery grave. Hindus revere the site because the sage Vashishta, from whose sacrificial fire the four original Rajput warrior clans first sprang, had his home here, and also because of its Nakki Lake, said to have been dug by the sage Balam-Rasiya using just his *nakkhs* or nails. Holy dips in the waters of Nakki are held to be as spiritually purifying as bathing in the Ganges. Great numbers of Jain pilgrims visit Abu too, primarily because of its world-famous Dilwara temples, perhaps the finest examples of Jain architecture to be found in India.

An important religious centre since the times of Ashoka and before, Abu acquired its principal architecture and stone carvings only during the Parmer period, which came to a sudden end between 1302 and 1311 with the invasion of the Chauhans. Much later (1917), the British purchased a site for a sanatorium here, but Abu remained largely undeveloped and uninhabited until the home-tourist boom started in the 1970s.

Abu is today the most Indian of all hill stations—a lively little place of ice cream parlours, omelette stalls, 'fun' shops, and an awful lot of ponies. There is a pretty lake, several good hill walks, a refreshing mountain breeze, and a festive party atmosphere. The sight of Indians abroad—laughing, joking, taking endless photographs, swarming to and from Sunset Point, generally having a ball—has western visitors completely mystified. It's not like India at all. It's just not like other hill stations: there's no hassle, no dirt, no drugs and no unemployed refugees. The very worst or best thing that can happen to you at Abu is being adopted by an Indian family and deluged with food and presents throughout your stay. They just love foreign tourists here, and their cordiality and friendship is infectious.

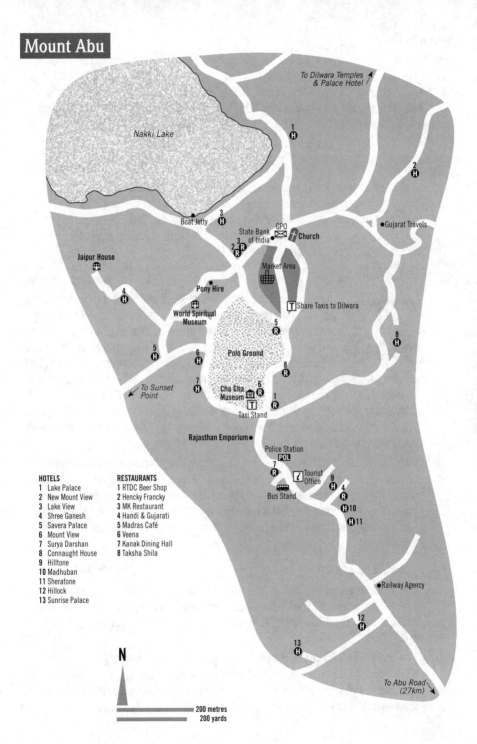

Mount Abu

To Dilwara Temples
& Palace Hotel

Nakki Lake

1 H

2 H

Boat Jetty 3 H

State Bank
of India

GPO

Church

Gujarat Travels

2 R
3

Jaipur House

Market Area

Pony Hire

4 H

Share Taxis to Dilwara

World Spiritual
Museum

5 R

To Sunset
Point

5 H

6 H

Polo Ground

8 R

7 H

6 R

Cha Cha
Museum

1 R

Taxi Stand

8 H

Rajasthan Emporium

Police Station
POL

7 R

Tourist
Office

Bus Stand

9 H

4 R

10 H

11 H

Railway Agency

HOTELS
1 Lake Palace
2 New Mount View
3 Lake View
4 Shree Ganesh
5 Savera Palace
6 Mount View
7 Surya Darshan
8 Connaught House
9 Hilltone
10 Madhuban
11 Sheratone
12 Hillock
13 Sunrise Palace

RESTAURANTS
1 RTDC Beer Shop
2 Hencky Francky
3 MK Restaurant
4 Handi & Gujarati
5 Madras Café
6 Veena
7 Kanak Dining Hall
8 Taksha Shila

12 H

13 H

N

200 metres
200 yards

To Abu Road
(27km)

When to Go

Abu is most pleasant from March to June and from September to November. Avoid the Indian holiday season of mid-May to late June and the Diwali festival of October/November. These dates are like D-Day and Christmas rolled into one, and you can't find a broom cupboard to sleep in. Late June to mid-August is tricky too, because of the monsoon. Aim for March/April, when it's quiet, relaxing and accommodation is available for half price.

Getting There

The normal approach to is by express bus or taxi from Udaipur. There are also bus services from other Rajasthan centres. Buses usually take you all the way up to Mount Abulf, however, you are dropped at Abu Road (27km down the mountain) or arrive here by train, you'll need a local bus (very regular service) for the final one-hour ascent up to Abu town.

Getting Around

 As hill stations go, Abu is very small and self-contained. You can get around very easily on foot, and walking is nearly all on the flat—there's none of that endless tramping up and down steep steps and winding declines that exhausts visitors to Darjeeling or Shimla. Also conveniently, most restaurants and hotels, and the post office, bus stand and tourist office, are all on the main road. This is directly in front of you as you step off the bus. At the bus stand, you'll be met by Abu's *baba-gadis* (porters) with their brightly coloured prams, eager to wheel your luggage off to your hotel for a few rupees. Later, their day's work done, they climb into their prams and go to sleep.

Abu's main sights and activities can be covered comfortably in a day—but stay a second day to pick up on the fun atmosphere. See all the pilgrimage places, including the Jain temples in the morning, by conducted tour (often crowded—book as soon as you arrive); leave the local walks and activities for the afternoon. Get around locally on foot, by pony, or by taxi/ambassador car (fixed charge for all journeys).

Mount Abu ℂ *(02974–)*   ***Tourist Information***

The **tourist office**, ℂ 3151, is opposite the bus stand (*open, in theory at least, 10am–1.30pm and 2–5pm*). If you can't get a **sightseeing tour** here, try Gujarat Travels near the bus stand. They run two tours daily, commencing 8.30am and 1.30pm.

The **State Bank of India** is near the **GPO** at the top of town. There are several **STD booths** for overseas calls, including one opposite the police station. If you're phoning *in* to Mount Abu and can't get through, try an extra 3 before the number. It sometimes works.

Tour of Abu and Nearby Sights

*By tour bus, morning; on foot, afternoon. Adhar Devi Temple–Guru Shikhar–
Achalgarh–Dilwara Jain Temples–Nakki Lake–Sunset Point.*

Abu town may be easy on foot, but all the surrounding sights are not. Every place covered on tour involves a stiff, steep climb. When you've had enough exercise, hire *dolis* (palanquin men) to carry you up.

First stop of the morning is **Adhar Devi Temple** 3km out of town, dedicated to the patron goddess of Abu. The climb up to this 500-year-old Durga temple involves 220 steps, a taster of what's to come. The black-faced deity at the top is secreted in a cave under the rockface, and you'll have to do a bit of potholing to visit her. This temple is considered the oldest place of pilgrimage in Abu. It is called *adhar* (without support) because Devi's statue is believed to be not man-made but rather a mystical manifestation, resulting from the fervent prayer of saints and sages. Set in pleasant woodland, full of the sound of singing crickets, it gives fine views down over Abu. Back at the bottom, try a plate of sliced tomatoes (popular thirst-quenchers) before reboarding the bus—they're delicious. A 15km drive then brings you to **Guru Shikhar**, the highest peak in Rajasthan at 1772m. There's a small Vishnu temple with a 15th-century brass bell at the summit, offering fine views of the surrounding valleys and hills. It's another 300 steps to the top, so hire a *doli* if it gets too much. Better still, return to Guru Shikhar at sunrise (taxi from Abu 5am, arrive 6am)—at that time the views are spectacular.

The next stop is **Achalgarh**, 11km out of Abu town, with its ancient Shiva temple (AD 813) and slightly less ancient Parmer fort (AD 900). Instead of the usual lingam, the main temple contains Shiva's toeprint (he once stood on Abu mountain to stop it moving away). This is at the bottom of a pit said to extend all the way down to the underworld. Pilgrims of three faiths pay their devotions here: the Hindus for the toeprint, and for the holy spring where the Devi goddess helped the 15th-century Rana to summon water from the rock and relieve a severe drought; the Jains for the richly-carved Jain arch and architecture; and the Muslims, because it was a Muslim warlord who built the new Shiva temple on this site after an attack of guilt over destroying the original one. There are lots of charming little temples and shrines containing bright-eyed gods, and also a fine brass Nandi and a huge old *champaka* tree in the courtyard. Outside, near the car park, is **Mandakini Kund**, a huge tank with a stone archer and three striking stone buffaloes. These figures face onto ancient cave dwellings of Jain monks, hidden up on the densely foliaged mountain-side. According to legend, the tank was once full of ghee, and three demons came in the form of buffaloes to drink at it each night. To stop them, the Parmer ruler Adipal killed all three with arrows. To see the pretty Jain temples above, take directions for the path up the hillside—another 10-minute climb.

Finally, you come to the small village of **Dilwara**, 5km above Abu town, with its five famous Jain temples (*open noon–6pm daily*). Two of these, the Vimal Vasahi and the Tejpal, represent the finest Jain architecture in India. Security at the entrance is stiff. Not only is there the usual ban on shoes and leather articles, which must be left outside, but women are warned that 'Entry of ladies in monthly course is strictly prohibited. Any lady in monthly course if enters any of the temples she may suffer.' Be prepared to be quizzed at the entrance—often in front of a crowd of inquisitive Indians. You can photograph anything inside except Jain deities.

See first the **Vimal Vasahi** (Adinath) temple, fashioned completely of white marble and dedicated to the first Jain *tirthankar*, Adinath. It is the earliest temple of the group, built in AD 1031 by the minister Vimal Shah for the Gujarat ruler Bhim Deva. Measuring 30m long and 13m wide, it took 1500 sculptors and 1200 labourers 14 years, working day and night, to complete. Entering via a series of 48 carved pillars, you'll come to a room full of marble elephants, on one of which is mounted Bhim Deva himself. The central courtyard, a vision of sublime ornamentation and sculpture, houses the large bronze image of Adinath, with eyes of precious stones and a necklace of gems. Around it are ranged 52 identical cells, each with its small resident Jain figure. Everywhere you look in this temple, there are beady-eyed cross-legged images staring right back at you. In a rear chamber, you'll find the ancient blackstone statue of Adinath, said to have risen from the earth from below a peepal tree. This was the original reason for a temple being built here.

Move on to the **Tejpal temple**, built in 1231 by Tejpal and Vastupal, two brother-ministers of the Gujarat ruler Viradhawaler, and dedicated to the 22nd *tirthankar*, Neminath. This has the same profusion of sculpture as the Adinath temple, but is notable for its technical perfection: every inch of marble is a masterpiece of intricate and delicate carving. Since each worker was paid in solid gold, and in direct proportion to the weight of marble covered, such attention to detail is perhaps not surprising. What is surprising is that this filigree fantasy-temple—with its cluster of translucent lotuses dripping from the porch dome, its glorious overhead panels of deities and attendants, its high-towered prayer hall and its massive statue of Neminath—were all carved from a single massive block of Makrana marble. The overall effect is stunning. Elsewhere, there are smaller temples to Adinath (14th century) and to Parsvanath (15th century).

Either take the tour bus back to Abu town (it stops only an hour at Dilwara), or stay longer—the temples are worth it—and return back down by shared taxi (Rs2, drops and picks up at the rank opposite Madras café in town).

In the afternoon, go boating on **Nakki Lake**, perhaps the finest hill station lake in India. It is an artificial sheet of water, studded with tiny islets, fringed by beautiful woodland, and overhung by the famous **Toad Rock** (a natural toad-shaped boulder). Paddle-boats are a waste of time—the currents are too strong. Hire a rowing boat, battle out to the centre of the lake, then relax. Back on land, you can take the path behind the boating point up to **Jaipur House**, the highest point in Abu. This decaying structure was once the summer residence of the Jaipur Maharajah and though very run-down affords first-rate views of the sunset and (if the caretaker lets you beyond the courtyard) over the lake and surrounds.

Dusk marks the great exodus of tourists out to **Sunset Point**, 2km west of Abu town. It's the accepted thing to do—now practically a tradition. To avoid the crowds, you can go there by pony, camel or even pram (!), all available from the pony rank at the top of town. This is great fun, and gets you noticed by every Indian tourist in town, many of whom are going to be far more interested in photographing you (with or without the pram) than the glorious sunset. It's at Sunset Point that you realize you're on a mountain, the open plains stretching out for miles below.

In the evening, Abu comes into its own. It is one of the few places in India with any claim to relaxed nightlife. People return from Sunset Point to take a long, leisurely evening promenade and the town streets are a mass of gaily twinkling electric lights. Sweet buns, ice cream, cold beers and 'genuine Bombay omelettes' are peddled on the roadside, and below the pony rank is a row of stalls brewing up Abu's famous ginger tea. Nearby, ladies can buy the attractive *mendi* patterns (henna palm-paintings, traditionally painted on, but here sold as stencils; the pattern lasts 5 days) or colourful bangles, bracelets and *bindi* beauty-spots. There are numerous street tailors, photography shops, *paan* stalls and cheap novelty-gift emporia. There's even a 'Character Building World Spiritual Museum', just up from the pony rank, where you can see how the world evolved and how Lord Shiva will manage things after it has been blown up.

Shopping

Abu's many 'fun' shops sell some of the worst tat in the world—plastic toys, ghoulish rubber masks, hideous plaster gods, and 'breakable educational zoological animals'. To see something better, visit **Rajasthan Emporium** near the bus stand, or **Khadi Gramodyog Bhavan** opposite the pony rank. To see something worse, visit **Cha Cha Museum**, Abu's biggest and oldest emporium. It's called a 'museum-like shop' because most of its bizarre curios and antiques hang around for ages before finding a buyer.

Leisure

Abu has more ponies than you can shake a crop at, so **pony rides** are an obvious relaxation. Otherwise, there's **boating** or pleasant **walks** to local viewpoints like Lovers' Point and Honeymoon Point. For the best views, take any of the paths leading up from behind Nakki Lake to the hilltop, a 30-minute climb. Abu also has a small **wildlife sanctuary**. To visit, contact the Forestry Office above the tourist office (*open 10am–5pm*).

Mount Abu © (02974–)   Where to Stay

Before the mid-April tourist rush, most of Abu's hotels offer generous 30–50% discounts. After that, prices soar and you can't (unless you advance-book) find a decent room for love or money. At any time of the year, the better hotels are full of noisy honeymooning couples, so take earplugs.

expensive (from US$30)

Abu's hotels are very much geared to Indian families, as you can tell from names like Hotel Kiddies Corner and Babyland Hostel. They are also heavily into self-glorification, as evinced by their brochures. One place claims to 'befit the cyber traveller' and to have 'the pride of place for propagating the philosophy of total guest satisfaction'. Rates quoted below are for the high season, which is any time of the year when Indian families are in town—i.e. Diwali, Indian holidays and most weekends. At any other time, room prices are slashed by up to 50%.

Close to the Dilwara temples, the **Palace Hotel** (ex-Bikaner House), © 3121, © 3674, is the ex-summer residence of the Maharajah of Bikaner. Nowadays it's very much the hill-station resort, with a private lake, lovely gardens, tennis courts and huge old-fashioned rooms packed with period furniture. The suites compete in size with the massive lobby, and as for the dining rooms, one can easily imagine sitting down to 'tiffin' with officers and ladies of the Raj. It's often sold out though, so book well in advance.

Even more Raj is **Connaught House**, © 3439, a quaint English-style stone cottage on the eastern outskirts of town. Formerly the private residence of Sir Donald Field (the PM of Jodhpur state), and now owned by the Maharajah of Jodhpur, it has 15 rooms surrounded by a shady terraced garden and is a virtual museum of pre-war memorabilia and furnishings. Meals are very 'English' and the old-world rooms, while smaller than those at the Palace Hotel, have a lot more atmosphere. For peace and quiet, ask for a room with verandah in the new block. For prestige, plump for Room 2 in the old block—this is where the Maharajah stays.

British India is again the theme at **Hotel Sunrise Palace**, set high on a ridge above Hotel Hillock, © 3573, © 3775. A marvel of Indo-Gothic architecture, this was originally the summer residence of the Maharajah of Bharatpur and was mainly used as a base for polo matches. Recently renovated, it is now a well-run place with efficient staff and lots of facilities. The multi-cuisine restaurant opens out to a wide terrace with views, and the huge geometric suites with their colourful 'theme' furnishings and sunrise views are possibly the best value in town.

Moving from traditional to modern, the new **Hotel Hillock** is on a rise to the south of town, © 3277, © 3467. This is Abu's classiest joint, with happy staff, a good restaurant, a complimentary shoe shine and the best pool around. Rooms are very swish and well-priced.

Almost as good is **Hotel Hilltone** near the bus stand, © 3112, © 3115. It's an older property set amid large lawns and gardens, with two restaurants, a bar, a pool and a health club. The best rooms are on the second floor, with sun balconies. There's also a pricey new cottage block, advertised as 'the place to get enchanted by your own silence, to rediscover your lost innocence and return to your own self'.

moderate (from Rs600)

You'll find **Mount Hotel**, © 3150, on the way up to the Dilwara temples. Originally owned by an English army officer, this is a something of a poor man's

Connaught House—a pleasantly run-down British bungalow with a quiet location, pleasant lawns and flower-bordered gardens. Present manager Jimmy Bharucha, along with Lucky Boy the horse and Spot the labrador, makes all his guests feel instantly at home. What he can't offer in style he makes up for in hospitality. This is the perfect place for a complete break.

The modern and central **Hotel Sheratone**, ✆ 3544, is just below Hotel Hilltone. It's a bit rough round the edges but is friendly enough and every room has a zippered TV on an elevated shrine.

Facing onto Nakki Lake, the **Hotel Lake Palace**, ✆ 3254, has a lovely situation and good recreational facilities, but is one to avoid at weekends and holidays when rooms are outrageously overpriced. At any other time, you can bargain for a comfortable double for Rs300/400.

On the way out to Sunset Point, **Hotel Savera Palace**, ✆ 3355, ✉ 3354, has pop '60s rooms, a pool, a steam bath, a skating rink and horse-riding on request. Needless to say, it attracts a lot of Indian families. The upstairs rooms are nicest, with balconies and views. Downstairs, there's a restaurant serving quality Punjabi food.

budget

Abu doesn't really cater for shoestringers, so cheap lodgings are pretty dire. An exception is **Hotel New Mount View**, ✆ 3320, with large, airy rooms for as little as Rs100 off season, Rs500 in season. The best ones are on the first floor, with a terrace and views. **Hotel Surya Darshan,** behind the taxi stand, ✆ 3147, is clean enough and has nice views of the polo ground from its top-floor doubles. These cost Rs500 in season, Rs150 other times, and cheaper rooms start at Rs80. Another find is the **Shree Ganesh** on the way up to Jaipur House, ✆ 3591. There are excellent views from the top terrace and the rooms are good value at Rs50/60 off season. All rooms, be warned, broadcast the English news daily from garbled wall-speakers.

One of the strange things about Abu is the lack of good hotels near beautiful Nakki Lake. The only budget choice is **Hotel Lake View**, ✆ 3659, with a Mediterranean sun terrace and bright, cheerful rooms, some with lake views, from Rs200 (Rs1000 in season!).

Mount Abu ✆ (02974–)   **Eating Out**

Abu's only traditional food (actually a Bombay import, like the omelettes) is *pau bhaji*—a savoury vegetarian snack of tomatoes, potatoes, spices and lemon tossed about in a banana leaf, generally eaten with buttered toasted rolls. Elsewhere, there are snack stalls and restaurants aimed at the town's wide cross-section of Indian tourists. Bombayites like their omelettes and *pau bhajis*, Tamils their *dosas* and *thalis*, Gujaratis their Gujarati *thalis*, Punjabis their tasty non-veg snacks at **Sher-Punjab**; and Rajasthanis their spicy 'desert' food.

Two good places for south Indian snacks and *dosas* are **Kanak Dining Hall** near the bus stand, and **Veena** restaurant further up the hill. Both do all-you-can-eat Gujarati *thalis* for Rs30. The long-running **Madras Café** next to Cha Cha Museum is well known for south Indian food and coffee, and has just opened a new section upstairs doing Punjabi and Chinese food. Also good for Chinese is the pure veg **Taksha Shila** at Samrat Hotel.

Ice cream parlours and juice bars abound on the approach to Nakki Lake. The most audible, with its pumping Indo-techno sounds, is **Hencky Francky**, which sells burgers, pizzas and shakes. **M K Restaurant**, opposite, has a competing sound system and does a mean *thali*.

For a big meal out, ring the **Palace Hotel**, ✆ 3121, and book one of their set lunches (Rs150) or dinners (Rs180). They're well worth going out of your way for.

The **Mayur** restaurant at Hotel Hillock has an excellent if amusing menu including 'Mouthful Nibblers', 'Vegetable Bullet' and 'Baked Weazle'. Less expensive are Hotel Hilltone's twin restaurants, the non-veg **Handi** for continental, Rajasthani and Chinese meals, and the **Gujarati** upstairs for pure veg south Indian food and delicious Rs30 *thalis*. Opposite the taxi stand, the **Government Beer Shop** does a brisk trade in beer and hard drinks from 10am to 10pm.

Moving On

By rail: The railhead for Mount Abu is Abu Road, 27km down the mountain. From here, the fast Ashram Express leaves for Ahmedabad at 8.10am daily, arriving at 12.40pm. There are also trains to Ajmer, Jodhpur, Jaipur and Delhi. For Bhuj, you have to go to Palanpur (2–3hrs down the line) and change trains. The tourist quota of tickets is held by the railway agency at the HP service station near Mount Abu's Tourist Bungalow (*open 9am–1pm and 2–4pm, Sun 9–noon*).

By road: Private deluxe buses from Mount Abu are quicker and more convenient than waiting for a train at Abu Road. They go to a variety of destinations—Udaipur (4½hrs), Ahmedabad (6hrs), Jaipur (12hrs), Ajmer (10hrs), Jodhpur (10hrs), Bombay, Aurangabad and Bhuj (17hrs each)—and should be booked at least a day ahead from Gujarat Travels near the bus stand, ✆ 3564. This agency also books and reconfirms air tickets.

By hired car (from your hotel or Gujarat Travels) it's only 3½hrs to Udaipur or 5hrs to Ahmedabad.

Chittorgarh
population 80,000

The ancient Mewar capital of Chittorgarh (or Chittor) represents the quintessence of Rajput valour and chivalry. Three times in its long and bloody history, faced by over-whelming odds, its menfolk dressed up in the saffron robes of martyrdom and rode out to certain death, while its women walked into the sacrificial bonfire and committed *jauhar* (mass ritual suicide). Carved marble memorials to heroes and *sati* victims litter the broken

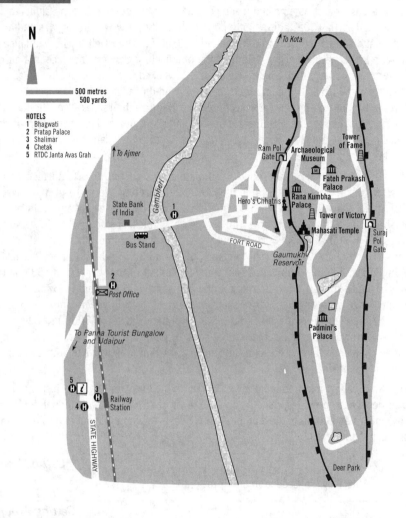

N

500 metres
500 yards

HOTELS
1 Bhagwati
2 Pratap Palace
3 Shalimar
4 Chetak
5 RTDC Janta Avas Grah

To Kota

To Ajmer

Gambheri

State Bank
of India

Bus Stand

FORT ROAD

2
Post Office

To Panna Tourist Bungalow
and Udaipur

5
3
Railway
4 Station

STATE HIGHWAY

Ram Pol
Gate

Archaeological
Museum

Tower
of Fame

Fateh Prakash
Palace

Hero's Chhatris

Rana Kumbha
Palace

Tower of Victory

Mahasati Temple

Gaumukh
Reservoir

Suraj
Pol
Gate

Padmini's
Palace

Deer Park

ruins, making this oldest and most famous of all Rajasthani fortress towns perhaps the closest to the warrior Rajput's heart.

A great deal of Rajasthan's history centres round Chittor. The origin of this powerful hilltop fort, situated on a 180m-high precipice, is shrouded in romantic mystery. The legend goes that it was a fort since prehistoric times, having been founded by the hero Bhim, one of the five Pandava brothers of the *Mahabharata* epic. Two Palaeolithic sites have been excavated at the nearby River Berach, but the fort probably only dates back to the 7th century AD. In the year 734 it was discovered as a strategic site by Bapa Rawal, founder of the Mewar dynasty, and was made his capital. It was Bapa Rawal who thought up the clever idea of calling himself the *dewan* (minister) of Shiva, which sidestepped any possible accusation of tyranny and made possible the unity of the clannish Rajputs under a single leader. In 1303, after a long period of steady growth, Chittor was suddenly attacked and sacked by the ruthless Ala-ud-din Khilji, Sultan of Delhi, who had fallen in love with its beautiful princess Padmini; after one fleeting glance of her face in a mirror he determined to have her, whatever the cost. He walked in on an empty fort—Padmini and all her royal ladies had committed *jauhar.* Ala-ud-din ruled Chittor for just 23 years before he was ousted by the valorous nobleman Hamir, who retook it for the Rajputs. Through this achievement, Hamir earnt himself and all his descendants the 'premier' title of Maharana—at Independence in 1947, there were 532 Rajahs and Maharajahs in India, but only one Maharana.

Chittor's glorious revival had one unfortunate repercussion: now confirmed as the ruling seat of the Rajputs, it became the lodestone attracting every prospective invader of Rajasthan. Only when they had conquered this city, could they lay any real claim to rulership of the state. For a time Chittor met all attacks successfully—it was quite impossible to storm, and its everlasting water supply from the fort's natural springs meant that besieging enemies had to camp out for months on the hot, bone-dry plains waiting for its food to run out. But then came two crippling defeats: first in 1535, at the hands of Bahadur Shah, the Sultan of Gujarat (a disastrous engagement—32,000 Rajput warriors were slain and 13,000 of their women went up in *jauhar* smoke); then in 1567, by the Mughal emperor Akbar (and the orange saffron of 8000 more warriors bled red). It was shortly after this final sack of Chittor that Maharana Udai Singh decided that enough was enough, and moved 110km westward to found the new Rajput capital of Udaipur.

Today, while a few hundred families still live on in the fort, Chittorgarh is just another of India's deserted ghost cities, a silent, lonely expanse of arches, gates, memorials and cenotaphs which stand testament to a proud, heroic people to whom honour and valour meant more than life itself.

Getting There

See 'Moving On' section in **Udaipur**, p.222.

Getting Around

Apart from the fort, there's little to see or do. It's best to arrive early from Udaipur, see the sights by auto-rickshaw or by the tourist office's morning tour (if operating), and arrange to be back in time for the afternoon bus on to Ajmer or back to Udaipur. Few people stay overnight.

Chittorgarh © (01472–)   ***Tourist Information***

The **tourist reception centre** (*open 8am–5.30pm daily exc Sun*) is in the RTDC Janta Avas Grah near the railway station, © 41273.

Tour of Chittor Fort

By tour bus/auto-rickshaw, half day. Rana Kumbha Palace–Fateh Prakash Palace–Tower of Victory–Gaumukh Reservoir–Padmini's Palace–Tower of Fame.

The ascent up to the fort, which contains all Chittor's interest points, is via a steep, winding 1km-long road. This takes you through seven gateways up to the western (main) gate of **Ram Pol** at the top. If you have your own driver, ask to stop at the **Hero's Chhatris**, where Jaimal and Kalla, two valorous victims of the 1567 conflict with Akbar, fell fighting.

Within the fort, see first the 15th-century **Rana Kumbha Palace**, with its Shiva temple, horse and elephant stables, and vaulted cellars where Padmini allegedly committed *jauhar*. In the more modern **Fateh Prakash Palace** opposite, visit the small and interesting museum with its collection of archaeological treasures recovered from the fort.

A short distance east, you'll find the **Tower of Victory** (Vijay Stambh), erected between 1458 and 1468 to commemorate Rana Kumbha's victory over the Muslim and Gujarat rulers in 1440. Climb this finest remainder of Rajput glory—nine storeys of noble yellow sandstone, rising 37m high—for fine views over the fort area. Outside, to the right, is the grim **Mahasati** area where *ranas* of olden days were cremated—note the several *sati* stones and tablets here. Straight ahead, and down some steps, is the **Gaumukh Reservoir**, a deep tank full of leaping fish situated right at the edge of the cliff. It takes its name from the carved cow's mouth which feeds the tank a constant supply of fresh spring water.

At **Padmini's Palace**, up on the eastern end of the fort, you can wander through the green gardens and flower-bordered courtyards to the balcony where Ala-ud-din got his fatal glimpse of the lovely Padmini, her face reflected in a silver mirror as she promenaded in the small water-bound island pavilion opposite. Then proceed by the **Deer Park** and the **Suraj Pol** to the **Tower of Fame** (Kirti Stambh), dedicated to Adinath, first of the Jain *tirthankars*. It was built in the 12th century, making it older than the Tower of Victory, by a wealthy Jain merchant. Covered in decorative nude figures of the Jain pantheon, it is a *digambara* or 'sky-clad' monument.

Chittorgarh ✆ *(01472–)*   ***Where to Stay and Eat***

RTDC's **Hotel Panna Tourist Bungalow** on the Udaipur road, ✆ 41238, has adequate rooms for Rs150–450. Something better is provided by **Hotel Pratap Palace**, between the bus stand and the tourist bungalow, ✆ 40099, ✉ 41042, with clean rooms around Rs250/300 air-cooled or Rs600/700 with air-conditioning. Both places are near the railway station and have good non-veg restaurants.

Moving On

Since this is the end of the route, you're probably looking to return by road to Udaipur and thence to Delhi by air, or to Ajmer for a few more days R & R in Pushkar. There are frequent buses and trains to both places.

Route 3: Valleys of the Gods

If you're doing this route, you're looking to spend some time in the mountains. You may be in search of a cool retreat from the heat-blasted plains of Uttar Pradesh, or you may just want to do some trekking. It's also possible, if you're on a long-stay visa, that all you want to do is head up to Manali for the holy ganja and to put in some serious relaxation. In any case, what you'll find in this part of India is a series of high-rise hill stations, each trapped in its own individual time-warp, which, even if you're not nostalgic for the glory days of British India, will nevertheless show you just how its officers and ladies spent their hot summers.

From Jammu, the winter capital of Kashmir, one enters the cool river valleys of Himachal Pradesh and drives up to Dalhousie, with its neighbouring hill towns of Khajiar and Chamba, or to Dharamsala, present home of the Dalai Lama, for mountain walks, funky shops and cafés, and bags of Tibetan atmosphere. Manali, at the head of the Kulu Valley or Valley of the Gods, is a hill resort of rare charm. This is another popular trekking base with direct access to the snow-clad Rohtang Pass. Nearby Kulu, the quiet hill town after which the valley is named, is host to Lord Jagannath (honoured by a vivid annual festival) and is famous for its woollen handicrafts. Shimla, by contrast, is the definitive British hill station resort, a place for scenic promenades and fond recollections of the Raj.

Itinerary

Jammu may be unstable (check the situation before going), so you could skip it in favour of a direct bus/flight from Delhi to Dharamsala. In this case, try the following route: Dharamsala (2 nights) to Kulu (1) to Manali (3) to Shimla (2), then a bus or a plane back to Delhi. Taking in Jammu and Dalhousie/Chamba, give yourself an extra couple of days. The places to stay longer, if you have the time, are Dharamsala and Manali.

Since late 1989, the Kashmir Valley, once a popular destination, has been disrupted by the increasing militancy of a popular movement demanding total independence from India. The ongoing politicial violence, coupled with the periodic abductions (and lately, executions) of foreign tourists, has dissuaded all but the hardy or foolhardy from visiting the area. Don't believe anyone, not even a tourist official, who says Kashmir is safe—until peace is declared, it remains a definite no-go zone.

It is still safe to visit Ladakh, though only by air from Delhi to Leh via Srinagar or by two-day bus journey (pretty but gruelling) from Manali. Readers wishing to make this trip are recommended to Lonely Planet's *India: a travel survival kit* (January 1996), where full information is given.

The best time to do this route is from April to October (temperature 14°–33°C), and December to February (0°–15°C). There are monsoon rains between July and September.

Gateway to Kashmir, Jammu is also the winter capital of the state. Situated on the banks of the river Tawi, this busy, prosperous town is surrounded by lakes and hills, temples and fortresses. Little is known of the city's origin. According to legend, it was founded by the 9th-century King Jambulochan on the site of Bahu Fort, which stands on the left bank of the Tawi. In 1730 it came under the rule of the Dogra chiefs of Rajput descent, and it was they who merged Jammu and Kashmir into one state in 1832 and continued to rule it until it acceded to India in 1947. Jammu has a fine artistic tradition, which culminated in the miniature court paintings of the 18th and 19th centuries.

Getting There

For the purposes of this route, Jammu is most easily accessed by air from Delhi. *See* 'Moving On', p.238, for more details. From the airport to the city centre (6km) is around Rs120 by taxi, Rs25 by auto-rickshaw; current rates are posted outside the terminal.

The fast 4645 **Shalimar Express** leaves New Delhi station at 4.10pm daily, arriving at Jammu Tawi station at 6.30 the next morning.

There are also cheap express buses from Delhi to Jammu, bookable from various lodges in Delhi. Jammu can also be accessed by bus from Dharamsala and by bus or train from Pathankot.

Getting Around

Delhi buses often drop passengers at the tourist office, which is close to the better hotels and lodges. Below it, down some steps, is the main bus-station. All this is in the old part of town. The railway station, several kilometres away across the river Tawi, is in the new town. To get to it, take a 'tempo' minibus from outside the main bus station (the stand is at the top of the bazaar). They leave about every half hour.

Taxis/rickshaws have fixed rates for all local tourist spots—they're posted outside the airport and at the tourist office. Bargain hard for short hops around town.

Jammu ℂ (0191–)   ### Tourist Information

The Jammu and Kashmir **Tourist Reception Centre** is above the bus stand on Vir Marg, ℂ 548172, and houses **Indian Airlines**, ℂ 542735, JKTDC tourist office (for **hotel bookings**) and the J & K Bank. There's a second Tourist Reception Centre at the railway station. The **State Bank of India** is in Hari Market and there's a convenient **post office** in Sahedi Chowk. **Modiluft** is at 48-C-C Green Belt Park, Gandhi Nagar, ℂ 532972.

If arriving by air, there's a **tourist information counter** inside the arrival hall, ✆ 531917. It's a lot more useful than the main tourist office.

Touring Jammu

The most common sights in town nowadays are military policemen, nervously fingering their carbines at street corners. Jammu has at least a morning's worth of decent sights, and while things remain so sensitive that's about all you'll want to give it.

City Tour

By rickshaw/taxi, 3–4 hours. Raghunath Temple–Kali Temple– Bagh-i-Bagh–Amar Mahal Museum–Dogra Art Gallery.

Start with a short walk down to the **Raghunath Temple**, just below the tourist office. Built in 1835, it is the centrepiece of a sizeable complex of small temples situated in the heart of the city. Make a short tour of the surrounding bazaars then catch a rickshaw/taxi up to the old **Fort**, 5km above the town. This is best visited on a Tuesday or a Sunday, when pilgrims gather in swarms to do *puja* to the tiny black-faced goddess in the **Kali Temple**, and to hire a goat. In olden days, the goats used to be sacrificed. Now they are just rented by the hour, earnestly prayed to in a small pen, and then sent back to live another day.

Below the fort lies Jammu's most pleasant feature, the lovely **Bagh-i-Bagh gardens**. This green, relaxing spot is constructed on a series of terraces, and gives fine views of the Tawi bridge and the river. You can pause here for tiffin at the small restaurant, before moving on to the **Amar Mahal Museum** (*open 10am–noon and 3–5pm, Sun 10am–noon only*), which is situated on a hill overlooking the Tawi River. Built in 1907, this French-designed palace is beautifully furnished and houses the art collection of Dr Karan Singh, the last Maharajah of Kashmir. The collection consists mainly of family portraits, but includes some rare Pahari paintings and fine soft-toned Kangra-school illustrations.

On a similar theme is the **Dogra Art Gallery**, near the New Secretariat in the Gandhi Bhavan (*open summer 7.30am–1pm, winter 11am–5pm, closed Mon*). Set up in 1954, this has an important collection of nearly 600 paintings (poorly lit but top quality), plus ancient tarleaf manuscripts, terracotta, sculpture and arms. Several of the miniatures depict scenes from the Krishna legend and are the work of the skilled Basohli and Pahari schools of painting which developed from the 18th century on. The schematic use of colours, with detailed Kangra brushwork, are the main characteristics of this delicate and refined school of art. Only a sample are represented, but you can ask to see more.

Jammu ✆ (0191–)   ***Where to Stay***

Few people stay overnight in Jammu, so there's a marked shortage of decent accommodation.

expensive (from Rs1000)

The best deal is the new **K C Residency**, next to the tourist office on Residency Road, ✆ 542773, ✆ 542779. This offers 5-star comforts at 2-star prices—lots of facilities including in-house movies, and centrally air-conditioned rooms at Rs1000/1200 double, breakfast included.

A little more expensive, but handy for the airport, is **Asia Jammu Tawi Hotel**, ✆ 535757, 🖳 5357576, with a nice pool and lawns, an open-air restaurant, and a useful travel agency.

moderate (from Rs350)

Try **Hotel Mansar** at Denis Gate, close to the tourist reception centre, ✆ 543610. There's a good restaurant and travel service, and rooms are well-priced at Rs350/410 or Rs425/510 with a/c.

On Gurdwara Sunder Singh Road, below the bus stand, you'll find **Hotel Swastik**, ✆ 543172, and **Hotel Swagat**, ✆ 466522, both asking Rs350/400 for rooms and Rs100 extra for central air-conditioning.

budget

Budget places near the bus stand include hotels **Sangam** and **City Top**, both with adequate doubles (bath attached) for Rs150/200. Most backpackers however favour the **Tawi View Hotel** at the bottom of the market (Maheshi Gate), with singles/doubles (bath attached) for Rs70/90. If you can't get in at any of the above, there's budget accommodation at both **tourist reception centres**, and retiring rooms (and Rs12 dorm beds) at the **railway station**.

Jammu ✆ (0191–)   **Eating Out**

The Premier Hotel, close to the tourist office, has two popular restaurants: the stylish **Princess**, with good multi-cuisine at moderate prices, and the kitsch **Victoria Junction**, which does a busy trade in burgers, pizzas, tandooris, sodas and shakes. This is a weird place, done up to look like a 19th-century train station, complete with gas lamps and railway carriage seats. The rooftop revolving restaurant at the **K C Residency** hotel has a great Indian/continental menu and the service is spot-on. For budget travellers, there are typical Kashmiri *waswan* (multi-dish) meals at the main **tourist reception centre**'s a/c cafeteria.

Moving On

By air: Indian Airlines and Modiluft offer daily flights between Jammu and Delhi. A new airline, KCV Airways, also covers this route, but only on Mondays and Saturdays.

By rail: From Jammu Tawi railway station, there are trains to Madras, Bombay, Calcutta and Varanasi. The fast train to New Delhi is the 2472 Jammu Tawi–Bombay Express, leaving 11.15am (Tues, Wed, Fri and Sat only) and arriving 9pm. If you're heading to Pathankot, for buses to Dharamsala/Manali, there are 6 or 7 trains daily—the fast 3.45pm departure gets you there in 2 hours.

By road: The bus to Dharamsala leaves the central bus stand at 5am daily. If you miss this one, as many do, there's one deluxe bus (dep 3.30pm, 2hrs) or numerous local buses (3hrs) to Pathankot. From here, there are regular buses up to Dharamsala (3hrs, last one dep 9pm) and occasional buses to Manali (10–12hrs), Shimla, and Dalhousie (4hrs). If you miss all these buses and are faced with an overnight stay in Pathankot (an awful prospect) consider a taxi—it's only Rs600 to, say, Dalhousie (2hrs).

Private deluxe buses to Delhi (14hrs), Manali and Kulu can be booked from Hotel Mansar. Taxis to Dharamsala (Rs2200) or to Manali/Shimla (Rs5500) can be hired from the airport or from outside the tourist office.

Dalhousie population 10,000

One of the least visited and quietest of northern India's hill stations, Dalhousie has retained much of its original character. It is located on a spur of the Dhauladhar range of the Himalaya at about 2000m, amid still well-forested hills. To the north there are spectacular views of the Pir Panjal mountains, and to the south, the rivers and plains of Punjab. When Punjab came under the control of British India in 1848, Dalhousie was developed as a sanatorium and later became a permanent military base. The land was leased from the Raja of Chamba, a nearby hill state, for an annual rent of Rs2000. By the 1860s Dalhousie was also a flourishing summer resort for the élite of Lahore—a sort of poor man's Shimla.

Since partition in 1947 and the loss of her traditional summer residents, Dalhousie has slipped into sleepy backwoods status but remains a nifty getaway from the heat and commotion of the plains below.

Getting There

There are buses to Dalhousie from Kulu, Shimla and New Delhi's ISBT bus stand. The nearest airport to Dalhousie is Kangra, 135km away.

Dalhousie ✆ (018982–)   ***Tourist Information***

The **tourist office**, ✆ 2136, is on the top floor of a building overlooking the bus stand. The **Punjab National Bank** is by the Aroma-n-Claire's Hotel.

Touring Dalhousie

Dalhousie is spread over five hills ranging from 1523m to 2378m, the most important of which are Pottreyn, Bakrota and Tehra (or Moti Tibba). Linking and encircling Pottreyn and Tehra is the Mall, on which many of the houses, hotels and shops are located. Part of the Mall remains closed to vehicles and is a popular walking area which winds through oak and conifer forests.

Dalhousie is not a town with great historical monuments or sites—for that you have to go to nearby Chamba, (*see* below)—but it is a wonderful base for both short and long strolls into the forest. Some 5km from the post office is the small village of **Lakkar Mandi**, from which paths lead to Dainkund Peak and to the nearby **Pholani Devi** temple, which affords spectacular views.

There's a small **wildlife sanctuary** at **Kalatope**, 8km from Dalhousie. The sanctuary has a good population of barking deer, a few Himalayan black bear and the occasional leopard, along with a great variety of birds.

Excursions from Dalhousie

Khajiar, 20km out of Dalhousie, is a large meadow fringed by pine trees, with a lake in the middle. It has a golf course and a 14th-century temple, notable for the quality of its woodcarvings. The surrounding forest, part of the Kalatope Sanctuary, still has plenty of wildlife. For overnight stays, try **Hotel Deodar**, with double rooms/dorm beds for Rs350/Rs45. There's also a **youth hostel** and a **PWD Rest House**.

Chamba, 55km down from Dalhousie, is an ancient hill state dating back to the 6th century AD and ruled by the same family right through to Independence in 1947. Easily reached by taxi/jeep (Rs600 return) or local bus (Rs18, 2hrs) from Dalhousie, it sits on a high ledge overlooking the river Ravi and invites comparison with a medieval Italian village. The town is a trading point for many surrounding hill peoples, and attracts many gaddis (traditional shepherds). On the banks of the river, next to the fire-damaged Maharajah's palace, is a complex of **ancient temples**, which have recently been restored by the Archaeological Survey of India. Three of them (including the large **Lakshmi Narayan Temple**) are dedicated to Vishnu and the other three to Shiva—they date from the 10th to the early 19th century.

The nearby **Bhuri Singh Museum** (*open 10am–5pm, closed Sun*) has a fine collection of 18th- and 19th-century miniatures from the local Pahari schools plus local stone carvings and brass images. There are two **HPTDC Tourist Bungalows** in Chamba: the moderate **Hotel Akhand Chandi**, ✆ (018992) 6363, and the slightly more expensive **Hotel Iravati**, ✆ (018992) 2671.

Dalhousie ✆ (018982–)   ***Where to Stay***

Dalhousie is best avoided during the mid-April to mid-July Indian holiday season, when hotel prices soar and decent rooms are at a premium. Accommodation is cheapest from mid-November to mid-December and from mid-January to early April. Don't expect anything fancy, though—most hotels are pretty run-down.

The top two places, both around the Rs600–1000 mark (low season), are hotels **Grand View** near the bus stand, ✆ 2623, and **Aroma-n-Claire's** on Court Road, ✆ 2199. The latter still has the ghost of the Raj clinging to it. The moderately-priced **Hotel Shangrila**, ✆ 2314, is a converted old house with fine views, a short walk up from Gandhi Chowk. The best cheap options are **Hotel Geetanjali** above the bus stand, ✆ 2155, with huge rooms for Rs190/250, and the friendly **youth hostel**, above the tourist office, ✆ 2189, with cheap dorm beds and a couple of top-view doubles for Rs40.

At Kalatope wildlife sanctuary, there's a **Forest Rest House**, which can be booked from the local forest officer.

Eating Out

Dalhousie is not known for its cuisine, and hotel food cooked to order is probably as good as any in the bazaar. There's a decent **Kwality** at Gandhi Chowk with good tandoori and Chinese items, and **Lovely Restaurant** nearby has Punjabi and south Indian meals at low cost.

Moving On

For Dharamsala and Shimla, it's quickest to get a bus back to Pathankot and take another from there. The same goes for Jammu.

Dharamsala   population 18,500

Like Dalhousie, this picturesque hill station lies on a spur of the Dhauladhar range, some 18km northeast of Kangra. Surrounded by snow-capped mountains, deodar and pine forests, hills and tea gardens, it offers beautiful scenery and some lovely walks. Dharamsala began life as a typical British sanatorium, but suffered a major tragedy in 1905 when it was levelled completely by an earthquake.

In 1960, it gained a new lease of life when adopted as the temporary headquarters of the Dalai Lama, Tibet's spiritual leader. In 1959, after eight years of trying to compromise with the Chinese in Tibet, he had fled—with 100,000 of his subjects—into exile in India. The journey was hard and tens of thousands perished *en route*. Granted sanctuary by Pandit Nehru, some 3000 Tibetans made their new home in Dharamsala, on McLeod Ganj. Since then, the hill station has risen to international fame as the 'Little Lhasa in India'. The Dalai Lama has become a major spokesman for world peace, with a central policy of perpetuating Tibetan religion and culture within Dharamsala itself. Here, children continue to be ordained as monks; senior lamas and reincarnates teach; and Tibetan medicine, education, arts and crafts are thriving once more.

Over the past 30 years, the Tibetans of Dharamsala have carved out one of the most successful stories of the rehabilitation of a people, vigorously maintaining their own identity whilst harmonizing with their new environment. They see the crisis which Tibet has undergone (25,000 Tibetans imprisoned in Chinese jails; all but 45 of Tibet's 6000 monasteries destroyed; only 1300 of their half-million monks and nuns still alive) as the result of bad karma from the past. In exile, their primary aim is to build up a collective fount of good fortune (or compassion) which will reinstate Tibet and oust the Chinese invaders.

In January 1989, one of Tibet's most holy men, the Panchen Lama, died. It was the responsibility of the Dalai Lama to name the child who would be the reincarnation of the Panchen, but no sooner had he done

To Triund (4km) &
Snow Line

To Talnoo

Dal
Lake

DHARAMKOT

Tushita Retreat
Centre

To Bhagsu

St John's
Church

FORSYTH
GANJ

Dip-Tse Chok Ling
Monastery

See McLeodganj
inset map

Mountaineering
Institute

McLEODGANJ

6

7

Tibetan Monastery

Dalai Lama's
Residence

Tibetan
Library

CANTTI ROAD

KHANIARA ROAD

5

OLD CHARLES ROAD

4

3

2

1

State Bank
of India

2

Tourist Office

Taxi Stand

Kangra Art
Museum

Bus Stand

GPO

LOWER
DHARAMSALA

1

To
Palampur

HOTELS
1. Dhauladhar View
2. Dhauladhar
3. Swagat
4. Chamunda
5. B Mehra
6. Bhagsu
7. Chonor House

RESTAURANTS
1. Dekyi Palber
2. Wow Taste Point

N

1km
½ mile

To Airport,
Pathankot
& Delhi

To Lower Dharamsala
(via Forsyth Ganj)

To
Dal Lake

To
Tushita Retreat

Yeti Trekking

1

1

Taxi Stand

Bus
Stand

2

4

2

To Bhagsu
(2km)

3

TEMPLE ROAD

JOGIBARA ROAD

3

5

Chorten &
Prayer Wheels

To Dip-Tse
Chok Ling
Monastery
(short cut)

6

7

State
Bank of India

5

4

TCV
Shop

6

Medical
Clinic

Bookworm
(shop)

GPO

To Monastery
& Dhauladhar
Travel

To Hotel
Bhagsu

To Tibetan
Library & Lower
Dharamsala

HOTELS
1. Seven Hill Lodge
2. Koko Nor
3. Green
4. Tibet
5. Om
6. Loseling Guest House
7. Tibetan Ashoka Guest House

RESTAURANTS
1. Lhasa
2. McLLo
3. Café Shambhala
4. Aroma
5. Yak
6. Ashoka

N

50 metres
50 yards

Dharamsala and Macleod Ganj

this than the child disappeared (July 1995). The Chinese have now enthroned their own choice, an act that could put the spiritual and politicial future of Tibet at stake. In Dharamsala, two questions are now foremost: first, will the child nominated by the Dalai Lama be hidden indefinitely or brainwashed against the Tibetans?; second, will his replacement be loyal to the Dalai Lama or become just a puppet for the Chinese government?

The Tibetan community in McLeod Ganj has now reached something of a crossroads. Regular injections of foreign cash together with funding from the Indian government have left it open to attack from many Indians, who see the Tibetans as rich, and rather too dependent on the West. As one resident put it: 'The Tibetans don't realize how lucky they are to be living in India. Here, they have a lot more rights, opportunity, money and security than if they were to return to Tibet. Presently, they are caught between their fear of being integrated into Indian values and society and their misplaced hope that by adopting western values, which are infiltrating rapidly, they will be better off in the long run. What they do not realize is that life as a refugee in the UK or the States would be far harder and more isolating than anywhere in India.'

When to Go

From New Year to early February is out—too much snow, and most hotels/restaurants are closed. The season really kicks off with the three-day festival of **Losar**, the Tibetan New Year, in February/March. Dharamsala is most pleasant from March to June, and from September to November. October is the best month of all—no rains, clear views and marvellous scenery. Whenever you come, bring some woollen clothing—it can get chilly at night.

Getting There

You can get to Dharamsala by air from Delhi (via Gagal airport, 15km away). Buses run to Lower Dharamsala and McLeod Ganj from Delhi, Shimla, Manali, Kulu and Pathankot. The fast 1077 **Jhelum Express** train from New Delhi (dep 9.50pm) arrives in Pathankot (Chakki Bank) at 8.25 the next morning.

Getting Around

The hill station divides neatly into two separate parts. Lower Dharamsala (1250m) is a dullish Indian-style township, with civic buildings, a bazaar, a few hotels, the tourist office and the main bus-stand. Upper Dharamsala is 700m higher up at McLeod Ganj, and is anything but dull. McLeod Ganj has Tibetan temples, chatty monks, psychedelic restaurants, '60s sounds, secondhand bookshops and crowds of chilled-out travellers.

Buses ply between Upper and Lower Dharamsala (45mins up, 30mins down, Rs4) every hour or so from 6.30am to 8pm. You can do the same trip by shared

For many, McLeod Ganj is the definitive freak centre of India—even more so than Manali, Goa or Pushkar. Westerners come here to study Buddhism, alternative medicine, and the merits of a ganja-based lifestyle— but mainly for R & R from India proper. The Dalai Lama is a big draw, and if you can't get a personal interview (he's booked out months ahead nowadays), you can at least catch one of his public audiences (get dates from his private office) or see a video of it later on. The best time to see him is at the end of Losar (*see* below), when he gives teachings over a 10-day period.

taxi/minicab for around Rs5 per person, or take a private taxi for Rs70. Walking up takes an hour, coming down (via the library) only 40 minutes.

Dharamsala ✆ *(01892–)*   ***Tourist Information***

The **tourist office**, ✆ 24498, is below Hotel Dhauladhar in Lower Dharamsala, and above **Jagson Airlines**, ✆ 4328. It opens and closes when it feels like it and is of no use whatsoever. The main **post office** is 1km further down the road, but most travellers use the small sub-office in McLeod Ganj. The Foreigners' Registration Office below the GPO in the lower town is a good place for **visa extensions**. The **State Bank of India** has branches in Lower Dharamsala and McLeod Ganj, but is open for foreign transactions from 10.30am to 1pm weekdays only.

McLeod Ganj's best **travel agent** is Dhauladhar Travels, just up from the Monastery, ✆ 23158, 🖷 22246. Run by friendly Rajiv, it offers a complete travel service—including cheap flights (e.g. Rs18,000 Delhi–London one-way; Rs12,000 Delhi–Bangkok return) and has an **STD phone/fax**.

Walking Tour

Full day. Tsuglag Khang–Tibetan Library–Tibetan Children's Village–Dal Lake–TCV Handicrafts Centre–St John's Church.

From McLeod Ganj bus stand, walk past the *chorten* wheels and fork right down Monastery Road until you come to the **Tsuglag Khang** (central cathedral) opposite the Dalai Lama's house. This is a lively, colourful temple draped with exotic *thangkas* (religious paintings on cloth) and housing a giant image of Avalokiteshvara, the 100-armed deity of Tibet. Built on the lip of the ridge, it commands fine views of the valley. Prayers take place around 4am and 8pm, and there's a Tibetan monastery and a small nunnery nearby.

Below the main temple, a steep hill-road leads down to the **Tibetan Library** (*open 9am–1pm and 2–5pm exc Sun*). To get there, you can either follow the road (45mins) or cut across it using goat tracks (20mins). It has an ancient manuscript room on the ground floor, where you can ask to see beautifully illustrated 1000-year-old volumes containing the teachings of Buddha. Upstairs, there's a small museum with a good collection of Buddhist images, ritual objects and crafts. The library also arranges lectures and can advise on meditation or Tibetan-language courses.

By the time you get back to McLeod Ganj, it should be time for lunch. Don't sit down too long, though—lunch often turns into supper. Back at the bus stand, a steep 15–20-minute hike up the hill-road via Yeti Trekking brings you to the Government Primary School, high up on the ridge. Here, you can either take the up-road to the pretty picnic spot of **Triund** at the foot of the Dhauladhar (4 hours' walk), or take the down-road following the water-pipe all the way down to Dal Lake. This is a pleasant 15-minute ramble, with an occasional flash of the Kangra valley appearing through the treeline. Just before the lake, you'll come to the **Tibetan Children's Village**. This was established in 1960  to care for the numerous orphans, semi-orphans and destitute Tibetan refugee children who flooded into India. Today, it provides Tibetan-style education and upbringing for some 1300 children, many of whom have individual sponsors from Europe and the US. From 7.30am to 1.30pm you can drop in for a chat with the children and teachers.

Just below TCV is the small pond surrounded by cedars which is **Dal Lake**. It's hugely popular with Indian tourists—a local Hindu deity is supposed to have materialized here. Above the lake, a metalled road leads up to **Mehr Ashram**, the only Hindu ashram in Dharamsala. A lot of westerners stay around here, studying yoga and meditation. Austerities start with the 4km hike up there. From the ashram, you can walk across to **Dharamkot**, a popular picnic spot affording panoramic views of Dhauladhar and its surrounding valley. There is a Vipassana meditation centre at Dharamkot village, with 10-day residential courses.

If you're feeling lazy, take the main road (left) from Dal Lake back to McLeod Ganj. Ten minutes' walk down the road, **TCV Handicrafts Centre** appears on your left. This was founded in 1974, to give crafts training and employment to Tibetan children who could

not continue formal schooling, or who had a talent for manual trades. At present, the centre has some 250 workers and is fast achieving self-sufficiency. It specializes in Tibetan hand-knotted woollen carpets, and there's a good workshop layout where you can see them and other crafts being produced. A short walk below the centre is the unexciting village of **Forsyth Ganj**. Here you have a choice of a bus ride or a 45-minute walk back to McLeod Ganj. If walking it, you'll pass by **St John's-in-the-Wilderness Church**, a typical English church in a peaceful glade of deodar cedars, with fine stained-glass windows and a cemetery with a monument to Lord Elgin, one of India's viceroys. The pastor has a good sense of humour and enjoys visitors; it's largely thanks to him that the old stone church is in such good condition.

Shopping

Between McLeod Ganj and Forsyth Ganj, **TCV Handicrafts Centre** (*open 8am–5pm exc Sun*) has the best range and quality of Tibetan produce. It's not cheap, but you'll be hard-pressed to leave without buying something. Popular purchases include handwoven shoulder bags, woollen jackets, brass-button cotton shirts, colourful *thangkas* on silk or cloth, rice-paper prints, semi-precious jewellery, and bright prayer-flags. TCV is particularly well known for its Tibetan woollen carpets, which incorporate tantric or dragon designs. The 'speciality' carpet measures 9m x 9m, depicts the sacred Kalchakra mandala, and can be made only with special permission from the Dalai Lama. There's another TCV shop, also fixed-price, in McLeod Ganj. Shopping anywhere else, be prepared to bargain hard. Tibetans aren't allowed to take jobs from native Indians so they have to charge high for their handicrafts.

One of the more interesting shops in McLeod Ganj is **Nowrojee & Sons General Merchant,** a fascinating old-fashioned store (with attached beer shop) which is one of the few genuine relics of the Raj to be found in any hill station.

Leisure

You can enjoy a beer at the McLLo restaurant or an 'English' film at one of the several **video parlours** in town, before heading out for some serious exercise.

Situated so close to the snowline, Dharamsala offers many possibilities for **trekking** and **mountain climbing**. Trekking in this region is far less exploited than at Manali. The best seasons are April to June and (especially) September to November. The going is generally tough, but there's a wealth of beautiful scenery to take your mind off tired muscles. With a good pair of walking shoes and a supply of water and biscuits (refreshments are limited in the hills), you can head off in any direction and be alone. One warning: if you stroll off the beaten track, don't go wandering into any dark caves—animals, even bears, may be sheltering there. For the best views, set out in the early morning. By around noon, the valley is often obscured by dense mist.

For short walks—say, up to Triund at the foot of the snow-clad Dhauladhar—you don't really need a guide. Beyond this point, however, you do. On treks above 3400m, you'll need to take it easy, as altitude sickness is a common problem. For organized treks, contact **Summit Trekking** above Ashoka restaurant or **Eagles Height Trekkers,** just up from the bus stand, © 24330. They both offer long-distance treks to Leh, Ladakh and the Spiti Valley, as well as short 4–5-day hikes to Kareri Lake (all year, except January/February) and marvellous seven-day treks (May to November) over the Dhauladhar to Bharmour, via the high Inderhara Pass (4610m). Charges are most reasonable: around Rs400 per day, inclusive of food, guide, porter and equipment. If you're feeling really adventurous, the **Mountaineering Institute,** a short walk north of McLeod Ganj, can arrange 8–10-day high-altitude treks (April to December) for around Rs2000 per person, all-inclusive, for a minimum of 10 people.

Medical Treatment

People (especially MS sufferers) come from all over the world to be treated by Dr Yeshi Dhonden, the former senior physician to the Dalai Lama. He has a clinic close to the Aroma restaurant, © 2461. Other private treatment is available from the Tibetan Medical Institute across from the Koko Nor Hotel, © 2484. The doctors obtain detailed diagnoses by pulse-readings, and the medicine prescribed is natural and effective.

Lower Dharamsala

There's only one half-decent hotel here: HPTDC's **Hotel Dhauladhar**, ✆ 24926/7, with first-rate mountain views from the sun terrace and an okay restaurant/bar. The management is slovenly, however, and even the £15 'deluxe' suites have dirty carpets, malfunctioning TVs, and monkey excrement littering the private balconies. It's popular mainly with Indian honeymooners.

The cheaper hotels **Padmini** and **Dhauladhar View**, ✆ 22889, are the first places you see coming up the hill by bus. Both have large but basic doubles with bath from Rs250, and you can walk up to the bigger hotel for meals and views. If on a budget, continue on up the hill until the road forks at a fountain. Bear to the right for hotels **Swagat** and **Chamunda** (Rs120/150 a night) and to the left for hotel **B Mehra** (large hovels for Rs40/50).

McLeod Ganj

Up here, most hotels shut down between New Year and early February, and are completely full by March (the busiest month). Don't worry about finding a room, though—there's always someone about to check out. A popular bet is the **Hotel Tibet**, behind the bus stand, ✆ 22587. It's not all that cheap, but £10/12 buys you a clean double with TV, hot shower and phone. The staff are friendly; there's a nice restaurant; and the views from the rooftop terrace are excellent. Two cheaper alternatives, both down an alley past the *chorten* wheels, are **Loseling** and **Tibetan Ashoka** guest houses. Both offer bright rooms from Rs50 to Rs250, and the monk-run Loseling has fine views from its 'breakfast' terrace. To the south of town, **Chinar Lodge**, ✆ 22006, ✉ 22010, has upmarket digs with TV/phone and room service for Rs800 a double. The HPTDC **Hotel Bhagsu**, opposite, ✆ 23191, is cheaper but not as cheerful. Down by the monastery, and up the steep road, there's the top-end **Chonor House**, ✆ 22006, ✉ 22010, with singles/doubles around Rs700/1000, a good restaurant, STD/fax facility and helpful staff. Many celebrities, VIPs, lamas and film crews stay here, and the rooms are beautifully done out with Tibetan wall murals.

Beyond McLeod Ganj

Of late, shoestringers have begun to shift up to the village of **Bhagsu**, a 20-minute walk up from McLeod Ganj bus stand. There's an interesting temple here, and a freshwater pond for swimming. In many ways, Bhagsunath resembles McLeod Ganj of ten years ago, with lots of little tea shops and cafés, and local people renting out clean rooms in their houses for Rs30–80 a night. A few guest houses have sprung up on the road to Bhagsu, including the **Green Hotel** and **Koko Nor Hotel** (both Rs40–100), also **Zilnon Monastery**, which has a good restaurant and simple clean rooms at Rs60/80. A separate fork above the bus stand leads up to **7 Hills Guest House**, in a quiet location and with good views and double rooms with bath for Rs80 (hot shower Rs10 extra). Just up from this one, a steep flight of stairs takes you up to **Kalsang Guest House**, ✆ 22609, and **Paljor Gakyil Guest House**. Both places charge between Rs140 and 250, and some rooms command spectacular views.

For a stay in style and peace, contact **Clouds 'n' Villa**, behind the Tibetan Medical Institute, on the way to the Tibetan Library, ✆ 22109. It has only seven rooms, priced around Rs800, but was once the Maharajah of Kangra's residence and is choc-a-bloc with antique furnishings and Raj memorabilia.

Another comfy place is **Glenmoor Cottages**, located on the road out to Dal Lake, about 1km north of McLeod Ganj bus stand, ✆ 4410, ✆ 23374. This has quiet and relaxing cottage-style accommodation from US$35/45, and is run by pleasant people.

If you really want to get away from it all, continue on down the same road, past Dal Lake, until 4km out of McLeod Ganj you come to **Talnoo**. This village has panoramic mountain views and is the starting point for many treks. To stay, ask around for **Annapurna Guest House**, which has cheap rooms from Rs100.

If you're looking to share the monastic way of life, make a beeline for **Diptse-Chok-Ling Monastery**. A camel track leads down to it from the main bus stand—just follow the signs. Rooms with bath are clean and comfortable, and there is no fixed charge—payment is by donation only.

Dharamsala ✆ *(01892–)*   ***Eating Out***

In Lower Dharamsala, the best food is still at Hotel Dhauladhar, even though it comes at you in sections. A few minutes' walk up the road, where it splits at the fountain, there's **Wow Taste-Point** to the left, with delicious juices, and **Dekyi Palber** to the right, with cheap local dishes. The **Monal** restaurant, just outside the Hotel Dhauladhar, does a wide range of tasty snacks (Chinese and continental) as well as Gujarati and Bengali fare.

McLeod Ganj is the place to forget you're in India and to tuck into as many quiches, pancakes, doughnuts and full fried breakfasts as you can handle. In terms of cuisine, as in so much else, this place is the nearest thing in India to Kathmandu, and few travellers leave without a doggie bag of goodies to consume on their way back to '*dhal* and rice' land on the plains below. Cafés and restaurants are opening and closing all the time, but a few—like the **Hotel Tibet**, the **Dol Kar** (opposite), the **Shambala**, the **Aroma** (down from the prayer wheels) and the mid-priced **McLLo** by the bus stand—should still be there when you arrive. Indian food is best at the **Ashoka Restaurant** in town and at the **Trimurti** in Bhagsu. For cakes and baked goods, it's the Hotel Tibet (again) and **Chocolate Log** on the road down to the library (take a room here, just for the breakfasts!). Tibetan/Chinese fare is tops at **Lhasa Restaurant** opposite McLLo, even though it takes forever to arrive, and at the **Himalaya** on Bhagsu Road. The small **Yak Restaurant** is famous for its veg or mutton *momos* (Tibetan dumplings) and the rooftop **Tsongkha Restaurant** for its tofu vegetarian dishes. Two other popular places, serving a bit of everything, are the **Om** and the **Shangri-La**. The tacky **Hot Spot Fast Food Joint**, in a brand-new three-storey building at the bus stand, has fresh biscuits, hummus and tabouli (great for a trek take-out) along with good ice cream and brown bread. Indians love it for its flash westernism.

Moving On

By air: From Gagal airport, 15km below Dharamsala, Jagson Airlines fly every Monday and Friday to Delhi, via Kulu.

By road: From the main bus stand in Lower Dharamsala (at the bottom of a steep flight of steps), there are daily buses to Kulu (10hrs), Manali (12hrs), Shimla (10hrs), Pathankot (3/4hrs) and Delhi (13hrs). The deluxe buses to Delhi and Shimla leave at 6am and 7.45pm respectively. There's only one bus daily to Dalhousie, leaving at 8.30am. To check timings, phone ✆ 24903.

From McLeod Ganj, there is one superfast bus to Delhi (12hrs), leaving 6pm every Sun, Mon, Wed and Thurs. Book tickets from **Dhauladhar Travels** near the Tibetan Monastery.

Taxis from McLeod Ganj charge Rs1600 to Kulu, Rs1900 to Shimla, Rs3300 to Delhi.

By rail: From Pathankot, taxis and auto-rickshaws run to Chakki Bank rail station (4km away) for fast trains to Delhi. The 1078 Jhelum Express (dep 9.45pm) gets into New Delhi at 10.15 the following morning.

Kulu   population 16,000

Kulu town is situated on the banks of the winding River Beas, looking down the beautiful 'Valley of Gods' from a cool altitude of 1200 metres. Though it is the administrative centre of the valley, it has not (unlike Manali) been developed for tourism. This means fewer facilities, but more peace and quiet.

Kulu is mentioned in Hieun Tsiang's travelogue, and changed hands many times over the centuries before coming under British rule in the 19th century. Much of its history is tied up in its principal landmark, the temple of Raghunath, dedicated to Lord Rama. The story goes that, in the mid-17th century, the rajah of the area fell sick and took the advice of his holy men to send out to the locality of Iyudya for the *murtis* (sacred images) of Raghunath (Rama). In thanks for his prompt recovery, he donated the entire valley to the gods, and made Kulu the permanent home of the holy icons, erecting the present temple for their safekeeping.

Like Manali, Kulu has a wide variety of hill and mountain people. The women wear mainly traditional costumes—woollen homespun dresses (usually cord-belted), embroidered shawls and leather moccasins. The men, compromising with western fashions, wear

Kulu caps and wool jackets along with Levi jeans and plastic anoraks. The people of Kulu, unlike in touristy Manali, are very open, friendly and keen to talk to foreigners. They are also very urbanized—a thriving chain of hi-fi, camera and electrical shops, and several video parlours, have sprung up between the old, tumbling wooden houses manned by grizzled tailors, dentists and fruit-and-nut men. Surprisingly, few of the 'locals' are local at all—most of them come from neighbouring valleys and other parts of Himachal Pradesh. The valley itself stretches northward for almost 80km from nearby Mandi at 750m all the way up to the Rohtang Pass at 3978m.

When to Go

Kulu is at its prettiest from April to June, and is best for trekking and views from September to November. The town itself really comes alive only during the important **Dussehra festival**, which takes place in October after the monsoons. The festival starts on the 10th day of the rising moon, and continues with mounting vigour for seven days. All over India, Dussehra is celebrated to commemorate Rama's victory over the demon king Ravana. But in Kulu, it is Raghunath as 'main man of the valley' who is the focus of festivities: some 200 gods from temples all over the valley are brought here to pay him tribute. The powerful goddess Hadimba is brought down from Manali to commence proceedings, and the festivities continue until she goes away again.

Getting There

You can fly to Kulu from Delhi, Dharamsala or Shimla. There are also fast buses from Manali, Shimla, Dharamsala and Delhi. *See* 'Moving On', p.252. for more information.

Kulu ✆ (01902–)   ***Tourist Information***

The **tourist office**, ✆ 2349, is on the ridge above the new-town bus stand. It is open 10am–5pm except Sundays and gives poor information in slow motion. It advertises tours it doesn't have and maps it doesn't sell. You'll find the **State Bank of India** above the tourist office, on the road out to Shimla.

Touring Kulu

Most of Kulu's sights, as in Manali, are natural ones, best seen on foot. A short 2–3-hour expedition is sufficient to gain the finest local mountain and valley views. The town is divided into two parts by the winding Beas River. The new town, with its modern bazaars, main bus stand and tourist office, lies above the quiet, archaic village of the old town. The long, narrow street connecting the two towns is a fiesta of Tibetan *dhabas*, Sikh jewellers, Hindu tailors, astrologer-palmists, bootmakers, and scores of shawl industries. The hi-fi/electronic shops keep a deliberately low profile in high season—handicrafts, not modern technology, are Kulu's main earner.

Unless you plan on staying over, a practical plan is to come into Kulu on an early bus from Dharamsala, drop your bags at the safe Bijaleshwar Hotel, spend a few hours looking around, and then hop on a late bus to Manali. Gruelling perhaps, but there are much better hotels and food in Manali.

Walking Tour

2–5 hours. Shiva Temple–Raghunath Temple–Vaishno Devi Temple.

This is a beautiful walk, offering some of Himachal's finest scenery. Start at the small pink-domed **Shiva Temple**, situated on the riverbank clearing between old and new Kulu. Opposite it is the **Kailash**, the only cinema in the valley. The temple is a modest affair. A small Nandi bull wearing a silk scarf faces into a tiled shrine. The five-headed marble image of the deity within is surrounded by fine floral wall-carvings. The small hut facing the shrine is where the resident priest hangs out, often in a huddle with other holy men and sadhus.

Walk back to the main road, and cross over. A steep stairway on the far side takes you up onto a cobbled path, which leads right up into the hills. Some 10 minutes after joining the path, you'll come across the **Raghunath Temple**—it's in a small courtyard, to the left of a stone archway. Unfortunately, it's only open from 5pm so, unless you're making a dusk visit, you can't go in or take photographs. You can, however, peer through the grid window and see Lord Raghunath sitting on his velvet-cushioned silver chariot, beneath four huge ceiling mirrors. Beside the grid, a charming sentiment invokes Shiva: 'As the fruit when ripened detaches itself from its limbs, so grant us the immortality liberating from the chain of transmigration.'

A few minutes further up the path, to the right, you'll spot a wonderful old Transylvanian-style mansion called **Raja Rupi Palace**. It's a private house, owned by one of the old ruling families of the valley, and is a remarkable example of Indo-Gothic architecture. A steep ascent of some 20 minutes further up the cobbled trail (actually a major pilgrim and trekking path) brings you out above the village and onto the high ridges, with breathtaking views down over the valley—the Beas River running along its length like a silvery snake. A misty mountain range, enclosing the narrow valley on both sides, provides the perfect backdrop. If you have the energy, another 45 minutes' climb up the rocky hill-path, following the other pilgrims, brings you to the quaint **Vaishno Devi Temple**, where the image of the goddess Vaishno (Durga) is enshrined in a small cave. Walking back down, you'll pass many friendly locals: shepherds, hill folk, even villagers carrying barn doors up the mountain on their shoulders. It's a complicated descent, though, so note your route on the way up to avoid getting lost.

Shopping

Kulu is famous for its fine, light woollen crafts—especially handloom shawls (*khaddi*). Genuine handwoven Kulu shawls are now, however, a rarity. Government taxes on wool have become prohibitive, and shawl-makers can no longer be sure of making a profit. If you're set on having one, avoid the dozens of shops in town selling fake shawls. The only place you can now be sure of getting the real thing (along with caps, mufflers, gloves and jackets) is the **Bhutti Weavers Co-operative Society**, 5km out of town on the road to Mandi, ✆ 5079. The standard shawl here measures 11.5m x 3m and costs anything from Rs200 to Rs2000. Pure *pashmina*, combed from the underbellies of Ladakhi *chigu* goats, is a particularly warm wool and thus very expensive—up to Rs3000 per shawl. Otherwise, try **Bug Boutique** at Hotel Shobla, which has 100% Kulu fabrics woven into pricey but fashionable clothing.

Leisure

Full trek information and guides are available at Raison, 14km from Kulu on the way to Manali. Raison is the base for many good **short-range treks** in this region.

Kulu ✆ *(01902–)*

Where to Stay
moderate (from US$20)

The new **Hotel Shobla**, opposite the new bus stand, ✆ 2800, 4646, has a fantastic location. Perched right on the edge of a cliff, it offers first-rate views of the surrounding rivers and valley from its rooftop restaurant-bar. The rooms are bright, the staff friendly, and the travel desk useful for flight ticketing, bus and taxi bookings, and fishing, trekking and white-water rafting trips. There's also an STD booth here, handy for international calls.

Out of town, choose between the smart new **Vaishali**, ✆ 4225/6, and the well-established **Silver Moon**, ✆ 2488, adjoining each other 1km from the new bus stand. Both hotels are warm and comfortable, with good restaurants and well-furnished rooms.

budget

Two good places, both at the back of the ridge behind the tourist office, are **Rohtang Hotel**, ✆ 2303, with a good restaurant, and **Bijaleshwar Hotel**, ✆ 2667, with a nice sit-out garden. The former charges Rs200/250, the latter Rs100/150, and both are friendly and clean.

Kulu ✆ *(01902–)*

Eating Out

Upmarket fare is available at hotels **Sarvari**, **Silver Moon** and **Vaishali**, all around 10 minutes walk from the tourist office. During the day, you can enjoy fine views along with your meal at **Hotel Shobla**, which also has the only beer-bar in town. If money is tight, there's cheap veggie fare at **Rohtang Hotel**, fast-food pizzas and burgers at **Hot Stuff**, and local snacks and good coffee at **Monal Café**. The last two are near the tourist office.

Moving On

By air: Archana Airways, ✆ 65630, fly daily between Bhuntar (10km from Kulu) and Shimla/Delhi, but often suspend flights out of season. Jagson Airlines, ✆ 65222, are more reliable. They fly daily to Delhi, every Monday and Friday to

Dharamsala, and every Tuesday and Saturday to Shimla. For more information, contact **Aggrawal Travels**, by the bus stand in Bhuntar, ✆ 65220.

By road: From the new bus stand by the tourist office, there are regular buses to Manali (2hrs) and to Shimla (8–9hrs), but only one bus daily to Dharamsala, leaving 8am. The fast deluxe bus to Delhi originates in Manali and is often full when it arrives in Kulu at 8am (at 7pm in the winter). Advance-book this one.

Taxis from the new bus stand charge Rs450 to Manali, Rs1700 to Shimla or Dharamsala, and Rs3500 to Delhi. To cut costs, ask to share.

Cars out to **Manikaran**, for the hot-water springs and the shawl factories, cost around Rs550 return (or go by Rs6 bus to Bhuntar, then another bus to Manikaran, 3hrs total). To stay, there's **Padha Family House** near the bridge (around Rs100) or HPTDC's **Hotel Parvati** (doubles for Rs300).

Manali
population 4000

The small, picturesque hill town of Manali lies at the head of the Kulu valley. Enclosed on three sides by calm mountains, it is surrounded by some of the loveliest meadows and orchards, rivers and terraced fields in Himachal Pradesh. Though a modern-day resort, it has been a holy site for over 1000 years, and pilgrims still come in large numbers both to visit the shrine of the saint Moni in old Manali village and to have a sacred dip in the nearby sulphur springs of Vashisht.

The name Manali was a British creation; until 1938 it was known as Dana Bazaar. The hippies found it—or rather its high-quality dope—in the 1960s, but it remained just a sleepy backwoods village until the late 1970s, when its tourist potential was discovered. At this time a new town sprang up, built downstream from Old Manali village, and a small iron bridge was built to connect them. Today, the new Manali is rapidly developing into a full-blown Indian holiday town, with 'Hot Byte' fast-food joints, noisy video parlours, screeching tannoyed music, and convoys of cars and jeeps full of hallooing party people. Its burgeoning reputation as the ideal holiday destination for Indian honeymooners is not the only reason for its current popularity, however; it also has much to do with the loss of Kashmir as a tourist destination. Hotels and trek operators know full well that this is as far north as foreigners wanting to see the mountains can go for the time being, and they have set up shop in a big way. The positive result is a far greater variety of sports and activities than before, including paragliding, river-rafting, mountain-biking and even heli-skiing.

The tourist office, inundated with tourists from all over India, has little time for foreigners. It does them all a big favour by packing them off to Old Manali, where it supposes 'hippies' belong. Few people object. Out of the noisy new town, Manali is still one of the most picturesque spots in India—a peaceful vista of dense woodland, yellow mustard meadows and red saffron paddy fields, inhabited by an exotic array of different hill and mountain peoples. In the spring, the valley is indescribably beautiful: there are rippling streams, pine-scented forests, meadows of violets and blue speedwell, and fields full of wild raspberries and strawberries. There is a lot to see, do and buy in Manali, and the walks and treks in this region really take some beating.

When to Go

Manali has a long tourist season. The flowers and meadows are at their best from mid-April to June; high-level trekking takes place between July and mid-November; mountain views are clearest during October and November (following the monsoons), and the skiing season is from December to February, culminating in the **Winter Carnival** of February. The most colourful occasion of the year is the big **Dussehra** festival of September/October, when people turn up from all over the valley, bringing their gods with them, for a riotous 10-day carnival of music, song and dance. Somewhat akin to an English country show, it's a great opportunity to see the wide variety of peoples inhabiting the Kulu valley decked out in all their traditional costumes.

The only time to avoid Manali is from mid-May to end-June—busloads of home tourists roll in, all accommodation soars in price, and the roads are clogged with screeching cars and jeeps. If coming in the winter, wrap up warm—there can still be snow about in March.

Getting There

The nearest airport is at Bhuntar, 50km away. From here you have a choice of local buses (from the stand just up from the terminal), or 5-person shared-taxis to take you up to Manali. You can fly to Buntar from Delhi, Dharamsala and Shimla. There are also daily buses from Shimla, Delhi and Dharamsala. *See also* 'Moving On' for more information.

Getting Around

Manali's one main street, the Mall, has the tourist office, the taxi stand, the bus stand, the better restaurants, and various handicraft shops. At the bottom of the Mall is the new Model Town, with several subterranean shopping precincts. The road up to Old Manali, 15 minutes on foot, starts from the top of the Mall, and is lined with hotels. Auto-rickshaws and taxis run visitors to Vashisht, Old Manali, and other local interest spots—off the meter. But Manali is essentially a place for relaxing walks and taking it easy. The old town has a large population of travellers who have doing nothing at all down to a fine art.

Manali ℂ (01901–)   *Tourist Information*

The **tourist office** at the top of the Mall, ℂ 2175, runs a close second to Bhubaneshwar's as the worst in the country—no maps, no printed information, and no time for foreigners.

The HP Marketing Office below the tourist office sells **sightseeing tours** by deluxe bus to the Rohtang Pass and Manikaran.

The **post office** is at the bottom of the Mall. The **State Bank of India** is opposite the tourist office. The **travel agency** just below the bank is the main booking

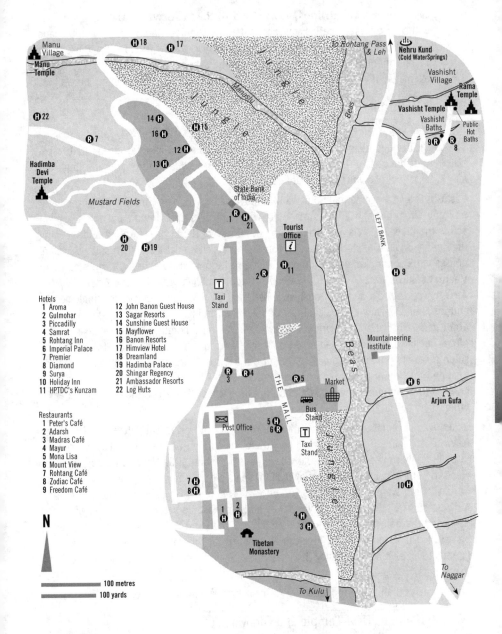

Manu
Village
Manu
Temple

H 18   H 17

To Rohtang Pass
& Leh

Nehru Kund
(Cold Water Springs)

Vashisht
Village

Rama
Temple

Vashisht Temple

Jungle

Jungle

Manshi

Beas

Vashisht
Baths

Public
Hot
Baths

H 22

14 H

R 7

16 H

R 15

12 H

13 H

Hadimba
Devi
Temple

Mustard Fields

State Bank
of India

9 R

R 8

R 1

R 21

Tourist
Office
i

H 11

H 20

H 19

LEFT BANK

H 9

Beas

Hotels
1 Aroma
2 Gulmohar
3 Piccadilly
4 Samrat
5 Rohtang Inn
6 Imperial Palace
7 Premier
8 Diamond
9 Surya
10 Holiday Inn
11 HPTDC's Kunzam

12 John Banon Guest House
13 Sagar Resorts
14 Sunshine Guest House
15 Mayflower
16 Banon Resorts
17 Himview Hotel
18 Dreamland
19 Hadimba Palace
20 Shingar Regency
21 Ambassador Resorts
22 Log Huts

Restaurants
1 Peter's Café
2 Adarsh
3 Madras Café
4 Mayur
5 Mona Lisa
6 Mount View
7 Rohtang Café
8 Zodiac Café
9 Freedom Café

N

100 metres
100 yards

Manali

2 R

Taxi
Stand

R 3

R 4

THE MALL

R 5

Market

Mountaineering
Institute

H 6

Arjun Gufa

Post Office

5
6 R

Bus
Stand

Taxi
Stand

Jungle

7 H
8 H

H 10

1 H

2 H

4 H

3 H

Tibetan
Monastery

To Naggar

To Kulu

255

agent for **Jagson Airlines**, ✆ 247, and **Archana Airways**. The cheapest STD booth for **overseas calls** is just above the tourist office. Bookworm, down the lane behind the taxi stand, is an excellent **bookshop** run by friendly Tibetans. Open 10am–6pm except Sundays, it has new and secondhand books for rent, sale or exchange. If you want to get into the spirit of Manali, you'll be coming here a lot.

Walk 1: Vashisht

Half day. Vashisht Baths–Vashisht Temple–Tibetan Monastery.

The small unspoilt village of Vashisht is famous for its natural mineral springs and (especially) for its hot sulphur baths. If you've just arrived off a sweaty bus or are returning from a trek, this should be your first port of call.

Vashisht is a very scenic half-hour walk from Manali town, best commenced in the early morning. From just above the tourist office, the road forks right down a hill and takes you across the River Beas via a bridge. On the other side of the bridge, turn left and, keeping the river and Old Manali mountain on your left, proceed up the track via rustic old Manali houses until, some 3km out of town, you hit a series of steps to your right, running up to **Vashisht Baths** (*open 7am–7pm; adm Rs40 for a small cubicle for max 2 people, Rs80 for a bigger one*). These are Turkish-style bath-houses, with tiled cubicles for single people and for families. They are exceedingly popular with Indian honeymooning couples, who don't generally get a lot of privacy elsewhere. Westerners enjoy them because they're often the first bath they've had in the country—a chance to lie back and let the bubbling sulphur waters (which are piped through from a natural spring) soak away all the grime, dust and tension of travel. You get about 30 minutes in the bath-house, which is quite enough for beginners: vertigo is a common after-effect. It's a good idea to arrive early when there are no queues.

Relax over a hot pot of tea outside, then make the 15-minute ascent (left) up to the village of Vashisht itself. On the way, you'll pass the highest mountain dairy in India, also several more old slate-roofed houses. In the village, visit the quaint little **Vashisht Temple**, dedicated to Lord Rama and allegedly over 2000 years old. At the temple, there's another set of natural hot water sulphur baths (*open 8am–8pm daily*). These are public baths—one for women and one for men. If you fancy a dip, choose between the ordinary baths for Rs40 and the deluxe ones for Rs80. The latter is tiled and the former isn't. Afterwards, back in town, drop in on the **Tibetan Monastery** at the bottom of the Mall—site of a famous carpet-weaving industry: it's one of the better places in town to buy carpets and handicrafts.

For information on accommodation in Vashisht, *see* 'Where to Stay', p.261.

Walk 2: Hadimba Devi Temple and Old Manali

For another morning, take the uphill road (bearing left) from the top of the Mall. A short walk takes you up to John Banon Guest House, where the road swings off to the left. A short way up this fork, opposite Rising Star hotel, a path cuts straight across the mustard fields (full of yellow blossoms in summer) and up into the dense pine forest. Some 15 minutes later, you'll come to a sign reading 'Dungri—population 140 souls'. You are now within striking distance of Manali's holiest shrine, the **Hadimba Devi Temple**. This famous pagoda-style temple, built in the 16th century by Raja Bahadur Singh, is constructed in the local architectural style of rough-cut stones alternating with bands of wood. The overhanging rock is capped by a four-tiered pagoda roof made up of beautifully fitted slats of deodar. The plinth is high and the pillars, door-posts and lintel—all exquisitely carved—are superb examples of the fine craftsmanship for which this valley is famous. Deer and markhor horns, donated by local hunters, flank the entrance, lending it a rather folklorish air. The interior is a natural rock cave and the shrine itself is a simple, unadorned slab of stone, on which sacrifices are offered. Under this is a shallow cave, where you can just about discern the footprint of the resident *devi* (goddess). There is no other icon.

Located in a peaceful wooded glade, the temple is dedicated to the goddess Hadimba Devi. According to popular myth, she was a mountain belle rescued from her evil demon-brother by the god Bhim, whom she later married. Today, she is revered as the mother goddess of the whole valley, and is regularly consulted in times of natural hardship or calamity (and by prospective brides and grooms). Most importantly, every Dussehra festival for centuries has been customarily opened and closed by Hadimba, in the presence of her *rath* or image. If (and this has happened) riots break out during the festival, it is taken as a sign that Hadimba is not amused, and the whole show is summarily cancelled.

Going back down, cut across to your left. This will bring you back to the main road and thence to John Banon Guest House. Turning left here, you'll soon come to the small bridge connecting New and Old Manali. In season, the landscape is a pastoral delight of colourful meadows, brick-house water-wheels, rushing mountain streams, and snow-capped peaks. Across the bridge and taking the path up to the left, you'll quickly come into the village of **Old Manali**, 3km from the new town. Here life proceeds much the same as it has for centuries. Bales of hay hang out to dry from barnyard rafters; smoke drifts up from stove-chimneys poking out from slate roofs; and stacked woodpiles prop up the sides of ornately carved traditional houses. Look out for the old **Temple of Manu** after whom the town was named—it's right at the top of the village, beyond the Dragon Guest House. Behind it, via damp cobbled paths, you'll find a ridge to the left with fine views of the winding river valley and of beautiful flowers and meadows.

Shopping

Himachal Pradesh is famous for its handicrafts, mainly metalcraft, silver jewellery, bamboo products, dolls and carpets. Popular buys are the hand-loom shawls of Kulu and the woodwork and walking sticks of Shimla. But Manali itself is famous for woollen goods—fancily embroidered Manali caps (circular box-hats, with Tibetan side flaps), gloves, socks, shawls and jackets. They are all reasonably priced and make excellent presents.

There are shawl emporiums all along the Mall where you can buy all this stuff, along with warm woollies (mufflers, gloves, socks etc.) for trekking. Manali new

The most amusing buys in Manali are ayurvedic medicines. These are often foul-tasting concoctions sold by street doctors who sidle up to unwary foreigners and offer them 'love potions'. To clinch the sale they proffer endorsements like the following:

This elixir benefits a man, can after use keep prolonged company with many a fair sex without feeling any sense of fatigue. He will have muscular energy like an elephant, he will be inflammable like fire, will have sweetness of voice like a peacock's, and will be noble like a horse. His eyes will be sharp as those of a vulture. His treasure of human potential fluid will be added in plenty. His heart would be amorous, and he would feel immense satisfaction after intercourse. It will bring him a sound undisturbed sleep. This may be taken by both the male and female partners. It is suitable in every season, and it will give them a healthy and handsome progeny.

town was only created in the '70s, so there is no bazaar tradition. The modern arcaded **Manu Market** lies below the tourist office and is often half-closed. You can, however, still find some nice Tibetan produce here, as well as at the **Government Charitable Shop** on the Mall.

Leisure
sports

Depending on the season, Manali is a marvellous base for trekking, skiing and fishing. The most popular activity by far is **trekking**, although be warned that the trails are not well marked, there are no lodges or eating places *en route*, and you'll need to hire equipment and a cook/guide. There are several trekking shops on the Mall, where you can pick up equipment and buy supplies. For maps and good information, contact Manali's **Mountaineering Institute**, 1½km above the Mall, © 2342. This place also offers courses in mountaineering, skiing, water sports and high-altitude trekking. There are several trek agencies in town, charging in excess of US$50 per day for long-range treks out to Lahaul, Spiti, Ladakh and Zanskar. If this is too much, then bargain yourself a private deal. People like Himalayan Adventurers, c/o Mayflower Guest House, can put together a marvellous 3–5-day 'local' trek up the valley for under £10 per head, inclusive of guide, porter, cook and ponies. Before you set off, let the tourist office know where you're going. No trekking permit is required, but you'll want someone to look for you in case of accident. Independent trekkers disappear with alarming regularity. If going solo, it's best to use Manali as a base camp and just venture out on short 2–3-day mini-treks. The most popular expedition is up to **Rohtang Pass**, which is the only crossover point between the Kulu and Lahaul-Spiti valleys. Situated 3915m above sea level, it affords some of the most spectacular mountain scenery in north India. Bear in mind, however, that after reaching the head of the valley (2 days) the steep inclines make crampons and full mountaineering gear obligatory. The pass is generally open only from June to November, but on the far side of it is a stark landscape of incredible beauty. If you haven't time to trek it, then take the bus from the tourist office, which plies up to the pass and over to the Buddhist village of Keylong, memorable for the resonant chanting of its monks, which echoes in a slow, deep rumble across the valley.

For a short, easy 3–4-day trek, opt for **Solang Nullah**, 13km out of Manali at the head of the valley. It has spectacular mountain scenery, a comfy mountain lodge, and the best **skiing** in the area. The best ski months are January/February, while **paragliding** usually takes place (also in the Solang) from June to August. For skiing, travellers recommend the 7-day course (around £50, all-inclusive) offered by **Northface Adventure** c/o Hotel Rohtang Inn in Manali. For **heli-skiing, paragliding, kayaking, river-rafting, and mountain-biking tours**, contact **Himalayan Journeys** near the State Bank of India, ✆ 2365.

Two short 1-day foot treks are to **Arjun Gufa**, a legendary cave near Prini village, and to **Nehru Kund**, a popular cold-water spring on the way to Keylong. A very easy 5–6-hour walk is to **Naggar**, 22km from Manali on the 'old road'. Scenery along the way is very pretty, and there are superb views from Naggar's **Hotel Castle**. You can stay here too, or at the cheaper **Hotel Poonam** down in Naggar town. Before going anywhere, though, look out a copy of *Trekking in India* (Gianchand and Manohar Puri) and the revised Lonely Planet guide to *Trekking in the Indian Himalayas* in Manali market.

In the trekking season, Manali tourist office runs people out to popular jump-off points (like Solang Nullah, for Rohtang Pass) in small minibuses. It's not that expensive to do the Rohtang Pass independently, by taxi from the rank above the tourist office. You get more space, and can hop out to take photos whenever you like.

There's good **fishing** for trout on the Beas River at Katrain (22km away), Raison, Kasel or Naggar. The season is from March to October, and permits are issued by the Manali tourist office. Equipment hire can however, be difficult.

nightlife

People go to bed early in Manali (it has a lot to do with the mountain air) so there's not much to do after dark. This said, July to September is party time. All the Indian tourists have gone home and the Goan freaks arrive in force and take over. Every Saturday there's a party at **Hotel Bhrigu** in Vashisht, and every Sunday there's another one at **The Clubhouse** in Old Manali. If you missed the '60s and want to see what all the fuss was about, you can catch them here.

From October on, the Clubhouse reverts to its normal function—a sedate recreation area, with billiards, table-tennis, lawn tennis, restaurant and bar. It costs Rs5 to get in and a little extra to use the games facilities.

Manali has really boomed in recent years. In the 1970s there were only 5 hotels; now there are well over 300. The only two months to avoid are May and June. This is the Indian holiday season, and every hotel doubles or even triples its prices. At most other times, notably March and April, you can get a nice room with attached bath, a TV, and even a private balcony with views (e.g. Woodlines Annexe) for as little at Rs100. All rates quoted below, therefore, are for the low season—which is basically any day of the year when there are not a lot of home tourists in town.

It's worth noting that many hotels and guest houses are closed from November through to February.

expensive (from US$30)

In September 1995, the River Beas experienced the worst flooding in 50 years. This caused devastating landslides which all but destroyed several luxury hotels on the Kulu side of the river. Despite repairs, this side of the river is still vulnerable to landslides, so if you want a peaceful stay of clas,s stick to the Manali bank.

Currently, the top hotels are (in order) **Holiday Inn**, ✆ 2262, ✆ 3312, **Imperial Palace**, ✆ 3330, **Sterling Resorts**, **Sagar Resorts**, **Ambassador**, ✆ 2235, and **Piccadilly**, ✆ 2152. These are all doing brisk business. Also good are the chalet-style **Banon Resort**, ✆ 2490, on the way up to Old Manali, and the **Shingar Regency**, ✆ 2251, ✆ 2553.

moderate/budget

New Manali

Most hotels in this category are Swiss-chalet style properties with quiet locations and good facilities. Worthy ones are **John Banon's Guest House**, **Mayflower Guest House**, ✆ 2104, and **Hadimba Palace**. The last two are both on the way up to the Hadimba Temple.

Of the several hotels on the Mall, the only one with any claim to class is HPTDC's new **Hotel Kunzam**, ✆ 3198, inside the tourist reception complex. Tastefully decorated in the colonial style, it has a real 'old-fashioned' ambience and the rooms are very cosy. Further down the Mall, **Rohtang Inn**, ✆ 2622, has some nice rooms at the top, with balcony views down over the town, but be warned: it's bang opposite the noisy bus station.

In Model Town at the bottom of the Mall, two quiet and cheap hotels are the **Gulmohar**, ✆ 2607, and **Aroma**, ✆ 3159—both asking Rs150/200 at quiet times.

There is now so much choice in this category that recommending any one place over another is pretty meaningless. If you're going to be here for any length of time, it's worth dumping your bags at the tourist office and going walkabout for an hour or two to find the best deal. Travellers in the know head straight up to Vashisht or Old Manali (*see* below)—both places are quiet and cheap, and there's far less chance of being busted for smoking the local weed (yes, it's growing all around but is still illegal!).

Old Manali

A good place to start looking is the road leading up from the Mall to Old Manali—here you'll find old favourites like **Woodlines Annexe** (down an alley, just before State Bank of India), **Hotel Tourist**, **Sunshine**, **Meadows** and **Rising Star** (*see* map). They all charge between Rs100 and Rs200 in the low season.

Just across the iron bridge separating New from Old Manali, three popular cheapies are **Hotel Dreamland**, **Himview Hotel** and **Hema Holiday Home**. All three have a lovely location overlooking the Manalsu River, but are often full. In Old Manali itself, the two 'quality' guest houses are **Diplomat** and **Dragon**, both charging around Rs200/300, but there are lots of cheaper places like **New Bridge View** and **Veer Guest House** where you can find a clean double for (out of season) Rs60/70 a night.

Vashisht

The two places to stay here are **Hotel Bhrigu** and **Hotel Valley View**. They're next to each other, just down from the village, and have good restaurants. If these are full, walk a few doors up to **Sanam Guest House**, or into the village itself for **Kalptaru** and **Prachi** lodges. Behind the temple, a steep series of steps leads up to **Dharma Guest House**, a simple place with fine views. Expect to pay Rs70–150 per night in Vashisht—double or triple that in high season.

Manali ☎ (01901–)   ***Eating Out***

Travellers hang out for hours on end at the **Mayur Restaurant** behind the Mall, and it's easy to see why. It has the best food, sounds and atmosphere in town. The longest menu too, including 'Bologanised Spaghetti' and 'Poulet Saute Hengroise' (sautéed chicken coated with hengroise sauce, and bed of rice garnished with chopeyed mushrooms on top), also great 'sizzlers' and tandooried trout. This place is often packed, so you may need to reserve a table. If nothing works, try the small **Mona Lisa** which is just as popular. Chinese/Tibetan food is best at **Mount View Restaurant** on the Mall or at the nearby **Chopstick Restaurant**, where you can enjoy noodles and *momos* along with a big-screen movie. For Indian food, try the non-veg **Adarsh** on the Mall or the pure veg **Madras Café** behind the Mayur. The latter specializes in south Indian snacks and does great coffee. Bakes and cakes can be found at **Superbake**, opposite the tourist office, and **Peter's** near the State Bank of India—both good places for pre-trek take-outs.

In Old Manali, popular cafés are **Moondance**, **Chinatown**, **Ish** and **Shiva**

Garden, all serving brown bread, apple pie, chocolate cake, tortillas, pizzas, and other yummy snacks.

There are lots of other eating establishments in town, though many of them are closed from late November right through to April.

For eats in Vashisht, try the **Freedom Café** (cheap) or the swank **Surabhai** (moderate) with its rooftop 'party' terrace.

If you've money to spend, **Hotel Piccadilly**'s restaurant in Model Town has a good reputation. For evening drinks, taxi out to **Span Resorts** at nearby Katrain. This has one of the top hotel bars in India, with over 250 different varieties of Scotch.

Moving On

By air: From Bhuntar, 50km below Manali, Jagson Airlines flies daily to Delhi, Mondays and Fridays to Dharamsala, and Tuesdays and Saturdays to Shimla. Archana Airways have daily flights to Delhi, but are not so reliable.

By road: The Himachal Pradesh Marketing Office, just down from the tourist office, sells daily deluxe buses to Shimla (dep 9am, 10hrs), to Dharamsala (dep 8am, 12hrs) and to Delhi (dep 5pm, 16–18hrs). In summer, there is an additional air-conditioned bus to Delhi, leaving at 6am. All these buses leave from outside the tourist office and are very popular, so book as far ahead as possible. Local buses to Kulu leave every 15 minutes from the main bus stand on the Mall.

Shimla   population 120,000

Former summer capital of British India, Shimla (commonly spelt 'Simla') is the largest hill station in the world and the one most associated with the old Raj. Spread over a high 12km ridge on the lower spurs of the northwest Himalaya, its cool heights (2100m) have always endeared it to foreign visitors. Favoured by politicians, army officers, writers (Kipling based his *Plain Tales of the Hills* on Shimla) and now tourists, it is a place designed for complete relaxation, with lovely views, a pleasant climate, and a plethora of old-colonial buildings. It is the least Indian of all hill stations, a probable hangover of the 'affectation that existed among officials of being very English', of knowing nothing at all about India, of eschewing Indian words and customs' (P. Woodruff, *The Guardians*).

Shimla probably derives its name from 'Shyamla', a title of the goddess Kali whose temple was found in the thickly wooded hill region of Jackoo in the early 19th century. Another possible origin is 'Shyeamalay', the blue-slate house erected by a fakir on Jackoo, the first nucleus of the settlement. However 'Shimlah', or 'Shumlah' as pronounced by the local hill-people, is probably the actual word from which the station takes its name.

Presently a peaceful holiday resort, Shimla was born out of the turmoil of the early 19th-century Gurkha Wars. Discovered by heat-weary British officers during the conflicts of 1819, its cool, healthy climate made it an ideal hill station on which to erect a summer village of military tents and bivouacs. Then, in 1822, young Major Kennedy started the

ball rolling by building the first permanent residence. Nurtured and popularized by the government, the élite and the traders, a town rapidly grew up, and Shimla became a highly fashionable retreat—particularly for place-hunting young officers who wanted to 'get on' by ingratiating themselves with the military high-ups holidaying here. It was popular also with those who had been banished from India for misconduct, who escaped to Shimla to build themselves a substitute life of parties and revelry. Most notable as a place to escape the heat of the plains, it was only when Lord Lawrence visited Shimla as Viceroy in 1864 that it was at last accepted as the official summer capital of the Raj.

In 1904 the construction of the remarkable Kalka–Shimla railway finally provided easy access to the hill station. By this time, Shimla had become a thriving town of English red-roofed cottages, Georgian-style houses and Gothic government buildings like Barnes Court, Kennedy House, the old Viceregal Lodge, and Gordon Castle. The palatial residences of the Governor and the Commander-in-Chief were the sites of regular summer balls where frenetic dance and revelry were the order of the day. Polo, cricket and tennis tournaments gave way in the evenings to packed houses at the Gaiety Theatre (built to look like the old Garrick in London), while twice-weekly gymkhanas and races in the spacious playground occupied any remaining free time. In its heyday, Shimla represented the most sophisticated seat of British high society in India.

Having moved from humble hill village to proud Imperial capital, in 1966 Shimla received its final crown of success. The new state of Himachal Pradesh was created out of the reorganization of the Punjab, and Shimla became its capital.

The days of the Raj may be over, but Shimla's attraction as a cool summer retreat, full of lovely walks and beautiful scenery, remains unimpaired. The town itself is busy, vital and very civilized—with marvellous hotels, restaurants and good tourist facilities—while outside it are calm, tranquil walks up into the green hills covered with fir, pine and Himalayan oak trees, red rhododendron and all kinds of mountain flowers, in between which are dotted the quaint old British-style houses and buildings which stand as a constant reminder of Shimla's imperial past.

When to Go

To see Shimla at its most colourful, full of wild flowers and greenery, visit in late September to end-October. December to March can be heavily snowbound, and are generally bad months to come; there are no sightseeing tours, and many hotels and restaurants are closed. The official summer season is mid-April to October, but wise travellers avoid the May/June home-tourist crush, and also the mid-July to mid-September rains. They come late March to early April for good weather and cut-price accommodation. Whenever you turn up, bring something warm; it can get pretty cold at night.

Getting There

Shimla can be approached by air from Delhi and Kulu. The most scenic approach, however, is by rail on the **Himalayan Queen** from New Delhi station. This leaves 6am daily and arrives in Kalka at 11.15am. Switching onto narrow-gauge track, it leaves Kalka at 11.45am, passes through 102 tunnels, and arrives in Shimla at 4.50pm.

If you want to suffer, there are overnight buses direct from Delhi, often involving a curfew stop at Chandigarh until dawn. More comfortable buses come in from Dharamsala, Manali, Delhi and Dalhousie.

Getting Around

Shimla is a lovely place, with lots to see and do, but it's the very devil to get around. Like Darjeeling, the town sprawls out over a wide ridge in a many-layered wedding cake of winding, twisting streets and honeycombed buildings. To reach each new layer involves steep, exhausting climbs or descents. The major roads have names, but where they begin or end is anybody's guess. Fortunately, most tourist facilities are on one level, the main thoroughfare called the Mall. Unfortunately, the Mall is right on the top of the wedding cake, and the bus and rail stations are way down below it, on Cart Road. In the day, there is no problem: the useful **tourist lift** ferries people up and down between Cart Road and the Mall (near Oberoi Clarke's Hotel) for just Rs2. If arriving at night, there is a problem. Screaming touts cling to the sides of the bus and thrust brass tokens in through the windows, shouting 'Porter! Government Porter!' They're on a winner here, because buses aren't allowed into the main bus stand complex—they stop about 1km short of it, and the tourist lift up to the Ridge (open 9am–9pm) is 2km beyond *that*. So you're left with three choices: a porter for the steep climb up to the Mall (Rs30), a long tedious walk to the tourist lift, or a rip-off taxi (Rs30/40) to the tourist lift. The first two take 20/30 minutes, the third 10/15 minutes, and all three put you in a bad mood. If you hire a porter, he'll stick to you like glue until you book into a hotel where he gets commission.

Leaving town, you don't need a porter. It's an easy 10-minute walk, starting at the steps next to Baljee's restaurant, all the way down to the main bus stand. From here, you can either stroll down Cart Road to the railway station (10–15 minutes) or take a taxi (Rs30).

You get round Shimla almost entirely on foot. The top two tiers of the ridge (the Mall and the level below it) are barred to all traffic. This makes for a very peaceful stay: no rickshaws, no taxis, no cows, no beggars and no hassle—but a leopard was seen on the Mall early one morning in July 1992. If you want to hire cars, taxis, rickshaws or take a bus, you'll have to go down to Cart Road taxi stand by the tourist lift. Hiring motorized transport can work out very expensive, largely owing to the very hilly terrain (slow going, high petrol consumption).

Shimla ☎ (0177–)   ***Tourist Information***

The **tourist office**, ☎ 214311, is on the Mall, open 9am–7pm daily. Like the one in Manali, it's overworked, understaffed and not interested in foreigners. The small information booth at the bottom of the Ridge, just before it dips down into the Mall, sells tours (the best one goes to Narkanda, for close-up views of the mountains). **Indian Airlines**, **Archana Airways** and **Jagson Airlines** have counters here, and there's an **STD phone** next door. The **GPO** is just up from the tourist office, on the Mall. It's open 10am–7pm except Sundays. Close by is the central telegraph office, with a **24-hour fax** facility. Also on the Mall are the **State Bank of India** and the better **travel agents**. Good **bookshops** are Asia and Maria Brothers on the Mall, and Badesh near the tourist lift.

Touring Shimla

Shimla is not a place for a whistle-stop tour. Life proceeds at a slow relaxed pace, and it's best just to go along with it. Sightseeing is very low-profile—people stroll off in any direction and don't much care whether they get anywhere or not, because the scenery is uniformly beautiful. The only priority is a good pair of shoes.

Walk 1: The Mall and Surrounds

1 day. Christchurch–Scandal Point–Himachal State Museum–Summer Hill.

Shimla is geared to relaxation, so spend your first day simply winding down. This is best done on the **Mall**, which is a sort of displaced Brighton, with bracing air, civilized promenades, English-style houses, ice cream counters and bright souvenir shops.

At the top of the Mall, on the Ridge, is the tall, yellow painted **Christchurch**, with a fresco over the chancel window designed by Lockwood Kipling. Its outward austerity

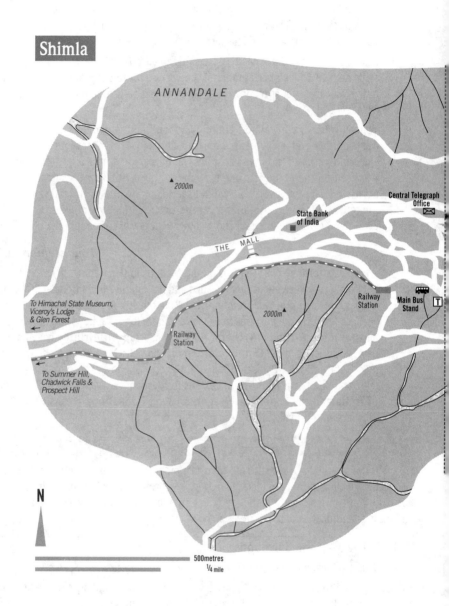

Shimla

ANNANDALE

▲ 2000m

Central Telegraph Office

State Bank of India

THE MALL

To Himachal State Museum, Viceroy's Lodge & Glen Forest

Railway Station

▲ 2000m

Railway Station

Main Bus Stand

To Summer Hill, Chadwick Falls & Prospect Hill

N

500metres
¼ mile

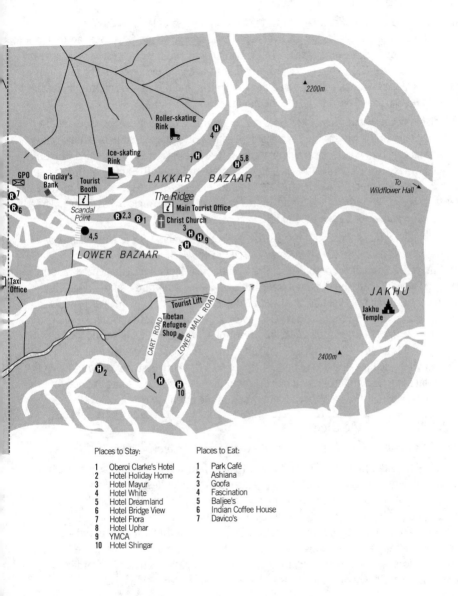

Places to Stay:

1 Oberoi Clarke's Hotel
2 Hotel Holiday Home
3 Hotel Mayur
4 Hotel White
5 Hotel Dreamland
6 Hotel Bridge View
7 Hotel Flora
8 Hotel Uphar
9 YMCA
10 Hotel Shingar

Places to Eat:

1 Park Café
2 Ashiana
3 Goofa
4 Fascination
5 Baljee's
6 Indian Coffee House
7 Davico's

conceals a rich interior of beautiful stained-glass windows (representing faith, hope, charity, fortitude, patience and humility), also murals, old oak pews and beamed ceiling, and interesting plaques to deceased army officers. It's worth attending the Sunday service if only to appreciate the rich, resonant organ.

The church leads out to **Scandal Point**, the large open area of levelled ground which is Shimla's main public meeting place. Ever since a young equestrian Casanova (an Indian prince) absconded with a young high-born British maiden from this spot years ago, this has been the favourite rendezvous of people wishing to air their views or exchange the latest gossip. It is always packed, generally with happy tourists, and the views from this point are excellent—on a clear day, you can see the mountains.

In British days, it was *de rigueur* to sip a cool beer at one of the hotels overlooking the Mall, generally after a game of golf or billiards. Today, it is enough to sit in one of its cafés or restaurants and to watch life slowly passing by. The lines of stately, oddly-titled English houses always arouse comment, especially the present **Tax and Excise building**—a bizarre gothic towered mansion. After a few hours here, most foreign visitors conclude that they are not in India at all, but in some kind of displaced Anglo-Swiss village. The general effect, once you've got used to it, is very pleasing.

From the Mall, you can take an hour's stroll down to **Himachal State Museum** (*open 10am–5pm exc Mon*) just above the now closed Oberoi Cecil Hotel. Set up in 1975, the museum has a fine collection of hill arts and crafts, particularly of Himachal Pradesh, together with Pahari-school miniature paintings, stone sculptures, and eye-catching embroidery and textiles. The hill-path leading down below the museum gives panoramic views of the city skyline. Past the new **Governor's Residence**, at the bottom of the hill, you can bear right (a 30-minute walk) for **Summer Hill**, the quiet and secluded suburb where Gandhi stayed on his visits to Shimla. It's also a very popular viewpoint. Follow the blue-and-white railings all the way up, until you reach the **University** at the top. Behind the last building (the Administration block), you'll find a forest trail leading back down to town (5km, 1 hour). The views are generally best in the morning.

Walk 2: Jakhu and the Glen

1 day. Jakhu Hill–Hanuman Temple–Glen Forest–Viceroy's Lodge.

The early-morning climb up to Shimla's highest point, **Jakhu Hill** (2438m), is practically a tradition. Many travellers wish it wasn't. The ascent is relentlessly steep and can take anything between 30 minutes (super-athletes) to an hour (the rest of us). Don't be shy of hiring a pony if you need one; they only cost Rs50 return. If you're blazing a trail on foot, start at the slope alongside the church on the Mall, walk up to Hotel Dreamland, then bear right and follow the blue-and-white railings. These peter out near the place selling 'monkey sticks', but the path onward is clear. At the top, your effort is rewarded with spectacular views down over the plains and across to snow-clad mountains.

Also at the summit is a **Hanuman Temple**. Inside, it's like Christmas—masses of glittering tinsel, balls, decorations and streamers. The resident fakir sits warming himself at a single-bar electric heater, his hot-water bottle dangling on a rusty nail in the corner. The

Writing of Jakhu temple in 1837, the commentator Gerard wrote of the curious sight 'of the old fakir in his yellow garments standing in front of the temple, and calling *ajao, ajao* to his monkey children'. They all had pet names, and one it seems fell from a tree while feeding. The *jogi* seemed much concerned at this unusual occurrence, but lost no time in making his apologies. 'Forty years ago,' he remarked, 'when I first knew that monkey, she could climb as well as any here, but even a monkey can grow old in forty years. Alas, poor Budhee!'

Mr C.J. French added in his 1838–9 journals:

> *Mount Jakko seems to be the pivot around which the Shimla community revolve in their morning and evening perambulations. While the evening is so often a scene of animation— sometimes the road is entirely taken up with conveyances— at this spot, in the morning it is generally one of perfect solitude.*

shrine is said to house the footprints of Hanuman, the monkey god, left when he paused here for a breather on his way over to Laxman, the injured brother of Rama, with some curative herbs. The temple itself is full of scampering (and very acquisitive) brown monkeys. If you're carrying any food, don't let them catch sight of it.

In the afternoon, try a pleasant walk down to **Glen Forest**. This pretty, secluded picnic spot is some 4km below the Ridge, beyond the cricket/polo-grounds of Annandale. One of Shimla's best walks, the Glen is famous for its lovely waterfall, best just after the monsoon, and for its rushing, ice-cold streams fed by melting mountain snows.

To get there, walk past the tourist office to the bottom of the Mall. Take the right-hand turning just past Cecil Hotel, then follow your nose. Allowing for scenery stops, the return journey should take around three hours. On the way back, you can turn left at Cecil Hotel for a peek at the old **Viceroy's Lodge**. This huge six-storey building, once the site of so many elegant balls and festivities, is now the province of the Indian Institute of Advanced Study, with a fine reception hall and library.

Other Excursions

Another good walk is to **Prospect Hill** (descend from Cart Road to Boileauganj, then it's a 15-minute climb), with its pretty temple of Karnana Devi. The temple commands excellent views of Shimla, Jutogh, Summer Hill and, if you're lucky, the toy train chugging past below. A couple of places best seen by car or bus are **Wildflower Hall** (13km) with spacious landscaped gardens and numerous varieties of wild flowers; and **Mashobra** (13km) with famous apple orchards (best in April), oak and pine-forested picnic areas, and a big annual fair in June.

Leisure

Shimla offers a lot more than just scenic walks. Go to Kulfri (16km) for **skiing** (best in January and February; equipment for hire); to Hatkoli (104km) for **trout-fishing**; and to Chail (45km) for **tennis, squash and golf,** and also to see the world's highest **cricket** ground. The best golf is on the scenic 9-hole course at Naldehra (23km). In Shimla itself, the better hotels arrange golf and tennis. In the winter (November to February), try Shimla's famous **ice-skating rink**, the only natural rink in India. You'll find it on the Ridge, down below ANZ Grindlays Bank. Also on the Ridge, near the church, you'll find a rank for **pony rides**. Lower Bazaar has a few **video parlours**, but most of them are dives. In season, you can enjoy a **show** or a **play** at the Gaiety Theatre on the Mall.

Shopping

For Shimla's one decent buy—woodcarvings—visit **Lakkar Bazaar** along the eastern fork from the Ridge. Rolling pins are popular souvenirs (husbands beware), as are carved walking sticks, bowls, spoons and toys. You'll find Kulu shawls and dolls everywhere. For something different, visit the **Tibetan Refugee Shop** just up from the tourist lift. It's particularly good for weavings and jewellery.

Shimla © (0177–)   ### Where to Stay

Shimla's hotels are very good, but there simply aren't enough of them. During the low season (November to mid-December and mid-January to early April), you should have no problem finding a 30–50% discounted room. By May, however, all hotels are full up and you'll be lucky to find a broom cupboard to sleep in. All prices below are for the high season and for double rooms since singles are scarce.

luxury (from US$130)

Hotel Oberoi Clarke's on the Mall, © 212991, @ 211321, has all the Oberoi tradition and more behind it. It launched M.S. Oberoi's career in 1934, and is still the hub of the city's social life. A pleasant combination of old-world charm and modern-day conveniences, it offers spacious and well-furnished rooms, each with an individual view of the city, and first-rate facilities, food and in-house recreations.

expensive (from US$40)

Two of Shimla's most pleasant places to stay are private homes. **Chapslee**, Lakkar Bazaar, © 78242, is one of Shimla's oldest surviving buildings. It was once the summer residence of the maharajahs of Kapurthala and has very pleasant rooms from US$45. The food, especially the afternoon teas, is excellent. **Woodville Palace**, 1½km past the Oberoi, © 72763, has large grounds, attractive rooms from US$40, and a homely atmosphere. Some say it's the most comfortable place in town. Two newer properties worth checking out are **Asia the Dawn**, © 231162, @ 231007, and **Hotel Eastbourne** close to Himland Hotel, © 77260.

moderate (from Rs200)

There are several good bets in this category. On the Ridge, behind the church, **Hotel Mayur**, © 72392, has excellent food, informative staff and very livable rooms from Rs500. When full, it sends people to **Hotel Shivalik**, ✆ 72435, a little out of town, or to **Hotel Shingar**, ✆ 72881, opposite the Oberoi. **Hotel White**, ✆ 5276, is still good, but has now upgraded itself and asks around Rs500 a night. In the same price range are hotels **Himland**, ✆ 3595, and **Gulmarg**, ✆ 3168, both recommended. HPTDC's **Hotel Holiday Home**, ✆ 212890, is a short walk down Cart Road from the tourist lift. It has good food, a fine location, and some rooms with a view.

budget

Many mid-range hotels become budget ones in the low season—there's a wide price fluctuation. Most travellers head for the clean, quiet, but very weird **YMCA**, located up a path behind Hotel Mayur, ✆ 72375, ✉ 211016. Rooms go for Rs90/130/200 (single/double/triple) and there's an extra Rs40 membership charge which includes breakfast. There are fine views from the terrace, British recreations such as billiards, badminton and table-tennis, and tasty *thalis* for Rs30/45 (veg/non veg). On the downside, it's not terribly friendly; there are rules about absolutely everything, and though there's a TV in the dining-hall, you're not allowed to watch it until breakfast-time!

You might do better to try hotels like **Uphar**, ✆ 77670, or **Dreamland**, ✆ 77377, on the north side of the Ridge; or even the good-value **Bridge View**, up some steps beside the Hotel Mayur. As a last resort, there's the new **Hotel Flora** in Lakkar Bazaar, ✆ 78027—though for the sake of a couple of quid, you might just as well move up a price category. Most budget places are cold and soulless.

Shimla ✆ *(0177–)*   ***Eating Out***

Shimla's cuisine has, as one might expect, a distinctly British flavour. Here you can still find tiffin, 'English breakfasts' and china-service tea. Alongside this is an increasing American influence—hamburger stalls, fast-food joints and ice cream palaces.

For quality fare, you have to go to the hotels. The **Oberoi Clarke's** has the finest food in town, but it's fixed menu and for hotel guests only. For a big meal out, try the restaurants at the **Woodville Palace**, **Asia the Dawn** and **Eastbourne**. Some of the mid-range hotels have good restaurants too, notably the **Himland**, **Gulmarg**, and **Mayur**. The latter has a cosy little dining area beside the lobby where you can watch Indian TV in the evenings. The flashy new **Ritz Restaurant**, above the Church on the Ridge, looks promising. If nothing else, it offers fantastic views.

Outside of hotels, Shimla has a surprising lack of decent places to eat out, in view of the number of tourists it gets. HPTDC has twin restaurants on the Ridge: the gloomy **Goofa** (reminiscent of a bomb shelter) for veg fare and *thalis*, and the flashier **Ashiana** for pizzas, sizzlers, soups, and Chinese ginger chicken—but you wait ages for service, and they're often crowded. Close to the fire station on the Mall, you'll find another twin eatery: **Fascination** upstairs (multi-cuisine, with a sprinkling of Italian and Thai fare) and **Baljee's** downstairs, with 'British' break-fasts (sausage, egg 'n' chips), good cakes and ice cream, fast service and good sounds. **Embassy**, close to the tourist lift, has fast-food combinations at mid-range prices. So does the new **Davico's**, further down the Mall, along with the best bar in town. A few doors down from Devico's, you'll find the **Indian Coffee Shop**, with dirt-cheap *dosas*, **thalis** and (of course) coffee, served by Raj-style waiters in turbans and cummerbunds. It's the most popular eating-place in town. To find decent Chinese food, you have to descend into the bazaar area (go down the steps opposite the Gaiety Theatre) and ask around for the **New Plaza** and **Malook** restaurants. Finally, don't miss the **Park Café**—it does the best pizzas in town (with real mozzarella cheese), along with great cappuccino, shakes, *lassis* and juices.

Moving On

By air: Jagson Airlines, ✆ 6810, flies to Delhi and Kulu every Tuesday and Saturday. Archana Airways, ✆ 203294, has flights to Delhi every Monday, Wednesday, Friday and Sunday. Taxis from Cart Road charge Rs300 to the airport.

By rail: The fun toy train leaves Shimla at 5.30pm daily, winds its way down the mountain to Kalka (where it changes onto broad gauge) and gets to New Delhi at 6am the next morning. If you miss it, you can get a taxi to Kalka (2½hrs, Rs550) and pick it up there before it departs at 11.30pm. To reserve a sleeper berth for the Kalka–Delhi leg of the journey, apply at least 24 hours in advance to the rail reservation office next to Shimla station.

By road: From the main bus stand down on Cart Road, there are daily deluxe buses to Delhi at 8.25am (8–9hrs), to Dharamsala at 8.30pm (10–12hrs) and to Manali at 8.30am (10hrs). There are slower buses to Delhi at 10am, 12.40pm, 6.30pm and 9.30pm, one bus daily to Dalhousie at 4.40am (14–15hrs), and hourly buses to Kalka. You can book tickets from the tourist office or the Hotel Mayur.

Taxis are cheapest from the main taxi stand down on Cart Road. Set fares are Rs2200 to Delhi, Rs1800 to Dharamsala/Manali and Rs1400 to Kulu, but you can always bargain them down a bit.

West India

Bombay

This is the most modern and developed part of India, albeit concentrated in the two centres of Bombay and Goa. Bombay is like London on Cup Final day, and in Goa you can imagine yourself on the Costa del Sol, complete with parties and power cuts. In contrast, Gujarat is rural and remote.

The west gives flexibility—from here you can go north to Rajasthan or south to Goa, with a possible side-trip to Gujarat to get away from it all.

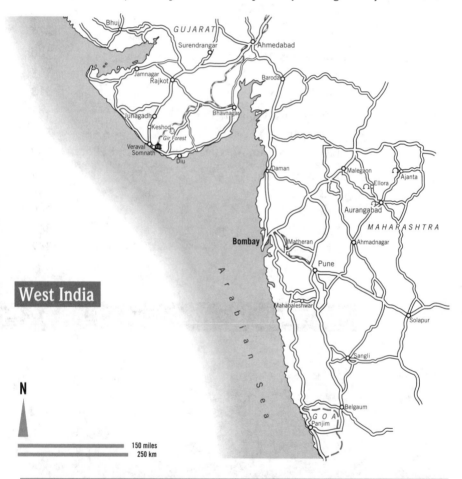

West India

Bombay

population 15 million

Bombay is a dynamic, go-ahead city of tycoons, skyscrapers, film studios and big business—the nearest thing to the West in the East, and the modern Gateway to India. In just 40 years, it has mushroomed from a small, though thriving, coastal port-town of 500,000 inhabitants to a crowded industrial metropolis of 15 million people. A futuristic vision of India, with gleaming luxury hotels, high-rise business houses, and air-conditioned shopping centres, it is an irresistible land of opportunity for the masses of homeless, jobless poor, and refugees that flood in at an average rate of 10,000 new families per day. They come in search of work or glamour or money, and most of them end up sleeping on the streets. The result is severe overcrowding and an appalling shortage of housing—a second city of ragged, squalid slum dwellings having grown up outside the modern business capital of gleaming plate-glass buildings.

Of late, Bombay has really cleaned up its act. Gone are the slums which once lined the road from the airport to the city; gone too are the heaps of garbage and boxes with people living on and in them (in the tourist areas, at least!); and gone are the tribes of pigs and cows which used to bring traffic to a halt. Most surprisingly, there is a near-absence of smelly auto-rickshaws polluting the roads with diesel fumes. Unlike Delhi, Bombay centre has no people lying around in the streets any more; they're all moving around and doing something, which is nice to see.

Bombay is, like Calcutta, a city of powerful contrasts, though it's not just all the problems of modern India that are highlighted here, but all her potential and brighter prospects too. Here there is hope, optimism, and great prosperity—for Bombay handles half the country's foreign trade, manufactures the same percentage of her textiles, and pays a third of her income tax. The affluent rich—a hardworking cosmopolitan mixture of Hindus and Parsis, Jews and Jains, Arabs and Sikhs—divert surplus revenue to the philanthropic construction of hospitals, schools, museums and rest houses. But it is Bombay's 'action' that draws everybody here—this is a city bursting with life, colour, noise and vitality. And you can almost smell the money.

History

All this has happened since the Second World War, since the rise of India's new business class following Independence. Up until the 18th century, Bombay was just a marshy, diseased quag of seven islands, inhabited by a simple fisherfolk called the Koli. Their name for the place was Mumbai or Bombaim, after their patron goddess Mumba Aai (Mother Mumba). This was later corrupted into Bom Bahia ('good bay') by the Portuguese. Ptolemy mentioned the islands as Heptanesia in the 2nd century AD, after which they faded from historical sight until occupied in the 13th century by the Hindu king, Bhimdev. The Sultans of Gujarat held the site briefly, and then the Portuguese arrived (1534). The first flush of Portuguese enthusiasm wore off—they saw its potential as a port, but the malarial swamps dissuaded them from developing it as a trading-post—and they offloaded it onto the British, as part of Catherine of Braganza's dowry when she married Charles II of England (1661). Charles didn't see its possibilities either, and he leased Bom Bahia, port and islands both, to the British East India Company for a nominal £10 per year in gold (1668). The Company's President, Gerald Aungier, became the founding father of modern Bombay, bringing in the influential Parsi merchant class and a host of assorted artisans and builders, to make possible the conversion of the port from pestilential swampland to thriving trading-centre. By his death, it was well on the way to becoming the centre of all west-coast trade in India. But it was in the mid-19th century that development suddenly became rapid—the railway arrived, as did the first textile mills and Bartle Frere's stately Victorian buildings. A series of large-scale land-reclamation projects took place (1862), the seven isolated mud-flat islands were joined into a single land mass, and Bombay's future success was assured. An excellent biography of Bombay, *City of Gold* by Gillian Tindall, was reprinted by Penguin India in 1992.

Today, the city is a single long peninsula island, a dynamic commercial and industrial centre, and a major international port and city. For the foreign visitor, it is probably the easiest place to acclimatize to India. Westerners tend to like its bright, brash quality (it certainly has more character than colourless Delhi), also its fine international facilities— quality restaurants, shops, bars and real luxury hotels. Also, because there are so many other foreign visitors, you just don't get the same hassle, stares or curiosity as in many other places in the country. Yes, there's still chronic overcrowding and teeming traffic, but it's always possible to escape into quiet environs, and many wise arrivals do just that: heading straight for the peaceful, elegant surroundings of Colaba at the southern tip of the peninsula and settling into India the civilized way—over a cocktail or a light meal at the famous Taj Mahal Hotel near the Gateway. After that, it's in with the earplugs, on with the smile and the money belt—Bombay is a pickpockets' paradise—and out into some of the most amazing street-life in the world.

Note: As of late 1995, Bombay has been officially renamed 'Mumbai' (its original Marathi title), though many residents would like to think it hasn't happened. Mumbai doesn't sound 'business-like' enough for them.

When to Go

The best time to visit Bombay is from October to February. It's very hot from March to June, and very wet from July to September. For a good festival, attend the post-monsoon celebration of **Ganpati** (Aug/Sept), held in honour of Bombay's favourite god, money-lucky Ganesh. The Holi festival of Feb/March is *not* a good time to come—hooligan crowds, lashings of red paint, and bewildered tourists diving for cover all over the place.

International Arrivals and Departures

Bombay is connected by air with most foreign countrie, and by air, rail, bus and even sea with most tourist destinations inside India. Wherever you are in west India, the relevant 'Moving On' section in this book will tell you how to get here (or somewhere close). *See also* pp.296–7.

Bombay has two airports: **Sahar**, 30km from Nariman Point in the city centre, for international flights, and **Santa Cruz**, 26km from the city centre, for domestic flights. The two terminals are 4km apart, and a shuttle-bus service runs between

Arabic Sea

Nehru
Planetarium
Amateur Riders'
Club
Mahalaxmi
Racecourse

Chinchpokli

Cotton
Green

Haji Ali Tomb

Mahalaxmi

CLERK RD

Byculla

Reay Road

Breach Candy
Swimming Club

Bombay
Central

BOMBAY
CENTRAL

JEHANGIR BOMAN BEHRAM MARG

Dockyard
Road

Towers of
Silence

Grant
Road

A PREMJI MARG

KAMATIPURA

MAULANA SHAUKATALI RD

Sandhurst
Road

Hanging
Gardens

Jain
Temple

KHETWADI

KHARA
TALAO

SARDAR VALLABHBHAI PATEL ROAD

All Saints'
Church

Kamala
Nehru Park

BHULESHWAR

PYDHUNI

MALABAR
HILL

GIRGAUM

Masjid

Chowpatty
Beach

Charni Road

Taraporevala
Aquarium

Walkeshwar
Temple

Marine Lines

Malabar
Point

Back
Bay

Marine Drive

Cross
Maidan

Victoria
Terminal

GPO

BANK ST.

Churchgate

FORT

Bombay Natural
History Society

University of
Bombay

Prince of Wales Museum

Nariman
Point

S. MAHARAJ MARJ

To Elephanta Island

ORMINSTON RD

Gateway of India

BHUSHAP MARG

COLABA

MERRIWEATHER RD

Bombay

CUFFE PARADE

SHADID BHAGAT SINGH ROAD

St John's
(Afghan) Church

Colaba
Point

Hotels :
1. Taj Mahal Hotel
2. Oberoi Hotel
3. President Hotel
4. Windsor Hotel
5. Salvation Army Hostel
6. Garden Hotel

Banks :
7. Canara Bank
8. State Bank of India

Main nightlife areas

N

2 km
1 mile

them every half-hour (free if you can show a connecting-flight ticket; Rs15 otherwise). Sahar is about an hour's drive from Bombay centre, and Santa Cruz about an hour and a half—more, if you travel in the rush hour.

Airport to city: Arriving from overseas, count on a good hour between touching down at Sahar and finally clearing the airport building. Do *not* leave the terminal without changing some money (for your bus/taxi into town) at the State Bank foreign exchange counter. Once you're outside, they won't let you back in. Ask for some low-denomination bills (nobody ever has small change) and count the money they give you before leaving; somehow, a Rs100 note always seems to go missing.

Pre-paid taxis from Sahar (24hr booth inside the terminal) cost Rs138 to Bombay Central railway station and Rs187 to Churchgate or Colaba. Baggage costs a few rupees extra. Having paid, give your slip to the taxi you've been assigned and don't get in until you're sure all your bags are securely locked in the boot. There is as yet no pre-paid taxi system at the domestic airport—only cowboys outside who rip you off for what they think you're worth. You can bargain a fare of Rs150/200 to Bombay Central/Colaba if you're lucky, but don't count on it.

The cheaper option, not only from Santa Cruz but from Sahar as well, is the airport bus service to the Air India building at Nariman Point. This runs every hour except between 1 and 4am, and costs Rs44/Rs36 from the international/domestic terminals. Tickets are sold inside the airports or on the bus, and baggage is Rs7 per piece extra.

City to airport: Taxis will generally (if you plead poverty) go *to* the airport on the meter. The airport bus service from Air India building, Nariman Point, runs every hour or so from 8am to 1am (i.e. not 1am–7am). For exact timings, ring ☏ 6124309. When booking your passage home, aim for a night flight: traffic out to the airport is much lighter in the evenings.

Notes: first, when flying out of Bombay, make sure you have the right airport. An alarming number of people miss flights by sitting dreamily in Sahar lounge waiting for a domestic flight (which never comes) or in Santa Cruz coffee shop waiting for an international one (likewise); second, late arrivals at airports can lose their reservations. Check-in is 75 minutes before departure at Santa Cruz and 3 hours at Sahar. But allow an extra hour for possible traffic delays; third, make sure that your flight ticket has been reconfirmed (do this on day one to save forgetting later) and that you have rupees left for your departure tax, payable on all international flights (pay *before* check-in): the tax is currently Rs300.

Getting Around

For a major capital, Bombay is quite easy to negotiate. This is because most tourist facilities are concentrated in one place—a narrow 3km strip running down from Churchgate to the bottom end of the island (Bombay is connected to the mainland by a series of bridges). This strip is bounded to the southeast by the Taj

Hotel in Colaba, and to the southwest by the Oberoi Hotel at Nariman Point. Colaba has most of the budget hotels, while Nariman Point is the ritzy part of town, where most of the airline offices, banks and upmarket hotels/restaurants are located.

By taxi: in the absence of auto-rickshaws (they're banned from the city centre), the fastest way of getting around town are black-and-yellow taxis. They are metered, but since the rates change every time there's a petrol-price rise or a devaluation of the rupee, the meters are always out of date. At the time of writing, you need to multiply whatever's on the meter by ten to arrive at the correct fare. The initial reading will be Rs1.00 (you pay Rs10), then Rs1.10 (you pay Rs11), and so on. If in doubt, ask your driver to produce his current rate card. For general reference, it should cost Rs12 from Colaba to Nariman Point, Rs16 from Colaba to Fountain, and Rs35 from Nariman Point to the top of Back Bay.

Note that there is *no* additional 'night charge' for taxis, no matter what the driver may say. Going out in the evening, you pay what's on the meter and not a paise more. Secondly, be aware that *hotel* taxis have a different rate card, with accelerated charges. Thirdly, this is not Delhi. *Never* ask a taxi 'How much?' to your destination—just tell the driver to set his meter, and he usually will.

By horse-drawn carriage: if you fancy a relaxing evening promenade up and down Marine Drive, hire a horse-drawn carriage or 'victoria' from outside the Oberoi Towers Hotel. You'll be asked Rs50 (or more) for the round-trip, but it's worth it. There's a similar joy-ride possible from the Taj Hotel (and up and down the Bunder) but you don't get the same sunset views.

Bombay ✆ (022–)   **Tourist Information**

Bombay is only a notch behind Delhi as an information-gathering point, so whatever your itinerary, get all the maps, timetables and printed matter you can here.

The Government of India **tourist office**, ✆ 2033144, ✉ 2014496, is at 123 M Karve Road, across from Churchgate railway station. It's open 8.30am to 6pm weekdays, until 2pm on Saturday and public holidays, closed Sunday. The staff are very helpful, and since they're fully computerized, you can give them a list of all the places you're going to, and they'll run off up-to-date print-outs for you. A useful handout to ask for is 'Tours in and around Bombay', giving details of current dance and drama programmes, also (on the back) updated travel and tour information.

The office sells two half-day tours of the city, starting at 9am and 2pm daily except Mondays; also a full-day Suburban Tour (starting at 9.15am daily except Mondays) to Juhu Beach, Kanheri caves, a Lion Safari Park and 'Fantasy Land'). There are other GOI counters at Sahar airport (✆ 8325331, open 24hrs) and at Santa Cruz (✆ 6149200, closes after last flight).

The Maharashtra Tourism Development Corporation (MTDC) is also worth a visit. It runs tours similar to the GOI office's, and has a head office at Express Towers (9th floor), Nariman Point (✆ 2024482, ✉ 2024521), and a nearby branch office at CDO Hutments, Madame Cama Road (✆ 2026713, ✉ 2852182).

banks

For quick, efficient foreign exchange, there's **American Express** next to the Regal Cinema on Colaba's Shivaji Maharaj Marg (open 9.30am to 7.30pm daily) and at 364 Dr D Naoroji Road, or **Thomas Cook** on Dr Naoroji Road, near Flora Fountain (open 11am to 3pm weekdays, 11am to 1pm Saturdays). If you're stuck with rupees at the end of your trip, don't forget there's a bank inside the international airport.

books and libraries

Good bookshops include the **Nalanda** in the Taj Hotel, **Strand Bookstall** just off Sir P Mehta Road (Fort) and **Bookpoint** on R Kamani Marg in Ballard Estate. The street bookstalls under the arcades along Dr D Naoroji Road and M G Road (south) are also good for a browse.

If you want to read the British newspapers, pop along to the British Council Library (ℰ 223530) at Mittal Tower A Wing (1st floor), Nariman Point. It's open Tuesday to Friday from 10am to 5.45pm and Saturday from 9am to 4.45pm.

foreign consulates

Among the many countries represented in Bombay (listed in the telephone directory) are the **UK**, Maker Chambers IVB (1st floor), 222 Jamnalal Bajaj Marg, Nariman Point (ℰ 2833602, ℻ 2027940); **USA**, Lincoln House, 78 Bhulabhai Desai Marg, Cumballa Hill (ℰ 3633611, ℻ 8223611); **France**, Data Prasad Building (2nd floor), N G Cross Road, off G Deshmukh Marg (Peddar Road), Cumballa Hill (ℰ 4950918); **Netherlands**, 16 M Karve Road (ℰ 2066840); **Japan**, 1B Dhanukar Marg, Cumballa Hill (ℰ 4934310); **Germany**, Hoechst House (10th floor), Nariman Point (ℰ 2832422); and **Australia**, Maker Towers (16th floor), E Block, Cuffe Parade (ℰ 2181071).

international airline offices

Offices in Bombay include **Aeroflot**, 241/242 Nirmal, Nariman Point (ℰ 221682); **Air France**, Maker Chambers VI (1st floor), Nariman Point (ℰ 2024818); **Air India**, Air India Building, Nariman Point (ℰ 2024142); **Alitalia**, Industrial Assurance Building, Veer Nariman Road, Churchgate (ℰ 222144); **British Airways**, Vulcan Insurance Building, 202B Veer Nariman Road, Churchgate (ℰ 220888); **Cathay Pacific Airways**, Taj Mahal Hotel, Apollo Bunder, Colaba (ℰ 2029112); **Gulf Air**, Maker Chambers V, Nariman Point (ℰ 2024065); **Iraqi Airways**, Mayfair Building, 79 Veer Nariman Road (ℰ 221399); **Japan Airlines**, 2 Raheja Centre (ground floor), Nariman Point (ℰ 2874936); **KLM**, Khaitan Bhavan, 198 J Tata Road, Churchgate (ℰ 2833338);

Lufthansa, Express Towers (4th floor), Nariman Point (✆ 2023430); **Pakistan International Airlines (PIA)**, 7 Brabourne Stadium, Veer Nariman Road, Churchgate (✆ 2021598); **Singapore Airlines**, Taj Mahal Hotel, Apollo Bunder (✆ 2870986); and **Swissair**, Maker Chambers VI, 220 Nariman Point (✆ 2872210).

medical services

If you need urgent **medical** help, phone ✆ 102 for an ambulance.

Two good central hospitals are **St George's Hospital** (✆ 2620301) on P D'Mello Road and the **Bombay Hospital** (✆ 2863343) on V Thackeray Marg.

post offices and telephones

The stately **GPO** is off Nagar Chowk, close to Victoria Terminus (VT) station. Most counters are open from 9am to 7pm (some to 8pm). The *poste restante* (counter 93) is open 9am to 6pm Monday to Saturday. You can't collect mail unless you bring your passport. If you want to send a parcel, there are boys outside who'll wrap them for you.

The **parcel post office** (open 9am to 7pm daily except Sundays) is up some stairs behind the main stamp counters.

It's easy to phone home from Bombay—there are lots of air-conditioned **STD booths** in town, notably at the GPO and opposite the Apollo Hotel in Colaba. The charge is Rs80 per minute, double that if you phone from a big hotel. Several larger hotels now have a fax facility, but it's expensive.

travel agents

For upmarket travel arrangements, try **Mercury Travels** (✆ 2025757, ext 6335) at the Oberoi Towers Hotel, or the travel shops at Thomas Cook/American Express (*see* banks).

For cheap flights, visa assistance, student travel service, etc., contact **Venture Travels**, three doors down from the Café Mondegar in Colaba, or **Transway International** (✆ 2626066, ✉ 2623518) at Pantaky House, 8 Maruti Cross Lane (off Maruti Street), Fort. The latter can be hard to find, being on the 3rd floor of a decrepit ruin, but is worth the effort.

visa extensions

The Foreigners' Registration Office (✆ 2620446) is on Dr D Naoroji Road, close to the Police Commissioner's Office. Visa extensions (up to the maximum stay of 6 months) cost Rs625 and take at least 24 hours to process. You'll need to bring 4 passport photos.

Bombay is not a tourist destination—it is a commercial centre, much like Tokyo or New York. The sights are very spread out and not up to much. You can do them all, if you have the stamina, in a one-day city sightseeing tour; and then follow up with a half-day trip to the Elephanta caves.

Tour 1: Bombay City

By tour bus, 4 hours. Gateway of India–Aquarium–Mani Bhavan–Jain Temple–Hanging Gardens–Kamala Nehru Park–Prince of Wales Museum–Jehangir Art Gallery.

For a good introduction to Bombay, and to avoid the crowds, take the MTDC morning tour. The buses are comfortable, the guides are good, and you are given some background history of the city. This said, insufficient time is allowed for each stop and you may well wish to backtrack to one or two places later. *Note:* the order in which the sights are covered varies from tour to tour, so don't be surprised if you see them back to front.

At **Colaba,** named after the Koli (Bombay's original fisherfolk who are still here), you'll see **Apollo Bunder**—the traditional reception point for dignitaries visiting India in the days of sea travel. In 1911 a very important dignitary stepped ashore here—King George V, accompanied by Queen Mary. To mark the occasion (it was the first time a reigning monarch had made a state visit to India), a hasty decorative arch of white plaster was erected on the edge of Bunder pier. Later, in 1927, a proper monument—the present **Gateway of India**—was built to commemorate the historic occasion. Designed by a government architect, George Wittet, it is now Bombay's principal landmark. Built of local yellow-basalt, the 26m-high gateway is an architectural oddity: designed in the 16th-century Gujarat style, it also incorporates traditional Hindu and Muslim features, notably minarets and *jalis* (the trellis stonework in the side-hall arches which eliminate tropical sun-glare yet allow cool sea breezes in). Return to the Gateway in the evening—it's a popular after-work promenade spot for Bombayites, and a nice relaxing spot to end the day. The ebony-black equestrian statue you see facing onto the gate depicts the mighty Maratha emperor, Chhatrapati Shivaji, who became the bane of the Mughal Aurangzeb. It was set up soon after Bombay became capital of Maharashtra state in 1961.

From Colaba, the tour moves into the city via **Flora Fountain**. Situated at the top of Mahatma Gandhi Road, this is the business heart of downtown Bombay, the home of most of the city's major banks and offices. Nearby is the imposing Gothic structure of **Victoria Terminus** (VT), the largest railway station in the East; also the Cathedral of St Thomas, begun in 1672 by Gerald Aungier, yet opened only in 1718. Then to the seafront, for a beautiful drive up **Marine Drive** (uninspiringly renamed Netaji Subhash Road) which was built on land reclaimed from the marsh in 1920. It sweeps up, in a long elegant arc, from Nariman Point to Chowpatty Beach at the top of Back Bay, and is another favourite promenade spot.

Below Chowpatty, the tour makes a stop at **Taraporewala Aquarium** (*open 11am–8pm daily except Mon; adm Rs3*). Opened in 1951, this aquarium (one of India's finest) houses a wide selection of interesting marine life—giant lobster, batfish, shark, sea-turtle, stingray

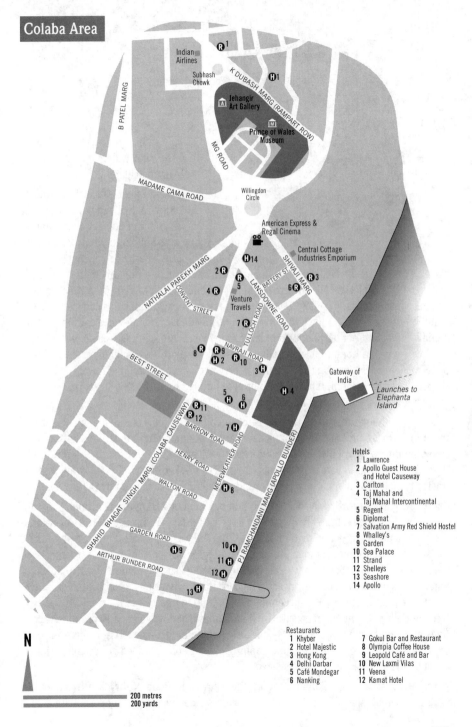

Colaba Area

Indian Airlines

Subhash Chowk

K DUBASH MARG (RAMPART ROW)

B PATEL MARG

R 1

H 1

A Jehangir Art Gallery

M Prince of Wales Museum

MG ROAD

MADAME CAMA ROAD

Willingdon Circle

American Express & Regal Cinema

Central Cottage Industries Emporium

NATHALAI PAREKH MARG

CONVENT STREET

H 14

R 2
R 5
R 4

Venture Travels

BATTERY ST

SHIVAJI MARG

R 3
R 6

LANSDOWNE ROAD

TULLOCH ROAD

R 7

BEST STREET

R 8
R 9
H 2
R 10
H 3

Navraji Road

H 4

Gateway of India

Launches to Elephanta Island

SHAHID BHAGAT SINGH MARG (COLABA CAUSEWAY)

R 11
R 12
H 5
H 6

BARROW ROAD

H 7

HENRY ROAD

MEREWEATHER ROAD

WALTON ROAD

H 8

GARDEN ROAD

H 9

ARTHUR BUNDER ROAD

P J RAMCHANDANI MARG (APOLLO BUNDER)

H 10

H 11

H 12

H 13

Hotels
1 Lawrence
2 Apollo Guest House
  and Hotel Causeway
3 Carlton
4 Taj Mahal and
  Taj Mahal Intercontinental
5 Regent
6 Diplomat
7 Salvation Army Red Shield Hostel
8 Whalley's
9 Garden
10 Sea Palace
11 Strand
12 Shelleys
13 Seashore
14 Apollo

Restaurants
1 Khyber
2 Hotel Majestic
3 Hong Kong
4 Delhi Darbar
5 Café Mondegar
6 Nanking
7 Gokul Bar and Restaurant
8 Olympia Coffee House
9 Leopold Café and Bar
10 New Laxmi Vilas
11 Veena
12 Kamat Hotel

N

200 metres
200 yards

283

and turbot—supplied with fresh sea water via an underground pipeline.

At **August Kranti gardens**, 1km above Chowpatty, you'll find one of Bombay's most important buildings: **Mani Bhavan** at 19 Laburnum Road (*open 9.30am–6pm daily; adm Rs3*). This was Mahatma Gandhi's residence during his visits to Bombay between 1917 and 1934. From here, he launched both his *satyagraha* (non-violence) and civil disobedience campaigns (1919 and 1934 respectively) and inside is an exact reconstruction of the room he lived in—his simple pallet-bed, spinning-wheel, walking-stick, sandals and quaint old telephone (kept just as they were during his life) along with his few religious texts–the Koran, Bible and Gita. On the floor, there's a beautifully crafted tableau of 28 model panels depicting key events in the great man's history. If you want to see and learn more about Gandhi, return later to browse through the extensive library or to see one of the regular film-shows held in the auditorium.

Next stop (although this place may not be covered by your tour), at the top of Back Bay, is the **Jain Temple** on Bal Gangadhar Kher Marg. Take time out at this colourful shrine to study the intricate carvings on its exterior walls—they're quite something. Then climb to the upper storey and watch the monks (their faces masked to avoid swallowing insects) tracing complicated mandalas in powder and ash before the image of their *tirthankar*.

On the heights of nearby Malabar Hill are Bombay's famous **Hanging Gardens**. They are not as exotic as they sound, being simply a terraced garden, landscaped in 1881 over three reservoirs supplying water to Bombay city, but they compensate with a truly terrific topiary of tidily trimmed 'animal' hedges. The popular flower-clock in the garden is close to 'elephant'. Hidden behind a wall beside the Hanging Gardens is the **Tower of Silence**, where the Parsis leave out their dead to be consumed by vultures (probably hawks nowadays). The bulk of the tiny Parsee community, 83,000 in total, presently reside in Bombay. Despite their small numbers, a surprising amount of them have risen to prominent positions in society, including the first Field Marshal of the Indian army. The towers are closed to visitors, and the only recent photographs of them to be published got the magazine in question (*Time-Life*) summarily censored.

Across the road from the gardens, there's the pleasant **Kamala Nehru Park**. Laid out in 1952 and named after Pandit Nehru's wife, this is a colourful, touristy place with a children's playground and a giant Old Woman's Shoe. Ignore the jibes and climb it for spectacular views down over Marine Drive and Chowpatty Beach—especially good around sunset.

The tour generally ends at the **Prince of Wales Museum**, off Willingdon Circle in Colaba (*open daily except Mon 10.15am–6pm; adm Rs5*). This beautiful Gothic structure— designed by Wittet in the Indo-Saracenic style, and with an imposing dome—was built in 1905 to commemorate the first visit of George V (then Prince of Wales) to India. It stands in oriental splendour in spacious palm-decorated gardens, and reminds many visitors of Monte Carlo. Within, you'll find one of the finest collections of art, archaeology and natural history in the country. Start off in the 'key gallery' just inside the entrance. This introduces all the other galleries in the museum, and exhibits the choicest specimens from each one. If your time is short (and it will be if you want to rejoin the tour), use this gallery to choose a couple of selected areas. On the ground floor, you'll find sculpture and stonework, much of it Buddhist, and some huge ceiling slabs from Chalukyan temples in northern Karnataka, dating back to the 6th century AD; on the first floor, there's some excellent ceramics, pottery and necklaces; and on the third floor, the unmissable Purshottam Vishram Mawji collection of art, a worthwhile Tibetan/Nepalese gallery, and fine exhibitions of Continental pottery and Victorian glassware. One of the jewels in this marvellous museum is the manuscript gallery with illustrations of Hindu texts, Mughal miniatures including the magnificent portaits of Jahangir and Dara Shikoh, and the collection of later Pahari school paintings from the hill-states of Punjab and Himachal. Bags must be deposited at the entrance, which is a nuisance; only your camera, passport and money are allowed inside.

Just a few yards down from the Prince of Wales, the air-conditioned **Jehangir Art Gallery** (*open 11am–7pm daily*) holds regular exhibitions of modern Indian art. It's a good place to wind up the day; you'll find toilets, telephones and a pleasant café here.

Note: If you're not into sights (or don't like tours) at least drag yourself over to the Prince of Wales Museum. It's only 10 minutes' walk from Colaba, and you won't regret it.

Tour 2: Suburban Sights

> By tour bus, full day. Kanheri Caves–Lion Safari Park–Juhu Beach–
> St John's Church–Chowpatty Beach.

If you enjoyed tour 1, there's a second MTDC (or GOI) tour out to **Kanheri Caves**, 42km from Bombay. This is one of the largest groups of Buddhist caves (109 total) in western India. They are set high up on a hill, in a forested enclave of the Borivali National Park. Dating from around the 2nd to 9th centuries AD, the earlier (*Hinayana*) caves have been excavated from a huge circular rock. Most of them are simple monks' cells of limited interest, but caves 1, 2 and 3 are noteworthy for their massive pillars, sculptures and stupas. Cave 3 is the famous **Chaitya Cave** with icons and a long, pillared colonnade.

The tour continues on to a nearby **Lion Safari Park** (*open 9am–5pm daily except Mon*), where you get a short tour by minibus. After this, it's on to **Juhu Beach**, 18km from the city centre. This is a 5km-long beach, fringed with palms and coconut trees, with lots of big hotels and beach entertainments at weekends. Only trouble is, you can't swim in the sea–it's too polluted.

My suggestion would be to leave this tour at Kanheri and make your own way back to Colaba. Take a taxi down to **Sassoon Dock** (a great place to watch fishing boats unloading their catch around dawn) and walk 10 minutes south to Colaba's most significant monument, the elegant **St John's (Afghan) Church**. Built in 1847, in memory of British soldiers who died in the first Afghan War, its tall spire has become a familiar landmark for sailors out at sea.

By now, you're probably toured-out—time perhaps to relax over a high-rise cocktail at Oberoi's roof-top Malabar restaurant and to watch the sun set gloriously over Back Bay. After this, if you're up to it, take a cab up the causeway to **Chowpatty Beach** (4km from the centre) and join all those tired Bombay businessmen who are winding down, along with their friends and families, after a hard day's making money. While you're here, tuck into typical Bombay snacks like *bhel puri* (a spicy mix of puffed rice, peanuts, onions, potatoes and chutneys) and *chaat* (fruit and veg tossed in a banana leaf). One end of the beach is a regular meeting-point for Bombay's gay community. The rest is lined with expert masseurs, kneading the strain out of stressed-out stockbrokers. Chowpatty is a good place to come for authentic local atmosphere, and for the famous view of Malabar Hill, beautifully illuminated after dusk. This is the renowned 'Queen's Necklace' around the 'throat' of Back Bay. You can't go swimming though—the water's as filthy as at Juhu.

Note: The above-mentioned tour now makes two calls (at a leisure park and an observation point) before reaching Kanheri. If you're short on sleep, stay on the bus.

Tour 3: Elephanta Island

By boat, 4 hours.

This is a good way to spend a Monday (when most other sights are closed), a Sunday (when the rest of Bombay is closed), or any other day when you need a break from the heat and noise of the city. What you'll see are four rock-cut **cave temples**, dating from AD 450–750, situated on Elephanta Island some 10km northeast of Apollo Bunder. To get there, you've a choice of a luxury launch (Rs50) or an ordinary boat (Rs35), tickets for which are sold at the small office opposite the Gateway of India. Go for one of the luxury boats—they have good guides (all archaeology graduates) and they really bring the place alive. Both categories of boat leave hourly from 9am and 2.15pm, and the voyage takes one hour. A new catamaran service is now in service, running to Elephanta in just 45 minutes and costing Rs100. It leaves 10am daily, returns at 2pm, but has (as yet) no guide on board.

Elephanta has the longest historical pedigree of any of Bombay's seven islands. While the others were still boggy marshes, it was being developed (between the 7th and mid-8th centuries) as the capital of an ancient Hindu dynasty. At that time, it was known as Gharapuri, the Fortress City. Much later, the Portuguese landed on the rear side of the island, found a massive stone elephant there (presently residing in Bombay's Victoria Gardens), and renamed it Elephanta. Later, as disenchantment set in, bored Portuguese gunners spent long, hot monsoon months using its beautiful cave temples as cannon fodder.

The caves themselves are a testimony to the faith of those who excavated them. Some contain 8m-high friezes of astonishing workmanship and figurative detail. Despite cannon-damage and loss of much of the original paintwork, the quality is quite as fine as that of the more popular caves at Ellora.

Arriving at the island, it's a gentle climb up 125 sloping steps to the main cave, dedicated to Shiva. On the ascent, keep an eye out for acquisitive monkeys—they go for food and bright jewellery. Hire a palanquin if you don't like exercise, and rejoin the guide at the top for an instructive talk.

The main cave, carved out of the hard, durable blackstone around the middle of the 7th century, comprises a pillared hall and a small shrine with four entrance doors, flanked by *dvarapala* guardians. The architectural style is a combination of Chalukyan (cushion capitals and graceful sculptures) and Gupta (mountain, cloud, nature imagery) influences. The cave itself features a series of large sculptured panels, the finest of which, the 5.8m-high *Trimurti* monolith, depicts Shiva in a rare triple role as creator, protector and destroyer (the Hindu Trinity). The gentle, feminine face on the right shows him as a young man holding a lotus blossom (Brahma/creator), the central panel has him as a middle-aged man with a wise Mona Lisa smile (Vishnu/preserver), and the face on the left depicts him as a ferocious old man brandishing a skull (Shiva himself, in his common role as destroyer). It's an exquisitely balanced piece of work.

Nearby is one of the finest sculptures in India—Ravana lifting Mount Kailash. This portrays the epic story of the Lankan king, Ravana, often shown with ten heads to denote superior intelligence, who took advantage of Shiva's deep slumber to try and displace his mountain home. In the nick of time, Shiva woke up and (using just his toe) pressed the teetering peak back into place again, burying the demon king beneath it for 10,000 years. Such is the skill of the sculptor here, that you can actually see the strain on Ravana's rippling shoulder and back muscles as he does battle with the mountain.

To the left of the Trimurti is another masterstroke—Shiva as *Ardhanarisvara*, or half-man/half-woman. This piece represents the combined force of masculine spirit and feminine creativity. Viewed from the centre, the bisexuality of the figure's form and features appears quite harmonious—a remarkable achievement. The female side of the face is looking into the mirror of *maya* or illusion.

Other important panels show Shiva playing chess with Parvati on Mount Kailash (surrounded by awed domestic servants), performing the earth-shaking Tandava dance (*Nataraja*), and demonstrating the discipline of yoga (*Yogisvara*). If you're lucky, your guide on the boat over will demonstrate the Tandava for you—it's a hoot.

Shopping

Most Bombay shops are open 10am to 7pm daily except Fridays. Bazaars and hotel shopping arcades often stay open till 9pm. Government and state emporiums run from 10am to 6.30pm and close on a Sunday.

Hong Kong and Korea are becoming expensive, so many people are looking to India, and particularly to Bombay, for international brand-name clothing. Labour is cheap and cotton is readily available. A lot of surplus (reject) clothing, especially cotton shirts and jeans, ends up in

Bombay, and you can find much of it (at throw-away prices) at the sixty or so shops in **Fashion Street**, close to the Central Telegraph Exchange on M G Road. Prices are lowest on a Sunday and it's best to turn up at around 11am, before it gets too crowded. If you're in search of a sari, you could walk (or take a short rickshaw hop) to nearby Queen's Street, where there's a wide selection from £15 to £500. The **Breach Candy** area near Cumballa Hill now has a few good department stores, offering a wide variety of quality items at fixed prices, including silk and cotton men's shirts (mainly brand names) as well as saris and costume/fashion jewellery to suit all tastes. The **Colaba** area is quickly filling up with shops selling Levi/Wrangler jeans and Bally/Reebok footwear—all very cheap, but they're already running into copyright problems. Several stalls along Colaba Causeway sell 'seconds' clothing and accessories; the prices are so silly, it's not even worth bargaining.

The best general buys in Bombay, apart from fashion clothing, are raw silk and cotton furnishings (especially cushion covers and bedspreads), leather shoes and accessories, and carpets. To get an idea of what's available and how much it should cost, drop in on the **Central Cottage Industries Emporium** just up the road from the Taj Hotel, or **Swadeshi** at the Fountain. What you get here is a wide cross-section of Indian handicrafts from blockprinted bedspreads and soft furnishings through to brassware, jewellery and leather bags—all at fixed prices. Also worth a visit are **Fantasia** on the 1st floor of the Oberoi Towers Hotel and **Anokhi** at Kemp's Corner. They specialize in quality Rajasthani fabrics and textiles, and charge accordingly. The Towers also has top-quality leather shoes, purses and bags, and you *are* allowed to bargain. Elsewhere, buy leather only from reputable shops like **Metro** (shoes only), **Rasool Bhai** and **Adamji** in Colaba. Many other places sell synthetic 'lookalike' leather which is hard to tell from the real thing.

There are lots of state emporia in Bombay, selling regional goods from all over the country. The Rajasthani one (for hangings, bedspreads and chunky jewellery) is up by the Fountain, while the Kerala one (good for sandalwood carvings and brass) is close to the Oberoi Towers. The Uttar Pradesh emporium specializes in embroidered goods and is at Cuffe Parade. Nearby, at the World Trade Centre, you'll find emporiums for Madhya Pradesh, Himachal Pradesh, Maharashtra and Jammu & Kashmir (best for carpets). If these places can't ship stuff home for you (most will), try Perfect Cargo Movers (℗ 2873935), 56 Abdullabmia Currimjee Building (4th floor), Jamabhoomi Marg, Fort. They're supposed to be reliable.

The centre for traditional jewellery and diamonds is **Zaveri Bazaar**, open daily except Sunday. The main retail street is Sheikh Memon Street, but it's not called 'duplicate Mall' for nothing. A lot of the silver sold here isn't silver at all. You'll pay more at reputable places like **Chida Kashi** (behind the Regal cinema in Colaba) and at the Oberoi Towers shopping arcade, but at least they give you a written guarantee with your purchase.

Close to Zaveri Bazaar is the old **Crawford Market** (founded 1867), now renamed Mahatma Phule Market. Raw, bloody and vital, you get a real feel of India here and it's a photographer's dream. There's not much to buy (except meat, fish, fruit and vegetables) but it's where half of the city goes shopping. If you want to avoid the crowds (and the pickpockets), turn up at around 7pm.

Nearby **Chor Bazaar** ('thieves' market') is a good place to scout round for leather shoes, antiques and smuggled goods. The favourite anecdote here is that you can be sold spare parts from your own car.

Leisure

Going to the **cinema** in Bombay is a must—it's not only the film capital of India, it also produces more movies than any other city in the world, Hollywood included. There are literally hundreds of cinema houses in town, most of them air-conditioned and very comfortable. To tune in to Bollywood movie-madness, pick up a *Star and Style* magazine (full of juicy screen gossip) and a local rag to see what's on. If you want to just chance it, head down the street opposite VT station, where you'll find three good cinemas—the Excelsior, Empire and Sterling—showing a mixture of Hindi/Marathi epics and recent-release Western movies. Later, ask the tourist office to arrange a visit to one of the film studios, where you can have a chat with the stars and watch them playing three different parts in three different movies on the same day. Meet them again later in the 1900s **disco** at the Taj Hotel on a Saturday night—if, that is, you can blag your way in. It's *the* place to be seen in Bombay, and only hotel residents or invited members get past the golden gate.

Something you *can* do at a big hotel without feeling awkward is go for a make-over. The Oberoi Towers gets glowing mentions from ladies who have used its beauty parlour. 'You go in and spend 30 dollars,' said one happy customer, 'and you come out feeling like a million! I had three or four people working on me for a whole hour—pedicure, manicure, hair-dye, eye-brow tweezering, the full works. They certainly know how to pamper you!'

For a spot of culture, pop along one evening to Taj Hotel's Tanjore restaurant where you can enjoy a **classical dance** programme (starts 7.45pm) along with a good Indian meal. If you want to see something more professional, there are several **dance, drama and music** events advertised in GOI tourist office's free fortnightly handout. This also has details of upcoming **art exhibitions** at the city's many galleries and **star-gazing shows** at the Nehru Planetarium.

When it comes to sports, Bombay is rather exclusive. Top hotels like the Taj, Oberoi and President can arrange **tennis, golf** and **squash**, also **sailing, horse-riding**, and **buggy-rides** round town, but only if you stay with them. **Horse-racing** at the Mahalaxmi Race Course, opposite Haji Ali Mosque, takes place every Sunday and public holiday from November and March. The big meets are in February/March and the cream of Bombay society turns out to be seen.

Swimming in the sea round Bombay is a health hazard. The water is badly polluted, and even locals don't dip their toes. The only half-decent beach is at **Manori**, 40km out of the centre. To visit, get a suburban train from Churchgate to Malad, then a 272 bus to Marve ferry, cross by ferry and walk to the mid-range **Manoribel Hotel** (℡ 2833918). This is in Manori's quaint fishing village, with the beach only a short walk away. Closer to home, you can have a cool dip at the **Breach Candy Club** (℡ 3674381), 66 Bhulabhai Desai Marg, 1km north of the

No visit to India is complete without seeing at least one Hindi movie. Here's what to expect: 'It was non-stop colour and excitement. Every few minutes, the action would stop for a song and a dance. The hero and heroine were both plump, which struck us as reflecting the ideal in a country where most people were very thin. It must have been an old movie too, because kissing was still not allowed on-screen. As a compromise, the two lovers moved toward each other, the music heightened to a crescendo and at the last possible moment the film broke off into a montage of glorious symbolic scenery. Taken as a whole, it was a fascinating blend of Hitchcock, James Bond and 1930s screwball comedy. The intermission was quite brilliantly managed, an unseen pair of hands pushing our stout heroine over a cliff, the curtains closing and the lights coming on all in the same moment. We returned to the cinema after the break to find the leading lady resting safely in a hospital bed—no clue was given as to how she had avoided her watery grave.'

Many cinemas also show matinée performances of English-speaking films, often spicy Western imports with 'lots of killing' and 'hot sexy encounters'. Advertise-ments for them in local newspapers are often as entertaining as the films themselves, for example: 'Sahara!—Irresistible Brooks Shields and bare-bodied sheikhs! Super cars and stallions! Passions and adventure!'

Hanging Gardens. This has a large pool in the shape of India before Partition, and Ceylon is the kiddies' pool. The non-member fees (Rs200 per day, Rs300 on weekends) include access to the pool, the volleyball courts, the bar and the snack-bar, but you'll need your passport to get in.

Behind Fashion Street market on M G Road is **Cross Maidan**, where you can watch a game of Sunday **cricket**. These urban gardens are overlooked by Bombay University (a wonderful gothic horror, dominated by an 80m-high clock tower) and are a popular haunt of Indian families at weekends. There's nearly always something going on here—a circus, a fun-fair or an offbeat show—and if you want to see how Mr & Mrs Bombayite (and their tribe) relax out of work, turn up on a Saturday night.

Bombay © (022–)   ***Where to Stay***

Living in Bombay is very expensive, and good rooms are hard to come by. With housing such a problem, decent hotels are often fully booked, and the few habitable budget lodges packed out. In the former instance, make advance reservations; in the latter, arrive very early in the morning to snap up any rooms going. The most difficult time is the November to February high season. Check-out at most hotels is at noon; at some it's at 10am.

As in Delhi, Bombay's top hotels are all gearing themselves to the business traveller, so you don't (apart from a few ethnic touches in the lobbies) feel like you're in India at all. This said, they're okay if you have money to burn and need a couple of days to acclimatize to the (often intense) climate and street-life. Interestingly, you have a much better chance of getting a luxury room at the weekends—the bigger hotels cater mainly to domestic business travellers from Delhi or Bangalore, who often go home on a Friday night. Weekends are also a good time to arrive in Bombay—far less traffic and much more peaceful than during the week.

luxury (from US$225)

More an institution than a hotel is the **Taj Mahal Hotel**, with its new addition the **Taj Mahal Intercontinental**, on Apollo Bunder, © 2023366, ✆ 2872711. The older building is one of Bombay's major landmarks; it opened in 1903 and features on every other postcard of the city, alongside the Gateway of India. Accorded the accolade of being one of the world's twelve best hotels, it is now a major focal point of all visitors to Bombay. Rooms start at US$275/295 (15% less at the Intercontinental) and the best ones, if you have a choice, overlook the sea. A wide range of facilities include 4 restaurants, 3 bars, coffee shop, discotheque, business centre, beauty salon, fitness centre and swimming pool.

The only other place to stay, if you're this well-off, is the soaring **Oberoi Towers** at Nariman Point, © 2024343, ✆ 2043282. Efficient and personal, it is the tallest building in India (with 35 stories) and overlooks the Arabian Sea on all sides. Rooms start at US$225/250 and the views get better the higher up you go. Next door is the **Oberoi**, ✆ 2025757, ✉ 2041505, charging US$275/300 or (with sea-view) US$305/330 for rooms. This is the newer hotel of the two, and what it doesn't have in the way of high-rise views, it certainly makes up for in style and opulence. Taken together, the Oberois now run parallel—in facilities and prestige—with the more fêted Taj.

If you need to stay near the airport, there's the **Centaur Hotel** outside the domestic terminal, ✆ 6116660, ✉ 6113535, and the plush **Leela Kempinski**, 1km from the international, ✆ 8363636, ✉ 8360606. The latter has rooms from US$225/245, the former from US$90/100, and both have good pools and deluxe facilities.

expensive (from US$70)

Rather more in the range of the general traveller—though prices have doubled everywhere in the last three years—is the warm and personal **Hotel President** at Cuffe Parade, ✆ 2150808, ✉ 2151201. It scores high on service, food and atmosphere, and the rooms are well-priced (for Bombay) at US$195/215. The only other contenders are the **Ambassador** at Churchgate, ✆ 2041131, ✉ 2040004, with rooms for US$120/140 and a rooftop revolving restaurant (but no pool), and the Arab-favoured **Fariyas** at Colaba, ✆ 2042911, ✉ 2834992, off Arthur Bunder Road. The latter has a nice restaurant, garden-pool terrace, health club, and the oldest 'English' pub in Bombay. Rooms are good value too, at just Rs2400/2800.

moderate (from US$30)

The top spot in this category is the **Hotel Apollo** on Lansdowne Road, ✆ 2020223, ✉ 2874990, behind the Regal Theatre. It's an informal, friendly place with a good restaurant, helpful staff and pleasant a/c rooms with TV from Rs1100/1327 (inc taxes). There's a wide choice, so see a few. Also in Colaba (*see* map), and similarly priced, are hotels **Regent** at 8 Best Road, ✆ 2871854, ✉ 2020363, **Diplomat** at 24–26 Mereweather Road, ✆ 2021661, ✉ 283000, and **Garden**, ✆ 2841476, ✉ 2044290. They're all very popular though, and should be pre-booked well in advance. At the Diplomat, go for a superior room at around Rs1200. The cheaper ones, though air-conditioned, are dingy.

Three other options, all close to each other on the Bunder (200 yards up from the Taj), are the **Sea Palace**, ✆ 2841828, ✉ 2854403, **Shelley's**, ✆ 2840229, ✉ 2840385, and **Strand**, ✆ 2841624, ✉ 2041160. They also fall into the US$30/40 bracket and have some sea-view rooms.

Finally, there are two old backpacker favourites to which renovation has been kind: first, the 3rd-floor **Hotel Lawrence** on Rope Walk Lane, ✆ 243618, off K Dubash Marg at the back of the Prince of Wales Museum; second, the **Chateau Windsor** at Churchgate, next to the Ambassador Hotel, ✆ 2043376, ✉ 2851415. Both charge around US$20/30 and are worth a look.

The loss of old freak haunts like Rex-Stiffles (now the Regent Hotel) and Dipty's Juice Bar spelt the end of an era, and one look is all it takes for many second-timers to jump on a bus to Goa. Nevertheless, downtown Colaba remains the backpacker centre of the city and a handful of cheap guest houses have hung on stubbornly in the backstreets behind the Taj Hotel. Space and hygiene are still at a premium though, so you'll have to be up with the birds if you want to get a decent room.

For maximum comfort (not saying much) stay at **Whalley's Guest House**, 41 Merewether Road, ✆ 2821802, ✆ 2834206. It's grubby on the outside, but the rooms are large and clean, and you get a fair breakfast thrown in with the rate (Rs350/450). The better rooms have aspirations to air conditioning. Nearby, at 30 Mereweather Road, the ever-popular **Salvation Army Red Shield Hostel**, ✆ 241824, has dorm beds for Rs70 (breakfast included) and for Rs100 (full board); also shared rooms at Rs125 per person and large doubles for Rs300. Check-out time is 9am, and you've got a chance of getting in here, since nobody can stay more than a week. A few doors down is the decrepit **Carlton Hotel** at 12 Mereweather Road; Rs300 buys you a hovel with common bath, but travellers seem to like it. They also favour **Apollo Guest House**, ✆ 2045540; **Hotel Causeway**, ✆ 2020833 (same building as Apollo); and **Hotel Shilton**, ✆ 2044368, all on Colaba Causeway (*see* map). Of the three, the Apollo is certainly the most tuned into travellers' needs (ask for Kamal) and is the cheapest too. Ask around for other Colaba options like **Janta Guest House**, **India Guest House** and **Hotel Gateway**, mentioned in descending order of awfulness.

Given the difficulty of finding rooms in Colaba at high season, you might do well to stay in the city instead. There are two good bets here, very well-located for the post office, tourist office, VT station and the better cinemas. Try first **Hotel City Palace** at 121 City Terrace, ✆ 2615515, ✆ 2676897, opposite the GPO. With friendly people and spotless rooms (with bath/TV) around the £10 mark it's one of the best buys in town. Air conditioning costs Rs100 extra. If this is full, settle for the **Railway Hotel** at 249 P D'Mello Road, ✆ 2616705, ✆ 2658049, just up from the GPO; it's similarly priced and has larger rooms.

The tourist office keeps a list of paying-guest accommodation, with rooms from Rs300 to Rs3000. It's worth checking out if you're still on the streets with nowhere to go.

Bombay ✆ *(022–)*   ***Eating Out***

Bombay has an amazing choice of restaurants at all levels so you're not going to starve, no matter what your budget. Food is expensive by Indian standards, but there's a host of fast-food joints and the star hotels offer some great deals to the penny-conscious traveller.

A case in point is the excellent **Shamiana** coffee shop at the Taj Mahal Hotel, often the first place Westerners go when they want good food. Not only is it air-conditioned and a wonderful place to cool off from the initial blast of city heat, but it has all-you-can-eat buffet breakfasts for Rs275 (7–10am), including unlimited coffee. Best of all, you don't feel like an alien if you turn up in jeans and trainers— though of course you don't win any points either. This place serves à la carte throughout the day for around £5 per head and has a special buffet brunch every Sunday (11am–2.30pm) for Rs325. In the evening, you can return for a *biriani* or *thali* supper (around £10 per head) at the Taj's sophisticated **Tanjore** restaurant, tying in perhaps with one of its cultural dance programmes at 7.45pm, 9.45pm and 10.45pm. If your wallet runs to it, you can finish off afterwards with a glass of wine or a cocktail at the same hotel's rooftop **Apollo Bar**, which has live music along with fondues and soufflés. All in all, a very pleasant night out.

The Taj also has the oldest tea lounge, the oldest bar and the most prestigious restaurant, the **Zodiac Grill**, in the city. The Zodiac (at lobby level) has a very elegant ambience, a rather formal atmosphere (smart dress required) and offers top-notch Continental fare with prices to match. The only place that gets close to it is Oberoi Towers' **Café Royal**, a very select Parisian-style eatery where every item of food is specially flown in from France. The menu here incorporates prize-winning dishes from international food festivals, and you can enjoy escargots, smoked salmon and lobster along with a wide choice of vintage wines. Other recommended restaurants at the Towers are The **Outrigger**, a Polynesian restaurant with good-value lunchtime buffets, the 24-hour **Palms** coffee shop (another place 'to be seen' in Bombay) with excellent buffets, and the exclusive **Mewar**, specializing in Rajasthani cuisine. Next door at the **Oberoi**, the French **Rotisserie** restaurant has popular executive lunches, the 1st-floor **Kandahar** authentic Northwest Frontier food, and the **Brasserie** English-style breakfasts/lunches. None of these places are as expensive as you might think, especially if you opt for the buffets.

Elsewhere, you're spoiled for choice. Not only are Bombay's restaurants far more interesting than Delhi's, but there are many more of them. This is because city residents eat out a lot—their prime concern is making money, and cooking is low priority. As in New York, people go out to be seen and, because most accommodation is so cramped, they prefer the space of restaurants. If Bombayites choose a hotel restaurant, it's usually for something of value (like the buffet lunches at the Taj-run **Rangoli**, Nariman Point) or something fancy (like pizzas, pastas, and serenading musicians at President Hotel's delightful **Trattoria**). But in the main, they stick to local restaurants with family atmosphere—fast-food joints like the **Pizzeria** on Marine Drive (quick pizzas, cold beers), **Open House**, **Sundance Café** and **Croissants**, all close to Churchgate station (burgers, fries, hot dogs and pastries), **Mahesh Lunch Home** and **Krishna** near Jehangir Art Gallery (seafood), and not far from these two, **Chetna** for *thalis*.

Chinese food seems to have become part of Indian cuisine. The **Golden Dragon** at the Taj is famous for it, if rather expensive. So is **Chinese Garden** at Kemp's Corner and **Ling's Pavilion** behind the Central Cottage Industries in Colaba. More afford-

Indian restaurants have become very multi-faceted of late. They usually have a very extensive menu which is divided into sections: Indian, Chinese, and Continental. In general, the smaller the restaurant the longer the menu is, and the less likely it is that you can order anything. In Manali, for instance, I found an eatery with 96 items on the menu. I went right through them with a waiter, and found only 9 dishes actually available. This was, he explained, because the 'old cook' who had prepared the menu had died, and his replacement couldn't even read it, let alone make any of it. You'll come across a lot of this kind of thing in India, but don't let it get to you. It's all part of the experience, and you'll laugh about it later (honest).

able are places like the **Nanking** and **Hong Kong** on Shivaji Maharaj Marg, Colaba. If you go up to Churchgate area, you'll find half a dozen cheaper places specializing in Cantonese and Szechwan dishes. Your hotel can usually recommend one.

Continental food is not so easy to find—Bombayites like their food spicy, not bland—so if you want steaks, sizzlers and Western-style baked dishes, you're restricted to 5-star hotels like the Taj, the Oberoi and the President. Or, if you want to spend a little less, there's the very popular **Society** restaurant (*the* place to go for steaks, as well as for French food) in the 3-star Ambassador Hotel at Churchgate. A little far out, but worth it, is a place called **Sizzlers** up at Kobe, near Chowpatty, which is a meat-eater's paradise—burgers, steaks and 'sizzlers', all reasonably priced.

Indian food is well sampled at the non-veg **Khyber**, 145 M G Road. It's not cheap, but has top-quality north Indian fare backed up by stylish stuccoed decor and first-class service. They're a bit stuffy though, so dress to impress. From here, it's down in style and price to the **Delhi Durbar** on Colaba Causeway, which is where most travellers have their first Indian meal. Air-conditioned and affordable, it does a brisk trade in milk shakes, ice-creams, and meat-based *tandooris* and *dhansaks*. Rather more trendy is **Gaylord's** on Veer Nariman Road, where you can chill out in a/c comfort and rap with the waiters (fun, like the menu) while you wait for your chicken korma or fish and chips. Top marks for this one; lots of bubbly atmosphere.

For cheap 'travellers' food', head back to Colaba. Like Paharganj in Delhi or Sudder Street in Calcutta, this area has any number of funky places catering to the anti *dhal*-and-rice brigade. The only difference is, this being Bombay, they've all gone yuppie. Take the long-running **Leopold's** on the Causeway for example— totally revamped, it now looks like a typical New York diner, with a TGIF menu, a Dayvilles-style ice cream parlour, and a single red rose on each table. It's a good place to drop in for a Western breakfast or a cold beer, and to watch the whole cross-section of Bombay's cosmopolitana drift in and out.

The nearby **Food Inn**, a few doors down, also does good business but doesn't serve beer. Also close by is the unmissable **Café Mondegar** opposite the Hotel Apollo. Full of 'cool dudes' and 'happening chicks' (local wannabees!), this is a glitzy pub-bar with Anglo-Indian snacks, wild wall-murals, and the only CD jukebox in town. It's full by 9pm and rocks on until midnight.

Less hectic are cheap veggie places like **Hotel Majestic** opposite the Mondegar, **Veena** and **Kamat** down from Leopold's, and **New Laxmi Vilas** in Navraji Road. Try **Bagdadi** on Tulloch Road for non-veg (around Rs30 per head) and the opposite **Gokul** for ice-cold beers. The latter is like a 1920s speakeasy, with subterranean decor, dim lighting and huddles of Indians whispering secretively in alcoves. You half-expect your bottle to come in a brown paper bag.

Moving On
by air

Air ticket reservation, confirmation and cancellation is best done through a travel agent. Many offices, especially Air India and Indian Airlines are best avoided (the queues never move). Ask the Mercury Travel desk at Oberoi Towers or the Air India desk in the Taj hotel to do the work for you. Alternatively, wait until you reach a quieter centre (Goa, Cochin or Trivandrum) where you can do it quickly yourself.

Damania (Skyline NEPC), 17 Nehru Road, Vakola, Santa Cruz, ✆ 6102525, flies daily to Bagdogra (for Darjeeling), Bangalore, Calcutta and Goa, 6 days a week to Madras, 5 to Ahmedabad, 4 to Cochin, and 3 to Delhi and Jaipur.

East-West Airlines, 'Sophia', 18 New Kantwadi Road, off Perry Cross Road, Bandra, ✆ 6436678, flies daily to Bangalore, Cochin, Delhi, Hyderabad and Madras, and 5 days a week to Madurai, Mangalore and Trivandrum.

Indian Airlines, Army & Navy Building, M G Road, ✆ 2023031, flies daily to Ahmedabad, Bangalore, Calcutta, Cochin, Delhi, Goa, Hyderabad, Jaipur, Madras, Mangalore and Trivandrum. It also has 6 flights a week to Udaipur, 4 to Aurangabad, Coimbatore, Gwalior, Jodhpur, Madurai and Rajkot, and 3 to Varanasi.

Jet Airways, Amarchand Mansion, Madame Cama Road, ✆ 8386111, flies daily to Ahmedabad, Bangalore, Calcutta, Cochin, Coimbatore, Delhi, Goa, Hyderabad, Madras and Mangalore.

Moduluft, Akash Ganga (2nd floor), 89 Bhulabhai Desai Marg, Cumballa Hill, ✆ 3635380, flies daily to Bangalore, Calcutta, Cochin, Delhi, Goa, Jammu, Jodhpur and Udaipur.

NEPC Airlines, Hotel Bawa International, Nehru Road, Ville Parle, ✆ 6107068, flies daily to Aurangabad, and 2/3 days a week to Bangalore, Keshod, Pune and Rajkot.

Sahara Indian Airlines, ✆ 2832446, has daily flights to Delhi only (as yet).

All the above airlines have offices at the domestic airport, and regularly add new places to their routes. It's worth ringing around before finalizing your flight arrangements within the country. Sample flying times are 45 minutes to Aurangabad, 1 hour to Goa and Ahmedabad, and 2 hours to Delhi, Varanasi and Trivandrum.

by rail

Between them, Bombay's two railway systems cover all major tourist destinations. **Central Railways** services the east and the south—Calcutta, Aurangabad, Goa,

Gujarat etc.—and a few places to the north. Computerized reservations are from the a/c reservation centre behind Victoria Terminus, ℂ 26175750. **Western Railways** services most places north and west—including Delhi and Rajasthan—from Churchgate and Bombay Central stations. Bookings are from the Western Railways office, ℂ 2038016, ext 4577, next to the GOI tourist office opposite Churchgate (open 8am to 8pm, till 2pm only on Sunday). Tourist quota tickets can be purchased here (9.30am to 4.30pm weekdays, till 2.30pm only on Saturday), along with Indrail passes. At VT, it's window 22 (ground floor) for tourist quotas and Indrail passes (9am to 4pm); but window 21 on a Sunday (8am to 2pm).

Tourist-quota tickets are available one day before departure only; in high season (October to February), all rail tickets should be booked a few days ahead.

Useful trains from Bombay Central station include the 2951 **Rajdhani Express** to Delhi (dep 4.55pm, 17hrs) and the 9101 **Gujarat Mail** to Ahmedabad (dep 9.25pm, 9hrs). From Victoria Terminus, fast trains include the 1065 **Ratnagiri Express** to Varanasi (dep 5.05am, 27hrs), the 2123 **Deccan Queen** to Pune (dep 5.10pm, 3½hrs), the 2859 **Gitanjali Express** to Calcutta (dep 6.05am, 33hrs), the 6529 **Udyan Express** to Bangalore (dep 7.55am, 24hrs) and the 7517 **Tapovan Express** to Aurangabad (dep 6.10am, 7½hrs).

The fast train to Madras, the 6063 **Chennai Express** (dep 7.50pm, 24hrs) leaves from a third station called Dadar, to the north of Bombay. Tickets can be booked from VT or Central stations.

For Goa, you'll need to check with Central Railways. The new Konkan rail-line from Bombay to Mangalore may be finished by the time you read this, in which case you're looking at just 10 hours' travel (plus a bus at the other end) before you hit the beaches.

by bus

Most long-distance buses leave from the **state transport bus depot** opposite Bombay Central station, but you'd be mad to book tickets there (biblical chaos). Travellers in the know use MTDC, who have two offices (*see* 'Tourist Information', p.279). MTDC offer a number of daily deluxe buses to useful destinations like Aurangabad, Panjim (Goa), Hyderabad, Bangalore, Madras, Delhi and Calcutta. Check the departure point though, since it varies. For destinations like Udaipur, Mt Abu and Ahmedabad, which may still not be covered by MTDC or state buses, you may have to check out private bus companies at 9th and 11th lane, Khetwadi.

by boat

Damania Shipping now offer an air-conditioned 'hydrofoil' service between Bombay and Goa. It leaves Bombay (Baucha Chakka ferry wharf) at 7am daily and arrives at Panjim 7 hours later. Coming back, it leaves Panjim at 3pm and arrives at Bombay around 10.30pm. The US$35/50 (economy/club class) fare includes food, refreshments and a recent-release Hollywood movie. To book, contact Damania at the ferry terminal, ℂ 6102525, ✆ 6104219, or any of their regional airways offices (*see* under 'by air' for Bombay office, p.296).

Matheran

If you want to escape the heat of the city, a cool day excursion is up to the nearby hill station of Matheran. To get there, take the fast Deccan Express (dep 6.40am) or the Miraj Express (dep 8.45am) from Bombay VT station to Neral Junction. These early trains connect with the scenic toy train up to Matheran itself. All trains must be booked in advance as they are very busy. There is not much to see or do in Matheran—this is a typical Indian hill station—but the town is famous for its honey and *chikki* (sugary toffee/nut confection), and from Porcupine and Louisa Points (both within easy walking distance) there are fantastic views over smoggy Bombay and the surrounding terrain.

Pune

Another worthwhile day excursion (for speed freaks only) is to Pune, connected to Bombay by express (but often full) commuter trains (4hrs). Pune is the site of the big **Osho Commune International Ashram**, founded by Bhagwan Rajneesh and a continuing success story despite the Bhagwan's death in 1990. It is an amazing place, with a vast zen garden, swimming pool, sauna, massage/beauty parlours, tennis and basketball courts, and even a bistro. If visiting for the day, take advantage of the 45-minute tours (Rs10) which run between 10.30am and 2.30pm. The ashram is also touched on by the 4-hour government bus tours of the city, which can be booked on arrival at the railway station (from the MTDC desk), and which leave the railway station at 8am and 2pm daily. Those who want to stay in Pune longer can stay at the expensive **Hotel Sagar Plaza**, © (0212) 622622, ✆ 622633, 1 Bund Garden Road, off Moledina Road; the moderate **Hotel Gulmohr**, © 622773, 15 A–1 Connaught Road near the railway station; or the cheap **Hotel National**, © 625054, 14 Sassoon Road, opposite the railway station. Foreign exchange is best at Thomas Cook, Thacker House, G Thimmaya Road. The GPO is on Connaught Road. If you want to stay at the Osho Commune itself, you must be prepared for an on-the-spot HIV test and to arrange your own accommodation.

Dawn mists,
Western Ghats.

Route 4: Golden Goa

Most people end up going to Goa at some point—if not the first trip to India, then definitely the second. It's not just that it's *the* beach destination in the country, it's just surrounded by so much hype. Like the Taj at Agra, you hear so much about it that if you haven't been there, you feel like you missed out on Shangri-La.

Goa is a long narrow 100km of coastline running between the Arabian Sea and the Western Ghats. It has some of the best beaches in the world and is India's favourite winter resort. The Mediterranean feel of the place (it was Portuguese territory up until 1961) adds to its charm, making it a favourite. And Goa is not just beaches. Within striking distance of Panjim, the charming capital, are a variety of picturesque forts, churches, temples and market towns. A short drive away, there's the impressive ghost city of Old Goa, with its haunting Roman Catholic churches. And everywhere you travel inland, you're surrounded by lush green fields of rice, coconut and cashew—an inheritance of the cropwise Jesuits.

Itinerary

Peaceful and serene, with a wide range of activities, Goa is less a 'route' than a fully self-contained holiday resort, with most people staying longer than originally planned, or at least wanting to. Unless you're on a direct charter from abroad, your best plan of action is a flight (or catamaran) from Bombay, followed by a short stay in Panjim for bus tours out to North and South Goa. Not only do these 2-day tours give you a quick overview of the whole territory (and there's a lot of it) but you get to see all the main beaches, and can decide which to revisit. How much time you allow for Goa is up to you, but don't linger too long—there are more beaches further south at Gokarn (*see* p.583) and Kovalam (*see* p.488). If travelling on to Bangalore, you could visit Hampi (*see* p.543) on the way.

History

The origins of Goa are lost in legend. The popular myth is that it was reclaimed from the sea by the sixth avatar (incarnation) of Vishnu. Historically, it is datable to the 3rd century BC, when it formed part of the Mauryan Empire. Later, it was ruled by the Chalukyan kings of Badami (580–750), and by the Kadambas (who allegedly settled the site of Old Goa in the mid-11th century). In 1469 it was seized from the Vijayanagar kings by the Bahmani Muslims, and in 1510 it was taken from the Bijapur kings by the Portuguese.

With its natural harbours and broad rivers, Goa made the ideal base for the trading, seafaring, evangelical Portuguese, bent equally on spreading Catholicism and controlling the eastern spice route. They named it *Goa Dourada*, or Golden Goa, and began a systematic programme of building churches while destroying Hindu temples. With the conquistadors came Jesuit and Franciscan missionaries, who achieved spectacular success in converting most Goans from Hinduism to Roman Catholicism—largely an achievement of the Inquisition, which arrived in 1560. The Jesuits also introduced the first cashew saplings to Goa and Kerala, and developed the art of cultivating coconut trees, which became Goa's primary crop.

Portuguese control began in Old Goa, and gradually extended to include most of the territory, displacing a succession of local Hindu rulers in the process. Old Goa remained their capital until a terrible outbreak of plague in 1738 prompted a gradual move to Panjim. Portugal's power then began to fade in Europe, reflected by a brief spell of British occupation of Goa during the Napoleonic Wars. Nevertheless all three pockets of Portuguese power in India—Goa, Daman and Diu—remained essentially intact right up to December 1961, when they finally returned to Indian control.

The last 35 years of Indian rule have hardly touched Goa's old Portuguese character and flavour, and have brought it considerable benefits. The Portuguese did little for Goa—until 1961 there were no bridges, no roads (outside of Panjim) and no electricity. The Indians built bridges over Goa's principal rivers, the Mandovi and the Zuari, and Panjim was at last connected up with north and south Goa. They also developed Pilar Harbour—a vast natural harbour backing onto a rich mountain of iron ore—and Goa became wealthy overnight.

Finally, having constructed paved roads, modern buildings and hotels, and proper communications, the Indian Government prepared Goa for tourism. The potential was always

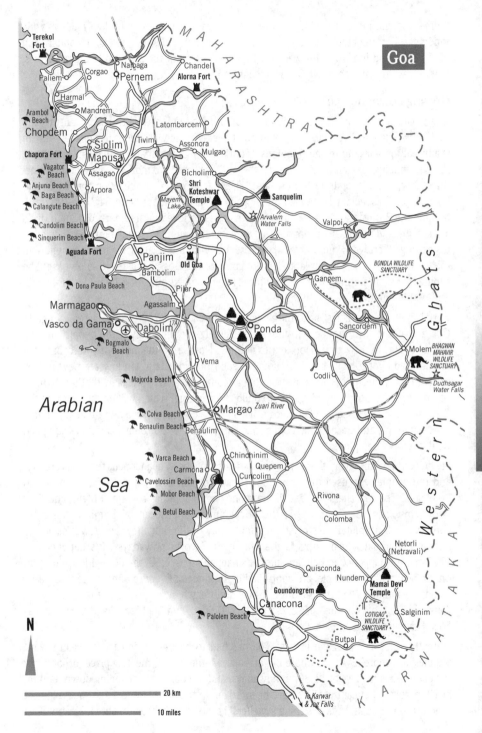

Goa

Terekol Fort

MAHARASHTRA

Paliem
Corgao
Nalbaga
Chandel
Pernem
Alorna Fort
Harmal
Arambol Beach
Mandrem
Latombarcem
Chopdem
Tivim
Assonora
Mulgao
Siolim
Assagao
Bicholim
Mapusa
Chapora Fort
Vagator Beach
Shri Koteshwar Temple
Sanquelim
Anjuna Beach
Arpora
Mayem Lake
Baga Beach
Arvalem Water Falls
Valpoi
Calangute Beach
Candolim Beach
Sinquerim Beach
Aguada Fort
Panjim
Old Goa
BONDLA WILDLIFE SANCTUARY
Bambolim
Dona Paula Beach
Pilar
Gangem
Agassalm
Marmagao
Sancordem
Vasco da Gama
Dabolim
Ponda
Bogmalo Beach
Molem
BHAGWAN MAHAVIR WILDLIFE SANCTUARY
Vema
Codli
Dudhsagar Water Falls
Majorda Beach

Arabian

Margao
Zuari River
Colva Beach
Benaulim Beach
Benaulim
Varca Beach
Chinchinim
Carmona
Quepem
Sea
Cavelossim Beach
Curcolim
Mobor Beach
Rivona
Betul Beach
Colomba

Netorli (Netravali)

Quisconda
Nundem
Mamai Devi Temple
Goundongrem
Salginim
Canacona
COTIGAO WILDLIFE SANCTUARY
Palolem Beach
Butpal

N

20 km

10 miles

KARNATAKA

Western Ghats

To Karwar & Jog Falls

there—the charming little villages with their sunny piazzas, the unbroken miles of wide sandy beaches, the pretty whitewashed churches and chapels, and the exotic combination of the Latin and Indian. But it was only in the 1960s, with the arrival of the first hippies, that its vast tourist market was at last recognized.

Goa-ing down the Pan?

The Goans are not particularly keen on tourism, feeling it a threat to their culture and traditions. The past five years have seen rapid over-commercialization. Goans feel tourism is a threat to their culture and traditions. 'Tourism brings degradation,' was one comment. 'Drugs, pimping, gambling, touting—all these things come around. Police are doing something now, but it is too little and too late.' There's an even fiercer reaction against 'Indian big business', especially since Goa finally gained her own identity on 31 May 1987 and became the 25th state of the Indian Union. As one aggrieved local remarked, 'The Indians are coming and taking all our land. Over the last ten years, our population has doubled—it's getting all crowded, not only with tourists but with financial sharks from elsewhere in the country buying up all our land. It's not good for the Goan people, you know. We'll be submerged as a minority. Even our culture is being wiped out. After twenty years, you'll find nothing of it.'

Certainly, the place is fast becoming over-commercialized. You used to be able to go to Goa and bump into the locals, who are extremely friendly, easy-going people, and be invited to stay in their houses for next to nothing. Now, from the moment you fly in to the moment you get to your hotel, all you can see from your taxi window are new hotels, restaurants, timeshares and other buildings going up. There's a plan that's just been accepted by the Goan administration to build a 7-star hotel which will extend out into the sea, using the latest sea-pol technology. It will have its own airstrip and heli-pad, private boat moorings, an international conference centre, and 1100 rooms, each one equipped with its own video-phone.

Few Goans go fishing any more. The paddy fields have been abandoned, the wells are dry, and the people who used to work the land are now taxi-drivers, waiters, cleaners and hotel staff. The real shame is that all the money coming in has corrupted them, and they know this. They also know that the development sponsored by Bombay/American concerns will ultimately destroy their simple way of life, but they feel powerless to do anything about it. Clearly this is the way of the world nowadays—it's happened in Thailand, it's happened in Bali, and now it's happening here. All the little girls selling stuff on the beaches, for example, are controlled by racketeers. Every so often some Goan thug comes up and takes half their takings. If they don't pay him, he just takes their stuff away. A traveller got that on video. He asked the guy 'Do you own the beach?' and the reply was 'Yes. Have you got a problem?'

With the arrival of package flights, Goa has had to change its image. It doesn't want 'hippies' any more. Even the Shore Bar at Anjuna—the regular meeting place for long-stay travellers—has to close at 11.30pm nowadays, and the police are clamping down hard on beach parties. The real travellers have been driven to the northernmost and southernmost beaches and, though Anjuna is still a travellers' beach, its days are numbered. Nearby Baga and Calangute tell the story—here you could easily imagine yourself at Koh Samui in Thailand: congested hotels, blaring music, loudly-revving motorbikes and bored couples sitting in sterile restaurants, munching fish 'n' chips and chicken in baskets.

This is the reality of Goa '96. If you go on a package, you're going to be locked into one hotel at one beach, and you should know what to expect. As an individual traveller, you've at least got the freedom to find the *real* Goa—or what's left of it—by hiring a motorbike and touring the beaches until you find one (and there are a few) where you can truly relax and be at peace. The one *good* thing about Goa, remember, is that it is big, big place. The developers can't overrun it all at once—so enjoy it while you can!

Food and Drink

A delicious mixture of Asian and Western cooking, Goan cuisine is a popular escape from the usual Indian diet of thalis, dosas and dhal. Repeat visitors flock here for the continental-style beach restaurants, with their pancakes, spaghetti, baked beans on toast, and chips. New arrivals, unaware of the pigs' diet, try the traditional Goan pork sausages (*chourisso*) or classic pork dishes like vindaloo (marinated in toddy vinegar, very spicy) or even *sorpatel* (pig's liver pickled in hot savoury sauce). *Xacuti* is a biting-hot coconut/masala preparation of chicken or mutton, and rich, layered *bebinca* is a very filling Goan sweet made of coconut and jaggery. The other main fare is, of course, seafood. The Arabian Sea lapping Goa's coastline yields a variety of delicately flavoured fish and shellfish, including crab, oysters, king prawns, massive shark steaks and snapping-fresh lobsters.

Goa also has the cheapest beer in India as well as the famous *feni*, a raw, potent brew (usually distilled just once) made from either the cashew apple or the coconut palm. The local Goan wines are also popular and cheap, this being one of the few places in India where 'wine' shops actually sell wine, not just whisky.

Most of Goa's best restaurants are isolated from tourist centres. Try **Martin's Beach Corner** at Caranzalem, a 3km ride out of Panjim on the way to Dona Paula. This is a fabulous place, famous for its fresh seafood prepared straight off the beach.

O Coqueiro's at Porvorim, 4 km out of Panjim on the Mapusa road (hire motorbike-taxi from Patto bridge), used to be *the* place for top-notch Goan cuisine. It still has a good atmosphere. **O Pescador** at Dona Paula (8km) is better, and serves primarily Polynesian cuisine. For delectable Indo-Chinese food, there's **Goenchin** restaurant (© 5718) near Mahalaxmi temple in Ponda—the Mandarin fish is special, but watch the incandescent sauce. Another recommended Chinese restaurant is **Riverdeck** near the Panjim jetty.

When to Go

Temperatures in Goa range from a pleasant 19° to a steamy 33°C. The best time to go is from late October to the end of February. You'll find fewer crowds in March/April, but then it's already getting hot. By May, it's unbearable and the beaches are packed with Indians on holiday. The June to mid-October monsoon is pretty miserable though most hotels, especially on the beaches, offer generous discounts.

The Goans are a basically simple, devout people, happiest when celebrating the feasts of their saints or deities; the population is pretty equally divided between Catholics and Hindus. The big festival is Christmas/New Year, celebrated here as nowhere else in India. This is one time when not even the police can stop the beach parties.

Getting There

Goa is accessed by domestic flights from Bangalore, Bombay, Calcutta, Cochin, Delhi, Madras and Trivandrum—also by international charter flights from the UK, Germany, Finland and Denmark—with France, Portugal, Sweden and Austria in the process of negotiation.

The airport is at Dabolim, 27km from Panjim. It has desks for most major airlines and hotels, as well as (in the departure lounge) a post office, bank and upstairs restaurant. Many of the bigger hotels operate free coach transfers for incoming guests. Just inside the terminal, there's a prepaid taxi booth—sample fares are Rs275 to Panjim, Rs380 to Baga, and Rs200 to Colva, with up to 5 passengers allowed to share costs. If you really want to save money, hire a motorcycle taxi from the airport to the main road (Rs6), then a local bus to Panjim (Rs5) or Vasco da Gama.

In the UK, travel agents like Lunn Poly and Inspirations handle charter packages to Goa.

From Bombay, the quickest approaches are by air to Dabolim or by high-speed catamaran (8hrs) to Panjim (*see* p.297). Trains from Bombay to Vasco da Gama (for Bogmalo beach) and Margao (for buses to Panjim) take a long 20–22hrs, though the completion of the Konkan railway should greatly reduce travel time (*see* p.323). Taxis from Bombay cost around Rs6000 (14hrs) and are a lot comfier than slow buses (16–18hrs).

Trains run from Delhi, Pune and Bangalore into Miraj, and from Hubli (near Hampi) and Mysore into Londa. From Miraj and Londa, there are buses into Panjim.

Getting Around

Goa is a surprisingly big place. It may look like just a dot on the map, but actually comprises 3702 sq km (1428 sq miles) of lush, attractive landscape dotted with hundreds of churches and chapels, fringed with an endless expanse of paddy fields and palm groves, all of it saturated with history. The unique mix of Portuguese and Indian cultures is apparent everywhere—stately Catholic churches and charming terraced bungalows existing alongside traditional Hindu temples and Indian-style dwellings. While most of Goa's action is on the beaches, most of her sights are inland—and they are well worth appreciating at leisure before getting out the sun-oil.

There are four main towns: **Panjim** in the centre (with its 'local' beaches of Miramar and Dona Paula); **Mapusa**, above the Mandovi River, which services the northern beaches of Vagator/Chapora, Anjuna/Baga, Calangute and Aguada; **Margao**, below the River Zuari, which connects to the southern beaches of Majorda, Colva/Benaulim, Betelbatim and Betul; and **Vasco da Gama**, near the Dabolim airport, the gateway to the exclusive luxury beach of Bogmalo. Some useful distances are: Panjim to Vasco (30km), Panjim to Calangute (16km), Panjim to Vagator (33km), Panjim to Tiracol (42km), Margao to Dabolim (29km), Vasco to Dabolim (3km) and Vasco to Margao (30km).

For short hops between these towns, there are either local buses (Rs1–5 to any destination, from Panjim's Kadamba bus stand, near Patto Bridge) or shared taxis, which can work out just as cheap. Motorbike 'taxis' pick up from the bus-stand and from the post office, offering cheap rides up to Altino Hill. Panjim is just 20 minutes (12km) from Mapusa, and 1 hour (33km) from Margao, for the northern and southern beaches respectively. Motorbikes are available for hire at most beaches. They're a good way of touring around (and relatively cheap at around Rs250 a day), but can be dangerous.

Panjim (Panaji)   population 100,000

Until it replaced Old Goa as capital of Portuguese India in 1843, Panjim or Panaji ('land which does not get flooded') was only a small fishing village. Today, it is one of India's smallest and most pleasant capital towns; also one of the least 'Indian'. Its Portuguese heritage lingers on in its whitewashed, red-tiled houses and narrow, winding avenues dotted with cafés, bars and tavernas. Situated on the southern bank of the Mandovi river, Panjim is the obvious base from which to discover the rest of Goa, not simply because most tourist facilities (Indian Airlines, banks, post office, boat jetty) are concentrated here, but also for the two Goa sightseeing tours running from Panjim's tourist office—useful both for checking out the major beaches and viewing the better inland sights.

Touring Panjim

Panjim is a place for gentle, relaxing evening promenades and cosy evening drinks in jolly tavernas. You can see its few sights in a couple of hours on foot or by auto-rickshaw. Start in the main thoroughfare, Dayanand Bandodkar Road, at the **Tourist Hostel**. Turn right (facing the river) and stroll past the small sub-post office with its distinctive striped postbox to the statue of **Abbé Faria**, an 18th-century Goan churchman, believed to be father of hypnotism. Opposite this is the **Secretariat** building, the old palace of Adil Shah (of Bijapur) which in 1759 became the residence of the Portuguese viceroys.

Turning right here, you'll come presently to Church Square (Communicada Street), with its beautiful white **Church of the Immaculate Conception**, built in 1600. A short walk behind this is the 18th-century **Jama Masjid** and the **Mahalakshmi Temple**, an interesting Hindu shrine. Next, make the 20-minute ascent up to **Altino Hill**, with its stately **Patriarch's Palace** (where the Pope stayed during his 1986 Goa tour) and its panoramic views over red-tiled Panjim and the glittering Mandovi river spilling over into the Arabian Sea beyond. On the walk down, note the bungalows and colonnaded houses, with their

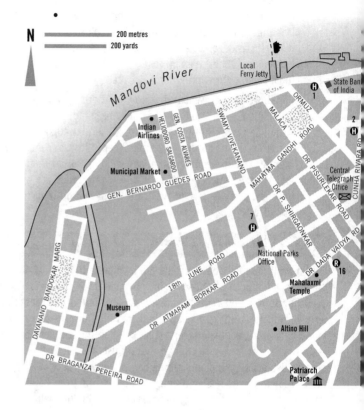

flower-decked windows, overhanging balconies and verandahs. This is the oldest, most Latin, quarter of town—the terraced hillock of Altino being the original site around which the city was built.

Panjim © (0832–)   ***Tourist Information***

The **main tourist office**, © 225583, is in the government-run Tourist Home, just across Patto Bridge. Closed at weekends, it has only one good handout (the Goa Tourist Directory) but sells the two day-tours of Goa, north and south (9.30am to 6pm, Rs60) along with a couple of interesting river cruises (dep 6pm and 7.15pm daily, Rs55). *See* 'Leisure'. You can also hire taxis and guides here.

The Tourist Hostel opposite Ferry Wharf sells the same tours, together with buses to Bangalore and Pune and bus/catamaran tickets for Bombay.

The helpful **Government of India tourist office** (© 43412) is in Communidade Building, Church Square. Other tourist offices can be found at Dabolim airport, at

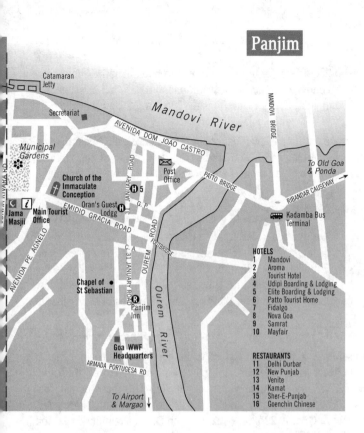

Panjim

Catamaran Jetty

Secretariat

Mandovi River

MANDOVI BRIDGE

AVENIDA DOM JOAO CASTRO

Municipal Gardens

Church of the Immaculate Conception

Post Office

PATTO BRIDGE

To Old Goa & Ponda

RIBANDAR CAUSEWAY

Oran's Guest Lodgg

Main Tourist Office

EMIDIO GRACIA ROAD

G. P

H 5

Kadamba Bus Terminal

Jama Masjii

AVENIDA PE AGNELO

C. A. 31 JANUARY ROAD

OUREM ROAD

FONTBRIDGE

Chapel of St Sebastian

Panjim Inn

Ourem River

Goa WWF Headquarters

ARMADA PORTUGESA RD

To Airport & Margao

HOTELS
1 Mandovi
2 Aroma
3 Tourist Hotel
4 Udipi Boarding & Lodging
5 Elite Boarding & Lodging
6 Patto Tourist Home
7 Fidalgo
8 Nova Goa
9 Samrat
10 Mayfair

RESTAURANTS
11 Delhi Durbar
12 New Punjab
13 Venite
14 Kamat
15 Sher-E-Punjab
16 Goenchin Chinese

Margao's Tourist Hostel, at Mapusa's Tourist Shopping Complex, and at Panjim's bus-stand.

Money can be changed at the **State Bank of India** (10am to 1pm weekdays, till noon on Saturdays) or at **Thomas Cook** (9.30am to 6pm, closed Sunday). The **GPO** and **poste restante** is open 9.30am to 1pm and 2pm to 5.30pm, closed Sunday. There are several **STD booths** around town for overseas calls. Visa extensions are possible at the **Foreigners' Registration Office** in the town centre, but not if you dress like a hippy. International **flights** can be reconfirmed at Air India in Hotel Fidalgo, or at travel agents like Aeromundial (✆ 224831) in Hotel Mandovi or Georgeson & Georgeson (✆ 228470) opposite the GPO.

There are good **bookshops** at hotels Mandovi and Fidalgo, with a wide range of international magazines.

In case of motorbike **accident**, bone and brain scans can be done by (respectively) Dr Bale's X-ray clinic (24 hrs) at Porvorim, 4kms out of Panjim on the Mapusa road, and Salgonkar Medical Research Centre (℅ 0834-512524) in Vasco da Gama, 30 kms from Panjim.

Leisure

From the tourist office or Panjim bus stand, you can book daily half-hour river cruises along the Mandovi River (see Tourist Information), also full moon cruises (8.30pm to 10.30pm) and evening cruises to Santa Monica. All boats have refreshments and Portuguese folk dances take place on deck.

The best place to see traditional Goan dance is a large house called **Festa Feira**, close to the toll booth at the end of Patto bridge. This has recently started open-air cultural programmes (along with dinner) every Monday evening—though only in the non-monsoon months.

Panjim ℅ (0832–) **Where to Stay**

Note: in peak season, all the hotels below have 100% occupancy, so it's wise to advance-book. All hotels in Panjim—and in Goa generally—discount tariffs during April/May (semi-season), and especially between June and October (low season). All rates quoted below are for the high season months of November to March.

expensive (from Rs600)

Apart from its usefulness as a base from which to discover Goa, there's little reason to stay in Panjim itself. Most hotels are noisy, even the comfy **Hotel Mandovi**, ℅ 224405, ✆ 225451, on Dayanand Bandodkar Rd. This has rooms from Rs750/1000 (some with river views) and a fine 1st floor restaurant. Slightly less costly are hotels **Nova Goa**, ℅ 226231, ✆ 224090, on Dr Atmaram Borkar Rd and **Fidalgo** ℅ 226291, ✆ 225061, with a swimming pool.

At Dona Paula, 5km out of Panjim, is the 5-star Cidade de Goa, ℅ 221133, ✆ 223303, offering top cuisine, good water-sports and deluxe double rooms for US$140. Nearby **Prainha Cottages by the Sea**, ℅ 227221, ✆ 229959, have popular rooms from Rs650 (or Rs850 a/c) and cottages from Rs675/725.

moderate/cheap

Choose between **Hotel Aroma**, Cunha Rivara Road, ℅ 224330, ✆ 224330, with clean rooms from Rs200/350 and good tandoori food, and the **Tourist Hostel**, ℅ 227103, with spacious rooms from Rs250/330 (Rs370 a/c), a terrace restaurant, a bar, a bookshop and a shopping complex. The Tibetan-run **Panjim Inn**, ℅ 226523, is a lovely 300-year-old house with TV lounge, gardens, good food and popular rooms for Rs315/410. Also worth a look are hotels **Mayfair**, ℅ 46174, and **Samrat**, ℅ 223318, both on Dr Dada Vaidya Road. Best of a grim bunch of budget places are **Patto Tourist Home** below the bus stand (dorm beds for Rs30/40) and **Elite Boarding & Lodging** in the old part of town (basic rooms at Rs70/80).

Goan food and seafood is best experienced at Hotel Mandovi's **Riorico** restaurant. You can eat well here for Rs250, including a glass of wine. Just as popular are **Sher-e-Punjab** at Hotel Aroma (tandoori), **Delhi Durbar** on M G Rd (Mughlai), **Goenchin** off Dr Dada Vaidya Rd (Chinese), **Kamat** south of Municipal Gardens (vegetarian), **Juicy Corner** opposite the Secretariat (fruit juices) and **Pastry Cottage** near Hotel Nova Goa (cakes and pastries).

A couple of kilometres out of Panjim, on the Mapusa road, you'll find popular eateries like **Casino's**, **Village Nook**, O Cajuairo and O Coqueiro—all specialising in Goan food, but with less spicy Continental dishes also.

Tour 1: North Goa

By tour bus, full day. Altino Hill–Mayem Lake–Bicholim–Mapusa–Northern Beaches

This tour is worthwhile, but if you're short on time or impatient to get to the beaches make do with the South Goa tour—that one visits Old Goa, the main inland attraction. Both tours use buses, and you'll need a front seat to hear a word the guide's saying, but the sights and glorious scenery speak for themselves. Sufficient time is allowed at the beach spots to check out the current accommodation situation.

The North Goa tour winds up to **Altino Hill**, Panjim, for the spectacular view of the city, then proceeds inland through acres of paddy fields and palms to the natural lake resort of **Mayem**, a popular picnic spot with lovely gardens of bougainvillaea, crimson cana orchids and china roses, together with peaceful lake views. Mayem is a wide basin lake encircled by green hills and dense palm groves. From here you'll move on to **Bicholim** to see a couple of Hindu temples, before arriving at **Mapusa** for lunch. Mapusa is the crossroads of northern Goa, and is famous for its Friday market (8am–6pm). Hordes of locals do their weekly shopping here, and you can buy anything from a glass bangle to a water-buffalo. After the market, take a taxi/rickshaw out to the **Haystack**, 5km from Anjuna, on the Mapusa road, for live music, folk dances and buffet (Friday nights 8.30 pm to very late).

To stay over, try the pleasant **Tourist Hotel** with cheap rooms and a pleasant roof-top bar/restaurant, or **Hotel Satyahera**. Eat out either at **Sanbhaya** restaurant (superb seafood and Goan curry) or at the **Haystack**. Mapusa's useful little tourist office is housed in the Tourist Hostel.

In the afternoon, the tour covers the **northern beaches**—first **Vagator**, then **Anjuna**, **Calangute**, and finally **Aguada** resort, marked by its 17th-century fort (now converted into a jail). There's just time at each place for a quick dip.

Tour 2: South Goa

By tour bus, full day. Miramar Beach–Dona Paula–Old Goa–
Mangesh Temple–Margao–Colva Beach–Marmagao

First stop on this tour is **Miramar Beach**, popular for its wide golden sands and lovely sunset views. Located just 3km out of Panjim, it's the ideal place to come for a swim, if staying in the capital. Unfortunately, everyone else in town has the same idea. **Dona Paula**, a further 5km up the road, is much quieter. A sheltered palm-fronted cove, with enchanting views of Marmagao Harbour and Zuari river estuary, this is another pretty sunset spot. The sophisticated O Pescador restaurant and exclusive Hotel Cidade de Goa are both located here.

Driving into the cathedral ghost-town of **Old Goa** (9km out of Panjim), you'll immediately detect the strong Latin influence. The priests of Rome were the real rulers here, not the Portuguese conquistadors, and the religious arrogance of the old conquerors is reflected in the grandiose complex of churches, monasteries and convents, many rivalling in size and scale the great churches of Renaissance Europe. The Portuguese arrived here in 1510, bearing a sword in one hand, a crucifix in the other. Goa Velha, as Old Goa was then called, became a city of great splendour and power, dominated by the huge ecclesiastical buildings which replaced the old mosques and temples of former Muslim rulers. Then came a series of devastating plagues (1543, 1635 and 1735), which decimated 80% of the population. In 1835 Old Goa was abandoned, and the administrative capital transferred to Panjim. Today, it is just a small village built round the ruined hulks of huge convents and churches dedicated to the zeal of Christianity. At present, only six of the town's original 14 churches remain in good condition, their red laterite structures eroded by centuries of wind and rain. They're a complete contrast to Hindu temples and shrines: much more reminiscent of small Portuguese towns than anything out of India. If returning for a longer look, come in by local bus from either Panjim (10 minutes) or Margao (30 minutes). Old Goa really should be appreciated at leisure—one can spend hours wandering round the vast, deserted cloisters and corridors of these decaying old buildings. For full information on the monuments, buy a copy of *Old Goa*, by S. Rajagopalan, available from the Archaeological Museum in Old Goa.

On tour, you'll first visit the **Basilica of Bom Jesus**, Goa's most popular and famous church (*open 9am–6.30pm daily; mass is at 7am and 8am weekdays, 8am and 9.15am on Sundays. No photography is allowed*). Built between 1594 and 1604, the rather dim interior is enlivened by the gilded baroque high altar, with elaborate screens and spiral columns, and by the huge, gaudy statue of St Ignatius Loyola, the founder of the Jesuit order. To the right of the altar is the Basilica's big attraction—the silver casket enshrining the mummified remains of **St Francis Xavier**, Goa's patron saint, who spent his life spreading Christianity among the Portuguese colonies. Murals of events from the saint's life run round the walls of the Italian-marble sarcophagus enclosing the casket. One of the most well-travelled corpses in history, Xavier was taken all over the place after his death in China in 1552, and came to rest here only in 1613. During his posthumous wanderings, one of his toes was bitten off by a Portuguese holy-relic hunter (1554). Later, as the grisly process of dismemberment continued, he lost a hand to the Japanese Jesuits (1619), had various sections of intestine removed, and suffered a broken neck after being stuffed in an undersized grave. Today, what's left of his corpse is remarkably well preserved. If you don't believe it, you can peer at Xavier's bald, mottled head—illuminated within the casket by a naked bulb—or, for a donation, view his silver-encased toes. Every 10 years, the shrivelled cadaver is given a public veneration (the next occasion will be 2004), when the town becomes a stadium of hysterical devotees. The same thing happens, to a lesser extent, at the annual commemoration on 3 December of the saint's death. Behind the casket, steps lead up to a small museum housing various portraits and relics attributed to St Francis Xavier, his life and times.

Across the road is the huge **Sé** or **Cathedral** (1562–1652). Dedicated to St Catherine of Alexandria, a pagan girl who embraced Christianity and was martyred on the same date that the Portuguese took Old Goa from the Muslims (25 November), it is one of Asia's largest churches, having 15 altars. The harmony of its façade was destroyed in 1776, when lightning demolished one of its twin bell towers. The remaining tower houses the famous 'Golden Bell' which once announced the death-knell of burning heretics during the Inquisition, and now sounds over a deserted city (three times a day: 5.30 am, 12.30 pm, 6.30 pm) to a distance of 10km. Walking up the crumbling staircase to view it is highly unsafe. The grand Renaissance Cathedral within is built in the Portuguese-Gothic style—the Corinthian interior being a baroque riot of carvings, with a vast barrel-vault ceiling and a glittering, gilded main altar (featuring painted scenes from the short life of St Catherine) which is the finest of India. Look at the 'miraculous' stone cross in one of the 14 side-chapels. According to the guide, it 'grew' so high over the centuries that the ceiling had to be raised. Nowadays it's protected by a sturdy wooden support to stop holy-relic hunters chipping away souvenirs. Undeterred, they chip away at the wood surround instead.

The nearby **Convent and Church of St Francis of Assisi**, notable for its two-storey façade crowned with twin octagonal towers, is one of Old Goa's most fascinating buildings. On the site of a small Franciscan chapel (commenced 1517), the present structure was constructed in 1661. It is notable for its richly carved woodwork, ancient murals, and flooring of 16th-century gravestones. The **Archaeological Museum** to the rear (*open 10am–5pm, except Friday*) has a model Portuguese caravelle (poorly lit), an entertaining portrait gallery of Portuguese viceroys, and various Hindu sculptures recovered from Goan sites.

If you want to make a day of it at Old Goa, leave the tour at this point. There's no problem getting back to Panjim: buses run back there at regular intervals (15–20mins journey). When you've had enough of dusty old churches, it's time to visit **Diwar Island**. This is a wonderful little demi-paradise, with empty beaches, shady palm bowers, and rustic old Portuguese houses. To get there, walk down the road behind the Cathedral to the pier, catch a ferry (regular service) over the Mandovi River, and hop on the connecting bus into the island interior. A short, strenuous climb takes you up to the top of the island, with memorable views from the church. Return down for a relaxing afternoon on the beach. Don't forget to bring a packed lunch.

Old colonial architecture, Margao

Staying on the tour, you'll continue on to the **Ponda** district, to see the 15th-century **Shri Mangesh Temple**, one of the few Hindu shrines in Goa to survive Muslim and Portuguese iconoclasm. Attractively situated on a hillock surrounded by green hills, it's a simple yet elegant structure dedicated to Shiva. The temple musicians here are astonishingly good. Set in an open courtyard, the shrine is notable for its glass chandeliers and blue-china murals. At nearby Mardol, you'll see the Shri Mahalsa Temple, one of Goa's oldest temples, dedicated to Vishnu. It was shifted here from its original site when Muslim persecution threatened its survival. You may also see the **Shanta Durga Temple** at Kavlem, with its impressive idol of the Goddess of Peace (Shanta Durga) flanked by Vishnu and Shiva.

Lunch is taken at **Margao**, Goa's southern centre and a thriving commercial metropolis. It has parks, modern buildings, and a very Latin flavour. Here are some of the area's most beautiful old Portuguese mansions, with balconies, patios, terraces and red-tiled sloping roofs—still lived in by descendants of the families who built them 400 years ago. There is not much for the tourist here—most folk just pass through on their way to Colva Beach. Cheap rooms and food are available on your way in from the south by train. The pleasant **Tourist Hostel** at the top of the main square has mid-range accommodation, as does the **Goa Woodlands** opposite the bus-stand on Miguel Loyola Furtado Road. **Casa Menino** and **Longhino's**, opposite the Municipality building, are both excellent for Goan food, while nearby **Gaylin** is famous for Chinese. Margao's tourist office is in the Municipal Building. To get here from the airport, take a bus to Vasco, then another here (total journey time 1–1½hrs). Regular buses serve Benaulim (5km) and Colva (10km) from Margao.

A pleasant hour at **Colva Beach** is followed by a visit to **Marmagao**, one of India's finest natural harbours. Here you can see mountains of iron ore (crushed from the cliff directly over the harbour) and fleets of tankers loading up 1000 tons of crude oil per hour. Located close to busy, modern **Vasco da Gama** (the airport gateway to Goa), you'll be shown Marmagao's massive refinery and shipping port, ostensibly for its fine views over the surrounding coastline, but more (one suspects) to demonstrate the new-found industrial muscle of this previously poor, agricultural state.

If you're not into such propaganda, leave the tour at Colva and spend an altogether more enjoyable afternoon on the beach.

Goa's beaches are world famous—long, idyllic sweeps of silvery sand overlooked by undulating palms and the calm blue Arabian Sea. The hippies discovered them in the early '60s, domestic tourists flocked to them in the '80s (mainly to see the hippies), and package charters have arrived in the '90s.

Over 80% of tourist traffic is now heading to the northern beaches—the south has virtually no infrastructure and hardly any parties. The party scene is concentrated on Anjuna beach, and to some extent on Baga and Calangute, but don't expect to rave on every night. All parties now have to be licensed, and only when you get into December—and particularly around Christmas and New Year—can you enjoy regular all-nighters with DJs and pumping sound systems. Full moon parties still occur, but not all the time—check at Anjuna's **Shore Bar** or Baga's **Brito's** for upcoming events. Failing that, ask any taxi-rickshaw wallah. The three luxury beaches of Majorda, Aguada and Bogmalo may have the best facilities, but are only good for couples and families (few laughs here). Colva and Benaulim, the extensive southern beaches, are for those in search of complete peace and quiet: here you can walk the whole day (*not* busy weekends though) without seeing a soul. This is even more true of Terekol and Palolem, respectively the northern-most and southernmost beaches, though facilities are still basic.

For the beach, you'll need sun-oil, flip-flops, sunglasses and a face-mask for snorkelling. You'll also need the right attitude—relaxed, yet not too switched-off (sunburn and theft are common). You can buy sun-oil and sunglasses on the beach, but the oil is often local concoctions in discarded bottles. Sleeping on the beach is not a good idea—robbery is rife. If money is really tight, you can still find rooms with local families (quieter beaches only) for a few rupees per night. As for entertainment, when you've had enough of sunbathing and bodysurfing, hire a motorbike or a taxi for the day—cruise up and down the beaches by day, scout out a party or bar to go to later on.

The simple message with **drugs** is: *don't*. In a country like India, where hashish, opium and cannabis are readily available and where valium and morphine can be bought over the counter (even at Delhi airport), you may be misled into thinking that their public consumption is tolerated. Nothing could be further from the truth. Up until recently, Indian policemen used to pray for a posting to Goa, where they could extort the maximum of l million rupees (£20,000) from hapless tourists having a quiet smoke on the beach. The same went, to a lesser extent, for high-risk hippy havens like Manali, Pushkar and Kovalam beach. Since 1980, over 500 travellers have been arrested in Pushkar alone—and with life imprisonment being enforced for possession of just 20 grams of hash, a lot of them are still in jail. The informers who put them there, it is worth noting, are often the same people who sold them the drugs in the first place. In Goa itself, police are now refusing kickbacks in favour of eradicating 'hippiedom' and sanitising the place for package tourism. So if you must have a puff, be discreet—there may be only 12 foreign drug offenders in Aguada jail right now, but who wants to be the unlucky 13th?

Nude bathing may have been the rage in the '60s, but is not smiled upon nowadays—particularly at 'family' beaches like Calangute and Colva. There's no actual ban on it, but all those camera-clicking Indians do make you feel like a caged exhibit. And Western women lying around exposed on public beaches write of appalling hassle.

Motorbikes are a popular way of beach-hopping and can be hired from many resorts (notably Baga/Calangute) for Rs150/200 per day—rather more in December/January. Nobody will ask you for an international driving licence—except for policemen collecting easy spot fines. If you want to tour the beaches or interior by **taxi**, expect to pay in the region of Rs700/day—more, if you travel over 100 kms. Bicycles can be rented from many places, the rate varying from Rs3 to 5 per hour or Rs20 to 40 per day.

Northern Beaches (all ✆ code 0832–)

Fort Aguada/Sinquerim–Candolim–Calangute–Baga–Anjuna–Vagator–Chapora–Arambol/Terekol

Fort Aguada/Sinquerim

This jet-set resort, notable for its 17th-century fort and apparently endless expanse of white sand, has the best water-sports, the best coastal views and the most famous beach hotel in India. This is the Taj group's **Fort Aguada Beach Resort**, ✆ 276201, ✉ 276044, built right inside the old fort walls. Rooms here go for US$125/135, with off-season discounts from April to September. The best ones, with excellent views from large terraces, are in the main block. Leisure facilities include water-skiing, wind-surfing, para-sailing, fishing, scuba-diving and 'hydrotherapy with sauna'. Right next door, also with access to small **Sinquerim Beach**, is the rather cheaper **Taj Holiday Village** (same ✆/✉) which offers charming beach cottages designed like Goan homes, in a private, romantic setting. It has a good water-sports centre. The third Taj property, overlooking the other two from a nearby hillside, is the deluxe 20-villa **Aguada Hermitage** (same ✆/✉) which was built for the Commonwealth Heads of Government conference in 1982. Exclusive villas start at US$215/325 and require a serious talk with your bank manager at the height of the season (Christmas/New Year).

Fort Aguada itself was built by the Portuguese (1612) to guard the mouth of the Mandovi River and commands wonderful hilltop views, especially from the old lighthouse. The caretaker will show you the dungeons, but expects a big tip. The new lighthouse is worth a look (4 to 5.30pm, adm Rs1) but photography is banned. To visit drug-offending foreigners in nearby **Aguada Jail**, you'll first need to contact your embassy.

Candolim

Slightly north of Aguada is Candolim, a pleasant beach with long palm-fringed sands. Independent travellers avoid it (too windy, too many Indian tourists) but there's some good resorts with pools like **Dona Alcina**, ✆ 276266, **Whispering Palms**, ✆ 276141, also mid-rangers like **Marbella Guest House**, ✆/✉ 276308, **Casa Sea Shell** and **Xavier Beach Resort**. The best 'cheap' lodges are **Lobo's** and **Pretty Petal**, with doubles around Rs300.

To eat, there's **Sea Shell Inn**, **Joe Joe** or friendly **Spice Garden** with a breezy open-air section, juicy steaks and live music every evening. For a big meal out, it's a short ride back to the **Banyan Tree** at Taj Holiday Village, which specialises in Thai and Chinese cuisine.

Candolim/Sinquerim is connected by bus with Mapusa (17km) and with Panjim (30 km).

Calangute

Some 5km north of Candolim is Calangute, the old 'Queen Beach' of Goa, where coconut palms once shaded a mile-wide stretch of tranquil orange sands. All that's left now is a bare, polluted beach fronting a fully fledged Indian holiday resort (grey, noisy and commercial) with wall-to-wall hotels, shops and restaurants. It's still the most heavily-booked beach in Goa, but only because package tours send people here who don't know any better. The main drag is full of pushy Kashmiri salesmen and blaring traffic, and the only two things to recommend the place are the shopping (lots of choice) and the nightlife.

Lively restaurants like **Planter's** offer traditional Goan folk dancing every night (along with fine food) and hacienda-style bars like **Capricorn** and **Oceanic Bar** are good places to hang out and sample every tipple known to man. You can hear the discos a mile away, but the 'real' party scene has shifted northwards, and I'm going to suggest that no independent traveller in their right mind will want to stay here. Those who do stop for a night—at high-class resorts like **Falcon,** ✆ 277327, 🖅 277330, mid-range options like **Varma's,** ✆ 276077, or cheapies like **Tourist Hostel** and **Hotel Mira**—are generally on their way to Baga the next morning.

There are frequent buses between Calangute and Panjim/Mapusa, though only up until 7pm.

Baga

Overlooked by a high promontory, Baga is (with the exception of Arambol) the best of the northern beaches—long, clean and safe for swimming. With the arrival of package tourism however, it has changed beyond belief and is now only for those who like Torremolinos-style 'action' (and all the blaring music, revving motorbikes and twinkling fairy-lights that go with it) or for the determined party-goer. If this is your kind of scene, then book a US$40/50 room at the **Hotel Ronil,** ✆ 276101, 🖅 276068, a US$15 double (US$25 with a/c) at the quieter **Hotel Linda,** ✆ 276066, 🖅 276599, or at **Sunshine Beach Resort,** ✆ 276003, 🖅 277474. All these places have pools and restaurants. Good moderate deals are the new **Lua Nova** and the **Hacienda,** ✆ 277348, with excellent food and rooms around Rs400/700. The Linda has outdoor barbecues and live entertainment on Wednesdays and Saturdays. Elsewhere in this area, there's a nightly sound-clash between local Portuguese bands and pumping rave-techno music—this goes on till around midnight. Away from the main drag, things quieten down a bit. Up near the bridge connecting Baga to Anjuna (5km away), **Baia de Sol,** ✆ 276084, has beachside rooms/cottages around Rs700/900 and good food/service. Below the bridge itself (surely the ugliest construction in the world) is the well-appointed **Riverside,** ✆ 276062, overlooking the river. Simple but clean rooms go for Rs500/600 and the breezy open restaurant is known for its seafood. North of this one (2km) is the new **Resorte Marinha Dourada**, ✆ 276780, 🖷 276785, with spacious apartments from Rs1000 and a free shuttle service to and from the beach. Facilities include pool, restaurant, health club, tennis courts and live music every night. Budget lodges are changing all the time (or upgrading themselves to package status), so there's no point listing names. There's a few solid places—**Villa Fatima** near the church, ✆ 276059, **Joseph D'Souza** by the Casa Portuguesa restaurant, and **Nani's Bar** across the nasty bridge, ✆ 276313—but advance-book to ensure a room. Otherwise, ask around for rooms or houses to rent at bar-restaurants like **Brito's, Jack's, Electric Cats** and **Cavala**.

Popular meeting places in Baga are **Tito's** by the beach (hippie gone yuppie, but fine sounds and dancefloor) and **Brito's** (good bakery, pumping tunes, favourite travellers' hangout). Both venues have pleasant sit-out sections with tasty fare and friendly atmosphere. Upmarket eateries like **Valerie's** at Hotel Baia de Sol and **Casa Portuguesa** below the church have superb seafood, but avoid the pork. Between these two (on the main road) is the excellent **Cavala** with a varied menu (most of which you can actually find) and a charming open-air garden section. There's a genuine Portuguese feel to this place, and the food and service are spot-on. Give the nightly barbecue a try and don't leave without trying one of the (superb) cocktails—the mango juice/coconut *feni* is out of this world! Other Baga favourites are **St Anthony's** (fish), **Goan Delight** (Portuguese), and **Chinese Kitchen** (Chinese). A friendly bar, away from all the hype, is **Alex's** just up from Brito's. If nothing else is going on, head into Calangute on a Saturday night and let off some steam at one of the popular discos.

Baga is about 3km north of Calangute—20 minutes by foot or Rs20 by share-taxi. From Baga to Anjuna is around 10km—Rs100 by taxi (up to 4 passengers) or a one-hour stroll along the beach. Once the new Siolim/Mandrem bridge is completed, you'll be able to get all the way up to Terekol from Baga in 1½ hours. Every Wednesday, regular boats leave Baga beach for Anjuna's flea market.

Anjuna

Anjuna is a small rocky beach overlooked by a palm-laden promontory. The sea is very suitable for swimming—except in the afternoon, when it is swept by strong onshore breezes. At this time of day, walk round to the quiet, protected coves between Anjuna and Baga which are beautifully secluded. In the town is the splendid 1920s **Albuquerque Mansion** (open 10am to 5pm weekdays), a massive Portuguese villa-cum-museum, still partly inhabited. If you want to go **parascending**, sign up for a course at the Shore Bar.

Anjuna has a small market every day, but the big one is the colourful **Flea Market** on Wednesday (9am till sunset). This is like Woodstock on the beach, with astrologers, tarot-readers, massage tents, throbbing sound systems, good veggie eats, and lots of people sitting around on grass mats, just taking in the scene. The best thing about the flea market is not the shopping nor the colourful mix of traders (mainly Kashmiris, Tibetans, and Gujarati tribals) but the whole buzz of the place. Arrive early to avoid the heat and cruise around for a while. Then sit down somewhere and start chatting to people—or simply enjoy the atmosphere. The market itself is not cheap (bargain till you drop!) but is *the* place to buy your mirrored topi hat, your funky beachwear, your hippy bag and beads, and your chunky ethnic jewellery. The idea here is to make yourself look like you've been in India for 6 months and not just 6 days. To add the final touches, pay a visit to the body-piercing and tattoo tents.

Anjuna has no big hotels, only small guest-houses and lodgings—mainly for long-stay travellers. At the bus stand, there are **Poonam** or **Sonic** guest houses, but they're often full. Better places appear back up the Mapusa road—the expensive **Bougainvillea**, ✆ 273271, 🖷 274370, and the mid-range **Tamarind**. Close by is **Grandpa's Inn**, ✆ 273270, with rooms from Rs250 to 400; also cheapies like **Cabin Disco** and **Coutino's Nest**. If all else fails, contact the Shore Bar—they may know a local family with a room or house to rent.

For eats, Westerners favour **Guru** and **Fernandes** bars at the bus stand. They also like nearby **Paraiso de Anjuna**, a pub-restaurant with attached nightclub. Set back from the beach (take directions), there are popular food places like **White Negro**, **Martha's Breakfast Home**, **Pussy Cat** and **German Bakery**—the last being the current trend. The **Shore Bar** at the southern end of the beach (near the flea market) is the main meeting point for the young crowd—a good place to catch the sunset over a beer or two and to learn the latest on the party scene. Most parties take place around Christmas/New Year, but you can generally count on something going on at Full Moon and on Wednesday evenings after the flea market. If things are dead, try the **Primrose Café** up at Vagator or ask a local taxi-driver—they're normally tuned in to what's happening.

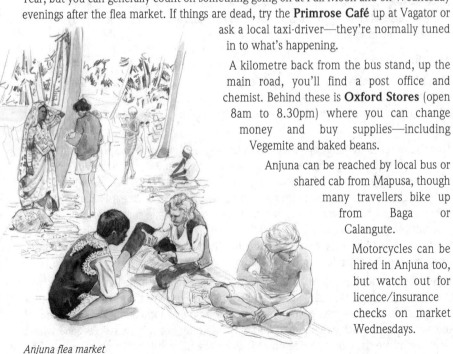

A kilometre back from the bus stand, up the main road, you'll find a post office and chemist. Behind these is **Oxford Stores** (open 8am to 8.30pm) where you can change money and buy supplies—including Vegemite and baked beans.

Anjuna can be reached by local bus or shared cab from Mapusa, though many travellers bike up from Baga or Calangute.

Motorcycles can be hired in Anjuna too, but watch out for licence/insurance checks on market Wednesdays.

Anjuna flea market

Vagator/Chapora

Vagator is on a high rise and affords the best sunset views of any beach, especially if you walk up to the old ruined **Chapora Fort** (1717) on the headland. It has a better beach than Anjuna too—a long crescent bay with silky-soft sand—and a funky little village with tiny bars, shops and supply stores. More than anywhere else in Goa, it shows you how things used to be 10 years ago. The only commercial part of it, for the time being at least, is the excellent **Sterling Holiday Resort** hotel, ✆ 229943, though anyone paying US$50/70 here is bound to feel ripped off when they walk outside and consume a big meal at a beach café for 80 cents! The top half of the hotel is time-share and geared to families, so go for the lower half—or the hillside chalets with views of the sea through palm trees. Every Saturday night, the hotel lays on a barbecue with a Goan band. The restaurant is the best in the area.

In direct contrast to the above is a Rs60–80 room in a Goan family house at the fishing village of **Chapora**, on the other side of the headland. If you go for this option, be prepared for *very* basic living and to share (often inedible) meals with the family. Cheap rooms are available at **Julia's**, **Dr Lobo's** and **Noble Nest**, though not often in the high season. The first two places have good restaurants, and the third a useful travel service. Chapora is a major hangout for shoestringers, who have all sorts of accidents for lack of a torch (no streetlights here). There's a tiny beach below the village, but it's not safe for swimming.

The easiest approach to Chapora is by bus, motorbike or shared taxi from Mapusa (11km). There are also local buses to/from Vagator and Panjim. Anjuna is only 3km away, a scenic stroll along the headland.

Arambol/Terekol

Arambol is the final retreat of the hippies and the place to get really away from it all. If you come only for the day, you'll wish (as I did) that you'd decided to stay longer. The only other place in Goa with this kind of natural beauty and perfect peace is Palolem, 90km to the south.

There's not much to the village itself, just a few lodges and restaurants, but then you find the beach which is beautiful. Swimming is good and safe, but don't leave your clothes or valuables lying around (theft is common) and watch out for plain-clothes policemen on drug searches. If you face the beach and turn left, you'll find the **Oceanic Bar**, with good information and nice cheap rooms. Behind it, set back from the coconut groves, there's a group of comparable lodges run by friendly, honest people. Facing the beach and turning right, you'll find hut-restaurants like **Morning Star**, **Palm Beach** and **Om Bholanath**. Apart from the first, service is funereally slow.

If time is short, don't stay long at the main beach. Walk on past the restaurants, cross over the rocks, and follow the coastal path for about 15 minutes. Give the (unsafe) guest houses along the way a miss—they're for long-stay travellers with nothing to lose. At the end of the path you come across something you don't see often—a narrow strip of sand with a clean freshwater lake on one side (inland) and a beautiful little beach on the other. The general plan is to take a swim in the sea first and to wash off in the lake after—you don't need a shower. Don't worry about being hassled; the only other people likely to be around are freaks getting back to nature. Most of them live in hammocks around a huge banyan tree, just 15 minutes walk inland, following the stream which feeds the lake. If you see large birds flying overhead, they're just travellers parascending down from the surrounding cliffs. To join them (Rs800 for a half-hour), ask for Guy at **Lake's Paradise** restaurant—and while you're waiting, try the cheese kofte.

Arambol is 3hrs by bus from Mapusa or 4hrs from Panjim—a long trip involving a ferry crossing from Siolim to Chopdem. You leave the bus at Chopdem and get a share taxi to Arambol (15km) via Mandrem. This final leg takes 30 minutes and offers beautiful scenery.

Note: As soon as the Siolim-Mandrem bridge is completed (probably 1997), you can expect this whole area to develop rapidly. They're already planning a 5-star resort complex, complete with a golf course.

A final ferry-ride north of Arambol (from Querim), **Terekol** beach marks the northern boundary of Goa's coast and has a fine Maratha fort, captured by the Portuguese in 1776. The only place to stay is the overpriced **Hotel Terekol Fort Heritage**, ✆ (0834) 220705, ✉ 283326, inside the fort (Rs1750 suites better than Rs800 doubles), and the only thing to do is visit the small church here (if open) and take in the views from the ramparts. This said, Terekol does have a nice sandy beach and makes a pleasant day outing by motorbike. For a quick dip along the way, stop off at deserted **Querim** beach above Arambol.

Southern Beaches (all ✆ 0834–)

Bogmalo–Colva–South Colva/Benaulim–Cavelossim/Varca/Mobor–Betul–Palolem.

To get from the northern to the southern beaches by bus, you need to go to Panjim first, then head down to Margao.

Bogmalo

This is one of Goa's best beaches, a secluded crescent-shaped cove with calm, safe waters for swimming (a contrast to the powerful breakers of the more open beaches) and a friendly fishing village. It is an exclusive beach, presided over by a single luxury hotel, the **Bogmalo Beach Resort** (✆ 513291, ✉ 512510). This is 5 minutes' drive from the airport and is currently under renovation. Whether it will match up to the high standards of the Oberoi hotel chain (who recently abandoned it) is yet to be seen, but prices remain high: US$180/190 for rooms, US$250–450 for suites.

Colva

Goa's longest beach is 20 unbroken kilometres of virgin white sand. Like Calangute to the north, Colva has been spoiled by progress: food and lodgings are overpriced, street-hawkers are aggressive, and busloads of Indians turn up at weekends to leer at Western women. The town itself receives thousands of package tourists every year, and is no longer for the backpacker. This said, you only have to walk 2km in either direction to have the beach all to yourself. The waters are warm and calm, and the only people you're likely to see are local fishermen.

There are a few pleasant shops at the bus stand, including Damodar for second-hand books (reading is the main occupation on the beaches, so stock up) and Navneeta for beach clothing. On the beach itself, you'll be offered lacquer boxes and painted shells—good little souvenirs.

The bus stand is near the sea, separated from the beach by a small bridge. Close by are Colva's two resort hotels: the disappointing **Penthouse**, ✆ 221030, and the better **Silver Sands**, ✆ 221645, both with pools, restaurants and a/c rooms around Rs750. Also round here are cheapies like **Vincy, Rodson's, Skylark** and **Maria**, all asking Rs150/250 a night. Back up the road from the bus stand, you'll find **Hotel Ben**, ✆ 722009, with spacious rooms for Rs200 or Rs350 with a/c, and **William's Resort**, ✆ 221077, with pool, swank restaurant and doubles for Rs650 or Rs850 with a/c. To get away from all the beach hype, try budget lodges like **Rosman, Micky** and **Barbarosa** out on the Colva–Benaulim road. To stay on the beach itself, top choice is **Longuinho's Beach Resort**, ✆ 222918, with sea-facing rooms (some with balconies and a/c) from US$20 and splendid food. Water sports and day trips can be arranged.

Most Colva residents eat at one of the ramshackle (but good) beach restaurants situated right on the shoreline. Current favourites—all serving excellent seafood in addition to pseudo-western fare—are **Rastafarry, Connie-M, Falcon** and the new **Kentuckee**. Come here to enjoy tasty fish dishes, spaghetti 'sizzlers' and a nightcap *feni* after a hard

day's sunbathing. Get your sunset table early though—they're often taken. Upmarket cuisine is best at **Silver Sands, Longuinho's** and **Penthouse** hotels, who often offer big buffet dinners, with a live band. For late-night action, check dance-spots like **Splash** and **Castaway** near the roundabout. Popular breakfast joints are **Men Mar Inn** and **Johnny Cool** (close to William Resort), also **Umita Corner Restaurant** (above Johnny Cool). Around 9am every morning, a small crowd gathers around the kiosks by the roundabout; this is when the hot doughnuts arrive.

Most big hotels change travellers' cheques (there's no bank) and the post office in Colva village has a poste restante service. Cycles and motorbikes are easy to hire, but you have to bargain a fair price. A cheap, direct way of getting up to the northern beaches from Colva is the Wednesday bus to Anjuna's flea market (Rs75); it's advertised in many beach restaurants.

Colva is most easily reached from Margao—by local bus (regular service, 30 mins), by auto-rickshaw (Rs40/50) or by share taxi from behind Karmat Magdoot restaurant, east of Margao's Municipal Gardens.

South Colva/Benaulim

South Colva is a small beach between Colva proper and Benaulim, just 1km along the sands from Colva bus stand. Long-stay travellers like it because it's so quiet and peaceful. **Furtado's, Camilson's** and **Xavier's**—all right on the seafront—provide cheap and simple accommodation (Rs100/150) and tasty seafood. The longer you stay, the cheaper they get, so they don't have many vacancies.

Another 10-minute stroll brings you to secluded Benaulim beach. There's not much to see or do, but it's a good place to wind down completely. Few people stay near the beach— it's too shadeless and windswept—though **L'Amour Beach Resort**, ✆ 223720, has some nice new a/c rooms for Rs750 (cheaper ones at Rs400) and tasty tandoori food. Across the way is **O Palmar**, with simple beach cottages for Rs250. In Benaulim village itself, about 1km walk up from the beach, ask around for **Rosario's Inn, Kenkre/Liteo** cottages, or **Falika**. They're all cheap, though the latter has a few a/c doubles at Rs375. Also tricky to find are cosy **Carina Beach Resort**, ✆ 221147, with a/c rooms for US$15, and cheaper **Palm Grove Cottages**, ✆ 222533—though any rickshaw driver should know the way.

For refreshments, try **Malibu** and **Casy Rose** bar-restaurants in the village (good places to ask about rooms) or **Pedro's, Patrose** and **Karibu** on the beach. The Karibu has the best sounds, food and atmosphere. Set back from the sands are **Domnick's** and **Johncy's** bars—with information on parties and boat trips down the coast to Palolem.

To get around Benaulim, hire a motorbike or cycle in the village. Or hop on an auto-rick-shaw—they'll take you anywhere for a price.

Cavelossim, Varca and Mobor

These three adjacent beaches are really just extensions of Benaulim's long, lonely south-ward sweep of sand down towards Betul. Varca is 5km south of Benaulim, Cavelossim 7km below this, and Mobor (where the road ends) a further 2km. All three villages

(Varca's, 2km back from the beach; Cavelossim's, 3km inland; Mobor's, right on the beach) are serviced by buses, auto-rickshaws and taxis from Margao (less than an hour away), and are reached along the main road from Benaulim.

Accommodation is mainly package-style resorts, full of people looking a little bored and wondering where the famous zest of Goa can have disappeared to. The hotels themselves are better than average though, and may be just the ticket if you want complete isolation. They're a particularly good deal in the off-season, when you can bargain for really big discounts.

At Varca, you'll find the quiet **Resorte de Goa**, ✆ 245066, ✉ 245310, with nice rooms at Rs1500 and better suites at Rs2000; also the plush 5-star **Goa Renaissance Resort**, ✆ 245200, ✉ 5225, offering truly luxurious rooms around US$150. Both places have good pools, restaurants and water-sports; the Renaissance even has a 6-hole golf course.

The best hotel at Cavelossim is the **Holiday Inn Resort**, ✆ 746303, ✉ 746333, with full 3-star facilities (including pool) and doubles/suites from US$100/180. The 'cheap' option is **Gaffino's Beach Resort**, ✆ 246319, with rooms from Rs300 and a well-priced restaurant. This is where all the package tourists from the bigger hotels come to eat.

Mobor has the premier beach resort of Goa—the **Leela Beach**, ✆ 246373, ✉ 246352, with its private beach and all conceivable 5-star facilities/recreations. Built around an artificial lagoon, near the mouth of the estuary, this attractive property looks onto an immaculate stretch of sand, shaded by palm trees.

Betul

An hour's walk down from the Leela (or boat across the estuary from Mobor), Betul is a lovely beach offering total seclusion and unspoilt scenery. The only place (so far) to stay is **Oceanic Tourist Hotel**, ✆ 221860, with friendly people and doubles from Rs150. You'll find it north of the village, close to the harbour. The developers have their eye on Betul, but for the time being it remains the perfect little getaway for the peace-loving beachcomber.

Palolem

Palolem is becoming very popular: not only is it quiet, but there's a pretty little village and you can hire fishing boats to go out and see the dolphins. Most people day-trip here from Colva/Cavelossim or get a share taxi from Margao/Panjim (1/2 hrs). Taxis expect you to stay overnight and to pay a small waiting charge, since they don't want to go home empty. The lone hotel is the **Palolem Beach Resort**, ✆ 643054, with breezy safari tents from Rs200 and chalet-style rooms around Rs300. **Jackson's**, the shabby bar/store along the Canacona road (50 yards south of the turn-off for the beach), charges Rs80 for rooms, but can show you places for half that much. The resort hotel has good food, and there are a couple of beach-restaurants to provide some variety.

By air: from Goa, Indian Airlines, ✆ (0832) 223826, flies daily to Bombay, Cochin, Delhi and Trivandrum, and 3 times a week to Bangalore and Madras. **Damania/ Skyline NEPC**, ✆ (0832) 46196, has daily departures to Bangalore, Bombay, Calcutta and Pune, and (except Monday) to Madras. **Modiluft**, ✆ (0832) 227577, services Bangalore, Bombay and Delhi daily, and **Jet Airways**, ✆ (0832) 221472, has one flight a day to Bombay.

By catamaran: bookings for the catamaran service to Bombay (dep 3pm, arr 10pm) can be made at the Damania office opposite the steamer jetty in Panjim, ✆ (0832) 228711, or through any of the company's airline offices. It's expensive though—US$35 economy, US$50 club class—and bad weather can disrupt services. For an extra Rs15/20, you might as well go by plane.

By rail: the whole rail situation is about to change, with the 760km Konkan Railway line from Mangalore to Bombay (via Goa) close to completion. This will link with the new station east of Panjim, reducing the present 20–24-hour trip to Bombay from Miraj/Londa (*see* 'Getting There') to just 10 hours.

The 2479 **Goa Express** currently leaves Vasco da Gama station (Castle Rock) at 4.45pm daily, proceeding via Londa (45mins), Miraj (5½hrs), Pune (11hrs), Gwalior (30hrs), Agra (32hrs) before terminating at Delhi's Hazrat Nizamuddin station (36hrs).

For Karnataka, your best option at the moment is a state-run Kadamba bus out of Panjim or Margao to Hubli (6hrs), followed by a train to Bangalore (20hrs), to Hospet (for Hampi) or to Badami/Bijapur. Again, this is all going to change in the near future—contact the Goa/Bombay tourist offices for an update.

In Goa, rail bookings can be made at the KTC Terminal in Panjim, and at Margao and Vasco railway stations. Only these last handle Indrail Pass bookings.

By road: private buses run out of Panjim, Mapusa and Margao for Bombay, Bangalore, Pune and Mangalore. State-operated buses go from Panjim's Kadamba bus stand to Bombay (16–20hrs), to Mysore (16hrs), to Mangalore (11hrs) and to Pune/ Bangalore. There are also daily state buses from Margao to Bombay and Mangalore. Most buses to Bombay leave around 3/4pm and run overnight, so bring a torch and a good book.

Route 5: Lost Wonders of the Wilderness

Once on the major trade routes between central India and the western coast, the dry Deccan plateau received visits from communities of wandering monks—Buddhist, Hindu and Jain—who were among the most skilled sculptors and painters India had ever seen. Patronized by local kingdoms, they immortalized their devotion in stone, creating beautiful examples of rock-cut cave architecture—and then, quite suddenly, they left. For hundreds of years afterwards, their achievement lay buried and forgotten. Then, not too long ago, they were rediscovered—living masterpieces in stone, completely untouched by time.

What you have here are three separate centres of sculpture, plotting the history of religion and architecture in ancient India. Though most notable for its Mughal monuments and famous silks, **Aurangabad** has its own caves, raw and primitive, situated on a high hillside shelf. The caves of **Ellora** are the finest rock-cut examples in the world, and are unique in showing the singular harmony existing between the Hindu, Buddhist and Jain faiths of the period. But it is the caves of magical frescoes and wall paintings at **Ajanta**, still fresh after all these centuries, which inspire the most awe and admiration. Here, in the depths of a forgotten wilderness, a tiny time capsule of India's spiritual and cultural heritage lives on.

Itinerary

This route is best done as a short detour from Bombay before heading down to Goa. A few days in the hot, dusty Deccan certainly gives that first beer on the beaches a special zing.

Allow 4 days to see everything. Fly into Aurangabad from Bombay (far quicker and more comfortable than bus or train) and use this town as a base for sightseeing. See Aurangabad's caves by tour bus on day 1, travel out to Ajanta and Ellora on days 2 and 3, and put aside day 4 for shopping and a late flight out again.

Aurangabad   population 700,000

Originally known as Khadke, Aurangabad was later renamed after the Mughal emperor Aurangzeb. Despite being the largest city in northern Maharashtra, it's a lot quieter and less hassle than many other Deccan towns and has a number of much-underrated sights, including several fine monuments and a series of interesting Buddhist caves.

When to Go

The area is coolest and greenest during the post-monsoon months of October and November. It remains pleasant but dry right up to March, but becomes unbearably hot by April/May. This is one place to have a water-bottle handy at all times.

By air, you can get to Aurangabad from Bombay, Delhi, Jaipur and Udaipur (*see* 'Moving On' sections). Fast trains here include the 1004 **Devagiri Express** from Bombay VT (dep 10.30pm, arr 7am next day) and the 7064 **Secunderabad– Aurangabad Express** from Hyderabad (dep 7.30pm, arr 9am next day). Overnight MTDC and MSRTDC buses from Bombay are long, hot and uncomfortable (12hrs).

Indian Airlines, ✆ 24864, and East-West Airlines, ✆ 23407, are en route to the airport, which is 10km east of Aurangabad town.

Getting Around

Aurangabad is a small, relaxed town alongside the Kham River. For easy reference, the railway station, budget hotels and tourist office are all close together, 1½km south of the bus stand on Dr Ambedkar Road. Most people get around on foot, though you can rent a bicycle from near the bus stand or hire (metered) auto-rickshaws.

Aurangabad ☎ (02432–) **Tourist Information**

The **Government of India tourist office**, ☎ 31217, is on Station Road West, open from 8.30am to 6pm weekdays (till 11.30am Saturdays). It's much better than the **state tourist office**, ☎ 31513, in MTDC Holiday Resort, Station Road East (open 7am to 7pm). The **GPO** is at Juna Bazaar, with a *poste restante* open daily (except Sunday) from 10am to 5pm.

Cave Tour

Full day.

Set aside a morning (coolest) to see Aurangabad's caves. There are six in the Western Group, four in the Eastern Group, and they are all Buddhist excavations of the 3rd to 7th centuries AD. Their isolated situation (3km out of town) and their uncompleted status mean that few tourists visit, but they compare favourably with the more popular caves of Ellora and Ajanta, and serve as a useful introduction to them.

Getting to the caves is best by auto-rickshaw—a bumpy 20-minute journey across the arid desert plateau. Unless you want to pay a heavy waiting charge, let the vehicle go on arrival—the stroll back down is very pleasant.

Aurangabad's caves are hacked into a high hillside rock-cleft, and afford spectacular views down over the Deccan plains. Ask to be dropped at the **Western Group** (Caves 5–10), where there is usually a guide with an 'illuminating' mirror waiting. Start with a climb up the walkway leading off to the right. This takes you up to **Cave 10**, the last one to be worked on and the most incomplete (Buddhism was well on the way out by the 7th century). It is of interest only as an illustration of how each cave began its life—as a large chamber of rough-hewn pillars supporting a low rock-cut ceiling. All the sculptures came later.

Cave 9 features a large image of Buddha (left-hand chamber), surrounded by large-breasted women, cobra-mantled attendants and fat, dissolute bodhisattvas (aspirant-Buddhas)—all indicative of Buddhism's later period of decline. The carvings themselves are superb.

Pass by **Cave 8** (just a hole in the rock) to **Cave 7**, the finest example of the whole group. This has the giant figure depicting Siddhartha as a near-Buddha on his way to enlightenment, praying for deliverance from eight fears—fire, sword, chains, shipwreck, lions, snakes, mad elephants and the demon of death. The theme of 'seven', recurrent throughout this cave, is most notable in the central shrine, with its seven handmaidens and seven bodhisattvas ranged around the large Buddha figure.

Cave 6 is a real curiosity—a mixture of Hindu and Buddhist sculptures. The gradual reabsorption of Buddhism into mainstream Hinduism is here reflected by the sole Buddha figure (right) supporting elephant-headed Ganesh (centre) and seven other Hindu deities, including Shiva (left). The sculptures of women are notable for their ornamentation and exotic hairdos. From the cave entrance, enjoy superb views over the surrounding plains.

Out of the western caves, it's a 20-minute walk right round to the other side of the hill. Here, at the top of a crumbling stone stairway, you'll find the **Eastern Group** (Caves 1–4). For best appreciation, start at the far end with **Cave 1**. This is incomplete, but has beautiful lotus carvings on its pillars and imposing 'guardians' bearing studded clubs, who flank the two humble Buddha figures in the side shrines. This cave also has fine views down over the plateau. Moving on to **Cave 2**, you'll find an army of exquisitely carved mini-Buddhas, each with two mini-bodyguards, set into the enclosing wall running around the main shrine. Within the shrine is a massive Buddha attended by supplicant spirits, animals and lesser deities.

The exterior simplicity of **Cave 3**—a square structure supported by 12 highly ornate columns—belies its inner charm and beauty. Within is an interesting series of sculptures depicting scenes from one of the *jatakas* (Buddhist fables), and also the finest Buddha image of the whole Aurangabad group, attended by a large retinue of devotees kneeling in prayer. The walls are covered with figures of women (the whole group has a distinctly female emphasis), clad in little else but heavy jewellery.

Cave 4 is the only *chaitya* (temple) of the group, all the others being *viharas* (monasteries). A silver casket *stupa* (memorial mound) containing Buddhist relics sits beneath an awesome ribbed ceiling, carved in the style of a Gothic church. Outside, a stone Buddha sits in his chair and prays to the sun. **Cave 5**, the last in this group, is disappointing—the principal sculptures have all been plastered over.

The walk down to Aurangabad from the foot of the cave steps is not as long or as daunting as first appears. There's also a real sense of desert isolation and timelessness in the 30-minute trek across the flat, stark plains to the gleaming dome of the **Bibi-ka-Maqbara** (*see* p.333) at the northern end of town.

Shopping

Aurangabad is famous for its *himroo* shawls, cotton brocade (still woven in gold or silver thread on silk), *bidri* ware and Aurangabad silk. For the best selection, visit **Silk Loom Fabrics** at the bottom of Station Road (near the railway station) or **Himroo Factory Emporium** close to the bus stand.

Aurangabad ✆ *(02432–)*

Where to Stay
expensive (from US$35)

Best value is the impressive new **Taj Residency**, ✆ 335015, ✉ 331223, on the road out to Ajanta (9km from the airport). This is a beautiful property, with Mughal palace-style architecture, 5 acres of landscaped lawn, a pool and a restaurant-cum-bar. Rooms are very well-priced from US$35/50. Similar facilities

with less style are provided by the town's other 5-star hotels: the **Ambassador Ajanta**, ✆ 485211, ✉ 484367, and Welcomgroup's **Rama International**, ✆ 84441, ✉ 84768.

moderate (from Rs150)

Along Station Road East, choose between **Hotel Great Punjabi**, ✆ 25598, MTDC's **Holiday Resort**, ✆ 34259, and **Hotel Nandavan**, ✆ 23311. The Punjabi has a travel counter and room service, the other two, pleasant outdoor restaurants-cum-bars. If you don't have your own mosquito net, stay at MTDC.

budget

The obvious place in this category is the **Youth Hostel**, ✆ 29801, between the bus stand and the railway station. It's immaculately clean and the people are very friendly. Double rooms go for Rs70, dorm beds for Rs27 (less for YHA members), and all meals are available. Checkout time is 9am, and there's a 10pm curfew.

Decent fallbacks include hotels **Natraj** and **Tourist's Home** on Station Road West, **Hotel Printravel**, below the bus terminal, ✆ 29707, and the new **Hotel Ashiyama**, just off Station Road West, ✆ 29322. The Printravel has a particularly good restaurant.

Aurangabad ✆ (02432–)   ***Eating Out***

The new Taj Hotel has memorable Indian/continental food, good for a big night out. The **Rama International** offers a reasonable buffet, including live music. Try **Bhoj** on Dr Ambedkar Road for mid-range vegetarian fare (especially south Indian), and Hotel Printravel's **Petang Restaurant** or the **Youth Hostel** for *thalis*. For tandoori meals, there's **Chanakya** or **Food Wala** restaurant-bars, both on Station Road East. MTDC **Holiday Resort** is good for a beer in the garden, but nothing else.

Moving On

By air: From Aurangabad, **NEPC Airlines** flies daily (and **East-West** 4 days a week) to Bombay. **Indian Airlines** flies 4 times a week to Jodhpur/Jaipur via Bombay and Delhi.

By rail: The two daily direct trains to Bombay are the 7518 **Tapovan Express** (dep 3.20pm, arr 11pm) and the overnight 1004 **Devagiri Express** (dep 7.25pm, arr 5am). For Hyderabad, catch the 7063 **Aurangabad–Secunderabad Express** (dep 7.30pm, arr 9am next morning). These trains are very popular though, so book well ahead.

By road: MTDC Holiday Home sells luxury overnight buses to Bombay (12hrs), also daily tours to Ajanta caves (8am to 5.30pm) and to Ellora–Daulatabad–Aurangabad (9.30am to 5.30pm). MSRTDC offer ordinary buses to Pune (6hrs) and to Bombay, also daily 'tourist buses' to Ellora and Ajanta from the main bus stand (dep 8am). To backtrack from Ajanta to Ellora, there are regular buses daily, via Phulambari.

Ajanta

By MTDC tour bus, full day. Caves open 9am–5.30pm; adm Rs0.50; bags can be checked in at the 'cloakroom' for Rs1, and you can hire multi-lingual guides from the entrance. Only hand-held cameras are allowed, and flashes are prohibited.

Ajanta's caves should be seen before those of Ellora's, which they mainly predate, in order to keep the chronological sequence. Avoid weekends and public holidays though—crowds of domestic day-trippers make enjoyment impossible.

Many travellers rave about Ajanta, saying it's the best thing they've seen in India, while others can't see what all the fuss is about. The once-bright Buddhist frescoes and wall paintings are rapidly fading away. Everybody suggests bringing a flashlight, for the caves are very poorly lit—a deliberate device, to keep the sunlight from damaging the murals any further. If you don't have your own lighting, you can buy a Rs5 'light ticket' whereby the caves with the most exciting paintings are illuminated. You'll certainly need a guide for Ajanta; the tours provide good ones, but don't lose them. If you're here on your own, try tacking onto a group—guides are very reluctant to shine their lights on paintings for solo travellers. To stay overnight, take a local bus down to Fardapur village (5km from the caves) and buy a Rs200/325 room or Rs15 dorm bed at the clean and comfortable MTDC **Holiday Resort**, ✆ (026353) 430, which also has beer and food.

The 30 rock-hewn caves of Ajanta are full of vivid sculptures and wall paintings, many of them still glowing in their original colours. They represent the finest achievement of the Buddhist monks who arrived here in the 2nd century BC, and reflect the zenith of ancient Indian art and architecture. Chiselled into a steep horseshoe-shaped rock gorge, the caves appeared in two distinct phases over a 900-year period. Most of them were carved in one continuous burst of energy from the 2nd century BC to the 2nd century AD, the remainder in erratic spurts from the 5th to 7th centuries AD. After that, the site was suddenly abandoned, the monks transferring their building activities to nearby Ellora. Only in 1819, after a millennium of obscurity, were Ajanta's beautiful cave paintings dramatically rediscovered by a British hunting party out in search of tigers. Their isolated situation had contributed greatly to the remarkable state of preservation in which they were found. Poor initial restoration work led to some sad deterioration in their quality, but expert Italian restoration in the 1920s halted their rapid decline. Today, work is constantly going on to ensure that as many visitors as possible will be able to enjoy this unique group of cave paintings.

The principal interest of the caves is their depiction of eight centuries of religious development, specifically Buddhism. Here can be seen the development of Buddhist art, thought and belief from the simple, ascetic Hinayana school, reflected in the older, centrally located Caves 8, 9, 10, 12 and 13, with their emphasis on the abstract and symbolic, through to the popularist Mahayana 2nd century BC offshoot in the more modern caves, on either side of the older Hinayana structures, which favour the rich, realistic mode of art. The central theme of the frescoes and sculptures is however consistent throughout the group—the life and times of the Buddha, along with tales of his previous earthly incarnations. Here he presides over a miniature cosmos of caparisoned war-horses and elephants, colourful monkeys and peacocks, bejewelled princes and princesses, spirited musicians and players—sometimes smiling, at other times meditating or dejected. The dominant theme of the paintings may be religious, but they are also a vivid portrayal of a civilization over a thousand years old.

As you tour the caves, you'll notice that most of them were designed to catch the full flood of sunlight at certain times of day. The mood and meaning of each painting alters according to which angle it is viewed from.

Like Ellora's Kailash cave, those in the Ajanta group are all monolithic—each one carved from the bare rock alone, with no additions, and methodically chipped away from the ceiling down to reveal pillars, monks' beds, façades and massive back-room Buddhas. The technical feat is staggering.

Cave 1 is the biggest, best and most recent of the Ajanta caves, with the finest murals. Its large central hall has notable sculptures (including one of four deer with a single head) and fine paintings of the 'black princess', the 'dying princess', *jataka* depictions of the Buddha's previous lives, and portraits of various bodhisattvas. Along with Caves 2, 16, 17 and 19, it has the very best paintings. **Cave 4** is the largest *vihara* cave, supported by 28 pillars, with fine sculpture scenes of fleeing people seeking protection from Avalokiteshvara (Buddha's disciple) against the 'eight great dangers'. Along with Caves 17, 19 and 26, it has the best sculptures in the group. The oldest cave of all, **Cave 10**, was also the first one stumbled upon by the British officers who rediscovered Ajanta.

Ellora and Other Sights

By MTDC tour bus, full day. Daulatabad–Grishneshwar–Ellora–Khuldabad–Bibi-ka-Maqbara–Panchakki.

This absorbing tour covers not just Ellora, but a number of interesting spots in and around Aurangabad. If you decide you need more time at Ellora, stay overnight at **Hotel Kailas**, ✆ (2347) 41063, near the caves. This has a range of rooms from basic doubles at Rs100 up to pleasant cottage-style rooms for Rs700 (a/c, with views of the caves). The attached restaurant does good Indian/Chinese food.

Halfway to Ellora from Aurangabad, the tour stops at the remarkable hilltop fortress of **Daulatabad**. Built by Bhilama Raja in 1187 and named Devagiri or 'hill of the gods', it later gained fame as the place selected by mad Muhammad Tughlaq (the then Sultan of Delhi) as his new capital. He force-marched all his subjects here in 1327, renamed the fort Daulatabad or 'City of Fortune', and then—just 17 years later—marched them all the way back to Delhi again. It was a long, long march (1100km) and many people perished en route.

Daulatabad is the only raised point in an otherwise flat wilderness and sits perched on top of a 200m-high pyramidal hill. Surrounded by 6km of thick walls, equipped with massive spiked gates (against elephant charges), dead-end ambush alleys, overhead channels (for pouring boiling oil on invaders), steep, gravelled slideways and a crocodile-infested moat,

Ajanta Caves

Muhammad's new capital really was a masterpiece of security. The only weakness was its water supply, which gave out during a siege; the invading forces then bribed the Sultan's guards to let them in by the front gate.

The tour round the fort is fascinating, but you'll need a flashlight. Just inside the entrance gate is the huge **Chand Minar** pillar. Built in 1435 as a Victory Tower, it soars to a height of 60m and is surpassed only by Delhi's Qutb Minar. It faces onto a small mosque erected over an old Jain temple. Across the moat (now a dry gully), you begin a half-hour climb up to the fort. On the ascent, look out for the **Chini Mahal** (the blue-tiled palace where Golconda's last king spent his final 13 years imprisoned) and the massive cannon cast from five different metals and engraved with Aurangzeb's name. Near the top there's a pitch-black, spiralling tunnel used to unleash burning coals on univited guests. Use your flashlight here, and then enjoy fine views from the bastion summit.

Moving on, the tour calls in at **Grishneshwar**, an 18th-century Shiva temple housing one of the 12 ancient *jyotirlingas* (major Shiva shrines) where 'visitors wishing to achieve *dharvana* with the deity must take off their clothes'.

At last you come to **Ellora**, site of the finest examples of rock-cut caves in all India. This place is the meeting-point of three faiths—Jain and Hindu structures having risen alongside each other as the original Buddhist impetus slowly tailed off. There are 34 caves in all—12 Buddhist (*c.* 600–800), 17 Hindu (*c.* 750) and 5 Jain (*c.* 800–1000)—and they are numbered in that order, running south to north.

You'll normally be shown the **southern (Buddhist) caves** first. Ten of these belong to the Mahayana sect (which favoured statue-worship) and contain images of the Buddha; the remaining two (**Caves 1 and 7**) are the work of Hinayana monks (who preferred relic-worship) and contain only stupas. They are all *viharas* or monasteries, except for **Cave 10**, which is the only *chaitya* (temple) of the group. Known as the Carpenter Cave (owing to its ceiling ribs, which resemble wooden beams) it contains a gigantic Buddha figure seated in meditation on a lion throne, flanked by attendants and flying figures. The image is fronted by a 9m-high stupa. To take any photos in the dimly lit chamber, you'll need the services of a guide with a mirror. Moving on, **Cave 5** is the largest *vihara* in the group, its title of 'Assembly Hall' being suggested by the rows of stone benches within. **Cave 12** is a large three-storey edifice, used as a training/sleeping area for student monks. The top floor has eight large Buddha figures, all exceptionally fine, and the walls are carved with attractive reliefs. **Cave 16** is the only **Hindu** example covered on the tour. This is the world-famous **Kailash Temple**, dedicated to Shiva and built to represent his Himalayan home of Mount Kailash. A stupendous edifice, with dimensions twice the area of the Parthenon in Athens—81m long by 47m wide and 33m high—it was carved from one enormous rock. Unlike all the other caves, which were cut at ground level and took an average of 50 years apiece to fashion, the Kailash was begun from the top of the rock and worked slowly down to the floor—creating gateway, pavilion, courtyard, vestibule and tower along the way—in an amazing flourish of creative zeal which, according to one estimate, took 7000 labourers over 150 years to build. Lavishly carved, and sculptured with epic themes throughout, it is the world's largest monolithic structure. Attributed to the Rashtrakuta kings of the mid-8th century, the temple is a testimony to the skills and imagination of those who built it.

Entrance to Kailash is via a bridge, leading through an enclosure to a large courtyard. To the front of the enclosure, two large stone elephants with flagstaffs flank the Nandi pavilion, which faces into the main shrine. Of the many strikingly carved frieze panels, perhaps the most famous is that depicting the demon king Ravana trying to lift Mount Kailash, while Shiva, unimpressed, presses it down again with just his toe. There are many such episodes from the *Ramayana* epic depicted here.

Caves 13 to 29 are Hindu excavations, mostly Shaivite in character, and to see these you will have to leave this tour at Ellora, or visit independently.

The group of five **Jain temples** (slightly north of the others) mark the final phase of Ellora architecture. They lack the dynamism of the better Hindu caves, but compensate with exceptional attention to detail. You'll be shown **Cave 32**, the **Assembly Hall of Indra**, which is the best of the group. The ground floor is a simple, rather plain imitation of Kailash, but has exceptional ceiling carvings. The upper storey, reached by a small stairway, is notable for its rich decorations. Inside the shrine is the seated Mahavira, last of the 24 *tirthankars* and founder of the Jain religion. The lotus-design detail-work on the Jain columns is the finest of the whole Ellora complex.

After lunch, you'll visit the small market town of **Khuldabad** ('heavenly abode'), 3km out of Ellora. Fortified by Aurangzeb, it was once an important centre, and remains the Karbala or holy shrine of Deccani Muslims, containing the tombs of many historical figures. Here you'll find the simple bare-earth grave of Aurangzeb, last of the great Mughal emperors, surrounded by a decorative marble screen. Renowned for his puritanism, the emperor stipulated that only money that he himself had earned by copying out the Koran should be used to pay for his tomb. It was his way, it was said, of atoning for the financial excesses (including the Taj Mahal) of his spendthrift predecessors. Even the screen round his grave was a later addition, donated by the wealthy Nizam of Hyderabad.

Back in Aurangabad, the tour takes a look at the **Bibi-ka-Maqbara**, built by Aurangzeb's son for the emperor's wife. Popularly known as the 'poor man's Taj', it was erected in 1679—just 25 years after the Taj Mahal itself—and pales in comparison. But its low cost of 68,000 rupees (300 times cheaper than the Taj) doubtless commended it to the parsimonious Aurangzeb. It differs from the Taj in three major respects: the four corner minarets are actually higher than the central mausoleum dome; it is built of plaster-covered common stone (not marble) set on a marble base; and the carvings and decorations are far simpler, less ornamental, than those of the Taj Mahal.

Last stop is the **Panchakki**, overlooking Aurangabad's Kham River. Built in 1624 to honour the memory of Baba Shah Musafir, a Sufi saint who was Aurangzeb's spiritual mentor, it is a massive water-wheel named after a mill once used to supply grain for visiting pilgrims and holy men. A small dam releases water through the mill gates into a large fish-filled tank, at the rear of which is a magnificent 500-year-old banyan tree.

Gujarat exists out of time. Untouched by tourism, it extends a warm, rather surprised, hand of welcome to the visitor who really wants to get away from it all. Nowhere is this more true than on the southern coast of the state. Here a small triad of nascent resorts provide the perfect escape from mainstream India. The central attraction, the 16th-century ex-Portuguese port of Diu, is a small idyllic town of Mediterranean charm, with a fort, beaches and Catholic churches. Life here is slow and peaceful, and you can relax over a cold beer in one of the several bars and tavernas. Close by is Somnath, a major Hindu pilgrimage centre, with a famous shore temple (seven times destroyed and rebuilt) and another fine beach. At Sasan Gir, one of the finest wildlife sanctuaries in the country, the Asian lion roams his last natural refuge on earth. Travelling this virgin territory, frequented by few foreign visitors, you'll feel like a stranger in paradise.

Itinerary

The main reason Gujarat gets so few foreign visitors, apart from its total ban on alcohol (Diu and Daman excepted!), is its remoteness. It's a huge state and—apart from the three places covered here—its main points of interest are very spread out and very time-consuming to cover by local bus.

The beauty of this route is that it lies exactly midway between two others—Rajasthan and Bombay/Goa, and makes the perfect interlude between them. You can fly in from Bombay to Keshod (the nearest airport to Diu) and then hire a car/take a bus up to Ahmedabad for Rajasthan. Or take a car/bus south from Rajasthan to Sasan Gir/Diu, via Ahmedabad, and continue on to Bombay.

Either way, you'll need at least six days. A week in an Ambassador car, hired from Udaipur (best) or Mt Abu, shouldn't cost more than £150, as long as you specify that you want a daily rate of £20, inclusive of 300km per day travel. It works out quite cheap if there's two of three of you to split costs with. The car should come with a good English-speaking driver who knows where he's going.

From Udaipur/Abu, it's only 4/5 hours by road to Ahmedabad. After a night here (day 1), the most cost-effective route would be south to Sasan Gir (days 2/3), east to Diu (day 4), back to Sasan Gir, via Somnath (day 5), and back to Ahmedabad (day 6). If you can afford it, allocate an extra day apiece to Diu and Bhuj. From Ahmedabad, you can fly back either to Delhi or on to Bombay for the south. Flights should be booked well ahead, and recon-firmed at least 3 days before departure.

Note: Local buses from Diu to Bombay are horrendously long and uncomfortable. The author took one once, and spent the whole night fending off drunks and pickpockets. He arrived in Bombay so distraught and dishevelled that the Taj Hotel took one look at him and said 'We don't let in hippies.'

When to Go

Gujarat is hot and dry for most of the year, but receives the rains from June to September. The best time to visit is between October and March, when temperatures are an acceptable 14° to 29° C. After this comes the April/May heatwave (27° to 41° C) and you'll want to be somewhere else.

<table>
<tr><td>

Diu
</td><td style="text-align:right">

population 40,000
</td></tr>
</table>

The small ex-Portuguese island of Diu is linked to the Gujarat coast by a bridge and a slip of a road over salt pans. Though only 13km from end to end, it offers a couple of striking churches, a 16th century fort (which doubles as a jail) and a pretty and unspoilt beach at Nagoa. The town itself is a picture postcard of pastel houses, clean cobbled streets, colourful locals selling fish and vegetables, and back-to-back bars and tavernas. Sleepy and relaxed, everything about Diu is pleasantly Mediterranean.

Diu derives its name from the Sanskrit word 'Dweep' island. Between the 14th and 16th centuries it was a busy and important seaport and naval base, used by merchants all over the world as a trading point with India. When the Portuguese set their heart on it in the mid-16th century, Diu was under the rule of the Sultans of Oman. Nuno da Cunha (the then Portuguese governor), launched the first offensive on it in 1531, but failed. A short time later, Bahadur Shah (the Sultan of Gujarat) was forced to let the Portuguese build a fortress on the island, in return for their armed help against Humayun, the Mughal emperor. The massive Diu Fort was completed in 1547 and gave the Portuguese the foothold they needed to seize the whole island from the Shah, as well as the opposite coastal village of Ghoghla. For the next 350 years, Diu was administered by a Portuguese governor. Only on 19 December 1961 did it return, along with the other Portuguese pockets of Goa and Daman, to Indian rule, after 450 years of foreign rule.

Since liberation, Diu has gained a number of new schools, roads, bridges and communications which have brought it slowly back into line with modern India. Yet it retains much of its old Portuguese charm, and is never anything less than completely relaxing. As a coastal fishing-town, the first thing you'll notice here is the powerful reek of fish— perfectly natural, since most of Ghoghla/Diu's population make their living from the sea. They are a happy, colourful and multi-national people, most of whom speak Gujarati and follow the Hindu faith. They are tuned in to Westerners, and you won't for once feel either odd or conspicuous. The only time you'll remember you're in India is at weekends when busloads of Gujaratis from far and wide come over for a party. With Daman, Diu is the only place in 'dry' Gujarat they can get a drink.

When to Go

For comfort, visit during the comparatively cool season of November to February. It's still pleasant in March–April, but a bit too warm for most. Avoid coming in May–June at all costs: swarms of Indian tourists hit the beaches, and you can forget all about peace and quiet.

Diu is best reached by road from Veraval (80km), which has overnight train services from Ahmedabad (*see* p.343), or by plane to Keshod (94km) from Bombay (*see* p.340). If coming in by bus, you'll normally be dropped off at Una, 10km away. From here, there are half-hourly buses to Diu (Rs6, 6.30am to 8.15pm) or auto-rickshaws for Rs50. Some STC buses now go direct from Veraval to Diu bus stand. Be sure to have your passport ready for checking at the Diu border.

 You can hire bicycles (back of the town square) and mopeds (next to Hotel Sanman) in Diu town, though the latter are unreliable. Auto-rickshaws cost Rs5 anywhere inside Diu town, Rs25 to Nagoa beach (7km), and Rs15 to Sunset Point. Local buses go to Nagoa (dep 7am, 11am and 4pm) from the stand next to the town square, opposite the petrol pump on Bunder Rd. They come back again at 1, 5.30 and 7pm (Rs2), from the stand near Nagoa's police post.

Note: don't expect much action between noon and 4pm. This is siesta time (another Portuguese legacy) and the whole island winds down.

Diu ☎ (028758–)

Diu's helpful tourist office, ☎ 2653, is on the waterfront a little way down Bunder Road from the town square (opposite the customs office). It has a full listing of current accommodation, sells a decent map of the island and is open 9am–6pm except Sundays. The State Bank of Saurashtra is just up from the post office on the main square. The Jethibai bus stand for out-of-town buses is just before the bridge (Diu side) leading over to Ghoghla and the mainland.

Touring Diu

By cycle/moped, half-day. Diu Fort–Don Nuno da Cunha–Ancient Diu Church–Bazaar–St Paul's Church.

Diu is one place to see at leisure and by bicycle. From the town square, turn right (facing the sea) up Bunder Rd until, some 10 minutes later, you come to the huge battlemented **Diu Fort**. This is the double-moated 16th-century Portuguese bastion, largely ruined today but worth an hour-long wander. Within, walk up to the vantage-point lighthouse, approached by a stone ramp, which gives prime views of the town, churches and coastline. From here, you can well appreciate the fort's strategic importance to the Portuguese; though rapidly crumbling today, it was in olden days near-impregnable. Round the lighthouse quadrant, looming over the stone buttresses, are some beautiful old cannon with reliefs of human faces moulded into the cast. Returning down into the courtyard of the jail, you'll find the arrogant, strutting statue of **Don Nuno da Cunha**, a bronze life-size oddity surrounded by heaps of old cannonballs. Several have been

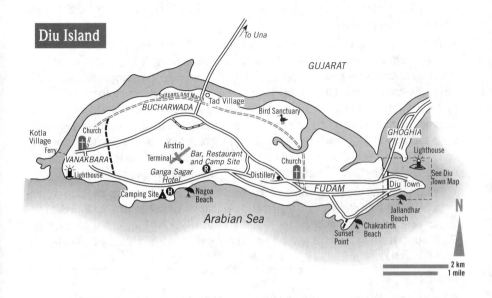

Diu Island

To Una

GUJARAT

Saltpans and Marsh

Tad Village

BUCHARWADA

Bird Sanctuary

GHOGHIA

Kotla Village

Church

Airstrip

Terminal

Ganga Sagar Hotel

Lighthouse

VANAKBARA

Ferry

Bar, Restaurant and Camp Site

Church

Distillery

Lighthouse

Diu Town

See Diu Town Map

Camping Site

Nagoa Beach

FUDAM

Jallandhar Beach

Arabian Sea

Sunset Point

Chakratirth Beach

N

2 km
1 mile

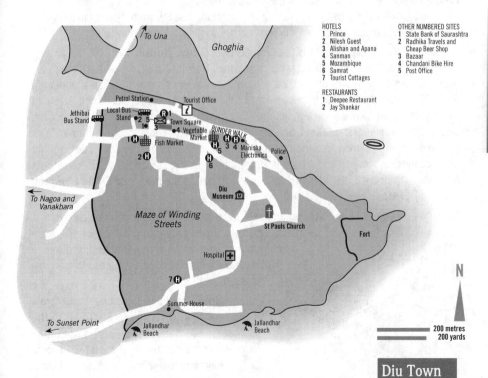

HOTELS
1 Prince
2 Nilesh Guest
3 Alishan and Apana
4 Sanman
5 Mozambique
6 Samrat
7 Tourist Cottages

RESTAURANTS
1 Deepee Restaurant
2 Jay Shankar

OTHER NUMBERED SITES
1 State Bank of Saurashtra
2 Radhika Travels and
  Cheap Beer Shop
3 Bazaar
4 Chandani Bike Hire
5 Post Office

To Una

Ghoghia

Petrol Station

Tourist Office

Jethibai Bus Stand

Local Bus Stand

Town Square

Vegetable Market

BUNDER WALK

Manisha Electronics

Police

Fish Market

To Nagoa and Vanakbara

Diu Museum

Maze of Winding Streets

St Pauls Church

Fort

Hospital

To Sunset Point

Summer House

Jallandhar Beach

Jallandhar Beach

N

200 metres
200 yards

Diu Town

employed as decorative borders to the flower-beds. The fort closes at 5pm daily; nobody stops you taking photographs.

Behind the fort, visit the three old Catholic churches on view from the lighthouse. They can be seen in any order. Only a handful of Indian Roman Catholic families remain in Diu, and these churches are no longer places of worship, little visited and largely ruined. Of the three, the **Ancient Diu Church** has been turned into a school—the imposing architectural style of its façade plus intricate interior woodwork contrasting strangely with the gleaming lunar module in the courtyard playground. The second, though notable for its stone springs and depictions of phases in Christ's life, has for the past 300 years doubled up as the town's hospital (convenient for casualties of the cricket games going on in the square below). The third—most peculiar of all—has now become a badminton club.

Walking or cycling back into town, drop in on the small but lively town **bazaar** (tucked away behind the market square), then take directions for nearby **St Paul's Church**. This is a towering structure, built in 1691, and dedicated to Our Lady of the Immaculate Conception. It is notable for its magnificent carved gates, and for its beautiful altar made of solid Burma teak.

Beaches

Nagoa beach is a wide crescent of golden sand nestling within a quiet protected cove—an idyllic spot for sunbathing, swimming or just taking a break from 'real' India. They've just started speedboats and water scooters though, so it's not as quiet as before.

The only place to stay and eat is the **Gangasagar Guest House**, ✆ 2249, which gets mixed reports. Everyone gets on with the owner, Haridas Samji, who likes to take his guests fishing. Nobody gets on with his wife, who has a very short temper. Small rooms go for Rs75/150, and larger family rooms for Rs225/300. Bathrooms are common, but with the Arabian Sea on your doorstep, who needs a private one? Ask for room 14, facing the sea. Meals are served at set times, and if you're late or want food at any other time, that's your problem. It's a good idea to bring some food of your own, just in case. There's a bar here (open to non-guests) and a palm-laden garden patio to enjoy drinks on. If this place is full, take a two-person tent (Rs250, with light and fan) at the next-door **Oasis Camping Site** until a room is free.

From Nagoa, you can now cycle on to **Vanakbara** at the extreme west of the island, and see its church, lighthouse, bazaar and fishing fleet. A ferry goes from here over to the pretty little fishing village of **Kotla** on the mainland of Gujarat, outside the jurisdiction of Diu.

Other beaches that have come up—in the wake of the new road connecting Diu Town to the southeast of the island—are **Jallandhar** (stay/eat at the good-value **Tourist Cottages**, ✆ 2654), **Chakratirth** and beautiful **Sunset Point**. All three places are poised for further development.

Shopping

The main thing to buy is booze. Although it is illegal to smuggle it out of Diu into 'dry' mainland Gujarat, everybody does it. It's no big deal if the police find it at the exit checkpoint; they'll just confiscate it and drink it themselves. If you're in a car, your driver will probably be smuggling some out himself and will offer to hide your bottles in a safe place.

Leisure

Entertainment is limited, but who cares. In Diu, life is a beach and people make their own amusement. This generally means hanging out at the town's innumerable bars and cafés (but treat the local rum and IMFI—'Indian Made Foreign Liquor'—with respect). The Aradhana **cinema** at the back of town shows the odd English film alongside the usual Hindi melodramas.

Diu ✆ (028758–) ### Where to Stay

Diu still caters mainly to the backpacker crowd, but has lately come up with some decent mid-priced accommodation too. This is just as well, since travellers looking for a bit of comfort were previously restricted to the Indian jet-set beach of Ahmedpur Mandvi (near Ghoghla on the mainland), which is strictly for Gujaratis on a booze binge.

In town, travellers favour **Hotel Mozambique**, ✆ 2223, with a range of rooms from Rs80 (double) up to Rs 200/300 for family rooms. The **Samrat**, ✆ 2354, a couple of blocks back from the main square, has very clean rooms at Rs250, or Rs550 with a/c. There's a couple of VIP suites for Rs900. **Hotel Sanman** (ex-Fun Club), ✆ 2273, an old Portuguese villa on Bunder Road, has double-bedded rooms from Rs100 to Rs250. Nearby, the more modern **Apana**, ✆ 2112, has Rs150 doubles and Rs550 a/c; also dorm beds for Rs60. The **Alishan**, ✆ 2340, and **Prince**, ✆ 2265, have rooms at Rs200 ordinary, Rs250 de luxe. The **Nilesh**, ✆ 2319, asks Rs60/Rs120 for singles/doubles, and some larger rooms cost Rs200; also dorm beds for Rs30.

Eating Out

For non-vegetarian food, try the restaurant at **Hotel Samrat** behind the main square. It does delicious tandoori chicken, Chinese dishes, and has an a/c bar. For dosas and vegetarian snacks, there's **Deepee**, once the town's only restaurant. A small omelette stall sets up at the back of the square around dusk, and does a very busy trade. On Jallandhar beach you'll find the friendly (though unlicensed) **Jay Shankar**, where delicious food is miraculously produced out of a tiny kitchen.

By air: Diu's tiny airport, just below Nagoa beach, is 7km from the town centre. It is serviced by Gujarat Airways, which flies in from Bombay and back again every Tuesday (US$66), and by East-West Airlines who have three flights a week from Bombay. The agent for East-West is Oceanic Travels, ✆ 2180, ✉ 2372, in Diu's town square (Bunder Chowk).

By road: leaving Diu, there's a small group of private bus companies in and around the main square offering half-hour minibuses to Veraval (2½hrs), to Junagadh (4hrs), and to Rajkot (7hrs); also overnight buses to Ahmedabad (dep 7pm, 11hrs) and Bombay (dep 10am, 22hrs). The Bombay bus is sold by Goa Travels, ✆ 2191, on the town square. Tickets should be booked at least 24hrs in advance, and you should check whether buses are leaving from the main square or (as is usual after 8am) from the new Jethibai bus stand at the Diu end of the bridge crossing over to Ghoghla. If it's the latter, it will cost you Rs5 by auto-rickshaw to go there.

There are no direct buses to Sasan Gir. You have to go back to Una (Rs50 by auto-rickshaw) and catch a bus from there. The slow alternative is the 1.30pm train from Delwada, near Ghoghla, which pulls into Sasan Gir around 5.30pm before continuing on to Junagadh. The train passes through the wildlife park and, if you're lucky, you might see a lion or two.

Somnath

Somnath, also known as Prabhas Patan, has one of India's most revered temples, along with a beautiful (if unshaded) beach. Somnath Temple, the main tourist magnet, has one of the 12 sacred *jyotirlingas* (Shiva shrines) and is extremely old. Legend has it that the first temple on this site was built by Somraj, the Moon God, after Shiva kindly cured him of consumption. This first structure was built of gold. Subsequent versions were of silver (donated by Ravana); of wood, donated by Krishna to mark the spot where he 'lost his body'; and of stone, by Bhimdev.

By the 6th century AD, Somnath was the richest temple in all India. Its wealth was so great that when the acquisitive Mahmud of Ghazni descended on it in 1024, even his vast caravanserai of elephants, camels and mules couldn't take it all away. What he destroyed was probably the first historically recorded version of the temple, built in the 1st century AD. Over the following 700 years, Somnath Temple was knocked down and rebuilt six more times. Finally, after Aurangzeb the Mughal iconoclast set his demolition team on it in 1706, the builders gave up and left it in ruins. Only in 1950 was the temple finally restored. This present version is an interesting, if not quite successful attempt at a modern Hindu temple incorporating traditional styles.

For comfort, visit Somnath between November and February. After that, it's too hot. Festival-lovers will enjoy **Kartika Poornima** (November–December), a vibrant village fair and performing arts gala, with lots of folk theatre, dance and chanting of Vedic hymns.

Also worth a visit is the big festival of the year, **Mahashivratri** (February–March), patronized by thousands of pilgrims from all over India. Both celebrations take place at the historic temple.

Getting There

The **Girnar Express** from Ahmedabad arrives in Veraval (4km up the road) at 7.45am daily. The **Somnath Mail**, also from Ahmedabad, goes only as far as Junagadh, arriving at 7.45am. From Junagadh to Veraval is 2hrs by STC bus. Also *see* p.355.

If you miss direct buses from Diu (1½hrs), it's 30 mins to Una, then 2½hrs to Veraval. Regular local buses ply back and forth between Veraval and Somnath (Rs4) or you can hire an auto-rickshaw for Rs20. If you leave Diu early, you can cover Somnath and be in Sasan Gir before dark.

Somnath ☎ (02876–)   ***Tourist Information***

Information can be obtained from the manager of the **Temple Trust**, ☎ 21200, though he's not always there. Next to the temple, there's a Vadilal ice-cream joint with an **STD** facility for long-distance calls. Adjoining this is a **Central Bank of India**. If this won't change money, the State Bank of India in Veraval (close to the railway station) will.

Touring Somnath

On foot, 2–4 hours. Somnath Temple–Jain Temple–Prabhas Patan Museum.

Coming into Somnath from Veraval by bus, look out for the richly carved Mai Puri, which used to be a Sun Temple, and the Junagadh Gate 1km further on. This is the ancient triple gate that Mahmud of Ghazni stormed to enter the temple town.

The **Somnath Temple** has a magnificent location, overlooking the Arabian Sea and a long stretch of grey but sandy coast (*open 6am–9.30pm*). Just inside the entrance, a richly raimented Nandi bull faces onto the Shiva shrine, shielded by a pair of massive silver doors. A small fee gains you access to the upper storeys. Bypass the first floor with its boring wooden boxes containing faded photos, bits of rock, dusty neon tubes, and climb to the good second-floor museum. This has an interesting photographic exhibition describing the history and archaeological background to the seven versions of Somnath temple. Slip over to the balcony for fine views of the coastline, and of the temple's beautiful upper-storey carvings. These show a definite Orissan influence, especially the carvings of (now extinct) Oriyan lions.

For the best sneak-preview of the Somnath Temple, climb to the top of the pink **Jain Temple** opposite the museum. The small government-run **Prabhas Patan Museum** (*open 8.30am–12.30pm and 2.30–6.30pm, closed Wed and every 2nd and 4th Saturday of the month; adm Rs0.50*). This is a small, grubby place, more like a warehouse than a museum, with lots of uncatalogued rubble lying around the central courtyard. Enough is left of the 11th-century, fourth-version temple to give you an idea of its original magnificence, and you can climb onto the courtyard parapets for decent views of the sea. There's a strange collection of holy and not so holy waters in little bottles, collected from famous rivers all over the world—from the Nile to the Danube and the River Plate. If you're staying over in Somnath, the best time to visit the temple is at sunrise or sunset, when Shiva is invoked in a lively, elaborate ceremony called *arti.*

Photography is not allowed inside the temple, and all cameras and electronic devices must be left at the cloakroom outside (get a receipt).

Walking away from the temple, past the Hotel Mayuram, you can walk 1km to a viewpoint marked by the confluence of 3 rivers. It's a popular picnic spot, and a good place to escape from the dust of the town.

Somnath ✆ (02876–) **Where to Stay**

Somnath is not geared to mass tourism, so accommodation is limited. Just below the temple is the new **Hotel Shivam**, ✆ 20999, with rooms from Rs100/150 or Rs300/350 with a/c. It's far and away the best place in town, so book to avoid disappointment. A couple of minutes down from this is **Hotel Mayuram**, ✆ 20286, with double rooms with bath for Rs150. Close by, opposite the bus stand, you'll find the **Sri Somnath Trust Guest House**, with monastic cells for Rs40 double and Rs60 triple.

Eating Out

Somnath is a good place to go on a diet. The only place of consequence to eat (though try the Hotel Shivam) is the pure vegetarian **Dwarakadhish** near Somnath Trust, which does a generous all-you-can-eat Gujarati thali for Rs20. If you want something better, go to Veraval.

The small port town of **Veraval** is a noisy, dusty place which (when the wind is in the wrong direction) simply reeks of fish. The only hotel worth a light is the new **Hotel Aradhana**, ✆ 21334, near the clock-tower. It has a pleasant manager and large clean rooms with bath and TV for Rs175, or Rs515 with a/c. Hotels **Satkar** and **Kasturi** near the bus stand ask Rs100/Rs150 or Rs300/400 with a/c, but are depressing.

Food is best at **Jill's** restaurant above Veraval bus stand (heading to the clock tower) or at the nearby **Sagar** and **Foodland** restaurants. If sleepless in Veraval, either visit the semi-interesting port where wooden dhows can be seen sailing off to the Middle East, or escape into the Aradhana **cinema**, next to Hotel Aradhana, for a happy Hindi epic.

By rail: the fast overnight **Girnar Express** leaves Veraval for Ahmedabad at 7.15pm daily.

By road: there's a row of sleepy travel agencies along the road leading away from the temple, offering deluxe buses to Bombay (18hrs), Ahmedabad (9hrs), Junagadh, Rajkot, Diu and Keshod. Try Kishan Travels; it's more lively than the rest.

From Somnath, there are only two useful buses a day to Diu (dep 6.30am and 1.45pm), though check at the bus stand for others that may have come up. The Somnath–Una road is very pretty—lined with palm trees and lush vegetation. It's a real slice of Kerala in the heart of Gujarat.

From **Veraval**, 44km up the road, there are more regular buses to Diu (2½hrs) and Junagadh (2hrs). For private buses, contact Mayur Travels opposite the state bus stand.

Sasan Gir

The Gir Forest is one of the largest continuous tracts of land in India reserved for the conservation of its wildlife, and contains an amazing abundance of animals, birds and flora. The terrain is extremely varied—open scrub country, dry deciduous and tropical thorn forest, and evergreen corridors along the river beds. Gir had an original spread of some 5000 sq km, but by 1969, when it was designated a wildlife sanctuary, this area had dwindled to just 1400 sq km. The interior core of the forest (258 sq km) was constituted a national park in 1975.

Sasan Gir is the last natural refuge in the world of the majestic Asiatic lion *Panthera leo ersica*, which in ancient times roamed the forests and open grassland as far afield as Greece in the west and Bengal and Bihar in the east. But human pressures led to a sudden, dramatic decrease in numbers. By 1884 there were no sightings of Asiatic lions outside the Gir Sanctuary. And by the turn of the century, the pitiful remainder of just 100 lions had been completely driven off their natural territory and confined to the very heart of the forest.

At this point, their fortunes revived. In 1900, the Nawab of Junagadh invited Lord Curzon, the then Viceroy of India, to join him for a lion shoot at Gir. Curzon accepted the offer, but soon had occasion to regret it. An anonymous protest in a British newspaper, angrily complaining of the impropriety of a VIP doing further damage to an already endangered species, not only persuaded Curzon to cancel his trip, but moved him to ask the Nawab to protect the remaining lions. The Nawab agreed, but it wasn't till much later that concerted conservation efforts began. In 1948 hunting in the area was banned but in 1974 there were still just 180 lions in the sanctuary. However, with continuing efforts to save the species, the numbers have now climbed to just over 300. Sightings of leopard, which now number 270, are more common than in any other sanctuary in India.

When to Go

If you're here to see lion, the best months are April and May. It's a bit hot during the day (40°C), but so are the lions and they come out of hiding in the cool dawn or dusk to drink from the few remaining water-holes or to prey on other wildlife which have had the same idea. From mid-June to mid-October the park is closed completely, and when it reopens the grass is generally too high to see any animals until later November. Early December is good, but from mid-December until New Year the place is packed out with domestic tourists and there's nowhere to stay, unless you've advance-booked. Visibility is good from January right through to late June, when the monsoon starts. If you're into ornithology, come for the rains. A whole host of migratory birds visit the park each year.

Getting There

The nearest airports to Sasan Gir are Keshod (80km away) and Rajkot (160km), both accessible from Bombay. If you can't make the Tuesday/Sunday NEPC flights to Keshod, Indian Airlines fly four days a week to Rajkot, and NEPC the remaining three. Taxis are available at Keshod airport and cost Rs350/400 to Sasan (1½hrs). From Rajkot, it's a stiff Rs700/800 (3hrs). If this sounds a lot, get a bus to Junagadh and a second one on to Sasan.

Sasan Gir can be also be reached by bus from Una and Veraval (see Diu/Somnath). The **Somnath Mail** train from Ahmedabad goes only as far south as Junagadh (65km away), though STC buses take you on to Sasan Gir in just 2hrs. *See also* pp.347 and 355.

Sasan Gir ☏ (02877–)   ### Tourist Information

For information, contact the Forest Manager at the Forest Lodge. His office is no.8 in the complex, open 8.30am–12.30pm and 2.30–5.30pm. He often hangs around until late though, chatting to friends. If you miss him, try Mr Singh at the Gir Lodge.

Phoning home is cheapest from the **STD** booths in Sasan village. Connections to the US or UK are amazingly clear.

Touring Gir

The main attraction at Gir is the Asiatic lion, a magnificent beast averaging a full 2.75 metres in length, and with a larger tail tassel, bushier elbow tufts and more prominent belly folds than his African cousin. He also has a smaller mane, and is a lighter brown in colour.

The sanctuary is also home to many other predators (notably the powerful leopard, capable of climbing up a tree with a full-grown stag in its mouth) and animals like bear, *langur*, barking deer, *chousingha* (four-horned antelope), fox, hyena and blackbuck. There is a large population of *nilgai* or blue bull, a species of antelope which, like the peacock, has enjoyed a considerable degree of natural protection by virtue of its religious associations (it resembles the sacred cow). The forest is also known for its many reptiles, including cobra, python, viper and marsh crocodile.

Had Gir not been designated a lion sanctuary, it surely would have established itself as a major bird sanctuary. In all, there are over 200 different varieties of birds to be seen, including green pigeon, oriole, partridge, painted sandgrouse, rock bush-quail, paradise flycatcher and India's national bird, the peacock.

You can't go on safari in the park without a permit, which must be applied for in advance. Even if you turn up at the Forest Lodge office (room no.8) as late as 7pm the night before, you'll get one. Permits cost Rs15 and are valid for one day only. Government jeeps cost Rs6 per km and take up to six persons. There are three main trails in the park, and five lesser ones. It's up to you which one(s) you go on, but since jeeps go down the smaller trails—where you are far more likely to see lion—it makes sense to do these first. You can comfortably cover two small trails (25/30km) in a day or, if you are really burning rubber, three of four (40/45km), though this is expensive. Should you fail to see at least one lion (and this is rare) you can always go back the next day and try a different route. A lot depends on the guide allocated to your jeep. His Rs25 charge (per jeep, not per person) should be supplemented by a tip only if he's made a real effort to look around and find you

Wild asses

things to see. Guides have supposedly been trained to 'talk in international languages', but have apparently forgotten all of them. If you're lucky, you may get one who can say, 'Look, lion!'

The park is open from 7 to 11am and from 3 to 6pm daily. Last jeeps out leave around 9.30 in the morning and around 4.30 in the afternoon. There are also minibuses for hire, but they hug the main trails and you often don't see anything. In general, your best chance of seeing wildlife—not just lion, but bear, deer, hyena and antelope—is just before dawn and around dusk.

Note: at present, Sasan Gir is the only wildlife park in India where noisy, polluting diesel jeeps and buses are allowed. The Taj Hotel is however setting up its own safari operation for visiting the park, complete with a fleet of 10 comfortable open-top (petrol-based) Gypsy vehicles plus a resident naturalist, who will brief hotel guests on what to look out for before they set off. Charges won't be unreasonable—around Rs1000 per 6-person jeep for a 3hr tour—and routes will be completely different to those used by the five existing Government jeeps.

Something else to do is visit the recently established **Gir Interpretation Zone**, where you can go on a minibus mini-safari (Rs70, including a guide) and see lion and a whole cross-section of Gir's wildlife in what is effectively a big zoo. The zone is a 6.5sq km enclosed area of natural forest, located 13km from Sasan at Devalia. To go there, you'll need a jeep from the Forest Lodge (Rs150 return, 4 to 6 persons) which will wait while you do your one-hour tour. Safari buses go into the zone from 7am to 9.30am and from 3 to 5pm daily, except Wednesdays.

In Sasan Gir village itself, just below the bus stand, you'll find the **Crocodile Breeding Centre**, where baby crocs are hatched out and then released into their natural habitat. You're allowed to handle them, but watch out for those 66 baby teeth! The centre was established in 1976 to counter the sudden decline in marsh or 'mugger' crocodiles and now has 700 specimens, some of them quite large. Eggs are collected from nearby Kamleshwar Dam and brought here to be artificially hatched. Official opening hours are 7 to 11am and 3 to 6pm, but they're not strict about timings and you can wander in at any time of day.

Sasan Gir ℂ (02877–)

Where to Stay
luxury (from US$55)

Three cheers for the Taj Group! Like an oasis in the desert, its brand new **Gir Lodge**, ℂ 5521, ✉ 5528, has appeared to give Gujarat its first modern luxury hotel outside Ahmedabad. It's built in the style of a jungle lodge, though with modern features successfully incorporated. Standard a/c rooms cost US$55 and the two a/c suites US$110 apiece. There's a cool pool and a restaurant, though the fixed buffet meals (served to residents only 9am–8.30pm) leave a lot to be desired. Before you try one, order a back-up meal at the Forest Lodge; you may need it. Manager Nagendra Singh is an experienced ranger, with lots of knowledge about

Gir and its environs. Bring a torch if staying here—walking to and from the village at night can be tricky in the dark.

moderate (from Rs150)

The government-run **Sinh Sadan Forest Lodge**, ✆ 40, is in the village itself, about 10 minutes' walk from the railway station. This has 20 or so clean, well-kept rooms ranged around a central garden courtyard with illuminated fountain. The best rooms (Rs450) have TV and a/c, though the cheaper rooms (from Rs150) are comfy enough and have mosquito nets. There are also dorm beds for Rs50 and two-person tents for Rs100. Like the Gir Lodge, it has fixed meals—Rs25 thalis or Rs90 non-vegetarian dinners—from 8 to 9.30am, 1 to 2.30pm and 8 to 9.30pm, though all food must be ordered ahead. A free video about the park is shown every evening at 7pm.

A new place with a beautiful location inside the park (2km from the village) is **Maneland Lodge**, ✆ 5555. It's run by a pleasant Indian couple from Ahmedabad and has ten cottage-style rooms for Rs1000.

Moving On

By air: from Keshod airport (80km away), NEPC Airlines flies twice a week (Tuesday/ Sunday) to Bombay. It comes back on the same days.

By rail or road: by car, you have a choice. Either see Somnath (1.25hrs) on the way to Diu (2½hrs), or go straight to Diu from Sasan Gir (3hrs) and see Somnath on the way back. Regular buses go from Sasan Gir to Veraval (40km, 1½hrs) and to Una for Diu (80km, 3hrs). There's also one bus a day to Keshod airport. For timings, contact the Forest Manager.

If you're heading back to Ahmedabad, get a taxi from Sasan Gir railway station (Rs250/300) or a cheap deluxe bus to Junagadh (2hrs), then the **Girnar Express** train (dep 9pm daily), which gets to Ahmedabad at 6.10am the following day. The slower **Somnath Mail** (dep Junagadh 7pm) arrives too early (4.20am next day) to start looking for a hotel.

Ahmedabad
population 4 million

According to legend, Ahmedabad was built on the ruins of the ancient township of Karnavati, founded by King Karna Solanki in the 11th-century AD. In historical terms, however, it traces its origin to Sultan Ahmed Shah (after whom it is named), who decided to build a town here.

Ahmedabad, with its rich pre-Mughal and Mughal architecture, was rightly called 'The handsomest town in Hindoostan, perhaps in the world' by Sir Thomas Roe, an early British envoy to India. The city was a favourite of the great Mughal Emperors Jahangir and Shah Jahan.

During the 15th and 16th centuries a unique fusion of styles from Hindu and Muslim schools of architecture came together here to create what is now known as the Indo-

Saracenic style. In Ahmedabad this is reflected in the mosques and mausolea (in mellow, honey-coloured-sandstone) built during this period—particularly in the arches, domes, vaults and pillars. A few centuries later, rich merchants of the Jain and Hindu faiths built a number of temples, which still form a distinct part of Ahmedabad's architectural landscape.

Modern Ahmedabad boasts of several public and private buildings designed by leading Indian and international architects like Charles Correa, Louis Kahn and Le Corbusier. This is a city where ancient architectural marvels survive among the modern; where traditional values and a modern outlook coexist in peaceful harmony; where progress hasn't meant the uprooting of all the ingrained customs and moral values.

This said, Ahmedabad is one place to get in and out of as quickly as possible. Like Delhi, it is noisy, polluted and overcrowded. Unlike Delhi, it has no definite centre or landmarks and so defeats the efforts of even hardened travellers to get to grips with it. Hardly anyone speaks English either, so anyone coming in from cosmopolitan Bombay is in for a big surprise. The people are however very friendly and eager to help foreigners.

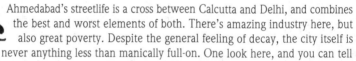

Ahmedabad's streetlife is a cross between Calcutta and Delhi, and combines the best and worst elements of both. There's amazing industry here, but also great poverty. Despite the general feeling of decay, the city itself is never anything less than manically full-on. One look here, and you can tell where all those Gujaratis working in the West get their energy from!

When to Go

April through to June can be quite hot, rising from 23°C to 43°C. There is no particular high season, as this is the commercial and industrial capital of Gujarat and has a busy stream of visitors throughout the year.

Getting There

There are Air India flights to Ahmedabad from the UK and US, though few Westerners use them. Domestic airlines service Ahmedabad from Bombay, Delhi, Calcutta, Jaipur, Madras and Pune. There is as yet no flight from Udaipur—a big pity. From the airport to the city centre costs Rs100 by auto-rickshaw, around 30 minutes if traffic is light.

Fast and frequent trains link Bombay with Ahmedabad via the beautiful university city of Vadodara (Baroda), and the daily **Ashram Express** from Delhi's Sarai Rohilla station is quick and convenient (dep 6pm, arr 12.40pm next day). Some travellers pick it it up at Ajmer (arr 2.30am) or at Abu Rd (arr 8am). State transport buses go to Ahmedabad from many centres including Bombay, Rajkot, Sasan Gir and Delhi (via Udaipur/Jaipur). Hired car from Udaipur/Mt Abu are very quick (4/5hrs).

Ahmedabad

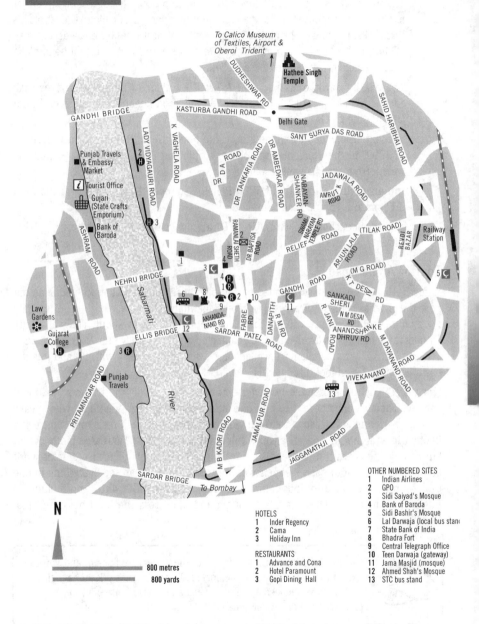

To Calico Museum
of Textiles, Airport &
Oberoi Trident

Hathee Singh
Temple

DUDHESHWAR RD

GANDHI BRIDGE

KASTURBA GANDHI ROAD

Delhi Gate

SANT SURYA DAS ROAD

SAHID HARIBHAI ROAD

LADY VIDYAGAURI ROAD

K VAGHELA ROAD

DR D A ROAD

DR TANKARIA ROAD

DR AMBEDKAR ROAD

NARAYAN SHANKER RD

JADAWALA ROAD

AMRUT K ROAD

Punjab Travels
& Embassy
Market

Tourist Office

Gujari
(State Crafts
Emporium)

Bank of
Baroda

ASHRAM ROAD

RAMANLAL RD

SHETH

DR BAPTISA ROAD

RELIEF ROAD

SWAMI NARAYAN TEMPLE RD

ARJUN LALA (TILAK ROAD)

REVDI BAZAR

Railway
Station

NEHRU BRIDGE

Sabarmati

(M G ROAD)

KT DESAI RD

GANDHI ROAD

SANKADI SHERI

N M DESAI RD

Law
Gardens

Gujarat
College

ELLIS BRIDGE

AKHANDA-NAND RD

FABRE RD

SARDAR PATEL ROAD

DANAPITH

R M RD

R JANI ROAD

ANANDSHANKE DHRUV RD

M DAYANAND ROAD

PRITAMNAGAR ROAD

Punjab
Travels

River

VIVEKANAND

M B KADRI ROAD

JAMALPUR ROAD

JAGGANATHJI ROAD

SARDAR BRIDGE

To Bombay

N

800 metres

800 yards

HOTELS
1   Inder Regency
2   Cama
3   Holiday Inn

RESTAURANTS
1   Advance and Cona
2   Hotel Paramount
3   Gopi Dining Hall

OTHER NUMBERED SITES
1   Indian Airlines
2   GPO
3   Sidi Saiyad's Mosque
4   Bank of Baroda
5   Sidi Bashir's Mosque
6   Lal Darwaja (local bus stand
7   State Bank of India
8   Bhadra Fort
9   Central Telegraph Office
10 Teen Darwaja (gateway)
11 Jama Masjid (mosque)
12 Ahmed Shah's Mosque
13 STC bus stand

The friendly but useless Gujarat Tourism office (☎ 449683) is at H K House, down a sliproad off Ashram Rd. It's open 10.30am to 5.30pm (with a short break for lunch) and is supposed to have a great monthly periodical called 'The Choice is Yours' (Rs3)—though the author never saw it. What it *does* have is a decent map of Gujarat (Rs8) and a current copy of *The Times of India* with current train/plane timings, though you can get these anywhere.

The nearby **Bank of Baroda** on Ashram Rd changes money and gives cash advances on Visa cards. It has a second branch on Relief Rd (western end), not far from the GPO.

Visa extensions can be applied for at the **Foreigners' Registration Office** (☎ 333999) in the Police Commissioner's office on Balvantraj Mehta Rd, on the way north to the Calico Museum.

Indian Airlines, ☎ 353333, is on Relief Road, open 10am to 1.15pm and from 2.15pm to 5.15pm, closed Sundays.

A good bookshop is **Sastu Kitab Dhar**, opposite and along from the Relief Cinema.

Touring Ahmedabad

Ahmedabad was originally surrounded by a fortified wall built by Sultan Ahmed Shah but now the city has spread out across the river Sabarmati. The newer portions of the city were built according to plan, so it is fairly easy to find one's way about. The walled city with its maze of lanes, is divided into self-contained quarters locally known as *poles.* Each comunity of weavers, merchants, jewellers or goldsmiths had their own *pole* and it is still possible to wander on foot through this area.

Not that this is recommended however—nowhere in India is the traffic so mad and chaotic. The challenge here is to find one auto-rickshaw wallah, just one, who speaks even a smattering of English, and to hang onto him for dear life. Do all your sightseeing in one trip with this guy, because you won't easily find another! Taxis are slightly better, but hailing one down in the street is equivalent to jumping off a cliff. Hotel taxis work on an 4 or 8-hour tour basis—expensive, but worth it if you can see everything in one day. Municipal corporation bus tours are much cheaper (Rs30, 4hrs) and include an English commentary. They leave at 9.30am and 2pm from the local bus stand (Lal Darwaja).

 Taxis in Ahmedabad are metered, but the meters are ancient and you can expect to pay double what the final reading is. You can ask to see their rate card, but you'll need a degree in Gujarati to make sense of it, so just agree a price with the driver beforehand.

City Tour

By car/rickshaw, 8hrs; by tour bus, 4hrs. Jama Masjid–Teen Darwaza–
Bhadra Fort–Sidi Saiyad Masjid–Rani Rupmati Masjid–
Hathee Singh Jain Temple–Shaking Minarets–Dada Harini Dev Baoli–
Mata Bhavani Baoli–Kankaria Lake–Calico Textile Museum–
Utensils Museum–Sarkhez Roza–M.K. Gandhi Ashram.

A good place to start is the **Jama Masjid**, situated almost at the centre of the walled city. This mosque, built in 1423 by Sultan Ahmed Shah in the Indo-Saracenic architectural style, is outstanding for its grand scale, superb proportions and exquisite workmanship. Fifteen domes of varying elevations are supported by over 300 pillars, and one of the achievements of the design is the successful filtering of light so no direct sunlight falls into the building. The 'shaking minarets' of this mosque were destroyed in an earthquake in 1818. (Similar minarets survive in the Sidi Bashir Mosque, *see* below.) Immediately to the west of the mosque is **Teen Darwaza**, a triple-arched gate, erected by Sultan Ahmed Shah to serve as the royal entrance to the Royal Square (Maidan Shah) of his eponymous city. Further west of Jama Masjid is the ancient citadel now known as **Bhadra Fort**. The foundations of this fort were laid in 1411 but it takes its name from the temple to Goddess Bhadrakali, built inside by the Marathas in the 18th century. Near the post office and court, which occupy an old palace next to the fort, is the **Sidi Saiyad Masjid** completed in 1472 by a slave of Ahmed Shah. The mosque contains famous filigree stone windows—note particularly those on the west wall. A little to the north is the **Rani Rupmati Masjid**, just below the Grand Hotel. Built between 1430–40, this mosque was named after Rani Rupmati, the Hindu queen of Sultan Mahmud Shah Beghara. Richly ornamented with carvings and finely crafted marble screens, it presents a fine example of the synthesis of Hindu and Muslim architecture. **Hathee Singh Jain Temple**, just north of Delhi Gate, was built in 1550 by a rich merchant. Constructed of pure white marble and decorated with rich carvings, this temple rivals the famous Jain temples of Mount Abu in beauty.

The **Shaking Minarets** form part of the **Sidi Bashir Mosque**, constructed 2½km from the city centre, and can be swayed by a little force applied to the top-most arch. When one minaret is shaken, the vibrations are communicated to the other minaret via a stone-bridge, and the second minaret starts shaking. A similar pair of minarets existed in the Rajabai Mosque but were damaged in the 19th century.

A characteristic architectural feature of Gujarat is the step-well or *baoli*. Many were built next to temples and provided a ready source of water, as well as a cool retreat in the hot, dry summer months. The **Dada Harini** step-well was built in AD 1501 by one of the ladies of Sultan Mahmud Shah Beghara's court. This has a spiral staircase leading down to the central reservoir. The walls' steps and supporting pillars are splendidly carved. A little to the north is the older **Mata Bhavani Baoli**, also some 800m northeast of the Daryapur Gate. Sultan Qutb-ud-din had the **Kankaria Lake**, to the southeast of the city, constructed in 1451. There is an island in the centre containing a summer palace known as Nagina Wadi and it is possible to hire a boat for a few rupees to reach it.

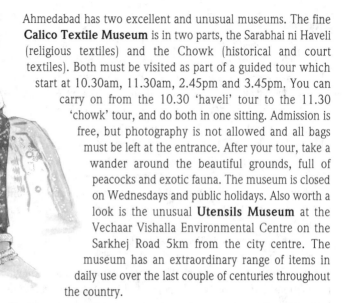

Sewing mirrorwork,
Gujarat

Ahmedabad has two excellent and unusual museums. The fine **Calico Textile Museum** is in two parts, the Sarabhai ni Haveli (religious textiles) and the Chowk (historical and court textiles). Both must be visited as part of a guided tour which start at 10.30am, 11.30am, 2.45pm and 3.45pm. You can carry on from the 10.30 'haveli' tour to the 11.30 'chowk' tour, and do both in one sitting. Admission is free, but photography is not allowed and all bags must be left at the entrance. After your tour, take a wander around the beautiful grounds, full of peacocks and exotic fauna. The museum is closed on Wednesdays and public holidays. Also worth a look is the unusual **Utensils Museum** at the Vechaar Vishalla Environmental Centre on the Sarkhej Road 5km from the city centre. The museum has an extraordinary range of items in daily use over the last couple of centuries throughout the country.

One of the architectural marvels of Ahmedabad is the **Sarkhez Roza** at Sarkhej about 8km southwest of the city. This group of structures built around a large tank include the large tomb of the Muslim holy man, Ahmed Khattu Ganj Bakhsh, the spiritual guide and advisor to Sultan Ahmed Shah, built in 1445 a huge but simply designed mosque constructed in 1454; and the tombs of Sultan Mahmud Shah Beghara and his queen Rajabai (1460). Much later on, the Dutch East India Company founded an indigo factory here.

About 6km from the city, on the banks of the Sabarmati river, is the **Ashram** founded by Mohandas Karamchand Gandhi, on his return from South Africa (1917). This quiet retreat was to grow into the nerve centre of the Indian freedom movement and was the starting point of Gandhi's 385km march to Dandi in 1930, when 90,000 people demonstrated against the government Salt Tax.

Other places covered by municipal bus tours are: **Adalaj Vav** (17km), a fine example of the traditional step-well; and **Lothal** (80km), where remains of Harappan Civilisation have been excavated recently. At **Modhera** (106km) on the road north to Abu and Udaipur, are the remains of a fine Sun Temple built in AD 1026 by Bhimdev I of the Solanki dynasty. **Nal Sarovar** (71km) is a bird sanctuary which acts as the winter host to various species of migrant birds—including rosy pelicans, Brahmin duck and flamingoes. **Patan** (130km) is home to the families who weave the famous Patola silk saris sold in Ahmedabad (from **Gurjari**).

Shopping

Gujarat is famous for its bright and colourful old embroideries, and there's nowhere better to shop for them than **Law Gardens**, off C.G. Road. Here, village people sit by the side of the road and sell traditional clothing, furnishings and jewellery from 5.30pm though to midnight. Prices aren't cheap, however, especially if you're a foreigner, but you can generally expect to clinch a deal at 50% of the first asking price.

For antique jewellery, boxes and curios, visit **Manak Chowk**, close to the railway station in the old city. Even if you don't buy anything, there are some old houses in the area worth seeing.

Two decent government places for handicrafts are **Gurjari** and **Handloom House**, both on Ashram Rd.

Leisure

Entertainment is not Ahmedabad's long suit. Apart from dance programmes at the **Darpan Academy**, ✆ 445189, on Ashram Rd, and music evenings at the **Cama Hotel**, this city is a cultural desert. If you want to use a hotel swimming pool, you have to be a resident.

Ahmedabad ✆ (079–) ### Where to Stay

Ahmedabad's image as a hellhole, with mad traffic and little to see or do, is hard to shake. Most travellers stay only one night, on their way down to Gujarat or up to Rajasthan. If the city had a few more hotels, they might stay longer.

Luxury/expensive hotels have a split rate tariff—you can either pay a high rate in foreign currency, in which case you avoid luxury taxes of up to 29%, or you can pay a slightly lower rate in rupees (only if you have an encashment certificate changed in Gujarat state). It works out far cheaper to pay in dollars or pounds.

---

luxury (from Rs2500)

If you're coming in by air and are only staying one night, the brand new 5-star **Oberoi Trident**, ✆ 7864444, ✉ 7864454—only 2km from the airport—is your obvious option. The hotel opened in October 1995 and has an executive centre, a pool and health club, and friendly, personal staff. Tariffs are US$95/100 and there's a short-day rate of US$65.

The **Holiday Inn**, ✆ 5505505, ✉ 5505501, on Lady Vidyagauri Road, near Nehru Bridge, is an anonymous high-rise hotel with all mod cons, including an indoor pool, jacuzzi, sauna etc, but with zero atmosphere. Rooms start at US$70/85, suites at US$200, and you don't want one overlooking the riverside slums.

The 4-star **Cama Hotel**, ✆ 5505281, ✇ 5505285, on Lady Vidyagauri Road, Khanpur, has palm-strewn lawns, a good restaurant and coffee shop, the nicest pool in the city and well-equipped rooms from Rs1195/1700. It's quite an old property, a bit flaked round the edges, but the people are friendly and the atmosphere very warm. The hotel's liquor shop is open 10am to 5pm (closed Sunday). Like the Holiday Inn, check-out time is a miserly 9am.

The **Inder Regency**, ✆ 6425050, ✇ 400407, is opposite Gujarat College at Ellisbridge. There is no pool, and the rooms are smaller (but more modern) than the Cama (from US$35/45), but it offers centrally a/c, 24-hr coffee shop, a good restaurant and all mod cons.

The **Rivera Hotel**, Khanpur, ✆ 5504201, ✇ 5502327, has deluxe rooms for Rs750/900, and a restaurant serving Indian, continental and Chinese dishes.

Most of the cheap hotels are situated around the railway station or near Relief Road. The friendly **Hotel Natraj**, ✆ 350048, near the Lal Darwaja local bus stand, has rooms overlooking the gardens of Ahmed Shah's Mosque for around Rs100/150. Or you could try the **Plaza**, ✆ 353397, behind the Hotel Capri. There's a range of comfortable rooms from around Rs100, all with bathroom. Both these hotels have cold water only in their bathrooms, but you can request a bucket of hot water.

Ahmedabad ✆ (079–)   **Eating Out**

The Oberoi Trident is a long way to go for a quality meal, but is ideal if you're close to the airport and need to fill up before or after a flight. The coffee shop has lunchtime buffets weekdays and all day at weekends. The main **Narmada** restaurant has a good name for kebabs and birianis, and serves speciality Gujarati, Rajasthani and Punjabi thalis (Rs200) on silver plates.

The Cama Hotel's **Aabodaana** is excellent for *à la carte* (especially steaks) and offers live music most nights from 7.30 to 10.30pm (a Western-style cover band on Mondays and Thursdays; Indian *ghazals* and instrumental music all other days). The attached coffee shop is a good place for a continental snack (vegetarian/non-vegetarian club sandwiches, burgers and tacos) in between

As elsewhere in Gujarat (apart from Daman and Diu), Ahmedabad is 'dry', so if you want a beer you'll have to go down to the excise office, buy a permit, go to the liquor shops at hotels Cama or Rivera, buy your 'quota' of alcohol and consume it in the privacy of your room. The only alternatives are to bring your own booze from out-of-state, or go without.

sightseeing. Also recommended is the **Timbuktu** on C J Road with good multi-cuisine and a jukebox with CDs. The next-door **Cakewalk** bakery is handy if you have a sweet tooth.

For a totally ethnic night out, try the well-rated **Vishalla**, ✆ 403357, a Gujarati village-style eatery in Vasana, on the southern outskirts of town. It's the single most popular restaurant in Ahmedabad, and must be booked well in advance.

For excellent thali, try the **Gopi Dining Hall**, just off the west end of Ellis Bridge, near the hospital. Dinners cost from Rs35. The **Advance** restaurant, opposite the cinema of that name, and the nearby **Cona**, are both good places for breakfast. The **Hotel Parmount** serves continental, Chinese and Indian cuisine under a huge crystal chandelier.

Moving On

By air: Ahmedabad is an international airport, with flights on to the UK and US via Air India. The airport has an upstairs restaurant with good cheap eats (decent dosas for Rs12, 'grilled veg slabs' for Rs10 etc) and fast, friendly service.

From the domestic terminal, **Indian Airlines**, ✆ 305599, have daily flights to Bombay and Delhi, and 3 a week to Bangalore and Madras. **Damania/Skyline NEPC**, ✆ 6426295 city, ✆ 786881 airport, fly daily to Pune daily, 6 times weekly to Bombay, Calcutta, Madras and Aurangabad, and 3 times a week to Madurai, Bangalore, Cochin and Coimbatore. **Jet Airways**, ✆ 401290, services Bombay and Delhi daily, and **Modiluft** flies to Delhi 3 times a week. New services out of Ahmedabad include **Sahara India** to Delhi/Jaipur, **VIF** to Pune/Hyderabad and **East-West.** to Bombay/Hyderabad.

By rail: the **Girnar Express** goes south to Veraval for Somnath (dep 9.10pm, arr 6.10am next day). The **Somnath Mail** only goes as far south as Junagadh (dep 11pm, arr 8.30am next day). Tourist quota tickets are easy to obtain from the computerized booking office (counter 12) at the railway station, open 8am to 8pm (only till 2pm on Sunday).

From Junagadh, there are taxis and jeeps to Sasan Gir. Also cheap local buses (2hrs) which leave the STC stand at regular intervals. In Junagadh, Raviraj Travels below Hotel Vaibhav has deluxe minibuses to Veraval (2hrs) for Somnath and to Una (4hrs) for Diu, as well as minibuses back to Ahmedabad (7hrs).

For Delhi/Rajasthan, there's the **Ashram Express**, which leaves Ahmedabad at 4.30pm and goes to Delhi (arr 10.15am next day) via Abu Road and Ajmer. The centrally air-conditioned **Shatabdi Express** leaves for Bombay at 2.25pm every day.

By road: Shree Nath Travels, ✆ 339155, and **Pankaj Travels**, ✆ 449777, are both in Embassy Market, a short walk from the tourist office. They both offer daily deluxe buses to Delhi via Udaipur (22hrs), to Mt Abu, to Jaipur via Ajmer (14hrs), to Udaipur (6hrs), to Jodhpur (10hrs), to Junagadh, for Sasan Gir (6½hrs), to

Veraval, for Somnath (9hrs), and to Rajkot (4hrs). The express bus to Bombay leaves at 8.15pm, arriving 12hrs later. All buses should be booked at least 24hrs in advance.

By car, it's 380km (8hrs) to Sasan Gir, via Rajkot and Junagadh. Popular destinations by car are Mt Abu (5hrs) and Sasan Gir (7hrs). The tourist office and the bigger hotels offer car hire at km or package rates.

Jagannatha Temple
Puri

East India

The east of the continent, bordered by the vast eastern sweep of the Bay of Bengal, contains the magnificent Orissan temples of the eastern triangle, the spiritual buzz of Calcutta, and the old British hill stations of Darjeeling, and Gangtok in Sikkim.

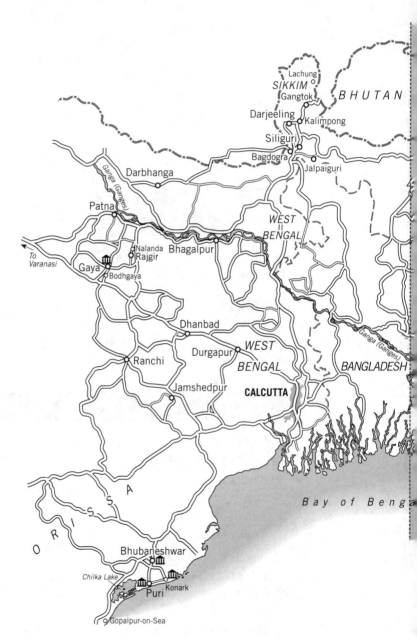

ARUNACHAL PRADESH

Dibrugarh

HUTAN

Guwahati

BANGLADESH

Imphal

DHAKA

Chittagong

East India

MYANMAR

N

150 km
100 miles

Calcutta is concentrated India. The capital of West Bengal, it is the second-largest city in the country—intense, vital and overcrowded—and one of the most populous cities in the world. Here are gathered India's finest artists and musicians, scholars and poets, and her most desperate, poverty-stricken slums. Full of holy men, gurus and street temples, Calcutta has been called the soul of India, but it is also her conscience. The contrasts between rich and poor, educated and ignorant, old and new, are here more stark and discordant than in any other Indian metropolis. The grand old monuments of the Raj—the Victoria Memorial, the High Court, even the Writers' Building—tower in frightening relief above a grey backdrop of shanty-towns and shattered pavements. Crumbling Georgian mansions look over narrow, festering bazaars. Dust-red London buses crawl alongside hand-drawn rickshaw carts through teeming highways. Busy coffee houses, buzzing with sophisticated literary debate, look out onto streets littered with uneducated poor. And just down the road from modern Chowringhee, with its glittering Western-style hotels and shopping arcades, there is primitive Kalighat, with its filth, ordure and animal sacrifices. Calcutta is the distillation—good and bad—of India, and no visit to the country is complete without seeing it.

History

The first settlement here was in 1690, when the British East India Company, abandoning their earlier trading post at upriver Hooghly, sent their agent Job Charnock south to occupy the three fishing villages of Sutanati, Govindpur and Kalikata. The name of the last was later corrupted to Calcutta. In 1696, with the construction of a small fort here—Fort St William, near present Dalhousie Square—the British Empire in India was born. It grew steadily for a time, then was attacked in 1756 by the Nawab of Murshidabad. The young Robert Clive raced up from Madras in time to save the fort, but too late to save a number of its residents from suffocating to death in an underground cellar, later known as the Black Hole of Calcutta. In 1772 the strengthened fort and town became the capital of British India, and received its first Governor, Warren Hastings. During the later 19th century it advanced rapidly as a commercial and political centre, becoming the Second City of the British Empire, then a focus of agitation for Indian independence. This sparked off the move of the British Raj to Delhi in 1911, and Calcutta lost its political throne. Soon after, during the Second World War, it lost its trade supremacy also—to the industrial new-boy Bombay—and began to crumble and decay.

Today, all that remains of its glorious past is a series of yellowing classical palaces and more British clubs than any other Indian city. But Calcutta remains a major centre of art, letters and industry, and its vital colonial heritage of political/intellectual activity remains intact. The fundamental problem is one of overcrowding: hordes of new refugees pour in daily, and there is nowhere for them to live. They spill out onto the street, and traffic and communications grind to a halt. Municipal maintenance is a thing of the past, and Calcutta's reputation now rests not on the might of empire but on the horrors of over-urbanization. Floods, famine, pollution, power-cuts, labour-strikes and unemployment are regular hazards tolerated, even expected, by the city's burgeoning population, yet few of them would prefer to live anywhere else. 'We're used to seeing Calcutta the way it is,' commented city poet Shakti Chattopadhyay, 'There *will* be dirt, traffic jams and garbage—if 50,000 people depend on garbage as a source of livelihood, then arrangements shouldn't be made to dispose of the rubbish; actually, it is a blessing that the slums are still around; you can get cheap domestic help here, unlike in Delhi!'

Most of the city's burgeoning population live on the bottom, bottom line, struggling daily for survival. Some will approach you for money, under the guise of being a tourist guide, a student wanting to improve his English, or a collection agent for a non-existent charity. They are best deflected—those who really need your help are either too tired or too proud to ask for it. Whatever, don't be deterred from going walkabout and discovering the real 'city of joy'. Talk to the people and pick up on their great sense of humour. They're famous for it. But don't dawdle; legions of undesirables rise up from the pavement the moment you look lost, so keep a third eye out for touts and pickpockets. More than anywhere else in India perhaps, Calcutta demands a split mentality—simultaneously open to friendship and deaf to time-wasters.

St Andrews. Calcutta

Despite its notoriety, Calcutta comes as a pleasant surprise to many foreigners. Americans seem to enjoy it because it reminds them of New York—big, brash and action-packed. Australians tend to hate it for precisely the same reasons. There are many long-stay travellers here, either working for Mother Teresa and her Sisters of Mercy in the slums, or receiving tuition from Calcutta's top sitar and tabla musicians. Tourists passing through find the noise and crowds either stimulating or overpowering, but they generally feel safe. The Bengalis are a civilized, friendly people; busy and familiar with foreigners, invariably polite, and keen to help when you're in a spot. The only thing they don't like is visitors pointing cameras at the poorer sections of their community. Wandering the packed streets, you'll need to be sensitive to this; for alongside scenes of courage, laughter and simple natural beauty there are harrowing scenes of human tragedy and suffering. Simultaneously beautiful and ugly, Calcutta leaves nobody unaffected.

When to Go

Close to the sea, and at low altitude, Calcutta suffers a lot of humidity. It is best visited from November to February, though for colour, spectacle and culture come for the three-week **Durga Puja** festival of September–October. But Calcuttans hold festivals and holidays on any excuse, and it is rare to arrive without something going on. After the **Holi** feast of February/March, the city becomes uncomfortably hot. Later on, during the July to September monsoon, it is often subject to torrential floods. For the best coverage of routes in this guide, aim to arrive in late February (after visiting Orissa), then do a couple of side-trips to Bodhgaya/Varanasi before heading up to Darjeeling/Sikkim around late March to escape the heat.

International Arrivals and Departures

by air

Calcutta is serviced from abroad by a growing number of international airlines (British Airways have recently started twice-weekly flights from London, via Delhi), as well as a wide network of domestic air, rail and bus links (*see also* 'Moving On', p.379).

Calcutta's **Dum Dum** airport (named after the bullet invented nearby) has adjoining domestic and international terminals. In an amazing burst of energy, between May and October 1994, the domestic terminal was totally renovated by the Oberoi hotel chain and is now the most modern and attractive of its kind in the country. It has two air-bridges, a business centre, a post office, a VIP lounge and (upstairs) a huge a/c restaurant/bar serving '*haute cuisine à la* Oberoi'. The international terminal is expected to follow suit in 1997/8.

The new domestic terminal has desks for Air India and Indian Airlines, as well as independents like Sahara, Jet, Moduluft and NEPC/Damania. If you need to make a choice, go for Moduluft—the others tend to fly only when they have enough passengers.

Airport to city: transport to the city (16km, 30/40 minutes) is cheaper here than in any other Indian capital. You have a choice of a/c car rental (currently Rs350), prepaid taxis (Rs70–90) and an EATS city-coach service which leaves every hour or so (from 8am to around midnight, Rs20) and which drops at all the better hotels (as well as Sudder Street) on its way to the Indian Airlines office.

No matter how you go to the airport, avoid peak-time traffic from 4 to 7pm, and take account of possible strikes. Calcutta has one or two labour strikes every month (political protests against the Marxist government) and all roads into or out of the city are blocked. Check with your hotel as to whether a strike is likely on the day of your flight home. If it is, either change your flight date or stay overnight at ITDC's Airport Ashok Hotel (*see* 'Where to Stay', p.377); it's drab and overpriced, but at least you'll catch your plane!

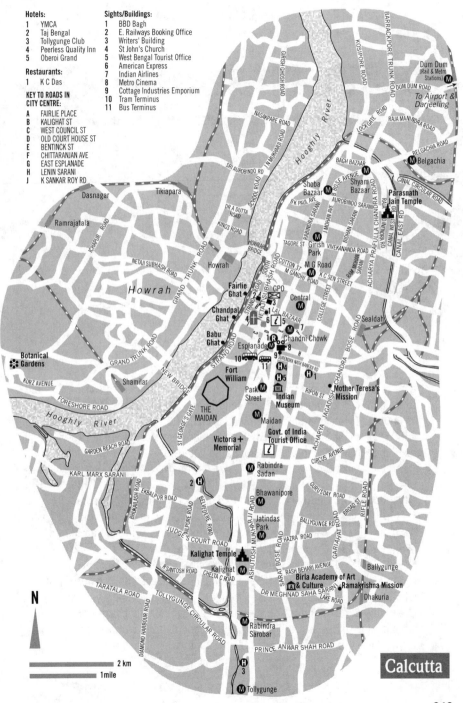

Hotels:
1 YMCA
2 Taj Bengal
3 Tollygunge Club
4 Peerless Quality Inn
5 Oberoi Grand

Restaurants:
1 K C Das

KEY TO ROADS IN CITY CENTRE:
A FAIRLIE PLACE
B KALIGHAT ST
C WEST COUNCIL ST
D OLD COURT HOUSE ST
E BENTINCK ST
F CHITTARANJAN AVE
G EAST ESPLANADE
H LENIN SARANI
J K SANKAR ROY RD

Sights/Buildings:
1 BBD Bagh
2 E. Railways Booking Office
3 Writers' Building
4 St John's Church
5 West Bengal Tourist Office
6 American Express
7 Indian Airlines
8 Metro Cinema
9 Cottage Industries Emporium
10 Tram Terminus
11 Bus Terminus

Calcutta

363

City to airport: the cheapest way back to the airport from town—apart from the irregular ex-serviceman's coach service (5.30am–5.30pm, but ring Indian Airlines, ✆ 260810, for exact timings)—is by Metro train (Rs5) to Dum Dum station, then a Rs25 taxi to the airport. Otherwise, you're looking to pay around Rs120/130 by taxi (up to Rs500 if you take one from a big hotel).

Getting Around

Central Calcutta is a compact, congested area sprawling up along the west bank of the Hooghly River, from the Zoological Gardens in the south up to Howrah Bridge some 5km north. Over the bridge are some of the worst slums and the beautiful Botanical Gardens. In the city centre is the large open expanse of the Maidan, hugged by BBD Bagh (Dalhousie Square) to the north (for the GPO, West Bengal Tourist Office, American Express, etc.), by Chowringhee/Jawaharlal Nehru Road to the east (for the better hotels/restaurants, airline offices and GOI tourist office), and by the Victoria Memorial, Birla Planetarium and other major sights to the southeast.

Calcutta is notoriously difficult to get around. Not only does it have a confusing duplication of street names—nobody knows whether to use the old (Raj) or new (post-Independence) names—but hardly any of the city's main roads have pedestrian footpaths, so human traffic just spills over into motorized traffic. With a mind-boggling average of 50 per cent of Calcutta's population (against a national average of 20 per cent) on the streets at any one time, it's a picture of sheer chaos.

Of late however, there have been a couple of improvements. First, a second bridge over the River Hooghly was opened 2km down from the congested Howrah Bridge (1992), and then the underground Metro railway was completed, all the way from Tolleygunge to Dum Dum airport (1995). The two projects were respectively 18 and 7 years behind schedule, but their completion has greatly eased the pressure of human and motorized traffic on the roads.

By taxi and rickshaw: local transport in Calcutta is unlike any other Indian capital. Not only can you still find man-powered rickshaws alongside auto-rickshaws (though both are banned from the city centre and can only be found in quiet areas like New Market, Free School Street and Sudder Street), but taxis can still be hired off the street. They do have meters, but use them only reluctantly in tourist areas. The meters are out of date anyway, and even when you do find one that 'works' (they start at Rs6 and go up in Rs1 increments) there's a 50 per cent surcharge on the usual reading. If in doubt, ask the driver for his printed conversion sheet. If you're in a hurry, just bargain a price before boarding. And have your hotel card handy (with the address written on the back in Bengali)—a lot of taxi drivers don't understand English.

Hiring a car for the day will cost you around Rs500 and will cover you for up to 100km of travel.

By horse-drawn carriage: horse-drawn carriages or 'Victorias' are still available from a few places—notably outside the Victoria Memorial—and are a good (if expensive) way of touring around at leisure.

By Metro: the underground Metro is a very cheap and convenient mode of transport (trains every 15 minutes from 8am to 9.20pm; from 3pm to 9.20pm on Sunday), but do avoid peak-time traffic from 9 to 11am and 6 to 8pm—it's bedlam. Also, don't be a litterbug; the station is immaculately clean (a total contrast to the streets above) and if you drop a sweet-wrapper passengers will pounce on you and make you pick it up.

By bus: bus travel is to be avoided. Not only do passengers cling onto the sides of buses (regular Indian procedure), but passengers cling onto passengers clinging onto the sides of buses. If you do make it on board, stand near the door if you ever want to get off again. The same goes for the city's tired trams, which trundle hopelessly around town like survivors of a nuclear holocaust.

banks

The **State Bank of India** has a special branch for overseas visitors at Chowringhee Road and a 24-hour counter at the airport. Like **Thomas Cook** at 230 AJC Bose Road, ☎ 2474560, ✆ 2475854, and **American Express** at 21 Old Court House Street, ☎ 2484464, ✆ 2488096, it can change travellers' cheques.

bookshops

Calcutta is *the* place for bookshops. The better ones are in Park Street, and include **Oxford** and **Cambridge**. A good monthly publication, available from many street stalls along Park Street, is *Travel Links*. This gives full up-to-date information on trains, hotels and airlines—not just for Calcutta, but for Bombay, Delhi and Madras too.

The one book to read if you're in Calcutta is *City of Joy* by Dominique Lapierre. It's slow to start, but 50 pages in, you'll be hooked. If you don't find it (or Geoffrey Moorhouse's excellent *Calcutta*, published by Penguin) in Park Street, try **Wheeler's** bookshops at either Sealdah or Howrah station, or swap with another traveller.

The official book centre is College Street, opposite the university, though most of the tomes sold here are cram-course books aimed at wannabe businessmen.

consulates

Foreign consulates with addresses in Calcutta include the **UK**, 1 Ho Chi Minh Sarani (☎ 2425171); **France**, 26 Park Street, inside the courtyard to the right of Alliance Française (☎ 290978); **Germany**, 1 Hastings Park Road (☎ 4791141); **Italy**, 3 Raja Santosh Road (☎ 4792426); **Japan**, 12 Pretoria Street (☎ 242241); and the **USA**, 5/1 Ho Chi Minh Sarani (☎ 2423611).

The **Nepalese Embassy** at 19 Sterndale Road (☎ 4791003) is open 9.30am–12.30pm and 1.30–4.30pm, and issues visas on the spot. Visas for Thailand are best arranged through a cheap-flight agent (*see* below), since the embassy is hard to find.

For visas to Burma and Bangladesh, you'll have to go to Delhi or Kathmandu.

international airline offices

International airlines with offices in Calcutta include **Aeroflot**, 58 Chowringhee Road (☎ 2429831); **Air France**, 41 Chowringhee Road (☎ 290011); **Air India**, 50 Chowringhee Road (☎ 2422356); **Bangladesh Biman**, 1 Park Street (☎ 292844); **British Airways**, 41 Chowringhee Road (☎ 293453); **Cathay Pacific**, 1 Middleton Street (☎ 403211); **Japan Airlines**, 35A Chowringhee Road (☎ 298370); **KLM**, 1 Middleton Street (☎ 2474593); **Lufthansa**, 30A/B Chowringhee Road (☎ 299365); **Qantas**, Hotel Hindusthan International

(✆ 2470718); **Royal Nepal**, 41 Chowringhee Road (✆ 293949); **SAS**, 18G Park Street (✆ 747622); **Singapore Airlines**, 18G Park Street (✆ 299293); and **Swissair**, 46C Chowringhee Road (✆ 2424643).

For domestic airlines, *see* 'Moving On', p.379.

medical services

A good hospital, in case of medical emergency, is **Woodlands** in South Calcutta, near the zoo. It's run very much on Western lines and has standards to match.

A good doctor, recommended by several consulates, is **Dr Watt** in Short Street. To find him, take directions from US Travels in Stuart Lane.

post offices and telephones

The huge **GPO** is on BBD Bagh, ✆ 2203150. It has a *poste restante*, a 24-hour counter for stamps only, and a philatelic section for collectors. Most travellers use the more convenient post offices at New Market (near Sudder Street) and in Park Street (next to the Park Plaza). The latter has a good **parcel-packing service**. Over at the GOI tourist office, there's a popular **message/mail-receiving service**.

You can phone home from the **Central Telegraph Office** just down from the main GPO, or from various **STD booths** in the Sudder Street area. Rates are cheap from **Gossip** at 3 Sudder Street, especially between 7pm and 6am. Some countries now offer a collect-call service—dial ✆ 186 to enquire.

travel agents

For flight bookings and upmarket travel arrangements, use a recognized IATA travel agent like **Mercury Travels**, 46C Chowringhee Road, ✆ 2423555, or **Trade Wings**, 32 Chowringhee Road, ✆ 299531.

Cut-price air tickets are offered by various travel agents in and around Sudder Street. Try **US Travels**, ✆ 2451683 (open 9.30am–6.30pm) in Stuart Lane, opposite Modern Lodge. Run by the genial Mr Ghosh, it offers a wide range of services—free left-luggage facility, emergency phone use, passport-loss advice, tourist visas for Thailand, visa-extension advice for long-stay travellers wishing to study music and dance in Calcutta, and cheap one-way flights to Bangkok (from US$110), London (from £230), New York (from £670) and Sydney (from £475). Return flights are an even better deal. If paying in rupees, you don't need an encashment certificate.

visa extensions

The **Foreigners' Registration Office** at 237 AJC Bose Road, ✆ 2473301, handles visa extensions and permits. For quick service, turn up at 9.30am (any weekday), armed with your passport and four photographs.

The Government of India tourist office, ✆ 2421402, is at 4 Shakespeare Sarani, ✆ 2421402, open 9am to 6pm weekdays, till 1pm on Saturday. It has helpful staff, good handout information and a useful mail-receiving facility. Get computerized printouts for all places on your itinerary here, and ask for a 'Calcutta This Fortnight' handout, full of upcoming cultural events. Also come here to book government-approved guides (Rs200 per day) and city tours (dep 7.30am and 8.30am daily, except Monday). The new Darjeeling counter (information and hotel bookings) makes unnecessary a separate visit to the **West Bengal tourist office**, ✆ 2488271, at 3/2 BBD Bagh—unless, that is, you want to book one of their 2/3 day trips to Sunderbans Wildlife Sanctury (October to March only). Sunderbans has around 300 tigers, who eat an estimated 30 people each year, but you'll be lucky to see one. To get a permit, go to the Writers' Building (*see* Tour 2 below).

Permits for Darjeeling, Sikkim and Assam are no longer required; both the above tourist offices have desks at the airport, and West Bengal at Howrah station.

Touring Calcutta

Calcutta's unique traffic situation is perhaps the main 'sight' of the city—a vast, heaving bedlam of horn-crazy cars, brightly painted lorries, double-decker buses, bullock carts, commuters and trolley buses. The combined impact of all this noise, dust, crowds and traffic is enough to put many sightseers off altogether. Persistence is the key. Expect to spend three times longer getting anything done as elsewhere in India, and start out slowly. Spend your first day getting your bearings and then, if you don't have time to cover the sights at leisure, brace yourself for a full-day conducted bus tour. They're not up to much: the guide's talk is drowned out by traffic, too much time is spent in the bus, too little at interesting places, but at least you'll get out and about a bit, and certain sights, notably Howrah, really are best experienced from a bus window.

Tour 1: City Sights

By tour bus, full day. Howrah Bridge–Botanical Gardens–Belur Math–
Ramakrishna Temple–Dakshineshwar–Kali Temple–Parasnath–Jain Temple–
Indian Museum–Nehru Children's Museum–Victoria Memorial–Zoo.

Don't do this tour on a Monday—the best thing on it, the Indian Museum (and Victoria Memorial), is closed. As the order of sights covered by tours is not fixed, don't be surprised if you see things back to front.

More often than not, the tour bus leaves the bus terminal in the city centre via the **High Court** building (1872) and the oldest Catholic church in Calcutta, **St Mary's**. A half-hour later, it comes to the single-span cantilevered **Howrah Bridge** (built 1943) and promptly grinds to a halt. Over a million people cross this bridge daily, and you have to wait your turn. Originally a marshy swampland (the origin of its name), Howrah is now Calcutta's most congested area. A tidal wave of human and motorized traffic washes over and around the bus, and if this doesn't tell you what Calcutta's about, nothing will.

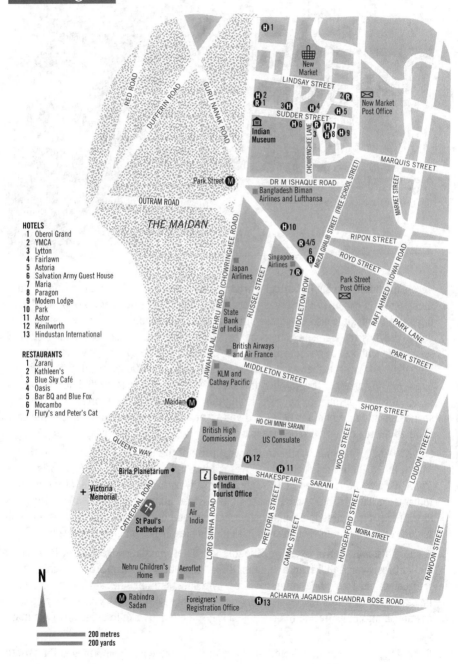

Chowringhee

HOTELS
1 Oberoi Grand
2 YMCA
3 Lytton
4 Fairlawn
5 Astoria
6 Salvation Army Guest House
7 Maria
8 Paragon
9 Modem Lodge
10 Park
11 Astor
12 Kenilworth
13 Hindustan International

RESTAURANTS
1 Zaranj
2 Kathleen's
3 Blue Sky Café
4 Oasis
5 Bar BQ and Blue Fox
6 Mocambo
7 Flury's and Peter's Cat

New Market
LINDSAY STREET
New Market Post Office
SUDDER STREET
CHOWRINGHEE LANE
Indian Museum
MARQUIS STREET
MARKET STREET
Park Street
DR M ISHAQUE ROAD
OUTRAM ROAD
Bangladesh Biman Airlines and Lufthansa
THE MAIDAN
RIPON STREET
MIRZA GHALIB STREET (FREE SCHOOL STREET)
Singapore Airlines
ROYD STREET
RAFI AHMED KIDWAI ROAD
Park Street Post Office
JAWAHARLAL NEHRU ROAD (CHOWRINGHEE ROAD)
RUSSEL STREET
Japan Airlines
MIDDLETON ROW
PARK LANE
State Bank of India
British Airways and Air France
PARK STREET
MIDDLETON STREET
KLM and Cathay Pacific
SHORT STREET
Maidan
HO CHI MINH SARANI
WOOD STREET
LOUDON STREET
British High Commission
US Consulate
QUEEN'S WAY
Birla Planetarium
Government of India Tourist Office
SHAKESPEARE SARANI
Victoria Memorial
CATHEDRAL ROAD
St Paul's Cathedral
Air India
LORD SINHA ROAD
PRETORIA STREET
CAMAC STREET
HUNGERFORD STREET
MOIRA STREET
RAWDON STREET
Nehru Children's Home
Aeroflot
Rabindra Sadan
Foreigners' Registration Office
ACHARYA JAGADISH CHANDRA BOSE ROAD

N

200 metres
200 yards

Great Banyan
Shivpur Calcutta

Across the bridge are the **Botanical Gardens**. The largest and oldest of their kind in India, they were laid out in 1787. Spread over 270 acres and housing over 30,000 varieties of trees and plants, it is also Calcutta's principal lung. The gardens are famous as the place where Assam's and Darjeeling's famous teas were first developed, and are home to several species of bamboos, palms, succulents and exotic plants gathered from five continents. But their main attraction is the world's largest banyan tree, over 200 years old, with a circumference of 417 metres. The 'mother' tree died from fungal decay in 1925, but the 2000 or so aerial roots continue to flourish, giving the tree the aspect of a forest. The tour bus spends exactly four minutes here, so if you want a closer look you'll have to come back another day (take a ferry from Chandpal or Babu ghats—quick and cheap).

Some 10km further north, still on the west bank of the Hooghly, you'll come to **Belur Math**, the headquarters of the Ramakrishna Mission (*open daily 6.30–11am and 3.30–7pm*). This was established in 1898 by Swami Vivekananda, in memory of the popular Indian sage Ramakrishna, who preached the essential unity of all religions. Reflecting this ideal, the **temple** here looks like a church, a mosque or a Hindu temple, depending on where you view it from. The mission itself is a medical help centre for the poor.

A short distance north, over the Hooghly via Vivekananda Bridge, a visit is made to **Dakshineshwar Kali Temple** (built in 1847), the place where Ramakrishna achieved his spiritual vision. Tour guides impress visitors by telling them that the saint's name has been invoked here continuously for 20 years. The great appeal of Ramakrishna's religion is its cosmopolitanism, its free and liberal tolerance, something which free-thinking Calcuttans can readily identify with.

Returning south, some 3km from the city centre, the tour ends the morning at **Parasnath Jain Temple**, arguably the most interesting temple in all Calcutta (*open daily 6am–noon* *and 3–7pm*). Built in 1867 and dedicated to Sitalnathji, 10th of the 24 Jain *tirthankars* (prophets), this exquisite structure overlooks beautiful gardens and houses an elaborate blend of glass mosaics, mirror-inlay pillars, and stained-glass windows. Primary features are the gilded dome ceiling, floral-design marble flooring from Japan, and ornate chandeliers from Brussels and Paris. It's unusually flamboyant for a Jain temple.

In the afternoon you'll see the **Indian Museum**, at the junction of Sudder Street and Chowringhee (*open daily exc Mon Mar–Nov, 10am–5pm; Dec–Feb 10am–4.30pm; adm Rs1, free on Fri*). Built in the Italian style of architecture (1875), this is the largest museum in India with one of the finest collections in Asia. Wandering around the dusty mothballed halls, look out for the following highlights: the immense **Bharhut Stupa**, depicting the 500 incarnations of Buddha prior to his enlightenment (archaeology department); two giant prehistoric skeletons, a double-coconut tree which blossoms once a century, and a preserved goat with eight legs and four ears (anthropology); a whole roomful of meteorites (geology); and an excellent display of miniature paintings (top floor). The whole place is dim and dusty with age, but this somehow adds to its appeal.

The **Nehru Children's Museum** at the bottom of Jawaharlal Nehru Road (*open daily exc Mon 11.30am–8.30pm; adm Rs2, or Rs10 for shows*), is a novelty stop with an over-rated scale model of Amritsar's Golden Temple and various electronic/scientific games. Its big attraction are the 1500 miniature models depicting India's longest epic poem, the *Ramayana*. This tells the story of King Rama who defeated the many-headed demon king of Lanka, Ravana, to retrieve his abducted wife Sita.

Next stop is the majestic **Victoria Memorial**, picture-postcard symbol of Calcutta (*open daily exc Mon Nov–Feb, 10am–3.30pm; Mar–Oct 10am–4.30pm*). Built between 1906 and 1921 at a cost of 7.5 million rupees, this gleaming white marble palace stands at the southern end of the Maidan, a living reminder of the might of British India. Often compared to the Taj Mahal, with its four rudimentary minarets, gleaming white dome and exterior of solid Makrana marble, it was conceived by Lord Curzon both as a tribute to Queen Victoria and a triumphant depiction of her reign in India. Playing on Henry James' lament on hearing of the Queen's death—'We all feel a bit motherless today'—Curzon appealed to popular sentiment and raised the money for this fabulous reliquary entirely from voluntary subscriptions. Fully reflecting the pomp of empire, the Empress of India sits at the entrance flight of marble stairs, enthroned in bronze, clad in the regal robes of the Order of the Star of India. Further symbol of her greatness is provided by the 49m bronze Angel of Victory, spreading its wings skyward, high atop the central dome.

Inside is the finest collection of Raj memorabilia anywhere under one roof. The Royal Gallery on the first floor has paintings of all major events in Victoria's life: her coronation, marriage to Albert, the christening of son Edward VII, celebrations of golden and diamond jubilees. Also, the museum's pride, the rosewood baby-grand piano on which the young princess played, together with her personal writing-desk and embroidered armchair. The largest painting in the gallery, indeed the largest oil painting in India, is the work of the Russian artist Vassily Verestchagin, and depicts all the pageantry of the Prince of Wales' (the future Edward VII's) visit to Jaipur in 1876. Nearby, in the portrait gallery, you'll find

Calcutta

a rare collection of ancient Persian manuscripts, including illuminated writings owned by the 'Tiger of Mysore', Tipu Sultan. The walls of the gallery are lined with pictures of key figures in the development of British India, including a pensive-looking Robert Clive, General Stringer Lawrence (father of the Indian army) and the Duke of Wellington. The adjoining gallery has an arms and armour collection dating back to the times of medieval Indian combat.

Beyond Robert Clive's cannon-fronted statue you'll find the Memorial's focal point, the magnificent **Queen's Hall**, with its graceful figure of the newly crowned girl queen. This is overlooked by 12 large frescoes depicting major events in her long life. Back on the entrance balcony, you can enjoy fine views out onto the Maidan.

It's worth returning to the memorial in the evening for the excellent *son et lumière* show. The English version starts at 8.15pm (daily except Monday) and admission is Rs5 or Rs10.

If you want to spend more time at the Victoria, leave the tour here. Otherwise, follow it on to the **Zoological Gardens** south of the Maidan (*open sunrise–sunset; adm Rs1*). The zoo is a depressing one, full of animals living in prison conditions, but is well placed for a relaxing sunset stroll around the **Maidan**. This large area of not-so-green parkland was cleared from the jungle around the old **Fort St William** to allow cannon an unobstructed line of fire. Today it is a popular early-morning yoga spot for city-dwellers heading into another day of urban stress. The only time it comes alive is during the **Dharamtolla ka Mela** fair on Sundays. This takes place near the **Ochterlony Monument**, and features all sorts of weird and wonderful entertainments.

Tour 2: Sights Round-up

Full day. St John's Church–Writers' Building–Birla Planetarium–St Paul's Cathedral–Kalighat Temple–Mother Teresa's Mission–Birla Academy of Art.

For day two, see a number of places that should be covered by tours but aren't. Start early (to miss the crowds) with a cool promenade across elegant BBD Bagh (opposite the West Bengal Tourist Office, north of Maidan). At the back of the square, walk ten minutes left down Council House Street to find **St John's Church**, modelled on London's St Martin-in-the-Fields. Built in 1784, this old stone church served as a temporary cathedral (1814–47) until St Paul's Cathedral was completed. Inside you'll see Zoffany's painting of the Last Supper and some charming wicker seats overlooked by marble memorials to imperial servants. Outside in the graveyard (Calcutta's first burial site) there's the octagonal mausoleum of the city's founder, Job Charnock, and the tomb of Admiral Charles Watson, who helped Clive retake Calcutta from the Murshidabad Nawab.

Twenty minutes' walk back up to, and just beyond, the rear of BBD Bagh you'll find the **Writers' Building**. This is where foreigners come for a **Sunderbans Tiger Reserve permit** (G Block, 6th floor, bring passport) or simply for some entertainment. Marvel here at the rows and rows of tables, piled high with files, with a small space cleared by each occupant for his newspaper and his cup of tea. As one visitor remarked: 'It was classic India. I went for a Sunderbans permit and was told to apply to the 'rosy-coloured boy' upstairs. This turned out to be a middle-aged man wearing a rose-coloured shirt. He was sitting at his table, snowed under by papers, staring up at the ceiling in a mystic trance. So was everybody else. The building was full of people doing absolutely nothing, or just reading newspapers.'

If you're lucky, you'll reach the **Birla Planetarium,** just below Victoria Memorial, just in time for one of its daily English-speaking shows. Your best chance is a Sunday, when there are three shows (presently 10.45am, 3.30pm and 6.30pm), but timings vary so it's a case of pot luck. In any case, this is the one of the largest planetaria in the world, and Rs8 buys you a cool air-conditioned escape from the heat outside.

Before or after this star-gazing show, drop in on **St Paul's Cathedral** (*open 9am–noon and 3–6pm*), two minutes' walk down the main road. Built between 1839 and 1847, this distinguished Gothic structure is the oldest Church of England cathedral of the British Empire. It is notable for its striking murals and frescoes, stained-glass windows, and coloured altar reredos.

From here, it's a rickshaw/taxi ride south to the notorious **Kalighat Temple**. Dedicated to the 'black goddess' Kali or Kalika (another possible origin of Calcutta's name), and considered the chief Kali temple in India, the present structure is an 1809 version of an

Volunteers wishing to work for Mother Teresa are generally encouraged to come between September and March, when it's not too hot. If you write from London, you'll receive a letter back telling you when to go. Otherwise, simply turn up at the Missionaries of Charity's House, 54A AJC Bose Road (ex-Lower Circular Road) to be employed on the spot. Mother Teresa generally sees visitors from 8.30 to 11.30am and from 3.30 to 5.30pm daily, though this depends on how busy her schedule is. It's a good idea to phone ahead (© 2447115) to see if she is in town or not. If she isn't, and you're here to offer your services somewhere, contact Dr Jack's clinic in Middleton Road. He helps mainly the poor and the homeless, and receives visitors/helpers from 8am onwards daily.

early 17th-century original. The gruesome legend attached to it is that Vishnu chopped up the body of Shiva's wife Devi, and one of her severed toes fell here. Today, because Kali demands daily sacrifices, it's goats and sheep who get the chop—bloody sacrifices taking place in the courtyard used for local cricket. Don't come here if you're squeamish—even Gandhi couldn't take it—but do go next door to **Mother Teresa's Hospital for the Dying Destitutes** (*visitors welcome early morning or 4–6pm*). The caring, unstinting help extended by this iron-willed yet gentle champion of the sick, poor and dying has provoked worldwide admiration. A short visit to see the results of her work is always rewarding.

Mother Teresa

To finish off, take a quick taxi over to the **Birla Academy of Art** at 109 Southern Avenue (*open daily exc Mon 4–8pm; adm Rs1*). It has fine sculpture and contemporary art sections. The Indian Society of Oriental Art and other cultural bodies run regular exhibitions here, all the paintings being well lit, catalogued and presented.

Shopping

Calcutta hasn't the choice or variety of goods found in Delhi or Bombay, but if you're looking for silk and saris, there's a wide choice—and excellent value for money—at the **Central Cottage Industries Emporium** at 7 Chowringhee Road, just up from the Oberoi Hotel. For fabrics, home furnishings and pottery, go to the **West Bengal Government Emporium** at 7 Lindsay Street. Actually, both emporia do just about everything, but they're closed on Saturday and Sunday afternoons.

Everyone in India wears real gold jewellery—22 carat if they can afford it, 18 carat if they can't—and while it costs more than in the West the quality is very high. There are some spectacular pieces, with and without stones, to be found at **P C Chandra**, 83 Chowringhee Road, and traditional Bengali jewellery (and modern styles) at **A Sarkar**, 171/1 Rash Behari Avenue, south of Park Street. Both places are supposedly fixed-price, but there is some leeway for bargaining.

For semi-precious jewellery with garnets, turquoise, lapis lazuli etc., go to **New Market** (closed Sunday) behind the Oberoi Hotel. Here you can get anything from a 50-paise pin to a 5000-rupee sari, and (in amongst all the meat and vegetables) there are lots of bargains to be found. Many stalls here sell the same things, so take time to compare prices before buying anything. The idea is, you hire a red-coated porter at the entrance for a few rupees (don't give him more) and he follows you round the market putting all your purchases in a basket on his head. It's Calcutta's answer to a Safeway's trolley.

Avoid street touts offering you cheap bargains 'just around the corner'. You'll often walk miles for no result.

Leisure

Calcutta is *the* place for **clubs**—there are around 15 major clubs in town, and 'everybody who is anybody' *must* be in one of them from Saturday afternoon through to Sunday. Entrance is always restricted to members, but at clubs like the **Tolleygunge**, 120 Deshpran Sashmal Road, ✆ 4732361, you can go across to the office and get a temporary membership, which varies from ten days to three months. The Tolleygunge is an ideal club, because it has a nice blend of everything—golf, tennis, squash, swimming, riding and billiards. It's best at weekends (dead during the week) and is run by Bob Wright, who is something of a legend in his own lifetime. If you know Bob, doors open all over town.

The same goes if you're a Western woman and even remotely attractive. All you have to do is sit on the verandah outside the Fairlawn Hotel (or the Lytton Hotel bar) and wait for some local playboy to pick you up and whisk you off to club-land.

Swimming at the pools of the bigger hotels is at the discretion of the management. Dress smartly and expect to pay a daily charge. Currently, your best bet is the Hindusthan International Hotel, which asks Rs150 per day. Otherwise, apply for temporary membership at the **Tolleygunge Club** (above), the **Saturday Club**, 7 Wood Street, ✆ 2475411, or the **Calcutta Swimming Club**, 1 Strand Road, ✆ 2482894—all three have decent pools and accept foreign visitors. The Saturday Club is a very homely place, with a good restaurant/bar and lots of facilities.

Discos are restricted to the larger European-style hotels, and you need to be a resident, a member, or invited by either, to get in. If you're staying at a good hotel like the Oberoi and want to hook into another hotel's nightspot, the hospitality lady will generally introduce you over the phone. Right now, the top disco is Taj's **Incognito** with a spacious dancefloor and great, if booming, acoustics. Hindusthan Hotel's **Anti Clock** is another goodie—mainly for the young set—and then there's Park Hotel's **Some Place Else**, which is more like a pub really, with a tiny dancefloor and fun atmosphere. It's the only place in town you can get draught beer and is best at weekends. Entrance is free before 9pm.

Set aside at least one evening to enjoy Calcutta's rich heritage of **music, dance and theatre**. Two good intros to classical dance are the 'Dances of India' show, held next door to the tourist office (6.30pm start, weekdays only) and the similar show at Hindusthan Hotel's Kailash restaurant (starts 5pm daily). Photography is allowed, so bring your camera. The principal culture halls—for professional music and dance programmes—are at **Rabindra Sadan** and **Academy of Fine Arts**, both in Cathedral Road. For full details, pick up a copy of *Calcutta This Fortnight* from the tourist office or buy a *Statesman* or *Sunday Telegraph*. Both papers also carry full **cinema** listings—the Lighthouse, the Globe and the New Empire all show English-speaking films.

Vina: classical instrument

A favourite leisure activity of Calcuttan ladies, as well as Western women who want to pamper themselves, is a complete make-over at Oberoi Hotel's **Silhouette beauty parlour**. Here you can get everything—manicure, pedicure, haircut, waxing, and a full facial—for under £25. If this is beyond your budget, try cheaper parlours like **Sunflower** on Russell Street or **Cecilia's** on Free School Street.

Calcutta ✆ (033–)   **Where to Stay**

As in Delhi and Bombay, rooms are expensive and getting more so all the time. If you're on budget, you'll need to listen hard to the travellers' grapevine; if not, you're still wise to advance-book your accommodation (especially in high season) to be sure of a room. Calcutta has relatively few good hotels in the upper bracket, and they're often full with VIPs and business people. The best deals are during the April–September hot season, when many places offer generous discounts. Prices quoted below do not include taxes.

luxury (from US$195)

There are only two hotels which merit a 5-star luxury rating. If you want to stay in the heart of the city, there's the **Oberoi Grand**, ✆ 2492323, ✉ 2491217, at 15 Chowringhee Road. If you don't, there's the **Taj Bengal**, ✆ 2483939, ✉ 2481766, in the quiet and green residential area of Alipore. Neither place is cheap, especially when 22.5% taxes are taken into account, but they're both aiming at the VIP/corporate market, not the leisure traveller. The Grand still scores high for style and food (ask for a room overlooking the palm-fringed pool), but it's the Taj that has the better service and facilities—bigger, brighter rooms too.

deluxe (from US$130)

The revamped **Park Hotel**, ✆ 2493121, ✉ 2497343, at 17 Park Street is a smart and friendly place, with lots of facilities, including a pool and a popular bar-cum-disco. It is highly recommended. Rather less so is the **Hotel Hindusthan International**, ✆ 2472394, ✉ 2472824, with a good pool and disco, but variable service and overpriced rooms; request one away from the noisy main road.

expensive (from US$40)

Hard to find, but worth it, is the newly renovated **Peerless Inn**, ✆ 2430301, ✉ 2486650, at 12 Chowringhee Road, just down from the Oberoi. This is a 4-star property with 3-star rates—only Rs1350 for a single, Rs1750 for a double, and Rs2300 (US$65) for a suite. No pool, but the service and facilities are fine, and with rooms so cheap (and only a notch down from the Oberoi's) it's my hot tip for the best value in town. Book ahead though; it's often full.

The old-style **Kenilworth Hotel**, ✆ 2428394, ✉ 2425136, at 1/2 Little Russell Street has more atmosphere and a popular barbecue restaurant and open-air coffee shop. The rooms need new carpets but are otherwise spotless and good value at US$60/70.

In the same price range is ITDC's **Airport Ashok**, ✆ 5529111, ✉ 5529137, outside the airport (*see* p.362).

moderate (from US$30)

The **Lytton Hotel**, ✆ 2491872, ✉ 2491747, at 14 Sudder Street is a real favourite with Westerners. The staff go out of their way to be helpful and the rooms are clean and comfortable—very attractively priced too, from Rs1000/1400, breakfast included.

The **Astor Hotel**, ✆ 2429957, at 15 Shakespeare Sarani has a peaceful location and is also well priced, from Rs750/950 (air-cooled). This is another older property, with lots of character and extremely cosy rooms. Even if you don't stay here, come for the pleasant sit-out restaurant (cum kebab house) and serenading musicians.

Rather overpriced, but worth the experience, is the time-warp **Fairlawn Hotel**, ✆ 2451510, ✉ 2441835, at 13A Sudder Street. This is a real period piece, with Noël Coward furnishings, ostentatious lounges, and a wonderfully eccentric manageress (Mrs Smith). Air-cooled rooms cost US$35/45 (ask for a double) and the tariff includes all meals. Things to savour are the pseudo-Western menus (fish fingers for starters?), the po-faced waiters in cummerbunds and turbans (amusingly rude) and the twinkling fairy-lights (put up one Xmas, never taken down again) which go off only when the gong sounds for dinner. Travellers are fascinated, and collect each evening to play out their parts in a kind of weird Raj-style soap opera.

Rather less strange is the central and convenient **Astoria**, ✆ 2449679, at 6/2 Sudder Street (facing onto Stuart Lane) with large, clean air-cooled rooms (TV/bath) at Rs550 single, Rs690 double. The **VIP Guest House** in Free School Street has so-so rooms at around Rs500, but you'll need earplugs.

The most popular cheapies—**Paragon**, ✆ 2442445, and **Modern Lodge**, ✆ 2444960—are at nos. 1 and 2 Stuart Lane, off Sudder Street, and are reserved exclusively for foreign tourists. Both have rooms around Rs100/150, dorm beds around Rs50, and differ only in that the Paragon has a relaxing rooftop section (good for snacks and meeting people) and Modern Lodge has a much better dormitory. When these places are full—as they often are—shoe-stringers flop at the nearby **Maria**, ✆ 2450860, or **Salvation Army**, ✆ 2450599, guest houses until a room comes free. Two other choices are the clean **YMCA**, ✆ 2492192, at 25 Chowringhee Road (Rs250/300, breakfast included) and the nearby **Lindsay Guest House**, where you have to walk up seven flights of stairs when the lift isn't working. There are several other places; just ask around.

Calcutta ✆ (033–)　　　　　　　　　　　　　　　　　　**Eating Out**

Calcuttans tend to eat out a lot, so there's a great choice of restaurants in the capital—especially Chinese ones. This is because many Chinese escaped here after the Revolution and never went home. There's a major Chinatown on the outskirts of the city called Tangra and—if you can ignore the smell from the local tanneries—this is *the* place to sample cheap and authentic Cantonese dishes. Take a rickshaw to South Tangra Street, off the East Metropolitan bypass, and choose from 20 or so soup kitchens. They vary in quality, but since most of them are basic and unclean you're advised to do as the Calcuttans do, and bring your own cutlery, glasses and drinks.

In the hotels, Oberoi's **Ming Court** is reputed to have the best Szechwan food in Asia, though it can be a bit hot for Western palates. Other recommended places, like the **Zen** at Park Hotel, the **Dynasty** at Lytton Hotel, and the **Chinoisserie** at Taj, are less spicy but the Chinese dishes are often Indianized and lacking in true oriental flavour.

When it comes to continental fare, Oberoi's **Rotisserie** is in a class of its own. This is a very stylish place—though ministers and VIP's do rub shoulders with local Indian families—and there's good live jazz music every evening. Famous for grills and steaks, as well as for seafood, it opens at 7.30pm and is often packed out within minutes. If you can't get in here, try the adjoining **Brasserie** which also offers air-conditioned buffet breakfasts (Rs150) with free newspapers. Over at the Taj, there's the 5th-floor **Chambers**, serving the best French food in town, and the 24-hr **Esplanade** coffee shop, offering good-value breakfast and lunchtime buffets for Rs125 and Rs195 respectively. Finally, there's Park Hotel's **Some Place Else** pub where you can enjoy Western snacks (lunchtimes only) like fish and chips, chicken in a basket, and steak and kidney pie. It's a very cosy informal place and everything—including beers and cocktails—is very reasonably priced.

The city's premier Indian restaurant is Taj's **Sonargoan**, which specializes in Northwest Frontier cuisine. It has pleasant village-style ambience, unsurpassed service and quality of food, and is *the* place to go for that special occasion. Only a notch down, **Zaranj**, ✆ 2499744, at 26 Chowringhee Road is very strong on North Peshwari dishes—mainly lamb, chicken and fish—and is definitely one to advance-book. Oberoi's **Mewar** is due to open soon, and will be offering top-drawer Rajasthani cuisine (plus tandoori items) in a typical 'royal Rajasthani' setting.

Park Street is 'food street', full of restaurants and bars. You can get good Chinese at **Blue Fox** or **Bar B-Q**, Indian food and 'sizzler' dishes at **Peter Cat**, vegetarian fare at **Kwality**, cakes and pastries at **Flury's** and multi-cuisine at **Oasis** and **Mocambo's**. The **Olympia** is shady and run-down, but it does have the best pepper steaks in Calcutta. On a Saturday afternoon all the 'bright lights' in the city converge here for a meal—it's a tradition.

Cheap travellers' fare is widely available from many places in and around Sudder Street. Current favourites are **Blue Sky Café**, **Curd Corner** and **Jo-Jo's**. **Kathleen's** now has an upstairs air-con bar/restaurant in addition to the bakery/confectionery at the entrance. **Kastury** on Free School Street is a good cheap Indian restaurant with a name for seafood.

For evening drinks and cocktails, try the stylish **Chowringhee bar** at the Oberoi or **The Junction** at the Taj. Park Street has a lot of good bars too, but you needn't go there for a drink. Calcutta is the only city in India (with the possible exception of Bangalore) where alcohol is freely available—even from streetside drugstores.

There's a surprising shortage of restaurants offering typical Bengali cuisine. **Suruchi's** at 89 Elliot Road is still good for it (especially fish dishes like smoked *hilsa* and cheap *thalis*), but the new **Aaheli** inside the Peerless Inn hotel does the same stuff better. For Bengali sweets, try **Ganguram's** at 46C Chowringhee Road or **K C Das** at the junction of Esplanade and Chowringhee Road. Specialities include milk and curd-based *rosogolla*, *mishti doi*, *indrani* and *sandesh*, all made to melt in your mouth.

Moving On
by air

From Calcutta, **Indian Airlines**, ✆ 269810, flies daily to Bangalore, Bhubaneshwar, Bombay, Delhi and Madras, and less frequently to Hyderabad (6 days a week), Bangkok and Kathmandu (4), Bagdogra for Darjeeling, Patna for

Bodhgaya, and Varanasi (3). There are daily flights on **Damania-Skyline NEPC**, ✆ 4759652, to Bagdogra, Bangalore, Bombay, Goa and Madras, on **Jet Airways**, ✆ 408192, to Bangalore, Bombay and Hyderabad, and on **Modiluft**, ✆ 299864, to Bombay and Goa. Modiluft also lays on 4 flights a week to Agra and Khajuraho, and 3 to Ahmedabad. **Sahara India**, ✆ 2472795, flies 4 times a week to Delhi and Goa; **NEPC Airlines** twice weekly to Bhubaneshwar, Patna and Varanasi.

by rail

Calcutta's two busy rail stations are **Sealdah** (east of the Hooghly river) which services Darjeeling, and **Howrah** (just across the Howrah bridge) which covers nearly everywhere else. Fast trains out of Howrah include the 2860 Gitanjali Express to Bombay VT (dep 12.30pm, 33hrs), the 2305 Rajdhani Express to Delhi (dep 1.45pm, 18hrs, air-con only), the 2841 Coromandel Express to Madras (dep 2.10pm, 27hrs), the 2303/2381 Poorva Express to Patna/Varanasi (dep 9.15am, 8/11hrs), and the 8007 Puri Express to Bhubaneshwar/Puri (dep 10.15pm, 7/10hrs). The 6322 Guwahati–Trivandrum Express leaves Howrah at 10.35pm and draws into Trivandrum exactly 24 hours later. The overnight 3142 Darjeeling Mail leaves Sealdah station (*not* Howrah!) at 7.15pm and travels up to New Jaipalguri in just under 12 hours.

For up-to-date train timings, buy a copy of *Trains at a Glance* from a Park Street bookstall. Rail reservations are now computerized, and you can book tickets anywhere (and any class) from the tourist railway booking office on the 1st floor at 6 Fairlee Place, close to BBD Bagh. It's open 9am to 1pm and 1.30pm to 4pm (till 2pm only on Sunday) and you should arrive early to avoid queues. Bring exchange certificates if you intend paying in rupees. To tap into the tourist quota (bring your passport) ask for the railway tourist guide—he's there from 10am to 5pm every weekday.

Warning: A lot of tourists 'lose' their baggage at Howrah station and on trains going to Puri and Varanasi. Be especially wary of people wanting to be your 'friends', and keep an eye on your bags at all times.

by bus

Few travellers go anywhere from Calcutta by bus; trains are far quicker and more comfortable. Don't take buses to Puri (full of vomiting villagers) or to New Jaipalguri (real kidney-shufflers). Most buses leave from the Interstate Bus Stand at the top end of the Maidan, where you'll also find most of the private bus companies. The terminus is impossibly congested though, and finding the bus you want a major achievement. To be sure of a seat, book at least 2 days in advance.

Orissa is not just cheap, but full of attractions—a majestic temple city at Bhubaneshwar, a funky seaside beach resort at Puri, and an unparalleled Sun Temple, the finest achievement of medieval Orissan sculptors, at Konark. Here you can truly be at peace with India, with beautiful country scenery all around and no touts or map-sellers to disturb your mood. Even better, unlike more fêted monuments like the Taj Mahal, hardly any of Orissa's myriad temples have been defiled by local vandals or diminished in stature by ugly graffiti.

But the mystery remains: why does this fantastic 'Eastern Triangle' get only 5 per cent of foreign tourist business, when the far more expensive, crowded and polluted 'Golden Triangle' of Delhi, Jaipur and Agra grabs a massive 50 per cent? One reason must be that Western travel companies—in the absence of direct charter flights to the state—relegate Orissa to the back page of their holiday brochures. Second, the Indian tourist board treat it as some kind of poor relative with no potential other than as a power supply for the rest of east India. Third, most first-time visitors to India are so distracted by the convenience of Delhi as an arrival point and so drawn by the irresistible lure of the Taj Mahal in Agra that the thought of flying on to Orissa just doesn't occur to them. This is fair enough, but if you're a second-timer to the country, or have a spare week this time round, you really shouldn't miss it.

Orissa is a very rich state as far as natural resources are concerned. Geologists and mineralogists—foreign and domestic—flock here in search of oil, coal and semi-precious stones. Five years ago, when the present government came into power, it decided that, in order to survive, it had to open up the whole country to foreign investment. At this point, it realized that a lot of commercial sectors had to be developed—particularly coal, steel and electricity—and that it had to attract corporate, as opposed to leisure, travellers. As a consequence of this, there's been a rapid development of infrastructure aimed at the new influx of business visitors, and prices have been pegged at a deliberately low level. In Bhubaneshwar, for example, you can still stay at the best hotel in town (the 5-star Oberoi) for £40 a day—less than a third of what it would cost you at a corresponding hotel in Bombay or Delhi.

Itinerary

Orissa tags on nicely to Calcutta, though more and more budget travellers are coming up from the south. They hop on a train from Madras/Hyderabad to Puri, spend a few days at the beach, do the obligatory temple trips at Konark and Bhubaneshwar, and continue on to Calcutta by train. On this basis, one could happily spend up to two weeks in Orissa. If you're watching the clock, however, you may only have time for a short 'taster' tour—a flight from Calcutta, 2 days in Bhubaneshwar, a 1-day bus tour to Puri/Konark, and out again by air. As a swift 4-day package, the route works best with a US$500 'Discover India' flight ticket via Indian Airlines (*see* p.12). This could get you three-quarters of the way round the country—from Bombay to Goa, Bangalore, Madras, Hyderabad, Bhubaneshwar, Calcutta and Delhi—in just 21 days. It's a very good deal.

Climate-wise, the best time to visit Orissa is between October and mid-March. After this it's too hot and, from July to September, too wet. Temperatures range from 27° to 49°C in summer, and from 5° to 16°C in winter.

Bhubaneshwar
population 450,000

Capital of Orissa, Bhubaneshwar is popularly known as the Temple City of India. At one time, some 7000 sandstone temples are supposed to have stood on the site of the sacred Bindu Sagar Lake alone. Most of them were built between the 7th and 15th centuries, when Oriyan Hindu culture reached its zenith. Temple building began as a status activity of the wealthy, and was carried on with vigour by ensuing kings and rulers. But then came the Mughal conquest of the 16th century, and all but 500 or so of these distinctive beehive-shaped temples were destroyed. Today, there remain only 100 'living' temples (shrines where the gods' lifeforce is maintained by regular devotions), and only a small group of 30 of these can be said to be well preserved. Despite the ravages of time, these few noble survivors testify to the glory of an ancient civilization that in terms of art and culture was perhaps the finest that India ever produced.

In ancient times, Orissa formed part of the powerful kingdom of Kalinga. At that time, Bhubaneshwar was known as Ekamrakshetra and was one of five religious centres in the state. It became a major place of pilgrimage and was considered a favourite resort of Lord Shiva—just as holy as his first preference, Varanasi. Here at Bhubaneshwar, Shiva was, and still is, worshipped as Tribhuvaneshwara (Lord of the Three Worlds) or Lord Lingaraj, and from this title the city derives its name.

At the peak of their power, the Kalinga kings suddenly came into head-on collision with Ashoka, the powerful Mauryan emperor. Around 260 BC, Ashoka dealt them such a crushing blow that, appalled by the carnage he had caused, he turned his back on violence forever and embraced the Buddhist faith of peace and compassion. To mark this event, he left many sets of rock edicts; including one at Dhauli, 8km south of Bhubaneshwar.

Buddhism quickly faded and, under the rule of Kharavela (the third Chedi king), Jainism was restored as the faith of the people. It was during his reign that the twin hills of Udayagiri and Khandagiri, west of Bhubaneshwar, became important Jain centres and the famous caves were created.

Under successive 8th-century kings, the temple for Lord Jagannath was built at Puri. In the 9th century, the worship of Shiva (Shaivism) replaced Jainism and many temples were erected at Bhubaneshwar. The cult of Surya, the Sun God, became strong in the 13th century, resulting in the creation of the famous temple at Konark.

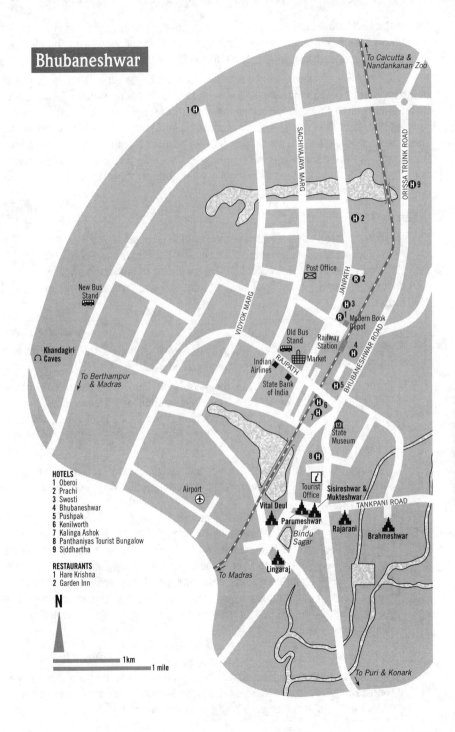

Bhubaneshwar

To Calcutta &
Nandankanan Zoo

SACHIVAJAYA MARG

ORISSA TRUNK ROAD

JANPATH

VIDYOK MARG

New Bus
Stand

Post Office

Khandagiri
Ω Caves

To Berthampur
& Madras

Old Bus
Stand

Railway
Station

Modern Book
Depot

BHUBANESHWAR ROAD

Indian
Airlines

RAJPATH

Market

State Bank
of India

State
Museum

Airport

Tourist
Office

Sisireshwar &
Mukteshwar

TANKPANI ROAD

Vital Deul

Parumeshwar

Rajarani

Brahmeshwar

Bindu
Sagar

To Madras

Lingaraj

To Puri & Konark

HOTELS
1 Oberoi
2 Prachi
3 Swosti
4 Bhubaneshwar
5 Pushpak
6 Kenilworth
7 Kalinga Ashok
8 Panthaniyas Tourist Bungalow
9 Siddhartha

RESTAURANTS
1 Hare Krishna
2 Garden Inn

N

1km
1 mile

Muslim incursions from both the northwest and the south (Golconda) led at last to the overthrow of the Hindu rulers. Thereafter, Orissa was held successively by the Muslims, the Afghans, the Marathas, and from 1803, by the British.

Bhubaneshwar today is remarkably unlike a major state capital. It is clean, fairly free of traffic but spread out, and it backs onto large expanses of lush meadowland and green fields. A new city of modern buildings has recently sprung up to the north of the old temple town, but there is no real sense of contrast. Ancient sandstone temple spires soar above new hotels and restaurants, and modern paved roads fade into dusty old dirt-tracks. But Bhubaneshwar's progress is taking place in the context of its old traditions and culture, and it is almost impossible to believe that this small, relaxed, semi-rural city administers the affairs of 35 million people.

When to Go

Bhubaneshwar's main festival is **Ashokastami**, which takes place over five days at the end of March (at Lingaraj temple). It's nothing like as grand as Puri's Rath Yatra, but you still get the spectacle of Lord Lingaraj being towed round town by thousands of delirious devotees. If you miss this one, there's a smaller tribal fair in late January.

Getting There

Bhubaneshwar is connected by air, rail and bus with Calcutta, Hyderabad and Madras. *See* relevant 'Moving On' sections and p.391.

The two fast trains from Delhi are the 8476 Neelachal Express and the 2816 New Delhi–Puri Express. They leave New Delhi station on alternate days, both at 6.35am, the Neelachal arriving at Bhubaneshwar at 4.35pm, the Superfast at 12.15pm. Both trains continue on to Puri, getting there at 7.30pm and 2.45pm respectively.

The airport is 4km from town—free by transfer bus (Oberoi or Garden Inn guests only) and Rs50–80 by taxi (book from the tourist booth inside the terminal).

Getting Around

Auto-rickshaws are not metered—the official rate is Rs3 per kilometre, but you'll have to fight to get it. Taxis can only be found at the airport or at the larger hotels. They hire out on a 4- or 8-hour programme basis, and are mainly useful if you want to do the Bhubaneshwar, Puri and Konark circuit in one day. The charge is Rs320 (or Rs600 a/c), which covers you for up to 80km travel. Anything over that costs extra.

Bhubaneshwar ☏ (0674–)   ***Tourist Information***

The **Orissa tourism office,** ☏ 431299, is down a lane by the Pantha Niwas Tourist Bungalow (*open 10am–5pm, closed Sun and 2nd Sat of each month*). It ranks with Kulu as the worst office in the country and has (or at least had) only one map of the city, glued together with somebody's breakfast. You'll get far more out of the information desk inside the railway station (very friendly) or the 24-hour one at the airport. Tours of Bhubaneshwar and of Konark/Puri (both 9am to 5.30pm daily) are sold at the Pantha Niwas Tourist Bungalow, where you can also **hire cars, coaches and even yachts** for sightseeing. Close by is a **Government of India tourist office**, ✆ 432203 (*open 9.30am–6pm weekdays only*).

The only place you can find decent maps, along with a good selection of western books, is **Modern Book Depôt**, ✆ 402373, opposite the railway station. Or there's **Wheeler's** bookshop on the station platform, which is not so good.

The best **travel agents** are Sita on Rajpath, Swosti Travels at the Swosti Hotel, and Mercury at the Oberoi. **Indian Airlines**, ✆ 400544, is opposite the old bus stand, but Arya Travels at Hotel Prachi, ✆ 416668, does Indian Airlines bookings quicker.

Touring Bhubaneshwar

Bhubaneshwar new town, with its hotels, shops, restaurants and bus station, lies to the north of the central railway line; the old temple town lies to the south. Cycle-rickshaws offer '5 temple' tours for Rs30, or you can take the day-tour from the Tourist Bungalow, which has a good reputation. Many travellers prefer to see the temples at leisure and on their own. This is best done in the early morning, when it's cool and quiet.

Tour 1: Temples

Half day. Brahmeshwar–Rajarani–Mukteshwar–Parumeshwar–Lingaraj–Sisireswar–Vital Deul Temples.

From the new town, it's a short rickshaw ride (or long walk) across the railway track into the old city. Some 15 minutes' walk down Tankpani Road (*see* map), will bring you to a huge old banyan tree. Turn right here for a short walk/ride to the 11th-century **Brahmeshwar Temple**, 2km from the town centre. This is situated in the quietest of settings: a pastoral clearing right on the outskirts of the old city. Nearly all Bhubaneshwar temples are dedicated to Shiva, but this one is different. Shiva is the presiding deity, but the temple itself is the home of Brahma. As a local quaintly explained: 'Father Brahma live here to be quiet. All rest of noisy family—Shiva, Ganesh and Parvati—live in big Lingaraj temple.' Apart from the elaborate ribbed architecture of Brahmeshwar, which is a feature of the whole group of temples, there's lots to appreciate, especially the beautiful carvings of dancing women and Orissan lions on the exterior walls.

Returning down Tankpani Road, **Rajarani Temple** looms up on your left, just across the canal. This 9th-century monument is set in green gardens and features unique erotic carvings of women and couples. The interior is very plain and the temple has long ceased to be in worship. It is, however, a fine example of the Orissan architectural style come to maturity.

A few hundred yards further up the road is the 9th-century **Mukteshwar Temple**, one of the most refined temples in Orissa. Small and compact, it is famous both for its ornate entrance arch and for its rare interior carvings. On the ceiling of the inner shrine can be seen lotus carvings and (in relief) the whole pantheon of Hindu gods. Mukteshwar is set in

Muktesvara temple
Bhubaneswar

a compound of several temples, ringed by mango and jackfruit trees, and is favoured by most of Bhubaneshwar's small population of temple beggars.

The ancient **Parumeshwar Temple**, built in the 7th century, is located at the top of Tankpani Road, near the northern edge of Bindu Sagar Lake. Ganesh lives here, along with his warrior brother Muruga (Parumeshwar). Renowned for its simple charm and for the dense volume of its carvings (note the beautiful latticed windows), this is the best-preserved example of the early group of Orissan temples. It comprises a flat-roofed rectangular pillared hall attached to the central sanctuary or *deul*, which contains a small lingam (don't trip over this in the gloom). The temple appears on the left-hand side of the road, and is easy to find. It is marked by a huge old mango tree, often with a bus driver or a security guard sound asleep under it.

Skirting the Bindu Sagar Lake, keeping to the left bank, see last the most notable of Bhubaneshwar's temples, the 11th-century **Lingaraj Temple**, dedicated to Shiva as Lingaraj or Lord of the Universe. Built during the reigns of three kings, and soaring to a height of 54m, it contains one of the 12 prized *jyotirlingas* or symbols of Shiva's creative power. These are of great antiquity and represent the quintessence of the Kalinga style of temple architecture. The vertical lines of the strongly drawn ribs, of which two on each side of the walls show miniature replicas of the whole, create an illusion of great height. The temple comprises four structures: the *deul* sanctuary, the *mandapa* or great hall, the dancing hall and the hall of offerings. The last two were added later by the Ganga kings. Sadly, the massive temple compound is completely walled round, and no non-Hindus may enter. To compensate, there's a small viewing platform beside the northern wall—originally erected for Lord Curzon—where you can peer over and take photographs. So-called priests ask for donations, as at most other temples nowadays, and you may have to give them a couple of rupees to get some peace. From the wall, you can see the lions overcoming elephants, which is said to symbolize the final-bell comeback of Hinduism, after going nine proverbial rounds with Buddhism.

The Lingaraj is the only temple in the Bhubaneshwar circuit where the whole family of gods reside (apart from Brahma, who does solitary back at Brahmeshwar). The big festival here is **Mahashivratri**—the night of the Feb/March new moon—when hordes of devotees light a candle to Shiva.

To complete your tour, head up the road running alongside the eastern wall of Lingaraj and then bear right until, on the far side of Bindu Sagar, you come to the small **Sisireshwar Temple**. This very decorative 8th-century structure closely resembles the Parumeshwar in architectural form and has fine carvings. It adjoins the famous **Boital** or **Vital Deul Temple**, also from the 8th century, which has particularly well-preserved carvings of the demon goddess Durga. The name *boital* derives from the word for 'spirit' and harks back to the days when a few temples were used for tantric practices, and when human sacrifices were made to the presiding eight-armed Chamundi deity. Dedicated to Durga, this is one of Bhubaneshwar's few non-Shiva temples. The goddess sits within like one of the witches in *Macbeth*, garlanded with skulls and sitting on a (hidden) corpse. The double-storey 'wagon roof' overhead harks back to Buddhist cave architecture.

Tour 2: Other Sights

*By tour bus, full day. Khandagiri and Udayagiri Hills–Nandankanan Zoo–
Dhauli Hill–Lion Safari Park–Botanical Gardens–State Museum.*

These places are well-covered by day-tour from the Tourist Bungalow. This tour also
includes the temples, so if you've just seen them and don't want to see them again, ask
that they be made the last stop of the day. The driver is generally amenable.

The **Khandagiri** and **Udayagiri Hills**, a few kilometres west of Bhubaneshwar, are
honeycombed with ancient caves. These were excavated by monks during the reign of
Kharavela, the Kalinga emperor, around the 1st and 2nd centuries BC. Udayagiri has 44
caves, all carved out of sandstone. Their entrances are decorated with monkey (Hanuman)
or elephant (Buddha) motifs, and are often adorned with Pali inscriptions. Several caves
functioned as monks' sleeping quarters and contain bare rock-beds. The central **Hathi
Gumpha** (Elephant Cave) exhibits the best example of Pali records so far found in India—
a full listing of Kharavela's religious, military and civil achievements during the first 13
years of his reign. An ingenious underground water supply runs right through the caves,
originating from a central reservoir.

Above and to the left of Udayagiri are the group of 19 Khandagiri caves. On top of
Khandagiri hill, you'll find 24 beautiful Jain statues in the 18th-century temple of **Mahavir**
(founder of the Jain religion). There are nice views from the summit too, but be quick—
the bus will already be revving up by the time you reach the top.

Nandankanan Zoo, 20km out of Bhubaneshwar, is an attractive botanical garden and
zoo set amid the forest and lakes of Chandaka (*open summer, exc Mon, 7am–6pm;
winter 7.30am–5pm; if visiting on your own, there are hourly buses here from
Bhubaneshwar*). The largest lion safari park in India, it is also the first zoo in the world
where white tigers have been bred naturally in captivity. The animals live in semi-tropical
splendour, often in quarters superior to those of their human visitors. They include rhinos,
monkeys, gharials, pelicans, pythons, brown bear, and crocodile. In March, there's a
colourful host of wild butterflies. For a quick orientation round the zoo grounds, take a
ride on the toy train which circles the perimeter. Alight at the new **Lion Safari Park**, and
take a bus out to see African lions (often asleep) in the vast 50-acre reserve. Then take a
pedalo or rowing boat on the lake, or pay a brief visit to the **Botanical Gardens** north of
the zoo, with their wide variety of indigenous and exotic plants.

The bright-white Japanese peace pagoda on top of Dhauli Hill, 8km south of Bhubaneshwar,
can be seen for many miles. Bedecked with gilded lions, this **Santi Stupa** has a five-tier
'umbrella' representing the five Buddhist virtues of faith, hope, compassion, forgiveness and
non-violence. It overlooks the vast plain where Ashoka destroyed the might of the Kalinga
empire, and then dedicated himself to peace. At the foot of Dhauli hill, look out for the
famous **Ashoka Rock Edicts**, inscribed by the repentant emperor after being converted to
Buddhism by a resident monk. Above the edicts, there is the earliest known sculpture in
Orissa. The forepart of an elephant (representing Buddha) hewn out of a huge rock. Dhauli is
a quiet, scenic spot with beautiful views in all directions. At the top of the hill, behind the
white-domed pagoda, is a small Hindu temple reconstructed in 1992.

The **State Museum**, opposite Hotel Kalinga (*officially open 10am–5pm exc Mon, but closed for lunch 1–2pm although not advertised, and no adm after 4pm*), is a large sprawling building with a rich collection of tribal art and many interesting archaeological finds. It's sadly run-down nowadays, and power cuts have plunged the (often excellent) exhibits into dim limbo. Photography isn't allowed, and even it were, you'd need a guide dog. The assistant curator, Mr Mallia, is helpful.

Shopping

Bhubaneshwar offers an extremely good choice of fabrics, textiles and crafts. The royal Mauryan textile workshops (established over 2000 years ago) began a lineage of spinners, weavers and embroiderers which has continued to the present day, with temple towns like Bhubaneshwar becoming the bases for several weaving communities. The result is a wide variety of silk, tussar and cotton fabrics, many with vibrant tribal, traditional or modern designs. The best crafts originate from the village of **Pipli**, 20km out of Bhubaneshwar on the Konark road. Here you can find cigar boxes, jewellery, decorative trays with intricate silver filigree work, folk paintings, brassware, papier-mâché masks, and colourful appliqué handicrafts. Also worth a visit is **Raghunathpur** village, 2km outside Puri, which has delightful *patachitra* paintings on cloth and a large range of local crafts. Prices are low if you bargain hard.

In Bhubaneshwar, there are beautiful handicrafts—silk saris and lungis, Pipli crafts and palm-leaf illustrations—at **Utkalika Handicrafts Emporium**, behind the government bus stand in Rajpath (closed Thursday). Utkalika also has a small shop at the airport, good for last-minute buys. **Little Shoppe** has two branches, at the Kenilworth Hotel and at the Tourist Bungalow, selling, among other things, interesting brass curios and artifacts.

Leisure

Bhubaneshwar has no nightlife at all. To relieve the boredom, pay a visit to Oberoi hotel's bar—it's cosy, friendly, and popular with expats. Some people get invited to parties, others chance upon one of the hotel's traditional dance shows (laid on only for groups). More regular **dance displays** are held at the air-conditioned **Rabindra Mandap** on Sachivalaya Marg. They usually take place on Saturday, Sunday and Monday evenings, but phone ahead, ✆ 417677, to check. Kasori, opposite, is the best **cinema** in town.

Bhubaneshwar ✆ *(0674–)* **Where to Stay**

Nowhere else in India, except perhaps for Khajuraho, can you live so well and for so little as here.

luxury (from US$30)

Small but luxurious rooms at the high-class **Oberoi**, ✆ 56116, ✆ 56269, cost just US$60 a night. This is the city's only 5-star property, 4km north of the town centre, with a lovely pool and grounds, fabulous Oriya temple-style lobby, and an unusually warm manager, Mr Rajat Chhabra. Together with Halla, his charming wife, he takes personal care of all his guests and, when he has time, he even introduces them to the local expatriate party scene, of which he forms the hub. If you're in town for any length of time, this is *the* place to be.

Down a side-lane off Janpath, just below the Prachi, you'll find the spanking-new **Garden Inn** hotel, ✆ 414120, ✉ 404254, with very spacious rooms from US$30/50 and family-size suites at US$70. Facilities include a nice pool, classy restaurant and useful travel desk. It's very glitzy on the surface, and the staff are friendly, but service is already on a gentle slide.

expensive (from US$20)

Most hotels in this class have tried upgrading themselves to 4-star level, with generally poor results. The best deals are the old-block rooms (a bit musty, but only Rs600/700) at the **Kalinga Ashok** on Gautam Nagar, ✆ 431055, ✉ 431056. This has the usual Ashok interior, dark and dingy, but good facilities and restaurants. Rooms in the new block are not worth the double tariff—all you get is a bigger carpet. A few steps away, the **Kenilworth**, ✆ 411723, ✉ 411561, has a good pool and facilities but small, indifferent rooms. On Janpath, **Hotel Prachi**, ✆ 402328, ✉ 403287, has changed from a rickety old-colonial hotel to a boring modern one. Stay here only for the pool. The nearby **Hotel Swosti**, ✆ 404178, ✉ 407524, is better, with acceptable rooms and a fine restaurant.

moderate

Top choice is the peaceful **Hotel Siddhartha**, 3km out of the centre on the Cuttack–Puri road, tel/fax 413496. It has a nice pool, gardens and a/c restaurant, and cheerful rooms for Rs350 or Rs600 with a/c. The more expensive rooms have private balconies. If full, try **Hotel Sahara** opposite Hotel Kenilworth, with big, clean rooms from Rs125/225 (from Rs375 with a/c). Ask for a room with private balcony overlooking the temples. Next down the list is **Pantha Niwas Tourist Bungalow**, ✆ 54515, with clean, popular rooms from Rs150 or Rs350 with a/c. The overpriced **Bhubaneshwar Hotel** on Cuttack Road is now a last resort, charging Rs375 for rooms which put Alcatraz to shame.

budget

At this level, be prepared to bring your own mosquito net—few lodges have decent protection. If you can get a room at **Hotel Blue Heaven**, on Babuji Nagar, ✆ 414979, count yourself lucky. It can get noisy, but there's nothing wrong with the rooms (wide choice, from Rs100/150) and the friendly manager has just added a restaurant. Rickshaw-men will show you other places, including **Hotel Pushpak** near the railway station, but you won't like them.

Bhubaneshwar ✆ (0674–)   **Eating Out**

Oberoi's multi-cuisine **Pushpanjali** is well worth a trip out of town, especially if you're a carnivore. It has everything from hot dogs to burgers and the steaks are

Bhubaneshwar is a Hindu temple city, so the cow is sacred. This said, don't be surprised if, when tucking into your *filet mignon* at a certain big hotel (*no name, to protect the chef), your waiter leans over and whispers confidentially: 'Good choice! This is *cow* meat, not buffalo!' It's only a matter of time before he says it to the wrong person.

out of this world. Meals are exceptionally cheap—only Rs150 for *lobster thermidor* with all the trimmings, and Rs100 for an all-you-can-eat breakfast buffet. Oberoi's other eatery, the **Chandini**, will shortly re-open with a Mughlai theme.

In town, the **Swosti Hotel** is indeed the 'cosiest restaurant in town', with stylish ambience, attentive service, delectable cocktails, and great cakes. It's not expensive either. Over at the **Garden Inn** hotel, there's another fine restaurant (very flash) with a menu to suit all palates. The **Ashok** hotel has well-priced food at its restaurant/coffee shop, and there's a bar attached, open 11am to 11pm. Resident expats recommend the bars at the Oberoi, Swosti and Prachi hotels.

The new **Cook's Kitchen** at Hotel Blue Heaven in Bapuji Nagar is popular with locals, and does excellent Indian food at moderate prices. Vegetarian meals are good at both the **Modern South Indian Hotel**, off the bottom of Rajpath behind Hotel Rajmahal, and **Hare Krishna Restaurant**, opposite the railway station.

Moving On

By air: From Bhubaneshwar, **Indian Airlines** flies daily to Calcutta and Delhi, and less often to Madras (4 days) and Hyderabad/Varanasi (3). NEPC Airlines have a desk at the airport, and offer two flights a week to Calcutta and Madras.

By rail: The quick and convenient Rajdhani Express leaves Bhubaneshwar at 8.50am daily, proceeding first to Calcutta (7hrs) and then to Delhi (24hrs). The Coromandel Express (dep 9.37pm) goes to Madras in 20hrs, the 1020 Konark Express to Hyderabad in 21hrs, and the 2815 Puri–New Delhi Express/8475 Neelachal Express (dep 10.52 am on alternate days) to Varanasi in 20/22hrs. The last-mentioned trains originate from Puri, leaving at 9.15am and reaching Bhubaneshwar at 10.45am.

Fast trains go from Bhubaneshwar to Puri at 12.15pm (2hrs) and at 4.45pm (2½hrs).

By road: From the new bus terminal 5km north of town there are several overnight buses to Calcutta. Buses to Puri and Konark (1½hrs) still leave from the old bus stand in the town centre—for Konark, you may have to change buses at Pipli. The Tourist Bungalow offers bus tours to Puri/Konark and hires out taxis.

Puri is one of the four holiest Hindu cities in India, and an upcoming seaside resort. The religious and cultural life of the town centres round the huge 12th-century Jagannath Temple, home of the Formless God, Lord Jagannath, who is said to represent the primordial essence of the universe.

Ten years ago, the Orissan state government had a dream: to promote Puri as a beach resort, along the same lines as Goa. Then they came up against a few harsh realities. The sea at Puri is not as calm as Goa—in fact it is extremely choppy, and the undercurrents pretty dangerous. Added to this, a fair chunk of the beach has become a public toilet. You now have to walk a fair stretch away from the fishing village to find somewhere clean to sunbathe. On the plus side, non-development has left Puri both cheap and unspoilt, and it's a great place to unwind for a few days before heading back into India proper.

Don't leave town without seeing at least one sunrise and sunset—they're something else.

When to Go

At the spectacular **Rath Yatra** (Car Festival) of June/July, Puri is invaded by zealous armies of pilgrims who gather from all over India to worship the images of Jagannath, which are dragged through town on massive wooden chariots. It's the most intense demonstration of religious fervour anywhere—an impossible madhouse of swaying crowds—and well worth going out of your way for. Puri also has an annual beach festival from 5 to 11 November, featuring a local crafts fair as well as a cultural programme, firework display and boat races.

Getting There

Puri is serviced by trains and buses from Bhubaneshwar, local buses from Konark, and trains from Madras and Hyderabad (*see* relevant 'Moving On' sections).

The ride out to Puri is beautiful in spring—mile upon mile of lush, green rice paddies and violet water-hyacinths, interspersed with temples, semi-tropical jungles and rustic farming villages.

Getting Around

Getting around Puri is easy—either hire a bicycle (from the budget lodge area) or let yourself be driven around by cycle-rickshaws. These charge Rs10 for the short ride between the beach hotels and the bus stand. **Tribe Tours** hire out scooters and motorbikes for around Rs300/350—booking and payment must be made a day in advance.

Puri © (06752–)   ### *Tourist Information*

The poor **tourist office**, © 22664, is on Station Road (*open 10am to 5pm exc Sun*). Better information is available from the Tourist Bungalow, which also sells the ambitious see-the-whole-of-Orissa-in-one-day tour—covering not just Konark, Pipli, Dhauli and the Udayagiri/Khandagiri caves, but all the Bhubaneshwar temples too! It runs from 6.30am to 5.30pm daily, and costs Rs75/105 by bus with/without air-conditioning. A far less stressful tour goes to Chilka Lake every Monday, Wednesday and Friday for Rs85/120.

The airport has a tourist information counter, open 24 hours. **Money-changing** is quickest at the Punjab Bank next to Holiday Resort. Loknath Bookshop on C T Road is a good place to rent/sell **secondhand books** and to buy postcards.

Touring Puri

At Puri, it's a 1km walk up from the bus stand to the **Jagannath Temple**. Even on a quiet day, the town's broad central avenue is total mayhem—packed solid with jostling beggars and ganja-sellers, bullock carts, cycle-rickshaws and itinerant cows, with shell-shocked Indian families staggering between tour bus and temple. Tin shacks and wooden stalls deal furiously in cold drinks, silverware, vegetarian food and all manner of cheap religious paraphernalia. In the background, temple bells clang an insistent invitation to devotees.

The Jagannath Temple, built in the 12th century by the Kalinga ruler Chodaganga Deva, is the tallest and most magnificent monument in Orissa. Its pinnacle rises to a formidable height of 65m and dominates the skyline for miles around. The temple itself divides into four parts: the central main hall, the hall of audience, the dancing hall and the hall of offerings.

Walking round the temple perimeter, you can see some of the original fine carvings on the exterior walls, slowly being revealed as a result of patient conservation work. Worthy of special mention are the four temple gates, each of which has an animal theme—horse (south gate), elephant (north gate), tiger (west gate) and lion (east gate). It is by the lion gate that pilgrims make their entrance, to visit Lord Jagannath and commune with his qualities of light, power and wisdom. In front of this main gate stands a 16-sided monolithic pillar called **Aruna Stambha**, which once stood in front of Konark's Sun Temple—it was brought here in the 18th century. Around the gates are the temple money-changers, the only people in town with a ready supply of small change.

Non-Hindus aren't allowed into the Jagannath Temple, but you can peer over the walls from a nearby viewing platform. This is on the roof of the library opposite (*open 9am–noon and 4–8pm*), and on the way up you'll be given a stick against monkeys. Looking down from the top, you can fully appreciate the sheer power and majesty of this huge temple, which looks like a spaceship. You also have a clear sweep of chaotic Puri town. Off the roof, stop in at the library's first-floor museum to see its interesting collection of rare palm-leaf manuscripts, some dating back 350 years. Many are written in ancient Sanskrit, scratched out by quill-pen, and are beautifully coloured. The curator is keen to show you copies, and even keener to sell you some.

If you're on tour, you'll head from the temple to the Tourist Bungalow for a *thali* lunch. After that, you can walk along the long, sandy beach or go for a swim. The sea is very salty and very brisk (don't go out of your depth: many people have drowned here). Nothing, however, deters pilgrims from their dip in the holy waters. If you decide to join them, be prepared to be adopted by local fishermen, who lassoo hesitant bathers with rubber rings. Swimming is safest between October and March, when the currents are least hazardous. The beach

pollution is worst around the Penthakota fishing village, but not bad if you walk 1km along the sands to the Mayfair Hotel area. It's okay to change on the beach—leaving your togs with an Indian family—and you can shower off afterwards at the Tourist Bungalow.

Shopping

Check out the many seaside shops selling soapstone carvings, horn/wood articles and palm-leaf paintings. They make great little gifts.

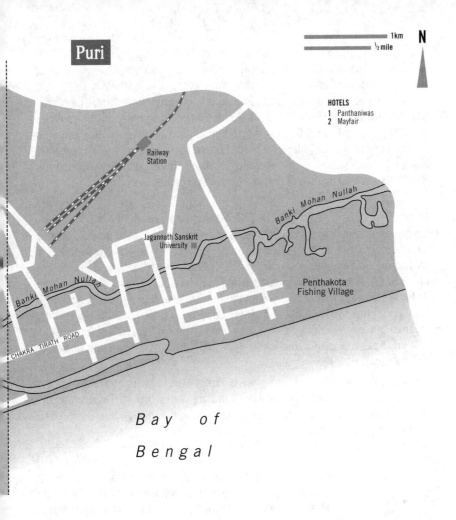

Puri

Railway
Station

Jagannath Sanskrit
University

Banki Mohan Nullah

Banki Mohan Nullah

Penthakota
Fishing Village

CHAKRA TIRATH ROAD

B a y   o f

B e n g a l

1km

½ mile

N

Puri ☎ (06752–)

Where To Stay

During the October to January high season, and especially at weekends, Puri's few decent hotels are packed out with visiting Bengalis. Travellers tend to stick to 'their' end of the beach (near the fishing village) where digs are cheaper and there's a wider choice of food.

expensive/moderate (from Rs400)

The 'Indian' end of the beach, near the top of Chakratirtha (or C T) Road, has Puri's best hotel—the **Mayfair Beach Resort**, ☎ 24041, ☎ 24242. This place is set in beautiful gardens and overlooks a clean stretch of beach. Choose from elegantly furnished sea-facing a/c suites (from Rs1650), cottages (from Rs1350) and rooms (from Rs1200), all with private sit-out and balcony. The full range of luxury facilities are on offer—including watersports and Puri's only swimming pool—and there are two excellent restaurants specializing in seafood. The nearby **Vijaya International**, ℂ 22702, ✆ 22881, doesn't compare, but has popular doubles for Rs400 or Rs700 with a/c. 'We monopolise service with a smile', it claims, but I never saw one. The South Eastern Railway Hotel has become very run down. Instead, try the breezy **Pantha Niwas Tourist Bungalow**, ℂ 22740—at least you won't grow a beard waiting for your food.

budget

Most cheap places, even the popular **Z Hotel**, at the bottom of C T Road, ℂ 22554, have poor protection against mosquitoes—so bring some cream (**Odomos**) or your own net. The Zed (not Zee!) is a lovely old-colonial style bungalow with a relaxing TV lounge, relaxing gardens and family-size rooms (far better than the cheaper ones) at Rs300. It's always full, though, so ring ahead to book. Right next door is the small **Traveller's Inn**, a pleasant place with rooms (bath attached) for Rs85. A minute's walk back up the road, you'll find **Hotel Love & Life**, tel/fax 24433, a friendly Japanese-run place with big clean rooms (bath attached) from Rs100 and a useful ticketing service. Manager Lutu has lovingly compiled maps on Puri, Bhubaneshwar and Calcutta, and is very helpful.

On the beach itself, the premier place is **Pinky House**, with good views and a restaurant. Double rooms go for Rs100 and are well worth it. There are many other cheapies in this area, but don't let a rickshaw-wallah show you them—he'll collect a large commission.

Puri ℂ (06752–)   ***Eating Out***

Puri is famous for seafood, particularly tuna steaks and (if available) lobster. Good upmarket fare is available from the **Mayfair Hotel**, while a set dinner at the **Railway Hotel** is a real experience. The cheap restaurants are **Mickey Mouse**, **Xanadu**, **Harry's Café** and **Peace**—all close to Z Hotel and all offering the usual travellers' fare. The latter two get the most business—mostly on account of their 'special' cakes and apple pies. The **Blue Heaven** behind Puri Hotel is less tacky; it serves delicious kebabs and Chinese dishes.

Moving On

From the bus stand next to Gundicha Mandir, quick minibuses go to Bhubaneshwar (1½hrs) and big buses to Konark (1hr). Puri has direct trains to Bhubaneshwar (*see* p.391) and to Calcutta.

In its heyday, Konark was the centre of Orissan culture and commerce. Today, it is a small village with half an ancient temple standing in isolated splendour among desolate sand dunes. It remains, however, a major pilgrimage centre. Every year, at the important **Chandrabhaga Mela** festival in February, thousands of pilgrims arrive to honour the Sun God, Surya. At dawn on the seventh day of the festival, they all troop down to the beach—originally at the foot of the Sun Temple, but now 3km distant from it—and take their ritual bath in the sea; then they anxiously await the rising of the sun; afterwards, they return to the Sun Temple to visit the nine planets installed there. This ceremony, which has been observed ever since the temple was constructed, is believed by all those who participate to erase the entire sum of their past misdeeds.

Konark derives its name from the Sanskrit language, and roughly translates as 'sun's corner'. According to popular myth, it was here that the tradition of sun-worship began, some 5000 years ago. Krishna, offended by a negligent son-in-law called Samba, afflicted him with leprosy and advised him to do penance to the Sun God for 12 years. Cured of his disease, the grateful Samba erected a small temple to Surya—much added to and many times reconstructed in later centuries—by the banks of the sacred river. In the mid-13th century, after the Sun God granted his prayer for a child, Narasimha Deva I of the Ganga dynasty built the present massive structure. It is said to have taken a total of 1200 artisans, assisted by 12,000 labourers, 12 long years to complete (AD 1243–55).

The Sun Temple is beautifully illuminated between 6 and 9pm at night, providing the perfect backdrop to traditional dance shows held at the nearby open-air theatre. The big one is in November, the other in February, and both transform the normally sleepy village into a mini-metropolis of feverish activity—with a funfair, lots of stalls, and a local co-operative craft show.

Konark ℗ (06752–)

Tourist Information

The **tourist desk** at the Pantha Niwas Tourist Bungalow is very helpful, but often deluged with home tourists.

Touring Konark

Konark is best visited as a day-trip from Puri or Bhubaneshwar. It's included in day-tours from these towns. If you prefer to travel independently, there's an express bus from Bhubaneshwar (dep 10am) which takes 1½hrs and is quicker than local buses. Buses and minibuses (crowded) take an hour or so from Puri.

Konark's **Sun Temple** (*open sunrise–sunset daily*) is a masterpiece of design and construction—built in the shape of a huge chariot, pulled along by seven racing horses (one for each day in the week) on 24 intricately carved stone wheels (one for each fortnight of the Indian year). The idea of the sculpture was to recreate the magnificent progress of the Sun God, Surya, through the heavens, and it was designed so that the first rays of the morning sun, every single day of the year, would strike first the dancing hall, then the hall of audience, and finally the head of the Sun God in the main temple, charging it with new energy and lifeforce. Originally, the temple had a huge spire, projecting to a height of 70m, but this collapsed some 400 years after its construction. In olden days, this soaring beacon was an important landmark for mariners navigating the passage to Calcutta. They called it the 'Black Pagoda' to distinguish it from the 'White Pagoda' of Puri's Jagannath Temple.

Before entering, buy a *Sun Temple, Konark* booklet from the small museum outside the temple enclosure. The museum (*open 10am–5pm exc Fri*) has many finely carved chlorite panels and khondalite images recovered from the temple excavations. You can get a good guide outside for Rs20.

To appreciate the educative function of this temple, do a circuit of the huge **Hall of Audience**—a 40m leviathan filled in with sand to prevent collapse by the British in 1903. The fine wall carvings divide into three distinct sections: elephant and animal motifs run round the baseline and lower levels, erotic carvings decorate the central level, while the top layer has depictions of various gods and goddesses. Even better carvings are concentrated within the massive spoked wheels of the chariot. Climb the stairs at the rear of the temple to see the three life-size images of the Sun God, carved out of polished blue-granite. These depict the rising, noonday and setting sun respectively; another explanation is that they represent youth, middle age and old age—or Brahma, Vishnu and Shiva. The empty dais in the sunken chamber once contained the seated statue of the Sun God, now housed in the British Museum. Note the beautiful elephant panels in this section, and return to admire the entrance doors of the **Hall of Audience**, which feature seven different carving styles, one for each spectrum of the rainbow (the Sun God's seven different 'lights'). Facing the doors is the **Dancing Hall**, still used on special occasions for classical Orissan dance displays. Looking down at your feet, you'll see a unique feature of this temple complex—its stone flooring, comprising solid massive blocks of stone joined with iron rivets. At no point was cement or mortar used. And the work still goes on. Industrious teams of stone-cutters are constantly at work on the site, carrying on time-honoured traditions of temple building and renovation. Despite the ravages of time, Konark remains Orissa's finest achievement.

From the temple, it's a 3km walk (or cycle-rickshaw ride) down to **Sun Beach**, a long unbroken sweep of golden sand considered by many to be Orissa's finest beach. It's certainly a lot cleaner than the one at Puri, though the currents are just as strong. If you do swim here, don't go out too far.

Where to Stay and Eating Out

Konark has a trio of cheap government hotels, catering mainly to holidaying Indians. The two best ones are **Yatri Niwas**, © 8820, and **Pantha Niwas**, © 8831, both with rooms around Rs120/180. Third comes **Traveller's Lodge**, © 8823, with a few a/c doubles for Rs300.

There are a few private hotels like **Labanya Lodge**, **Sunrise** and **Banita** with rooms from Rs60 to 75.

The nearest thing to *haute cuisine* is Pantha Niwas's **Geetanjali** restaurant, but don't expect anything special. Cheaper fare is available from the **Yatri Niwas** and from the rash of small restaurants below the Sun Temple, notably **Shanti Hotel** (good for a cold beer) and **Sun Temple Hotel**.

Chilka Lake

If you want to get off the beaten track, take a local bus/taxi (or even a tour bus) to **Chilka Lake**, some 30km south of Puri. Chilka is the largest lagoon of its kind in the country, measuring some 70km long by 15km (on average) wide, and is an excellent venue for bird-watchers. During the winter season (December/January), it receives flocks of exotic and rare migratory birds, some from as far off as Siberia.

From the small Tourist Bungalow here, © 488, one can take a boat into the lake at the crack of dawn, and float quietly for hours through the vast marshes, lowlands and back-waters of Chilka—perhaps visiting Nalaban Island, where great numbers of birds come to roost. Fishing, swimming and yachting is good in this area, and it's wonderfully quiet.

Gopalpur-on-Sea

South of Chilka Lake is the ancient seaport of Gopalpur, now a run-down but charming beach town. To get here, take a local bus (5hrs) from Bhubaneshwar to Berhampur, then another bus (45mins) or taxi on to Gopalpur. While arranging transport at Berhampur village, visit the silk-weavers lining the street beside the main temple.

Gopalpur is a miniature seaside haven with a charming club-style hotel, the Oberoi Palm Beach, right on the beach. Swimming, however, is not always safe. Depending on the season, there can be some tricky undercurrents. The beach itself is lovely, clean and very long. It looks out onto the Bay of Bengal, and borders a lush, green network of backwater creeks and sleepy lagoons.

Best here is the **Oberoi Palm Beach**, ℃ 82021, the pre-World War II resort choice of holidaying Calcuttans. A beautiful whitewashed building, it has good watersports, relaxing gardens, and a real old-colonial flavour. Lots of artists and dilettantes have made a pilgrimage here, and Satyajit Ray spent a month or so at the hotel every time he needed to get away and plan a new film. Rooms go for US$40/70 (or US$50/80 with a/c) and are generally excellent value.

Gopalpur has very little infrastructure as yet, but there are a few cheap places to stay and eat. Try either **Pantha Niwas Tourist Bungalow**, on the rise at the end of the main street, ℃ 21482, or **Hotel Uphar**, near the bus stand, ℃ 21558. Most of the cheaper places are grim.

A mid-19th century creation of the Raj, Darjeeling is one of the major hill resorts of north India—and certainly the most spectacular. Perched 'on the roof of the world', this charming hill station lives in the shadow of the majestic Kanchenjunga peak and is surrounded by snow-capped mountains and dense conifer forests, plummeting down into an enchanting valley below. The busy little town is a maze of steps and terraces, a melting pot of exotic hill and village peoples, full of bazaars, markets and shops selling colourful handicrafts, and of course the famous Darjeeling tea.

Rich in flora and fauna, the surrounding countryside is a paradise for nature-lovers with over 4000 species of flowers, 600 varieties of birds, and many animals and reptiles. A major base for trekking in the eastern Himalaya, Darjeeling also has a variety of recreational facilities including golf and fishing. Nearby is Tiger Hill, with unforgettable dawn views of Mount Kanchenjunga, and Ghoom Monastery where is enshrined a figure of the Tibetan 'Buddha to Come', Maitreya. Of all the hill stations of India, Darjeeling has perhaps the most to offer the foreign visitor with its cool charm, lovely scenery and unique atmosphere.

Darjeeling district was ceded to the British following a dispute with the rajah of Sikkim in 1828, and the small protectorate of Sikkim joined India as the 22nd State of the Union in 1975. Much of southern Sikkim is now open to tourists, and a visit to Gangtok, the capital, or a short trek along the border with Nepal makes an interesting and worthwhile extension to a stay in Darjeeling.

Itinerary

This is straightforward. You head up from Calcutta and you return the same way. Some people take a plane on to Delhi from Bagdogra (close to Darjeeling), but it's expensive and you fly over important places like Varanasi and Bodhgaya. Allow a week for this route—4 days minimum for Darjeeling and 2/3 days for Sikkim. There's also an option for a 1/2 day side-trip to Kalimpong. Permits are still required for Sikkim (*see* p.414).

The best months to visit are mid-April to mid-June and September to November. Temperatures range from 6° to 17°C, with monsoon rains from June to September (sometimes to late October).

Darjeeling   population 80,000

Ruled first by the rajahs of Sikkim until the start of the 18th century, then by the Gurkhas of Nepal, who invaded Sikkim in 1780, and subsequently returned to the rajahs by the East India Company, Darjeeling had a chequered history before being 'discovered' in 1828 by two British officers on a fact-finding mission. At that time, it was called Dorje Ling or 'Place of the Thunderbolt'. This was the mystic thunderbolt of Lamaist religion, representing the sceptre of Indra (Lord of the Gods) said to have fallen here—on the site presently known as Observatory Hill. The town of Darjeeling grew up around the ex-Buddhist monastery of Dorje Ling, which had been built on this hill.

The two officers quickly appreciated Darjeeling's strategic importance as a possible access to Nepal/Tibet and its recreational potential as a hill resort. They reported back to the Calcutta authorities, who put pressure on the rajah to grant the site to the British in return for an annual fee of Rs3000. Darjeeling quickly developed as a trading and a tea-growing centre, and despite much opposition from Tibetan lamas and merchants, whose own fortunes were threatened, the British strengthened their hold. In 1849 they annexed the whole territory between the present borders of Sikkim and the Bengal plains, making Darjeeling, previously just an isolated enclave within Sikkimese territory, part and parcel of other British territory further south.

The British arrived to find Darjeeling reclaimed by forest, the once large and busy village almost completely deserted. They began a rapid development programme, which by the early 1840s had produced roads, houses, a hotel, a health sanatorium and several tea plantations using bushes smuggled out of China. Not only British army officers and their wives, but also British families working and living down on the plains (mainly in Calcutta) began to use Darjeeling as a summer 'health' resort. The only problem was transport, visitors taking nearly a month to get up there from Calcutta—cruising up the Ganges, crossing the plains of Bihar and Siliguri, and proceeding up the old Hill Cart Road by bullock cart or

Foreign visitors to Darjeeling are often struck by three things: the cool climate, the dense greenery of the place, and the amazing diversity of cultures and peoples. Darjeeling, like Kathmandu, is a real pot-pourri of different racial types and groups—Tibetan *lamas* in their yellow robes, Tibetan ladies in striped aprons and brocades, Gurung farmers from central Nepal, Gurkhas from eastern Nepal, fair-skinned Lepchas and Bhutias from Sikkim, Drukpas from Bhutan, Sherpas from the mountains, and all manner of foreign and domestic tourists.

buggy. The prohibitive cost of this journey led to the construction of the famous 'toy train' miniature railway, completed in 1881, which reduced the journey time from Calcutta to just two days.

Since Independence, much of Darjeeling's prosperity comes not from high-class British sponsorship nor from its renowned tea trade (which is greatly suffering today, due to soil erosion and little replanting of new tea trees) but from the local tourist market and from its schools, where well-to-do Indian children receive a 'proper English education'. In this quaint quest for western-style knowledge, they progress from kitsch kindergartens like Mini-land and Love-Bud to impressively named academies like North Point, St Paul's and Loreto's.

Despite the recent appearance of gum-chewing young Nepalis and of soft-porn video palaces, Darjeeling remains one of India's most pleasant, fascinating hill stations. The old guard, mainly street pedlars or hotel staff with fond memories of the Raj, still address western women as 'memsahib' and take tourists home for 'tiffin' and endless cups of tea. The atmosphere is relaxing and beguiling, the architecture a curious blend of pre-war British buildings and tin-roofed wooden local shacks. In amongst the bright-green park benches, the civilized town squares and the neat ranks of ponies, rows of little wrinkled ladies sell rugs, shawls and acrylic sweaters hand-over-fist to shivering Indian tourists.

In the late 1980s, friction between the GNLF (Gorkha National Liberation Front) and the West Bengal government transformed this once-lovely 'queen of hill stations' into a bomb-blasted tourist wasteland. The situation has now settled with the establishment of the Gorkha Hill Council, which gives the people of Darjeeling and Kurseong districts a degree of self-government within the state of West Bengal.

When to Go

Darjeeling has two tourist seasons. Mid-April to mid-June is popular as a cool escape from sticky Calcutta, and to see the area at its most green and beautiful; September–November attracts just as many visitors for its clear mountain views, though rain can still be teeming down at the end of October. Evenings are cool throughout the year, so warm clothing is essential. The biggest festival of the year is Buddha's birthday (1 May), celebrated here as nowhere else.

Getting There

From Calcutta (*see* p.380), there are trains to New Jalpaiguri; from there it's 3/4hrs to Darjeeling (Rs40 by bus/jeep or Rs70 by share-taxi). Planes fly from

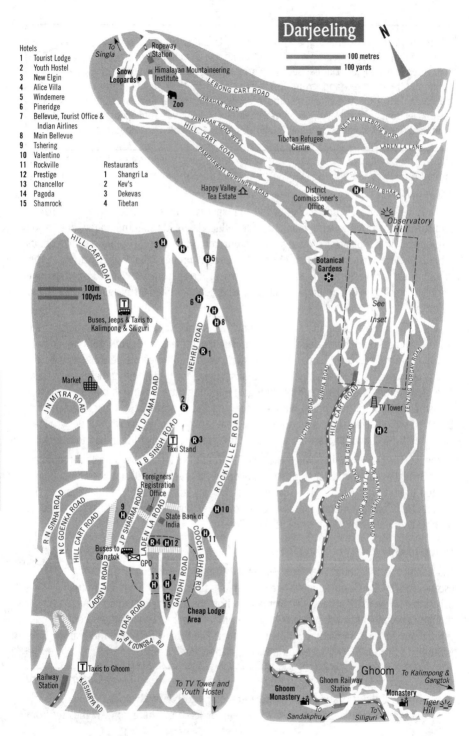

Darjeeling

N

| | 100 metres |
| | 100 yards |

Hotels
1 Tourist Lodge
2 Youth Hostel
3 New Elgin
4 Alice Villa
5 Windemere
6 Pineridge
7 Bellevue, Tourist Office & Indian Airlines
8 Main Bellevue
9 Tshering
10 Valentino
11 Rockville
12 Prestige
13 Chancellor
14 Pagoda
15 Shamrock

Restaurants
1 Shangri La
2 Kev's
3 Dekevas
4 Tibetan

To Singla

Ropeway Station

Snow Leopards

Himalayan Mountaineering Institute

Zoo

LEBONG CART ROAD

JAWAHAR ROAD

JAWAHAR ROAD WEST

HILL CART ROAD

PAMPHAWATI GURUNGRI ROAD

WESTERN LEBONG ROAD

LADEN LA LANE

Tibetan Refugee Centre

Happy Valley Tea Estate

District Commissioner's Office

BHAN BHAKTA

Observatory Hill

Botanical Gardens

See Inset

TENZING NORGAY ROAD

SINHA ROAD

VICTORIA ROAD

HILL CART ROAD

D B GIRI ROAD

DR ZAKIR HUSSAIN ROAD

A J C BOSE ROAD

GANDHI ROAD

TV Tower

HILL CART ROAD

100m
100yds

Buses, Jeeps & Taxis to Kalimpong & Siliguri

Market

J N MITRA ROAD

R N SINHA ROAD

N C GOENKA ROAD

HILL CART ROAD

H D LAMA ROAD

N B SINGH ROAD

NEHRU ROAD

ROCKVILLE ROAD

Taxi Stand

Foreigners' Registration Office

State Bank of India

J P SHARMA ROAD

LADEN LA ROAD

COOCH BIHAR RD

GANDHI ROAD

Buses to Gangtok

GPO

Cheap Lodge Area

LADEN LA ROAD

S M DAS ROAD

S B K GONGBA RD

Taxis to Ghoom

Railway Station

KUSHARYA RD

To TV Tower and Youth Hostel

Ghoom

To Kalimpong & Gangtok

Ghoom Monastery

Ghoom Railway Station

Monastery

Tiger Hill

To Sandakphu

To Siliguri

Calcutta to Bagdogra, which is 3½hrs from Darjeeling by airport bus (Rs55). If the toy train is operating, it's worth getting a taxi from New Jalpaiguri to Siliguri (5km away) and catching the 9am train up to Kurseong (5hrs). A Rs10 bus or Rs30 share-jeep from Kurseong will get you to Darjeeling by sunset.

Getting Around

Darjeeling is a large, widely dispersed complex of steep steps, deep declines, heaped buildings and winding streets (few of which are properly signposted) strung out over a wide ridge like a flattened, many-tiered wedding cake. As in Shimla, it takes days to figure out (and inches off your waistline finding out), though the scenery takes your mind off the constant ascents and descents. When you've had enough of walking, there are cars for hire from the tourist office and taxis/Land Rovers from the taxi stand. It's fun to go on a pony-ride from Chowrasta (the town square), which costs Rs25 per hour.

Darjeeling ☎ (0354–)   ### Tourist Information

The **tourist office** adjoins the Hotel Bellevue at Chowrasta, ☎ 54050, and is open (in theory at least) from 10am to 4.30pm except Sunday. The staff are helpful but often busy, so go armed with precise questions. Come here to book buses to Bagdogra airport (Rs55), sunrise tours to Tiger Hill (dep 4.30am daily) and good guides, though trekking information is better at the Youth Hostel.

The **GPO** and **State Bank of India** are both on Laden-La Road in the centre of town.

Touring Darjeeling

Spend a day getting used to the altitude and the cool, crisp mountain air, then try the recommended walks. These take the tourist office as their starting point and cover the central, northern and southern sections of Darjeeling respectively. They can be done in any order—though to get the mountain views, you should visit Tiger Hill at the very first sign of clear weather.

The toy train, built between 1879 and 1881, is a brilliant feat of Victorian engineering. Its 88km-long track winds in and out of the scenic mountain valleys to culminate in the famous Batasia Loop, just short of Darjeeling. You get exactly the same views by bus (the road follows the train track most of the way up) but not the same experience. The alternative, if you miss the train, is to wait until you're in Darjeeling itself and take the short but scenic half-hour run to Ghoom, the highest station on the line at 2222m.

Walk 1

Full day. Bengal Natural History Museum–Botanical Gardens–Victoria Falls–Ava Art Gallery–Tenzing's House.

Coming up Nehru Road to Chowrasta square, turn left for the **Bengal Natural History Museum** in Meadowbank Road (*open daily exc Wed 10am–4pm, Wed 10am–noon; adm Rs1*). This was set up in 1903 to give visitors some idea of the wildlife of the district, and houses a comprehensive collection (4300 exhibits) of pattern-board butterflies/insects and stuffed animals. The latter include hang-gliding Himalayan squirrels, surprised-looking tigers and buffaloes, and the tusks and legs of an Indian elephant. It's an interesting display, very well presented.

Further down Meadowbank Road, cut left into Cutcherry Road and then down into Cart Road. Ten minutes' walk to the left brings you to the **Botanical Gardens** (*open 6am–5pm daily, adm free*), situated just below the Market Motor Stand. Opened in 1865, these pretty, peaceful gardens contain a representative collection of flora of the Sikkim Himalaya. The charming terrace has alpine plants, arum-lilies, geraniums, azaleas, rhododendrons, tree ferns and various conifers. Inside are over 2000 different species of orchid and a herbarium. The hothouses are supposed to be a feature, but are disappointing out of season.

Take the south exit out of the gardens into Victoria Road (ask the way) and proceed left on a pleasant half-hour hike down to **Victoria Falls**. The falls only crash down in October/November, after the monsoon, but the walk's the thing. A short distance further down Victoria Road, turn up left into Uday Chand Road, then onto Cart Road. Just to your right is the **Ava Art Gallery** (*open daily 8am–6.30pm*). This houses a fine exhibition of art and embroidery work belonging to Mrs Ava Devi. Opposite the gallery, 5 minutes' walk up D B Giri Road, pay a visit to **Tenzing's House**, home of the famous mountaineer (he conquered Everest with Hillary in 1953), before taking the long Gandhi Road back to the tourist office.

Walk 2

Full day. Happy Valley Tea Gardens–Himalayan Mountaineering Institute–Zoological Park–Passenger Ropeway–Tibetan Refugee Self-help Centre.

Proceed down by the Cart Road, and follow the road signed 'Ropeway' (leading off the top of Chowrasta square) to the **Happy Valley Tea Gardens**, 2km from the centre of town (*open 8am–noon and 1–4.30pm exc Mon and Sun pm; 2–3-hour tours sometimes on offer, Rs10/15*). The estate makes good viewing only from April to November (the plucking season). Of the 70 or so tea gardens in this hill region, this is one of the nearest to town. It still produces tea by the orthodox method, whereby the fresh tea leaves are placed in a withering trough and dried out with high-velocity fans, then successively rolled, pressed and carefully fermented on a conveyor belt. After a final drying process, the tea is sorted into grades: Golden Flowery Orange Pekoe (unbroken leaves), then Golden Broken Orange Pekoe, Orange Fannings and Dust (broken leaves).

Turning left out of the tea gardens, it's a 10-minute walk down Paphawat Gurungi Road to the **Himalayan Mountaineering Institute** on Jawahar Road West (*open 9am–1pm and 2–4.30pm*). This unique institute, set up to train mountaineers, has a marvellous museum full of photos, exhibits and equipment relating to various attempts on Mount Everest. You can see a film show here, or get a close-up of Kanchenjunga through a telescope presented to a Nepalese king by Adolf Hitler. There's a vegetarian restaurant nearby, just next to Tenzing's statue.

The adjoining **Zoological Park** (*open daily 8am–4pm; adm Rs1*) is spoilt by the quite awful conditions in which its animals (Siberian tiger, Himalayan black bear, rare red panda etc.) are kept. It merits a visit only for its excellent snow leopard enclosure (*open 9–11am and 2–4pm*), which is separate and on the way out to the ropeway.

Darjeeling has the first **passenger ropeway** (cable-car) to be constructed in India. It's 5km long and connects Darjeeling with Singla Bazaar, a beautiful picnic and fishing spot at the bottom of the valley. This is a lovely excursion, so long as you have a head for heights, and is the perfect way to finish off the day. The trouble is that everyone else feels the same way—so advance-booking (in person) is essential. Also, long-standing power problems have left only the first 2km of the route operational. On this basis, the return trip (Rs30) takes around an hour. Cars leave every half-hour from 8am to 3.30pm, but not on Sundays and holidays.

If time permits, pay a visit to the **Tibetan Refugee Self-help Centre** (*closed Sun*) a sturdy half-hour trek back towards town along the Lebong Cart Road. Established to rehabilitate Tibetans who came to India with the Dalai Lama in 1959 (in the wake of the Chinese invasion), this large and well-organized centre produces marvellous carpets, woollens, leatherwork, wood carvings, curios and jewellery. Prices tend to be fixed, but bargaining is always fun. Take time out to see the weaving and dyeing shops, and to chat with the workers—they're very friendly. Before leaving, ask directions for the stiff, demanding half-hour climb back up to Chowrasta square.

Walk 3

Overnight stay. Tiger Hill–Ghoom Monastery.

Situated 11km out of Darjeeling town at an altitude of 2610m, **Tiger Hill** is internationally famous for its dawn views over Mount Kanchenjunga and the great eastern Himalayan peaks, including Mount Everest.

A noisy convoy of Land Rovers ply up there around 4am every morning but are cramped and cold. You're far better off going up there on foot. Set aside a full day, and stay overnight at the cheap and simple **Tiger Hill Lodge**, beautifully situated on a scenic plateau facing directly onto Kanchenjunga. Note, however, that this lodge may be closing—check with the tourist office before departure.

Set off early afternoon, taking a jeep to Ghoom from the rank at the bottom of Laden-La Road, or a train from the nearby station. Alighting at **Ghoom's Jore Bungalow**, start up the hill-road rising above the train track. Two minutes later, strike left up the narrow, high path leading to a small Buddhist temple—this is a short cut, taking you along the mountain ridge all the way up to Tiger Hill Lodge in just 1 hour—far better than the dull 2–3-hour slog along the main road. On a clear day, the views from the ridge are spectacular: deep, dipping valleys of conifer, magnolia and rhododendron, set against a dramatic backdrop of gleaming-white mountains.

Up at Tiger Hill, enjoy a good *thali* supper at the lodge and request an early-morning call. You'll need to rise a good hour before dawn. Have a flashlight handy in case of power cuts and bring warm clothing—it can get very cold at night.

In the morning, it's a stiff, steep 30-minute ascent to Tiger Hill viewpoint. Walking up the dark road, keep your flashlight waving all the time, to avoid being mown down by fleets of Land Rovers full of droopy-eyed tourists. Don't begrudge them the easy ride. They'll be frozen at the top, but you'll be as warm as toast—the walk will see to that.

At sunrise, the massive peak of Kanchenjunga rears up in spectacular fashion, flanked by Mounts Kabru and Pandim. To the far left is Everest, surrounded by Markalu, Lhotse and several other summits. Before descending, struggle through armies of local tourists to the viewtower (*adm Rs2, or Rs7 in the warm VIP lounge*) for the obligatory photograph. Then return to the lodge, take breakfast and return down the short-cut hill-path to the **Jore Bungalow** (40mins).

Next stop is **Ghoom Monastery**, the oldest and most famous of Darjeeling's monasteries. A road goes up there (signposted) from just above the Jore Bungalow, passing through a small, colourful village before reaching a plateau of fluttering Buddhist prayer-flags which herald your arrival at the monastery. Established in 1850 by a famous Mongolian astrologer-monk, it belongs to the Yellow Hat Sect and houses a massive image of Maitreya (the Buddha to Come) which sits in a dark, dusty shrine, illuminated by a single beam of light from a ceiling window. It's typically Tibetan and very atmospheric. Photographs are allowed and a small donation is customary.

If it's running, you can take the toy train back to Darjeeling from Ghoom station, 5 minutes' walk above Jore Bungalow. At the station itself, enjoy strange signs like "Don't be afraid of unnecessarily—keep a strict watch around yourself.' The ride takes 30 minutes and provides breathtaking views.

Shopping

The handicrafts of Darjeeling show marked influences of Tibetan, Nepalese, Sikkimese and Bhutanese art and culture. The main products are woollen blankets, hand-knitted garments and woven fabrics, also woodwork, bamboo fretwork, copper-plate curios studded with red and blue stone (or engraved with religious emblems), bedroom slippers and rope-soled shoes, hanzu coats (made from handloom cloth) and masks. The main shopping centres are the **Bengal Emporium** in Nehru Road, near the tourist office (good for Himalayan crafts and Bengal fabrics at fixed prices), **Hayden Hall** in Laden-La Road (for handknitted woollen carpets), and the various tourist shops in Chowrasta (bargain hard for attractive wood carvings and local jewellery). The **Cart Road Market** sells novelty bamboo umbrellas and patterned woollen sweaters. Note that Darjeeling's main markets are closed on Thursdays, and its shops on Sundays and Saturday afternoons.

The best buy, of course, is tea. Real Darjeeling tea has a completely distinctive taste and aroma, greatly superior to the so-called "Darjeeling' teas sold abroad, which are often mixed in with Assamese teas. The top-quality tea is unbroken leaves of Golden Flowery Orange Pekoe (from Rs600 per kg), though you're best off, unless a connoisseur, with ordinary Golden Flowery at half the price. The traditional way to grade tea is to place a pinch in your closed fist, breathe on it to moisten the leaves, and then judge the quality from the aroma. If nothing else, it looks good. The best place to buy tea is Chowk Bazaar, off Cart Road, near the Botanical Gardens. This is also an interesting place to shop for spices, jewellery, curios and handicrafts.

Leisure

During the Raj, Darjeeling residents spent their spare time collecting flora and fauna, creating botanical gardens, playing sports, laying out tea plantations and scaling mountains. Today, visitors have a choice of **walking, trekking, pony-riding,** or playing **golf** at the **Senchal Golf Course**, near Tiger Hill. This enjoys the reputation of being one of the highest golf courses in the world, at 2484m. During the spring and autumn seasons, there is horse-racing at the **Lebong Race Course**. Good **fishing** can be had at the Rangeet River at Singla (8km away), with a permit issued by the District Forest Officer (enquire at the tourist office).

The **Darjeeling Gymkhana Club** on Bhanu Sarani West is great fun. Once a snobby social club, it is now full of travellers playing snooker and billiards, and Indian kids rumbling around on roller-skates and clambering over tennis courts. Membership costs Rs15 per day, and tennis (mornings only) costs Rs5 (extra for racquet hire). In the evening, choose from the masses of backstreet video parlours that show Western releases (often rude/violent). Folk dances can be seen in the monasteries at festivals such as the **Tibetan New Year** in mid-February. Local community groups hold their own celebrations, though these are rarely seen by tourists.

Darjeeling's treks are short, scenic and not too hard going. They are most pleasant in April–May, when all the flowers and shrubs are in bloom, and in October–November, when mountain views are clearest.

If you want an organized trek, complete with porter, guide and food, try **Himalayan Adventures** near Tshering Denzongpa Hotel or **Juniper Tours** on Laden-la Road, close to the clock tower. Otherwise, go off trekking on your own—the trails are well marked and there are good cheap lodges all along the way. A popular short trek is up to Sandakphu (3536m), which gives fantastic views of Everest and the whole range of Kanchenjunga mountains. The journey there and back takes 4 days, starting with a jeep or taxi ride from Darjeeling to Manebhanjang (26km) and proceeding to Sandakphu via Tonglu (3070m), following the Nepalese border the whole way. The full trekking circuit takes 8 days—past Sandakphu to Phalut (3600m) with its close-up views of Kanchenjunga, then down through lovely terraced cultivations to the beautiful village at Lodhama River, and returning through several tea gardens, beautiful rhododendron, silver fir, camellia and magnolia forests via Bijanbari (762m) to North Point above Darjeeling.

For further details of these and other treks, contact the helpful tourist office in Darjeeling. Potential trekkers are also advised to visit the Youth Hostel before setting off: you can get cheap trekking gear here, as well as lots of useful tips from previous trekkers in the visitor's book. Two agencies in town with better (and more expensive) equipment are **Trek-Mate** on Nehru Road or **U-Trek** on N B Singh Road. Guides and porters are available from the tourist office or the Youth Hostel, but are not essential.

Darjeeling ✆ (0354–)   **Where to Stay**

Darjeeling has a wide range of hotels, the better ones offering lovely mountain and valley views, the worst ones no water or heating. Before taking a room, always check if there's a) a back-up generator in case of power cuts and b) water to wash and shower in. Tariffs fluctuate wildly throughout the year and can be discounted as much as 75% in the low season—though not by as much in the big hotels. Prices quoted below are for the high-season months of mid-March to mid-July and mid-September to mid-November.

expensive (from US$35/55)

For comfort and style, stay at the **Windamere Hotel**, up on Observatory Hill, ✆ 54041. Nearly a century old, and once used as a British officers' club, this is a real period piece. Eschewing modern conveniences like TVs and central heating, it entertains with string quartets in the drawing room and a pianist at dinner, and warms its guests with log fires and hot-water bottles. Rooms are quaint and functional, and the US$58/87 tariff includes all meals. Raj-style entertainments include badminton and miniature golf, and all around are dotted amusing signs like 'lie supine on the hearth or sleep behind the settees, lest unintended offence be given to others'. If you fancy an evening tipple, there's a bar.

The more modern **Hotel Sinclair's** at 18/1 Nehru Road, ✆ 3431, has good views, central heating, a restaurant-bar, and comfy rooms with attached bath. Tariffs are a third less than the Windamere, and include breakfast and dinner. The food here is generally excellent.

In the same price bracket, and a popular fallback, is the **New Elgin Hotel** on H D Lama Road, ✆ 2182. This is another old-style place, also good for food, with lots of British touches and TVs in all rooms. The unattractive but friendly **Hotel Chancellor**, ✆ 2956, is opposite the GPO, and will do if needs must.

moderate (from Rs350/500)

The popular **Bellevue Hotel** on Chowrasta, ✆ 2221, is both central and well-kept. It's run by a friendly Tibetan family, and all rooms have bathrooms, heaters and hot water. For the best views, ask for No. 49. Breakfast and snacks are available from the attached café which overlooks Chowrasta. Don't confuse this place with the quieter and older **Main Bellevue Hotel**, just up from it, ✆ 54178. Across the road is the comfortable **Pineridge Hotel**, ✆ 54074, while down on Laden-la Road you'll find two restaurants, the **Shangri-La** and the **Dekevas**, with a few good rooms with views.

Elsewhere, there's **Hotel Tshering Denzongpa** on J P Sharma Road, ✆ 3412 (run by friendly Sherpas), **Hotel Alice Villa** near the New Elgin, ✆ 54181, and **Central Hotel** on Robertson Road, ✆ 2033—all reasonably priced and reliable. The government-run **Tourist Lodge**, ✆ 54411, is some way out of town, next to the Gymkhana Club, but is clean and comfortable. Rooms go for Rs520/785 (breakfast/dinner included) and have views, heaters and hot water. Most reports say you can eat well here.

budget

You need good legs to reach the **Youth Hostel**, above Dr Zakir Hussain Road, ✆ 2290. It's right at the top of the ridge—a stiff 20-minute hike up the hill from the railway station. Only come here if your main purpose is trekking (first-rate information) and/or you're on a shoestring (dorm beds for Rs25). The place is running down fast, and the dormitory often receives icy winds. Travellers often prefer the **Triveni Guest House** opposite (Rs25 dorm beds, Rs60 double rooms) or the nearby **Aliment Restaurant and Hotel**, with a few rooms for Rs40/60. Further along the ridge is **Hotel Tower View** with fine sunrise views and cheap dorm beds/rooms. Take directions for this one though—it's not easy to find.

Neither are the plethora of budget places in town, though most of them lurk on or just off Laden-la Road. The best two are hotels **Shamrock**, ✆ 3378, and

Prestige, ✆ 2699, both up some steps beyond the post office. The nearby **Hotel Pagoda** isn't bad either and (like the other two) has hot water. More expensive, but with better views, are hotels **Crystal**, **Rockville** and **Capital**, above the taxi stand on Nehru Road. The Rockville asks Rs330 (or Rs440 with hot water) but you feel welcome.

Darjeeling ✆ *(0354–)*   ***Eating Out***

Local Tibetan-style food is cheap and simple. The most interesting items are Tibetan bread (delicious with honey or jam) and traditional *momo* mincemeat balls, flavoured with onion and ginger and cooked in steam. Finding good food is a problem, though, and many people eat in their hotel. Darjeeling has few restaurants, mainly just small speak-easies where patrons secretly consume their food in tiny partitioned boxes. Not only does this stop you meeting people, but a curtain is often drawn to stop you even seeing them.

There are several small places like this along Laden-la Road, though some of them are starting to experiment. Where they used to do just local dishes, plus omelettes and chips for travellers, they're now branching out into Chinese, Indian, Kashmiri and Punjabi—a real mix of things. The **Shangri-La** is a good example, as is the **New Embassy** in the Hotel Valentino (Rockville Road), though most travellers take breakfast western-style at **Kev's** (Keventer's Snack Bar) and at **Dekevas** across the road.

At tea time, you want to be at **Glenary's**, just up the hill. Pots of real Darjeeling tea (Rs15) are delivered by cummerbunded waiters onto freshly starched tablecloths, and with a bit of imagination you can see yourself back in the Raj. Good Indian meals (and beer/wine) are served in the restaurant until 7.30pm, while people queue up at the bakery in the early morning for delicious cakes, doughnuts and brown bread.

If you don't want to eat in a hole-in-the-wall, there are lots of mid-range restaurants to choose from, where you can get a decent meal, plus a beer, for around Rs100/150. The standard menu is Indian and Chinese, and is best sampled at the **Park Hotel**, just below Kev's, **Hotel Sinclair's** near the Capital Cinema, and **Polynia** below the Mall. For upmarket continental/Indian fare, ring ahead to the **Windamere Hotel**, ✆ 54041, and book their Rs310 set dinner—it's a real blow-out.

Moving On

By air: from Bagdogra, 90km below Darjeeling, Indian Airlines flies every Monday, Wednesday and Friday to Calcutta, and every Monday, Wednesday, Saturday and Sunday to Delhi. Damania/Skyline NEPC offer daily flights to Calcutta, Delhi, Bombay and Madras. Indian Airlines have an office in the Bellevue Hotel, Chowrasta, ✆ 2355. To book Damania, try a travel agent.

The airport bus (Rs55, 3½hrs) connects with Bagdogra flights and leaves from opposite Hotel Alice Villa. Tickets must be bought in advance from the tourist office.

By road and rail: for Calcutta, the quick option is bus/jeep/taxi (4hrs or less) down to New Jalpaiguri, then the Darjeeling Mail to Sealdah station (dep 6.45pm, 14hrs). There are direct buses to Calcutta, but it's a long, uncomfortable journey—not recommended. Some companies in Darjeeling offer 'direct' buses to Kathmandu (Rs275) but you have to change buses at Siliguri, 4 hours down the mountain. Other agents sell flight tickets from the border (Bhadrapur) to Kathmandu with Everest Air or Royal Nepal. If you need comfort, it's US$100 well spent.

For Gangtok in Sikkim, there are private buses from the bus stand, share taxis for Rs80, and one minibus daily (dep 1pm, Rs60, 7hrs) from Sikkim Nationalised Transport below the GPO on Laden-la Road (book early to avoid disappointment). Car hire is available from several travel agents.

Kalimpong

Kalimpong is another Raj-style hill station, set high up on the Himalaya at a cool altitude of 1250m. Jeeps and buses come here from Darjeeling's Bazaar bus stand at regular intervals between 7.30am and 3pm. It's a 2½ hour trip either way, and you'll enjoy it far more by jeep (Rs35) than by bus. By car, Kalimpong makes a perfect half-way stop between Darjeeling and Sikkim.

Once the property of the Sikkimese rajahs, Kalimpong passed briefly to the Bhutanese in the 18th century before the British took control of it in the 19th century and made it part of West Bengal. Up until 40 years ago, it was the centre of India's wool trade with Tibet. Now it is just a quiet place to enjoy mountain views, bird-watching and scenic hill-walks. There's not much to see in town—just a couple of monasteries and churches—but the trip there and back has fantastic views.

Kalimpong is best on Wednesdays and Saturdays, when the market brings the normally sleepy town into semi-interesting half-life.

Kalimpong ☎ (03552–)   **Where to Stay and Eating Out**

For comfort, put up at the wonderful old-stone **Himalayan Hotel**, ☎ 55248, run by friendly Tim and Nilam McDonald. You'll get all the help and information here to make the best of your stay, and the rooms (Rs850/1300) and food are excellent. You can also book this place in Darjeeling, via the Windamere Hotel, ☎ 54041, 🖷 54043. The mid-priced **Park Hotel**, ☎ 55304, 🖷 55982, is a pleasant alternative, with colonial-style decor, good-value rooms (Rs450/600), and a bar-restaurant attached. Like the good, cheap **Deki Lodge**, ☎ 55095, it's about 10 minutes walk from the bus stand.

The state of Sikkim is situated to the north of Darjeeling, surrounded by Tibet in the north, Bhutan in the east and Nepal in the west. Though measuring only 100km from north to south and 60km from east to west, it has a wide range of elevation (from 244m to over 8500m) which gives it an extraordinary range of flora and fauna. The most dominant feature of Sikkim is Mount Kanchenjunga, the third-highest mountain in the world, soaring to a height of 8603m. The Sikkimese consider the mountain to be their protective deity—their 'mother' goddess.

Among the first people to settle in Sikkim were the tribal Lepchas and other small farmers. After them, in the 15th and 16th centuries, came Tibetans tired of the religious wranglings of various Buddhist sects in Tibet. While the Yellow Hat (Geluk-pa) sect gained control in Tibet itself, the Red Hat (Nyingma-pa) sect became foremost in Sikkim and, with the departure of the nature-worshipping Lepchas to remote regions, they assumed spiritual leadership of the area. Up until quite recently, Buddhism was the state religion and the Chogyal (king) a devout Buddhist.

In the early 19th century, Gurkhas from Nepal occupied a large part of Sikkim. They were eventually defeated by the British and signed the Treaty of Titaliya in 1827, by which all Sikkimese territories were ceded to the British. Though these lands were later returned to the erstwhile king, the British retained Darjeeling hill in return for an annual payment.

Unlike other parts of India, Sikkim displays very little evidence of the Raj. It was on Darjeeling that the British concentrated their attention. Sikkim became an independent kingdom in 1947 although, by agreement, India became responsible for its defence. Ethnic conflict between the minority Lepcha and Bhutia communities on the one side and the Nepalis on the other forced the king to rethink matters, however, and in 1975 Sikkim merged with India to become its 22nd state. At present, some 75 per cent of the population are Nepali, the remaining 25 per cent being a mix of Lepchas, Bhutias and various Indian minorities. There are now more Hindus (60 per cent) than Buddhists (30 per cent), but religious disagreement is rare.

When to Go

Sikkim is best visited from March to late May, and from October to end-December. Temperatures vary from 14° to 22°C in summer, and from 4° to 15°C in winter, so warm clothing is a must. Visiting Gangtok is a bad idea during the 10-day festival of **Durga Puja** in October—hordes of Bengalis roll up from the plains and all hotels are booked solid.

Permits

Standard 15-day permits to visit Gangtok (as well as Rumtek and Phodang monasteries) are issued while you wait at the Foreigners' Registration Office in Calcutta (237 A J C Bose Road, ℗ 2473301). You can get them in Darjeeling too—go to the District Commissioner's Office (11am–1pm and 2–4pm weekdays only), then to the FRO in

Laden-la Road for an endorsement, then back to the DC to collect your permit. In either instance, the whole process takes an hour. Permits can also be issued in London, with a tourist visa, but for west Sikkim only; the procedure takes 10 days.

Trekking in west Sikkim (not covered by this book) requires a separate trekking permit from the permit office in Gangtok (inside the tourist office). They are issued only to groups of four or more people, and only to those who have made a trek booking with a recognized travel agent.

Gangtok
population 85,000

Capital of Sikkim since the 19th century, Gangtok sits on a high ridge (1574m) alongside the Ranipool river. The small modern town has lost much of its charm, but offers spectacular views, especially of majestic Kanchenjunga, and a number of worthwhile excursions.

Getting There

Gangtok can be accessed by road from Darjeeling (*see* p.413) and Kalimpong. The nearest airport is Bagdogra, near Siliguri, which has regular bus and jeep connections with Gangtok (4½hrs).

Getting Around

It's an easy walk from the bus stand to most hotels and cafés. The post office, tourist office and Foreigners' Registration Office are all nearby. Cars can be hired from the tourist office and taxis from the taxi stand.

Gangtok © (03592–)   **Tourist Information**

The **tourist office** is in the bazaar, © 22064 (*open 8am–4pm exc Sun*). In season, it sells irregular tours to local sightseeing spots.

The **Foreigners' Registration Office** is open 10am to 1pm weekdays only. There is a **Sikkim information desk** at Bagdogra—useful if you're coming in by air. You can make **overseas calls** from the post office and **change money** at the State Bank of India opposite the tourist office.

Touring Gangtok

Most of the town can be seen on foot in a morning. Start at **Tsuklakhang**, the royal *gompa* (chapel) of the Chogyals (ex-rulers of Sikkim) in the grounds of the **Royal Palace**. This was once the most important *gompa* in Sikkim—site of royal coronation and marriage ceremonies, and of celebrations to mark national and religious festivals. Tsuklakhang is a very elegant structure in typical Sikkimese style, with carved and painted woodwork, murals, wall hangings and priceless Buddhist treasures. Among the important festivals still celebrated here are *Pang Lhabsol*, held in mid-September to honour Kanchenjunga (the guardian deity of Sikkim), *Kagyat* in early December, when Buddhist monks enact a colourful dance-drama, *Loosong,*, the Sikkimese New Year (also around this time), and *Losar* in February, celebrating the Tibetan New Year. It's only at Losar, unfortunately, that the building is open to visitors.

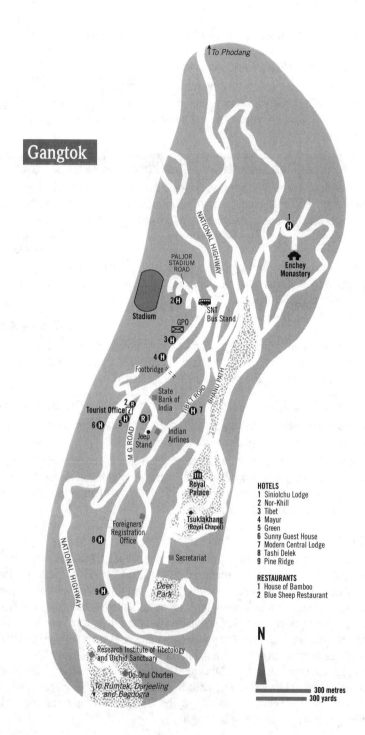

Gangtok

To Phodang

NATIONAL HIGHWAY

PALJOR
STADIUM
ROAD

Stadium

2 (H) Nor-Khill

SNT
Bus Stand

GPO

3 (H) Tibet

4 (H) Mayur

Footbridge

State
Bank of
India

Tourist Office

2 (R)

6 (H) 5 (H) R 1

Jeep
Stand

Indian
Airlines

TIBET ROAD

BHANU PATH

7 (H)

1 (H) Siniolchu Lodge

Enchey
Monastery

Royal
Palace

Tsuklakhang
(Royal Chapel)

Foreigners'
Registration
Office

8 (H)

Secretariat

M G ROAD

NATIONAL HIGHWAY

9 (H)

Deer
Park

Research Institute of Tibetology
and Orchid Sanctuary

Do-Drul Chorten

To Rumtek, Darjeeling
and Bagdogra

HOTELS
1 Siniolchu Lodge
2 Nor-Khill
3 Tibet
4 Mayur
5 Green
6 Sunny Guest House
7 Modern Central Lodge
8 Tashi Delek
9 Pine Ridge

RESTAURANTS
1 House of Bamboo
2 Blue Sheep Restaurant

N

300 metres
300 yards

A little way south, next to the Secretariat, is the **Deer Park**, a popular viewpoint on the edge of the ridge. Look out for the gilded statue of Buddha in teaching mode—a replica of the one at Sarnath. From here, take the winding road down to the **Namgyal Institute of Tibetology** (*open 10am–4pm exc Sun; adm Rs2*). Established by the last Chogyal in 1958, this is the only institute of its kind in India, with several rare Lepcha, Tibetan and Sanskrit manuscripts, statues and *thangkas*, together with other priceless objects.

Next door is an **Orchid Sanctuary** (over 200 varieties of Himalayan orchid), with the impressive **Do-Drul Chorten** (built 1945) only a short walk south. The large gold-topped *chorten* is encircled by 108 prayer wheels which are spun in rotation by circuiting pilgrims. The adjoining monastery has huge statues of Guru Padmasambhava, who took Buddhism to Tibet, and of his manifestation, Guru Snang-Sid Zilzon.

In the afternoon, take a bus, jeep or taxi 14km south to another **Orchid Sanctuary**. Most of Sikkim's 500 or so species of orchid can be found here, and whenever you visit, at least half of them will be in bloom (visit April/May to see the full display). Tours to Rumtek Monastery (*see* below) generally stop here on the way.

For the same or another afternoon, visit the 200-year-old **Enchey Monastery**, 3km out of town above Siniolchu Lodge. Blessed by a lama who'd (allegedly) mastered the power of tantric flight, this place is an important centre of the Nyingma-pa Buddhists. You'll see better monasteries elsewhere, but the views down over Gangtok from the ridge are special. In January, monks perform the masked religious dance of *chaam*, which depicts the age-old battle between good and evil.

Tashi View Point on the North Sikkim Highway, about 8km from Gangtok, offers a spectacular view of the various monasteries on the surrounding hills, as well as of the famous Siniolchu mountain peak. Take a jeep or taxi here to see the sunrise or sunset.

Rumtek Monastery is the largest of its kind outside Tibet and is the seat of the Kagyu-pa order of Tibetan Buddhism. Situated 24km southwest of Gangtok in a lower valley, it is almost an exact replica of the original Kagyu-pa headquarters in Tibet. Though a quite recent structure, it houses several unique religious art objects and is famous for its murals. The best time to visit is the late afternoon, when you can join the prayer and chanting sessions, and even get a cup of salt-butter tea. Tour buses come here, as do local buses (dep 4.30pm, return 8am next day, 1hr), share-jeeps (Rs25) and taxis (Rs250 return, 1 hour stop) from Gangtok. If you want to stay near the monastery, try the budget **Sangay Hotel** or the mid-priced **Shambala Hotel**. Both places are friendly and serve meals.

Smaller but less touristy is **Phodang Monastery** in Thumlong, 40km north of Gangtok. Of Sikkim's 70 or so monasteries, Phodang is one of the most important. The building itself is fairly new, but you'll enjoy the (nightmarish) murals inside and the views into the valley below. To get here, take a share-jeep from the jeep stand in Gangtok (one a day, dep 6.30am—you'll need to pre-book), or take a local bus.

To see the older **Labrang Monastery**, 2km up the hill from Phodang (40 minutes walk), you may have to stay overnight. There are two budget options: the **Yak & Yeti** or **Hotel Northway**.

Yellow Hat Lamas.
Sikkim

Shopping

There are many craft shops in town, but only one—**Charitrust** in the Hotel Tibet—which is non-profit. Most proceeds go to incoming refugees.

Where to Stay

expensive (from US$35/50)

For a traditional stay with all the trimmings, try **Hotel Tashi Delek** on M G Road, ✆ 22038. The staff are friendly, the views from the roof garden/restaurant excellent, and the rooms comfortable. Tariffs include meals and there's a bar. The more modern (and more pricey) **Nor-Khill Hotel** above Paljor Stadium, ✆ 23187, is also recommended. Again, rooms include full board and there's a bar and restaurant. It's particularly good value in low season, when discounts are offered.

moderate (from Rs200/250)

Everyone tries to stay at the **Hotel Tibet**, ✆ 22523, which is far and away the best choice in this bracket. It's centrally located on Stadium Road(next to the GPO) and has fantastic views of Kanchenjunga from its rear rooms. The multi-cuisine restaurant and bar are exceedingly popular and all rooms are well decorated in the traditional Tibetan style. Hot water, TV and heating are supplied, and rates are discounted by 30% off-season.

If this is full, settle for the nearby **Hotel Mayur**, ✆ 22825. It costs half as much as the Tibet (Rs200/250) and has hot water, a bar and a restaurant.

budget

Travellers favour the **Modern Central Lodge** on Tibet Road, ✆ 23417. Run in friendly fashion by two Sikkimese brothers, it offers well-priced rooms (with or without bath), 24-hour hot water, good food, and a snooker hall. The same people also run the new **Pine Ridge Hotel** above the Tashi Delek, which is another good choice.

It's a long haul up to the **Siniolchu Lodge**, just below Enchey Monastery, ✆ 22074. The rooms are bland, and there's no heating, but you do wake up to the best views in town. Taxis go there from the centre for Rs15.

Two popular places, both near the private bus stand, are **Sunny Guest House**, ✆ 22170, and **Hotel Orchid**, ✆ 23151. The former has hot water and views (some rooms only); the latter has hot water and great views from the upstairs bar-restaurant.

There are no views at all at the **Green Hotel** on M G Road, ✆ 23354, but it has hot water (from buckets), a good bar-restaurant, and lots of loyal fans.

Eating Out

The better food is in the hotels—notably the **Tashi Delek** (Chinese/Indian buffet dinners for Rs160), the **Hotel Tibet** (great sizzlers and multi-cuisine), and the **Modern Central Lodge** (western-style breakfasts). Elsewhere, there's the **House** of **Bamboo** for Tibetan/Chinese fare and the **Blue Sheep** for Sikkimese and sizzlers. Both places are on M G Road.

The local tipple is *chang*, made from fermented millet seeds. Mildly intoxicating, and often drunk in huge quantities, it is available from many shops in the market.

Moving On

By air: for flights out of Bagdogra (the nearest airport), contact the Indian Airlines agency on Tibet Road, ✆ 23099.

By rail: trains for Calcutta and Delhi out of New Jalpaiguri/Siliguri can be booked from the railway booking office at the SNT bus stand. It's open 9.30am to 11am and 1.30 to 2.30pm, closed Sunday.

By road: Sikkim Nationalised Transport run daily buses to Darjeeling (7hrs), Kalimpong (3hrs), Bagdogra (4½hrs) and Siliguri (5hrs). These leave from the SNT bus stand and should be pre-booked (9am–noon and 1–2pm) as far ahead as possible. The same goes for private buses, which go to the same places from the private bus stand.

For Siliguri and Kalimpong, there are regular jeeps from the private bus stand.

South India

In recent years the south has become increasingly popular—especially the beaches of Gokarn and Kovalam, and historic Cochin. Since the loss of Kashmir as a holiday destination the scenic attractions of the backwaters of Quilon and Alleppey have to some extent replaced those of the mountainous north. The region also boasts some the country's most important wildlife sanctuaries, and excellent trekking around Ooty and Coorg.

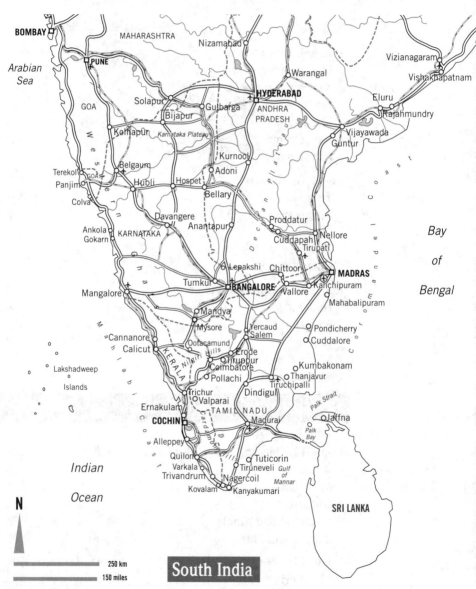

South India

250 km
150 miles

Capital of Tamil Nadu, Madras differs from the larger Indian capitals of Delhi, Calcutta, and Bombay in three major respects. First, it is a home of the ancient Dravidian civilization, hardly touched by the invasions from the north, and often claimed to be 'pure' Indian. Next, it is still unusually spacious, at least away from its main commercial centre—a wide, green and airy 80 sq km of parks and gardens, beaches and esplanades—with very few built-up areas. Last, it has managed to grow from rural village to modern metropolis in 360 years without losing much of its simple charm. All three factors have combined to give Madras, and the south in general, growing popularity as a tourist destination.

History

An important port, Madras has a long history of association with other cultures. The names of many of its streets—Armenian Street, China Bazaar Road, Portuguese Church Street and so on—reflect its early days of international trading importance. Even before the British arrived, its precious cargoes of handlooms, fabrics, silk and hides had attracted European interest, leading to the establishment of a small Portuguese settlement at Sao Tomé.

Madras was also the first English settlement in India. The East India Company arrived here in 1639, and was granted by the Rajah of Chandragiri the small village of Chennapatnam (later the city of Madras), located between the ancient towns of Mylapore and Triplicane in the south and Tiruvottiyur in the north. On this site, in 1641, the Company constructed Fort St George and began exporting cloth back to England. To the north of the European fort arose a second town, called Madraspatnam or 'Black Town' for the Indian community, which later (following King George's visit in 1911) became the present Georgetown. Following its grant of a municipal charter in 1688 by James II, making it the oldest Municipal Corporation in India, Madras became a battleground for competing French and British trading interests in the 18th century, and was even occupied by the French for a brief spell (1746–9) before the young Robert Clive ousted them at the Battle of Arcot in 1751. Though replaced a short time later by Calcutta as the primary British settlement (1772), Madras continued to be one of the four major seats of British Imperial power in India throughout the 19th century. Under the Madras Presidency, the city expanded rapidly outwards, giving birth to a relaxed, open garden city of clubs, churches, parks and elegant Victorian monuments. Today, Madras is abandoning its traditional textile-based economy in favour of rapid industrial and technological development, but it remains a pleasant, semi-rural town, a unique blend of the old and the new.

Many feel Madras is the most pleasant introduction to India—far less noisy and crowded than Bombay or Calcutta, and nowhere near as touristy as Delhi. The people are very friendly too—dark-skinned and insatiably curious Tamils with an obsessive love of foreigners. Here, a casual enquiry for directions will attract a vast swaying crowd of helpful locals within seconds.

When to Go

They haven't named a curry after Madras for nothing. Like the south in general, it has only three seasons—hot, hotter and hottest. It's also humid for much of the year, there being two monsoons—light rains from June to August, and heavy ones from September to November. Travellers normally come for the 'cool' season of December/January (20°–28°C), when it's not so sticky. A good time to be in town is the spring harvest festival of **Pongal** (mid-January), when everyone paints themselves, and their sacred cows, in bright colours and goes beserk for a week. The more sedate **Dance and Arts Festival** of mid-December is another big draw. Madras has any number of minor festivals, each one of them a near-riot.

Food

The staple diet, as elsewhere in the south, is either a tray of assorted vegetables, spices and rice, called *thali* or 'meals', or a folded pancake filled with spiced vegetables called *masala dosa*. Both are cheap (around Rs5) and extremely nourishing. There's also the famous south Indian coffee, generally served in two beakers. The scalding brew is 'cooled' by pouring it back and forth between the two utensils from increasingly high elevations until it's fit to drink. Losing half of it down your lap is an appalling loss of face—and very painful! Since *thalis* and *dosas* may be all you'll find elsewhere in Tamil Nadu, it's worth eating as well as you can in Madras.

International Arrivals and Departures

Madras airport is 17km south of the city centre and has two adjoining terminals—**Anna** for international flights (including British Airways from London) and **Kamarajar** for domestic ones. From the airport, you have a choice of PTC and Aviation Express mini-coaches into town for Rs10/15 or (if you're not prepared to wait for them to fill up) there's an a/c flybus service from the domestic airport for Rs60, luggage free. Prepaid taxis cost more—Rs150 to Anna Salai (Mount Road), Rs180 to Egmore—so you can try bargaining a rate for an auto-rickshaw outside the terminals, but they can be extortionate. From the city to airport is slow by a/c flybus (picks up from several hotels, including Broadlands Lodge), faster by auto-rickshaw (Rs70–100, bargain hard) and quickest by taxi (Rs150–200). The cheapest option is a rickshaw to Egmore railway station, then a suburban train (one every 5 minutes, 4.15am–11.45pm) to Trisulam station, followed by a stroll across the road to the airport—total cost around Rs30! You can use this method *into* the city from the airport too.

Getting There

Madras is the Gateway to the South, and can be reached by air, rail and road from most destinations in southern India. Flights come in from abroad (London, Frankfurt, Bangkok, Singapore, Colombo, and Kuala Lumpur) and from most inland centres, including Bombay, Bangalore, Calcutta, Cochin, Delhi, Goa, Hyderabad, Ahmedabad, Madurai, Pune, Bhubaneshwar and Trivandrum. For more information, *see* p.436.

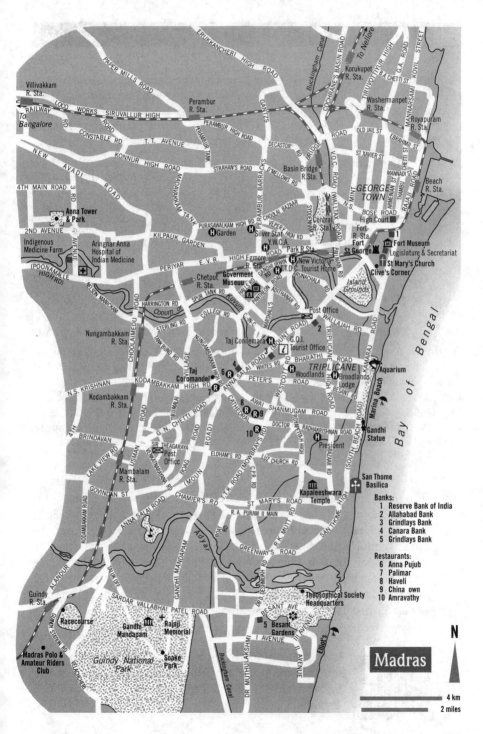

Banks:
1 Reserve Bank of India
2 Allahabad Bank
3 Grindlays Bank
4 Canara Bank
5 Grindlays Bank

Restaurants:
6 Anna Pujub
7 Palimar
8 Haveli
9 China own
10 Amravathy

Madras

N

4 km
2 miles

banks

Cash/travellers' cheques are best changed at **Thomas Cook**, 45 Ceebros Centre, Montieth Road (open 9.30am to 6pm, not Sundays) or **American Express**, G–17 Spencer Plaza, Mount Road (open 9.30am to 7.30pm daily). The **State Bank of India** has branches at Rajaji Salai, Georgetown, at 103 Mount Road, and at both airport terminals. For Sunday transactions, try **ANZ Grindlays Bank**, Padmanabha Nagar, Adyar, open 8.30am to 10.30am only.

books and libraries

There's an awesome range of reading material at **Landmark Books** in the basement of Apex Plaza, 3 Nungambakkam High Road. Also worth a visit are **Higginbothams**, 814 Mount Road, the **Oxford Bookhouse** in Cathedral Grounds, also off Mount Road, and the foyer shop of the **Taj Coromandel Hotel** at 17 Nungambakkam High Road. All bookshops are closed on Sundays.

consulates

USA: 220 Mount Road, ✆ 8273040; **UK**: 24 Anderson Road, ✆ 8273136 (closed at weekends).

international airline officess

Air India, ✆ 8274477, and the domestic **Indian Airlines**, ✆ 8277977 enquiries, 478333 reservations, are both at 19 Marshalls Road, Egmore; **Air France**, 769 Mount Road, ✆ 88377; **Air Lanka**, 758 Mount Road, ✆ 8524232; **British Airways**, 26 Commander-in-Chief Road, ✆ 8274272; **Delta Airways**, 163–4 Mount Road, ✆ 88493; **Lufthansa**, 171 Mount Road, ✆ 8269095; **Malaysian Airlines**, 189 Mount Road, ✆ 868625; **Qantas**, 112 Nungambakkam High Road, ✆ 8278680; and **Singapore Airlines**, 167 Mount Road, ✆ 8521872.

Fast trains into Madras include the 6063 **Chenna Express** from Bombay (dep 7.50pm, 24hrs), the 6042 **Alleppey Express** from Cochin (dep 4.38pm, 14½hrs), the 2676 **Kovai Express** from Coimbatore (dep 2.20pm, 7½hrs), the 2622 **Tamil Nadu Express** from New Delhi (dep 8.30pm, 33½hrs), the 2841 **Coromandel Express** from Howrah, Calcutta (dep 2.05pm, 27½hrs), the **Mangalore Mail** (dep 12.40am, 6hrs) from Mangalore, and the 6320 **Trivandrum Mail** from Trivandrum (dep 1.10pm, 17½hrs). See pp.561 and 542 for the Shatabdi Express from Mysore/Bangalore.

Getting Around

Madras divides into three main sections: busy, commercial **Georgetown** to the north (with GPO, American Express, bazaars, budget hotels in and around Netaji Subhash Bose Road); **Egmore** in the city centre (for bus/rail terminals, airline offices,

medical services

The **Apollo Hospital**, ✆ 8277447, at 21 Greams Lane offers a 24hr emergency service.

post offices and telephones

Though the main **GPO** is on Rajaji Salai, most travellers find the smaller post office in Anna Salai more convenient (8am to 8.30pm, Sundays 10am to 5pm), not just for mail but for poste restante (10am to 6pm, closed Sundays), for practical packing/sending, and for 24hr international phone calls. There are **STD/ISD** overseas call booths all over town, and you can use Videsh Sanchar Bhavan, 5 Swami Sivananda Salai, for reverse-charge (collect) calls and faxes (7am to 7pm daily).

travel agents

The best travel agents are **Mercury Travels**, 191 Mount Road, ✆ 8522993 (plus a desk at Oberoi Trident Hotel, ✆ 2344747 ext 3395), and **Sita World Travel (P) Ltd**, 26 Commander-in-Chief Road, ✆ 8278861. **Travel Corporation India** (**TCI**), 734 Mount Road, ✆ 868813, is good for car and flight bookings (contact Charlene). One-day car tours are best arranged through small independent agents such as Hotel Shri Lekha, 48 Anna Salai, ✆ 830521. Oberoi recommend them for excursions to nearby places like Mahabalipuram, which costs only Rs600 return (bigger agents such as Clipper Holidays would charge Rs1000 or more). Use **Clipper Holidays** (Flat BS17, Basement Floor, Gems Court, 14 Khadar Nawaz Road, ✆ 8232645), rather, for long-haul tours.

visa extensions

These can be applied for at the Foreigners' Registration Office, ✆ 8278210, at the back of Shastri Bhavan annexe (ground floor), 26 Haddows Road. Turn up at 9.30am sharp (weekdays only) for quick service and bring your passport and one photo.

consulates, tourist offices and decent hotels/restaurants, in and around Anna Salai/Mount Road); and **Guindy/Adyar**, the quiet, semi-rural 'green belt' (with wildlife park, beaches and the Theosophical Society) to the far south.

Getting around Madras presents you with two problems: first, all the streets were renamed following Independence, and the new names haven't stuck (everybody still calls Anna Salai, Madras's chief thoroughfare, by its old title of Mount Road); second, transport round town is very hit-and-miss. The inner city is crowded with unemployed auto- and cycle-rickshaws who'll do anything, even climb the pavement, to get your business. Few of them speak English, however, and even fewer of them know where they are going. Auto-rickshaws charge Rs5 for the first 2km, then Rs1 for each subsequent km. There are no metered taxis in Madras, only cars which can be booked from the tourist office, the better hotels and travel agents. They are not metered, but work on a half (Rs500) or full-day (Rs1000) package basis. If you're staying in the city centre, there's a 24-hr taxi service outside the Taj Connemara Hotel in Binny Road—useful for airport drops (Rs160). Most travellers see Madras by **bicycle**, which can be hired from guesthouses like Broadlands for around Rs10 per day.

Tourist Information

Madras' **Government Tourist Office**, 143 Mount Road, ✆ 840752, is open from 10 to 5.45 daily, and round the clock for tour bookings. It's the most useful and helpful tourist office in southern India. Here you can pick up brochures, a complimentary copy of *Hallo Madras* (full of useful tips), and advance-book TTDC accommodation throughout Tamil Nadu. You can also book tours for Madras city (dep 8.30am and 1.30pm; Rs65 non a/c, Rs100 a/c) or for Kanchipuram, Thirukalikundram and Mahabalipuram (dep 6.20 to 7pm; Rs 160 non a/c, Rs260 a/c).

TTDC also has an information counter at the central railway station, open 6am to 9pm, while the more general and under-staffed **Government of India Tourist Office** is at 154 Mount Road, ✆ 8524295/8524785, open 9.15am to 5.45pm weekdays, 9am to 1pm Saturdays); it sells a good city map for Rs5.

Touring Madras

Madras is a huge, sprawling giant of a city and its few interesting sights are very spread out. Take a conducted tour bus for quick, cheap orientation, then go exploring by car or bicycle. Madras has one of the longest beaches in Asia—a good place to head when sightseeing is over.

City Tour

By tour bus, 4 hours. Fort St George–St Mary's Church–Fort Museum–
High Court–Government Museum–National Art Gallery–Valluvar Kottam–
Guindy Snake Park–Kapaleeshwara Temple–Sao Tomé Basilica

From the tourist office, it's a straight run up Anna Salai (Mount Road) to the birthplace of Madras, **Fort St George**. Still surrounded by cannon-proof walls (in whose guardhouses tailors and barbers have now set up shop), the fort was rebuilt several times between 1642, when its original bastions were completed, and 1749 when the French left. Despite this, it remains—moats and all—pretty much the same today as when it was first made the seat of empire. Declared a national monument in 1948, most of its buildings have been converted into government offices, notably the Legislature and Secretariat. The fort was at various times the home of Robert Clive, Elihu Yale and Sir Arthur Wellesley (later Lord Wellington). Inside it, visit the sturdy little **St Mary's Church** (*open daily, 8.30–5.30*), the oldest Protestant church east of Suez and the first Anglican one in India. Built in 1680 from voluntary contributions of the Fort's English inhabitants, it gained its spire in 1710 and was completely renovated in 1759. Designed by a British gunner (and built to last, with walls 4ft thick and a roof 2ft thick), this church is noteworthy for its total brick and stone composition: no wood was used anywhere. The three aisles, arched with brick and stone, have a bomb-proof vaulted roof. The gallery has a finely carved nave, with two curved outer staircases. The walls are dotted with memorials to the East India Company's 18th-century administrators and soldiers who died at Madras. Few of these made it past the age of 50, giving an insight into the conditions of those choleric and malarial times. In the courtyard are some of the oldest British tombstones in India; a few have been moved inside and are now beneath the altar. The Renaissance painting above the altar was painted by an unknown artist and was brought here from Pondicherry in 1761. Famous people who married in St Mary's include Lord Cornwallis, Elihu Yale (an early Governor of Madras, who later founded Yale University in the US) and Robert Clive. Clive House, behind the church, is another reminder of the great empire-builder who started out as a humble clerk within this fort.

The nearby **Fort Museum**, (*open daily, 9–5, except Fri, adm free*) is now housed in the Fort's Exchange Office (built 1780–90). The museum has 10 galleries with many exhibits telling the story of the East India Company's activities in south India. The top floor has some good French porcelain, clocks and glass, and, of most interest, some 19th-century prints of Madras. The ground floor has East India Company memorabilia, including officers' medals, tea-sets and cutlery. The weapons gallery has some good curiosities, including early 19th-century mines, mortars and chainshot—two iron balls linked by a chain, fired from a light cannon and designed to rip, literally, through massed ranks of soldiers. Next door is an old palanquin used by the pre-Raj Nawabs, and a scale model of the fort. However, the museum's real treasure is back in the weapons gallery—a weird little wooden cage in which a huge, whiskered officer called Captain Philip Anstruther spent a month after being captured by state guards in China in 1840 while on Company business. Anstruther was chained inside the cage, with a split open head, and displayed for the derision of the local Chinese until he received a miraculous pardon and was set free. For some reason, he asked to keep the cage. Local stories about the man are not confined to this incident. Apparently Anstruther was something of a character in his own right. One story reports that he once gave a beggar a gold sovereign in the street, exclaiming, 'Good God Man, you're the first man I've seen who's even uglier than me!'

Just north of the fort is the magnificent **High Court** (built 1861), reputed to be the finest example of Indo-Saracenic architecture in India. It's worth returning to later on (as you only get a fleeting glimpse from the bus) for a leisurely tour around its stately corridors, courts and staircases. There are several interesting paintings here too, and a 'lighthouse' tower which was in use until 1977. You can climb to the top.

Returning to the city centre, the tour makes a worthwhile visit to the beautiful, if decaying **Government Museum** in Pantheon Road (*open daily 8–5, except Fri*). A classical structure with faded red walls and a delightful internal labyrinth of staircases and interconnecting galleries, the museum is notable for its annexe, which houses an unequalled collection of fine bronzes, mainly from the early Pallava, Chalukya and Vijayanagar periods. Of particular beauty is a dancing 8-armed Shiva (in the act of creation), which occupies the central position in the gallery. In the main museum, the

Itinerant fortune teller, Pongal festival

largest exhibit are the panels from the *c.* 200 BC **Amaravati Stupa**, said to have been erected over Gautama Buddha's relics, which occupies a whole gallery. It was discovered, and later excavated in 1816, by Colonel Colin Mackenzie who found the panels being used as building material. One warning: the museum staff may encourage you to take photographs of exhibits, and then immediately demand *baksheesh*. You don't have to pay, so say no.

Attached to the museum (and included in the same admission ticket) is the **National Art Gallery**, a fine Indo-Saracenic building with a good collection of Mughal and Rajput miniatures, glass-paintings from Tanjore and assorted 11th–12th-century metalware. Note the paintings of early 19th-century rajahs and ranis, fat, baby-faced caricatures, and the disturbing miniature of Jains being impaled during the south Indian persecution of the sect in the 18th century.

Down in Nungambakkam (the Hollywood of south India and full of film studios) there's an overlong stop at **Valluvar Kottam**, a memorial dedicated to the poet-saint Thiru Valluvar. Opened in 1976, its massive auditorium is one of Asia's largest, containing 4000 seats, and is an important cultural centre. Inscribed on the polished granite are 1330 of the poet's verses from his epic *Thira Kural.* Outside, there's a 'temple chariot' in stone, a vast rectangular terrace and extensive gardens.

Guindy Snake Park (*open daily, 8.30–5.30*) is 6km further south, close to the Governor's House or Raj Bhavan. It's a small, interesting reptilium of snakes, iguanas, crocodiles and spiders. Here you can go chameleon-spotting, investigate the curious 'Snake Worship Anthill', and watch the hourly (from 10am) demonstration of unfanged-cobras being handled. You are also allowed to handle the snakes but this is not recommendable! The Snake Park backs onto 300 acres of parkland supporting herds of blackbuck, many *chital* (spotted deer) and monkeys. For a pleasant day here, return via urban train, or by no.45 bus from Anna Square in the city centre.

Off R K Mutt Road, in the old Mylapore district, you'll proceed next (if on a tour bus) to **Kapaleeshwara Temple**. Dedicated to Shiva, the temple's legend (Parvati as a peacock, praying to Shiva for deliverance after some domestic transgression) is portrayed in sculpture within. The 40m-high *gopuram* tower, festooned with richly coloured deities, is a distinctive feature of Dravidian temple architecture. You'll see more of these throughout Tamil Nadu. Their principal purpose was to guard the inner shrine from attack, either spiritual or temporal. Considering how few south Indian temples suffered damage over the centuries, they seem to have been remarkably effective. Here, as with other 'living' temples in Tamil Nadu, non-Hindus are not allowed into the inner shrine.

After a brief visit to Elliot's Beach (just enough time for a paddle), the tour finishes off at **Sao Tomé Basilica** on South Beach Road. This is a Gothic-style Catholic church said to house the remains of St Thomas, the 'Apostle of India', who died at nearby St Thomas Mount in AD 72. Despite being miffed at finding the Indian Christian Church (known as the Syrian Orthodox) alive and well—and older than their own—the early 16th-century Portuguese missionaries quickly went about catholicizing St Thomas (he was an apostle after all) and built a church here in 1504. However, the Renaissance structure was sadly replaced by the present late-Victorian edifice in 1893.

Triplicane

There are a few places in busy Madras to stroll around and take in the street life. One exception is the old residential quarter of Triplicane, located south along Anna Salai (Mount Road), about 2km from the town centre. For easy orientation, jump into an auto-rickshaw and ask for Broadlands Lodge, an ex-Nawab's town residence (now a budget traveller's hang-out) in the heart of the area. For a while, you'll wonder why you've come. Past the usual chaos of filth, livestock and beggars and people going hurriedly about their business, creating an atmosphere which, though full of busy charm, is little different from that of any other Indian town, however, look up above the shop fronts and you will notice many fine designs on the buildings, with balconies and rooftop terraces peeping over onto the squalid streets. This is the clue to the real Triplicane, for behind these fine, yet dirty fronts lie cool quiet courtyards with trees and gardens and a traditional south Indian town life that has remained unchanged for centuries. Visit Broadlands Lodge for a glimpse of one of these interiors (*see* p.435). Triplicane also has a plethora of cheap, clean eating houses, and is a good place for a cool walk before supper.

Beach Excursion

By bicycle, full day. Marina Beach–Theosophical Society–Elliot's Beach–Golden Beach

This is the ideal follow-up to the hot, sticky city tour—a cool, relaxing ride by bicycle down the city's long seafront to a couple of its nicest beaches.

From the centre of town, it's a 10/15-minute bike ride down to **Marina Beach**, by the Aquarium. This 11km strip of fine sandy shore is known as the 'pride of Madras'. A favourite evening resort of locals, it is fronted by garden-fringed promenades dotted with statues and parks dedicated to prominent Tamil writers and educators.

Turn right down South Beach Road until you come to **Gandhiji Statue** (after 2km). Just behind this is the new **Lighthouse**, where you can climb 150 feet for marvellous views of the coastline. You can swim here, though it's less rough farther south down Marina Beach.

A scenic half-hour journey takes you on via Sao Tomé Basilica (turn off right here down Sao Tomé High Road) to the quiet, rural Adyar precinct. Past the derelict **Ayappa Temple** (on the left, a mile inland), turn left into Dr Durgabai Deshmukh Road, and cross over the wide **Adyar Lake**. Over the bridge, turn left into Besant Road for the **Theosophical Society** (*open weekdays, 8–11am and 2–5pm; Sat 8–11am; gardens open sunrise–sunset*). The approach along pretty country lanes is the perfect introduction to the 270 acres of beautiful gardens within the Society's grounds. Established in New York in 1875 by Madame Blavatsky and Colonel Olcott, the Theosophical Society moved to Madras in 1882. It was formed to promote the study of comparative religions, philosophy and science. After migrating to Madras, the society was run by Annie Besant. The vast campus, spread over 1750 acres, has shrines to all faiths and houses a superb library with 17,000 manuscripts. It is also the site of one of the world's largest banyan trees.

Elliot's Beach appears on your left just 10 minutes' ride past the Society. For a quick, quiet swim try the beach off V Avenue Road. Friendly fishermen take it in turns to 'guard' you and mind your clothes and belongings while you're in the sea.

The best stretch of sand in Madras area, **Golden Beach**, lies a further 10km south. If you're not up to cycling it, you can get a bus from Elliot's Beach, and return here to pick up your bike later on. Alternatively, be at Kapaleeshwara Temple for the sunset over Adyar River. To get there, go straight ahead at the end of Dr Durgabai Deshmukh Road and up R K Mutt Road for a mile. The evening lights over the small lake are beautiful—so is the evening ceremony of *aarti* when the gods are brought out and shown the setting sun, with musical accompaniment.

Shopping

For silk, the best buy, visit **Co-optex** just past the museum on N S R Bose Road or reputable shops like **Kumaran Silks** and **Nalli's** in Thinagaya area. Co-optex is a huge place, with a whole ground floor of quality silks and fabulous south Indian handloom fabrics. All prices are fixed. Go with your purchase to the basement shop at **Spencer's Plaza** and get the material made up by the tailor there. It helps to bring along a pattern and, if possible, an Indian woman to advise on styles and to bargain for you. **India Silk House (P) Ltd**, 846 Mount Road, ✆ 844930, is one of many emporia on Mount Road which specialize in fabrics, which can be better than Co-optex. For general handicrafts, try the interesting **Indian Art Museum**, at 151 Mount Road, which does nice jewellery and sandalwood carvings.

Spencer's Plaza, on Mount Road, is a good place to shop for Western-style garments and leather items. Latest-design leather articles are also available at the in-house arcades of the **Taj** and **Connemara hotels**. Madras is a major centre of the leather boom and the city is full of *haute couture* leather boutiques, offering good quality briefcases, handbags, jackets, coats and shoes at knock-down prices. For flashy, flamboyant stuff, try **Iguana Boutique**, at the WelcomGroup Adyar Park lobby. For soft leather in more subdued styles, go to **Fashion 'n' Gems** on

Nungambakkam High Road. Silver is not good quality in Madras; you're best off waiting until you get to Delhi or Rajasthan to buy it. **Fashion n' Gems** is, however, a good shop for both gold and silver jewellery. If you've got time for only one shopping outing, head for **Victoria Technical Institute (V T I)**, at 765 Mount Road. This has practically everything under one roof, and prices are fair.

For people who want to buy food and self-cater, there's a massive range of fresh produce available from the new **Nilgiri's** supermarket.

Leisure

Apply to the **Cosmopolitan Golf Club**, Mount Road, ✆ 849946, for use of its sandy but shaded 18-hole course. The **racecourse** near Guindy rail station holds meetings most weekends from November to March. The **Madras Riding Club** offers hacking and lessons on the Madras racecourse throughout the year with the exception of June, when it's too hot. For temporary membership apply to **Madras Race Club**, ✆ 431171. For squash, tennis and indoor games, apply in writing to the Secretary of the **Madras Gymkhana**, ✆ 447863.

There's instant membership for guests at the **Boat Club**. You can find luxury **pools** at both at the New Woodlands (7.30am to 12noon and 2 to 4.30pm) and the nearby Hotel Savera, for a small charge. If you want to swim in the sea (not recommended though), the cleanest and safest stretch is at Mylapore Beach, near Mahatma Gandhi's statue on Beach Road. Avoid crowded Sundays though.

Madras is the centre of *Bharatnatyam*, possibly the oldest **classical dance** form in India. Traditionally performed by young girls dedicated to south Indian temples (*devadasis*), it is today performed by women who describe not only passages from religious texts, but also the moods of a girl in love. Madras has a dozen good cultural centres—notably **Kalakshetra Centre** at Thiruvanmiyur, and **Music Academy**, T.T.K. Road, Alwarpet. To plan your entertainment programme—dance and culture shows, cinemas, drama and tourist fairs, temple celebrations, music exhibitions, craft presentations and even circuses, buy a Friday edition of the *Hindu* or the *Indian Express* newspapers which carry a full listing of upcoming events. Otherwise, spend an evening at Taj Coromandel's **Raintree** restaurant—there's a great *Bharatnatyam* programme every evening from 8 to 9.30pm.

The best **cinemas** are Devi Paradise and Woodlands; they both carry English films as well as Hindi ones.

Madras is surprisingly short on **nightlife**, compared to Bombay or Delhi, but Oberoi have recently started monthly discos with a 'zodiac' theme; ring for dates and details. In town, there are weekend discos at hotels **Sindoori** (off Anna Salai) and **Park Sheraton**, though entrance is normally restricted to residents or invited guests.

Madras has surprisingly few good hotels for a big city, and the better ones are (in season) constantly full. Whenever possible, book your rooms in advance. For convenience, most people stay in the central Mount Road–Egmore area, though this is where good rooms are scarcest (November to February especially). If arriving around Christmas/New Year, reserve well in advance or be prepared to sleep on your pack.

luxury (from US$100)

The 5-star hotels do very well, mainly because their tariffs are so much lower than Delhi's or Bombay's. They are particularly attractive in the hot, humid months of May to July, when rates are discounted.

Until the new Oberoi opens up on Mount Road (1997/8), the nearest thing to Western-style luxury is the stylish **Oberoi Trident** at 1/24 G S T Road, ✆ 2344747, ✆ 2346699, on the way to the airport (2km). It's a bit far out for sightseeing, but is useful for early morning flights. Set amidst five acres of tropical gardens, it has three speciality restaurants, a pretty pool, an efficient travel desk, handy car-rental service, and very livable a/c rooms around US$100/120. Staff are friendly, and can arrange golf, badminton, tennis and riding. The hotel's only weak link is its reception desk.

Far more central than the Trident is Taj's **Connemara** in Binny Road, ✆ 8520123, ✆ 8523361, a lovely old property (owned originally by Lord Connemara) with beautiful gardens and very comfortable rooms from US$100. Ask for one of the 'old colonial' ones—the only rooms in Madras which are not discounted at any time of the year! Recently renovated, it now has a popular restaurant, a 24-hour coffee shop with live band, a business centre and the largest pool in the city. The **Taj Coromandel** at 17 Nungambakkam High Road, ✆ 8272827, is more expensive, has less character, and is geared to the business traveller. The upper-storey rooms offer good views and the Indian restaurant is superb. The new **Park Sheraton Hotel Towers**, though, is a totally renovated hotel in a quiet residential area at 132 T.T.K. Road, ✆ 4994101. Rooms are spacious but rather bland.

expensive (from US$25)

The **Ambassador Pallava** at 53 Montieth Road, ✆ 8554476, is a good place to meet the Madrasi upper classes (especially in the quality Chinese restaurant), but is rather overpriced at US$40/55. Slightly more costly, but generally better value, is the **Savera**, 69 Dr Radhakrishnan Road, ✆ 8274700, ✆ 8273475, with a pool, many facilities, and very well-appointed rooms.

moderate

It's in the mid range category that Madras runs into serious problems. The only thing 'new' about the much-fêted **New Victoria**, 3 Kennet Lane, ✆ 8253638, is the lobby. The surrounding streets are one big slum and the rooms are way-over-priced at around US$20. It's handy for the railway station, though, and the staff are friendly. Cheaper and cleaner is the **New Woodlands Hotel** at 72/75 Dr Radhakrishnan Road, ✆ 8273111, ✉ 8260460, next to the Savera Cinema in Mylapore. This offers spacious air-cooled rooms from Rs250/500, popular a/c cottages from Rs850, and top-value deluxe suites at US$20. It's the only place in this range worth the price, and scores with helpful staff, a billiard room, and an excellent a/c bar-restaurant. A couple of second-stringers are **Nilgiris Nest** (a few doors down at no.58, ✆ 8275222, and **Hotel Kanchi** at 28 C-in-C Road, ✆8271100.

inexpensive

Everyone heads for the same place—**Broadlands Lodge** at 16 Vallabha Agraharam Street, opposite Triplicane's Star cinema, ✆ 845573/848131. Like the Taj Connemara, this was one of the town residences of the old Nawab of Arcot in the 19th century but was acquired by the government after Independence. Unlike the Taj, this place has retained its period charm and is an Arabian Nights-style confusion of galleries, courtyards and rooftop terraces, with 44 rooms to choose from. Run by the genial Mr Kumar, it has the sort of things you'd like to see in *every* budget lodge in India: good information, nice gardens, a sun-roof, filtered water and room service. Here you can hire a cycle, use the library, and chill out in the shaded gardens. Rooms go for Rs140 single, Rs280 double, the two best ones being no.18 with its famous graffiti wall-paintings, and no.44, the roof cottage. If full, staff will give you a dorm bed or, failing that, a mattress on the roof. If you're in Madras just for the day, you can dump bags here while you go sightseeing. You can also (for a small charge) leave excess luggage whilst travelling elsewhere in the south.

A good fallback, if Broadlands is full, is the new **Hotel Comfort**, just up the road at 22 Vallabha Agarwal Road, ✆ 845117, with rooms for Rs175/225. Other options are the **Tourist Hotel**, ✆ 416001, on Andhra Mahila Sabha (Adyar Bridge Road), the **Shree Krishna** on St Peter's Road, ✆ 8522897, or the **Sornam International** at 7 Stringer Street, ✆ 563061, worth staying in for its rooftop restaurant.

budget

Cheap accommodation in Madras is mostly confined to the YMCAs, which are often full. The two most popular are the **YWCA Guest House and Camping Ground**, 1086 Poonamallee High Road, ✆ 39920, and the **YMCA** in Westcott Road, ✆ 811158, opposite Royapettah Hospital. Try also the **TTDC Youth Hostel**, on E.V.R. Road, near the Central Railway Station, ✆ 589132, or the **YMCA** on N.S. Bose Road, opposite the city bus stand, ✆ 58394. Many travellers use the **Salvation Army Red Shield Guest House** at 15 Ritherdow Road, ✆ 5321821.

For high-quality Chinese food, it's a toss-up between the speciality restaurant at **Oberoi Trident** and the **Golden Dragon at** Taj's Coromandel. Both claim to be the best in town—decide for yourself!

For a real splurge, try the Taj Coromandel's **Pavilion** coffee shop (12.30 to 3pm daily) or the open-air **Raintree** restaurant at the Connemara, which serves authentic *Chettinad* south Indian cuisine (very hot and pungent). A meal at the Raintree costs around Rs500 per head, and you'll need to arrve at 7.30pm sharp to grab a table near the stage—the excellent classical dance show starts at 8pm. In the same hotel is the city's only French restaurant, with excellent personal service and an elegant ambience.

Over at the Chola Sheraton, the equally exclusive **Peshawri** is Madras's only eatery serving Northwest Frontier food—a last repast of tasty *tikkas*, *tandooris*, *birianis* or marinated meats before you plunge into the vegetarian heartland. The Peshawri is open from 12.30 to 3pm and from 7.30 to midnight, a standard meal costing around Rs400 per head.

Cheap places selling *thalis* (vegetable tray and rice) and *masala dosas* (spicy veg-filled pancakes) are all over town. If you're heading into the south and haven't tried these two dishes yet, the place to start is **Hotel Maharaja**, just round the corner from Broadlands Lodge in Triplicane. This is a dark but popular hangout, favoured by Indians and travellers alike, with a cool a/c section and the news in English on TV. There's an extensive menu, including Rs12 *thalis*, Rs8 *dosas*, sandwiches, and tasty tandoori items.

Another popular joint is the **Fiesta** restaurant at Spencer Plaza on Mount Road. Rich Indians come here for chilled filter-water and for baked beans on toast. Westerners turn up for good Indian/Continental food and for milk shakes—or just to sit in the shade. They also like **Dasaprakash** ice-cream parlour, 806 Mount Road, for cheap veg snacks/salads and ice cream. The best mini-splurge in town is still Hotel Connemara's excellent lunchtime buffet (Rs200). The pastry shop at lobby level is definitely worth a visit.

Over at 67 Mount Road, the long-running **Chungking** restaurant serves a wide variety of mid-priced Chinese dishes, including chicken, chips and spring-rolls for Rs100. Rather cheaper for Chinese is **Tom's Place**, just round the corner from GOI tourist office.

Very big with travellers is the vegetarian restaurant at the **New Woodlands Hotel**, famous for its tandooris/*dosas* and surprisingly inexpensive.

by air

Madras has flights to other countries (*see* 'Getting There', p.424) as well as to many places within India.

Indian Airlines, ✆ 8251677, flies daily to Bombay, Calcutta, Delhi, Hyderabad and Trivandrum; less often to Bangalore (daily except Sunday), Coimbatore (4 days a week), Goa, Ahmedabad, Madurai, Mangalore, Pune and Cochin (3), and Bhubaneshwar (2). **Damania/Skyline NEPC**, ✆ 8280610, flies 7 days a week to Delhi, Calcutta, and Bagdogra; less frequently to Bombay (6), and Bangalore (3). **NEPC Airlines**, ✆ 458650, has increased its network to include Cochin, Coimbatore and Madurai (daily flights), Bangalore and Hyderabad (6), Pune and Mangalore (3), and Bhubaneshwar (2). **Modiluft** and **Jet Airways** offer daily services to (respectively) Delhi and Bombay.

by rail

Madras has two stations—**Egmore**, for destinations in Tamil Nadu (right down to Kanyakumari), and **Central**, for everywhere else. Both stations are close to each other, off Poonamallee High Road, and you can use suburban trains to get around Madras itself—say, up to Fort St George or to Madras Beach, or down to Guindy for the National Park.

Fast trains out of Madras Central include the 2007 **Shatabdi Express** to Mysore (dep 6am, 14hrs) via Bangalore (5hrs), the 6064 **Chenna Express** to Bombay (dep 7am, 24hrs), the 2842 **Coromandel Express** to Hyderabad (dep 8.10am, 28hrs), the 2621 **Tamil Nadu Express** to New Delhi (dep 9pm, 34hrs), the 6059 **Charminar Express** to Cochin (dep 7.35pm, 13½hrs), and the 6319 **Trivandrum Mail** to Trivandrum (dep 6.55pm, 17hrs).

Seat reservations are easy, and you can tap the tourist quota by going to the Indrail office, 2nd floor, inside Central Station. It's open from 10am to 6pm and you don't need an Indrail Pass for reservations, just your passport.

by road

TTC state buses go to all major points in Tamil Nadu, notably Mahabalipuram (2hrs), from the Express bus stand on Esplanade Road, Georgetown. You can buy tickets in advance from the upstairs reservation office, open 7am to 9pm daily. Also come here to reserve out-of-state JJTC buses to Bangalore (8hrs), to Madurai (10hrs), to Kodaikanal (12hrs), and to Hyderabad, Trivandrum, Ooty and Kanyakumari (all around 15/16hrs). Use local kids to get you on the right bus; the terminal is sheer chaos.

Cars can be hired from hotels, travel agents and TTDC tourist office for day-tours to Mahabalipuram (Rs680 return) or Kanchipuram (Rs900). A/c cars cost around double.

Route 9: Tamil Nadu

Relatively unspoilt by foreign invaders, Tamil Nadu is home to the ancient Dravidian people who today consider themselves the only 'true' Indians. In this southernmost state, many of the country's original customs and traditions survive in their purest form.

Tamil Nadu is essentially a land of temples, thousands of them. This route plots the course of their evolution— form simple unadorned beginnings at **Mahabilapuram** (with its famous Shore temple and lovely beach) to towering, sophisticated examples at silk-centre **Kanchipuram**, to the culmination of the sculptor's art at the Sri Meenakshi temple complex of **Madurai**. Dotted between these sites are a trio of interesting diversions—the old French settlement of **Pondicherry**, the scenic hill-station of **Kodaikanal**, and the Land's End of India, **Kanyakumari**— where 'templed-out' travellers can rest up and recover.

Itinerary

You'll need a good fortnight to see Tamil Nadu properly. Allow 4 clear days in Madras—2 to explore the capital, 2 more for quick day-tours to nearby Mahabalipuram and Kanchipuram. If you're short on time, use day 5 for a flight from Madras to Madurai, followed by 3 nights in Madurai (one to see the temple city, two for the slow trip up to Kodaikanal and back again). To complete the circuit, there are buses from Madurai to Kanyakumari (one night), then another back to Madras. Pondicherry is something to do either as a third day trip from Madras (followed by a bus to Madurai) or as a diversion from Madurai on the way back to Madras.

If this sounds complicated, it needn't be. Few travellers see Tamil Nadu as a self-contained route. Most of them do Madras—Kanchipuram—Pondicherry—Madurai—Kodai—Madurai—Kanyakumari in a straight run by bus. This takes 10–14 days, and is usually followed by a short bus hop up into Kerala for Kovalam Beach.

The best time to go is from November to March, avoiding the monsoon in October–December (in the western hills, also June–September). The climate is around 18°–43°C.

Mahabalipuram (Mamallapuram)

Situated on the shore of the Bay of Bengal, Mahabalipuram was already a famous seaport in the 1st century AD, at about the time Tamil Nadu's recorded history begins. It was later adopted by the empire-building Pallava kings (600–800), who turned it into a major trading port to service their nearby capital of Kanchipuram. They also used the town as a workshop for their temple-building schemes—the 7th century AD marking a move away from monolith rock-cut cave architecture to free-standing, structural temples. The seven 'rathas' or temple chariots, and the seven pagoda-style shore temples they built here at Mahabalipuram are the earliest known examples of Dravidian architecture, and were

India's best temples are in the south. The ones in the north are largely modern reconstructions, modelled on originals destroyed by successive waves of Muslim and Aryan invaders. There are certain exceptions of course—like Khajuraho, which escaped mutilation owing to its isolated situation—but if you want to see temples, the earliest free-standing examples are found only in the deep south. These date back to around AD 600 and were the work of two rival dynasties, the Chalukyas of the Kanarese districts and the Pallavas of the Tamil country. They started out with a very simple design, just a small *vimana* or shrine surmounted by a modest gateway tower. This *gopuram* was comprised of a series of diminishing pavilion-type ornaments around a central block, on which images were carved.

The prototypes of these temples can be seen at Mahalipuram, together with fascinating examples of the transition, in the early 7th century, from monolithic caves to small structural temples. At nearby Kanchipuram, where the architects moved next, the art of temple-building came to maturity. Over the next 1000 years, right up to the fall of the Vijayanagar empire around AD 1600, temples became more and more elaborate. During the late Chola period (AD 1100–1350) the *gopurams* became immense and pillars began to appear, decorated with lotus or cobra ornaments. By the early 17th century, spacious halls or *mandapas* came in and the upper sections of the *gopurams* were profusely decorated with stucco figures. All this effort culminated in Madurai, famous temple city of the south, with the creation of Sri Meenakshi temple—once seen, never forgotten.

constructed over a period of just 100 years, starting in the reign of Narasimha Varman I (630–68). For some reason, the large complex of caves, temples, bas-reliefs and friezes—covering a huge hump-back hillock in the town centre—was never finished. As at Ajanta and Ellora, the architects suddenly and inexplicably deserted the site, and its rich treasure of ancient art and sculpture lay lost and forgotten.

Now a small, thiving beach-resort, Mahabalipuram attracts a regular trickle of travellers wanting a break from mainstream Tamil Nadu. Here, the pace of life is slow and relaxed, and when you've had enough of (yet more) temples, you can jump in the sea or enjoy a plate of fresh lobster fresh off the beach.

When to Go

Mahabalipuram has a year-round season, but is most pleasant from November to February. Try to avoid busy weekends.

Getting There

Regular buses go to Mahalipuram from Madras, Kanchipuram and Pondicherry. There are less frequent services from Madurai and Bangalore. A day-trip from Madras by car (*see* p.437) is a good idea—arriving around 10am, seeing the temples before lunch, relaxing in the sea in the pm, and seeing the town in the early evening. Leaving around 8pm (to avoid the rush hour), you can be back in Madras by 10pm.

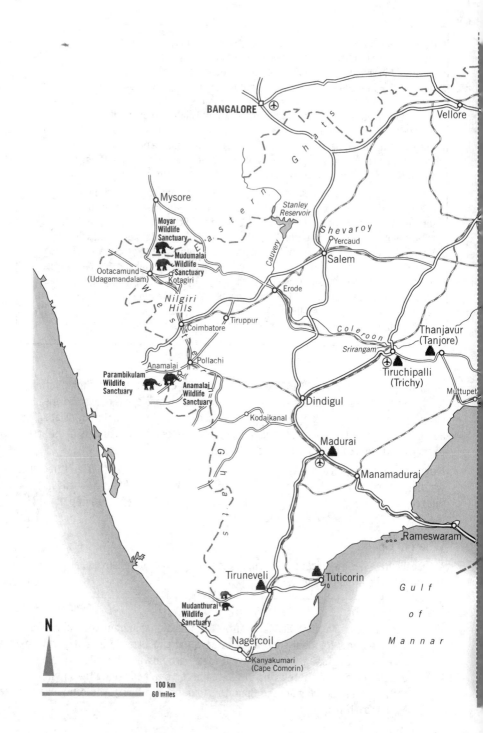

Tamil Nadu

Tourist Information

The tourist office, ☎ 42232, is near the post office on East Raja St, open 9am to 5.45pm daily. Come here for current bus timings and for directions to agencies who handle train bookings out of Madras. Money and travellers cheques can be changed at the Indian Overseas Bank to the north of town (closed Sundays).

Touring Mahabalipuram

This is an ideal tourist situation—everything worth seeing is within easy walking distance. You can hire auto-rickshaws off the street, or cars/motorbikes from JRS Travels opposite the tourist office, but few people bother. The best plan is to do the sights in the cool of the morning and then to flop on the beach. Doing it the other way round is fatal—you'll never see anything!

Mahabalipuram

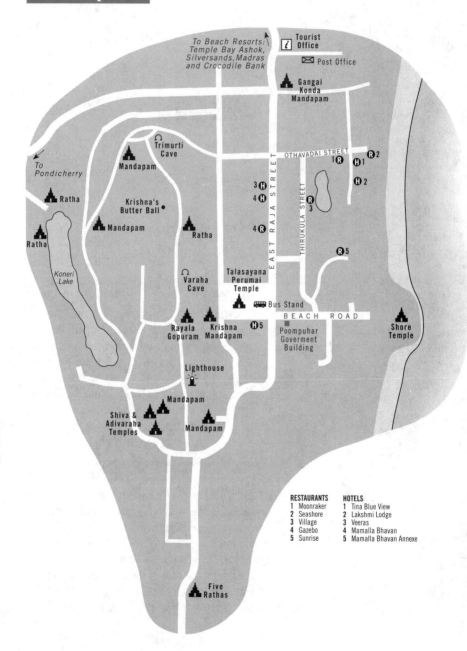

To Beach Resorts:
Temple Bay Ashok,
Silversands, Madras
and Crocodile Bank

Tourist Office

Post Office

Gangai Konda Mandapam

OTHAVADAI STREET

EAST RAJA STREET

THIRUKULA STREET

Trimurti Cave

Mandapam

To Pondicherry

Ratha

Krishna's Butter Ball

Mandapam

Ratha

Ratha

Koneri Lake

Varaha Cave

Talasayana Perumai Temple

Bus Stand

BEACH ROAD

Rayala Gopuram

Krishna Mandapam

Shore Temple

Poompuhar Goverment Building

Lighthouse

Mandapam

Shiva & Adivaraha Temples

Mandapam

Five Rathas

RESTAURANTS
1 Moonraker
2 Seashore
3 Village
4 Gazebo
5 Sunrise

HOTELS
1 Tina Blue View
2 Lakshmi Lodge
3 Veeras
4 Mamalla Bhavan
5 Mamalla Bhavan Annexe

442

Temple Tour

On foot, full day. Shore Temple–Krishna Mandapam–Descent of the Ganga–Five Rathas

Time and tide have washed away all but one of Mahabalipuram's seven famous seashore temples. To see the single surviving example, take a 5-minute stroll down Beach Road (left out of the bus stand). Built in the final phase of Pallava art by Rajasimha (700–28), the **Shore Temple** sits perched on the very edge of the sea, sheltered from the pounding surf only by a sturdy rock barrier. This, of course, only adds to its romantic charm. The temple has been undergoing excavation for the last 100 years, and new treasures are continually coming up. In 1992, for instance, they discovered an ancient swimming pool—used by the Pallavas to bathe in before going in to pray—along with two new statues.

A simple, elegant structure with a layered pagoda roof, this is one of the oldest temples in south India. It is unusual in that it houses shrines for both Shiva and Vishnu—the larger of the two spires (facing east) containing the shrine to Shiva, the smaller one (facing west) that to Vishnu.

For a proper appreciation of this spectacular monument, hire a guide at the entrance (Rs25–30). They speak good English, and treat their subject with warmth. Entering the temple enclosure, note the series of guardian bulls (Nandis) on the surrounding wall, and (within the frontal shrine) the bas-relief of Shiva, attended by Parvati (his wife), Brahma (as wisdom), Vishnu (as eagle-god) and Ganesh (as good fortune). In a second chamber you'll find the 2.5m-long monolith of Vishnu in the attitude of repose. The rear chamber has an ancient, much-prized lingam, only a shard of which now remains. The carved cow facing the shrine represents a permanent sacrifice to the presiding deity.

To get the full effect of the shore temple walk down the beach and view from a distance (best in the late afternoon). If going for a swim, watch out for strong currents. Drying off, be prepared to entertain the 'lobster man', the 'coconut man' and a procession of hopeful youngsters hawking seashells and stone carvings. To get some peace, keep walking until you find a quiet stretch of sand.

Back at the top of Beach Road (facing Mamalla Bhavan Lodge) bear left for **Krishna Mandapam**. Mahabalipuram has eight such mandapams (rock-cut cave temples), each one an exquisite study in bas-relief portraying various vivid episodes from Hindu legend or mythology. This one depicts Krishna using the umbrella of Mount Govardhan to shield his flocks of cows and shepherds from the rage of the rain god, Indra. It is noted for its realistic representation.

Nearby is the world's largest stone bas-relief, **The Descent of the Ganga**. This amazing piece of sculpture represents the earliest work of the Pallava sculptors, undertaken during the reign of Narasimha Varman I, after whom the town was named (he earned the title of Mamalla or 'Great Wrestler'). The megalith itself is a massive whaleback-shaped rock, split down the middle with a fissure, the whole face of which is covered with relief sculptures. Measuring 27 metres long by 9 metres high, this vast stone frieze faces out to the sea. It pictures over a thousand sculpted deities and animals, each one a separate work of art.

Mahishasuramardhini Cave

Dominated by a procession of elephants, two of which are 5 metres long, it portrays a dynamic world of gods, demi-gods, angels, men, animals and birds, all apparently rushing towards the cleft in the rock's centre. It is said either to represent the *Mahabharata* fable in which Arjuna, the emaciated figure seen standing on one leg, did penance to Shiva (after fighting alongside Krishna and killing many fellow human beings) or the 'descent of the Ganga' from Mount Kailash, the holy river seen flowing down from Shiva's matted locks. In this story Bhagiratha, a mythical hero, beseeched the gods to send down the celestial waters of the Ganges, to carry the ashes of his ancestors to *nirvana*. But he unleashed a mighty flood, only contained when Shiva mopped up the waters with his hair. Whatever the meaning, this is a masterpiece.

A huge granite hillock overlooks the *Descent of the Ganga*. The path up there leads past a number of interesting rock-cut caves and peters out near **Krishna's Butter Ball**, an immense boulder delicately poised on the crest of the hill. Like the Shore Temple, you can't imagine it staying there much longer. Behind it, pause for the beautiful view over **Koneri Lake**, a pretty inland lagoon with one of the ancient *rathas* (chariots) situated on the far bank. Then proceed, via the colonnaded **Sthalasayana Perumal Temple**, to the high **Lighthouse**. You can climb to the top (*2–4pm only*) for a glorious view over the town and surrounds, though photography is not (officially) permitted. Below the lighthouse is the **Mahishasuramardhini Cave,** with a famous frieze of Durga (Kali) destroying the buffalo-headed demon Mahishasura. In the background, oblivious to all this activity, there's Vishnu in one of his famous 'cosmic sleeps'.

From the hillock, it's a 10-min walk down to the enclosure of the **Five Rathas**. Eight monolithic 'temple cars' (the main five being named after the Pancha Pandava hero brothers of the *Mahabharata* epic) are the 7th-century prototypes of all Dravidian temples to come. Each of these miniature temples displays the familiar *gopurams* (gatehouse towers), *vimanas* (central shrines), *mandapams* (multi-pillared halls) and sculptured walls so characteristic of later temple architecture. The rathas themselves are simple, unadorned structures, each of a different style, but all are *viharas* (monastery buildings). They are either square or oblong in plan and pyramidal in elevation. Adorned with rampant lions, elegant pillars and sculpted divinities, they stand (unfinished) in lonely, isolated splendour, guarded by three life-size stone animals—a lion facing north, a central giant elephant looking south and a bull to the east.

Be sure to return to the Shore Temple before 7pm (when it is closed off) to enjoy the illuminations (weekends and holidays only) and to take some moonlight shots.

Excursions from Mahabalipuram

Tirukkalikundram

By bus, taxi or motorbike, half-day.

This semi-interesting little Shiva temple, situated atop Vedagiri Hill, is located 14km out of Mahabalipuram. It's covered on the one-day tour to Mahabalipuram sold by TTDC in Madras, but is a worthwhile cycle excursion from Mahabalipuram itself.

Tirukkalikundram has a famous and popular hilltop sanctuary where two eagles (apparently the reincarnations of two famous saints) fly in around noon daily. Ostensibly this is for a rest on their holy flight between Varanasi and Rameshwaram, but in fact they just grab a free meal from the temple priest. Before tackling the tiring 565-step climb to the top (in bare feet) check that the birds are actually up there. Other attractions at Tirukkalikundram include a large tank (to the southeast of town) with alleged curative powers, and a marvellous temple complex at the back of the town.

Madras Crocodile Bank

Another 15km cycle trip (or bus ride) from Mahabalipuram is this sanctuary and breeding centre for large reptiles (*open daily 8.30am–5.30pm*). It was set up by an English herpetologist and eccentic called Romulus Whitaker, to protect a shy, fish-eating and endangered giant lizard called the gharial (the same size as a crocodile but with a snout too thin to attack man or beast). Whitaker's breeding programmes have since expanded to include snakes, crocodiles (Nile, Indian and Australasian), caimans and monitor lizards, and a fascinating hour can be spent watching them bask by their man-made pools.

Vedantangal Bird Sanctuary

Another worthwhile excursion, though it has to be done by motorbike or private car, is to this major waterfowl sanctuary 45km west of Mahabalipuram. From November to February, the wetland reserve throngs with migrants. Vedantangal is best visited at dawn and dusk, so it's a good idea to spend the night in the forest rest house. Bookings must be made in advance (best through a travel agent) via the Wildlife Warden, 50 Fourth Main Road, Adyar, Madras, ✆ (044) 413947.

Shopping

The town's stonemasons, drawing on the skill of centuries, now produce only tat in alabaster (which scratches, unlike marble). If you're going to do any shopping at all, save your money for **Poompuhar Government Emporium** (*closed Tues*) on Shore Temple Road. This has an interesting assortment of ceramics, handicrafts, perfumes, cut glass and dolls at more or less fixed prices.

Leisure

Swimming in the sea can be fun (especially for body-surfers), but don't go out of your depth—the waves are rough, and the under-currents strong.

For evening entertainment, drop over to the Silversands hotel. During the season, they often have classical dance performances or magic shows. The non-resident admission fee is steep (Rs80), but it's the only show in town.

Mahabalipuram ✆ *(04113–)*   ### Where to Stay

The town's tourist season runs from November to February, and during these months (especially Xmas/New Year) the quality accommodation is often booked out.

luxury

The only real luxury option is Taj Group's **Fisherman's Cove**, ✆ 44304, 🖹 44303, some 10km north of Mahabalipuram at Covelong. This beautiful property occupies the site of a 17th-century Dutch fort and is set in a secluded cove, overlooking a private beach. The sea is still brisk here, but there's a separate pool and facilities for sailing and wind-surfing. Rooms go from US$90, and beach cottages from US$100 but if you're here for a treat, opt for one of the sea-facing cottages from US$120.

expensive

A number of resort-style hotels have sprung up in and around Mahabalipuram itself. The best of these, ideal if you want to snooze on a private beach, is the quiet **Shore Temple Bay Resort**,✆ 42235, some 3km out of town. This has a good pool and restaurant, large bright rooms, and a few a/c cottages. Closer to town, the large **Silversands**, ✆ 42228, 🖹 42280, offers a wide range of rooms from ordinary singles/doubles for Rs500 to a/c suites/family cottages for

Rs2000. Food and facilities are good, and room-rates are heavily discounted (like everywhere else) during the off-season.

moderate

In the village itself (along the main drag), choose between two adjoining properties—**Mamalla Annexe**, ✆ 42260, and **Veera's** Hotel, ✆ 42288—with spotless rooms from Rs300/400 and pleasantly air-conditioned restaurants. Again, rates fluctuate according to the season.

budget

TTDC's **Youth Hostel and Cottages**, on the way to the Shore Temple, is a well-run place with clean rooms at Rs170 and a clean Rs30 dormitory. **Mamalla Bhavan** by the bus stand, ✆ 250, has more basic doubles from Rs60 and a good vegetarian restaurant downstairs. **Tina Blue View**, in the fishing village, has clean rooms from Rs130 and tasty food. **Lakshmi Lodge**, near the beach, has sea-facing rooms for Rs180 and cheap dorm beds.

Eating Out

Silversands still has the best (and the priciest) food in town, with fresh grilled lobster the speciality. Seafood is generally very good in Mahabalipuram, the best-known establishment being the **Gazebo**, on the main street, just 100km north from the bus station on the west side, with meals from Rs75 per head. **Tina Blue View**, on the quiet back road leading down to the fishing village, is another favourite. In the same street are the **Village Inn** (good seafood), **Moonraker** (popular with shoestringers), and **Seashore** (on the beach, good for full moon parties). At many of these places you can choose your own crab, lobster or king prawns—but always ask the price first!

The **Sunrise** rooftop restaurant, also on the way down to the Shore Temple, offers tasty grilled and boiled lobster with all the trimmings at Rs200, grilled jumbo prawns at Rs75 and a whole giant swordfish at Rs350. It's a popular meeting place. Nearby, the **Rose Garden** is popular for toasted sandwiches and chocolate milk-shakes, while **Village Restaurant** offers fresh lobster from Rs150, Madras Chicken at Rs20 and Western breakfasts at Rs20. **Bamboo Hut**, near Sunrise, has a regular clientèle of laidback gourmands, though less patient diners head up to **Shore Temple Bay Resort** to get some food in under an hour.

Moving On

Mahabalipuram's bus stand is opposite the Mamalla Bhavan hotel. Daily services run to Kanchipuram from 5am to 7.30pm (2½hrs) and to Madras at 6am, 12noon, 2.30pm, 3.45pm and 5.15pm (1½hrs), but they are hot and overcrowded. Taxis to both places cost Rs400 and Rs500 respectively. There are also daily buses to Bangalore (7–8 hrs), and one each to Madurai (10hrs) and Pondicherry (with one change). There's no need to advance-book tickets; you can buy them on the bus.

Kanchipuram is one of the seven sacred cities of India (the others are Varanasi, Mathura, Ujjain, Hardwar, Dwarka and Ayodhya), and the only one associated with both Shiva and Vishnu. It is famous both for its temples, many of them remarkable well preserved, and for its handwoven silks.

It was the empire-building Pallavas (6th to 8th centuries AD) who turned the ancient holy town of Kacchi into the wealthy capital of Kanchi. Under the artistic Mahendra Varman I (600–630 AD), a sudden surge of cultural and building activity took place, starting the traditions of silk-weaving, temple building and Bharat Natyam dance for which Kanchipuram later became renowned. In this period, Dravidian architecture developed from modest simplicity, as exemplified by the Mahabalipuram *rathas*, to wildly extravagant maturity. The development of the *gopuram* temple-towers into soaring stone leviathans dripping with tiny dancing deities was particularly dramatic.

All this zealous religious activity attracted flocks of artists, educators and musicians to Kanchipuram, and it became a major centre of art and learning. But then, in the 9th century, the Pallava dynasty fell, and the city's power and influence rapidly faded. Under subsequent rulers—the Cholas, the Vijayanagar kings, the Muslims and eventually the British—it returned to being just a typical country town, enlivened by constant parades of devout pilgrims.

Kanchipuram today is a noisy, dusty place, with a definite shortage of good hotels and restaurants. The fever-pitch noise and bustle may come as a bit of a shock after tranquil Mahabalipuram but (like Varanasi) the authentic spirituality of the place lies just beneath the surface.

When to Go

The cool season to visit is November to January, but many brave the heat for the big **Car Festival** of February to March. Subsequent festivals in April and May are hot, crowded and uncomfortable.

Touring Kanchipuram

There are around 1000 temples in and around Kanchipuram. About 200 of these are in the city itself and (with one exception) the best examples are all conveniently close to the bus stand. If you're short on time, hire an auto-rickshaw for a quick morning tour of the temples for around Rs100–150. If you've a full day to spare, do all your sightseeing by bicycle; there are many hire places around.

Most of the temples are open only from sunrise to 12.30pm and from 4pm to sunset.

Getting There

There are regular buses in and out of Kanchipuram from both Madras and Mahabalipuram. All are a mad scramble and you'll have to fight tooth-and-nail for a seat. *See also* 'Moving On', p.452.

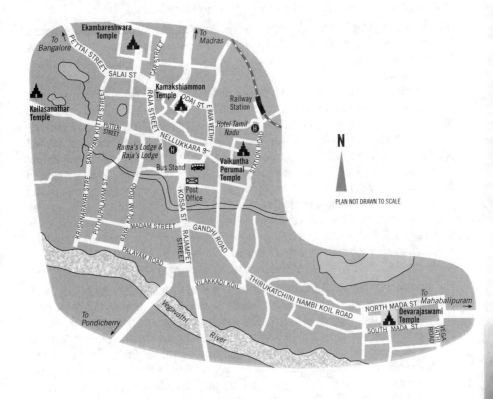

Kanchipuram

Ekambareshwara Temple

To Bangalore

PETTAI STREET

SALAI ST

CAR STREET

To Madras

Kamakshiammon Temple

ODAI ST

RAJA STREET

E RAJA VEETHY

Railway Station

Kailasanathar Temple

SANTHAM KUTTAI STREET

PUTTERI STREET

NELLUKKARA ST

Hotel Tamil Nadu

Rama's Lodge & Raja's Lodge

Bus Stand

STATION ROAD

Vaikuntha Perumal Temple

KRISHNARAYAR STRE

PUTHUPALYAM ST

RAYA KOLAM ROAD

Post Office

KOSSA ST

N

MADAM STREET

GANDHI ROAD

RAJAMPET STREET

PALAYAM ROAD

VILAKKADI KOIL

THIRUKATCHINI NAMBI KOIL ROAD

To Pondicherry

Vegavathi

River

NORTH MADA ST

Devarajaswami Temple

SOUTH MADA ST

To Mahabalipuram

VEGA VATHI ROAD

PLAN NOT DRAWN TO SCALE

Kanchipuram ☎ (04112–)   **Tourist Information**

The **tourist office** is at the Hotel Tamil Nadu. The Archaeological Survey of India office, opposite Kailasanathar Temple, is helpful, but often closed.

The **post office**, on Kossa Street, is just below the bus stand.

For **foreign exchange**, the State Bank of India is on Gandhi Road.

Temple Tour

By bicycle/rickshaw and bus, 4–6 hours. Kailasanathar Temple–Ekambareshwara Temple–Kamakshiammon Temple–Vaikuntha Perumal–Varatharaja Temple.

A short 15-minute cycle ride down Nellukkara and Putteri Streets takes you to the west of town and the 8th-century **Kailasanathar Temple**. This lies in a garden clearing and the giant Nandi bull in the grounds shows it's a Shiva temple. The structure itself is very early Dravidian architecture—with the exception of the front, which was added later by Mahendra Varman III. Delightfully simple and elegant, it has none of the decorative ostentation of the later Chola and Vijayanagar building styles. Built in sandstone, it has some beautiful carvings and sculptures (several of which are well-renovated) and remnants of bright frescoes still cling to a few of the 58 small shrines running round the inner courtyard, giving an idea of the temple's original magnificence.

Just to the left of Nellukkara and Putteri Street junction, you'll find **Ekambareshwara Temple**, marked by its towering 192 foot-high *rajagopuram*. Inside, there's an extensive temple compound surrounded by a massive stone wall, added by Krishna Devaraja (a Vijayanagar king) in AD 1500. Ekambareshwara probably derives its name from 'Eka Amra Nathar'—Shiva, as 'Lord who was worshipped under the Mango Tree'. The ancient mango tree in one of its compounds which, according to local tradition, is over 3500 years old, is where Parvati is said to have done penance to Shiva, after misguidedly closing his eyes and plunging the whole universe into chaos. Pilgrims troop around the tree all day long, and will (after you've paid your camera fee) urgently insist that you join them. Actually, you are not allowed to see much more—Ekambareshwara is a living temple (the god still lives here, in the mango tree) and many of the other shrines are off limits to tourists. No matter, you can still climb the central *gopuram* for marvellous views down over the temple complex. Ask permission first from the temple curator found behind the **Thousand Pillar Temple** inside the compound. This particular temple does have a thousand pillars, a colourful display of temple chariots, and images of the various animal carriers who accompany the gods of the Hindu pantheon. Allow yourself a good hour at Ekambareshwara.

The most popular temple, **Kamakshiammon** (5 minutes left out of Ekambareshwara), is dedicated to Parvati and is the site of the February/March Car Festival. As one of the three holy places of Shakti (Parvati as bride of Shiva), it is considered particularly auspicious for marriage-blessings and up to 25,000 people show up at the larger festivals to supplicate the goddess for happy nuptials. Show up around 8pm on Tuesday or Friday evening for fireworks and music, caparisoned elephants and vast, swaying crowds—the Golden Chariot cruises slowly round the temple grounds, and the moaning hordes part like the Red Sea in the Cecil B. de Mille movie. It's a spectacle. By day, Kamakshiammon is surprisingly quiet and relaxed; a few visiting pilgrims stare appreciatively at the resident elephant, and you're free to wander around unmolested. In its present form, the structure is a 14th-century temple of Chola construction, its central ghat overlooked by watchtower *gopurams*.

A short ride away, you'll come across **Vaikuntha Perumal**. This is one of the oldest temples in town, dedicated to Vishnu and built by Parameswar Varman in the 8th century AD. It is most notable for its cloisters within the outer wall which are prototypes of the 1000-pillared halls seen at later temples like Ekambareshwara. There's an interesting bas-relief circling the main shrine, which portrays battle scenes between the Pallavas and the Gangas/Chalukyas, as well as various depictions of Vishnu sitting, standing and lying down.

A rather alarming bus ride from the Nellukkara Street stand, just up from Raja's Lodge, takes you 3km across town to **Varatharaja Temple**. Recently renovated, this temple is in fine condition and features one of Kanchipuram's finest *gopurams*. The views from the top are stunning. There's also an agreeable temple elephant contributed by the Elephant Shed Foundation, which will take you for a short ride round the grounds.

Pay your camera fee and head for the central 100-pillared **Marriage Hall**. The pillars are notable for fine base-carvings, of Vishnu (warrior-horses), Parvati, Ganesh, Brahma, Shiva and Buddha. The raised plinth within is the marriage platform, with seating space for wedding guests. In the corner lives the gloriously painted wooden chariot of Varatharaja (Vishnu). It is carried round town on festival days. Beyond the marriage hall is the large temple ghat and two small shrines. The small stone marquees dotted round the marriage hall are for pilgrims to relax under, tucking into popular temple sweets like lemon-rice *laddoo*.

Shopping

With a weaving tradition dating back to the Pallava era (when silk was the royal cloth) Kanchipuram is justly famous for its particularly fine silk saris, embellished with stunning patterns. There's no problem finding shops— over 5000 families are currently engaged in the weaving industry—but there is a problem finding ones which speak English or don't rip off tourists. Avoid expensive private emporia and stick to the cheap government cooperatives. Places like **Murugan** in Railway Road; **Srinivas and Co**, 135 Thirukatchi Nambi Street; **Thiruvallur Cooperative Society** 207 Gandhi Road; or **Kamatchi Co-optex**, 182 Gandhi Road, have a good name. For shopping advice and to see top-quality Kanchi silk being produced on the looms, call in on the **Handlooms Weavers Service Centre** at 20 Railway Road, just up the road from the post office. Open on weekdays only from 9.15am to 5.45pm.

Kanchipuram ☎ (04112–)

Where to Stay

Kanchipuram is a typical temple town, with lots of pilgrim *dharamsalas* and hardly any tourist hotels.

budget

The TTDC **Hotel Tamil Nadu**, 78 Kamatchiamman Koil Street, ☎ 22553/4, is a pleasant place, with clean, comfortable rooms and a reasonable restaurant. Also try **Raja's Lodge** and **Rama's Lodge** which adjoin each other in Nellukkara Street, close to the bus stand. Both have clean rooms with hard beds and boisterous Indian neighbours. The Rama is the better deal, with its pleasant sunroof and a vegetarian restaurant.

Eating Out

There is not a great choice: *masala dosa* (the traditional south Indian snack of spiced vegetables within a thick pancake envelope), *thalis* and precious little else. For something slightly more thrilling, take a rickshaw over to **Saravana Bhavan** (Gandhi Road), ☎ 22505. If you're happy with local food, try either **Hotel Tamil Nadu** or **Sri Rama Café** next to Raja's Lodge. This has good value Rs7–10 *dosa* dinners and an air-conditioned lounge where you can practise 'cooling' coffee the Tamil way.

There are regular buses to Madras and Mahabalipuram, which are always crowded. There is only bus operating to Madurai (journey time about 10hrs). Alternatively, you can travel by local bus (every 5mins) to Chengalpettu (50 km, 2hrs), from where every 30mins there are buses to Madurai (9hrs).

Madurai

Mad, mad Madurai: the largest, busiest and most aggressive of Tamil Nadu's temple towns comes as something of a shock to the traveller used to the more mellow pace elsewhere in the state. However, even if you don't visit any other temple town, to miss Madurai's temples is to miss one of the India's architectural wonders. The town's atmosphere is that of a medieval fair: un-put-offable touts will drag you into their shops and hotels, music blares from every corner and you will be kept awake by the thumps and giggles that come through the walls of the cheap hotels, many of which double as brothels. You will also have to contend with fierce heat, pugnacious rickshaw drivers and teeming crowds.

For all this godlessness, Madurai is a sacred site, the special abode of the goddess Meenakshi, 'the one with eyes like fish'. The vast temple complex built here in her honour is perhaps the finest achievement of the Dravidian architects and still remarkably intact. The nine soaring *gopurams* of Madurai are the first thing most visitors see, whether coming in by air, rail or road.

Over 2500 years old, Madurai takes its name from *mathuram*, the nectar which Shiva let fall from his flowing locks after Kulaskera, a Pandyan ruler, began praying for a new capital. The Pandyas, great patrons of Tamil art, architecture and learning, ruled 'Nectar City' from as early as the 6th century BC, right through to the 13th century AD, apart from a short period of Chola rule during the 11th and 12th centuries. After the Pandyas came the Delhi Sultans and the Vijayanagar kings but it was left to the enlightened Nayak rulers, who governed Madurai from AD 1559 to 1781, to build the city in its present form. It was laid out in the shape of a lotus flower, with the impressive Meenakshi temple at the centre, in accordance with the Shilpa Shastras (ancient laws of architectural science). In 1781 the British ousted the Nayaks, razed the old fort and converted the surrounding ditches into broad avenues known as *veli* (outer) streets. From then on, the growth of the modern town outside the temple walls was rapid.

When to Go

Full of colourful bazaars, itinerant street tailors, thronging pilgrims, academics and joyful religious processions, Madurai today is a small, bustling town which attracts up to 10,000 visitors each day. For fun and spectacle, come for the month-long **Chithrai Festival** in April and May. People have been known to pass out in the heat and crowds but it really is a glorious pageant. Otherwise, there's the cooler **Teppam** (Float) **Festival** of January and February. Madurai is popular all year round but the climate is most pleasant from October to January.

Indian Airlines flies Madras–Madurai daily, Trichy–Madurai daily. There are also connections to Bangalore and (with East-West) to Bombay. From Madurai airport it's a 6.5km ride into the city centre by airport bus or taxi (Rs30–40).

The fast *Vaigai Express* from Madras gets to Madurai in just 8 hours, stopping at Trichy on the way. Other links are to Quilon, Trivandrum, Tirupati and Tuticorin.

Buses going to Madurai leave Kodai, Kanyakumari, Madras, Trichy, Trivandrum and Kottayam.

For more information, *see* 'Moving On', p.460.

Two small cities in one, Madurai is easily negotiable by foot or by cycle. The central Meenakshi Temple, aptly named a 'city within a city', is enclosed by the old town, which is itself enclosed by the four Veli Streets. The newer town, 1.5km north over the river Vaigai, is of little interest but has the better hotels. All the budget lodges, restaurants and tourist office are in the old town and so is all the action. Whenever possible sightseeing is best done on foot. But don't jaywalk round the temple area unless you want to be mown down by crazed cyclists. You can hire auto- or cycle-rickshaws for around Rs10–15 for short hops but most people only use them for out-of-town trips. Allow at least 2 days to see the sights.

Madurai ✆ (0452–)   **Tourist Information**

TTDC, West Veli Street, ✆ 34757, has good information and is very helpful. There are also tourist information counters at the railway station (though this one is notoriously *un*helpful) and at the airport.

The **post office** is in Scott Road, near the railway station. **Indian Airlines**, ✆ 541234/541795, is at Pandyan Building, West Veli Street. For **foreign exchange**, the State Bank of India is also in West Veli Street. **Higginbotham's bookshop**, selling a useful city guide and map, is in the railway station.

City Tour

By foot or by rickshaw/taxi, full day. Sri Meenakshi Temple–
Thirumalai Nayak Palace

From either the bus or rail station, it's a 15-minute walk up Town Hall Road to the **Sri Meenakshi Temple** (*open daily, 5am–12.30pm, 4–10pm, avoid Friday when hordes of pilgrims pour in*). This is one of the biggest temple complexes in India—258 long by 241 metres broad. Most of it was built in the reign of Thirumalai Nayak (1623–55), though it was substantially added to by later rulers. It is a rectangular twin shrine: the southern temple dedicated to Meenakshi (a Pandyan princess who lost her embarrassing third breast when she met Shiva up on Mount Kailash), the other dedicated to Sundareswarar

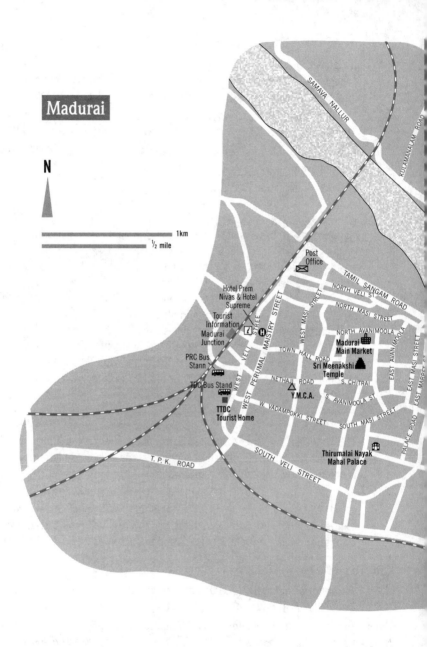

Madurai

N

1km
½ mile

Post Office

Hotel Prem Nivas & Hotel Supreme

Tourist Information

Madurai Junction

PRC Bus Stann

TDC Bus Stand

TTDC Tourist Home

TAMIL SANGAM ROAD

SAMAYA NALLUR

KULAMANAKAM ROAD

NORTH VELI ST

NORTH MASI STREET

WEST MASI STREET

WEST VELI STREET

WEST PERUMAL MAISTRY STREET

NORTH AVANIMOOLA

Madurai Main Market

Sri Meenakshi Temple

TOWN HALL ROAD

S. CHITRAI

EAST AVANIMOOLA

EAST MASI STREET

EAST MARKET

NETHAJI ROAD

Y.M.C.A.

S. AVANIMOOLA ST

W. VADAMPOKKI STREET

SOUTH MASI STREET

PALACE ROAD

Thirumalai Nayak Mahal Palace

T. P. K. ROAD

SOUTH VELI STREET

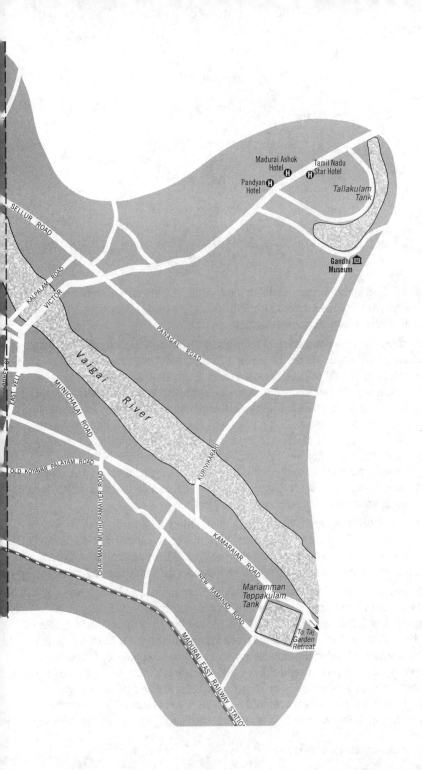

(Shiva himself). Dominated by four enormous outer *gopurams*, the usual entrance point is the Ashta Sakthi Mandapam on the east side. Within, are five smaller *gopurams*, enclosing the two small golden *vimanas* or central shrines.

Meenakshi temple is a constant buzz of noise and activity, especially around the East Tower Bazaar, full of exotic stalls selling bright clothes, jewellery, incense and spices. Enter the temple by the official gate, at the end of Town Hall Road where you must deposit your shoes outside. Just inside the entrance, bearing right, there's usually a row of fortune-tellers. Just past these are a couple of 'classrooms' where, in the early evening, you can hear tuneful songs and prayers being practised. Turning left, you'll find the **South Tower**. It used to be possible to climb to the top of this soaring *gopuram* and to enjoy spectacular views over the whole temple complex. But then someone fell off the top and the tower was temporarily closed to the public. It is worth asking if it is again open. If not, you'll find plenty of local touts eager to guide you to the tops of local buildings which just happen to double-up as handicraft emporiums—beware!

Continuing anti-clockwise, you'll come across the **Golden Lily Tank**, used by pious Hindus for sacred dips. The legend goes that any book thrown into it will sink if worthless (this guide is a rare exception!). Surrounding the tank is a pillared portico, its walls decorated with paintings from Hindu mythology and verses from the Tamil classic, *Tirrukkural*.

Beyond the nearby mural of Meenakshi's wedding to Shiva are the two single-stone sculptures of the temple's 12th-century founder and his chief minister. Behind the tank is the gate-facing shrine of **Sri Meenakshi Sannath**, guarded by two huge *dwarabhalagas* (door-keepers). Through the entrance gate of **Sundareswarar Sannathi**, you'll find the beautiful hall of **Kambathadi Mandapam**, notable for its excellent sculptures of Shiva. Next, wander over to the nearby **Thousand Pillar Hall**, which actually has only 985 superbly carved pillars. Two small temples stand on the space intended for the other fifteen. Much of the rest of the hall has been given over to the extensive **Art Gallery**—a fascinating, if poorly lit, exhibition of Tamil temple art and architecture. Outside again, take directions for the **Puthu Mandapam**, opposite the Eastern Tower. Built by Thirumalai Nayak in honour of Sundareswarar, this is noted for its sculptures and for its imposing pillars, on which are carved representations of the four Nayak rulers. Sadly, it is now open to the public just twice a year (ten days on each occasion) for marriages. The surrounding tailors may however slip you in after dark, subject to a small tip to the nightwatchman; bring a torch. Just east of this is the **Rajagopuram**, a massive 54-metre tower base which, had it been completed, would have been the tallest tower in south India.

In April 1995, after two years' work, the whole temple complex was renovated. This was not necessarily a good thing, since the grey layers of age which lent the *gopurams* their stately air of antiquity have been garishly overpainted with bright rainbow colours, which reduce them in many Western eyes to a Disneyesque circus attraction.

Don't feel obliged to follow this route to the letter; people often enjoy just wandering round Sri Meenakshi at random. The most enjoyable time of day to visit is the early evening, when it's relatively quiet and cool. There's normally some musical entertainment going on (informal and inspired) at the Golden Tank from 6.15 to 7.30pm and from 9 to 10pm. If you're at the South Tower around 9.15pm, you can see Shiva being 'put to bed'. Photographs are only allowed inside the temple from 1 to 4pm daily (camera fee Rs5) but you can pick up some good black and white prints in the bazaar, very cheaply.

In the afternoon, take an auto-rickshaw (it's complicated on foot) down to **Thirumalai Nayak Palace** (*open daily, 9am–1pm and 2–5pm*). This palace, built by Thirumalai Nayak in 1636, fell into ruins and was partially restored by Lord Napier, Governor of Madras from 1866 to 1872. The original palace was four times larger than the existing building, though enough remains to make a visit worthwhile. There's an excellent sound-and-light show in English here, commencing 6.30pm daily. Tickets are Rs5 or Rs7. The cheaper tickets are best—you see far more.

Enter via the magnificent granite portico into the rectangular courtyard, flanked by huge, tall colonnades. Walk up to the northwest of the building, to see the splendid Main Hall. Originally Thirumalai Nayak's bedroom, it measures 41.5 metres long by 20.9 metres wide. It was also used as a theatre, where dancers, musicians and court magicians used to entertain the king and his guests. On the west side of the courtyard, visit the Celestial Pavilion (Swarg Vilasa). The large central dome is supported by 12 columns but appears to lack any support whatsoever. The fine decorative stucco *chunnam* (shell-lime work) on both the dome and its arches are a characteristic of Tamil ornamentation. The Celestial Pavilion is approached by a flight of steps guarded by a group of damaged, carved mounted horsemen.

Sights Round-up

By local bus, full day. Thirupparankundram–Mariamman Teppakulam Tank–Gandhi Museum–Government Museum.

From the PRC bus stand, catch a no.5 bus (they leave every 10 minutes) for the remarkable rock-cut temple of **Thirupparankundram** (*open daily 5am–12.30pm, 4–10pm, adm free*), 8km out of town. This temple, carved into the side of a mountain, is one of the six sacred abodes of Subramanya, second son of Shiva, and celebrates his marriage to Deviyani, daughter of the rain god Indra.

Entrance to the innermost shrine cut from solid rock is denied to non-Hindus but there's lots to see in the preceding series of *mandapas* or halls. These are generally packed to capacity with devotees preparing to go into worship. The head of each family distributes small lamp-lit bowls of coconut, fruit, rice and incense to his group and marks their fore-heads with the lines of Shiva in red or grey powder. You can follow them on their way into devotions, as far as the door leading to the inner chamber. Just beyond the door is a small courtyard, containing 'Shiva's Postbox', where incinerated prayers drift up to the god through the soaring wicker-tower roof. In the centre of the courtyard is a brightly painted triumvirate of Nandi (Shiva's bull), a peacock and a rat fashioned out of black granite. The surrounding pillars are surmounted by fierce stone lions and the ceiling decorated with beautiful murals. Following the pilgrims out of the shrine, you'll see them making offerings of boiled rice to the schools of leaping fish in the temple ghat. Out in the street again, sit awhile over a cup of *chai* and enjoy the colourful flow of people: pilgrims, priests, holy men and Indian families on their way to prayer.

Back at PRC bus stand, catch bus no.4 or hire a rickshaw to **Mariamman Teppakulam Tank**, 5km east of the city. Measuring about 305 square metres, this tank is almost as large as the Meenakshi Temple. Built by Thirumalai Nayak in 1646, it is the site of the big **Float Festival** held on the night of the January/February full moon. The central pavilion, **Mayya Mandapam**, houses a small temple and can be reached by boat, for a rupee or two. The tank is connected to the nearby Vaigai river by underground channels.

From here, take bus no.6 to the **Gandhi Museum** (*open daily 10am–1pm and 2–6pm, closed Wed*), 5km north. It's a 5-minute walk from the Collector's Office in the new town. The museum contains various relics, photos and material relating to Mahatma Gandhi, a crafts exhibition of Khadi and Village industries and a south Indian handicrafts display. Also here is a relatively new, if rather scruffy **Government Museum** (1981) (*open daily 10am–1pm and 2–6pm, closed Fri*). To return to the old town, you'll need a bus no.3 or 4.

Shopping

Madurai is a living bazaar—there are shops, stalls and markets every-where. Cotton and silk clothing are the best buys, followed by cheap costume jewellery. Buying silver is not a good idea; most of it has been directly imported from Jaipur and costs twice the price. There is no problem finding good clothes here. The streets are alive with salesmen carrying armloads of clothes and silver trinkets around, pestering tourists with irresistible sales patter.

All the best tailors hang out opposite the East Tower of Meenakshi temple in a huge indoor tailors' complex. Check out a man called 'Perumal' in Shop 100—several travellers have found him of great help. Both here and down by the South Gate, you can get clothes made up at very reasonable prices in under 4 hours (although Jaipur will charge about half the cost).

Poompuhar, the new government emporium opposite the train station, has a good selection of fabrics, wood- and stone-carvings, brass trays and cotton lanterns at fixed prices.

Leisure

Lakshmi Sundaram Hall, Gokali Road, Tallakulam, ✆ 530858, and **Raja Sir Muthiah Mandram**, opposite the district court, hold regular dance and music programmes. Near Gandhi Museum, there's a yoga centre and a swimming pool. Ladies' hours are 2 to 4pm.

Madurai ✆ *(0452–)*

Where to Stay
luxury (from Rs 1600)

Madurai's most interesting hotel is the **Taj Garden Retreat**, Pasumalai Hill, ✆ 601020, ✆ 604004, found on a hill 6km from the town. The house once belonged to the British manager/director of a large plantation and the steps to the upper level are still adorned with the antlers of the *sambar* deer he shot in the nearby mountains. The Taj Garden's grounds are extensively wooded and have superb birdlife; a circular walk is being planned through the woodland connecting the main accommodation area with the swimming pool. There are also well-maintained formal gardens and tennis courts.

Many of the other hotels are located in the new town, about 4km from bus and railway stations.

expensive (from Rs 1000)

The air-conditioned **Pandian** in Racecourse Road, ✆ 42470, has a good restaurant and fine temple views from its rooms. The **Hotel Madurai Ashok** in Alagarkoil Road, ✆ 42531, ✆ 42530, is rather more impersonal and expensive but its travel desk is very helpful. Also at the top of this price range is the **Hotel Supreme** on West Perumal Maistry Street, ✆ 543151, ✆ 542637.

moderate (from Rs 400)

For a really good deal, TTDC's **Tamil Nadu Star Hotel**, Alagarkoil Road, ✆ 42465, has spacious double rooms priced well within this category and a couple of large comfortable suites for less than the Rs700 maximum. The vegetarian restaurant is also good and you can get reliable travel information here. TTDC's **Hotel Tamil Nadu**, West Veli Street, ✆ 37471, is rather a disappointment with uncomfortable, overpriced rooms. You can stay in better comfort in the 'cheap' price range listed below.

budget

Madurai attracts a good crowd of budget travellers and there are many cheap lodges. Be warned however—Madurai is a money-making town, so don't be shocked if you find that some rooms in your lodge are being used by prostitutes. A few favourite backpacker hotels, with rooms around Rs75 single, Rs120 double, are **Hotel College House**, on West Perumal Street, near the Meenakshi Temple; **Hotel Prem Nivas**, at 102 West Perumal Street, ☎ 542532; **Ganga Guest House** opposite it; **Abinaya Lodge**, 198 West Masi Street; **P.S.B. Lodge**, West Veli Street; and **Aftab Lodge**, 12 Kakka Thopu Street.

Eating Out

Pandyan Hotel's **Jasmine** restaurant offers a superb Rs150 buffet lunch between 12 noon and 3pm daily. The *à la carte* is good too—a fine range of Indian, continental and (after 7pm) Chinese dishes at between Rs50 and Rs75. Helpings are huge. Two popular restaurants, close together in Town Hall Road, are the **Taj** and the **Mahal**. They both serve Western-style food in addition to standard Indian fare.

Old favourites like the **Indo-Ceylon** and the **Amutham**, also in Town Hall Road, are fairly drab now. More fun is the rooftop **Surya Restaurant** at the Hotel Supreme on West Perumal Maistry Street or the **Ruby Restaurant** on the same street, which has a pleasant outdoor terrace, set back from the temple crowds, yet close enough to take in the action. Prices here are between Rs20 and Rs35 per item.

The **New College House** continues to turn out the cheapest and best south Indian *thalis* in town. Similar fare can be had at the **Ashok Bhavan** opposite the tourist office, which serves 'special' lunches for Rs25–35 from 12noon to 2.30pm daily.

Moving On

By air: Indian Airlines fly to Bangalore a couple of times a week. East-West Airlines make daily flights to Bombay.

By rail: The morning Madras–Quilon Mail takes 8hrs to reach Quilon in Kerala and crosses the scenic Western Ghats. You're not supposed to be able to book seats in advance but it's often half empty. If you don't fancy just turning up on the off-chance, contact the TTDC information counter inside the station and see what they can do. Daily train services also run to Trivandrum in Kerala, Tirupati in Andhra Pradesh and Tuticorin in far southern Tamil Nadu.

By bus: Madurai has two main bus stands, adjoining each other off West Veli Street. The PRC stand is for Kodaikanal and for local city buses. The TDC stand is for Kanyakumari, Madras, Trichy, Trivandrum and Kottayam. With TDC buses, you must buy your tickets in advance.

Kodaikanal (Kodai)

Until a few years ago, Kodai was a quiet, charming hill station, visited only by a few day-trippers from nearby Coimbatore and travellers wanting to cool off from hot, dusty travels down in the plains of Tamil Nadu. Situated 2.5km up in the scenic Palani Hills, Kodai's temperate climate has remained but not, alas, its tranquillity. In recent years the town has been developed as a major day-trippers' and honeymooners' resort, with attendant road and hotel development, tacky souvenir stalls, noise and increased traffic. The part of town immediately around the lake is still worth seeing for its nostalgic colonial feel but nowadays it has to be said that unless you plan to use it as a base from which to trek into the wild and beautiful Palani Hills, 5km from town, you would be better advised to avoid Kodai and head straight for one of the smaller hill stations or wildlife sanctuaries.

If you do decide to visit, the bus trip up from Coimbatore across rugged mountains, plummeting valleys and terraced coffee plantations is spectacular. The countryside around Kodai is famous for hill-fruits and plums and its pride is the rare Kurunji flower, which blooms just once every 12 years. Unfortunately, it last flowered in 1992. The two tourist seasons, when the place is rampant with groups of drunken Indian men, are mid-November to mid-January and mid-April to the end of June. For better weather and 20–30 per cent discounts at larger hotels come in February and March or August and September. If visiting between November and February, bring warm clothing as it gets very cold at night.

Getting There

Kodai is linked by bus to Madurai, Coimbatore, Ooty, Bangalore and Kanyakumari. For more information, *see* 'Moving On', p.466.

Getting Around

The emphasis in town is on light exercise and recreation: walking, pony-riding and paddle-boating on the lake. Central Kodai overlooks the lake and is easily negotiated on foot. You can hire ponies and cycles by the hour or day down by the boat club on the lakeshore below the Carlton Hotel. There are also taxis but few people take them. Kodai is really just a place for long, invigorating rambles but in the hills away from the traffic and noise of the main roads. Allow 2 full days for the best walks and have a decent map handy (try Higginbotham's bookshop in Madurai).

Kodaikanal ℂ (04542–)   ### Tourist Information

TTDC **tourist office** is near the bus stand, open daily from 10am to 5pm, ℂ 41675. The **post office** is between the market square and the lake. The **State Bank of India** is just above the bus stand.

Walk 1

Full day. Coaker's Walk–Sacred Heart Church–Kodai Lake–Bryant Park–
Golf Club–Green Valley View–Pillar Rocks.

Rise at 5.30am, dress warmly and take a blanket for the sunrise over the mountains, Kodai's main attraction. A 15-minute walk up **Coaker's Walk** from the market-place brings you out on a plateau running along the steep southern face of the Kodai basin. The early morning scenery is glorious (though the crowds of holiday-makers are not) but late-comers be warned: the views are often lost in cloud by 9am.

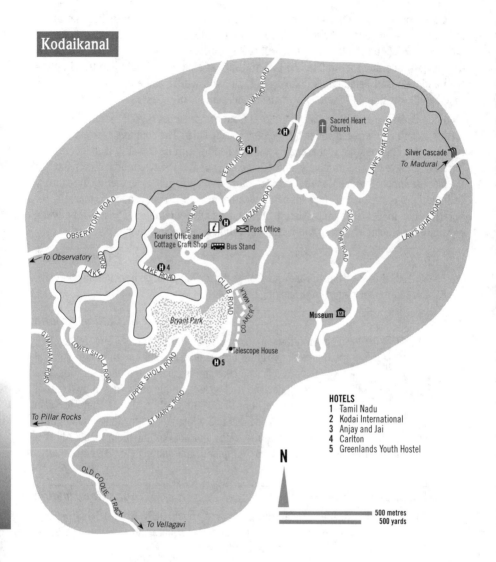

Kodaikanal

HOTELS
1 Tamil Nadu
2 Kodai International
3 Anjay and Jai
4 Carlton
5 Greenlands Youth Hostel

500 metres
500 yards

After breakfast, proceed east from the market place down to the lake. On the way, divert right for a brief visit to **Sacred Heart Church**. It has a touch of Surrey with stained-glass windows, Gothic arches, a mock-Tudor tower and a small English cemetery. If not for the Tamil hymn books, you wouldn't know you were in India at all. Kodai's famous star-shaped **Lake** was formed in 1863 by Sir Vere Levenge and nestles in a wide range of dense wooded slopes. Covering 60 acres, it is the focal point of all life on the hill station. Clean, tranquil and scenic on its waters, if not its shore (which is the general promenade for the visiting holiday-makers), the lake feels very 'English'. Its small Boat House, to the left, coming down from the Church, ✆ 315, hires out four-seater rowing boats from Rs50 per hour. For a choice of boats and no crowds, turn up early. Nearby, you can hire out one of the underfed ponies for about Rs60 per hour, looked after by ostlers who accept no responsibility for 'any accident those who riding themselves without horse man'. From the pony rank, it's a 10-minute walk to the east of the lake, (look out for the signs prohibiting 'eve-teasing'—the Indian expression for male-female sexual harrassment) where you can enjoy a picnic lunch in pleasant **Bryant Park**, noted for both its hybrid and grafted flowers. There's a popular horticultural show here each May.

Even if you are not a golfer, the 6.5km walk up to the **Golf Club**, ✆ 40323, is one of the best in the station. Take the road leading off the northern end of Bryant Park, ascend to the top of the ridge from where there are fine views down over the lake and whenever you hit a major fork, keep to your left. The walk is a continuous joy. Young boys may turn up to suggest 'short cuts' and they are reliable. You'll reach the golf club in around an hour. The course itself is beautifully kept and spans a succession of undulating meadows and hills. Cows are employed to keep the grass down. It's hardly ever used, except in May, when the 300 club members turn up for the annual tournament and, for a green fee of Rs100 and temporary membership of Rs200 per round or Rs1200 per week, you get clubs, balls, and the course practically to yourself. An extra Rs50 will hire you a good caddy and for another Rs20 you get a spare set of balls.

Alternatively, take directions at the club for adjoining **Green Valley View**, which commands a beautiful view of the entire Vaigai Dam or walk further on past the golf course for **Pillar Rocks**, three massive boulders standing shoulder to shoulder, measuring 106m and providing a plummeting view down into the valley plains. There's a pretty waterfall here too.

Walk 2

Full day. Observatory–Bear Shola Falls–Museum–Telescope House.

For day two, try a pleasant 40-minute stroll up to the **Solar Physical Observatory** (*normally open April–June daily, 10am–12noon and 7–9pm; check at the tourist office before visiting*), 3km from town, approached via Observatory Road, 5 minutes north of the Boat House. Founded in 1898 at the topmost point of Kodai at a height of 2347 metres, it gives panoramic views of the town, lake and surrounding Palani Hills. On the return walk, take the rugged, picturesque path left for **Bear Shola Falls** 1.5km from the lake, another popular view point and picnic spot (though now sadly defaced by graffiti).

In the afternoon, stroll back up Coaker's Walk for the **Shenbaganur Museum** (*open daily, 10–11.30am and 3.30–5pm*) near the top of the rise, on the left. This is famous for its collections of flora and fauna including 300 varieties of orchid and is well maintained by the Sacred Heart College. The **Telescope House** at the nearby observatory is a good place to be at sunset. If it isn't free and it often isn't, enjoy the sun going down from the small knoll below which is a sheer drop of 670m, with privacy guaranteed.

There are several other nice walks, notably **Prospect Point** (6.5km), **Fairy Falls** (5km) and **Silver Cascade** (1km), behind the Sacred Heart Church.

Trekking in the Palani Hills

Although the area immediately around town has been deforested, it is worth arranging treks into the wilder, forested Palanis, which begin about half an hour's walk from the edge of town. Although unprotected, the Palani forests are still home to elephant, *gaur*, leopard, wild boar, the occasional itinerant tiger and a host of smaller game and birds. It is essential to have a guide, as the area has no maps.

Short treks around the Kodai hills for about Rs100 per person per day are offered by Vijayan Soans at **A School in Nature Education**, c/o Greenlands Lodge, Coaker's Walk. These are easy-going nature rambles, geared to students and youth hostellers, which take place between May and June, September and November.

Longer treks of several days can be arranged through **Vijay Kumar's Nature Walks**, behind the Telephone Exchange building on Observatory Road. These cost around Rs100 per person for a trek of 5 hours but are well worth it as Vijay, the founder and guide, knows the area's flora and fauna intimately. He, along with several other prominent members of Kodai's ex-hippy community and International School staff (an unlikely mix but this is India), have formed the **Palani Hills Conservation Council**, aimed at getting the local eco-system the official protection it needs from the rabid developers of commercial Kodai. With funding now coming from Sweden's overseas conservation fund, it looks as though Vijay and his friends may well succeed in saving the area from an otherwise inevitable rape. A portion of your trekking fee will go to the council.

Shopping

There's a reasonable selection of weavings and local crafts at the **Cottage Craft Shop** near the bus stand. It's open from 9am to 12.30pm and from 2 until 6pm, Monday to Saturday. You'll find attractive Tibetan produce and local *coir* mats for sale on the road leading down to the lake.

Leisure

Apart from **golf, boating** and **pony-riding**, Kodai is a good area for **fishing**. Licences are issued by the Department of Fisheries on Observatory Road and cost Rs15.

Kodaikanal ✆ *(04542–)*

Where to Stay

expensive (from Rs 1500)

There's elegance and lake-view rooms at the **Carlton Hotel** on Lake Road, ✆ 40056/40071, ✆ 41170. At the top end of this price range, the room rate includes meals and during the low season of mid-January to March and July to mid-October discounts of 25% or more are given. This 'warm-hearted luxury hotel you and your family deserve', has good food and good facilities which include a health club with jacuzzi, sauna and massages, billiards and tennis. But it's often full.

moderate (from Rs 650)

Slightly less expensive properties include **Hotel Kodai International**, ✆ 40649, which offers a choice between comfortable rooms and cottages. **Sterling Resorts** at 44 Gymkhana Road, ✆ 40313, has cottages only. However, the best place to stay is undoubtably the **Trattoria Venice Guest House**, about 3km out of town along the Fairy Falls Road (reached via Observatory Road), ✆ 40775, ✆ 41288/40206. Owned by Ganesh, a local coffee-planter and conservationist and his Italian wife, the place is an old planter's bungalow with homely, old-fashioned rooms and superb Italian food. Tariff includes full board.

budget

Among the budget hotels is the **Hotel Jai** in Lloyds Road, which has the rather alarming advertisement: 'Be our cosy guest tonight—wake up Gay in the morning'. If that sounds too much of a risk try **Hotel Clifton** in Bear Shola Road, ✆ 40408/9, **Hotel Anjay** near the bus stand, ✆ 41089, or the **Hotel Tamil Nadu**, Fernhill Road, ✆ 41336/9. All offer clean, comfortable bases in the town centre. Backpackers favour the excellent **Greenlands Youth Hostel** right at the top of Coaker's Walk, with views out over the plains. Treks into the Palanis can be arranged from here: beautiful situation, lovely gardens, pleasant rooms. The other budget lodges up on Coaker's Walk are generally squalid, though the **Yagappa Lodge** has a few adequate rooms, as does the **Taj Lodge**.

Eating Out

The best food in Kodai is not its most expensive. Head straight for the **Venice Trattoria**, 3km from town, first up Observatory Road, then left onto Fairy Falls Road, where the owner, Ganesh, and his Italian wife prepare home-made pastas with fresh herbs that are as good as anything in Europe. A full meal is about Rs75–100.

Also very good, though in basic surroundings—a tin shack on Bear Shola Falls Road, 5 minutes' walk from the lake—is the **Manna Bakery**, run by the bearded, charismatic Israel Bhooshi. His home-made breads, pizzas, soups and apple crumbles make up possibly the best continental-style cuisine. Three courses here cost around Rs45.

Otherwise, there is a good range of Indian food at either the snooty **Carlton Hotel** or the **Hotel Tamil Nadu** for about Rs150 and Rs100 respectively—though only the brave can stand the Carlton restaurant's evening vibraphone player with his instrumental interpretations of old Beatles songs. The **Hotel Jai** does reputable non-vegetarian cuisine. The **Boat Club** restaurant is alright for snacks. Just below the market square are three good places: **Lala Ka Dhaba**, a *proper* Indian restaurant offering delicious Punjabi food in a tasteful setting; **J.J.'s Fast Food**, a busy pizza and burger joint run by jolly Vincent; and **Tibetan Brothers** with delicious vegetable *momos* (deep-fried dumplings), fair Chinese food and homely service. Prices are cheap—about Rs40 for a meal.

From Kodai there are regular buses to Madurai; two buses daily to Coimbatore (10am, 7pm); two buses daily to Ooty (9.30am, 8pm), two buses daily to Bangalore (6pm, 7pm via Salem) and two buses daily (via Madurai) to Kanyakumari. It's wise to book seats in advance.

Excursions from Kodaikanal

To reach either of these sanctuaries, you have to go back down to the plains (Coimbatore) and get a bus to Pollachi (5hrs), from where every 2hrs local buses will take you to the sanctuaries' entrances (50km, 2hrs). Anamalai particularly is worth visiting, for its elephant herds and a variety of other wildlife and birdlife.

Anamalai and Parambikulam Wildlife Sanctuaries

Anamalai is known for large herds of elephant which divide their time between the thick forests of the lower slopes and the high grasslands and *sholas* of the peaks and ridges. Trekking is possible here with a guide, (*insist* at reception) and there is a good chance of seeing sloth bear or leopard if you are willing to spend several days in the mountains. There are also *gaur*, a few visiting tiger, many wild boar and good birdlife, including hornbills and black-headed orioles. Crocodiles swim in the sanctuary's reservoir.

A local beauty spot and look-out point called **Topslip** lies inside Anamalai and attracts hundreds of day-trippers in the December holiday season. Avoid it then but pay it a visit in the drier months,

Muntjac

as elephants are often spotted near here. If no wild ones show up you can ride on a tame beast into the nearby forest, for the sanctuary keeps an elephant training camp here.

By contrast, almost nobody visits **Parambikulam** where denser forests make game viewing difficult. This is real rainforest, however and worth taking the trouble to get into. Beware of leeches in November and December. Parambikulam harbours the same game species as Anamalai. Trekking can be arranged at the reception office. Ask to speak to the chief conservator.

Accommodation in **Anamalai** is provided in several comfortable resthouses: at Topslip (often full), Varagaliar, Sethumadai and Amarathinagar. You are supposed to reserve these in advance via the District Forest Officer in Pollachi, ✆ 2508. If you do not have time, try your luck at reception. They may say they are full but are probably lying. Make a scene and you'll get a bed.

Accommodation at **Parambikulam** is more problematic. Unless you have arranged a forest trek—in which case you must put your sleeping bag down in the forest wherever the guide decides—you have to stay at one of the Anamalai rest-houses and travel over to Parambikulam by bus or jeep in the early morning.

Mudanthurai Wildlife Sanctuary

This is the southernmost accessible point in Tamil Nadu's Western Ghats, where a Project Tiger Reserve has been established in the dry forest zone of the eastern slopes. With a large reservoir at the centre of its 217 square km, Mudanthurai can be visited either by government jeeps, which leave from the reception office at around 7.30am and 5pm daily, or on foot with a guide. To take a guided trek involves some bureaucratic hassle (as it does in every wildlife refuge everywhere in the country) and you are supposed to apply in advance at the Wildlife office in Tiruneveli. However, just turning up and asking to speak with the chief conservator at Mudanthurai is more effective, providing you can convince him that your interest in the wild is genuine. The treks are by the day, returning each night to the (very basic) forest rest house near the reception area.

Mudanthurai's wildlife includes tiger, leopard, sloth bear, wild boar, *sambar* and *chital*, *nilgiri* and common *langur*, bonnet and lion-tailed macaque.

The easiest access from Kodaikanal is via Tiruneveli, 48km away (6hrs) by the one daily bus. From Tiruneveli buses leave for Papanasam (55km, 2hrs), and from here you can take a local auto-rickshaw or taxi to the sanctuary.

Kanyakumari (Cape Comorin)

Kanyakumari is the Land's End of India, a staggering 3200km south of Jammu. It is named after the Kumari (Virgin) goddess whom the gods tricked out of a marriage with Shiva because they needed a virgin to defeat the powerful demon Banasura. It's just the kind of poignant, tragic love story that devout Hindus adore and they turn up here in their thousands to console the dejected goddess in her temple and to seek her help. They also come because Kanyakumari is the meeting point of three great seas: the Indian Ocean, the Arabian Sea and the Bay of Bengal and bathing in the waters is believed to wash away all sins. Local tourists and foreign travellers come for the unique sunrises and sunsets which are most spectacular at full moon, when sunset and moonrise take place simultaneously.

Away from its temple and its beach, Kanyakumari is an unremarkable place which has somehow developed in the short space of a few years from a modest fishing village into a full blown Indian-style resort. And of all Indian resorts, this one is the most full of cheap tourist junk. It sells grass hats, funny masks, plastic whistles, plastic tropical plants and bags of coloured Kanyakumari sand. It even has a drive-in restaurant chicken corner. Noisy, well-to-do families clamber over the rocks, take invigorating beach promenades and wade into the shallows dressed in their best suits and saris. The high season months are from November to January and from April to June. For peace, quiet and a chance of a decent room visit between February and March. It's fairly cool then and you can enjoy the full moon.

There are two buses daily (via Madurai) from Kodaikanal. You can also arrive by bus from Trivandrum, Kovalam Madras, Trichy and Coimbatore. For more information, *see* 'Moving On', p.470.

Kanyakumari ✆ *(04653–)*   ***Tourist Information***

TTDC tourist office is near Gandhi Mandapam, ✆ 276, open 10am to 5.30pm except weekends. Staff regard Western visitors with undisguised shock and are generally too flustered to be really helpful. The **post office** and **State Bank of India** are both near the old bus stand.

This is a tiny seaside town, with one main street. Sights are few but walks are interesting. Stay for at least one sunrise and one sunset and during the day try the following jaunt.

Beach Tour

On foot, 3–4 hours. Sunrise Point–Kumari Amman Temple–Gandhi Mandapam– Fishing Village–Catholic Church–Vivekananda Memorial

Try to be up around 5am for the sunrise. This is best seen either from **Sunrise Point** down on the beach, or from your hotel roof. Every hotel near the shoreline has a roof and each one will be choc-a-bloc with jostling tourists. The sunrise itself takes place against an atmospheric background of Muslim muezzin-calls, Catholic prayers and picturesque fishing boats putting out to sea. Afterwards, you can go straight back to bed.

Later, take a walk down to the beach. Here you'll find **Kumari Amman Temple** (*open daily, 4.30–11.30am and 5.30–8.30pm; the sanctum is closed to non-Hindus*), dedicated to the virgin goddess who is now the nation's protective mother-figure. The deity sits in a small dark pavilion, flanked by four attendants. She used to look out to sea but her glittering nose-diamond lured so many sailors to their deaths (including the British vessel which purloined the original jewelled nose-ring) that the temple door was closed in her face.

Just west of the temple is **Gandhi Mandapam**, the rather bizarre monument erected to commemorate the spot where the Mahatma's ashes were kept before being immersed in the sea. It's worth a visit (have 10 *paisa* handy, or you'll never get in), if only for the coastline views from the top-storey balconies.

A total contrast to the touristy new town is the quaint little **fishing village** just down the beach. Here you'll find a warm and friendly community of fisherfolk living in the same way they have for centuries. Give them a hand with a fishing line, or help push out a dugout to sea and you'll be their friend. For around Rs20, they run parties of 3–4 people out to sea for 'fishing trips'. You don't get to do a lot of fishing but you do get stunning views of mainland India and Sri Lanka from 1.5km or so out. Sitting for 2 hours in a primitive five-plank catamaran leaves you very damp, so take a spare pair of trousers.

Beyond the village are lovely palm-fringed beaches: great for sunbathing, fatal for swimming. The coastal currents are generally dangerous. To swim in safety, use either the sheltered bathing ghat back in town, or the new pool on the shore built for visitors.

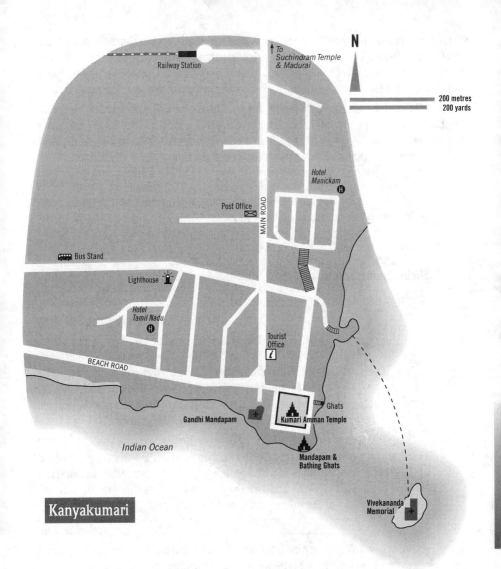

Above the village is the clean, white **Catholic Church**, established by St Francis Xavier in the 16th century. It's massive. So is the Disneyesque image of the Virgin Mary inside. She is the patron saint of the fishing community, afforded just the same reverence as is given the Kumari deity by the Hindu pilgrims across the bay. Since the congregation prefer to squat in the church, there are no pews.

Returning to the bathing ghat, take a boat (*daily departures from 7–11am, 2–5pm, except Tues, about Rs20 return*) out to **Vivekananda Memorial**, which lies on the two rocky islands 201yds offshore. Dedicated to the philosopher-saint Swami Vivekananda, who came here and meditated in 1892 before setting out to become one of India's leading religious crusaders. It is a relatively recent structure (1970) which attempts to blend all the architectural styles of India. The security is over-strict, in part to highlight the sanctity of the site. Smoking and eating are prohibited and shoes must be removed. The views of the mainland from it are excellent. Pilgrims visit the rock to view the Kumari goddess' footsteps.

Try to be back at the ghat around 6pm for sunset. This is often low tide and best views can be obtained by wading over to the small observation rock opposite. Take care coming back though, as the rising tide has a nasty habit of leaving unwary tourists stranded. At the April full moon the setting sun and rising moon appear side by side on the same horizon.

Shopping

Apart from seashells, plywood toy racing-cars and 'precious sand of three seas', there's nothing local that is worth buying.

Leisure

There is sea-fishing (bring your own tackle); also one cinema. At sunset, pop over to **Suchindram Temple**, a 10-minute auto-rickshaw ride away for the evening *arti*.

Kanyakumari © (04653–)

Where to Stay
moderate (from Rs 400)

 **TTDC Hotel Tamil Nadu** is just below the new bus stand, © 71257. Clean and friendly, it has the prime beach situation, with some lovely rooms overlooking the sea. The restaurant serves excellent South Indian fare. Cheaper dormitory accommodation is available. Or you could try the brand new **Saravana**, opposite Vivekananda pier; mainly favoured by Indians, it can be noisy.

budget

TTDC also run a **youth hostel** next to Hotel Tamil Nadu but this is often booked up. The better budget lodges are located down by the old bus stand. **Manickam**, North Car Street, © 71387, and **Lakshmi**, East Car Street, © 71570, have the best roofs for views of the sunrise and sunset and offer clean, basic rooms.

Eating Out

Again, you won't find anything exciting. **Hotel Saravana** has the best vegetarian restaurant in town. Hotel **Manickam**, © 71387, offers reasonable food for carnivores as well as vegetarians. Otherwise, it's back to *thalis*.

Moving On

By bus: Kanyakumari has a swish new bus station, with rest rooms, a restaurant and a shopping complex. Unfortunately, it's inconveniently situated; a long 1km walk up the hill from Vivekananda pier. From here, buses go 4 times daily to Trivandrum, Kovalam and Madras (each a 16 hour ride), 3 times daily to Madurai and Trichy (an 8hr journey), and at least twice a day to Coimbatore (about 10hrs) for connections with the Tamil Nadu mountains beyond. For Pondicherry, take a frequent local bus to Nagarcoil and from there a once-daily deluxe bus (12hrs).

Back on the coast, some 96km from Mahabalipuram, everyone suddenly speaks French, the drinks get cheaper and the English colonial influence, so strong up in Madras, disappears from both the architecture and the ambience. Pondicherry, until the 1950s a far-flung outpost of the French maritime empire, is so different to the rest of Tamil Nadu that the traveller immediately feels that he or she has entered another country. This busy coastal town is divided roughly into two: the old White Town of elegant French houses, restaurants and old administrative buildings focused around the low, clipped hedges and disciplined lawns of the Government Square; and the Black Town west of the canal, where India takes over again. The offensive colonial/racist overtones of the names of these *quartiers* persist, but the (now largely Indian) residential community appears to have little problem with them.

Pondicherry's Factions

Pondicherry society is divided—interesting for the traveller and endlessly absorbing for the townsfolk, who seem to talk about nothing else. The old French colonial community (supplemented by a fair number of more recent French émigrés come to enjoy the sun and cheap cost of living) keeps its distance from the upper-class Franco-Indian families who also live in the White Town. Both groups are regarded askance by the devotees of a large, intellectually based *ashram*, the Sri Aurobindo Ashram, founded in 1920 and now a major property owner in the town, which itself became divided in the 1960s when several European devotees went off to found Auroville, an experimental rural community about 9.5km out of town. Meanwhile, many of the local Tamil townspeople, farmers and fishermen feel, with some justification, that their land is not their own.

To understand Pondicherry it is necessary to know about these factions but, having highlighted them, it should also be stressed that there is no open hostility, such as fighting or insulting behaviour, between the groups: Pondicherry is a peaceful, fairly prosperous place and the atmosphere is a happy one.

History

In the very distant past (around 1500 BC), the semi-mythological sage Agastya is thought to have set up his hermitage here, and a small village called Agastishwara is supposed to have grown up around it. One (brief) millennium later, a Roman trading centre is known (from archaeological excavation) to have operated nearby in the 1st century AD and through the subsequent centuries, the settlement graduated from fishing and trading town to become the site of a university under the high Dravidian culture of the 9th century. However, the place remained small until the French landed there in the 1670s and decided to base their southern Indian trade from this hot, windswept Coromandel shore. From then until the late 18th century, Pondicherry was the centre from which the French tried to oust British rule in India.

Throughout this period, the energetic French governor Dupleix tried valiantly to achieve the usurpation of British rule, forming alliances with the anti-British Nawabs and

Maharajahs of southern India, including the great Tipu Sultan (*see* **History**) and fighting several campaigns at various locations in Tamil Nadu and Karnataka. Dupleix and his allies were eventually defeated, but following Tipu Sultan's death in battle in Karnataka and the gradual gathering of all south India under the Union Jack, the British were magnanimous enough to let the French keep Pondicherry. The little enclave subsequently outlived the British Raj, being voluntarily returned to India by the French in 1954.

Earlier this century, Pondicherry had achieved a limited international fame for reasons completely unconnected with empire. In 1908 an anti-British Hindu philosopher called Aurobindo Ghose came to Pondicherry after spending some 14 years studying in England. He chose Pondicherry because he wanted to follow in the antique footsteps of the sage Agastya and make the town his base. He founded an ashram whose teachings pioneered some of the ethics that were to flower, much later, into the Western Environmental Movement. Thinking of India, and thus the Earth, as a living entity ('the Mother' or *Shakti*, in ancient Hindu belief), Aurobindo attracted a wide circle of followers, many of them European, and taught a mixture of Hindu spiritualism and environmental ethics.

His most influential devotee was an aristocratic French woman called Mirra Alfassa, who later became known as 'the Mother' after Aurobindo's initial image of *Shakti*, and who helped from the 1920s onwards to bring Aurobindo's teachings to an international, though largely academic audience. She survived Sri Aurobindo, living until 1973 and helping to found, in the heady 1960s, the experimental agricultural community of Auroville, outside town, whose houses and central meditation centre were designed by a French architect and attracted many idealistic young European settlers.

Today the remains of both 'the Mother' and Sri Aurobindo are housed in the *ashram* in the old 'White Town', and both this and the now more-or-less autonomous Auroville community still attract a steady stream of visitors and pilgrims from all over the world.

When to Go

Despite being a largely Roman Catholic town, Pondicherry's Hindu residents observe several festivals throughout the year, mainly centred around the large Manaakulla Vinayagar Temple on Cathedral Street The most important is **Masi Magam**, a moveable feast celebrated at full moon in the Tamil month of **Masi** (late February/early March). Images of the various gods are taken from the Manaakulla temple (and from several smaller ones) to the sea for a ritual immersion. Holy men walking on red-hot coals mark the highlight of the ceremony. If you miss the ones at *Masi Magam*, other fire-walking events take place at various times through the year. Contact the Tourist Information Office on Goubert Salai for firm dates.

Getting There

Pondicherry can be reached by bus from Madras and all other main towns in Tamil Nadu and Kerala.

The railway station is on Lal Bahadur Street at the far west end of the Black Town.

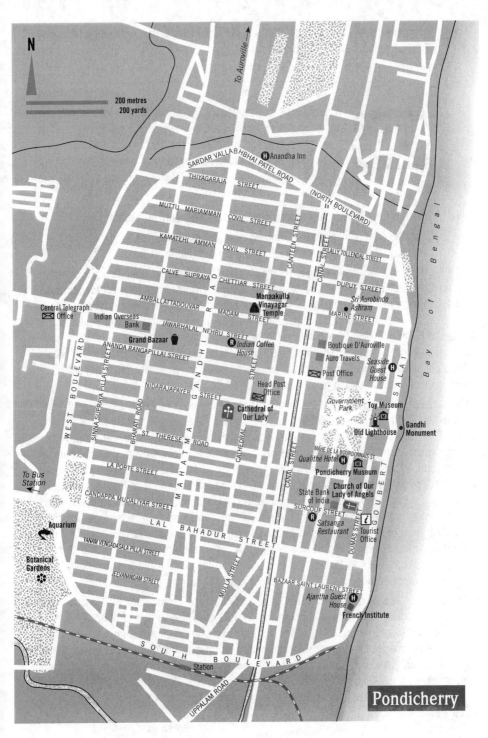

N

200 metres
200 yards

To Auroville →

SARDAR VALLABHBHAI PATEL ROAD (NORTH BOULEVARD)

Anandha Inn

THIYAGARAJA STREET

MUTTU MARIAMMAN COVIL STREET

KAMATEHI AMMAN COVIL STREET

CANTEEN STREET

LALLY TOLLENDAL STREET

CALVE SUPRAYA CHETTIAR STREET

DUPUY STREET

CANAL STREET

AMBALLATTADOUVAR

MADAM STREET

Manaakulla
Vinayagar
Temple

Sri Aurobindo
Ashram

MARINE STREET

Central Telegraph
Office

Indian Overseas
Bank

GANDHI ROAD

JAWARHALAL NEHRU STREET

Grand Bazaar

ANANDA RANGAPILLAI STREET

Indian Coffee
House

Boutique D'Auroville

Auro Travels

Post Office

Seaside
Guest
House

Bay of Bengal

WEST BOULEVARD

SINNA SUPRAYA PILLAI STREET

NIDARAJAPAYER STREET

BHARATI ROAD

MAHATMA GANDHI ROAD

ST. THERESE ROAD

Head Post
Office

Cathedral of
Our Lady

CATHEDRAL STREET

CANAL STREET

Government
Park

Toy Museum

Old Lighthouse

Gandhi
Monument

To Bus
Station

LA PORTE STREET

MAHE DE LA BOURDONNAIS ST.

Qualithe Hotel

Pondicherry Museum

GOUBERT SALAI

CANDAPPA MUDALIYAR STREET

Aquarium

YANAM VENGADASALA PILLAI STREET

Botanical
Gardens

JEEVANANDAM STREET

LAL BAHADUR STREET

MULLA STREET

State Bank
of India

SURCOUF STREET

Satsanga
Restaurant

Church of Our
Lady of Angels

DUMAS STREET

Tourist
Office

BAZAAR SAINT LAURENT STREET

Ajantha Guest
House

French Institute

SOUTH BOULEVARD

Station

UPPALAM ROAD

Pondicherry

473

Pondicherry is connected, via Villapuram, to Madras, Trichy, Madurai, Trivandrum and other major centres in the south.

For more information, *see* 'Moving On', p.478.

Getting Around

Walking is best in the White Town, but for excursions, you can hire **bicycles** at Jaypal on Gingee Salai (Canal Street) and at Snappy on Jawaharlal Nehru Street for around Rs35 per day. Motorbike hire can also be arranged at Snappy, for around Rs65–70 per day. Take taxis or auto-rickshaws between the White and Black Towns (but insist on a meter).

Walk through Old Pondicherry and the French Residential Quarter

Full day. Government Park–Pondicherry Museum–Beach Road–Jawamaz Toy Museum–French Institute–Sri Aurobindo Ashram.

Old Pondicherry is an excellent place for walking, its streets being neither dirty nor crowded (at least by Indian standards). The easiest place to start your exploration is **Government Park**, at the far east end of the White Town, just behind the seafront. Surrounded by quietly grand white stuccoed colonial buildings, the small park, with its low, cropped hedges and lawns, is in the Classical French style—planned as an octagon with short gravel walks radiating out from the centre. The measured calm of the place sets the tone for the whole atmosphere of the White Town, even at lunchtime, when the park becomes a meeting place for the town's office workers, who sprawl on the lawns, picnic and gossip.

On the south side of the park is the **Pondicherry Museum**, a real treasure house of dusty curiosities gathered from the ancient world, through the colonial period to the present day. The main room contains French 18th-century furniture and ornaments (all rather falling apart), including a big four-poster bed in which the French Governor Dupleix apparently slept. A faded early 19th-century oil painting of *La chasse à courre* ('Hunting to Hounds') hangs over the entrance doorway—calling to mind the later French governors' nostalgia for fresh autumn woods in Pondicherry's climate of feverish heat. At the east end of this main hall is a small sideroom where ceramic and stone artefacts (funerary urns, small carvings of the gods, ornamented oil lamps) from the nearby Roman trading settlement of Arikamedu gather dust in shabby glass cases stacked any old how. Some have been moved to make way for never-to-be-completed redecoration and are so jumbled as to make it impossible to see inside them without physically climbing over the others.

At the other end of the main hall, a small collection of French and Indian arms and armour includes, of all things, a boomerang which was used apparently on the battlefields of 18th-century India. Where and how this weapon developed is unclear: the piece is not of Antipodean workmanship and seems unique to Pondicherry. The arms and armour room gives onto another filled with indifferent wooden carvings, which in turn gives way to a small art gallery of paintings by local artists. With the exception of one or two fine landscapes, the work displayed is of a uniform garish awfulness—especially the Dali-esque abstracts.

The Sea Front

Having seen the museum, you can either walk back into town along the Rue Mahe de la Bourdonnais, which runs along the south side of the park, or up to the hot windswept **Beach Road** (Goubert Salai). The word 'Beach' is misleading here as there is none at all: Pondicherry falls to the sea in a tumble of jagged rocks and even if there was a beach, the water just here is too polluted with the town's waste for swimming; the real beaches are out at Auroville. However, it is fun to promenade along here in the morning or evening, when the sun is not too strong. The little **Pondicherry Café**, which sits right next to the **Gandhi Monument**, looks out to sea from the top of the short road leading back to Government Park. Have an ice cream or a coffee on the café's shaded (though windy) terrace with waves crashing on the rocks a few feet below. Just north of the café and memorial, by the **Old Lighthouse** on the landward side of the road is another eccentric museum, the **Jawamaz Toy Museum**, a one-room collection of painted dolls dressed in the various national costumes of India. Some of these seem indistinguishable from the others, but the dolls and their clothes are beautifully made. The little museum seems to have no connection with the town or region, or indeed to have any point at all, and this is somehow charming.

About 200m south along Goubert Salai (Beach Road) is the local **tourist information** office (one corner on the left after the junction with La Bourdonnais). A few minutes further on is the **Ajantha Guest House**, which has a shaded rooftop restaurant over-looking the ocean.

The French Residential Quarter & Aurobindo Ashram

Also south along the sea front 200m from the tourist information office, you eventually come to the Bazaar St Laurent, among whose fine colonial buildings is the **French Institute**. This is a good place to get local geographical or cultural information, as the insti-tute, originally set up to study these subjects, has an extensive library. If you have the time, take a browse through its section on Indian mythology.

If you turn right into elegant Bazaar Street Laurent, and then turn right (back towards town), you pass the French 19th-century **École Française de l'Extrême Orient**, which has a renowned archaeology and Sanskrit school. Walk 2 minutes further on and you reach Canal Street (Gingee Salai), where another right turn takes you for a 5 hot minutes up to Pondicherry's main east–west drag **Jawarhalal Nehru Street**, where most of the useful shops and cheap eateries are. On the corner of Nehru and Canal Streets are a collection of good bookshops. If you turn right (east) up Jawarhalal Nehru Street, left on Manakula Vinayagar Street and right again on the Rue de la Marine, you will come to the **Sri Aurobindo Ashram**. Here, in the peaceful, tree-shaded courtyards, you can talk to various *ashram* members and ask to view the marble vaults that house the remains of Sri Aurobindo and 'the Mother' (*see* 'History', p.472). Remove your shoes before entering the *ashram*, and don't arrive between 1 and 2 in the afternoon, when the buildings are closed to visitors. Those interested in more detailed information on the Ashram should visit the Auroshree shop, 2D Jawarhalal Nehru Street, or the Boutique D'Auroville at 12 Jawarhalal Nehru Street.

The Black Town

West of Canal Street is the 18th-century Indian quarter, among whose mostly Brahmin inhabitants the French Jesuits erected their high Baroque cathedral of **Notre Dame de la Conception**. The cathedral (built between 1691 and 1765) is on Saint Therese Road about five blocks southwest of the Sri Aurobindo Ashram. To ensure finding the cathedral open, go between 10 and 11am when morning Mass is being sung, or between 4 and 5 for evensong. St Theresa Street runs into Cathedral Street (also confusingly called Mission Street), where you can make international calls and faxes from the **Central Telegraph Office**. Another fine, but more recent, French colonial church is the **Église de Notre Dame des Anges** (built in 1855) on the corner of Surcouf Street and the Rue Roman Rolland, which runs south of Government Park. A number of late 19th-century religious paintings hang in the church, one donated to the colony by King Louis Napoléon III. The rest of the Black Town is Indian rather than colonial and has few sights beyond the usual colourful street of any Indian town, but is useful for shopping and cheap eating. Most of the shops and *thali* houses/cafés are located on the main commercial thoroughfare of Jawarhalal Nehru Street. Five minutes' walk to the west, in a large square between Jawarhalal Nehru and Nidarajapayer Streets (which both run east/west) and Mahatma Gandhi and Bharati Roads (which run north/south) is the **Grand Bazaar**. A hot, crowded general market, the bazaar's feverish activity makes a sharp contrast with the more measured (some would say sleepy) atmosphere of the rest of the town.

The Suburbs

Pondicherry's beautiful **Botanical Gardens** lie at the far western end of the Black Town, a 10-minute auto-rickshaw ride from the town centre via Lal Bahadur Street. The gardens, laid out in 1826 on the site of a fort that was razed by the British are designed according to the formal French style, with clipped trees, exotic flower beds, gravel walks and fountains. The old **Lieutenant Governor's Residence** sits amid the lawns and trees—a far nicer place to live than the old Governor's Residence on Government Park, which, despite the benefit of sea winds, has the heat of the town. Also in the Botanical Gardens is an **Aquarium**, where tanks display some of the more spectacular marine species from the Coromandel Coast and which has a small but rather dull museum on traditional fishing.

Shopping

Pondicherry's Auroville *ashram* produces some high-quality goods. At the Boutique D'Auroville on Nehru Street, hand-made jewellery, Western-cut clothes, incense, pictures and books are sold at reasonable prices.

Pondicherry © (0413–)

Where to Stay

expensive (from Rs 800)

The new **Anandha Inn** on S.V. Patel Road, © 30711, 📠 31241, is the only truly upmarket place in town. Although very comfortable, its location is slightly awkward, being a

10-minute walk, or a short auto-rickshaw ride, from the old White Town. However, it has two good restaurants, one northern Indian, one vegetarian, and the people on reception are very helpful with any travel arrangements you might need to make.

The **Pondicherry Ashok** on the coast at Chinakalpet, ✆ Kalapet 65160, also has a rather inconvenient location for those wanting to explore old Pondicherry, being on a private beach slightly out of town. Points in its favour are its small size (20 rooms), and its small stretch of clean private coastline.

moderate (from Rs 400)

Back in town, the **Hotel Mass**, on Maraimalai Adigal Salai, ✆ 37223, while reasonably comfortable is overpriced and lacks character.

budget

The most interesting hotels in Pondicherry fall into the 'inexpensive' category. Much cheaper, and with far more character than the expensive hotels, is the **Qualithé Hotel**, ✆ 34325, on the south side of Government Square. A fine piece of 19th-century colonial architecture, its rooms open onto a long verandah, and its beds—period pieces from the 1920s—come with optional mosquito nets. Run by a family of French-speaking Indians, the Qualithé has a restaurant, bar and an old function hall that, according to the owner, pre-dates the hotel building and served as a secret meeting chamber for the 18th-century French Governor Dupleix and Tipu Sultan during their many plottings against the British in Madras.

On the seafront (Goubert Salai) is the **Sea Side Guest House**, ✆ 36494, also occupying an old building. Though very comfortable, because it is owned by the Sri Aurobindo Ashram, guests have to be back by 10.30pm, which can limit things—even though there is nothing beyond the town's restaurants to distract the visitor at night.

Pondicherry does not lack cheap, good places to stay. To get the sea breezes, try the **Ajantha Guest House** on Goubert Salai, ✆ 38898, which has clean, airy rooms, and a rooftop restaurant overlooking the wide ocean. Also on Goubert Salai is the **Park Guest House**, ✆ 34412, with basic but comfortable single and doubles and cheaper dormitory accommodation.

For dirt cheap but reasonably clean accommodation, try the **G K Lodge**, ✆ 33555, on Anna Salai in the Black Town, or the **Tourist Homes** on Uppalam Road, ✆ 36376, where you can pay extra for an air-conditioned room. If you have a motorbike or are prepared to cycle half an hour, the **Youth Hostel**, ✆ 33495, north of town at Solaithandavan Kuppam, is a great place to kick back and relax in the middle of a traditional fishing village and right on the ocean.

ashram accommodation

Both the Sri Aurobindo Ashram in town and the Auroville community in the nearby countryside have guesthouses costing around Rs35–40 per night. The managements of both communities are not keen that just any old traveller should use their accommodation, but if you are genuinely interested in the *ashrams*, ask at one of their shops on Jawarhalal Nehru Street (*see* below) and you might be allowed to stay.

Accommodation in Auroville is available in guesthouses called Fraternity Youth Camp, ✆ 62357, Central Field Guest House, ✆ 62155, and Aspiration, 62283, costing Rs200–300 per day including meals. Write to the guest houses direct c/o Auroville.

Eating Out

Pondicherry has one very good French restaurant, the **Satsanga** on Surcouf Street in the White Town, ✆ 605001, which occupies a grand building that served as a brothel in the 18th century. You eat on the beautiful verandah among a mainly French-speaking clientèle. Rs150–200 will buy three courses and decent wine. In the same price range is **Le Rendezvous**, around the corner on Sufferen Street, which also caters to the French crowd in an air-conditioned colonial hall.

Cheaper options proliferate in the White Town. Try the rooftop restaurant at the **Ajantha Hotel** on Goubert Salai for good seafood at about Rs75 per head. Also in Goubert Salai is the **Café Pondicherry**, right by the Gandhi Monument. Waves lap at the foot of the outdoor terrace, where you can eat good pastas and *birianis* for Rs50. Tibetan food can be had at the **Snow Lion**, 22 Rue St Louis, and there is a good, if tiny **Vietnamese Restaurant** on Romain Rolland Street just south of the junction with Government Square. Prices for both the above are Rs50–100.

Much cheaper, though only open until early evening, is the **Ashram Dining Room**. Another rooftop affair, this is run by the Sri Aurobindo Ashram on Canal Street (Gingee Salai). A Rs35 ticket will buy you a light vegetarian meal.

In the Black Town, cheap *thali*-houses can be found on Jawarhalal Nehru Street and around the bus station on Lal Bahadur Shastri Street. All offer fresh, clean fare for around Rs20 per head.

Moving On

By rail: a small narrow gauge line runs two services per day between Pondicherry and Villapuram, from where main line connections can be had to Madras, Trichy, Madurai, Trivandrum and other major centres in the south.

By road: Pondicherry has two bus stands, one for long-distance travel and another for local hops, just 2 minutes' walk from each other on the north side of Lal Bahadur Street, near the train station at the far west end of town. Buses to Madras run all day, every half hour or so and there are daily direct services to other major towns in Tamil Nadu and Kerala, with a minumum of two buses per day. For the most efficient enquiries and bookings contact Auro travels, 12B Jain Street, ✆ 35560/35128. Buses out to Auroville can be taken from the local bus stand on Lal Bahadur Street (the local bus stand is the one closest to town).

A tropical paradise of undulating palms and warm, sandy beaches, Kerala is a narrow strip of coastal territory sloping down from the Western Ghats in a riot of green, luxuriant vegetation. Said to have been carved out by axe-wielding Parasurama, an avatar of Lord Vishnu, it is still a land of ancient charm and mystery. Kerala is also one of the richest states in India with forests and plantations of rubber, cashew, and coconuts everywhere. The meeting place of many cultures, Hindu and Muslim, Christian and Jewish, Kerala has a particularly rich heritage of dance and drama (Kathakali, Koothu and other temple arts originated here) and her people are among the most industrious and well-educated in the country.

Suddenly, Keralan tourism has begun to explode. The catalyst was the recent shutdown of Kashmir as a holiday destination. A group of private individuals got together and decided that, since tourists could no longer enjoy houseboat holidays at Srinagar's Dal Lake, they should fill the gap by selling a similar kind of experience on Kerala's backwaters.

Kerala's appeal lies in its calm, relaxed style of living, combined with its wide variety of scenic attractions. **Kovalam** is a picturesque beach resort which every traveller is loath to leave; nearby **Trivandrum** is capital of the state, with temples, palaces, art gallery and a good zoo. **Quilon** is the start of Kerala's famous inland waterways, where ancient 'pagoda' boats still ply the lagoons and Chinese fishing nets stand at the water's edge. Leisurely yet spectacular boat-trips up the backwaters to **Alleppey**, the Venice of India, and to **Kottayam**, age-old pilgrim centre of the Syrian Christians, lead on to **Periyar Lake**, one of south India's finest wildlife sanctuaries. Finally, at the old Portuguese/Dutch port of **Cochin**, the modern city of **Ernakulam** (centre of Kathakali dance-theatre, and handicrafts) vies for attention with Fort Cochin, the oldest European settlement in India—the site of historic churches, synagogues, museums and pastel Mediterranean buildings.

Itinerary

It's worth spending two weeks following this route. As well as visiting Trivandrum, Kovalam, Quilon, Alleppey, Kottayam, Periyar and Cochin, the route includes two 2/3-day excursions from Trivandrum to Neyyar and Agasthya wildlife parks, and two 3/5-day excursions from Cochin to the Munnar mountain range and one of the Kerala elephant festivals. The best time to visit is from November to April. The monsoon months are June–September/October, and the climate ranges from 21°–35°C.

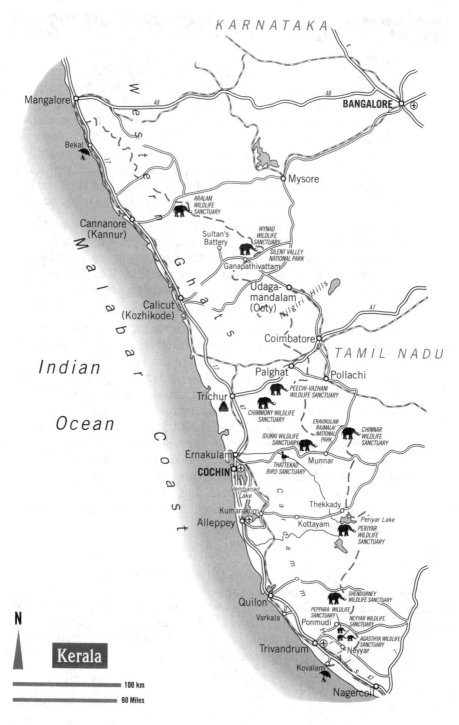

Most travellers begin their exploration of Kerala from Trivandrum on the coast, heading for the nearby beach resorts of Kovalam and Varkala, before starting to explore the backwaters and the mountains.

Hot, bustling Trivandrum is Kerala's state capital and has been so since the British ended the region's 500 years of warfare and made the local Travancore dynasty into regents in 1789. Yet, despite a few surviving monuments and palaces, Trivandrum doesn't look or feel like a state capital at all, having more the air of a large town than of a city.

But Trivandrum is the centre of Keralan culture: Kathakali dance, Kalaripayat martial art, Ayurvedic yoga, medicine and massage evolved here during the early Middle Ages. Many travellers stay in Trivandrum for weeks on end studying one or other of these ancient arts and sciences.

Built over seven hills, Trivandrum derives its name from *Thiru-Ananda-Puram* ('Home of the Serpent'), and is believed to be the home of Ananda, the sacred snake on which Vishnu reclines. Its official name, Thiruvananthapuram, is never used.

Getting There

The airport is 4 miles from the city centre, Rs1 by no.14 local bus. You can fly there from Bombay, Cochin, Goa, Bangalore, Hyderabad and Madras.

Trivandrum is connected by rail to Cochin, Quilon, Goa and Mangalore. There are bus links with Madurai, Kanyakumari, Coimbatore, Madras, Kumilly, Ernakulam, Quilon and Alleppey.

For more information, *see* 'Moving On', p.485.

Trivandrum ✆ (0471–)   ### Tourist Information

The **KSTDC Tourist Office**, ✆ 451085 is at Parkview, opposite the museum complex. It has very friendly, helpful staff and excellent published information, including a useful festival list for Kerala.

The **KSTDC Reception Centre**, ✆ 75031, is near the bus stand in Station Road opposite the railway station exit, open 6am–10pm. Also very helpful, it offers a number of tours: Trivandrum city sightseeing, Rs85; Kanyakumari; Thekkady (Periyar), Rs225. There is also an information counter at the **airport**, ✆ 71085.

The **GPO** is just off M G Road, between the bus and railway stations and the Secretariat. **Indian Airlines**, ✆ 66370, is at Mascot Junction. **Air India**, ✆ 64837, is at Vellyambalam. **Gulf Air** use Jet Air, Saran Chambers, Diamond Hill, ✆ 68003/67514.

A good travel agent is **Sheriff Travel**, Patan Palace Junction.

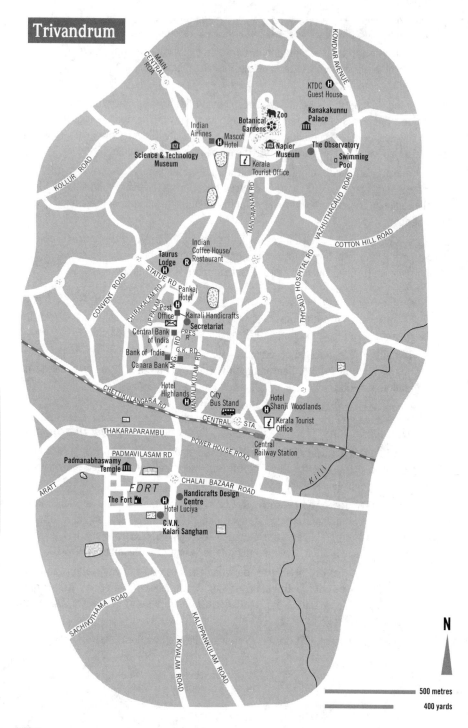

Trivandrum

KTDC Guest House

Kowdiar Avenue

Main Central Road

Indian Airlines

Mascot Hotel

Botanical Gardens

Zoo

Kanakakunnu Palace

The Observatory

Science & Technology Museum

Napier Museum

Swimming Pool

Kollur Road

Kerala Tourist Office

Nandavanam Rd

Cotton Hill Road

Vazhuthacaud Road

Thycaud Hospital Rd

Indian Coffee House/ Restaurant

Taurus Lodge

Convent Road

Statue Rd

Chirakalam Rd

Uppalam Rd

Pankaj Hotel

Post Office

Kairali Handicrafts

Secretariat

Central Bank of India

PRES R

G.K. Rd

Bank of India

M.G. Rd

Canara Bank

Manalikulam Rd

Chettikulangara Rd

Hotel Highlands

City Bus Stand

Hotel Shanji Woodlands

Kerala Tourist Office

Thakaraparambu

Central Sta.

Central Railway Station

Padmavilasam Rd

Power House Road

Kili

Padmanabhaswamy Temple

Aratt

Chalai Bazaar Road

FORT

The Fort

Handicrafts Design Centre

Hotel Luciya

C.V.N. Kalari Sangham

Sachivotham Road

Kovalam Road

Kalippankulam Road

N

500 metres

400 yards

City Tour

By auto-rickshaw/taxi, half day. Padmanabhaswamy Temple–Secretariat–Zoo and Botanical Gardens–Napier Museum–Sri Chitra–Art Gallery– C.V.N. Kalari Sangham.

Trivandrum city is bisected by a single long thoroughfare, M G Road. Getting to the museum, zoo, art gallery, main tourist office and Indian Airlines (all at the top of M.G. Road) from Padmanabhaswamy Temple, or the Kovalam bus stand (opposite each other, at the bottom of M.G. Road) is a long 15-minute ride by auto-rickshaw (Rs10–15) or taxi (Rs20). It is a good half-hour walk, or a Rs10 rickshaw ride from the main bus stand and rail station, opposite each other in Station Road, to the Secretariat and Statue Junction at the centre of M.G. Road.

The city's main landmark is the **Padmanabhaswamy Temple**, a fine example of south Indian architecture, constructed in the Dravidian style by a Maharajah of Travancore in 1733 and dedicated to Lord Vishnu, the presiding deity of Trivandrum. Its magnificent seven-storeyed *gopuram* is reflected in the placid temple pool, and the interior is decorated with intricate carvings and murals.

Unfortunately it is off-limits to non-Hindus. That said, some travellers have sought and gained permission to enter from the Ramakrishna Centre, near the temple. You must dress traditionally inside, in *dhotis* or *saris*. Even if you can't get in, the exterior view is fine, and there are many interesting old houses in the surrounding backstreets. At 4pm Vishnu is taken on his daily procession round the temple grounds.

Proceeding north up M.G. Road by rickshaw, look out for the white-stuccoed **Secretariat** on your right. It's an impressive building, fully reflecting the pomp of the British Raj. Much more impressive is the vast, landscaped museum complex to the north of town. Here are the spacious **Botanical Gardens** (*open daily 10–5, except Mon; adm Rs5, plus a further Rs3 to visit the art gallery. Camera fees are Rs5 extra*), 80 acres of beautifully laid-out lawns, lakes and woodlands. Numerous varieties of tropical tree can be found here. Within the grounds is the dingy and rather depressing **Zoo** (though it has to be said that the animals seem in reasonable health, and you can identify many species for later travel), the magnificent, Indo-Saracenic red-tiled **Napier Museum** housing a famous collection of bronzes and **Sri Chitra Art Gallery** with a modest display of Indian and Far-Eastern paintings. The complex is a good place to bring a packed lunch, and spend a relaxing day.

Back on the south end of M.G. road is the **C.V.N. Kalari Sangham** in the East Fort area. This is Trivandrum's oldest existing institute for both the Kalaripayat martial art, and for Ayurvedic medicine and massage. It operates partly as a clinic for the paying public, partly as a fighting school, and will take foreign pupils for courses of several months. Built of stone, its Kalaripayat training arena allows visitors in (6.30–8am) to see the warriors (who begin as young as 8 years old) perform their limbering exercises and fighting with the fourteen different weapons. You can also get a superb massage there and consult one of the doctors about any health problems. The institute's rather strange name derives from the late Sri C.V. Narayanan Nair, a fighting champion from the early part of this century who laid down a single system for Kalaripayat from the many then practised, and founded several schools across Kerala. To make an appointment or find out about training programmes call ✆ 74182.

Varkala

Less than 1 hour by train from Trivandrum (30 miles; 8 services daily from Trivandrum/ Quilon) or a 2hr journey by bus, this delightful unspoilt little seaside resort has a mineral-water spring, a Vishnu temple dedicated to Lord Janardhana with fascinating rituals, a beach that is empty except at weekends, good swimming and lovely country scenery. Apart from a minor problem with theft, the beach and its small village are mercifully free from the hassle of Kovalam: no groups of Indian tourists turning out to see European flesh, and few hawkers. Visit soon however, as Varkala's beauty has not gone unnoticed; the Taj hotel group is planning to build a huge resort hotel and golf course on the cliffs above the beach in the next few years.

Shopping

Popular buys in Trivandrum are carvings and curios, bell-metal lamps, screw-pine items, handloom fabrics, and Kathakali masks and dolls in *papier mâché* or wood. The two (good) government emporia are **Kairali**, ✆ 60127 at Statue Junction, and **SMSM Institute**, behind the Secretariat. Both are fixed-price establishments, offering the full range of local produce. Although some shops still offer ivory items, the sale and export of ivory is banned by both Indian and international law.

Leisure

Two troupes, **Kathakali Club** and **Drisyavedi**, give displays of traditional Kathakali 'story-play' dance twice monthly, usually at the **Karthikathirunal Theatre,** near to Padmanabhaswamy temple. Both outfits draw their players from the Margi School of Kathakali, near the West Fort, and if you turn up at the Fort High School behind Padmanabhaswamy temple in the early morning, you can make an appointment to watch classes the following day.

To reserve **boat trips** in the backwaters at Thiruvallam, contact Lagoona Beach Resort, ✆ 480049.

Instruction in yoga and Ayurvedic massage is given by Dr Pillai at the **Yoga Therapy Hospital** in Bazhuthacaud Junction. The doctor prefers you to take the full 3-month course, but if you've only a week to spare, he may decide he can do something for you.

Trivandrum ✆ (0471–)

Where to Stay
expensive (from Rs 700)

For modern, clean comfort, try the KTDC **Mascot Hotel,** ✆ 438990, well situated on Mascot Square at the top of M.G. Road, near the museum complex, with a pool and sauna. If you prefer something a little more eccentric, the new **Hotel Lucia**, East Fort, ✆ 463443, ✉ 463347, near the Padmanabhaswamy Temple, offers air-conditioned rooms and suites done up in a variety of styles, including Chinese and a ham-fisted half-timbered attempt at Olde English style. The **Madison Fort Manor**, Power House Junction, ✆ 70002, is centrally located, has a good travel desk and clean, airy rooms.

moderate (from Rs 400)

Least expensive in the range is the central **Hotel Highland**, on Manjalikulam Cross Road in Thampanoor suburb, ✆ 68200, which has air-conditioned rooms and a good restaurant. The modern, state-run **Chaitram** on Station Road, Thampanoor, ✆ 330977, is very near to the railway and bus stations. Again, air-conditioned rooms here are very good value—almost at the bottom of the price range. A little more expensive is **Hotel Pankaj**, opposite the Secretariat on M.G. Road, ✆ 76667, ✉ 76255. The least 'Indian' of Trivandrum's big hotels, it can be snobby (*very* reluctant to show backpackers rooms) and food is pricey, but there's good service, stylish rooms and a nice rooftop restaurant.

budget

The **Hotel Highland** (*see* above) has non air-conditioned rooms. Also good is the **Hotel Poorna**, ✆ 331315/331729, on M.G. Road south of the Secretariat. Within the price category are the **Hotel Safari**, ✆ 77202/72778, opposite the S.M.V. school on M.G. Road, the **Hotel Samrat** on Thakaraparampu Road, ✆ 463314 and the **Highness Inn** on Airport Road, Peruntanni, ✆ 450983.

Try the **Taurus Lodge**, located down Statue Road. It's run by 'George', one of those polite, informative lodge-owners who help make travel in India a joy, rather than a continual struggle. Rooms are clean and quiet and the best ones (nos.21, 24 and 25) are spacious, with good views. Whatever you want to know about Trivandrum, its culture, transport, entertainments or shopping, ask George. In the same price bracket is the small, clean **Omkar Lodge** on M.G. Road, ✆ 78503.

Eating Out

The best upmarket restaurants are at **Hotel Shanti Woodlands** (Thycaud) and **Hotel Pankaj**. Both offer mid-priced quality fare in air-conditioned comfort. For grills (burgers etc.) and Indian food, try **Kalayara Restaurant** near Taurus Lodge. The **Mayfair Hotel** opposite has a good bar. Two other popular restaurants with more local food are **Ananda Bhavan** and **Athul Jyoti**, both on M.G. Road, just along from the Secretariat.

Moving On

By air: from Trivandrum airport (6½km from the city centre, Rs1 by no.14 local bus) there are daily flights to and from Bombay, Cochin and Goa. There are less frequent services which fly to Bangalore, Hyderabad and Madras.

Trivandrum is also an international airport with Air India flights to Gulf cities including Dubai and Muscat. Some of these flights continue on to Europe and New York and there are plans to expand the airport to take more European air traffic over the next few years. Indian Airlines operates flights to Malé in the Maldives and Colombo in Sri Lanka. Air Lanka also operates to and from Colombo. Gulf Air operates from and to Abu Dhabi, Bahrain, Doha and Muscat with onward connections to Europe.

By rail: from Trivandrum railway station (opposite the bus station), there are four trains daily to Ernakulam (Cochin), via Quilon. The fastest train is the 6.15am *Parosaram Day Express*, which gets to Quilon, 45 miles away, in 1½ hours, and to Ernakulam in just 3 hours. It's a wonderfully scenic ride, cutting right through the eight creeks of Ashtamudi Lake. Best of all, you don't even need to pre-book: just hop on, and pay for your 2nd-class air-conditioned seat on the train.

The best train for Goa leaves Trivandrum at 11pm, arriving in Mangalore at 10am the next morning. Proceed immediately by auto-rickshaw to Mangalore's government (not private) bus stand, in order to catch the 11am express bus (10 hours) to Panjim. Don't miss this early bus as the next one bound for Goa is in the evening.

By bus: Trivandrum has two bus stands. Buses for Kovalam leave from the East Fort bus stand. Buses for all other destinations leave from the city central bus stand, opposite the railway station. Destinations include Madurai (many buses from 4.30 to 10am and from 5 to 11pm; 7 hours), Kanyakumari (10 departures a day; 2 hours), Coimbatore (6.30pm; 12 hours), Madras (12.30pm and 7pm; 17 hours) and Kumilly (8 hours). For all these long-haul destinations, you'll have to advance-book tickets: a real pain, in view of the long queues. Try to find a boy to queue up for you for Rs8–10 while you go sightseeing.

Fortunately, there's normally no need for advance reservations on the hourly buses to Ernakulam (4 hours) which run from 5am to midnight, calling at Quilon (1½ hours) and Alleppey (3 hours). Just toss your bags in the window and pay on the bus.

Excursion to the Cardamom Hills

The southernmost part of Kerala's Western Ghats are named after the wild cardamom that grows in the forests. Two small hill stations in these 'hills' (in fact, small mountains) can be easily reached from Trivandrum, both being about 56km (3 hours by bus) from the town. The first, **Neyyar Dam** is an interesting settlement in its own right, with a **Yoga Ashram**, open to outside visitors, a small market where local forest tribals come to trade, a dam, with shoreline gardens decorated with garish sculpture, where crocodiles swim, and a surrounding forest well populated with wildlife. Accommodation is cheap, both in the state-run **Agasthya House**, near which is a wildlife-viewing tower, and which has a small bar/restaurant, or at **Neyyar Guest House**, ✆ 04725 4493.

Neyyar town lies in the foothills of the Ghats, but the nearby **Neyyar Wildlife Sanctuary** extends up into the high mountains. Around the entrance about 100 yards west of the dam, there is a park with animals in open cages, whose inmates include

Asiatic lion. In the wild forest live elephant, tiger, leopard, sloth bear, bison, *sambar*, spotted deer. The reserve backs onto neighbouring **Mudanthurai Tiger Sanctuary** on the eastern slopes of the Ghats, so the game can migrate freely from the wet to the dry zone forests.

One of Kerala's best trekking routes runs through Neyyar reserve—the three-day hike up **Agasthya Peak**, a 6122 feet high (1866 metres) mountain that was the mythological home of the sage Agasthya. The trip must be arranged via Clipper Holidays, Cochin (*see* p.503). For those not trekking, accommodation in Neyyar Wildlife Sanctuary is at a rest house at the entrance. Day walks can be arranged at the office.

On the north side of Neyyar Sanctuary is **Agasthya Vanam Biological Park**, overlooked by the great peak of that name, and which protects the **Kottur Reserved Rainforest**. As yet there is no general access to the reserve, but trekking routes are set to be opened in 1996/7.

At the northern end of the Cardamom Hills (also 3 hours by bus from Trivandrum) is the tiny hill station of **Ponmudi**. Set on a

Sloth bear

high peak above an area of alternate forest and tea plantation, Ponmudi is a superb centre from which to trek or look for wildlife—the full complement of south Indian wildlife lives in the forests and grasslands here. You do not need prior permission to walk in the surrounding ranges, and you can venture into the forests either alone or hire a guide through one of the two rest-houses whose cottages and one main lodge comprise the entire settlement. Guides charge about Rs100 per person per day, and you can trek into the surrounding forests for up to 8 days, sleeping in caves. You take your own food, but your guides will cook for you.

Ponmudi has accommodation in the state-run **Ponmudi Tourist Complex** (run-down but fine views—rooms from about Rs40), up the hill from which there is a small restaurant/bar and the **Ponmudi Tourist Resort**, which has a small collection of equally basic bungalows, starting at Rs8 per night. If you walk 2km up the tar road from Ponmudi, you

, grazed by a resident herd of *sambar* (good photo-
lookout points that give spectacular views out over the
Western Ghats. One warning though: Ponmudi fills up at
unken day-trippers from Trivandrum. Go in the week only, or
t in the forests by the weekend.

, 7 miles from Trivandrum, was once the Arabian Sea beach resort of the court of
ajas of Travancore. Today, its two scimitar-sweeps of sand comprise the most popular
urist draw in southern Kerala. The place used only to cater for hippy backpackers but
now matches Goa for restaurants, hotels and shopping. However, despite a massive
increase in visitors (400 per week from London alone), Kovalam still has its soft yellow-
white sands, warm, clear waters, and wide views of the ocean horizon. Small beach
restaurants provide the laid-back tourist community with fresh seafood and slightly overpriced Western-style cuisine. Fishermen still put out to sea in their catamarans each
morning and most visitors find it very difficult to leave. The coolest and best months to
come are between December and March. In April the heatwave arrives, driving many
people north. The result (but beware sunburn and a few pre-monsoon showers!) is empty
beaches and cheap accommodation.

Getting There

Kovalam is linked to Trivandrum and Quilon by rail and bus. *See* also 'Moving
On', p.492.

From Trivandrum, bus no.9D (every half-hour, from 6am to 10pm) goes from the
city bus stand at East Fort (40-minute journey, Rs4 fare). Sometimes, auto-rickshaws
offer cheap 'share' rides (Rs25 per head) from the bus stand. The normal point-to-
point rickshaw fare is nearer Rs60. Taxis and hire cars regularly ply this route.

Kovalam ✆ *(0471–)*   ### Tourist Information

There is tourist information desk at the **Kovalam Ashok Beach Resort,**
✆ 480085, as well as a bank for changing money. **Indian Airlines**, **State Bank of
India** and the **post office** are in Trivandrum. To post letters, buy aerogrammes
and the like, use the small **sub post office** in Kovalam Village (a 20-minute climb
up the back of the beach, near the top of the headland).

The Beaches

Kovalam has two popular beaches, separated by a large rock outcrop extending
into the sea. The luxury beach, overlooked by the five-star Ashok Beach Resort
Hotel, is just below the bus stand. The main beach, with all the budget accommodation and beach restaurants, is a 1-minute walk through shady palm groves
from the bus stand. The end of this 'budget' beach is marked by the lighthouse up on
the headland.

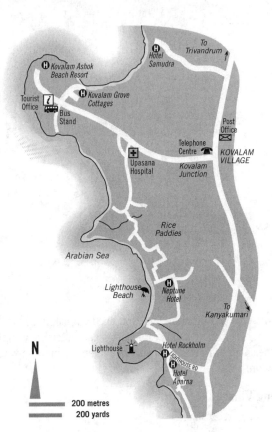

Kovalam Beach

Popular beach activities at Kovalam include snorkelling (easy to hire equipment), water-skiing (contact the Ashok Hotel), and body-surfing the big waves about 200 yards off the shore. Swimming is very pleasant in the shallows, which extend a long way out, but don't go much farther as the currents become dangerously strong.

One problem that women will encounter is unwanted attention from the crowds of Indian tourists who come down at weekends to see bikinied or topless Western flesh. You will have to be firm, if not abusive in getting rid of such company, but also use common-sense and don't go topless—remember that in India a bare breast (let alone a pair!) is something worth travelling miles to see. In high season, you will also be assailed by hordes of grinning salesmen selling fruit, seashells, silk lungis (but beware of low quality!) and soft drinks. For peace and quiet try the quieter cove directly behind the lighthouse, or wander up to the bay above the big Ashok hotel, which is often quite deserted.

Avoid drugs peddled by dealers on the beach, and take care not to doze off on the beach or you may wake up, badly sunburnt, to find all your belongings gone. Smoke drugs openly and you will also find yourself in trouble: there are police informers all over the place and an on-the-spot fine may cost you everything you have.

If inertia or boredom set in, and you need a break from the beaches, it's time to get out and about. For many people, this just means a leisurely stroll up onto the headland, to visit the shops in Kovalam Town. For something more rewarding, try the following short excursion.

Fishing Village

By foot, 2/3hrs.

This walk is a treat. Be down on the beach at 7am to watch the fishermen put out to sea, then take the high road running up from the lighthouse to the top of the headland. From here, it's a scenic 2km stroll, offering beautiful views along the coastline, to the small decorative Muslim shrine perched on the cliff edge. There's a path here, which takes you down to the beach again. Keeping to your left, you'll shortly arrive at the fishing village with its shiny new government-sponsored (motorized) fishing boats. A few of the traditional wooden dug-outs remain, however, and the way to introduce yourself (they don't see a lot of tourists) is to lend a hand with a fishing rope, net or boat.

At the back of the beach, you'll see the charming tiered Catholic shrine housing a red-faced Jesus and Mary, the community's patron saints. Climb the rise behind this for a cold drink and stunning coastline views. Then drop in on the village, an interesting collection of narrow, cobbled streets and thatched dwellings with wide courtyards for drying out the fish. Behind the village, back on the main road, you'll find the modern seaside town, with Portuguese-style bungalows, little knick-knack shops, a couple of cafés and lots of locals on holiday.

From here, it's a leisurely 45-minute walk back up the headland to Kovalam Beach for a well-earned rest in the sun.

Shopping

The most common buys at Kovalam are suntan lotion, funky beach clothes and mosquito repellent. You can find all this stuff, plus cigarettes and confectionery, at the small general stores by the bus stand. Good tailor-made clothes can be made up by K. Surash's Fashion Tailoring Shop, a little place next door to the second-hand book exchange on the road leading down to the first beach from Kovalam town. Suresh's prices are fair, but this cannot be said of the book exchange next door, which charges more than the new retail price for its second-hand stock. Seashells, sarongs and (fake) jewellery are hawked by children on the beach, but Kovalam just isn't a buyers' market. Like Goa, it's a place to sell things. Unload any unwanted film, cameras, Walkmans, and even snorkel equipment here. You'll have no problem swapping books either. Most people, remember, spend all day on the beach reading!

Leisure

Kovalam is full of places offering **Ayurvedic massage**, but of course there are also many charlatans. Head straight for **Medicus Massage** opposite the Rockholm Hotel on the Lighthouse road, a small clinic run by a husband and wife team, Drs. K.R.C. and Lalitha Babu. The clinic is opposite the Rockholm hotel.

Kovalam ℂ (0471–)

Where to Stay

Note: In all of Kovalam's hotels you may be able to bargain discounts of up to 50% in the low season (any time apart from November to February).

luxury (from US$380)

The prestige place to stay is the five-star **Kovalam Ashok Beach Resort**, ℂ 480101, ℮ 481522, with its superb location, water-sports, yoga and massage facilities, but the standard of service and food can be poor and the place looks somewhat shabby. The beach cottages are pleasant but, as the air-conditioning rarely works, are not recommended in the hotter months. The large balcony rooms, which cost 25% higher between mid-December and the end of February, have the famous sunset view. A new wing opened in late 1992 and the old Palace guest house on the hill above the resort has four suites.

expensive (from Rs 1200)

Try the well-appointed **Hotel Rockholm**, ℂ 480306, up on the lighthouse head-land. This has some lovely, breezy rooms overlooking the cliffs, and an excellent restaurant with open-air patio. KTDC's pleasant **Hotel Samudra**, ℂ 480089, a 15-minute walk north of the luxury Ashok hotel, is a modern building, tastefully done. In season, it has a good restaurant on the roof. Some rooms have balconies and sea views. You can also try the **Hotel Aparna** on Lighthouse Road, ℂ 480950/480951, which has rooms, again with some overlooking the sea.

Two hotels have rooms that fall within both categories. Directly behind the Rockholm on Lighthouse Road, is **Syama Lodge** with huge, well-furnished rooms which drop to half-price in the low season.

budget

There are now so many small, cheap, and generally comfortable lodges, either right on the beach, or set just back from it that recommending any one over another is a difficult exercise: they're changing all the time. Many have rooms from Rs100 per night and it is also possible to rent rooms with local families for Rs300 a week. Try the **Achuta Lodge Guest House**, the **Neptune Hotel** or **Holiday Home Guest House**—all on Lighthouse beach—or ask at any of the beach restaurants and you will soon find your way.

Eating Out

Kovalam has some excellent restaurants, although some of the old favourites on the beach have closed. Good Italian, French, Chinese and Malabar dishes plus the local seafood are all just a short, lazy stroll up the beach. Two popular restaurants on the road up the hill are the **Milky Way** and **German Bakery**. The **Rockholm** (℡ 480306) has excellent fish dishes, depending on what's available that morning in the market. While the menu includes some European dishes it is their seafood that excels. Lobster, crab and mackerel can be prepared to order. Meals cost anything from Rs60–250 a head depending on how many dishes of crab curry you can eat.

Moving On

There are half-hourly buses from Trivandrum to Quilon; journey time 1½ hours.

Quilon

The gateway to Kerala's beautiful backwaters, Quilon (also called Kollam) is a rather ugly town situated on the edge of the more beautiful Ashtamudi Lake, 'lake of eight creeks', whose shore are fringed with luxuriant coconut groves and cashew plantations.

An ancient commercial centre, the site on which modern Quilon stands was used by the Phoenicians, Persians, Greeks, Romans, Arabs and the Chinese. Even today, you can see the Chinese fishing nets, more commonly associated with Cochin farther north, dotted round the lakes here. Quilon town, established in the 9th century, is associated with the origin of the Malayalam-era 'Kollavarsham', which began in AD 825. In more recent times, its commercial wealth made it a bone of contention between Portuguese, Dutch and English trading interests. Today, it is just a sleepy market town divided into a picturesque quarter of red-tiled wooden houses and winding backstreets, and the usual scrubby Indian semi-industrial hellhole.

Daily trains stop at Quilon on their way between Trivandrum and Ernakulam (Cochin). Buses do the same; Trivandrum to Quilon takes 1½hrs (hourly departures).

There is a **tourist information desk** at the Government Guest House (✆ 76456). The **post office** and **Bank of India** are both at the top of Parameshwar Nagar, two thirds of a mile above the bus stand. Boats can also be hired from the **Quilon Boat Club** (✆ 72519) or through the tourist office.

The Backwaters

You need not linger in Quilon more than a day: the big attractions in these parts are the famous backwaters, best visited from December to February. By March, the heat and the mosquitoes are too oppressive. Budget travellers will need a mosquito net if sleeping in Quilon's cheap hotel rooms.

Arriving in Quilon, go straight to the boat jetty, a minute's walk below the bus stand, to check the departure time of the morning backwaters' boat. You'll need to arrive early to get a seat on this government-run, and therefore cheap, service. Private boat trips are more expensive at about Rs100–200, but can be booked through almost any hotel. Then use any free time in Quilon to stroll around the pretty part of town around the lakeshore, or to

visit **Thangasseri Beach** for its sands, lighthouse and Portuguese/Dutch fort ruins 2 miles away. For a short while Thangasseri was a British trading outpost.

The **Kuttanadu Backwaters** between Quilon and Alleppey are unforgettable. The 8½-hour boat journey takes you from narrow canals canopied by dense foliage out into large inland lagoons framed by dense tropical palm groves. Fishermen stand waist-high in the waters and cast their nets. Families of river-dwellers pass by in narrow punted dugouts. Wooden vessels with primitive Chinese sails drift up the waterways, stately and silent. Children run down from Portuguese churches and schools to welcome your approach. In the lush season (February), the boat carves a plough through canals carpeted with blossoming water hyacinths. At sunset, you chug across a huge lake into Alleppey harbour, a corridor of gently swaying coconut palms, backing onto brilliant green meadows. The trip is a delight. It leaves Quilon at 10.30am (report at the DTPC jetty at 10.00) and costs Rs150 per person. Take plenty of camera film (the views cry out to be photographed) and lots of food, because there are only two stops, at about 1pm and 4pm, for *thalis* and coffee. Try to get a berth on the boat roof; you're generally allowed up, depending on the mood of the crew, a short while after departure from Quilon. A couple of rupees baksheesh may be in order, but it's well worth it. Make sure you have a hat and plenty of sunscreen.

Backwater Alternatives

The Backwaters between Quilon and Alleppey are not the only ones available for exploration. Smaller, quieter waterways wind from Alleppey out to Kottayam (which has a fantastic lagoon resort for those who can afford luxury accommodation), as well as up to Ernakulam (Cochin) and into various backwaters around that city. It is possible to make some of these trips by government boat (information available from the Tourist Office at the boat jetty in Alleppey) but it is far, far more pleasant to go by **private houseboat** for a few days. These old Keralan craft are made of dark hardwood with impressive carved prows, have cabins of woven palm-leaf and can accommodate several people. Prices are expensive—around Rs2000 per boat per day, but you can split this between about four people. Contact Varkey Kurian at **Clipper Holidays** in Cochin, ✆ 0484 364453.

Quilon ✆ (0474–)   ***Where to Stay***

Note: all hotels have a problem with mosquitoes, so bring lots of repellent.

The **Sudarshan** on Hospital Road near the boat jetty, ✆ 444322, 📠 740480, has air-conditioned rooms (though only some) with attached, Western-style bathrooms and two restaurants. Private backwater trips to Alleppey cost about Rs100 and can be booked from here. The **Government Guest House**, ✆ 76456, is a former British Residency with lovely gardens, good Keralan-style food and a useful jetty. Boat hire is available from 10am to 4pm daily.

The most popular place among backpackers is the **Karthika** halfway up Main Road (also called Paika Road) from the station end, ✆ 76240. The Karthika has a reasonable-to-awful restaurant, a shop and, again, you can book a private backwater trip to Alleppey from reception. Also on Main Road, nearer to the bus station, is the **Lakshami Tourist Home**, ℂ 70167, which is a little cheaper, though it has a few air-conditioned rooms. Try also the **Iswarya Lodge** on Main Road, but further east, ℂ 77801.

Eating Out

For good Indian, Chinese and continental food, try the **Hotel Sudarshan** (two restaurants, plus an air-conditioned bar); for cheaper vegetarian meals, visit the **Hotel Guru Prasad** on Main Road. For a big breakfast before the boat trip (you may not eat again all day) try **Mahalaxshmi Lodge** opposite the bus stand. The **Indian Coffee House** on Main Road is good for snacks and coffee.

Alleppey

Far more attractive than Quilon, Alleppey is a small market town, built around a curious maze of bridges and canals. These have earned it the title 'Venice of the East'—a trifle far fetched, owing to its small size, which gives it a pleasantly intimate feel. The canals are surprisingly filth-free, often green with water hyacinth and, if you look closely, you will often see schools of young fish feeding near the surface. Kingfishers fly by in flashes of iridescent azure, and along St George's Street, which flanks the main canal, merchants load and unload directly from the long hardwood trading boats that ply the backwaters with cargoes of mostly yarn, rope and mats—for Alleppey is the centre of Kerala's famous *coir* products. The town merchants in their old Keralan houses, heap their wares in open 'go downs' (warehouses) at street level. Take a walk down St George's Road, which starts about 550 yards south of the boat jetty, to bask in the laid-back, yet prosperous atmosphere of the backwaters. Otherwise, especially if you stay in the tourist lodges near the jetty, you will never get a feeling of what this town is all about.

Once a year the town explodes into furious life for the spectacular **Nehru Cup Snake-Boat Race,** held on the second Saturday of August, when the 90 foot-long boats (paddled by 60 men) fly down the long backwater straights to the boom of drums and the roar of a crowd tens of thousands strong. Teams train and prepare throughout the year and up to 70 boats compete over a mile-long course. The Allepuzhans' enthusiasm and rivalry for the coveted trophy is similar to that of the Sienese of Italy for their famous *Palio* horse race and similar attempts by the different factions to undermine the boats and teams of the others' lend a euphoric ferocity to the whole proceeding.

Alleppey ℂ *(0477–)*

Where to Stay
moderate (from Rs 200)

Alleppey's only hotel in this range is the Western-style **Alleppey Prince**, ℂ 243752–57, ℻ 243758. The Prince has flexible rates, so do not hesitate to bargain. Situated halfway down A.S. Road, a long mile from the town centre, it works hard for custom. Touts selling this hotel board your boat just as it drifts into Alleppey. In fact it's worth reserving in advance to avoid the crush, such is its popularity;. the Prince has quiet a/c rooms, a superb Keralan restaurant and a pool.

inexpensive

The **Komala**, opposite the jetty, ✆ 243631/243632, has clean rooms and a good restaurant. The old travellers' haunt, **St George's Lodge** in C.C.N.B. Road near the boat jetty, ✆ 3373, is useful for its money exchange facilities (as is the Canara Bank in St George's Buildings). However, the food is not good.

budget

The **Karthika Tourist Home** on S.V.D. Road, ✆ 245524, over the bridge, one block north of the boat jetty. Good value, with some air-conditioned rooms, the place has a reasonably good travel service and an ayurvedic massage clinic. On the same side of the bridge is the **Kerala Hotel**, easily visible from the jetty, which has cleaner rooms with bathrooms attached.

Eating Out

Far and away the best place for food, drink and relaxation is the **Indian Coffee House**, a mile south of the boat jetty towards St George's Street, with Raj-style waiters and décor, cheap non-vegetarian food and excellent coffee. For good Rs10 *thalis*, you can try **Vijaya Restaurant** in Jetty Road. Otherwise check out the inexpensive vegetarian places near the Raja Tourist Home. The vegetarian **Arun Restaurant** at the Komala Hotel is considered by some to be the best in Alleppey.

Backwater Routes from Alleppey

For travellers, Alleppey is simply a jumping-off point for another amazing trip up the Keralan waterways. Many find the shorter 2½-hour journey from here to Kottayam far more satisfactory than the preceding trip from Quilon: you don't tend to get jaded with the scenery.

Furthermore, being so near to the extensive Vembanad Lake stretching north to Cochin, Alleppey is a major centre of inland water transport, so there's a good deal more to see on the lakes. It's a very scenic run, with many country craft, laden with *coir* goods and cashews, gliding up the canals. And there are some lovely inland lagoons, fringed by thin green necklaces of vegetation. The narrower stretches of water are often covered with a purple-green blanket of blossoming water-lilies. The final approach into Kottayam is down picturesque avenues of lush tropical trees.

There are a number of boats leaving for Kottayam daily, tickets Rs4.90. But for maximum comfort and superior scenery, an early morning or mid-afternoon departure is best.

Kottayam

About two hours by either train or backwater boat from Cochin and Alleppey, Kottayam is principally a springboard point for Periyar Wildlife Sanctuary in the mountains to the east, and for the expensive Coconut Lagoon backwaters resort. A prosperous commercial town (and thus now ugly and increasingly polluted at its centre), famous for its cash crops of rubber, tea, pepper and cardamom, it was developed as an educational centre by English missionaries. Indeed, Kottayam's Christian history extends back into antiquity: it was patronized by St Thomas (1st century AD), and the descendants of some of the wealthy Brahmins he converted later helped build some fine churches here, notably the 16th-century **Vallia Palli Church** some 3 miles northwest of the railway station. Mass is sung at 9am on Sundays. Vallia is notable for its Pahlavi inscriptions and for its Nestorian cross, which is said to have come from St Thomas' original church at Cranganore. Kottayam is an important centre for Syrian Christians in Kerala, as well as being the place where many of Kerala's leading newspapers are published.

Kumarakom

Much more pleasant then smelly old Kottayam, Kumarakom is the name for a thinly-spread set of fishing villages set around the massive Vembanad freshwater lagoon, about 7 miles from Kottayam. A superbly tranquil 'backwater' (pun intended), Kumarakom has a wooded, marshland **bird sanctuary**, through which you can walk, and has evolved a bizarre local method of fishing; the lagoon is no more than 4–5 feet deep in most places and a group of fishermen will wade in, two carrying a long rope, the others walking behind, dragging a small boat. The rope is dragged along the lake's glutinous floor, hitting the fish and causing them to burrow into the the mud for protection. The fishermen walking behind then dive down, feel around and grab the fish wherever they find them. These they then bring to the surface and chuck into the boat. It seems a time and energy-consuming way of catching fish but the fishermen are highly skilled and the local inhabitants are obviously well fed.

Where to Stay

Kottayam ✆ (0481–)

Stay at either the 'moderate'/'inexpensive' category **Anjali Hotel**, K.K. Road, 3½km from the railway station, ✆ 563661, with clean, comfy air-conditioned rooms. In the same price range is the the **Hotel Greenpark**, Nagampadam, ✆ 563331, and the **Hotel Vembadi** on the lake (2km outside town), with chalet-type rooms and a floating restaurant.

In the 'cheap' category is the off-beat **Tourist Bungalow**, a tricky but rewarding 15-minute walk/climb from the boat jetty. It offers spacious double rooms (originally British officers' quarters) with period furnishings.

Kumarakom *©* (048192–)

luxury

The recently established **Coconut Lagoon**, *©* 668221, *◈* 668001, is a private resort of antique Keralan houses imported from various parts of the state and built around a minor labyrinth of waterways on the shores of the lake. An outdoor pool, decent Indian and continental restaurant, ayurvedic spa (though the ayurvedic massage here is not the best in Kerala) and ultra-efficient service make up the attractions. There is also superb birdlife—not just at the bird sanctuary on the opposite island (the management runs a boat over to the sanctuary every morning), but also in the complex itself: egrets, black-headed orioles, bee-eaters, brahmini kites and a whole host of herons are just a few of the breeding species at Coconut Lagoon. The resort also offers boat rides on the surrounding canals amid rice paddies.

inexpensive

Fortunately, you don't have to be rich to stay on the lagoon. The **Kumarakom Tourist Complex** has a couple of houseboats that you can rent. The surrounding woodland and lake attract many species of birds.

Periyar (Thekkady)

Just outside the mountain town of Kumilly is the Periyar Wildlife Sanctuary (Tiger Reserve) at Thekkady. One of the main sanctuaries of southern India, it is also one of the largest in India. Comprising 300 square miles of lush, tropical forest, with a vast artificial lake in the centre, it is the natural habitat of an extensive range of wildlife. The huge Periyar Lake, measuring 10 square miles in area, was formed in 1895, with the completion of the Periyar Dam by the British government in Madras. Its original purpose was irrigation, but its conservation potential was soon recognized.

Getting There

From Kottayam or Cochin (and over the mountains to Madurai) there are several daily bus services that take about 4–6 hours. One direct service connects Kumilly with Kovalam and another with Kodaikanal in Tamil Nadu.

If staying in Kumilly, you can hire bicycles from most of the cheaper lodges to go in and out of the sanctuary (½hr ride to the boat jetty).

Thekkady (04868–) **Tourist Information**

Kumilly **tourist office** is located at the top of the main street, opposite Lake Queen Hotel. When open, it dispenses boat-trip tickets, maps and walking/trekking permits. The **Wildlife Preservation Office**, *©* 27, is at Periyar, overlooking the boat jetty.

Sanctuary Tour

By tour boat, half day.

The first game warden was appointed in 1923, the area was constituted a sanctuary in 1934, and it came under **Project Tiger** management in 1978. The rapid decrease in the population of tigers (from 40,000 at the turn of the century to just 1830 in 1972) led to the creation of Project Tiger, and the immediate management of 7 parks. Eighteen now come under the project, and the tiger population had increased to 4334 in 1989, 48 of them at Periyar.

Situated at a high altitude of between 914 and 1828 metres, Periyar has a comfortably cool climate between November and January. But to see the wildlife at close quarters, it is best to come during the 'dry' months of February to June, when the animals, deprived of the forest water-holes, come to water down by the lake.

Periyar has a rich variety of wildlife, notably tiger, elephant, leopard, *gaur, dhole, sambar, chital*, wild boar, monkey, and a few Malabar flying squirrels, among many mammal species. The extensive bird life to be seen includes heron, hornbill, jungle fowl, kingfisher and egret. The forests are dense jungles of creepers, spices and blossoming trees interspersed with some grassland.

To see the best of the wildlife, take the early 7am boat onto Periyar Lake (Rs20–30, tickets from the Wildlife Office, above jetty). Unless you are trekking, or are prepared to spend a couple of nights in one of the forest watchtowers, this is your best chance to see

elephants, *gaur*, deer and, occasionally, tiger at close quarters; they come to water only very early in the morning, and in the late afternoon. You will not see many animals at any other time of day. At weekends, a motorboat full of tourists will send most animals on the banks scurrying for cover, so you may be better off hiring a private launch, from the Wildlife Office at about Rs80 per hour.

The boat tour lasts 1½ hours, and is a useful introduction to the sanctuary's flora and fauna. To follow up, it is necessary to explore the surrounding forests on foot. The Wildlife Office runs 3-hour **forest group treks** (Rs50 per person) which, if the group is small and disciplined, is worthwhile. These walks are often good for bird-watching. Some people, disregarding the injunction not to wander into the forest unescorted, report alarming experiences, returning with tales of unexpected eyeball encounters with bull elephants. If you want to get into the deep forest, the wisest course is to hire a private guide from the Wildlife Office (Rs100 per day) who'll take you to the best hides in complete safety, or for an **overnight trek** to one of the **forest rest houses** (an extra Rs100 per night, and you take your own food), enabling close sightings of elephants, bison, snakes, monkeys and a rich array of bird life.

Persuade the wildlife officer at Periyar that you're not a typical tourist, that you've come here specifically to study wildlife, and he may just let you stay alone at one of the **observation watchtowers**. These stand in the heart of the forest, on stilts, and elephants come to rest in their shade. To get to them, you take the tour boat out onto the lake, then walk a couple of miles into the jungle along with the park ranger. Since there are only two watchtowers available, it's worth booking 3–4 days in advance. A flashlight, blanket, food, drinking water and mosquito repellent are essential.

Thekkady (04868–)   ***Where to Stay***

expensive

If staying in the nearby village of Kumilly (a short bike or taxi ride from Thekkady, 2 miles from the lake), stay at **Spice Village** (US$90) a new resort with well-furnished cottages, bookable through the Casino Hotel, Cochin, ✆ 340221, ✉ 340001. The food is very good, wild spice trees grow on the lawns, and there is a pool. The hotel can arrange all your transport into the sanctuary and can also put together treks, supply food etc. The plush **Lake Palace**, ✆ 22024 (Rs5000), is an island bungalow fairly deep within the sanctuary with nice gardens, a prime lakeshore situation, and pleasant rooms. Book through KDTC in Trivandrum, ✆ 61132. **Aranya Nivas Hotel**, ✆ 22023 (Rs1500–2000), also in the sanctuary, is a fair fall-back with dodgy food, but good facilities. Rooms face the lake. Pre-book through the KTDC office in Trivandrum, ✆ 61132.

moderate

The **Government Rest House** in the forest has three very comfortable rooms and they provide a servant to cook for you. Check availability with the tourist office in Kumilly.

The **Ambadi**, at the checkpost, near the sanctuary entrance, ✆ 22192, offers well-furnished, homely cottages, with rooms around Rs300. Another budget place is the **Lake Queen Tourist Home** opposite the tourist office, ✆ 22086. It has some nice first-floor rooms with views of the hills (around Rs150), but guests complain of the alarming 6.30am 'breakfast calls'.

For dirt cheap accommodation, the **Forest Rest House** inside the sanctuary costs well under Rs100 per night, but with only 3 rooms it's generally full. In Kumilly try the **Holiday Home**, ✆ 22016 and **Rani Lodge**, both of which are basic.

Eating Out

The best eating places are in Kumilly. **Hotel Vanarani** offers a fine range of south Indian cuisine, very cheaply; **Hotel Paris** is the best for Western food, with quick service; and **Hotel Ambadi** often lays on displays of Kathakali dance in its popular open-air restaurant. All the hotel restaurants are open to non-residents.

Cochin/Ernakulam

Portugal's original trading station in the East Indies, Cochin is one of Kerala's most beautiful places; a town built around a saltwater lagoon of the Arabian Sea. Unfortunately, to get here you have to pass through one of Kerala's least beautiful places, the mainland city of **Ernakulam** (*see* below). Once there, Cochin seems to be a city from the past come to life. It comprises the southern peninsula of **Fort Cochin** and **Mattancherry**, and the islands of **Willingdon**, **Bolghatty**, **Gundu** and **Vypeen**, all connected by a network of bridges and ferries. The scenic setting of its natural harbour, away from Ernakulam, is famous—surrounded by palm groves, green fields, inland lakes and backwaters. All this beauty has earned Cochin the title 'Queen of the Arabian Sea'.

Cochin has a rich maritime history and still ships Kerala's *coir*, rubber, seafood and pepper products abroad. Influenced at various times by the Arabs, Chinese, Dutch, British and the Portuguese, it was Cochin's Jews who founded the first strong community here, over 1000 years ago, one of the only places that the dispossessed children of Israel found tolerant enough to allow them to prosper during their wanderings of the early medieval period. However, their joyful isolation only lasted until the early 16th century when Vasco da Gama sailed to the East Indies and seized Cochin for the Portuguese in 1502. The port became the first European settlement in India and changed hands several times over the following centuries. Lured by its spices and ivory, the Dutch arrived (1602) and displaced the Portuguese (1663). In 1795 Cochin passed to the British. All of these conquerors left their mark, and present-day Fort Cochin/Mattancherry is a curious pot pourri of Jewish synagogues, Chinese fishing-nets, Portuguese churches, Dutch palaces and British cricket pitches. The atmosphere is perceptibly Mediterranean. But the climate is sub-tropical; hot and sticky for much of the year. The official season is October to March, but for comfort visit in December or January.

Chinese fishing nets

Getting There

Although plans are afoot to build an international airport on the mainland (but then such plans are always afoot in India), Cochin's present airport (Willingdon Island) is 4 miles from Ernakulam town centre, a Rs30 taxi ride, or Rs2.50 by bus to or from Ernakulam's Kallor city bus stand, just above Ernakulam Town railway station. You can fly to and from Bombay, Bangalore, Delhi, Madras and Trivandrum.

Ernakulam has two railway stations, linked to Alleppey, Kottayam, Quilon, Trivandrum, Madras, Mangalore, Bangalore and Ooty. There are buses to and from Alleppey, Quilon, Trivandrum, Trichur, Calicut, Kottayam, Bangalore, Madras, Madurai, Kanyakumari and Coimbatore.

For further information, *see* 'Moving On', p.508.

Getting Around

Fort Cochin and Mattancherry have the historical sites; modern Ernakulam has the bus and railway stations, the hotels, shops and restaurants as well as the filth, crowds and squalor. The real Cochin starts on Willingdon Island, the site of the airport, the two top hotels and the tourist office. Neighbouring Bolghatty island has its famous palace hotel, and Gundu its interesting *coir* factory. If peace and quiet are not your first priority, then stay in Ernakulam. It may be a busy, unrelaxing commercial centre, but it's certainly the most convenient base for sightseeing. All Cochin's islands are linked by a regular ferry service, operating from Ernakulam's three jetties. The main jetty charges a few rupees for trips over to Willingdon, Vypeen, Vallarpadam and Fort Cochin (either to Chinese Fishing Nets, or to Dutch Palace) islands. The High Court jetty, at the top of Shanmugham Road, has ferries to Bolghatty island. The Sealord jetty, near Sealord Hotel, is the venue for twice-daily KSTDC boat trips round all the islands (*see* 'Tourist Information' below). These excursions are an excellent way of covering Cochin's many sights in a single day.

To get around Ernakulam itself, you have a choice of **auto-rickshaws**, which don't use meters (establish your fare in advance) or **taxis**.

If staying out at Fort Cochin, which has limited but pleasant accommodation, the most enjoyable way of getting round is by cycle. There are several hire places, charging around Rs20 per day.

Cochin ✆ (048–)   ***Tourist Information***

The **Government of India Tourist Office**, is at Malabar Hotel, Willingdon Island, ✆ 340352, is open 9 to 5 weekdays, 9 to 12noon Saturday. It still enjoys the reputation of being the 'best tourist office in India'; hires out good approved guides (Rs50 half day, Rs80 full day) and the staff are invariably helpful. KTDC's **Tourist Reception Centre**, near Ernakulam jetty (Shanmugham Road, ✆ 353234) is open 8am–6pm daily, and sells the boat tours (9.30–1, or 1.30–5; Rs20) round Cochin and its islands. It also sells Jaico's monthly *Timetable*, an excellent little publication with up-to-date city information and local plane/train/bus timetables.

All other useful tourist addresses are in Ernakulam: **Indian Airlines** are at Durbar Hall Road, ✆ 370242. The main **post office** is in Hospital Road (8am–8am, Monday to Saturday, 10 to 6 Sunday).

A useful travel agent for bus/train reservations, and any other travel arrangements is **Clipper Holidays**, Convent Road, ✆ 364453.

Cochin Islands Tour

By tour boat, half day. Leaves from Sealord jetty, Shanmugam Road in front of Sealord Hotel.

Mattancherry Palace–Synagogue–Chinese fishing nets–St Francis' Church–Santa Cruz Church–Bolghatty Palace–Gundu Island.

Get a sun-deck seat aboard the 9.00am KTDC sightseeing boat leaving daily from Sealord jetty which is cooler than the 2.00pm departure. The tour passes by Willingdon Island, off which are moored giant cargo ships loaded with fertilizer, chemicals and palm oil, and makes its first stop at **Mattancherry Palace** in Fort Cochin. Presently administered by the Archaeological Survey of India, this large white, red-roofed structure has an interesting history. Built by the Portuguese *c.* 1555 and presented to Raja Veera Kerala Varma (1537–61) as a goodwill token in exchange for trading rights, it was later renovated by the Dutch in 1663 and gained the misnomer of the 'Dutch Palace' (*open daily 10–5, except Fri*). An interesting combination of Keralan and Dutch architectural styles, it stands in a walled garden enclosure fronted by a tank, backing onto mango groves and three Hindu temples. The palace is built on two floors and around a central quadrangle. Inside the palace, see the large central Durbar Hall, where the Cochin royal family held their coronation ceremonies. Here you'll find an assortment of their palanquins, weapons, dresses and turbans. The adjacent series of royal bedrooms and other chambers have some fine murals dating from the 17th century. The 45 murals depict scenes from the *Ramayana* epic, as well as the Puranic legends relating to Shiva, Vishnu, Krishna, Kumara and Durga. Vigorous, fresh and delightfully sensual; one can't help but notice Shiva's eight arms busily at work on eight grateful handmaidens. Unfortunately you cannot photograph them without permission from the Archaeological Survey of India, and there are no books or postcards for sale.

Just a few hundred yards south is the oldest **Synagogue** in the Commonwealth (*open daily, 10–12noon, 3–5, except Sat*). The present structure was built in 1568, destroyed by the Portuguese in 1662, rebuilt by the Dutch in 1664 and donated its distinctive clock tower by Ezekiel Rahabi, a wealthy Jewish trader, in the mid 18th century. He also provided its exquisite willow-pattern floor tiles, each hand-painted in a different design, brought from Canton in 1776. The synagogue interior is fascinating: 19th-century Belgian chandeliers, interlocking pews, a ladies' gallery, and a superbly crafted brass pulpit. The curator, Jacky Cohen, shows visitors around and gives full information. He can also sometimes be prevailed upon to show the synagogue's two most prized treasures: the Great Scrolls of the Old Testament, and the copperplate grants of privilege made by the Cochin Maharajahs (962–1020) to the Jewish merchant Joseph Rabban. Nowadays, the place has a rather empty feel: all but 27 of Cochin's Jews have left; many having migrated to Israel.

The tour boat proceeds to the northern tip of Fort Cochin, where huge, cantilevered **fishing nets** proclaiming the ancient trade connections with China are ranged along the water's edge like a string of filigree lace handkerchiefs. Probably introduced by traders from the court of Kublai Khan, these fascinating nets are still an efficient method of fishing. While not unique to Cochin, the nets flanking the opening to the harbour are perhaps the best place in Kerala to see them at work.

A short walk below the nets is **St Francis' Church**, believed to be the first European church to be built in India. The original structure built in 1503, presumably by Portuguese Franciscan friars, was of wood. Later, during the mid 16th century, it was rebuilt in stone. Over the years it has experienced a number of 'conversions' from Catholic Portuguese, to Protestant Dutch, to Anglican, before achieving its present status within the Church of South India. The exterior is notable for its impressive façade, and there's an array of interesting Portuguese and Dutch tombstones including that of Vasco da Gama, who died here in 1524, although his body was taken to Portugal 14 years later. Should you wish to leave the tour at this point, a short walk inland brings you to **Santa Cruz Church**. This is a Roman Catholic structure, built in 1557, with a brilliantly painted interior. Nearby, locals play polite games of cricket on the Surrey-style village green. Beyond this, walking up Calvetty Street, you'll find a medieval settlement of pastel houses, 16th-century Portuguese bastions and narrow alleys, and still more Catholic churches.

The tour continues on to **Bolghatty Island**, to visit the **Bolghatty Palace Hotel**. Set in 15 acres of lush green lawns, this palatial structure started life as a Dutch palace, built in 1744 and later became home of the British Resident to the Raja of Cochin after 1799. Presently run as a hotel by the Kerala Tourism Development Corporation (KTDC), it has a golf course, a bar and a restaurant. From here, it's just a short chug across the harbour to **Gundu Island** (look out for leaping dolphins), for shopping at its small **Coir Factory**. Here a busy cooperative workers' society produce doormats handwoven from rough coconut fibre (*coir*) (Rs50–200). The weaving process is worth seeing.

Back in Ernakulam, off the boat, it's a short walk to Durbar Hall Road for **Parishath Thamburan Museum** in the old Durbar Hall (*open daily 9.30–12noon, 3–5.30, except Mon*). This has 19th-century paintings, copies of murals, old coins, delicate chandeliers, sculptures, musical instruments and lovely chinaware. The main attraction is the collection drawn from the Cochin royal family treasury.

Shopping

Buy teas, spices (ginger, turmeric, cardamom, cumin and cloves) and cashew nuts along the roadside leading down to Ernakulam main market. Because these pavement vendors sell their produce in the open, they (unlike shops) can't adulterate them. Another good place to buy the famous Cochin spices at local prices is **Grand Bazaar** supermarket, at Abad Plaza Hotel in M.G. Road. For fabrics, rosewood, walnut, Kathakali props and masks, and assorted jewellery, try the various emporia and shops along M.G. and Broadway Roads.

Leisure

No visit to Cochin is complete without seeing a performance of **Kathakali**, the famous dance-drama of Kerala. Kathakali started out some 2000 years ago as a temple art form, depicting themes from the *Ramayana* and *Mahabharata* epics. More an elaborate sequence of yogic exercises than a dance form, Kathakali may seem slow and stylized compared to say, Bharatnatyam, but it has a grace and a charm all of its own. A unique 'language' of gestures has evolved over the centuries, any combination of which conveys a definite meaning. The eyes are especially important, suggesting an immense range of differing moods and emotions. The costumes, wigs and masks which are used are bright and flamboyant, all made from natural materials. Make-up is distinctive with several layers of paint being applied to the dancer's face to accentuate lips, eyebrows and eyelashes. The overall effect is highly dramatic.

At present, Cochin has three Kathakali dance companies. They are at the tiny **Cochin Cultural Centre**, © 353732, Durbar Hall Ground, D.H. Road; **See India Foundation**, © 369471, Kalathiparambil Lane; and **Art Kerala** on Ravipuram Road. All three places charge the same (Rs50, pay at the door), and shows start at either 6.30pm (Cultural Centre) or 7pm (See India and Art Kerala). Turn up early to see the dancers applying make-up backstage which you can photograph, and bring mosquito coils to place under your chair. Of the three, the Cultural Centre has the best reputation, though Art Kerala puts on a wide range of Keralan dances (not just Kathakali), and See India gives the fullest, clearest explanations preceding each dance.

Other recreations include golf (9-hole course, Rs60 green fees include caddy, balls and clubs) and English films in air-conditioned comfort at the **Sridhar** cinema, near the KSTDC reception centre in Shanmugham Road.

The cool air-conditioned **Devi** cinema (Cochin's best) in Mahatma Gandhi Road, Ernakulam, is an ideal escape on hot, sticky afternoons. So is the swimming pool at the Malabar Hotel on Willingdon Island, open to non-residents (except Tuesday and Friday) for a daily charge of Rs60.

Cochin ☎ (048–)

Where to Stay

luxury (from Rs 1600)

The two top hotels are on Willingdon Island near to the airport. The **Taj Malabar Hotel**, ☎ 666811, 🖷 668297, has an excellent location on the northwestern promontory of the island, overlooking Mattancherry and the Chinese fishing nets, with the Government of India tourist office on your doorstep. It has good first-floor balcony rooms in the original building and a nice swimming pool. The **Casino Hotel**, ☎ 668221, 🖷 668001, is slightly cheaper and has air-conditioned rooms throughout, a brand-new pool, informal (yet stylish) ambience, and two excellent restaurants. The Casino is linked by private ferry to the Coconut Lagoon resort, and is also the only place from which foreigners may book tours of the Lakshadweep Islands (*see* below). The spanking new **Taj Residency**, Marine Drive, ☎ 371471, 🖷 371481, is over the water in Ernakulam. Big, very comfortable, but rather bland, the Residency is close to the sea jetties on Shanmugham Road, and has fine views out over the bay.

expensive (from Rs 800)

One of Cochin's best hotels falls within this price range: over on Bolghatty Island, the KTDC **Bolghatty Palace**, ☎ 355003, is a rather run-down Raj-style hotel with large grounds, good recreational facilities, and lots of character. The massive old-wing rooms are not air-conditioned, while the newer air-conditioned rooms are not so attractive. The cottages down by the water's edge are often plagued by mosquitoes. In Ernakulam, stay at the **Hotel Presidency** on Paramara Road, ☎ 363100, 🖷 370222, which has air-conditioned, bland comfort, but offers low prices for an expensive hotel; the air-conditioned **Sealord Hotel**, Shanmugham Road, ☎ 352682, 🖷 370135, which has a good rooftop restaurant; or the **Hotel Abad Plaza**, ☎ 361636, 🖷 370729, on M.G. Road, clean, comfortable and well-located, with a nearby seafood restaurant and attached supermarket.

moderate (from Rs 500)

Top of this range is the **Woodlands Hotel** on M.G. Road, Ernakulam, ☎ 351372. It's a reasonably clean hotel, if tacky, with an air-conditioned vegetarian restaurant and ice cream parlour.

budget

In Fort Cochin, the **Hotel Sea Gull** in Calvetty Road, ☎ 352682, has a pleasant location between the two ferry stops, overlooking the harbour, and nice air-conditioned singles and doubles. The restaurant and bar are very popular. Facing the Chinese fishing nets in Fort Cochin, there's KTDC's **Subala**, a nice friendly place with cheap restaurant, helpful staff and comfy rooms. It's very convenient for the boat jetty and bus stand. Other decent cheap lodgings are **P.W.D. Tourist Rest Home** near the beach (spacious but spartan rooms) and **Hotel Elite** near St Francis' Church, with decent double rooms on the ground floor but cheaper, grimmer rooms upstairs.

In Ernakulam, many budget travellers enjoy **Biju's Tourist Home** in Market Road, opposite the main jetty, ✆ 369881, with a friendly and informative management and bright, spacious rooms. As a second string, try **Hotel Luciya** in Stadium Road, next to the bus stand, ✆ 366296, or the **Hotel Sea Rock** on M.G. Road, Palimukku (south of Shanmugham Road), ✆ 682016, or the **Hotel Yuvarani** at Jos Junction on M.G. Road in the same area, ✆ 681011.

Eating Out

The **Casino Hotel** on Willingdon Island has one of the most prestigious eateries in town, a seafood speciality restaurant called **Fort Cochin**. Service and food are excellent, and the lobsters unbelievably large. An average meal including dessert comes to around Rs300 per head. The Casino's other restaurant, the multi-cuisine **Tharavadu** features a daily lunch buffet for Rs175 and live music performances nightly. The Taj Malabar's **Rice Boat** prepares some excellent Malabar seafood from Rs350 per head.

There is good cheap food to be had in Fort Cochin. **Hotel Sea Gull** is good for non-vegetarian food, doughnuts and porridge, and KTDC's **Subala** has a nice breezy restaurant by the water, with cheap if rather unimaginative meals. The best treats are still at **Hotel Elite's** famous Parisian-style café with its choice of patisseries and refrigerated cheese.

Ernakulam has a wide choice of cheap eating places. The **Sealord Hotel** has a popular air-conditioned restaurant, with tasty Indian and continental food at around Rs40 per dish. For fast food and superb north Indian fare, try **Pandhal Restaurant** opposite Woodlands Hotel on M.G. Road. This is a relaxing air-conditioned place, with good lunchtime specials; *thalis* and Kerala-style curries from Rs20, 12 noon to 3 daily, except Sundays. For seafood, try the Rs70 buffet lunch (12noon to 3) at **Abad Plaza Hotel**, which serves squid, lobster and prawns. At **Subhiksha**, the stylish vegetarian restaurant attached to B.T.H. Hotel in D.H. Road, you can enjoy amazing lunchtime *thalis* for about Rs40 and incredibly cheap south Indian food with most dishes only Rs8 in air-conditioned comfort. Next door, there's a popular little coffee shop. Ernakulam has two **Indian Coffee Houses**; one opposite the main jetty in Cannon Shed Road, the other below the rail station in M.G. Road, which do good cheap breakfasts for under Rs20. Two reliable Chinese restaurants are **Malaya** on Bannerjee Road and **Golden Dragon** opposite Park Hotel. Chinese food is also available at the Sealord's rooftop restaurant and the Hotel Presidency.

Two good bakeries are **Cochin Bakery** opposite Woodlands Hotel, and **Ceylon Bake House** near the tourist office on the Broadway.

Moving On

By air: **Indian Airlines**, ✆ 370242, flies 3 times daily between Cochin and Bombay, and once daily to Bangalore, Delhi, Dabolim in Goa, Madras and Trivandrum. **East-West Airlines**, ✆ 363542, operates a daily flight to and from Bombay. **Jet Airways**, ✆ 369423, also flies twice a day to Bombay, as does **Modiluft**, ✆ 367740, while **NEPC**, ✆ 367720, flies to Bangalore and Madras.

By rail: Ernakulam has two rail stations—Ernakulam Junction and Ernakulam Town—both some 1½ miles from the main boat jetty. Ernakulam Junction is easier to deal with: the Area Manager here (office open 10 to 5) may be able to get you tickets at short notice, if you've failed to book in advance. There are daily trains to Alleppey, Kottayam, Quilon, Trivandrum, Madras, Mangalore, Bangalore. For Ooty, take the daily 9.25am *Tea Garden Express* (via Mettapulayam/ Coimbatore). The final leg of this 15-hour journey, as the pretty blue steam train huffs and puffs its way up the mountainside on the narrow-gauge track, presents some memorable scenery. Get a window seat on the right-hand side of the carriage and have a camera ready.

By bus: there are regular buses for Alleppey (1½hrs), Quilon (4hrs) and Trivandrum (5hrs), and for Trichur (2½hrs), Calicut and Kottayam (2hrs). Interstate buses leave from the KSTDC bus stand in Ernakulam for Bangalore (few express buses, 15 hours), Madras, Madurai (regular, but 8.15am is best; 10 hours; superb scenery), Kanyakumari and Coimbatore. The same trips are also run by private operators such as Conti Travels, Ashirwad Travels, Indira Travels, Sharma Travels, SP Tours, PK Transport and Yesbee; they usually depart between 5.30 and 7.30pm and travel overnight; bring earplugs—noisy video entertainment tends to continue into the small hours.

Excursion to an Elephant Festival

Also known as Thrissur, **Trichur** is a large temple town about 70km north of Cochin/ Ernakulam (a 2½hr bus ride). Unremarkable for most of the year, it is very much worth visiting in mid-January and mid-April for its two great **elephant festivals**. January has the better—Kerala's largest elephant festival, known as the **Great Elephant March**. This involves about a hundred temple elephants (as well as some borrowed from local forestry camps to make up the numbers) parading in full caparisoned regalia—including brass headpieces with gold bosses; orange-robed mahouts sitting under brightly coloured sunshades; brahmins standing on the elephants' backs waving wide, circular fans known as lotus plumes and *kavadi* carriers—devotees and pilgrims bearing huge, multi-coloured structures made of painted bamboo on their heads to offer to the gods in return for special favours. The procession is led by white-robed women carrrying oil lamps.

The whole procedure is repeated every day for four days, winding its way slowly from the town's central stadium up to a hillock where ancient tribal dances known as *theyyams*, thought to date from the Neolithic era, are performed to banish evil spirits.

Other Elephant Festivals in Kerala

Trichur has the state's biggest festivals but other, smaller ones (*Utsavams*) take place elsewhere throughout the year. There is even a Christian and a Muslim elephant festival. All festivals hold slightly different dates from year to year. The following is a rough timetable. Contact the tourist office at Cochin for the correct dates. All the above locations can be reached by bus from Cochin.

mid January	Trichur	Great Elephant March
early February	Ernakulam	Paramara Devi Temple Utsavam
end February/ first week March	Guruvayoor	Sree Krishna Utsavam (100km from Cochin)
mid March	Kottayam	Thirunakkara Mahadeva Utsavam
mid April	Trichur	Thrissur Pooram
mid May	Perandur	Sree Bhagavaty Utsavam (6km from Cochin)
mid August	Thiruvallam	Sree Parasurama Temple Bali (5km from Trivandrum on the way to Kovalam)
early September	Thripinthura	Athachamayam Procession (9km from Cochin)
early October	Pazhanji, Kunnamkulam	St Mary's Church Feast (110km from Cochin)
early November	Trivandrum	Sree Padmanabhaswamy Utsavam
early December	Thripunithura	Sree Poornathrayeesa Utsavam (18km from Cochin)
end December	Changanacherry	Puthur Muslim Juma-at Chananakumam (20km from Kottayam).

Munnar and the Annamudi Range

Kerala's highest mountains rear to the sky in a jagged line almost due east of Cochin. A tea-growing area of plantations almost entirely owned by the incredibly powerful, Parsi-run Tata Corporation (which seems to own and manufacture just about everything in India from cars to telephone directories), Munnar has a cool climate, bringing relief after Cochin's humid heat.

Munnar has access to the best **trekking** in Kerala, though into a tribal region that is very difficult to get permission for. There is also the superb **Rajamallai National Park** in the higher slopes near town, where India's largest herd of Nilgiri *tahr* (a species of ibex unique to the Western Ghats) is protected.

The Foothills Below Munnar

If coming to Munnar by bus or taxi from Cochin or Kottayam, try and stop for a day first at **Thattekad Bird Sanctuary**, about 55km east of the city. To cover the last leg of this journey, you and your vehicle have to cross the Periyar River, before arriving at the gates of the sanctuary, just outside a small village on the edge of thick forest. Although officially there to protect birds, Thattekad has other wildlife too: elephant have recently recolonized the forest, and tigers have been seen in the area for the past two years. Among the rare bird species found here are the Malabar hornbill, Malabar Shama, the grey-headed fishing eagle, the beautifully named fairy bluebird, crimson-throated barbet, night heron and the iridescent-feathered, tiny sunbird. You can go **trekking** with a Wildlife Department guide (don't go into the deep woods alone, as the elephant round here are known to be aggressive) and there is a rest house for accommodation.

Also in the Munnar area is **Idukki Wildlife Sanctuary**, reachable by bus from Kottayam or Cochin (both about 120km). Set in the foothills west of Munnar, Idduki is undulating forest country, home to a very large elephant population, tiger, leopard, sloth bear, *dhole* (wild dog), *gaur* (bison), *sambar*, spotted *chital* and muntjac deer, wild boar and a host of bird species.

Idukki has a large dam, with boating facilities, and **trekking** is an option in the forests, with rest house accommodation. Trekking and the rest house must be booked in advance, © Idukki 323/328. To get to Idukki, take a bus from Kottayam or Cochin to Cheruthony, Kattapana or Thodpuzha, and then go by local bus (about 1 hour) to the forest entrance.

From Thattekad or Idukki, the mountain road winds up a steep climb of several hours through cardamom and rubber plantations, until the high grasslands and tea estates announce that you are about to arrive in **Munnar** itself.

Munnar Town

Munnar is a strange little place—part olde worlde Raj survivor (it was developed by British tea planters in the 1920s, who left a church, some small but handsome government buildings made from stone and the tea estates), part truck-stop—for Munnar sits atop the commercial route between Coimbatore in Tamil Nadu and Cochin in Kerala, and there is a steady stream of lorries and buses going to and fro over the pass. The result is a scruffy little town centre on the banks of a mountain river choked with refuse, with, on the hills above, lovely winding lanes that lead to old British cottages, now the homes of Forestry and Wildlife Department officers.

To the northeast of town rises the great rock wall of Anamudi Peak, at 8828 feet (2695 metres) the highest in Kerala, while on every side green tea bushes march in neat close-set rows, pleasing to the eye, up towards the wilder hills where jungle and watershed grassland take over.

Getting There

Several buses run daily from Cochin and Kottayam in Kerala (journey time is approximately 5 hours) and from Coimbatore in Tamil Nadu, with a change a Gundulpet (approximately 6 hours).

Whether you take a day trip out to the national park (which has no accommodation of its own) or plan to get into the deep forest, you will have to stay in Munnar for a night or two.

moderate

If you can, stay at the **High Range Club** on the west end of town, ✆ 53—the old meeting point for the English planters that opened up the area. You are supposed to be a member but, unless the place is full, you can generally find a room. The **Edassary East End**, in the centre of town is modern, ✆ 30451, but you'd never know it. Built in the style of a planters' bungalow, it has self-contained cottages and a good restaurant. More tranquil (about 1½km out of town on the western side) is the **Hillview**, ✆ 30567, built by a river. Again, the hotel has a decent restaurant.

inexpensive

For about Rs100–150 per night, you can get a clean, basic room at the **S N Lodge**, also on the western edge of town, ✆ 212.

budget

For Rs 50–80, try the **Krishna Lodge** next to the bus stand. It's a little noisy, but clean enough, and there are some cheap *thali* houses and bakeries nearby.

The Munnar Ranges

The main reasons to visit Munnar are the **Erivakulam/Rajmalai National Park**, 10 miles northeast of town, and the **trekking** in vast areas of **reserved forest** on the eastern side of the mountains. This deeply wild area is still home to a variety of wildlife and to the fiercely independent **Munnuvan** tribe, who have managed to hang on to their traditional way of life, despite various kinds of government interference over the years.

Getting into the Forest Areas

This is one of south India's most problematic regions to enter: the Forest and Wildlife Department both require permission and this has to be obtained via Delhi, which takes some time. However, those really interested in getting into the Munnuvan region should contact Varkey Kurian at Clipper Holidays in Cochin, ✆ (0484) 682 035. On no account try to hire a local guide yourself and go into the forest: when the author was 3-days' trek inside the Munnuvan tribal area, he and his group ran into a police raiding-party looking for ganja plantations, which the Munnuvans allegedly cultivate in the jungle. Had we not had the necessary permissions, we would have ended up in jail and been heavily fined.

The Munnuvan Tribal Peoples

If you do manage to get permission for the Munnuvan region, it will be one of the most fascinating experiences you will ever have. The tribals will put up trekkers who come through a guide known to them, in their own villages, each of which has a guest house.

The Munnuvans worship an elephant god and live by planting wild cardamom under the towering forest trees and planting rice in small paddies in some of their hidden valleys. In the surrounding forests lives the full range of south Indian wildlife, and by night you can hear the whines of jackals and hyenas, and sometimes the deep rumble of a tiger, the dark spaces between the trees a-dance with fireflies.

The Munnuvans themselves have an interesting society. Although male-dominated, the men help to look after small children—it's a common sight to see the elders walking around with babies strapped to their hips—and both boys and girls are sent to live communally in school huts where they learn their rôles and provide a task force for the old and sick people in the village. All trekkers are accommodated in the boys' school huts.

The National Park

The more casual visitor wanting to get into the hills should take a rickshaw or bus from town up to Erivakulam/Rajmalai National Park. Although this is a huge wild area, tourists are only allowed into a 4-mile strip on the southern edge, running along the tar road from the entrance to a police hut at the top of the pass leading over into the Munnuvan territory. However, you can see a lot of wildlife in this short section, notably small herds of Nilgiri *tahr*, the ibex species unique to the Western Ghats. On sunny days, these have a pleasing habit of posing majestically on rocks, horns silhouetted against the sky, just as you walk by with your camera. If it's drizzly, as it often is, the *tahr* tend to keep to the forests, so if you want to take wildlife photos, wait for a clear day.

Chinnar Wildlife Sanctuary

On the eastern side of the mountains, about 3–4 hours' bus ride from Munnar, is **Chinnar Wildlife Sanctuary**, on the Kerala/Tamil Nadu border. This is a dry forest zone, so it is best to visit between November and January; after that most of the game migrates up to the wetter forests around Munnar. This is especially true of the tiger, leopard, elephant and *gaur*. *Sambar* and *chital*, *dhole*, wild boar and jackal may be spotted all year, and many people have reported good wildlife sightings from the reserve's **watchtower**, a few hundred yards from the sanctuary entrance and forest checkpoint. The main road from Cochin to Coimbatore passes through the reserve, and all traffic is stopped at a barrier to make sure nobody is smuggling out forest products like sandalwood or skins. There is dormitory accommodation, which is often full but, if you insist on staying, they'll generally put you up in one of the other buildings, and you can take guided walks, morning and evening, into the bush.

Chinnar has a beautiful river flowing just below the forest checkpoint, and the woodland along its banks is alive with exotic birds. Paradise flycatchers, black-headed orioles, kingfishers, bee-eaters and bulbuls are all common. Look out also for the giant grizzled squirrel among the riverside trees, and when picnicking, beware of fleet, thieving monkeys (bonnet macaques).

The Muslim conquest of India in the 13th and 14th centuries moved the power-centres of the south up to the Deccan. Present day Andhra Pradesh, is a historic land of temples and mosques, combining the age-old traditions of the south with the Muslim cultural heritage of western and Central Asia. Hyderabad, modern capital of the state, took over from Golconda, ancient capital of the Qu'tb Shahid kings, as the symbol of Muslim imperialism in the south. Today, it boasts glorious palaces and mosques, peaceful lakes and picnic spots, and the most outstanding zoological park in India.

The modern state of Karnataka comprises large parts of the princely state of Mysore, the Berar territories of the erstwile Nizam of Hyderabad's kingdom and a few areas that were controlled by the British. The area was unified in the 1950s on the basis of common language; in this case Kannada. In Karnataka, the Hindu kingdom of Vijayanagar resisted the Deccan Sultans for 200 years, before being overpowered in 1565. Its capital was Hampi, perhaps the finest and certainly the largest complex of ruins in the country today. In earlier centuries the area was the seat of powerful dynasties like the Kadambas, Hoysalas, Chalukyas and Vijayanagars. Under British influence in the 19th century the cool garden city of Bangalore was developed.

South of Karnataka are the Nilgiri hills; although in Tamil Nadu they are best reached from Bangalore and Mysore. In these hills, Ootacamund (Ooty) and Coonoor became summer resorts of the Raj. Ornate palaces, glorious parks and beautiful buildings appeared, often sponsored by local princes and maharajahs, and reflecting the might of empire. Bangalore, once a staid cantonment city, became the glorious 'Garden City of the South', and then a booming commercial capital of cinemas, restaurants, night clubs and fun activities. Mysore, famous 'City of Incense', gained the spectacular Maharajah's Palace and numerous public buildings, a magnificent zoo, and the famous Brindhavan Gardens. The lovely hill station of Ootacamund, bordering Karnataka and Tamil Nadu states, gained its large, scenic lake, its botanical gardens, and the coveted title 'Queen of the South'.

For relaxed, sophisticated elegance, away from the usual heat of the Indian plains, this route provides the perfect introduction to the south.

Bangalore is the most convenient base from which to see this lovely area. However, transport is such in the region that the city will inevitably become a base for excursions to the neighbouring places of interest, rather than a jumping-off point for a route. Hyderabad, although central in terms of influence and importance, is relatively isolated and should be visited separately at the beginning or end of your trip round the empires of the south. But whatever you do, don't miss it out.

Itinerary

This route takes about two weeks. Starting in Hyderabad, it includes a side-trip to Nagarjunasagar ruins and wildlife sanctuary from that city before going on to Bangalore. From here you make an excursion to Hampi. Then the route continues to Mysore, and finally to the hill station of Ooty; between Mysore and Ooty the Moyar area is good for trekking, and there is increasingly popular trekking around Ooty with the possibility of visiting tribes in the Nilgiri hills.

When to Go

The bes time to visit is October–April, avoiding the monsoon in June–October. The climate is in the region of 26°–35°C (summer), and 14°–25°C (winter). In Ootacamund the temperature is 12°–16°C year round.

Hyderabad

Now capital of Andhra Pradesh, Hyderabad is a beautiful city surrounded by lakes of great charm and tranquillity, and is itself sometimes known as 'The Lake'. It was founded in the late-16th century by the Qu'tb Shahi dynasty, a line of Muslim rulers famed for their magnificent monuments and mosques. The city was laid out in 1591 by Muhammad Quli when Golconda, the fortress city from which the Muslim rulers had ruled their Hindu subjects since 1512, fell prey to epidemics of plague and cholera, caused by poor water supplies. It was planned out on the grid system, and comprised two broad intersecting streets with the famous central Charminar Arch (described as the outstanding architectural monument of the Qu'tb Shahi period) at the crossing, and space for some 14,000 shops, schools, mosques and baths.

Successful trading in diamonds, pearls, printed fabrics and steel rapidly made Hyderabad one of the richest cities in India. Then, in 1650, the Mughal emperor Aurangzeb captured Golconda, and Hyderabad's short period of prosperity came to an abrupt end. Its importance as an administrative and financial centre declined, and the city fell into partial ruin. In the 18th century, with the disintegration of the Mughal empire, the Mughal Viceroys or Nizams of the Deccan seized power and in 1763 Hyderabad again became the capital of the area (under the Mughals, power had been wielded from Aurangabad). Commerce and construction rapidly resumed, and the city once more became a major business concern. The Nizams soon became some of the wealthiest individuals in the world, a position they maintained up to, and for a decade beyond, Independence in 1947.

Today, while Hyderabad, together with Bangalore, is the fastest-growing city in Asia, it has yet to find itself as a tourist centre. Its obvious attractions, its beautiful sights, good shopping, unique cuisine are largely offset by its remote location. But you can expect big changes in the near future. Hyderabad is rapidly equipping itself with tourist facilities, luxury hotels, better transport, shopping complexes, even a Rs100 *crore* Disneyland project around the Hussain Sagar—and is now patiently awaiting the expected boom.

There's been a big push to promote tourism recently, starting with Sound & Light shows at the Golconda Fort and Salar Jung Museum—but then came prohibition. A total ban on alcohol consumption, which came into force in January 1995, has seriously crippled the tourist trade. The only way one can get a drink now is to stay at a 5-star hotel, take a boring trip to the Customs & Excise office, and buy a Rs125 liquor permit. Many travellers—particularly Indians—can't be bothered and stay away in droves. The only solution, until government policy changes, is to bring your own booze from out-of-state, furtively drink it in a darkened room, and make sure you hide the bottle afterwards!

When to Go

Situated 610m above sea-level, Hyderabad has a very equable climate through much of the year. The coolest (best) time to visit is from October to February. From March onwards it is not so much the heat as the very dry air that has visitors reaching for the water bottle.

Getting There

From the airport to the city centre (10km) is around Rs120/140 by pre-paid taxi; rather less (if you bargain) by auto-rickshaw.

Hyderabad can be accessed by air from Bangalore, Bhubaneshwar, Bombay, Calcutta and Madras. It is more commonly approached by train or bus from Madras to Puri, or visa versa. A few people come in on the **Coromandel Express** train from Calcutta, or by bus from Bangalore or Bombay, but not many.

See also p.528, 'Moving On'.

Getting Around

Hyderabad has overcrowded city buses, crazed auto-rickshaws which stop for absolutely nothing (Rs5 for the first 2km), and a few maniacal taxis. Auto-rickshaws can be hired for around Rs50 an hour if you have a lot of places to see in a short time. Taxis can be found outside most of the better hotels and work on a 'tour' basis—a 4hr programme costing Rs255 and an 8hr one, Rs405. The traffic is suicidal; in the city centre, you need nerves of steel to get around on foot. 'Daydreaming is dangerous', cautions one traffic sign; 'Undertakers love overtakers' proclaims another. For worry-free travel, use the tourist taxi service offered by A.P. Travel and Tourism Dev. Corp., Gagan Vihar, Mukhram Jahi Road, © 557531, 556303, or your hotel. For out-of-town trips, cycling is pleasurable and cycles can be hired for Rs10–15 per day from several places; your hotel can advise. If biking around in town, make sure you have some decent insurance. City conducted tours are far too hurried, but they are a useful introduction and orientation. Then you should tour Hyderabad independently, allowing a minimum of 2 days for sightseeing and shopping. The traffic in the old city is often chaotic, and downright

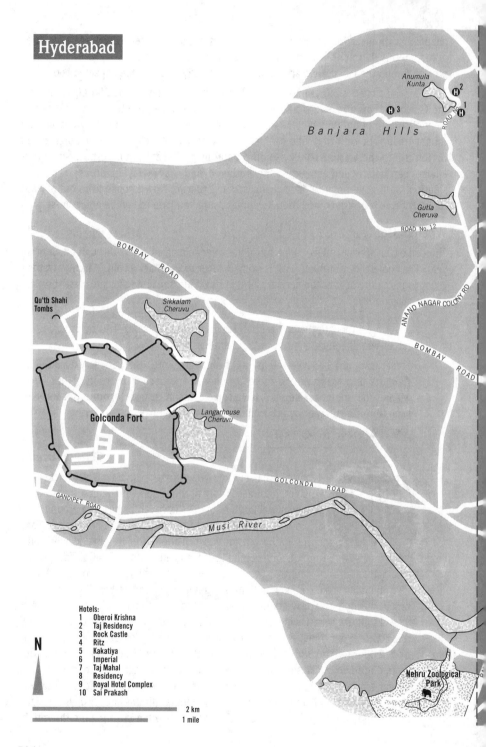

Hyderabad

Anumula Kunta

Ⓗ 2
1 Ⓗ

ROAD No. 1

Ⓗ 3

B a n j a r a   H i l l s

Gutla Cheruva

ROAD No. 12

Qu'tb Shahi Tombs

B O M B A Y   R O A D

ANAND NAGAR COLONY RD

B O M B A Y   R O A D

Sikkalam Cheruvu

Golconda Fort

Langarhouse Cheruvu

G O L C O N D A   R O A D

GANDIPET ROAD

M u s i   R i v e r

Hotels:
1 Oberoi Krishna
2 Taj Residency
3 Rock Castle
4 Ritz
5 Kakatiya
6 Imperial
7 Taj Mahal
8 Residency
9 Royal Hotel Complex
10 Sai Prakash

N

2 km
1 mile

Nehru Zoological Park

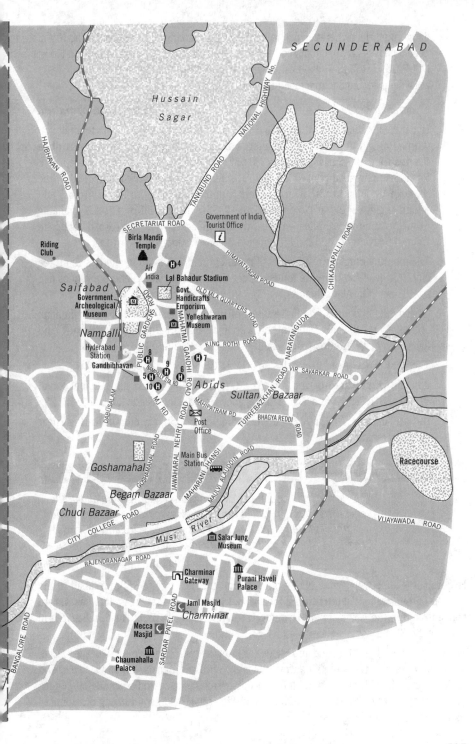

dangerous; ride wherever possible, and avoid walking across main roads. If you need a badge-carrying guide, contact A.P. Dept of Tourism, Gagan Vihar, 5th Floor, M J Road, ✆ 4732554 (you can also book them from the tourist information desks at Hyderabad and Secunderabad railway stations).

Hyderabad ✆ (0842–)   ***Tourist Information***

Hyderabad is still not used to foreign visitors, so expect tourist officers to greet you with gushing, but garbled, information. For tour bookings, go to the main **Andhra Pradesh (A P) Tourist Office**, ✆ 816375, at the Yatri Niwas guest house in S P Road, Secunderabad (closed Sunday). It sells the city sightseeing tour (Rs80), the 'Deccan by Dusk' tour, which covers Lumbini Park, Qu'tb Shahi tombs, and Sound & Light show at Golconda Fort, (Rs55). General information is available from the sub-tourist office on the 5th floor, Gagan Vihar, M J Road (opposite Gandhi Bhavan), ✆ 4732554/5 (open 6.30am–7.30pm).

The monthly **magazine** 'Channel 6' is full of useful information and tips about the city. It is available from the tourist office, airport, better hotels and bookshops like A.A. Hussain in Abids Road.

Outside the big hotels, the **State Bank of India** on Bank Street, or the main bank branches on M G Road above Abid Circle all exchange traveller's cheques and hard currency. **Thomas Cook** is out in Saifabad, ✆ 222 689.

The **post office** is on the south side of Abid Circle.

Reliable **travel agents** are Sita World Travels, Hyderguda and Chapel Road, ✆ 233638/235549, and TCI, 102 Regency House, Greenlands Road, ✆ 312722.

Indian Airlines, ✆ 236902 and **Air India**, ✆ 232858, are both in Saifabad near the Secretariat building.

Touring Hyderabad

> *The sides of the road are thick with crowds that take up all but the very centre, through which thrust and weave trucks and buses and all sorts of wheeled vehicles, right down to bicycles and a legless beggar, paddling a platform mounted on squeaky roller bearings.*

> Robin Brown, *Deccan Tamasha*

Hyderabad is effectively two cities in one, though the new city of Secunderabad to the north is of minimal tourist interest. All the sights, the hotels, the action and the bazaars are concentrated in the Abids area of Hyderabad town, directly south of Hussain Sagar, and north of the Musi River.

The city itself is a busy, bustling and sprawling complex where new multi-storeyed buildings and wide modern streets contrast strongly with the narrow medieval lanes and backstreets of the old town around the Charminar arch, and where the smoke of modern industrial factories meets the dust of busy roadside cottage workers, turning out some of India's finest handmade crafts.

Old City Tour

By auto-rickshaw/taxi, 4–6 hours. Golconda–Qu'tb Shahi Tombs–Mecca Masjid–Charminar–Salar Jung Museum–Birla Mandir Temple–Birla Planetarium.

Set out for **Golconda Fort** early in the morning before the heat of the day. It lies 11km west of Hyderabad, and takes about 40 minutes by rickshaw (Rs60–70 return, plus a waiting charge of Rs10 per hour while you sightsee). Going by taxi takes slightly less time but doubles the cost. The fort lies in a very dry, exposed situation, so wear a hat/scarf and long-sleeved shirts. There are about a dozen good English-speaking guides at the fort entrance. It's not a bad idea to establish their fee in writing before you set out; you can pay them more if they're worth it, which they usually are. The inner fort of Golconda is 25km around, and you can tour its various palaces, audience rooms, baths, armoury and mosques comfortably in 1½ hours. If you wish to wander round on your own, buy the good little Golconda guide book with map, printed by Commercial Book Depot, Charminar, and available in many Hyderabad bookshops. Every evening except Monday at 6.30 or 7pm, depending on the time of year, there is a spectacular Sound & Light show (English-speaking only on Wednesdays and Sundays). It lasts 2 hours, costs Rs40 and you can advance-book from the tourist office (10am–noon only) or pay on the spot.

Golconda Fort

Golconda is the biggest fort in south India. Constructed from solid limestone, it took several thousand labourers, working day and night, 62 years to build. Founded in the 13th century by the Kakatiyas of Warangal, it was originally just a small hilltop fort with mud walls. Its name derived from the words *golla* meaning 'shepherd' and *konda* meaning 'hill'. In 1512 it became the capital of the Persian Qu'tb Shahi kings, who expanded the original structure into a massive fort with battlements and crenellated walls of granite some 5km in circumference. The 8 sets of gates were studded with iron spikes as protection against war elephants, and it boasted its own freshwater supply.

Like so many Indian forts, Golconda finally fell to treachery rather than to arms, a treacherous Qu'tb Shahi general letting the Mughal emperor Aurangzeb in the front ('victory') gate in 1687 following an 8-month siege. Thereafter the legendary fort and its famous diamond market went into decline, and power passed to the new capital of Hyderabad.

Though partly in ruins today, this monumental fortress, erected on a picturesque granite hill some 120 metres high and surrounded by three tiers of loopholed and battlemented ramparts, remains the major tourist attraction of the Hyderabad area. Of its eight original gates, four are still in use. The fort also has 87 semi-circular bastions, each 15 metres high, and each built of huge blocks of masonry weighing several tons apiece.

Start your tour at the **Grand Portico** (entry gate). Here you'll come across its unique system of acoustics, one of the fortress's most interesting features. A clapping of hands in the centre porch can be heard at the fort's highest point, the Bala Hissar, 380 steep steps above. This device was contrived, it is believed, to convey any message regarding visitors to the topmost guards. Behind this echo chamber is a purple-blossomed tree, popular with local people who use its hard-wood bark for cleaning their teeth.

Your guide will take you up into the fort via the 'common passage', leading past the armoury on your left; the mortuary bath where dead royals had a ceremonial dip before being buried, to your right; and the bodyguard barracks, with adjoining two-storeyed building used by the court ministers Akkanna and Madanna, also to your left. An ascent of 360 steps now begins, leading up to the **Bara Dar** (General Assembly Hall). On the ascent you'll see various deep wells, water reservoirs and watering canals.

Halfway up, you reach the **Ramdas Kotha**, an old storehouse which became the 12-year prison of Abdul Hasan Tanah Shah's chief cashier, Ramdas. He was interred for dipping into official revenue to renovate a nearby temple. It's a dark, gloomy place, full of the handmade deities (Ram, Lakshman, Hanuman) and faded carvings/paintings of animals and plants which the bored Ramdas made to fill in his time.

Past the jail, and just above the **Barood Kotha** (gunpowder store), there's a charming little Hindu temple cut into a large natural boulder the shape of a Nandi bull. A little further up is the simple, elegant **Mosque** of the royal family, built by the third king of the dynasty, Ibrahim Quli Qu'tb Shah in 1550. In those days, the king prayed in the mosque and his Hindu chief minister in the small rock-cut temple below; it was an age of practical religious tolerance. From the eastern side of the mosque, there's a beautiful view down over Golconda and across to Hyderabad city. From the northern side, you can see the Qu'tb Shahi Tombs, fully reflecting the glory and pomp of the rich sultans of Golconda, whose last resting-place these are.

Finally, you'll reach the **Baradari** or Durbar Hall at the summit of Golconda. This is a 12-arched, three-storey pavilion, with a top terrace giving panoramic views of the surrounding fort, and an open-air stone throne called Shah Nashin. Here, the Qu'tb kings used to sit out on the open terraces, or hold meetings with the royal family or court ministers. The Durbar Hall also has a 8km long secret underground passage which was used in times of emergency or danger. It is here, from the topmost point of the fort, that your guide will show the effectiveness of the 'clapping' technique, signalling down to the entrance gate for a demonstration.

You'll probably return down via the **King's Way**, which leads to the royal palaces and harem area. In olden days, the king was transported down this path by *palanquin*. You won't be, but the descent on foot is a pleasant one. On the way, look out for the fort's unique water-supply system. Huge tanks filled with water diverted from the Banjara hills 6.5km away, and ingeniously raised to the fort by a system of laminated clay pipes and Persian wheels, which moved it all the way up to the gardens, waterfalls and hanging gardens near the fort's summit.

Below, in the beautiful **Rani (Zanana) Mahals**, the first thing you're likely to be shown are the royal bathrooms. Only then will your guide point out the other attractions of the site. This series of crumbling, complex ruins used to be full of painted, jewelled palaces, arcades, Turkish baths, flower gardens and bubbling fountains. Little remains either of the lovely harem palaces nearby, though the royal kitchen, on the site of the old Camel Stable, is still in good condition. While here, you may well smell a strong scent not unlike buttered popcorn, emanating from the darker recesses. Follow it, and the smell is reinforced by a high chittering sound. Go further and you find yourself standing under one of the largest colonies of bats in southern India. The popcorn smell is in fact their guano. Squadrons of the nervous, flapping creatures fly about continuously amid the din. For fun (if you have a flash on your camera), go as far into the darkness as your creeping skin will allow, point your camera roofwards and take a couple of shots. You'll be surprised at how many bats are illuminated in the prints when you finally get the prints back. Return via the armoury to the entry gate.

The Qu'tb Shahi Tombs

The grand domes of the Qu'tb Shahi tombs (*open daily 9am–4.30pm except Fridays, camera fee extra*) rise about 1.5km to the north of Golconda fort. To reach them, walk through the Banjara gate and head across the great maidan to where the ten tombs rise from their surrounding formal garden. Richly ornamented with religious inscriptions and the remains of mosaics of glazed tiles, the tombs were restored and the present gardens planted at the turn of the century. The monarchs that lie here are: Sultan Quli Qu'tb Shah, who murdered his own father and founded the dynasty (1518–43), Jamshid Quli Qu'tb Shah (1543–50), Ibrahim Qu'tb Shah (1550–80), Muhammad Quli Qu'tb Shah, founder of Hyderabad, (1581–1612), Muhammad Qu'tb Shah (1612–26), Abdullah Qu'tb Shah (1626–72) and Abdul Hasan Tana Qu'tb Shah (1672–87). The Princess Kulsum Begum (d. 1608), Princess Hayat Baksh Begum (d. 1677) and Pammati, favourite mistress of Muhammad Qu'tb Shah (d. 1664) also have tombs here.

Golconda Town

Before returning to Hyderabad, take some time to explore the old town of Golconda, situated within the outer fort walls. In times past, this small bazaar town was a splendid fortress city, famed for its cutting, polishing and marketing of diamonds. The unique *Koh-i-noor* gem, now part of the British crown jewels, is said to have come from here. Today, the town is small, yet well-populated, and there are lots of cheap knick-knacks and trinkets being sold.

Old Hyderabad, the Charminar and the Mecca Masjid

From Golconda, return to Hyderabad city centre for the impressive **Mecca Masjid**. This huge white mosque is the finest in south India, and the seventh largest in the world. Begun in 1614 by Muhammad Quli Qu'tb Shah, it was completed in 1687 by Aurangzeb, the Mughal invader. It derives its name from the few bricks brought from Mecca (and the stone apparently brought from Muhammad's birthplace) which are embedded in its walls.

Entering the mosque, beware of unsolicited guides. Most are difficult to understand but if you take one on, he should charge about Rs5–10. Just inside the wide courtyard you'll see a long enclosure full of small marble tombs to your left. This is where many of Hyderabad's wealthy Nizams are interred. The mosque itself is a marvellous structure. Its huge entrance façade is built of a single block of stone, richly inscribed with sayings from the Koran. Inside are Portuguese chandeliers, an antique French clock, and inlaid marble flooring. This mosque is the principal place of Muslim worship in the city, and every

Charminar arch

Friday up to 50,000 people gather for prayers. The huge 20 metre high interior can accommodate 3000 worshippers, the grounds a further 7000. On important religious days and festivals even the streets outside are filled with kneeling devotees.

Just across the road from the mosque you'll find the **Charminar** (Four Tower Arch) (*open daily 9am–4.30pm; illuminated 7–9pm*), Hyderabad's definitive landmark. This imposing arch, deriving its name from its four 55m high slender minarets, was built in 1591 by Muhammad Quli Qu'tb Shah, reputedly to commemorate the end of a plague epidemic. It stands a watchful guardian over the old city, serenely overlooking the surrounding chaos of anarchic traffic and crowded thoroughfares. A climb of 149 steps up a winding staircase brings you out near the top of the arch, at the tiny second-floor mosque. The high terraced balconies, notable for their profuse stucco decorations, balustrades and noble arches, offer superb bird's-eye views over the heart of Hyderabad city—busy, bustling scenes of battling rickshaws, thronging pavements, teeming mosques, and colourful bazaars of silversmiths, bangle makers, embroidery shops, perfume merchants and antique dealers.

The Salar Jung Museum

Continuing on by rickshaw or taxi, visit the Salar Jung Museum (*open daily 10am–5pm except Fri; free guide service every hour; photographs not allowed; adm Rs5*) on the south bank of the Musi River, whose green, cultivated banks make a pleasant, if incongruous relief from Hyderabad's grim urban feel.

The museum building houses the superb private collections of three Nawabs Salar Jung, successive *wazirs* or prime ministers of the Nizam of Hyderabad. Salar Jung III died in 1949 without an heir, and the collection was handed over to the Government of India in 1956. The 35,000 exhibits, gathered from all over the world, now fill 35 large rooms and form possibly the finest private collection of fine art and textiles in the country. The ornate entrance hall, with its beautiful chandeliers, leads into the ground-floor collection of textiles, Mughal glass, ivory, miniatures and a fascinating bell clock. On the first floor are Kashmir, Burmese, Chinese, Japanese and Western art, as well as a good selection of bronzes. The prize pieces of the museum are the ivory chairs and the turban of Tipu Sultan, and the swords and daggers of the Mughal emperors. Also of special interest are the small collection of Indian miniature paintings and the fine exhibition of jade. The Japanese ivory sculptures in the ivory gallery are humourous and exquisite—especially the miniature ones of demons and sages.

All exhibts are well lit and well presented, and though there's a lot of kitsch on display—particularly in the children's section with its grotesque tableau of Snow White and the Seven Dwarves (minus Snow White), its tacky doll's house with a negligéd girl posing provocatively at one of the beds, and a leering one-eyed negro flute player—this provides welcome light relief from the endless galleries of art treasures and priceless manuscripts.

If you still have the energy, finish off with a sunset visit to **Birla Mandir Temple** (*open Mon–Fri, 4–9pm, weekends, 7–11am and 3–9pm*). Set atop a rocky hill overlooking the southern end of Hussain Sagar, this modern Hindu temple, constructed from pure white marble, offers memorable views over the city at sunset. Nearby is the **Birla Planetarium** (English programmes at 3.30 and 6.50pm daily, plus an extra 11.30am show at weekends), arguably the best in India with its 'Japanese Technology Sky Theatre'. Pleasantly air-conditioned, it's the perfect place to cool off after a steamy day's sightseeing.

Nehru Zoological Park

Allow a full day to visit the Nehru Zoological Park (*open daily 9am–6pm, except Mon*), thought by many to be the best zoo in India. It lies in a huge 300-acre expanse of undulating, semi-tropical landscape, and is the home of some 1600 animals. Famous for its Lion Safari Park and for its many birds (over 240 species), its extensive grounds vary from attractive landscaped gardens to peaceful picnic bowers, from lush jungle forests to still, serene inland lakes. A Rs45 rickshaw ride from the town centre, the Nehru Zoological Park is located just outside the old city walls on the Bangalore Road, quite near to Charminar.

Visit early in the morning, when all the big cats are still fairly alert (by noon, they're comatose), and spend all day wandering around. There's enough here to justify it. Inside the entrance, you'll find a useful map. Straight ahead, there's the small toy-train track that runs right round the inner park perimeter, and the Rs1 ride is a good way of orienting yourself quickly within the large grounds.

Back at the park entrance, head left on foot. This takes you via the tiger, cheetah and camel compounds, and over to the ever-popular elephants and white rhinos. You'll note that all the animals are very well kept, and live in near-natural surroundings separated from their human visitors only by the most unobtrusive of barriers.

At the top of the park, a 20-minute walk from the entrance, you'll come to the **Lion Safari Park**. Crowded but cosy minibuses speed off in search of lions every 15 minutes or so, from 9.30am to 12.15pm, and from 2 to 4.30pm daily. When the bus finds some lions, it generally screeches to a halt for photographs; sometimes it breaks down, and the lions wander over to stare at the tourists instead.

Out of the Lion Park, strike left down the outer perimeter path to find deer, bison, gnu and monkeys. Just past the waterbuck compound, head into the centre of the park for *sambar*, crane, *nilgai*, bear, water-birds and more lions. There's a couple of snack restaurants here, and a pleasant picnic area where you can enjoy a relaxing lunch. During the hottest part of the day (1–4pm), visit the **Natural History Museum and Aquarium** (*open 9am–1pm, 2–5pm daily*), both by the entrance ticket-gate while the animals rest. Then see the **Prehistoric Animals Park** and nearby **Ancient Life Museum**, both a short walk from the entrance. Otherwise, visit the monkeys who never go to sleep.

Shopping

Not for nothing is Hyderabad known as the 'City of Pearls'. In olden days, the Nizams would settle for nothing less than the best of Gulf pearls. Today, while connoisseurs are content with beads from China and Japan, Hyderabad remains the only centre for their trade in India.

At a reputable pearl dealer like **Mangatrai**, Bashir Bagh, you can pick up old pearls from the Persian Gulf (known as Basra pearls) for as little as 20 per cent of current London prices. The cost of pearls varies depending on type and shape; be prepared to bargain. Both the above dealers offer rice pearls, seed pearls, round pearls and drop pearls. A medium-sized string of pearls weighs about an ounce. But don't have pearls strung and set in Hyderabad—have them done in Bombay where it is far cheaper.

If you can't afford pearls, shop around for the famous, sparkling Hyderabadi bangles, *nagans*—the main street selling them is the Chudi Bazaar, which leads west from the Charminar. Often embedded with semi-precious stones, they are made from pure lac, a resin secreted by beetles, and are extremely lustrous and durable—nip off down the side-streets and watch the artisans making them with a small coal fire to melt the resin. Prices range from Rs15–500 per pair.

Silver jewellery is available at many shops in Charminar, but it's not cheap. Bargain hard, or take an Indian friend along to haggle for you.

Charminar's many bazaars are among the most varied, lively and colourful in India; an exotic pot-pourri of antique shops, bangle makers, jewellers, chemists, bidriware craftsmen, pearl dealers and silversmiths. You can find practically anything here, and the atmosphere is quite remarkable. There are whole streets covered in old books and clothes, intriguing hairdressers and lots of local people wandering around in green Viking helmets and pilot goggles. Things to buy include traditional *bidri* work—shiny silver inlay designs on black gun-metal, *nirmal* lacquer toys, picture frames, trays and furniture, Himroo fabrics and brocades, gun-metal statuettes, and *kondapalli* sandalwood toys. Bidriwork is best bought at **Bidri Crafts** at Gun Foundry, at the top of Abids Road (in front of the State Bank of Hyderabad).

For a quick overview of what's available, pay a visit to **Lepakshi Government Handicrafts Emporium** in Gun Foundry. Then take a rickshaw down to **Lad Bazar**, Charminar, and go shopping at street level. There's not an awful lot to buy—unless you're into turbans, bangles, bamboo furniture and cooking spices—but the whole market is prettily lit up at night and there's a carnival atmosphere which has you reaching for your camera every few seconds.

There are good fabric shops on Nampally Road, and a **Flea Market** every Thursday morning near the Charminar which starts early. You can find saris at **Meena Bazar**. Prices on all goods are variable, and you're best advised to get a idea on what is fair at a reliable government emporium. Good ones are **Lepakshi Handicrafts Emporium** at Gun Foundry, **APCO Handloom House**, Sundar Estate (Abids) and **Handloom House**, Mukharam Jahi Road.

There are good opportunities in Hyderabad to see traditional craft processes. The ancient process of *bidri* ware may be seen at **Mumtaz Bidri Works Coop Society**, 22-1-1042 Darush Shifa or **Yaqoob Brothers**, 995 Habeeb Nagar. To see *nirmal* ware being made, visit the factory and showroom of **Nirmal Industries**, Raj Bhavan Road; left off the main road between Panjagutta and downtown Hyderabad in Khairatabad. When at the factory, ask for directions to the nearby *Himroo* weaving centre.

Try the **A.A. Hussain Bookshop**, Abid Road, which stocks Avion Escort's good city map/guide (Rs10). The tourist office sells M.A. Mahmood's excellent *Glimpses of Hyderabad. City of Legends* by Ian Austen (Viking, Penguin India 1992) is a popular history of the city. Another excellent book is *The Days of the Beloved*, an oral history of life in Hyderabad under the last Nizam collected by Harriet Lynton and Mohini Rajan; originally published by California University Press (1974), a local reprint by Orient Longman is available. The small pocket guide and map published by Sangam Books (Rs50) is locally available.

Leisure

Hyderabad has an **Amateur Rider's Club** in the Saifabad suburb (about 5km from the city centre on the road out to Golconda). A few years ago, the club had immediate access to the countryside, but the city has grown so rapidly that it is now completely hemmed in by buildings. However, the horses are well looked after, and if you can be content with riding in the ring, the facilities should suit. Amazingly, the horses are still hacked out on exercise (with the grooms riding one and leading one) through the thick traffic of the main Golconda road that runs past the club's entrance.

You can go **swimming** at the pools of the Oberoi (dress smartly to get in) or the cheaper Ritz.

There is nowhere at present to see **traditional dance** in the city, though the new top-floor restaurant at the Viceroy Hotel plans to feature live *ghazal* music nightly.

There are several **cinemas** in the Abids Road area; the programmes are listed in *Deccan Chronicle*.

As for **nightlife**, there isn't any. Andhra Pradesh is a 'dry' state and beer can only be bought by foreigners at big hotels, upon the filling-out of a tedious 'alcohol licence' form. The banning of alcohol in this Muslim-influenced state was only implemented in 1995. Since then the use of marijuana in Hyderabad has apparently increased dramatically.

Hyderabad ✆ (0842–)   **Where to Stay**

In Hyderabad, you have the choice of staying either in isolated splendour up in the Banjara Hills (formerly the heart of the city) 6.5km from the railway station, or in the seedier but atmospheric Abids/Nampally Road area of the town centre.

luxury (from Rs 2000)

The **Krishna Oberoi**, Road No.1, Banjara Hills, ✆ 222121, ✉ 223079, caters mainly to VIPs and diplomats, and is set in 9 acres of beautifully landscaped gardens, with many rooms overlooking the Hussain Sagar. Its palatial-style architecture is perhaps over-emphasized by the presidential suites that have their own swimming pools.

Far better value, and more accessible to the general travellers, is the new **Taj Residency**, Road no.1, Banjara Hill, ✆ 399999, ✉ 392218, just down the road from the Oberoi; it has good food, and a choice of rooms overlooking the lake (free boating facilities) or Golconda fort. Most rooms have balconies; standard ones start at US$70.

expensive (from Rs 900)

The **Viceroy**, Tank Bund Road, ✆ 7618383, ✉ 7618797, is a brand new hotel with 5-star facilities (including the best pool in town) at a 3-star tariff. Immaculate rooms at Rs1300 (double); avoid the smelly lake-facing ones. Try also the **Green Park**, 7-1-26 Ameerpet, ✆ 291919, ✉ 291900. Fraying at the edges, but still a comfortable option, is the fine old **Ritz**, Hillfort Palace, ✆ 233848. Built as a summer residence for one of the younger sons of the last Nizam but one, it sits in its own gated enclave at the far end of Hill Fort Road, just north of the Lal Bahadur Stadium. It is an ex-palace with Raj-style charm, lovely views, tennis courts and pool, but the service is variable. Rooms start at Rs1100 for a double.

moderate (from Rs 600)

The popular **Residency**, Public Garden Road, Nampally, ✆ 204060, ✉ 204040, is near the railway station, and has a/c rooms at Rs850 for a double. The **Rock Castle**, on Road No.6, Banjara Hills, ✆ 33541, is a small family hotel with pleasant rooms and cottages (some air-conditioned) set in a large garden. The **Sampurna International**, ✆ 40165, on Mukranjahi Road is more central and has two restaurants, a good travel desk and most rooms are air-conditioned. **Jaya International**, Nehru Road, Abids, ✆ 232929, is very central.

There's a good choice of clean, comfortable hotels in the inexpensive bracket, most of them catering to the recent influx of business visitors. The best of these is the centrally located **Sai Prakash**, Station Road, Nampally, ✆ 511726, ✉ 513355, which is reasonably priced at Rs325/425 single/double non a/c and Rs425/525 single/double a/c. Or head for the **Kakatiya**, ✆ 590200, ✉ 515713, on Nampally Station Road, just 5 minutes' walk eastwards from the railway station; rooms range from Rs140–400 and the attached vegetarian restaurant is a big plus. Up towards Abid Circle is the slightly overpriced **Sri Brindavan**, ✆ 203970 with large, breezy singles and doubles. **Rock Castle**, Road no.6, Banjara Hills, ✆ 399742, is a small family hotel run by friendly Mr Rodrigues. Spacious, if somewhat run-down, air-cooled rooms cost Rs300 double—great value, though in the absence of regular tourist traffic (he hasn't got a liquor licence), the owner has been reluctantly forced to let the place out more or less full-time to Indian film crews. Ring ahead first.

budget

Shoestringers don't often come to Hyderabad, which is just as well since there's a dearth of good cheap hotels. Inside the aptly named Royal Hotel Complex on Nampally Station Road, you'll find **Gee Royal Lodge**, **Neo Royal Lodge** and **Royal Home**. None of these places have a sniff of royalty; all they provide are spartan cells from Rs60–150 with a lightbulb, chair and bed. Typically, the only hotel in this complex *without* the word 'royal' in it is the best place to stay: the **Raj Mata**, ✆ 201000, with immaculate deluxe rooms with TV for Rs290 double. It's a step down again to the **Sri Durga**, opposite the Royal Complex, with drab but spacious rooms from Rs60–160. Finally, the often-full **Imperial** on Nampally Station Road, ✆ 202220, has large clean rooms for Rs130 double.

Eating Out

Hyderabad does fine southern Indian cuisine: *chat*, a delicious series of savoury/sweet hot snacks, tray-meal *thalis*, pancake-like *dosas*, rice and *dal idlis*, and flour-wafer *pappadams*. But the speciality dishes are *baghara baigan* (small eggplants stuffed with spices, cooked in tamarind juice and sesame oil) and *mirchi ka salan* (stuffed green chillies). Both are a bit hot for Western palates, so you may care to try the city's famous *birianis* or *tikka kababs* instead. Particularly recommended is *haleem*, a mildly spiced mutton and wheat preparation, followed by *khobani* (dried apricots cooked to a purée). Finish off with a pot of good rich south Indian coffee.

Rana, chef at the Oberoi's **Firdaus** restaurant, serves à la carte dishes at around Rs350–400 per head; or sample the good-value Rs250 lunchtime buffet served between 12.30 and 3pm. Popular European-style breakfasts and lunch buffets are served Monday to Saturday at the Oberoi's **Gardenia** restaurant, plus a special brunch on Sundays (11am–2pm, Rs200). The same hotel also has the **Szechwan Garden**, which features a lunchtime buffet (Rs250) and serves the best Chinese food in the city.

The Taj Residency's **Kabab-E-Bahar** is a lake-side open-air barbecue open each evening and famous for its (spicy) Indian kebabs. The same hotel has authentic Deccan plateau cuisine in its **Dakhni** restaurant; try the Rs150 lunchtime buffet. Or relax in the stylish ambience of the Taj's **Waterside Café**, which offers buffets (breakfast, lunch and dinner) and excellent service. Less upmarket, there's excellent Mughlai food at **Shahraan** opposite Charminar; it's very popular with the locals, so you often have to fight for a table.

The Green Park Hotel's **Tulip's** coffee shop serves excellent snacks, though the service can be indifferent. The same hotel serves popular lunchtime buffets (Rs140) in its **Once Upon a Time** restaurant—only for those who like spicy Mughlai cuisine. The hotel's **Memories of China** restaurant has a good Chinese dinner buffet (weekdays only, Rs95).

Outside of a hotel, the best places to go Chinese are **Hai King**, 3–6–276 Himayath Nahar and (much cheaper) **Nan King**, 105 Park Lane.

If you're stuck in town at the end of a busy day's sightseeing, there's nowhere better to eat and relax than **Palace Heights**, 8th floor, Triveni Building, Abid Road, a stylish place, with good mid-priced continental, Mughlai and Chinese cuisine. For vegetarian, try Sai Prakash Hotel's **Woodlands** restaurant.

In the Abids area, you'll find cheap and tasty vegetarian fare at Emerald Hotel's **Sapphire Restaurant**, Royal Hotel's **Laxmi Restaurant**, and **Annapurna Hotel**'s air-conditioned restaurant. The Annapurna is particularly well known for its ice cream.

For good cheap eating try the **Brij Vasi Chat Bhandar**, a strange little place down an alley (signposted) called Chirag Ali Lane, off M.G. Road a few blocks north of Abid Circle. The *chat* here is really good, and you can follow it up with soft ice cream, all for under Rs50. Below this price range are the usual south Indian *thali* houses, found on every street. Try the one at the Sri Brindhavan on Nampally Station Road (Abids end). **Baker's Inn** is recommended for burgers, cakes and pastries.

Moving On

By air: Indian Airlines, ✆ 236902, offers daily flights to Bangalore, Bombay, Clacutta, Delhi and Madras, also three flights a week to Bhubaneshwar. **Jet Airways**, ✆ 231263, flies every day of the week to Bangalore, Bombay and Calcutta.

By rail: the main railway station is Secunderabad, to the north of town, though you can board trains for Bangalore, Calcutta, Madras and Delhi at the more central Hyderabad station. The popular shoestringer train northeast is the 2714 **Secunderabad–Vijaywada Express**, which leaves Secunderabad at 4.45pm daily and draws into Puri 24hrs later. The 1019 **Konark Express** does the journey to Bhubaneshwar in an hour less. Other fast trains include the 7085 **Bangalore Express** to Bangalore (dep 8.20pm, 17hrs), the 7032 **Bombay Express** to Bombay (dep 8.20pm, 17hrs) and the 3.45pm **Madras Express** or the 6.40pm **Charminar Express** to Madras (both 14½hrs)—though nowhere is exactly 'fast' from Hyderabad.

Both Hyderabad's stations have a tourist quota of tickets, and both accept ticket reservations from 8am to 8pm, till 4pm only on Sundays. All long-distance trains should be booked well in advance—they're very busy.

By road: from Hyderabad's central bus depot, Gowliguda Road, there's one state bus daily to Madras (704km; 15hrs) and to Bombay (739km; 17hrs); plus 3–4 buses daily to Bangalore (560km). The above destinations, together with places like Aurangabad (600km) and Hospet, are also handled by private bus companies. You can, and should, pre-book seats.

Nagarjunakonda Ruins

The Indus Valley and Mesopotamia are generally regarded as the twin birthplaces of civilization, of settled agricultural communities and the first towns. However there were several other parts of Asia where the same forms of settlement were evolving, if somewhat out on a limb. Andhra Pradesh's **Nagarjunakonda** was one such site. For the last 400 years, Nagarjunakonda has not been inhabited, but archaeologists estimate that this stretch of the Krishna River has been settled for an estimated 200,000 years, and as recently as 6000 years ago, settled farming and village life had begun.

Getting There

By road: to get to the dam, you can either take a tour bus from Hyderabad, booking through A P Tourism (*see* p.518), or go independently: several daily services ply the 110 mile, 8-hour route to and from Hyderabad, with a change at Vijayapuri (9.5km from the dam).

By boat: a boat service takes tourists across the lake from the dam at mid-morning and mid-afternoon (about Rs30 per person).

Tourist Information

The **A P Tourist Office** is in the state-run Project House, ✆ 325.

History

Nagarjunakonda was 'discovered' in 1926 by the eminent Indian archaeologist A.R. Saraswathi. At first, great excitement was caused by his revelations that a 3rd-century Hindu-Buddhist empire once had its capital here. Then, further excavations revealed tools from the early Stone Age, closely followed by Neolithic cemeteries, stone circles and megaliths, evidence of early farming and metal working and finally of early towns—all in one continuous line of settlement. The greater part of the most ancient remains were submerged in the 1950s beneath the vast Nagarjuna dam. Only an island, what was the hilltop fort, remains, but fortunately many key finds were saved and relocated to the Nagarjunakonda hilltop and museum before the valley was flooded.

Thus the site was already ancient when the Ikshavakus, an early Hindu dynasty, established a fort on the hilltop, and began to lay out their own walled town around the existing mud and thatch settlements in the valley. The Ikshavakus were unique in south Indian history by actively encouraging both Hinduism and Buddhism in their kingdom, with direct patronage for both religions from the royal family.

The Ikshavaku hilltop city was called Vijayapur, or 'City of Victory'. There is some controversy over the origin of the city's present name: some believe that it refers to the 2nd-century Buddhist monk Nagarjuna, whose teachings were quoted in contemporary Buddhist texts from distant China. Others believe that the name simply means 'snake hill'. Whatever the origins of its present name, old Vijaypur was as prosperous as anything in contemporary Europe, and was known as far afield as Rome: Pliny wrote of a Roman trading post on the coast from which merchants came to Vijaypur to buy manufactured muslin cloth; the Roman coins and artefacts found on the site and now exhibited in the museum seem to bear this out. Before the valley was flooded, the archaeologists found an amphitheatre, laid out in the Roman style (and the only one of its kind in India).

Religious and secular building thrived under the Ikshavakus, who are credited by architectural historians with having developed one of the earliest, or 'archaic' forms of Dravidian architecture. Several Buddhist monasteries, Hindu temples, theological colleges, and even schools of sculpture and painting for both religions were found on the hillside and valley floor. Nine monuments were rescued before the flooding, and moved to the hilltop island where they have since been restored to something close to their original appearance.

It is possible the dynasty prospered too well and became a soft target—because the Ikshavakus were suddenly overrun in the 6th century by the Pallava armies of Tamil Nadu, and the town was sacked and abandoned—its distance from Tamil Nadu making it unfeasible for the Pallavans to garrison, but the ferocity of its fall being sufficiently great to cripple and ultimately kill the urban culture that had thrived there.

But Nagarjunakonda was too good a defensive site to remain unused for long. In the mid 7th century the Chalukyans took it over and at once began to build temples in their own heavily ornamented style next to the ruins of the starker Ikshavaku buildings. The Chalukyans held on to Nagarjunakonda until the gradual contracting of their great empire in the 12th century. From then, the town became a Vijayanagar outpost against the kings of Orissa, then against the Deccan sultans—first the Bahmanis, then the armies from Delhi. The hilltop fort continually changed hands between Hindu and Muslim warlords between the 14th and 16th centuries, but was again abandoned after the Vijayanagars were finally smashed by Golconda in the late 16th century.

Despite its strategic position and great cultural heritage, the site was never reoccupied, its ruins standing forgotten except by the local farmers who cultivated between the tumbled masonry of the valley and shunned the hilltop for fear of ghosts.

The Island

Now a World Heritage site, the island in the middle of Nagarjunakonda's vast dam (apparently the third-largest man-made lake in the world), can be visited by tourists. The restored buildings and ruins are not as spectacular as Hampi or Aihole in Karnataka (*see* pp.543 and 586) but the feeling of sheer antiquity has not been marred by the development of the dam; it rather increases the sense of eeriness and isolation. Few foreign tourists make it here, and you may well have the place to yourself if you visit on a weekday.

Among the restored buildings inside the late medieval Vijayanagar curtain walls of the old fort are a 2nd-century Vishnu temple, and several to Shiva, whose different architectural styles show the progression of Dravidian forms from the ascetic Ikshavaku beginnings to the Chalukyans' 12th-century high ornamentalism. There are fascinating sculptures too, including one that appears to be depicting the act of *suttee* (a widow throwing herself on her dead husband's funeral pyre); and some memorial pillars celebrating long-gone military heroes, with intricate depictions of their successful battles. Various Buddhist stupas from the early period have also survived, but there are few images of the Buddha, for the *Hinayana* form of Buddhism practised at the height of the Ikshavaku period always referred to the Buddha via symbols such as a swastika, a wheel or feet. The later form of *Mahayana* Buddhism did not have long to produce its art before the city fell to the Hindu Pallavas.

At the eastern end of the fort is the **museum** (*open daily, 10am–4pm, except Fri*), housing some of the more precious sculptures, including a huge 3 metre-high standing Buddha. Many of the early Stone Age and Megalithic artefacts found on the site are also displayed here.

Where to Stay
budget

Andhra Pradesh tourism runs several lodges near the ferry. There's the **Vijay Vihar Complex**, which is very good value with air-conditioned rooms and some self-contained cottages. Try also the nearby **Soundarya Tourist Annexe** hill colony which has the same facilities, but is a little more expensive, and the **Project House**, © 325, which has two floors of cheap rooms and a tourist office.

Nagarjunasagar Srisailam Tiger Reserve

The forested hills called the Malamallai, or 'Black Hills', surrounding the Krishna River Dam now harbour a vast wildlife sanctuary—at about 2978 square km it's the largest tiger reserve in India.

Unlike most of Andhra's other sanctuaries, Nagarjunasagar has good tourist facilites. You can arrange game-spotting drives or guided treks to and from *machans* (bamboo viewing platforms) built into the trees at various watering sites where the game comes to drink. Although there are no elephant here, visitors stand a reasonable chance of seing tiger, leopard, sloth bear, *dhole* (wild dog), wolf, striped hyena, jackal, *gaur* (bison), *nilgai* (Indian giant antelope), *chital* (spotted deer), *sambar* and muntjac deer, *chinkara* (Indian gazelle), blackbuck antelope, *chousingha* (the tiny, four-horned antelope) and a variety of langur and macaque apes.

However, because the forest is dense and there is a vast 'core' area where no human disturbance is allowed, visitors should aim to spend several days here if they intend to see game. There is accommodation in three resthouses by a set of ancient temples.

Bangalore   population 5.5 million

Capital of Karnataka state, Bangalore is a spacious, well-planned city with beautiful parks, some magnificent Raj buildings and long boulevards now sadly choked with traffic. One of Asia's fastest-growing cities (the population has grown six-fold since the mid-1970s), it has now lost many of the trees, private gardens and quaint bungalows that gained it the soubriquet 'Garden City of India', but despite this remains the nation's tidiest and greenest capital.

Kempe Gowda (1513–69), the founder of Bangalore, started building his capital in AD 1537. It soon developed into such as prosperous trading centre that a fort had to be erected around it to protect it against covetous neighbouring chieftains. The fort had four gates facing four directions, and was ruled by various dynasties over successive centuries, before being enlarged and rebuilt in stone by Hyder Ali in the late 18th century. Significant improvements to the new structure were made by his son, Tipu Sultan. The arrival of the British (1809) spelt further changes, and a spacious cantonment town, with parks and gardens, museums and churches, Gothic bungalows and colleges sprang up. Encouraged by the enlightened Maharajahs of Mysore, Bangalore swiftly became a leading educational and industrial centre and eventually replaced Mysore as the state capital.

Now a 'silicon city' of the '90s, Bangalore is well on its way to replacing Bombay as the cosmopolitan and commercial centre of India. Information technology is big here and the city now has its own software Technology Park and an Electronic City housing most of the country's microchip companies. Catering to the rapid influx of visitors (mainly business travellers) over the past five years, the city centre has totally recreated itself; it is now a modern, vibrant parade of shopping malls, fast-food joints, pubs, clubs and discotheques.

When to Go

Situated 1000m above sea level, Bangalore is cool most of the year. The most pleasant months to visit are Oct–Nov and Feb–May. To see the parks and gardens at their best, come in January or August.

Getting There

International travellers can now fly Air India to Bangalore from London, New York, Perth and Singapore. There's a change of planes at Bombay, but (fortunately) no immigration queues until Bangalore.

Bangalore is also serviced by air from Bombay, Calcutta, Delhi, Jaipur, Madras and Pune, by train (the **Shatabdi Express**, daily except Tuesday) from Mysore (dep

2.20pm, 2hrs) and Madras (dep 6am, 4.45hrs), and by bus from most centres in Kerala and Tamil Nadu.

The airport is 11km from the city centre, around Rs90–140 by auto-rickshaw/taxi—though you'll have to bargain for these prices. Hopefully, there'll be a prepaid taxi system at the terminal soon.

Getting Around

Walking is not really an option—this is a big city with heavy traffic, long (non-signposted) roads, and broken pavements. Use auto-rickshaws or taxis to get around. The former have calibrated meters, and the flagfall is Rs5 (which covers you for the first 2km). The latter are less prone to getting lost.

Bangalore ✆ (080–)   ### Tourist Information

The **KSTDC Tourist Office**, ✆ 2275883, is at Badami House, Narasimharaja Square. It gives information in slow motion, but is generally helpful (open 8am–2pm and 2.30–9pm daily). Come here to buy your city sightseeing tour (dep 7.30am and 2pm, 4hrs); also tours to Mysore, Belur-Halebid, Ooty and Nagarhole. Two other KSTDC offices—at 10/4 Kasturba Road, ✆ 2212901/2/3, and on the 1st Floor, F Block Cauvery Bhavan on K.G. Road, ✆ 2215489—are both open 10am–5.30pm, closed Sunday. There are also tourist counters at rail and bus stations. The **Government of India Tourist Office** is in the KFC Buildings, 48 Church Street (1st Floor), ✆ 5585417. **Higginbotham's** have a bookshop inside the railway station.

The essential *Bangalore this Fortnight* booklet can be picked up in most hotels. It's the best city guide in the country.

The **GPO** is on Cabbon St, open 8am–6.30pm (10.30–1pm Sundays). It has a poste restante open 10.30am–4pm (closed Sundays). **Foreign exchange** is best done at **Thomas Cook**, 55 M G Rd, near the junction with Brigade Road (closed Sundays). The **Indian Airlines** office is at M G Rd (✆ 2211211/2211914, airport ✆ 566233) and at Cauvery Bhavan complex, District Office Road (✆ 572605).

Higginbotham's bookshop is on M G Road, just before Brigade Road diverts into Church Street, and stocks a wide range of city/state guidebooks (they also have a branch inside the railway station). Just as good is **Gangarams,** also on M G Road.

Visa extensions can be applied for at the Foreigners' Registration Office on Infantry Road, a 10-minute walk from the GPO (open Monday–Saturday, 10am–5.30pm). They are issued in 24 hours.

A good place to take health problems is the **Mallya Hospital**, ✆ 2217979 on Vittal Mallya Road. Some rickshaw drivers still know it by its old name of Apollo Hospital. Women with gynaecological problems should ring Dr Shetty's private clinic, ✆ 3342233. She's very sympathetic.

N

2km
1mile

Bangalore

Southern Railway
Nagarbhavi Thotal
80 FEET ROAD
80 FEET ROAD
LINK RD
12th MAIN
MAGADI RD
MAGADI ROAD
City Railway Station
2nd MAIN ROAD
PLATFORM ROAD
LOOP R
City Bus Stann
DHANVANTHRI
KSRTC Bus Stand
TANK BUND RD
H Swagath
CHICKPET
DR T.C.M. ROYAN
BHASHYAM ROAD
City Market
MYSORE
Victoria Hospital
ALBERT VICTOR ROAD
1st RD
Tipu's Palace
KRISHNARAJENDRA
MYSORE ROAD
Kempambudhi Tank
VANIVILAS ROAD
To Bull Temple

534

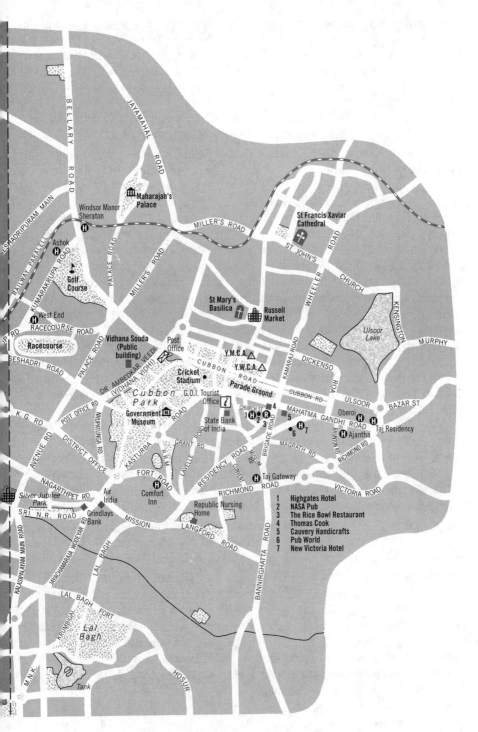

1 Highgates Hotel
2 NASA Pub
3 The Rice Bowl Restaurant
4 Thomas Cook
5 Cauvery Handicrafts
6 Pub World
7 New Victoria Hotel

All the major sights are kilometres apart. To see them all quickly, take a conducted tour. Follow this with a day of shopping (excellent) or discover the beautiful parks.

City Tour

By tour bus, half-day. Government Museum/Art Gallery–Tipu Sultan's Palace– Bull Temple–Lal Bagh–Ulsoor Lake–Vidhana Vidhi–Vidhana Souda

A short tour of the palatial buildings around Cubbon Park brings you to three museums in **Jayachamarajendra Park**. Best of these is the **Government Museum** (*open 10am–5pm, except Wed*), one of the oldest museums in India (established 1866). It has 18 sections housing fine collections of miniatures, inscriptions, coins and sculptures recovered from the Neolithic-period Chandraval excavation. The **Venkatappa Art Gallery** (*open daily, 10am–5pm except Wed*), forms one wing of this museum, and has well-presented exhibitions of water colours, plaster-of-Paris sculptures, bronze antiquities and works of art by the famous artist Venkatappa and other court painters. There are regular modern art exhibitions on the third floor. The adjoining **Technological Museum** is generally disappointing. Just down the road, opposite Queen Victoria's statue, is the **Aquarium** (*open 10am–7.30pm except Mon*), not covered by the tour, but worth returning to. South of town 1km from the City Market), you'll visit **Kempe Gowda Fort**, Hyder Ali's stone stronghold built in 1761 on the site of the original mud fort. While the fort interior is closed to the public, you can enter the first two courtyards and pass through an impressive gateway. The exterior view of the lovely 16th-century **Ganpati Temple** within the walls merely whets the appetite. Much more satisfying is **Tipu Sultan's Palace** (*open 8am–6pm, daily*), started by Hyder Ali in 1781 and completed by Tipu in 1789. One of three summer palaces built by the two Mysore rulers, it is (like the others) made entirely of wood, except for the internal pillar-supports. Within are gloriously painted walls, ceilings, balconies and soaring pillars of green, red, black and gold; also elaborate arches, surrounded by minarets and family paintings. The palace here has a small museum, illustrating the life and times of Tipu Sultan, who presented the British with their most stubborn resistance in the South.

Near the palace you'll see the **Venkataramanaswamy Temple**, built by the Wodeyar kings in the 17th century. An attractive example of Dravidian-style architecture, it was restored to them (along with their throne) after Tipu's death in 1799.

From the palace, it's a 1.5km drive south to the **Bull Temple** up on Bugle Hill. Here you'll find the fourth-largest Nandi bull in India, made of black granite and measuring 6.3m across by 4.6m high. Credited with miraculous 'growing' power, the Nandi is chiefly notable for being so much larger than its 'master', Shiva. You'll find Shiva's tiny image in the small temple at the foot of the hill. Also here is the strange **Ganesh Temple**, with its large elephant made of 528kg of strong-smelling butter. Donated by wealthy devotees, the butter is broken up every four years and distributed to pilgrims. Local philanthropists are then 'buttered up' to donate a fresh coating.

The beautiful botanical gardens of **Lal Bagh**, 2km southeast of the City Market, were laid out by Hyder Ali in 1760, and substantially added to by Tipu Sultan. Smaller than Cubbon Park, they are in every way superior—240 acres of trees and plants (1000 tropical and sub-tropical varieties, many of them rare), 19th-century pavilions and lamps, landscaped gardens and avenues, fountains and flower-beds, even an elegant glasshouse modelled on London's Crystal Palace! The best time to see the dahlias, marigolds, and rose gardens, as well as many other varieties of flowers here, is either January or August. Just up from the entrance, overlooked by Kempe Gowda's statue, is the flower-bordered **Lawn Clock** (completed 1983), which is accurate to three seconds each month. Just to the right of this is the area where visiting dignitaries/state leaders are invited to 'dedicate a tree.' (In olden days, they had expensive monuments erected to them. Nowadays, all they get is a shrub).

The last stop of the day is **Ulsoor Lake** on the eastern edge of town, 3km from the bus station. This is a pleasant boating lake with wooded islands, rose-pink water lilies and white-headed brahmini kites wheeling on the air above. The small **Boat Club** (*open 9.30am–5.30pm, daily*) has rowing boats for hire and a peaceful set of lawns called Kensington Gardens.

Around sunset, take an enjoyable promenade down **Vidhana Vidhi** (Bangalore's finest avenue) and admire its attractive selection of Greco-colonial style buildings. Start with the palatial post office (India's grandest) and walk down the tree-lined boulevard to **Attara Kacheri** ('18 Courts'), the stately red-brick structure housing the High Court. Recently saved from development it has now been restored to its original splendour.

Opposite this is the magnificent post-Independence **Vidhana Souda**, housing the Secretariat and the Legislature. Built in 1954, this four-storey ornamental structure of solid granite was designed in the neo-Dravidian style. It is notable for its soaring columns, charming frescoes and excellent carvings. Visitors are only allowed inside between 3.30 and 5.30pm, and must get permission from the public relations officer in the entrance lobby.

If you're around on a Sunday evening, between 7 and 9pm, you can see Vidhana Souda beautifully illuminated. Just down the road, at the bottom of Vidhana Vidhi, **Cubbon Park** has nightly illuminations and features a popular 'Fairy Fountain'.

Shopping

Next to Madras, Bangalore is the prime shopping centre of the south. It is famous for traditional Mysore silk saris and for rosewood, sandalwood, lacquerware, *bidri*ware and wooden-inlay items. The general shopping centres—Commercial Street, Brigade Road and M G Road—are all close together. In Brigade Road particularly, you could easily imagine yourself in Bangkok—wall-to-wall department stores, high-rise shopping malls and hi-tech emporiums.

Good places to see the **general crafts** range are the Cottage Industries Emporium and the Cauvery Arts & Crafts Emporium, both on M G Road. The latter is particularly good for hand-crafted rosewood furniture and sandalwood carvings, though prices are not cheap. If you're looking for **antiques** or replicas, Natesan's on M G Road is very reliable and not expensive.

Deepam's and **Nalli's** on M G Road are two excellent silk emporiums. For cheaper silks and textiles, there's the buzzy **City Market** in Chickpet, or the big shopping centre in M G Road.

The best gold and silver **jewellery** shops are on Commercial Street. **Krishna Sethi** is a very reputable place for gold.

Bangalore is home to one of the world's kitschest shops, inexplicably called **Big Kid's Kemp** and advertised as 'the world's greatest shopping experience'. A budget-style department store at the far end of M G Road (opposite the Oberoi), it sells everything from saris to radio-controlled aeroplanes and stays open until late at night. There is nearly always some kind of cheesy promotion stunt going on outside the front doors, usually people in cartoon animal suits dancing to Michael Jackson tunes.

Leisure

Bangalore is one of the few Indian cities with any real claim to **nightlife**. This centres around its 100 or so pubs which serve real draught beer (around Rs15 a glass) and which are open till 11pm. Pubs (with real beer on tap) in particular, have really taken off in recent years and the city centre seems to crawl, or rather stagger, with them. The most friendly is definitely **Pub World** on Residency Road which, despite terrible piped music (Bryan Adams a speciality), is a good place to chat with locals and play pool. Other goodies are **Cellar's** on Brigade Road and **Downtown Pub** opposite Pub World, with three full-size snooker tables. Amusing for its décor is the **Nasa** on Church Street, done up inside to resemble a spaceship. The **Guzzler's Inn** on Brigade Road is a more low-key place where people relax after work.

Live music and dancing in pubs was banned recently, to crack down on naughty cabarets and topless go-go dancers, but will doubtless sneak back again. In the meantime there are still 'secret' Saturday night discos at the **Concord Hotel**, on the way to the aiport, and at **The Club**, on the way to Mysore (15km). Entrance to The Club is free on Fridays, Rs150 on Saturdays.

As befits a film-making capital, Bangalore has numerous cinemas, some of them notably on M G and Brigade Roads, showing recent English-speaking releases, though these are usually soft-porn films that died quickly in the West. Programmes are advertised in local newspapers, *Deccan Herald* or *Indian Express*, along with details of music/dance shows at **Chowdiah Memorial Hall**, Sankey Road.

Bangalore's **Amateur Rider's Club** (*open daily except Monday*) is at the racecourse in the centre of town. Admission is Rs170, and you buy a coupon book for Rs250 which entitles you to 10 half-hour rides. Riding times are early morning and evening.

Coarse **fishing** is allowed at Hesaraghatta Lake or Chamarjasagar Reservoir (enquire at the tourist office). If you are a game fisherman, you can go after the mighty *mahseer* at the exclusive Cauvery River Camp 80km to the south. For all places, you need your own tackle.

The Windsor Manor, or West End hotels can arrange golf at the city centre's 8-hole course.

Bangalore ✆ *(080–)*

Where to Stay
luxury (from Rs 2600)

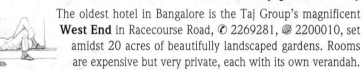

The oldest hotel in Bangalore is the Taj Group's magnificent **West End** in Racecourse Road, ✆ 2269281, ✉ 2200010, set amidst 20 acres of beautifully landscaped gardens. Rooms are expensive but very private, each with its own verandah. The newly renovated **Taj Residency**, 14 M G Road, ✆ 5584444, ✉ 5844748, caters more to the business than the general traveller, but has a good pool, gym and Chinese restaurant. The new **Oberoi Hotel**, M G Road, ✆ 5585858, ✉ 5585970, opened in August 1992 and is one of the most beautiful hotels in the south. It has very well-appointed rooms, well-trained staff and superb gardens surrounding a pool. Ask for a room away from the gardens (too many mosquitoes).

expensive (from Rs 1200)

The best value in town is Taj Group's **Gateway** Hotel at 66 Residency Road, ✆ 5544545, ✉ 5544030. This offers 4-star service at 2-star prices—rooms for only US$60, suites for $95. Welcomgroup's **Windsor Manor**, 25 Sankey Road,

✆ 2269898/2296322, ✉ 2264941, is a first-rate hotel, with exquisite decor, immaculate service, nice restaurants, and well-furnished rooms and old-fashioned courtesy. The **Comfort Inn Ramanashree**, 16 Raja Ram Mohun Roy Road, ✆ 223 5250, ✉ 221214, has very comfortable rooms and includes breakfast in the tariff. A 5-minute rickshaw ride away from M G Road is the **Capitol**, Raj Bhavan Road, ✆ 2281234, ✉ 2259933, with staff always eager to help and comfortable rooms from Rs2000 (a/c double).

moderate (from Rs 1000)

Centrally located, the **Harsha Hotel**, Park Road, ✆ 286566, ✉ 2865943, offers a multi-cuisine restaurant, a swimming pool, and double rooms From Rs790 (a/c). A little run-down, but cheaper and with much more atmosphere than the expensive hotels, is the late-19th century **Victoria Hotel** at 47 Residency Road, ✆ 5584077/ 5585028, ✉ 5584945, whose rooms still have their old (but basic) hardwood fittings. Built around a courtyard restaurant and bar (with famously inefficient service) the Victoria is walled off from the crazy outside traffic of Residency Road, and is something of a quiet haven. Much more modern is **Hotel Highgate** at 33 Church Street, ✆ 5597172, ✉ 5597799, with the cleanest, quietest and most comfortable (a/c) rooms in this bracket. The **St Mark's**, ✆ 2279090, on St Mark's Road gets good mentions, but ask for a room away from the street. The **Ivory Tower**, 12th floor, Barton Centre, 84 M G Road, ✆ 5589333, has large clean a/c rooms around Rs1000.

inexpensive

If you don't mind being above a department store, try **Nilgiris Nest** at 171 Brigade Road, ✆ 5588401, ✉ 5585348. This is a very cosy hotel with big spotless doubles for Rs450. **Ashreya** at 149 Infantry Road, ✆ 2261921, has rooms at Rs500/600 and two nice restaurants.

budget

There are still some decent cheaper hotels in and around the Chickpet area— handy for the railway station but costly if you want to get into town (20mins by rickshaw from M G Road). Best of a pretty poor bunch is **Sudha Lodge**, 6 Cottonpet Road, ✆ 605420, with a central situation, good information, hot and cold running water, and clean renovated rooms from Rs60–130. It's a great meeting-place but often full. If so, it's only a 5-minute walk to the **Swagath** at 75 Hospital Road (near Majestic Theatre), ✆ 2877200. This is clean and livable enough, with rooms from Rs300 or Rs450 with a/c. The **Sudarshan**, near the bus station, ✆ 72702, is a friendly place with cheap rooms.

Eating Out

Bangalore is well on its way to becoming the food capital of India. Even more than Bombay, there is a wide range of cuisine available outside of hotels. In order to compete, the hotels have themselves developed new restaurants.

Among the Indian restaurants, the **Karavalli** at the Gateway Hotel is now rated as one of the top five restaurants in the country; it's famous for its excellent Malabar, Konkan and Coorg food. Spicy seafood is the speciality; fixed menu lunches are Rs110 per head. The **Coconut Grove** on Church Street has an airy, palm-laden outdoor section where you can enjoy inexpensive dishes; very popular with locals. The **Windsor Manor Hotel** has the best Northwest Frontier food. A traditional Keralan restaurant, set in an old 1930s Raj Art Deco building, is **Koshy's Restaurant** on St Mark's Road, ✆ 221 3793, where you can go for either a beer and a snack (Rs35–50) or a full meal (Rs50–75). There is also high-class fare at **Tycoon's**, in Infantry Road. Cheaper Indian restaurants include the excellent **Ullas Refreshment Rooms** on M G Road—a 1st floor restaurant in a modern complex with an outdoor terrace serving *chaat* and vegetarian dishes for about Rs20 each; the **Chalukma** vegetarian restaurant on Racecourse Road, near the West End Hotel, and the **Plantain Leaf Brigades** on Church Street (serving traditional *thalis*), also with individual dishes at Rs20–35. At **Kamat Yatri Nivas** hotel, you can sample vegetarian dishes from all over south India for as little as Rs25 per meal.

On a slight variation, the **Garden Café** at the West End Hotel serves Anglo-Indian food, derived from the Anglo-Indian settlers. Try the Mutton Bowl curry. At the same hotel is the **Mermaid** poolside barbecue, specializing in Indian barbecue— the meat dishes are famous.

continental

Mid/high-price continental food is best at restaurants like the exclusive **Prince's**, 9 Brigade Road, ✆ 5580087 (book ahead), the **Peacock** in the Gateway Hotel, and **MTR** by the main entrance of Lal Bagh. The latter has a famous bar and is open from 7 to 11am and from 4 to 7pm. *The* place to go at the moment is **Sunny's**, in Kasturba Road off Lavelle Road, ✆ 2243642. It's run by two gay guys and serves Italian and French food in small but very airy surroundings.

Chinese/Thai

The **Szechwan Court** at the Oberoi Hotel is one of the premier Chinese restaurants in the city and definitely worth a visit. You can get cheaper Chinese at the **Continental**, the **Chung Wah**, or at the low-budget **Rice Bowl**, all in Brigade Road. A meal at **Memories of China** in the Taj Residency Hotel will cost around Rs150. The **Paradise Island** at the West End Hotel serves excellent Thai food and a multi-cuisine buffet at lunch time for Rs135 per head. The restaurant is set on an island in the centre of a lake and surrounded by acres of well-landscaped greenery—especially beautiful at night.

international

The Gateway has a **Pot Luck Café**, so called because the menu changes every day and you can pick and choose from a wide selection of international dishes—all the way from Indonesian *nasi goreng* to Malaysian chicken curry. The best deals here are the RS110 multi-cuisine breakfast and the 3-course 'express' lunch at Rs210.

Most restaurants in Bangalore serve draft beer and there are numerous pub lunches throughout the city. Tasty snacks for under Rs50 are served at **Excel Restaurant** in Tank Bunder Road, behind the bus station. This place has a well-stocked bar and lots of 'local' character. On Gandhi Nagar in Kempe Gowda, travellers favour **Hotel Blue Star** (opposite Tribhuvan cinema) for its 'well-experienced cook' and tasty chicken dishes at around Rs45–60. Nearby **Sukhsagar Food Complex** (opposite Majestic Theatre) has Gujarati/Punjabi food on the 3rd floor, south Indian meals on the 1st floor, and mouthwatering ice creams, sweets and juices on the ground floor. **Chaat Corner** on M G Road does light Indian snacks.

Two popular ice-cream parlours on M G Road are **Milk Bar** and **Chit-Chat**. The latter is one of the ritziest parlours in India, with chandeliers, musical fountains, and toffee-nosed waiters who won't serve you unless you sit on the ground-floor and look very rich. Less frosty is **Baskin-Robbins American Ice Cream** on Residency Road, just down from the Gateway Hotel. For fast food, try **Kentucky Fried Chicken** or **Wimpy** in Brigade Road.

Moving On

By air: Indian Airlines, ✆ 2211914, offer daily flights to Bombay, Calcutta, Delhi, Hyderabad and Madras, also less frequent services to Cochin and Trivandrum (4), Ahmedabad and Pune (3) and Coimbatore (2). **Damania/Skyline NEPC**, ✆ 558736, fly to Bombay, Goa and Pune on a daily basis, and to Madras and Ahmedabad 3 times a week. **NEPC Airlines**, ✆ 558 5678, fly Bombay, Pune, Cochin and Coimbatore 3 days a week, and Madras daily except Sundays. **Modiluft**, ✆ 582202, and **Jet Airways**, ✆ 5586095, both service Bombay and Delhi daily. New sectors are being added all the time.

By rail: The fully air-conditioned **Shatabdi Express** goes to Madras (dep 4.30pm, 4.45hrs) and to Mysore (dep 10.45am, 2hrs) daily except Tuesday. Other fast trains out of Bangalore include the 1014 **Kurla Express** to Bombay (dep 9.05am, 22.5hrs), the 6526 Kanyakumari Express to Ernakulam/Cochin (dep 9pm, 13hrs), the 6592 **Hampi Express** to Hospet (dep 9.55pm, 9.5hrs), and the 7086 **Hyderabad Express** to Hyderabad. The quickest train to Delhi is the 2429 **Rajdhani Express**, leaving at 6.45am daily (except Mondays) and arriving 34hrs later.

The railway station is a good half-hour's drive east of the central M G Road area, so allow sufficient time to catch your train. The booking office is on the left facing the station, open 8am to 8pm (Sundays, till 2pm only).

By road: Bangalore's efficient Central bus stand, directly opposite the city railway station, offers regular express buses to Mysore (every 20mins from 6am to 9.30pm, 3½hrs) and to Madras (8hrs). There are also buses to Bombay, via Belgaum (24hrs), to Ernakulam and to Hospet, as well as to Hampi direct (8–9hrs). There's also at least one bus daily to Ootacamund, to Kodaikanal, to Madurai, to

Pondicherry, and to Panjim in Goa. Most long-distance buses are heavily subsidized, so book at least 24hrs ahead.

Hampi (Vijayanagar)

It was a question of light, of entering the cave at a time when the rays of the sun, pouring through the irregular fissure in the roof, fell transversely across the rock chamber, illuminating the whole main wall...upon this wall, lovingly sculpted in frieze upon frieze, were Valmiki's gods and godesses.

Karmala Markandaya, *Obsesssion*

Up in the Central Deccan Plateau, about 184km east of Belgaum and 320km north of Bangalore lie the ruins of Hampi, once the greatest of all medieval Hindu capitals. Founded in 1336 by two local princes, Hari Hara and Bukka, it became the seat of the mighty Vijayanagar empire, which held sway over south India for more than two centuries. By the reign of Krishnadeva Raya (1509–29), generally considered the golden period of the empire, its rule extended from the Arabian Sea east to the Bay of Bengal, and from the Deccan plateau south to the tip of the peninsula. The Vijayanagar kings built up Hampi as a showpiece of imperial magnificence, and a definitive Vijayanagar style of architecture emerged, typified by lofty *gopurams*, stylized sculptures (often depicting scenes from the *Puranas* and the *Ramayana*), intricately carved columns, and separate shrines for goddesses.

The city itself had, and still has, a spectacular natural setting, enclosed on three sides by the Tungabhadra river and by rocky gorges, with huge boulders strewn across the landscape as if thrown there like pebbles from the hands of giants. The addition of seven concentric rings of massive fortifications made it almost invulnerable to attack. Hampi had a series of enlightened rulers who patronized the arts and education, cultivating it as a centre of learning and culture, as well as of the erotic arts, as many of the temple carvings illustrate. Meanwhile, a growing trade in spices turned its busy, colourful bazaars into an international centre of commerce. In its heyday, the city had a population of half a million, bolstered by a powerful mercenary army of an incredible one million soldiers. Such a large force was required to defend the supremacy of Vijayanagar against rival Muslim sultans and Hindu kings. In 1565, however, it was finally overcome by five allied Deccan sultans in the disastrous battle of Talikota. The king fled southwards, and the invaders spent six long months systematically sacking and looting the abandoned city, burning and pillaging without mercy. The empire lingered on for another century, but Hampi itself was never occupied again.

To miss Hampi is to miss one of the principal treasures of India. Now a World Heritage site, the ruins are well worth the 24-hour haul from Bangalore, Goa or Hyderabad, and you should allow at least three days here to get around the whole place and soak up the atmosphere. Many people stay for weeks, but as yet there has been no real tourist development at Hampi, so most of the visitors are hippies and independent travellers.

So well preserved is this fantastical abandoned city, and so vividly does it reflect a vanished glory, that Hampi has been termed 'The Pompeii of India'. Spread over a vast area of 6400 acres, including temples, pavilions, whole bazaars, bath complexes and palaces, the ruins are on a very grand scale. High *gopurams* rear to the sky, and some of the sculptures alone have been hewn from single blocks of granite up to 7 metres high. You can really sense a mighty civilization at work here. With only the slightest effort of imagination, you can easily visualize it. At present, the Government of Karnataka and the Archaeological Survey of India are trying to restore the capital to something of its past glory. An ambitious project perhaps, but not impossible. A great many of the ruins are in surprisingly good condition.

When to Go

Hampi has a very dry, exposed location and is best visited in the cool months of December to February. Travellers do trickle in as early as August and September, when the river is swollen by the monsoon and the surrounding countryside a rich lush green, and as late as March, but after that it's too hot for comfort.

Getting There

Hampi lies outside the town of Hospet. A regular local bus service covers the 21km between Hospet and Hampi. Otherwise, hire an auto-rickshaw or taxi (approx Rs75 round trip), or a bicycle (*see* below).

By rail: from Bangalore and Hyderabad there is one overnight train daily taking 8 and 13 hours respectively. From Bangalore the **Hampi Express** overnight train leaves at 9.30pm and reaches Hospet at 6.20am the following morning. From Hyderabad you have to change trains at Guntakal.

By bus: there are connections between Hospet and Bangalore, Hyderabad, Mysore and Goa.

For further information, *see* 'Moving On', p.550.

Hampi © (08394–)   ***Tourist Information***

The **KSTDC tourist office**, behind Hospet bus stand, is open daily from 10am to 1pm and from 2 to 5pm. It's fairly helpful and has a free map of the site, but **Malligi Tourist Home** has the better information.

There are **post offices** at Hospet, Hampi and Kamalapuram.

For **foreign exchange**, the State Bank of Mysore is next to Hospet tourist office.

Tour of the Ruins

By auto-rickshaw/taxi, 6 hours; by cycle, 8 hours. Vittala Temple Complex–
Virupaksha Temple–Vittala Temple–Narasimha–Sister Stone–
Royal Palace Complex–Kamalapuram.

If you're touring on foot, bear in mind that the complete round-trip (from Hospet to Hampi, round the ruins, and back) is 48km. Some people stay in Hospet, taking a bus to **Hampi Bazaar**, then walking up to the **Vittala Temple** complex, returning to the bazaar,

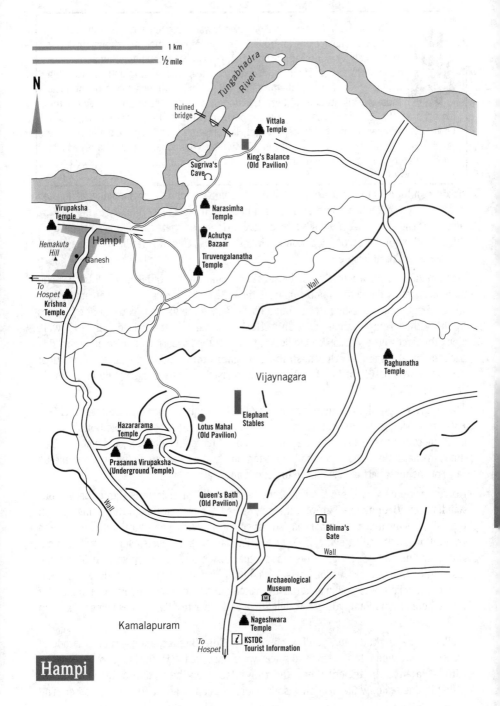

N

1 km

½ mile

Tungabhadra River

Ruined bridge

Vittala Temple

Sugriva's Cave

King's Balance (Old Pavilion)

Narasimha Temple

Virupaksha Temple

Hemakuta Hill

Hampi

Ganesh

Achutya Bazaar

To Hospet

Krishna Temple

Tiruvengalanatha Temple

Wall

Raghunatha Temple

Vijaynagara

Elephant Stables

Hazararama Temple

Lotus Mahal (Old Pavilion)

Prasanna Virupaksha (Underground Temple)

Queen's Bath (Old Pavilion)

Wall

Bhima's Gate

Wall

Archaeological Museum

Kamalapuram

Nageshwara Temple

To Hospet

KSTDC Tourist Information

Hampi

The police in Hampi are not well-disposed towards the hippy type of traveller and sometimes come looking for trouble. The commonest trick is to summarily arrest young men for not wearing shirts in the main bazaar, pulling them out of the restaurants and *chai*-shops with a great deal of shouting and some rough handling and hustling them off to the station. Although many of the local Indians walk around shirtless, this does not exempt Westerners. If so caught, expect a Rs100–300 fine, whether on the spot or in court at Hospet the following day. Obviously, if you are carrying any hashish (and Hampi is a smoker's mecca), the fine will be much more expensive. In two days, the author saw five young male travellers arrested and fined with the policemen doing their best to humiliate them in front of the local populace.

striking south to **Kamalapuram** (via the Palace complex), and finally plopping, exhausted into a mid-afternoon bus from Kamalapuram back to Hospet. They then try to mop up the remaining sights on a second day's forced march. However, there is no longer any need for this for although the accommodation in Hampi itself is basic, it is far better to stay there and see the ruins at leisure.

Opinion differs as to whether it is better to see the ruins by foot or bike. On foot you spend no money, you are free to scramble up to all the little rock temples, and you do not have to worry about your bike being stolen. But a bike covers more ground. You can hire bicycles by the Vittala Temple, then pedal up to Hampi Bazaar (via the Palace complex), walk along the river to the Vittala Temple (leaving bikes at the bazaar), and finish off with a ride back to Kamalapuram, via **Ugranasimha** and **Sister Stone**. Either way, if you start out at 6.30–7am (the best light for photos), you can be back at your lodge by midday before it gets too hot.

Alternatively, you hire an auto-rickshaw (Rs60–70 for up to 3 persons) or a taxi (Rs200–250) from Malligi Tourist Home in Hospet. This is the most comfortable option, but it lacks the romance of wandering the fantastic, boulder-strewn landscape, and coming upon the ruins naturally. Also, only the largest temples and palaces are actually accessible by car. For the most part, you still have to get out and walk.

However you decide to see the ruins, the best place to start from is Hampi Bazaar bus stand, at the **Virupaksha Temple**, the only sacred complex in Hampi still 'living' (still in worship). Dedicated to Virupaksha, an aspect of Shiva, it has two main courts, each entered by a towered gateway or *gopuram*. The larger *gopuram* is over 50 metres high, and looks incredibly new and gets a fresh coat of whitewash every year, at **Shivratri**. Inside the temple, look out for finely carved columns with rearing animals, and for the semi-erotic reliefs of temple maidens. Also watch out for hordes of acquisitive monkeys. If you're here around 7am, you can watch Shiva and other resident deities being woken up by the priests.

Walking up along the river, you'll soon come to **Sule Bazaar**, a long, ruined arcade of arched pillars, where fruit, gems and spices were once sold. Past this, up a low rise, is the **King's Balance**. In ancient times, the king established the wealth of his kingdom by sitting in one scale, while his rich vassals poured cash and jewellery into the other. The proceeds went to the temple brahmins. Enjoy the views here, then walk down to **Vittala Temple**, the finest achievement of Vijayanagar art. Constructed in the 16th century and currently being restored by the archaeological department, this is a delightful complex of structures set within a rectangular courtyard. The main temple is famous for its rearing animals and for its 'musical' columns. Each series of 16 columns is hewn from a single granite block, and each one plays a different scale of musical notes or phrases when struck. There are 250 pillars either side of a central path, which leads up to the Marriage Hall. Again, there

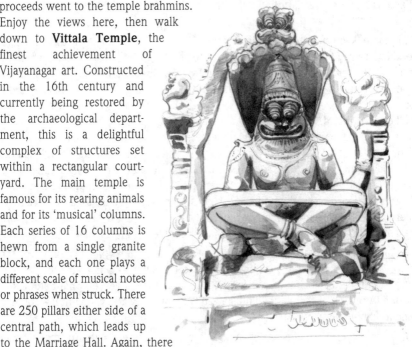

are some erotic reliefs on the pillars—though you have to look for them—some of which feature scarcely believable acts involving horses.

East of this hall is an exquisite, though huge **temple car** carved in stone. A faithful reproduction of a real temple chariot (as used in festivals), it is said to symbolize the ancient University of Gulbarga, 320km from Hospet. The miniature car houses Vishnu's vehicle, the *garuda*, and is drawn by a pair of stone elephants. Traces of the original bright paintwork still cling to the wheels. Out of the temple, walk down to **Purandaradasa Hall**, a low-ceilinged temple down by the riverside. According to legend, a famous 16th-century musician, Purandara, was turned to stone here, for singing a particularly divine song. A tiny figurine of him playing his mandolin is propped against one of the pillars. Opposite, there's a spectral group of stone pylons spanning the river. These once supported the old stone bridge which linked the two banks. You can cross Tungabhadra River in traditional 'coracle' boats (Rs5 per person).

On the other side of the river, a few scattered temples soon give way to a much wilder landscape. If you are camping, this is the place to pitch tent and wander among the boulders by night.

Back at Hampi Bazaar, a short walk south takes you up onto Hemakuta Hill. Best views are from the **Kadalaikullu Ganesa Temple**, notable for its unusually tall columns and huge image of the elephant god. Nearby, another Ganesh image stands with an open hall known as **Mustered Ganesh**. Off the hill, **Badavi Lingam** is a massive monolithic Shivalinga within a chamber, fed with water from a narrow roadside stream. Next to it is the famous figure of **Narasimha**, half man, half lion *avatar* of Vishnu, carved out of a single boulder.

Driving south, keep an eye out for **Sister Stone**, two huge boulders propped against each other like a pair of Siamese twins. They are apparently two of Shiva's sisters, whom he petrified after a family squabble. Down at the **Royal Palace Complex**, you'll find state archaeologists busily at work restoring the ruins. Walk inside the palace walls to find a large raised dais from which the king observed festival rites, various columned structures (for officers and guards), a roofless subterranean chamber (possibly the state treasury) and various civic buildings and watchtowers. Past these is **Lotus Mahal**, a beautiful two-storey pavilion with distinctive arches. It was built for the ladies of the court, in a skilful blend of Hindu and Islamic architectural styles. Nearby, there's a large step-well, extremely well-preserved, which served as a royal bath. Behind this is the **Queen's Bath**, a square water basin surrounded by a vaulted corridor. It was originally covered by a large canopy, supported by four pillars. This is now gone, and the walls are defaced by graffiti. But there's nice stucco work, and the remains of a narrow moat.

Also look out for the fine carvings, mainly of monkey figures, on the ceilings of the corridor. The tiny niches in the ceilings were for candles which illuminated the baths at night. Just outside the enclosure, to the east, look out for the largest **elephant stables** in the world. A row of 10 chambers with high vaulted roofs, they are symmetrically disposed around a central two-storey pavilion.

If you have bicycles, a rickshaw or taxi, it is worth making a side-trip from here to **Kamalapuram**. Built as a fort with circular bastions, this small town has an interesting **Archaeological Museum** (*open daily 10am–5pm, except Fri*) with many fine recoveries from the Hampi site. It has a good scale model of the ruins which is useful for orientation, if you're starting out from Kamalapuram by bike. The museum also sells the useful ASI booklet on Hampi.

Shopping

Hampi has no indigenous crafts, but there is always a stall outside the big temple gate in the main bazaar selling overpriced 'antique' bronzes (bargain down to at least half the asking price). The **Aspiration Store** in Hampi Bazaar has a wide range of produce from Sri Aurobindo ashram in Pondicherry; marble, silk fabrics, hand-made paper, postcards, even herbal bath powder. Good books to buy here are R. Sewell's *Forgotten Empire* and Longhurst's *Hampi Ruins*. Though most people get by with Michell and Fritz's *Hampi*, issued free at the tourist office.

Leisure

No stay in Hampi is complete without a trip down the river on an **inner tube**. Although there are signs up warning of whirlpools and drownings, the river is only dangerous at high water (August–October), after which the level drops to a safe, steady flow. You can hire tubes for about Rs25 per day from the Rao Guest House, or anywhere else on the bazaar that has put up a sign. Once you have your tube, walk up to the big temple, bear right and follow the path parallel with the river bank, just past a sign pointing to a shack called the 'Mango Tree Restaurant'—a *chai*-house set under a big wild mango tree. The path then leads down to the river through a short section of paddy fields. Sit inside and go. You can drift down for well over an hour. When you have had enough, paddle to the shore and walk home. Make sure you take sun-screen, and some money in a plastic bag to have a drink at one of the *chai*-shops on the riverbank as you return.

The safest **swimming** spot is reached by taking the side street off the main bazaar past the Ashok Restuarant and Guest House and down to the river—you will see where the local boys are splashing about. The river is deep and calm enough here to allow a decent swim, but try not to swallow the water: though fast flowing and not officially used as a human toilet, the local buffalo know no rules when it comes to water hygiene.

Hampi

budget

Hampi has some good, but very basic guesthouses, with rooms still under Rs100 per night. The most popular are the **Rao Guest House**, just around the corner from the bazaar bus stand, and the **Shanthi Lodge**, built around a central courtyard, and reached by turning right by the big temple at the top of the main bazaar and following the road for about a minute—the Shanthi is on the right. Partyers stay at the **Ashok**, the only place in town that serves beer (illegally). You can bargain for really cheap rates here. Both the Ashok and the Rao have cheap restaurants, and the Shanthi sells home-made banana bread.

In all the lodges, you will need a mosquito net at night.

If you want more comfortable, or air-conditioned accommodation, you'll have to stay in Hospet.

Hospet

moderate

Hospet has the new KSTDC **Hotel Mayura Vijayanagar**, © 8270, which has the best facilities and rooms—there is no air-conditioning but the rooms have good fans and mosquito nets are provided. There is a second KSTDC unit at **Tungabhadra Dam**, 6.5km away.

inexpensive/budget

The **Malligi Tourist Home**, 6/143 Jambunatha Road, © 8101, is a short rickshaw ride from the bus stand and good value. Friendly and comfortable, it has two air-conditioned doubles at the top end of its range, a good restaurant, bakery and ice-cream parlour, running hot water till 10am, laundry and money-changing facilities, small library and bookshop, TV lounge and cool gardens.

Malligi can arrange all local sightseeing and pre-book all onward travel. As a fall-back, try **Hotel Sudarshan**, ✆ (08394) 8574, on Station Road. Service is poor, but rooms are reasonably priced from under Rs100 (single, no bath) to more expensive clean doubles, with bath.

Eating Out

Hampi

The main bazaar has India's best restaurant—a simple outdoor (but shaded) affair called the **Krishna** which does great pancakes, watermelon juice, home-made pasta (yes, really) and, best of all, has a pet bull who comes in every morning and walks confi- dently between the tables to the counter where he is given a banana by the owner. Having eaten it meditavely, the great, stately beast then turns politely around in the narrow space, careful not to knock over any tables and chairs, and walks out. You can eat at the Krishna for under Rs40 per head, including drinks (no beer though).

If you want a beer with your meal, go to the **Ashok** down a side-street towards the river on the opposite side of the bazaar from the Krishna. The service is terrible and the food pretty poor, but the beer is cold.

Travellers also rate the restaurant at the **Rao Guest House**, which serves decent Western dishes and *thalis* under a shady tree for about Rs25–30 per head.

Hospet

Malligi Tourist Home has two good restaurants. The indoor **Nirmal** does cheap vegetarian fare, including tasty standard *thalis*. The garden restaurant, the **Eagle**, is the perfect spot to cool off after a hot, dusty day in the ruins. It serves a range of tasty non-vegetarian meals, and has a bar with ice-cold beers.

The Hotel Mayura has a restaurant and the **Shanbag Hotel**, next to the bus stand in Station Road, is famous for its vegetarian food, and is always crowded. Another **Shanbag,**, on the way to College Road, offers north Indian cuisine in comfortable and more relaxed surroundings.

In general you can eat out in Hospet for between Rs25 and Rs50 per head, going up to Rs100 if you have beer.

Moving On

By rail: the **Hampi Express** to Bangalore departs Hospet at 9pm and reaches Bangalore at 8am. For Hyderabad (13hrs) you have to change trains at Guntakal. At present, Goa only has bus services (10hrs travel plus the time between changes), but there are plans to re-open the railway line that used to run over the mountains to Hospet, once it has been built up to broad gauge—the projected opening date being some time in 1996/7.

By bus: there are 10 express buses daily from Bangalore (9hrs) and two from and to Hyderabad (11–12hrs). In addition, there are two buses a day to Mysore (10½hrs), and a few morning buses to Hubli, for Goa (4–5hrs). Hubli has one express bus to Panjim (departing at 11am, arriving 3pm), four slow buses to Panjim (7hrs), and one slow bus to Vasco da Gama (7–8hrs). There are also two trains (departing at 7am and 11pm) from Hubli to Goa. Gokarn, the jewel on Karnataka's coast, is 8hrs away by bus via Hubli, with several services daily.

Mysore   population 710,000

The golden age of maharajahs and princes may be over, but Mysore remains a splendid city of palatial buildings, beautiful gardens and handsome, tree-lined boulevards. There are 17 palaces here in all, and even the most common public buildings are adorned with domes, turrets, pavilions and vaulted archways. Many of the buildings are now in disrepair, but there is still a stately atmosphere to the place and Mysore's fame as the 'Sandalwood City' of the south remains undiminished. A major centre for the manufacture of incense, the air in its markets and bazaars is fragrant and sweet with the perfume of musk and jasmine, sandalwood and rose.

Mysore is the only state in the Deccan Plateau that managed to stay Hindu for almost all of its history. It derives its name from *Mahishasura*, the demon who wreaked havoc among the people in this area until destroyed by the goddess Chamunda. By the high Middle Ages, *Mahishuru* (town of Mahishasura), had become 'Mysore', the cradle of many great dynasties in the south. During the rule of the Hoysalas (12th to 14th centuries), art and architecture came to their peak, resulting in the famous sculptured temples of nearby Halebid, Belur and Somnathpur. Then, in the late 14th century, Mysore became the permanent capital of the Wodeyar Maharajahs. They lost it just once—to Hyder Ali in 1759—but regained it from the British after the death of Ali's son, Tipu Sultan, in 1799. Under the protection of the Raj, the Maharajahs had nothing left to fear and went into palace-building in a big way. Yet the coming of Independence in 1947 spelt the end of their power and of their many opulent palaces. The finest, Amber Vilas, was turned into a museum, another into an art gallery, and three more into luxury hotels. The tourist revenue coming in from these establishments is sufficient to guarantee the present Maharajah just as rich a lifestyle as that of his predecessors.

When to Go

Like Bangalore, Mysore is at a fairly high altitude (770 metres), giving it a pleasant climate throughout the year. It is most most temperate from September to January, but travellers drift in right up to May. The best two months are September and October, when the city is a post-monsoon spectacle of lush greenery and host to the 10-day festival of **Dussehra**. Turn up on the last day to see a victory procession of caparisoned elephants, jingling cavalry and (real) gold and silver coaches, accompanied by bands, floats and parading soldiers (all supplied by the present Maharajah), celebrating Chamundi's defeat of Mahishasura.

Most travellers come into Mysore from Bangalore, 2hrs away by **Shatabdi Express** train (not Tuesday). The same train takes 7hrs from Madras. Otherwise, there are regular bus services from Bangalore, Madras, Hospet, Ernakulam, Goa, Hyderabad, Mangalore, Ooty and Pune.

 Mysore is a compact town easily negotiable on foot. There is a lot to see and do in the centre, and some worthwhile excursion spots (Sriringapatnam, Chamundi, Somnathpur, Brindhavan) just outside it. Orientation is easy; you can walk from one end of the town to the other in about 30 minutes. Auto-rickshaws cost Rs5 for the first 2km, and because journeys are so short, you should never have to pay more than Rs15 anywhere, though you'll have to haggle and, if necessary, flag down the meter yourself. Local buses are useful for out-of-town destinations like Brindhavan, Chamundi, Sriringapatnam, Government Silk Weaving Factory etc., and leave from the bus stand near New Statue Square.

For a comprehensive viewing of the many sights, take one of the (good) city conducted tours. You can return to see the better ones another day.

Mysore ℂ (0821–)

KSTDC's **tourist office**, ℂ 22096, is open daily from 10am to 5.30pm, in the Old Exhibition Building, Irwin Road; waffly but helpful staff, poor handouts, but good information (hotels, tours) posted on various boards. KSTDC's **tourist reception centre**, ℂ 23652, is in Hotel Mayura Hoysala, open daily 6.30am–9pm. It sells the Mysore city sightseeing tour which includes Somnathpur (Rs85, 7.30am–8.30pm) and the over-ambitious tours to Belur-Halebid (Rs150, Tues, Wed, Fri, Sun) and to Ooty (Rs150, Mon, Thurs, Sat only). There are also tourist counters at the bus and railway stations. **Higginbotham's** have a useful bookshop inside the railway station.

Indian Airlines, ℂ 25349, is also in Hotel Mayura Hoysala complex, open daily 10am–1.30pm and 2.15–5.15pm except Sundays. In the likelihood of this office closing, you may have to do flight bookings/reconfirmations through private agents (like MITA, opposite the palace entrance) or via travel desks at hotels like the Metropole or Siddartha.

For **foreign exchange**, the State Bank of India is in St Mark's Road. Some of the local Canara Bank branches also change traveller's cheques, as will the managers at the Southern Star, if asked politely.

The central **post office** is in Ashoka Road.

The **Basapa Memorial Hospital** on Vinoba Road about 2km west of the Southern Star, and the huge colonial pile of the **Mary Holdsworth Hospital** on Sajaki Road in the town centre are recommended.

Mysore

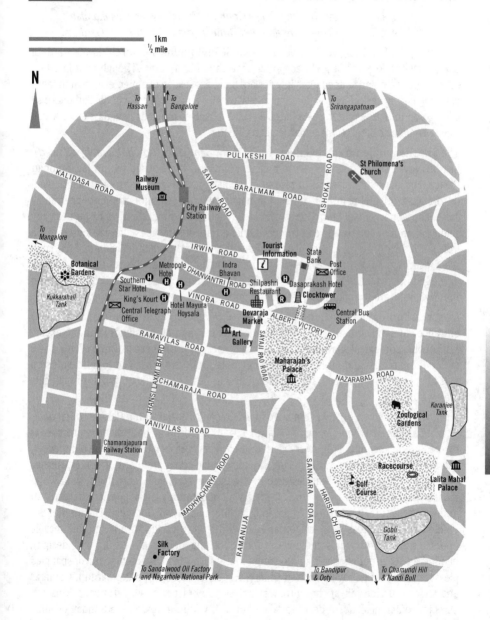

1km
½ mile

N

To Hassan
To Bangalore
To Srirangapatnam

KALIDASA ROAD
PULIKESHI ROAD
BARALMAM ROAD
ASHOKA ROAD
St Philomena's Church

Railway Museum
City Railway Station
SAYAJI ROAD

To Mangalore

IRWIN ROAD
Tourist Information
State Bank
Post Office

Botanical Gardens
Kukkarahalli Tank

Metropole Hotel
Indra Bhavan
DHANVANTRI ROAD
Shilpashri Restaurant
Dasaprakash Hotel
Clocktower

Southern Star Hotel
King's Kourt
VINOBA ROAD
Hotel Mayura Hoysala
Devaraja Market
Central Bus Station

Central Telegraph Office
RAMAVILAS ROAD
ALBERT VICTORY RD
SAYAJI RAO ROAD

Art Gallery

JHANSI LAXMI BAI RD
CHAMARAJA ROAD
Maharajah's Palace
NAZARABAD ROAD

VANIVILAS ROAD
Zoological Gardens
Karanjee Tank

Chamarajapuram Railway Station

MADHYACHARYA ROAD
RAMANUJA ROAD
SANKARA ROAD
HARISH CH RD

Racecourse
Golf Course
Lalita Mahal Palace

Gobli Tank

Silk Factory

To Sandalwood Oil Factory and Nagarhole National Park
To Bandipur & Ooty
To Chamundi Hill & Nandi Bull

City Tour, including Chamundi Hill

By tour bus, full day. St Philomena's Church–Art Gallery–Zoo–Maharajah's Palace–Chamundi Hill–Somnathpur–Sriringapatnam–Brindhavan Gardens.

If on tour, the first thing you'll probably see is **St Philomena's Church**, in the north of town. This is one of the largest neo-Gothic style churches in India. Though built in 1931, its lofty grandeur and stained-glass interior are more suggestive of a medieval than modern construction. Buses rarely stop long here (few of your co-passengers will be Catholics), so dash down into the crypt to see a life-size plaster image of the saint in a glass case. A side alcove contains a life-like image of the dead Christ.

The **Sri Chamarajendra Art Gallery** (*open daily, 8am–5pm, no photography allowed*), just off New Statue Square, is of more general interest. It is housed within Jaganmohan Palace, and contains treasures of rare musical instruments (mostly broken), exotic wall decorations, original paintings of Ravi Varma, a couple of beautiful mother-of-pearl inlay sofas, and a marvellous French musical clock (each second marked by a drum beat, toy soldiers march out on parade every hour). Other attractions include a life-size lobster made from carved ivory and grains of rice painted with microscopic pictures. Some of the landscape paintings are worth seeing—belonging to the Art Nouveau period, they owe much to the Indo-European version of that style. The late-Victorian life-size panels of scenes from the *Ramayana* are, by contrast, overly sentimental.

Mysore's **Zoological Gardens** (*open daily, 8.30am–5.30 pm; adm Rs8*), have their entrance gate on Lalitha Palace Road, 1km east of the central bus stand. With the exception of the zoological gardens in Hyderabad, these are the best in India. Over 1500 varieties of animals and birds live here, in near-natural surrounds. The tour doesn't stop half long enough, so come back another time (and early in the day, when the big cats are awake).

Dominating the town centre is the huge Indo-Saracenic **Maharajah's Palace** (*open daily, 10am–5.30pm; free tours every hour from 10am*), Mysore's main attraction. Entrance is by the South Gate only. Built over a period of 15 years (1897–1912) after the old wooden palace was razed by fire, this imposing structure, a gleaming profusion of domes, turrets, archways and colonnades, was designed by the English architect Henry Irwin, with workmanship by local artists. (The Hoysala-style wall decorations are of special interest.) An immense structure, it measures 74.5m long by 44m high by 47.5m wide. The interior is a Pandora's box of treasures—a Durbar Hall with jewel-studded throne, mosaic marble floors, crystal furniture, stained-glass domed ceiling (a miracle of art and design), hammered silver doors opening onto sumptuously furnished apartments, mirror-spangled pleasure rooms and a lovely portrait gallery. Hugely extravagant, but great fun. Cameras and shoes must be left at the entrance, unless you get permission from the Museum Director (office near ticket desk) to take photos. If you're in town on a Sunday evening between 7 and 9pm, return to the palace to see it brilliantly illuminated with thousands of tiny bulbs; the atmosphere is amazing.

The Maharajah's Palace

After your tour, walk round to the stables at the back of the palace, where the Maharajah still breeds thoroughbred horses. The grooms will be happy to show you around for a small *baksheesh*.

Chamundi Hill, 3/4km out of Mysore, has a cool altitude of 1072 metres and is a popular beauty spot with panoramic views. Once a royal summer resort, the hill is now a major pilgrimage and tourist centre. At the top, visit the 12th-century **Sri Chamundeswari Temple** (*open daily, 9am–noon and 5–9pm*), built in the southern Dravidian style with a distinctive *gopuram*. Inside there's an interesting pillar with silver panels depicting Ganesh, Nandi, and Shiva's trident, facing into the solid-gold Chamunda figure. In the open courtyard below it, you'll find the **Mahishasura Statue** (a giant technicolor pirate) erected in memory of Chamunda's slain demon.

To escape from the hype of the main temple complex, walk 800m down Chamundi Hill to the huge black granite monolith **Nandi Bull**—49m-high and the third-largest in India. The walk down affords beautiful views. If not on tour, you can walk from the bull down to the rickshaw stand at the foot of Chamundi Hill. Bargain hard for a Rs15 ride back to town (1km).

Out at **Somnathpur**, 45km from Mysore, there's one of the finest temples in the south (*open daily, 9am–5pm*). Built in 1268, and dedicated to Keshava, it is one of the three great **Hoysala Temples** of Karnataka. Covered with exquisite carvings portraying various scenes from the *Ramayana* and other epics (also numerous fascinating depictions of Hoysalan life and times), the temple is especially notable for the six horizontal friezes running round its baseline. The Rs1 entry includes a free guide service.

Next stop on the tour is the ruined town of **Sriringapatnam**, 16km out of Mysore. From this small island fortress-town, straddling the river Cauvery, came two brilliant Muslim leaders—Hyder Ali and his son Tipu Sultan—who ruled a powerful empire comprising much of southern India for 40 years. Tipu Sultan, the 'Tiger of Mysore', became the most dreaded foe of the British in the south, and inflicted two punishing defeats on the forces of the East India Company before being finally overcome in 1799. Tipu was killed and his town razed, but his elegant **Summer Palace**, or Daria Daulat Bagh (*open daily 9am–5pm*), remains intact. The British kept hold of it for their own use—Arthur Wellesley, later Duke of Wellington, lived here for a spell while serving as governor of Mysore.

Sriringapatnam is given insufficient time on tour. It's another one to see at leisure on another day. There are half-hourly buses to the town from Mysore, followed by a rickshaw or pony cart 2km out to the Summer Palace. The palace was built in 1784 (mainly of wood), and has a beautiful interior, painted in black, red and gold, and hung with portraits of Tipu's contemporaries. One of the murals commemorates Tipu and Hyder Ali's victory at Polilur, the plaque beneath mocking the opposing Deccan forces who arrived too late to help the British, with the taunt that 'they came like a boar and fled like a cow'. The superb little museum upstairs has a fascinating collection of engravings, family ink drawings, coins and prints illustrating Tipu's life and times, plus a number of his belongings. From the palace, take one of the waiting rickshaws 3km further on to the **Gumbaz**, burial place of Tipu and Hyder Ali.

A rickshaw from outside the Gumbaz (Rs15) will get you back to Sriringapatnam. Once here, walk in under the ruined gatehouse to the extensive fort ruins. To the right of these is the small plaque marking the spot where Tipu Sultan died in combat (or rather, where the British found him lying under a pile of redcoats he had killed). Nearby stands Tipu Sultan's mosque, the striking **Jami Masjid**, with its high minarets. Sriringapatnam gets a lot of tourists, but still has a lot of rustic charm—walking down the main street, you'll come to **Sri Ranganathaswamy Temple**, one of the oldest Dravidian temples in Karnataka (built 894). A prominent white blockstone structure, supported by hundreds of monolithic pillars, it houses a massive Vishnu reclining on a serpent and a soaring brass prayer column. Outside the temple are the town's *dhobi* ghats—stone steps leading down to the Cauvery River. The local kids collect unattended cameras and valuables, so keep these close to hand.

Note: Karnataka Tourism now runs **canoeing** and **white-water rafting** trips from Sriringapatnam down to the Cauvery Fishing Camp near the Biligiri Hills. These operate during the high-water season following the August rains. There is also a very good bird sanctuary some 2km southwest of Sriringapatnam (Rs20 return by rickshaw). Set in thick woods by the river, the **Ranganathittu Sanctuary** is home to vast numbers of heron, ibis, stork, spoonbill, tern and other waterfowl species. Boat rides around the waterways are available for a small extra cost. Crocodiles lurk by the marshy banks and you may spot an otter. Accommodation is provided at three riverside cottages, each with two double rooms, but these are usually full. The sanctuary levies a stiff Rs100 entrance fee from foreigners. In Sringapatnam, you can stay at cheap riverside cottages at the **Hotel Mayura River View**, ✆ 114.

Brindhavan Gardens

From Sriringapatnam to Mysore is a very picturesque ride, a continuous vista of palm-groves, paddy fields and sugar-cane plantations. For this journey alone, the bus tour is worthwhile. Last stop of the day is at the fabulous **Brindhavan Gardens**. Nineteen kilometres north of Mysore, these are among the best known of Karnataka's attractions. Beautifully terraced below the Krishnarajasagar Dam, Brindhavan's ornamental gardens take their name from an original series in Mathura, south of Delhi. Taking as their theme the pastoral frolics of Krishna with his 16,000 *gopis* (handmaidens), they are of enormous popularity among young Indian couples. In high season (April–May) up to 400 tour buses per day swarm up here. Weekends are also excessively busy. Arriving here around dusk, you'll have time to view the landscaped lawns, rose gardens, flower bowers and conifers in the vast southern section before the mass exodus starts via the central boating lake (Rs3 boat trips) to see the pretty musical 'dancing fountains' (*illuminated weekdays 7–8pm, weekends 7–9pm*). The gardens are also transformed into a colourful fairyland of cascading fountains and twinkling lights. The walk back to the tour bus is delightful.

For overnight stays, choose between the ex-palace **Krishnaraj Sagar Hotel**, *✆* Beluga 22, with rooms from Rs550 single, Rs700 double or the cheaper **KSTDC Tourist Home**, *✆* Beluga 52, with single and double rooms at Rs125 and Rs170. Both offer fine views, but are often full.

The Railway Museum

One sight rarely seen in Mysore is the marvellous **Rail Museum** (*open daily 9am–5pm, except Mon*) in Krishnarajasagar Road, just above the railway station itself. Almost as good as the one in Delhi, it houses antique engines, rolling stock, the Maharani's coach and a joyride mini-train.

Shopping

Mysore is famous for its incense and sandalwood, and these are the best buys. Other popular purchases are silk saris, printed silk, inlay work and jewellery.

To see the full range of **handicrafts**, visit **Kaveri Arts and Crafts Emporium**, (*✆* 21258), Sayaji Rao Road (closed Thursday), but avoid badly joined furniture and overpriced sandalwood. The best buys here are incense (*agarbathi*), rosewood (inlaid with deerbone, not ivory) and silk.

For quality **silks**, catch a no.4 or 5 bus out to the **Government Silk Weaving Factory** and **Karnataka Silk Industries Corporation Workshop**, both on Mananthody Road.

For pure **sandalwood**—carvings, powder, paste, dust, oil, incense and even soap —visit the small row of shops opposite the Zoo on Dhanvantri Road, round the corner from the Kaveri Emporium. These are a group of shops specializing in sandalwood and rosewood carvings; the town's best selection is probably to be found here. Compare prices from store to store before you begin bargaining.

If bargaining is too much of a hassle, head for the **Handicraft Sales Emporium**, ✆ 23669, where you can buy small sandalwood Buddhas or Indian deities from Rs200–300, bigger ones for Rs600–1200; sandalwood oil by the vial or bottle and sandalwood paste and powder by the ounce. The upstairs section does a fine line in gems and jewellery.

Apart from Jaipur, Mysore is the best place to buy semi-precious **stones** and **precious gems**. The rubies, garnets and lapis lazuli are of particularly high quality. But take care when buying a 'line' stone; the orientation is all-important. With moonstones, sapphires and rubies alike, the line *must* be central.

For **batiks** and good quality cotton *sulwars* (punjabi suits) try **Sarong** on Devaraj Urs Road. You can find good *khadi* fabric (handwoven cotton that breathes in the heat and keeps in the warmth) in the shops opposite the palace bus stand on Sayaji Road. If you buy some and want to get it made up, go to **Krishna**, a tailor specializing in Western-style clothes, whose shop is oppsite the entrance to the Shilpshri hotel and rooftop bar on Gandhi Square.

Mysore's **Devaraja Market** is probably the best fruit and vegetable market in India. It's certainly one of the largest, running all the way down Sayaji Rao Road from Dhanvantri Road to New Statue Square. There's one section devoted exclusively to bananas and their many varieties. You can wander round here all day, and not get bored. Nobody returns empty-handed. Good purchases here include colourful bangles, lacquerwork and crafted silver jewellery. Marvellous little souvenirs are the packs of 10 assorted incenses, sold for around Rs30. Be sure to pack these carefully.

Gita Book House, New State Square (near the bus stand), is possibly the only place in town which sells a decent Mysore map.

Leisure

There's a good **racecourse** below Chamundi Hill, with popular meetings on Wednesdays and at weekends during a three month season between September and November.

Karnataka Tourism offers 2–3 day trips **canoeing** down the Cauvery, starting at Sriringapatnam and ending up at the Cauvery Fishing Camp south of Mysore. For details contact Mysore's tourist office, ✆ 22096. You can also go white-water rafting on the Cauvery, starting from Sriringapatnam; ring ✆ 22906 for details.

Mysore has one of India's best **yoga** schools in the Lakshmi Puram neighbourhood, run by an 80-year old master who looks no more than 50. His particular brand of yoga, known as Asthanga Yoga, is much more physically demanding than the more traditional forms, as testified to by the superb bodies of the long-term yoga students who come from all over the world and pay in excess of US$300 a month for the daily tuition (Indians pay far less). Casual students are not allowed to take classes, only those staying for a month or more.

You can escape the heat by visiting the **pool** at the Southern Star—a regular meeting point for tourists and long-stay students. The non-resident fee (Rs150) is however stiff.

Though far more sedate than buzzing Bangalore, Mysore is quite sophisticated and offers much more in the way of **nightlife** than most Indian towns, with some reasonable bars and dance clubs as well as the more traditional forms of entertainment. The city's nightlife is starting to concentrate in and around Sri Harsha Road. Unfortunately, at the time of writing, there is a total ban on live music, but this is likely to be only a temporary measure.

Two **cinemas**, the Woodlands and the Ritz, show English films as matinées. Others, like the Shalimar and Sterling, show English films all day; they are both in the same building, a fair way out of town. All cinema listings can be found in the *Deccan Herald* newspaper.

Nightly *sitar* and *tabla* **recitals** are given to diners at the outdoor Park Lane Restaurant on Sri Harsha Road, just opposite Curzon Park, and at the Lalitha Mahal's restaurant. Regular **classical dance** performances are given at the theatre inside the Chamarajendra Art Gallery in the old Jagamohan Palace. Dates are advertised in the *Deccan Herald*.

Away from the big hotels, Mysore has two lovely rooftop **bars**, the Shilpashri, and the slightly more run-down Durbar, both opposite each other on Gandhi Square. The only **disco** in town takes place every Saturday night at the Southern Star.

Mysore ✆ (0821–)

Where to Stay

luxury (from Rs 3000)

The **Lalitha Mahal Palace**, T. Narasipur Road, ✆ 26316/ 27650, ✉ 33398, has some stylish rooms in a beautiful old building overlooking the city, but the service is poor. A little cheaper and in the centre of town, is the good **Southern Star**, ✆ 27217, ✉ 32175, on Vinoba Road, next door to the Hotel Metropole (*see* below). The Southern Star has excellent buffet breakfasts, but the rooms are bland. Rooms start at Rs1895 for a double.

expensive (from Rs 750)

Mysore's most stylish hotel is the **Metropole**, ✆ 520681, ✉ 520854, on the corner of Jhansi Lakshmibai Road and Vinoba Road. A colonial set-piece, its vast airy dining room is still presided over by the stuffed head of the largest tiger to be shot by the last Maharajah. In its small, shady bar, the waiter will bring you your bill in a little teakwood box and the rooms are still furnished with Victoriana. Non a/c doubles are around Rs850, a/c Rs990.

Hotel Dasaprakash Paradise, 104 Vivekananda Road, Yadavagiri, ✆ 515565, ✉ 514400, is in the suburbs, about 2km north of the railway station, but is the town's best Indian-style hotel, with a very good restaurant and a pool. Ask for 3rd-floor rooms overlooking the Chamundi Hills. A/c doubles cost around

Rs840. If you can't get in, try the comfortable a/c **King's Kourt**, ✆ 25250, ✉ 32684, on Jhansi Lakshmibai Road, opposite the Metropole. The staff aren't geared to foreigners, but the rooms (from Rs990 double) are clean and pleasant enough.

moderate (from Rs 300)

Most of Mysore's new crop of mid-range hotels in Mysore are in and around Sri Harsha Road. Best of the bunch is the **Viceroy**, ✆ 24001, ✉ 25410, close to the palace, with suite-size a/c rooms from Rs700, and warm and friendly staff. An enjoyable Indian-style hotel (actually an old hotel renovated to look like new) is the popular **Siddharta**, 73 Guesthouse Road, Nazarbad, ✆ 26869, with large carpeted rooms, tiled bathrooms and free newspapers. Doubles cost Rs450 (a/c). The **Lokranjan Mahal Palace**, ✆ 21868, on the eponymous Lokranjan Mahal Road is very good value for the price, with colonial-style rooms (some a/c), plenty of atmosphere and a pool. Otherwise, there's KTDC's **Mayura Hoysala** at 2 Jhansi Lakshmi Bai Road, ✆ 25349—very much a case of pot luck, but generally clean.

budget

There's not much in the cheap range, and what there is is often full. Opposite the railway station, in Dhanvantri Road, you'll find two old favourites: the dirt-cheap **New Gayathri Bhavan**, ✆ 521224, and **Indra Bhavan**, ✆ 23933, which is the most friendly, informative budget place in town, with quiet, clean rooms (mostly common bath), two good restaurants and an STD phone. The popular **Park Lane**, ✆ 30400, opposite Curzon Park on Sri Harsha Road, has clean but basic rooms (starting at Rs90) still decorated Raj-style, as well as one of the town's best open-air restaurants. Over at Gandhi Square, the **Durbar**, ✆ 520029, has okay rooms and two very popular restaurants, including a rooftop bar. The nearby **Srikanth**, ✆ 22951, is also worth checking out for its clean rooms with bath. The seedy but popular **Dasaprakash** (just around the corner from the Durbar) has a few rooms with shower from Rs100. Try also the **Govardhan** on Sri Harsha Road, a friendly place with a cheap vegetarian restaurant, and the **Cauvery** on Ashok Road, where many of the long-term yoga students stay.

Eating Out

The **Metropole** is the place to dine in style: a stately, palatial restaurant offering well-priced Indian, Chinese and continental cuisine and elegant service. Eat well here for Rs250. Then relax in the quaint **Planter's Inn** bar. Cheaper but equally stylish is the outdoor eatery at **Park Lane Hotel**, where you can sit in a tree-shaded courtyard, and enjoy an outdoor barbecue (nightly) for Rs60/70. A little red light bulb hangs above each table, which, if you pull the cord, immediately attracts a waiter suppressing a kind of desperate irritation at being so summoned. The **Lalitha Mahal Palace** is recommended for Indian food, but service is poor.

At the **Southern Star Hotel**, the main restaurant has extensive buffets (breakfast and lunch) for Rs125 and a 24-hour coffee shop. Over at the **Dasaprakash**, there's a famous vegetarian restaurant, with meals around Rs80–120 per head and a great ice cream parlour.

Two popular rooftop bar/restaurants in Gandhi Square are **Shilpashri**, ☎ 25979 (consistently good food, nice bar, but expect to queue), and **Durbar** (lots of shoe-stringers, tinny taped music). An evening at either will cost you around Rs100, including a beer.

Indian vegetarian food is at its cheapest and best at the backpacker hotels: the **New Gayatri Bhavan, Dasaprakash** and **Indra Bhavan**. A little more upmarket, the **Siddhartha** hotel offers all you can eat in a/c comfort for around Rs40 per head.

Indra's Fast Food on Devaraja Urs Road is inexpensive and serves the best *chaat* (south Indian snack dishes) in Mysore. It's also a hang-out for local students, eager to try out their English on you. **Samrhat** on Dhavantri Road does good north and south Indian *thalis* from Rs35, including *nan* and a drink, as does **Paras Café** on Sayaji Road.

Moving On

By air: the nearest airport is at Bangalore, but Indian Airlines have an office at the Hotel Mayura Hoysala, open 10am to 1.30pm and 2.15 to 5pm daily except Sundays.

By rail: few people go anywhere from Mysore by rail, most track in and out still being on narrow-metre gauge track and involving at least one long stop along the way. The only exception is the daily (except Tuesday) **Shatabdi Express** (dep Mysore 2.20pm), which stops at Bangalore (4.30pm) before continuing on to Madras (arr 9.15pm). You can buy your a/c chair-car tickets inside the railway station up to 1hr before departure.

By bus: the new Central bus stand to the north of town offers express buses to Bangalore (every 20 minutes; 3hrs), to Mangalore (7hrs), to Ooty (5hrs), and to Ernakulam (13hrs). Nearby, opposite Hotel Mannars, more comfortable private buses go to all the above places; also to Bombay, Hyderabad, Coimbatore (14hrs) and Pune. There's a useful cloakroom at the main bus stand where you can leave your bags if you're only visiting Mysore for the day.

Excursion from Mysore to Bandipur National Park

Bandipur is part of what is now called the Nilgiri Biosphere—a vast conserved wild area that includes Mudumalai National Park in Tamil Nadu, Wynad in Kerala and Nagarhole and Bandipur in Karnataka. The southernmost nature reserve in Karnataka, Bandipur is also one of its largest. Alas, it is also the most crowded, being within easy reach of Mysore. There are direct bus services connecting Bandipur's entrance office with Mysore, running roughly every hour between 7.30am and 3.30pm.

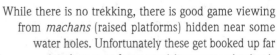

While there is no trekking, there is good game viewing from *machans* (raised platforms) hidden near some water holes. Unfortunately these get booked up far in advance so for most visitors game viewing is limited to big, rattling government vehicles (some jeeps, some minibuses) on a few shortish roads, and to even shorter elephant rides near the main office.

As most of the wildlife stays in the 'core' region of the park, where tourists are not allowed, serious wildlifers will find the place a bit frustrating, knowing that there are rare species like tiger, leopard and sloth bear in the forest. If you get lucky and see anything other than spotted deer, distant bison or perhaps elephant, the animal will quickly run away as the occupants of your vehicle shout and exclaim excitedly.

If you do visit Bandipur, do so between November and February, after the rains and before the hot season. In the summer (February–August), the deciduous forest (mainly teak, rosewood, and silk-cotton) loses its leaves. Most of the game then migrates over to the eastern slopes of the Western Ghats. You will certainly need a few days to have any chance of spotting something, so it is worth booking accommodation inside the park, if it's not full.

Where to Stay
inexpensive/budget

Bandipur has cheap dormitory accommodation near the park office at the main reception area, as well as several slightly more expensive lodges and cottages. If you can, book the one called **Venuvihar Lodge** up in the Gopalaswamy Hills, deep in the forest. It is hard to get accommodation in Bandipur and it must all be booked in advance, either directly through the Field Director of Project Tiger, Mysore, ℂ 20901, or through a travel agency specializing in wildlife areas. Try **Clipper Holidays** in Bangalore, ℂ (080) 5599032/34. Avoid visiting at weekends if you want to be sure of getting somewhere to stay in the park.

Former summer capital of the Madras Presidency (now Tamil Nadu), Ootacamund, often known by its shorterned name of Ooty, is popularly known as the 'Queen of Hill Stations', though the quiet charm it once had has been somewhat eroded over the past decades by its expansion into a small city with attendant crowds and dirt. Ooty now sprawls over several hills and into a wide valley of the Nilgiris (Blue Hills) near the junction of Karnataka, Tamil Nadu and Kerala, at an altitude of 2308 metres. Famous for being an eccentric place (snooker was invented here, the local army headquarters still keeps a pack of foxhounds and herds of wild ponies sometimes force you off the pavement), Ooty is within reach of some of India's most spectacular scenery and offers access to some of the Western Ghats most interesting tribal regions.

Ootacamund derives its name from a Toda term *Othakamanthu*, meaning 'village of huts'. The Todas, original settlers here before the British, are an aboriginal tribe who still own much of the wild grasslands of the countryside immediately north of Ooty. They still live in curved, wattle longhuts and worship a buffalo goddess, tending large herds of the beasts on the natural downlands. It is possible to trek into and sometimes to stay, in their settlements, as well as to other tribes of the area (*see* below).

The site for Ooty was discovered by the then Collector of Coimbatore, John Sullivan, who built first a residence (1819) and then created the lake (1823). The British quickly moved in, erecting stone cottages with flower gardens, laying the beautiful Botanical Gardens (1840) and developing facilities for golf, horse-racing, polo and tennis. In 1869, the hill station became the summer headquarters of the government in Madras, with a rigidly stratified social life centred on the exclusive Ooty Club.

Today, 'Snooty Ooty' is a rather rundown resort and retirement home for the rich. But it remains a popular watering hole for travellers, with a definite air of elegance and refinement still clinging to parts of it. There are Raj reminders everywhere, notably in the terraced Botanical Gardens, the English public schools, the churches and, above the town, the tea-gardens and eucalyptus plantations. At the centre of town is the huge (if scruffy) racecourse and in summer the stables here are still full of horses in training and racing meetings are held once a fortnight.

When to Go

Even the climate is British; cool and drizzly, even frosty, in the winter and one of the few places in India you'll need to bring warm clothing. Though most popular in September/October and April/May, it's far cheaper (low-season hotel discounts) and far less crowded in February and March. Ooty has its big **Summer Festival** throughout the month of May with tribal dances, live music and drama shows, held every evening at Anna Stadium. There's even a ballroom dancing competition when they can find enough people to participate!

Getting There

There are daily flights between Coimbatore (3hrs by bus from Ooty) and Bangalore, Bombay and Madras.

The steam train up and down the spectacular escarpment between Ooty and Coimbatore on the plains leaves from Ooty to Mettupalyam/Coimbatore at 9.15am and 2.50pm daily and back to Ooty at 7.40am and 9.30am. There are also connections to Madras, Madurai, Cochin and other major destinations.

Buses link with Mysore, Bangalore, Kodaikanal, Madras and Coimbatore.

For further information, *see* 'Moving On', p.569.

Getting Around

 Ooty is more a place to use as a jumping-off point for the Nilgiri wildlife and tribal areas, than a destination in its own right. However, the tens of thousands of Indian holiday-makers who come up here every year would say otherwise and the town is definitely geared for tourism.

If you decide to stay for a few days, there are still some lovely walks in the hills on the fringes of the town and the bazaar is worth exploring for its medieval feel. Many of the available walks climb to viewpoints over the town and surrounding country and, owing to the spread-out nature of these viewpoints, you'll need some sort of plan. The walking routes suggested below cover the main points of interest but there are several other mini-treks available.

In town, get around on foot, by cycle (hire bicycles in the market) or by auto-rickshaw (Rs10 for short trips). The focal point of the small town is Commercial Street and the Upper and Lower Bazaars, which run parallel with it. The tourist office and banks are on Commercial Street, while the jewellers, bakers and craftsmen are in the bazaars.

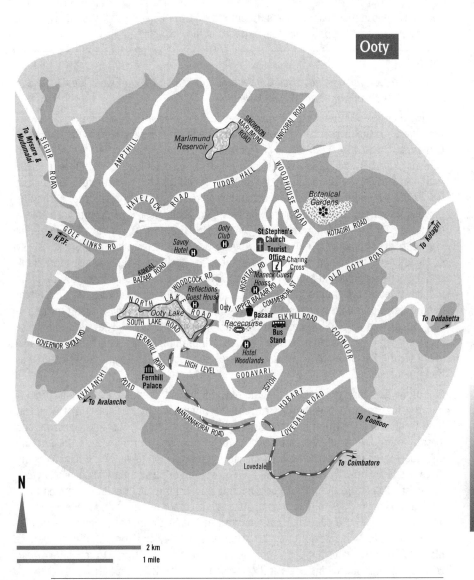

Marlimund
Reservoir

Botanical
Gardens

To Mysore &
Mudumalai

SIGUR ROAD

AMPTHILL

HAVELOCK ROAD

TUDOR HALL

SNOWDON
MARLIMUND
ROAD

ANICORAL ROAD

WOODHOUSE ROAD

KOTAGIRI ROAD

To H.P.F.

GOLF LINKS RD

Ooty
Club
H

St Stephen's
Church

Savoy
Hotel **H**

Tourist
Office

Charing
Cross

To Kotagiri

OLD OOTY ROAD

KANDAL
BAZAAR ROAD

WOODCOCK RD

HOSPITAL RD

Maneck Guest
House
H

UPPER BAZAAR RD

COMMERCIAL ST

Reflections
Guest House

NORTH LAKE ROAD

Ooty

Ooty Lake

SOUTH LAKE ROAD

Bazaar

Racecourse

ELK HILL ROAD

Bus
Stand

To Dodabetta

GOVERNOR SHOLA RD

FERNHILL ROAD

HIGH LEVEL

Hotel
Woodlands
H

COONOOR

AVALANCHI ROAD

Fernhill
Palace

GODAVARI

HOUSE

HOBART

To Avalanche

MANJANAKORAI ROAD

LOVEDALE ROAD

To Coonoor

Lovedale

To Coimbatore

N

| 2 km |
| 1 mile |

Ooty ☎ (0423–)   ***Tourist Information***

The **tourist office** at the Super Market building, Charing Cross, ☎ 396, organizes tours. There's far better information (and good sightseeing tours) at **King Travels** across the road, ☎ 3137, and **Blue Mountain Tours**, Nahar Shopping Centre, Charing Cross.

The **post office** is near the Collectorate and the **State Bank of India** overlooks Commercial Street. **Higginbotham's bookshop** has two branches: the main one is opposite Chellaram's department store in the Charing Cross area, while the other one is opposite the main entrance to the post office.

Walk 1

On foot, full day. Botanical Gardens–St Stephen's Church–Ooty Club–Ooty Lake–Golf Club–Wenlock Downs

From either bus or railway station on the east edge of the lake, it's a winding 2km walk northwest (via the racecourse, up busy, traffic-cursed Commercial Street) to the **Botanical Gardens**. Created by the Marquis of Tweeddale in 1847, these are 51 acres of terraced gardens and extensive lawns housing 650 varieties of plants. There's a big **Flower Show** here each May and visitors can buy flowers and seedlings from the Curator's office. Just below the mini-lake, check out the intriguing 20 million-year-old fossil tree. Ascending through gardens of ornamental plants, orchids, ferns, conifers and rockplants keep an eye out for the local Toda community (*see* 'The Nilgiri Hills', p.570) on the top levels—the closest tribal community to Ooty town. About 2000 of them live here, almost exclusively engaged in the cultivation of potatoes and weaving, having left behind their more tradi-tional practise of buffalo-herding to trade with the townspeople and tourists. However, the women at least have kept to their traditional look, boasting tattooed skins, wearing bright handwoven clothes, keeping their hair in distinctive plaited loops and running their fami-lies with an iron rod. Toda women, unlike Tamil, are very feminist. They used to practise polyandry, having up to four husbands apiece, all of them henpecked. Near the village, you'll see the **Raj Bhavan** (Government House), still used by the Tamil Nadu Governor as a summer residence.

Out of the gardens, turn right at the end of Garden Road, then make a hairpin turn left into Higgins Road to **St Stephen's Church**; a 20-minute ascent. The creation of a Captain John Underwood (1829), it is a typically English parish church, with Gothic exterior and Tuscan interior. Just below it is the select **Ooty Club**, well worth a visit for its amazing collection of Raj memorabilia (contact manager for permission to view) and famous as the place where snooker was invented in 1875. From here, it's a straight walk down to **Ooty Lake**: small, picturesque, with good boating and fishing facilities but crowded with raucous holiday-makers in season and flanked by syces, or horse-copers, desperate to get you up onto one of their underfed, overworked ponies for a short, expensive (Rs60–100/hour) ride. Still, get out onto the water on a hot day and you'll find it the perfect place to spend an afternoon messing about in boats. The **Boat House** here (*open 8am–6pm*) hires out rowing boats at Rs60 per hour (with a Rs35 deposit).

In the afternoon, try a lovely 6km walk (3 hours return) up to the **Golf Club**, bear right at the top of the Lake, then left at Finger Post into Golf Links Road. The scenery is very varied and picturesque and if you turn up at 9am sharp, you can usually get a game of golf (Rs150 green fee including hire of clubs and balls) on the expansive 18-hole course. A kilometre and a half further on, you'll come to **Wenlock Downs**, offering spectacular views down over the local Bodega villages, the Coimbatore plains, Ketti Valley, the Mysore plateau and the tea estates. The more adventurous among you will notice that there are many unmarked paths snaking away into the plantation forestry around here.

These are used by the local Bodega villagers for their firewood forages and make for lovely forest walking if you have a good sense of direction. In some of the glades you may surpise *sambar* deer or even *gaur* if you are out at either dawn or dusk and in some of the natural *shola* forest in the herat of these plantations, Nilgiri *langurs* still live among the evergreen trees.

Walk 2

By bus, then on foot, 5–6 hours. Dodabetta Heights.

This is a very pleasant excursion, best done in the afternoon. Take a bus (20-minute journey, regular service from Ooty bus stand) up to **Dodabetta Heights**, the highest peak (nearly 3000 metres) in the Nilgiris. There's an observation point with telescope at the top and on a clear day the views down over the hill ranges, plateaux and plains are superb. But the walk back down's a 3–4 hour, 9.5km descent through tea-gardens, terraced fields, wooded glades and pretty valleys. If you get tired, you can always hitch a bus for a quick lift back to town.

Other good viewpoints in the area include **Snowdon Peak** (panoramic view of Mysore), **Cairn Hill** (overlooking Avalanche River) and **Elk Hill**, which is just an hour's walk from Ooty. Further information, plus details of the many local treks available from the Trek Director, Department of Tourism, Government of Tamil Nadu, Madras (✆ 849803).

For real **trekking**, the Nilgiri Hills offer some of the most spectaculalr routes in India. A selection of these and their wildlife and tribal possibilities is included in the Nilgiri section on p.570.

Shopping

Tribal Toda jewellery, embroidered shawls and silver can be found at **Suraaj** in Main Bazaar, or **Suraaj Paradise** in Commercial Road. Prices are not cheap, so bargain hard. **Vimal Gems and Jewellery,** next to Nahar Hotel in Charing Cross, has a good selection of silver jewellery, semi-precious stones and Nilgiri spices and honey. Two government emporia nearby, **Poompuhar** and **Chellarams**, sell the full range of Ooty handi-crafts at fixed prices. Buy tea and eucalyptus oil, the two most famous local products, at **Idco Tea** next to the tourist office. Home-made chocolate is another Ooty speciality. There are shops all over town but the **Sugar Daddy** outdoor ice cream parlour on Commercial Street stands out, about three blocks towards the bus stand from the tourist office.

Leisure

If walking, pony-riding, boating and golfing are not enough, there's good **fishing** to be had (carp and trout) at Emerald and Parson's Valley and in Ooty Lake itself (contact the Assistant Director of Fisheries near the bus stand, ✆ 2232, for a licence). For **indoor games:** badminton, table tennis, visit Anna Stadium, below the Botanical Gardens. Of the several cinemas in town, the Liberty in Commercial Road is most popular.

NB: In Ooty's hotels, rates are heavily discounted in the low season but charge 25% more during the Christmas–New Year period and in the May–June holidays.

luxury (from Rs 1400)

There is a choice of deluxe rooms or cottages with verandah at Taj Group's reputable and elegant colonial-style **Hotel Savoy**, 77 Sylks Road, © 44142/3/4, ✆ 443318, the town's most famous Raj-era hotel. Good golf and poor quality horse-riding can be arranged here.

The Taj group have also recently taken over the **Fernhill Palace**, © 43910, tlx 08504, built in 1842 by the Maharajahs of Mysore and set in a large estate. Although less well renovated than the Savoy, Fernhill is much more attractive, with its own woods and extensive gardens and a fantastic view out over the hills. For about US$60 you can have the Maharajah's own suite. If you ask, log fires are lit in the bedrooms and there is more Raj memorabilia than you can shake a stick at—animal heads, framed photos of the Ooty hunt in its heyday, an antique, professional-sized billiard table and a great hall. A word of warning though—stick to Indian items in the restaurant, despite the tempting French dishes on offer. They sound better than they taste.

In the same grounds as Fernhill is the **Regency Villa**, © 43910, an attached shooting lodge and a smaller more intimate version of the palace. Prices are also a little lower and the food is good.

expensive (from Rs 1000)

The most atmospheric hotel in this range is the **Nilgiri Woodlands**, © 42551, which overlooks the racecourse on Ettines Road. This is a late-Victorian set-piece, a little run down but still handsome. Its lawns and verandahs are a blessed relief from the bustle of the main town and it has a decent restaurant. Choose between standard double rooms, self-contained cottages and old four-poster deluxe rooms. **Merit Inn Southern Star**, Havelock Road, © 43601, ✆ 43287, is in better nick but is a bland modern building.

moderate (from Rs 650)

Hotel Lake View, West Lake Road, © 43904/43580, ✆ 43579, has a nice location overlooking the wide lake and clean, comfortable double rooms. **Reflections Guest House** on North Lake Road, is about three-quarters of a kilometre north of the bus stand, © 43834, overlooking the lake. It has double rooms and cheaper dorms. The restaurant is good—both for Indian and Western food and you can eat on an outdoor terrace. Ask Douglas, the owner, to play guitar for you—he's a virtuoso.

budget

Ooty has some very good budget lodges. First choice goes to the Jain-run **Maneck Tourist Home**, on the Main Bazaar, © 43494, which has clean, double rooms overlooking the racecourse with small en suite bathrooms (Indian style) and a decent vegetarian restaurant downstairs. Also good value is the **Nahar Hotel**, Charing Cross, ✆ 42173, run by jolly Babuji. It's well run, well located and has a bakery, vegetarian restaurant and cosy rooms.

The **YWCA** on Anandagiri, Ettines Road, near the bus stand, ✆ 42218, caters for both men and women and has a few charming cottage rooms. **Vishu Lodge** in the bazaar has nice clean rooms, with bath.

Eating Out

For a real taste of the Raj, try to get invited to lunch or dine at the Ooty Club. If this is not possible dine out at **Fernhill Palace**. The palatial 'restaurant' features elegant but painfully slow service, romantic lighting and well-priced Mughlai/continental cuisine. Eat well for around Rs150 a head and have a chuckle over the menu.

Punjabi food is good at **Paradise Restaurant** in Commercial Road and the nearby **Tandoor** is reliable for non-vegetarian fare. Both cost from Rs60 per head. **Nahar Tourist Home** has a cheap vegetarian restaurant, popular with *thali*-lovers. **Shinkows** in Commissioner's Road (near the Collectorate) is best for Chinese food, while town residents favour **Kurungi** (near the tourist office) for local-style Indian meals. Of Ooty's many bakeries, **V K Bakery**, 148 Commercial Road, still makes just about the best piping-hot fresh bread, mutton puffs, coconut balls, pies and cakes in India!

For cheap but good value, the **Maneck Restaurant** serves very good, if rather limited Jain vegetarian food in the downstairs restaurant of the Maneck Tourist Home on the Main Bazaar. At **Reflections Guest Lodge**, on the road overlooking the lake, about three-quarters of a kilometre north of the bus stand, there is a decent, cheap continental menu. Otherwise, buy your supper from one of the many street-side bakeries at the bus stand.

Moving On

By air: **Indian Airlines** has daily flights between Coimbatore (3hrs by bus from Ooty) and Bangalore, Bombay and Madras.

By rail: the steam train up and down the spectacular escarpment between Ooty and Coimbatore on the plains leaves from Ooty to Mettupalyam/Coimbatore at 9.15am and 2.50pm daily and back to Ooty at 7.40am and 9.30am. From Coimbatore, there are regular mainline trains for Madras, Madurai, Cochin and other major destinations. To reach Mettupalyam directly from Madras take the **Nilgiri Express** which leaves Madras Central at 9pm and arrives at 7.20am in time to connect with the waiting **Nilgiri Passenger** to Ooty via stations with names such as Hill Grove, Coonoor, Ketti and Lovedale.

By bus: Ooty's smart, efficient bus stand has a handy reservation desk for buses to

Mysore (6.30am, 8am, 12.30pm, 1.30pm, 3pm; 4½hrs) and for Bangalore (10am, 10.30am and 10pm; 8hrs). There are also two buses daily to Kodaikanal and to Madras, and half-hourly buses to Coimbatore (3hrs).

The Nilgiri Hills

Trekking into wildlife and tribal regions can be done more easily in the Nilgiris than in any other part of the Western Ghats. At an average elevation of around 2133m, with some much higher peaks, the Nilgiris themselves also offer some of the country's most spectacular scenery. Their high downlands (properly referred to as Watershed Grassland) are reminiscent of British uplands, while in some places reservoirs and huge pine plantations give the landscape a North American feel.

The area has several tribal groups: the Bodegas, who farm the land around Ooty; the buffalo-rearing, feminist Todas, who use the downs for grazing and still live in longhuts; the Kotas, known for making musical instruments and the forest-dwelling Kurumbas of the north slopes of the Nilgiris, who have a reputation for making magic and who still, in some places, live by shifting forest agriculture and hunting.

Trekking into the Tribal Regions

Trekking into the Toda, Kota and Kurumba settlements can be arranged only through a guide known to and trusted by the tribals. If you try to go in independently, language is a problem and there is a general distrust of outsiders—they do not want hordes of people coming to gawp at them. Like tribal people all over India, those of the Nilgiris have had to fight hard to resist the appropriation of their land by local government and developers. By request of the tribal headmen consulted by the author, the location of settlements will not be detailed, only how to contact a guide known to them.

To organize a trek into the Toda, Kota or Kurumba settlements, this guide can confidently recommend one (rather eccentric) guide, who accompanied the author and is known personally to the villagers. His name is R. Seniappan (or 'Sini') and he can be contacted through his home on 137 Upper Bazaar, in Ooty. Or contact Habeeb Mustapha at 67 Grant Duff Road, Valley View, Lovedale, ✆ 43057. Be warned though—these can be hard treks and accommodation in tribal villages is necessarily basic. You will also be expected to eat any food offered—including buffalo curd and butter-milk (not to everyone's taste).

Other specialist treks, for botanic, tribal and wildlife interest can be arranged locally through R. Ranjeet, of 'Meghdoot', Bokkapuram, Masinagudi (south of Ooty towards Mysore), ✆ 216; or in advance through Ranjan Abraham at Clipper Holidays, Suite 406, Regency Enclave, 4 Magrath Road, Bangalore 560 025, ✆/✉ (080) 5599032/34/5599833. Ranjan, a conservationist himself, offers one of the only reliable services for eco-tourism in India.

The Tribes

Most accessible (even as a daytrip from Ooty) are the **Todas**, who own most of the grasslands north of town and have protected them against the creeping settlement that is ruining the southern Nilgiris. With the protection of their buffalo goddess and the wealth of their buffalo herds, the 1500 Todas who still live traditionally, look set to stay in their economically strong position. Not only do they differ from the Tamils in religion, they also do in custom, as the women more or less run things and the men tend to hover in the background, often being told to shut up when they interject. For India—a man's society if ever there was one, this makes a refreshing change. Marriages are simple but beautiful, the couple going off to a tree in one of the *sholas* and dedicating themselves to the spirit there, before returning, hand-in-hand, to the village. Although the Todas will allow their youngfolk to marry outsiders, those who do may never return to the village.

The Todas also look physically different from both the Tamils and the other Nilgiri tribespeople, having more Caucasian features and a way of wearing both their embroidered cloths—almost like togas—and their hair (the women hang theirs in ringlets) that differs greatly from anything else in south India. Tradition states that their ancestors were soldiers of Alexander the Great, who migrated down from the conquered territories of the Indus Valley sometime in the 3rd or 2nd centuries BC. Whether this is true or not, they certainly look more northern Indian/Middle Eastern than Dravidian.

By contrast, the Kotas and Kurumbas are much darker and more delicately featured. Also unlike the Todas, both tribes speak dialects of Tamil and their religions are loosely based around Hinduism. The **Kotas** cultivate a philosophy of peace—towards both animals and men and regard blood-letting of any kind as sacrilegious. In fact, their religion has many parallels with Jainism and it has even been suggested that other similar tribal ideologies of non-violence may have been the wellspring from which Jainism developed. More 'modern' than the Todas (meaning that they cultivate crops and sell them at local markets), the Kotas are nonetheless regarded less as farmers than as a distinct society of craftsmen: skills in musical instrument-making, metal-working, woodcarving and pottery are passed from father to son and the Kotas are in great demand for their musicianship at religious festivals throughout the region. There are about 2000 Kotas currently living in the Nilgiris.

The **Kurumbas** (the name means 'forest-dweller') were traditionally the shamen, or medicine-men, for the other Nilgiri tribespeople and were held in some fear. Their hunter-gatherer culture changed only recently—though it persists in some deep parts of the northern Nilgiri jungles—to working for the local forestry and agricultural companies and certain Toda and Badega groups still seek out Kurumba diviners to make contact with the spirit world. Like the Kotas, today there are around 2000 Kurumbas in the region.

Two other tribes inhabit the southern and eastern sections of the Nilgiris: the Irulas and Kasavas. The **Irulas** have a tradition of herbal medicine and also fulfil certain religious functions for the rest of the Nilgiri peoples, including officiating at a great outdoor festival to the spirits of virility (Rangasamy) on Rangasamy peak, in the Kota territory. Like the Kurumbas, the forest-dwelling **Kasavas** were hunter-gatherers until recently. Nowadays they are mainly plantain cultivators, though certain groups have gone back to the forest.

Far more primitive are the Chodaikanal or **Sholanaikan** tribe; semi-nomadic cave-dwellers and hunters who live in the jungles of the southwestern end of the Nilgiris, where they spill over into Kerala. However, access to this area is completely restricted and the tribespeople themselves have deliberately resisted western influences and wish for no contact with travellers. The Sholanaikan men gather wild honey and use fire-hardened bamboo spears to take small forest game, while the women provide the bulk of the food—roots and forest fruits.

Trekking into the Mountains and Wildlife Sanctuaries

More mainstream trekking in the Nilgiris is also very rewarding. The following is a list of routes and where to stay in Forestry and Wildlife Department resthouses. Bear in mind that you have to apply for permission to stay in these places and that this can be incredibly hard to obtain. Your best bet is to put it into the hands of either Sini or Ranjan (*see* 'Trekking into the Tribal Regions' above), or somebody recommended by them and to give them at least two weeks' notice to get the paperwork in order. Otherwise take a tent and make do for yourself but be ready to be cold at night and remember that you are not allowed to make fires in the Nilgiris.

Mukurthi Peak and Mukurthi National Park

This involves an overnight trek. Take a bus from Ooty to Anumupruram, near Pykara (about 40km) and hike the last 11km to the National Park. Accommodation is in a Wildlife Association hut but you take your own food and sleeping bag. Mukurthi Peak is a jagged, conical *arrête*, that the Todas refer to as the 'gateway to the world of the dead'. Rather, it is an idyllic landscape of high pasture, grazed by Nilgiri *tahr* and a pathway for roving bands of elephant migrating between Kerala and Tamil Nadu. The hidden rainforest of Silent Valley lies on the southwest part of the park but to get here you need to set aside at least three days.

Avalanchi

This is another high upland trek, with good possibilties of spotting Nilgiri *tahr*. Again, you should allow for at least an overnight stay; take a bus from Ooty to the Trout Hatchery, about 32km south of the town and hike the remaining 4.5km into the trekking region along the lake called Avalanche. Once in the wilderness area, you will travel though extensive areas of *shola* forest, where you stand a good chance of seeing Nilgiri *langurs*. Accommodation is in a beautiful Forest Department guest house near the Trout Hatchery. Built in the 1850s, its sound wooden walls still sport the trophy antlers of huge *sambar* deer. A guide for this trip is imperative, as there are no maps and the forest areas are too dense to risk getting lost in.

Upper Bhavani

You can trek into this region from Avalanchi or take a bus 59km from Ooty to Korakundah and hike the last 9.5km. Accomodation is in your own tent, or, if guided, in local tribal settlements. Like Avalanchi, Upper Bhavani has some huge tracts of *shola* forest, harbouring leopard, jackal and *langur*, between upland downs grazed by wild buffalo and Nilgiri *tahr*. There is a route into the Silent Valley rainforest from here but a good guide is essential.

The Moyar Wildlife Area

On the Mysore plateau to the north of Ooty and the Nilgiris is a vast area of dry deciduous forest divided into various areas of reserved forest and official wildlife sanctuaries. In the 48km stretch of wild country between the Nilgiris and the town of Masinagudi (itself on the edge of the huge Mudumalai and Bandipur Wildlife Sanctuaries) a number of wildlife lodges have sprung up in the reserve forest on either side the Moyar River. This is an area known for game density—particularly elephants, some of which have killed people, so don't walk off into the bush alone.

Langur

Offering a more intimate contact with the forest than the official sanctuaries, most of the lodges in the area offer guided wildlife and bird treks and sometime riding. It is rewarding to spend a week or so drifting between the different lodges: the scenery is spectacular, with the Nilgiris towering to the south and west, the forest alive with birds and insects and the game-viewing is better than anywhere else in the south.

By far the best of the lodges for seeing game is **Jungle Trails**, ✆ Masinagudi 56256, which has a few double rooms at around Rs350 per night and a dormitory with viewing platform at Rs100. Meals and drinks are extra. To get there, take the bus from Ooty to Masinagudi (a 1½ hour journey which negotiates 36 hairpin bends on its way down to the Moyar River area) and ask to be set down at the driveway. From there it's a 1km walk to the lodge. Be *sure* to do this before dusk, as elephant are very active in the area at night. From the verandah at Jungle Trails, you stand a good chance of seeing all the large and small south Indian game: sloth bear, bison and leopard as well as elephant among the regular visitors. There are also *machans* (bamboo viewing platforms) built into the trees on the Moyar's banks which allow great photo opportunities.

A few kilometres further along the road to Masinagudi is **Jungle Hut**, ✆ Masinagudi 56240. Although the game is not so plentiful in this immediate area as at Jungle Trails, Jungle Hut also has regular visits from wild elephants. As part of the package, guests are taken to the nearby Mudumalai Wildife Sanctuary for the official Wildlife Department game drives there at morning and evening. Jungle Hut also gives guided treks up into the montane forest between the Mysore Plateau and the upper Nilgiris. Guests have been known to meet elephants on these treks...

Jungle Hut's accommodation is basic but comfortable but the food—both Western and Indian—is superb and the tariff of Rs600 for a double room includes meals. To get to Jungle Hut, take the bus to Masingudi from Ooty or Mysore, then share a jeep taxi from the bus stand (about Rs50).

About 5km from Jungle Hut is the **Monarch Safari Park**, (access as for Jungle Hut). Not a safari park at all but a collection of cottages built on stilts as protection against snakes, centred around a central, open air restaurant, at the foot of the Nilgiris, it's not cheap (around Rs750 per double per night, meals extra) but it has some unique delights. Treks into the forest bordering on Mudumalai Wildlife Sanctuary are particularly rewarding for birdlife but Monarch's real attractions are its horses. The place has two stallions, a gelding and a mare of the Rajasthani breed. Similar to Arabians these crescent-eared, fiery horses are trained to dance—a system of movements evolved by the Rajasthani cavalrymen of the late Middle Ages, to make the horse completely obedient and manoeuvreable in battle. Being so well schooled, Monarch's horses are pure joy to ride. Because the game is less shy of horses than humans, you also have a good chance of seeing wildife while riding—especially the large herds of *chital* that live in the surrounding bush. For beginners, there are some good, steady ponies on offer and all rides are accompanied by a syce. Rides cost Rs150 per hour but are worth it for the quality of horse on offer. By night it is worth talking to Mahesh, the manager, who knows the area and its wildlife well and can arrange trips into Mudumalai Wildife Sanctuary.

The closest lodge to the sanctuary itself is **Bamboo Banks**, ℂ Masingudi 56222/56211, Rs840 per night for a double, meals extra. Within sight of Masingudi town, this place offers the best accommodation in the area and also serves excellent Western and Indian food. The proprietor Mr Kothavala is a brilliant raconteur and used to be Master of the Ooty Hunt. He still breeds Rajasthani horses and, like Monarch, Bamboo Banks offers good riding. Around the cottages are heavenly gardens, laid out by Zerena, Mr Kothavala's wife. The trees and flower beds are densely colonized by birds—black-headed orioles, tree pies, bee-eaters, brilliantly coloured woodpeckers and paradise flycatchers are all common.

Trips into Mudumalai are offered morning and evening and Bamboo Banks can arrange elephant rides there even when the staff there have assured you that there is 'no vacancy'. The rooms are pleasantly old-fashioned and you are given great privacy—something that is rather at a premium in India.

Mudumalai Wildlife Sanctuary

About 6km beyond Masingudi town the sanctuary begins. You can reach it by bus or by taxi or hired jeep from the town and there is basic dormitory accommodation for about Rs5 per bed per night, or accommodation in rest houses costing Rs40 for a double (contact Wildlife Warden, Mahalingam Building, Coonoor Road, Ooty, ℂ 44098. Trips into the forest—mostly teak—are offered at 7.30am and 5pm in Wildlife Department minibuses and trucks. This costs about Rs35 per person but limits your chances of good game viewing, as the vehicles stick to the same routes and make a lot of noise. However, during the dry season from February to August, large herds of elephant appear in the sanctuary and these will approach quite close. At any time of year you should see *gaur*, *chital* and *langurs* and giant squirrels in the tree-tops. If you are very lucky, you may see tiger or leopard, both of which are well represented here but they tend to stick to the core area of the reserve, where no tourists are allowed.

At the southern end of the sanctuary is an **elephant training camp**, where Rs100 elephant rides are offered on a short trail into the forest at the same time as the vehicle rides. These are very hard to get onto, however and the game viewing is limited as the trail stays close to the camp. You are better advised to visit in the evening when you can watch the inmates being fed and the trained youngsters doing *puja* at a small temple attached to the camp.

Every Wednesday at about 5.30pm, the elephant handlers put on an hour-long show for the tourists (Rs25) which includes an elephant football match and various acrobatic displays. While the show is going on, look out on the left for a big male wild boar who takes advantage of the elephant show to come and forage around the empty stalls. Sometimes he brings his family with him. They root about happily while the show is going on, then run off into the forest with alarmed squeals when the crowd disperses and wanders over to the elephant stalls to pat the giant performers. If you have a good lens, the wild boar visit during the show offers an excellent chance for a bit of wildlife photography.

Mudumalai is about as far north as it is possible to go in the mountain and wildlife area of Tamil Nadu. A few kilometres on from the sanctuary's office, you cross into the state of Karnataka at Bandipur, another great protected wilderness.

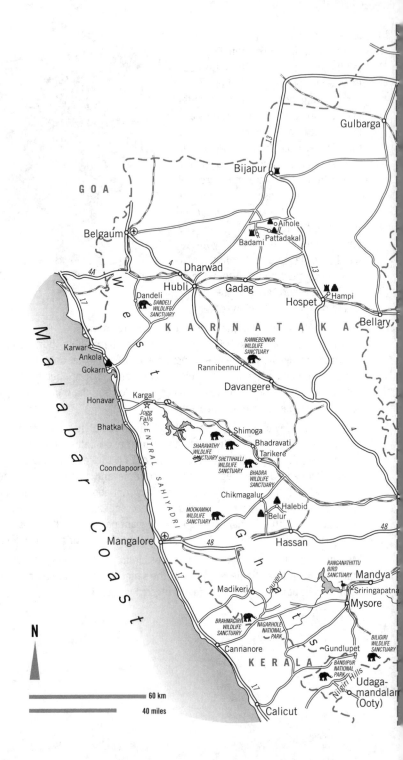

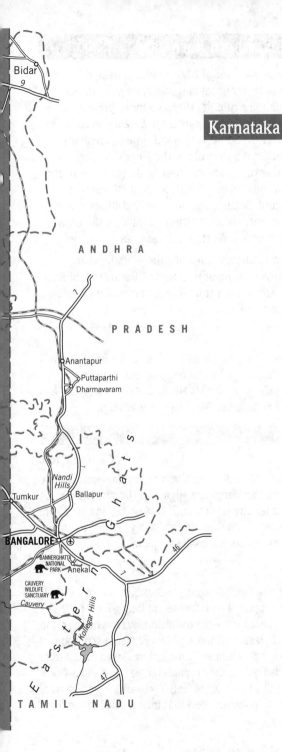

Karnataka

ANDHRA

PRADESH

Anantapur
Puttaparthi
Dharmavaram

Nandi
Hills
Tumkur   Ballapur

BANGALORE

BANNERGHATTA
NATIONAL
PARK   Anekal

CAUVERY
WILDLIFE
SANCTUARY
Cauvery

Kollegar Hills

TAMIL   NADU

Bidar
9

46

47

Route 12: Deccan Tour of Northern Karnataka

The old semi-independent princely state of Mysore was renamed Karnataka in 1973 after Kannada, the local language (*see* p.513). Although the Maharajahs no longer rule, it still has a more prosperous feel to it than anywhere else in the south apart from Kerala—even on the arid Deccan Plateau of the interior. Some very handsome towns have survived its turbulent history: during the rule of the Hoysalas (12th to 14th centuries), art and architecture came to their peak, resulting in the famous sculptured temples of Halebid and Belur. In the 17th-century came the coastal temple town of Gokarn, medieval walled Bijapur, and the romantically ruined city of Pattadakal, northern capital of the early medieval Chalukyan kings and now a World Heritage Site.

This route takes in the walled medieval cities of Aihole/Pattadakal, Bijapur and Bidar and the temple towns of Hassan and Belur/Halebid. In Puttaparthy, Sai Baba's huge ashram is a must-see for anyone interested in Indian mass personality cults.

Itinerary

Beginning at Bangalore, this route takes 7 days. Go by train to Hassan for Belur/Halebid (both day trips), then on by train to Mangalore, up the coast by bus to the unspoiled beaches of Gokarn, inland by bus to Pattadakal/Aihole via Hubli, on by bus to Bijapur and Bidar, then back to Bangalore by bus via Puttaparthy, Sai Baba's huge ashram.

Halebid and Belur

Getting There

These twin temple towns lie about 100 miles northwest of Bangalore and Mysore via the small town of **Hassan** on the Mangalore Highway. Hassan itself can be reached by bus or train from either city (approximately 4 hours) and also from Bangalore, Mangalore, Mysore, Hampi and Goa. Hassan has a variety of accommodation from which to base your excursions out to the temples.

Halebid

An hour's bus ride from Hassan through the Deccan countryside leads to Halebid, the 11-century capital of the (Hindu) Hoysala Empire. The Hoysalas are long gone—their city razed by the Northern Mughals in the 14th century—but the main **Hoysalasvara temple** still stands amid well-kept lawns. A small Nandi bull and a 30 foot (9 metre) Jain statue of Lord Gomateshvara stand outside. The temple entrance is flanked by carved friezes from the *Ramayana* while inside, squat rounded pillars, their capitals carved into various Gods, rise from a marble floor polished smooth by centuries of feet. There are no *gopurams* at Halebid, whose flat-roofed design has a more homely feel to it than is usual to the flamboyant Dravidian temple architecture.

A mile south of the main temple is a small Jain temple from an earlier period—the Hoysalas had converted to Jainism during the 10th century but abandoned it for Hinduism by the middle of the 11th. However, they did not raze their Jain monuments, but tolerated the practice of the religion despite the withdrawal of royal patronage. There are seldom any visitors at Halebid's Jain temple, unlike the Hoysalasvara temple where would-be guides assail you. The entrance to the Jain temple is guarded by two low stone elephants and there is a free-standing tower inside the compound with a beautiful carving of a prancing horse at eye level.

Belur

The original capital of the Hoysala empire, Belur was abandoned for Halebid during the 11th century. This loss of status proved fortunate; while only the temples at Halebid were left after the city was destroyed by the invading Mughals in the 14th-century, Belur, no longer of any importance, survived and remains a town to this day. Still a market centre for the surrounding Deccan villages, Belur sits beside the Yagachi river and has the superb **Chennakeshava Temple**, built in 1116 and dedicated to Chenna in commemoration of a great victory of the Hoysalas over the Cholas.

The temple does not look anything special from the outside, until you go up close and see the rows of friezes: processional elephants, dancing girls and musicians border scenes from the great Hindu epics, runnning all the way around the sides of the temple in a delicate tracery of stone. Inside is a central pillar, known as the Narasimha pillar, covered in almost microscopically intricate carvings of temple dancers. Apparently the pillar could once be rotated, but it now stands rooted to the floor.

A smaller temple complex, the **Viranarayana temple**, stands just a little to the west of the Chennakeshava temple.

Where to Stay

Belur ✆ (08172–)

The **Mayura Velapuri** is an inexpensive state-run guesthouse on Main Road, with clean but basic comfort.

There's a number of pretty awful budget guesthouses on Main Road, but they'll do for a night if you can't face getting back on a bus to Hassan.

Hassan ✆ (08172–)

expensive (from Rs 1000)

The **Hassan Ashok**, ✆ 68731, is a well-run place with a good vegetarian restaurant and air-conditioned rooms. You can arrange for transport out to the temples by taxi from here (round trip approx Rs250) and also check out the hotel's resident magician, who begs you to watch his performance as you go in and out of the entrance. His tricks include apparently swallowing a live coal and sending a live cobra down his throat to retrieve it, as well as regurgitating several pounds of old rusty nails. If you have a few minutes, it's worth watching him go through his repertoire.

Hassan has only one hotel in this category. The **Ambilee Palika**, on Racecourse Road, ✆ 67145, is just as comfortable as the Ashok but has no magician. It does have foreign exchange though, and a bar.

Try the **Vaishnavi Guest Lodge** on Church Road, ✆ 67413, or the **Satyaprakash Lodge** on Bus Stand Road, which has rooms from below Rs100.

Moving On

By train: the nearest access point is Hassan. Several daily services connect Hassan with Bangalore (4 hours), Mysore (3 hours) and Mangalore (8 hours over the mountains). The train station is a mile east of town on the Bangalore road.

By bus: buses run between Hassan and Bangalore (every half hour) and Mysore (every hour). Several services daily to Mangalore, Hampi, and Goa.

Local buses run from Hassan to the temple complexes at Belur and Halebid every half hour. The bus station is by Maharaja Park in the centre of town.

Mangalore — population 465,000

Getting There

Indian Airlines, Jet Airways and East West Airlines fly into Bajpe airport, about 23km from the town centre, and connect with Bangalore, Madras and Bombay. Mangalore is linked by rail to Madras and to all towns on the coast. There are two trains from Madras: the 6027 **West Coast Express**, which leaves daily at 12pm and arrives at 6.05 the following morning, and the 6001 **Mangalore**, which leaves Madras daily at 7.05pm and arrives at 1.15pm. You can travel by bus to and from Goa, Bangalore, Mysore, Madras, Madurai and all towns on the coast.

For further information, *see* 'Moving On', p.582.

Mangalore ✆ (0824–)   **Tourist Information**

The **Tourist Information** office, ✆ 421692, is currently located at Hotel Indraprastha, Lighthouse Hill Road; however, this hotel is expected to be demolished soon and a new location for the tourist office has not yet been decided. The complex housing the **GPO** and **Telegraph Office** is on Dr. U.P. Mallya Road downhill from the mosque. The **State Bank of India** is on K.S. Rao Road, as are most of the hotels and restaurants.

City Tour

Bunder–Milagres Church–St Aloysius Church–Kadri Caves–
Mangaladevi Temple–Mahatma Gandhi Museum–Santo Rosario Cathedral.

You won't find the natural splendours of the Karnatic coast in Mangalore, the coast's only large town. This humid, smelly port town has the usual modern Indian semi-industrial ugliness on its fringes and crowded, motor-horn honking stress at its centre.

You should use Mangalore only as a brief rest-stop before going on up the coast to discover the beauty of the region. But while in Mangalore it is worth exploring the small part of town that centres around the old port or **Bunder**—still a working labyrinth of 100-year-old 'go-downs' (warehouses), their piles of merchandise piled in cool shade away from the glaring sun. The port is run partly by Indo-Portuguese Christians (Mangalore was one of the few points of the Karnatic coast developed by the Portuguese traders) and partly by white-robed Muslims (this is the Arabian Sea after all); it would be hard to say which community is the more prosperous. The Bunder is therefore a strange architectural mish-mash of old Catholic churches, carved wooden mosques in the Keralan style, wizened labourers bent double and straining under huge loads of coffee—the Bunder handles 75 per cent of Karnataka's annual harvest—*coir*, spices, forest hardwoods, cotton, cashews, or fish. Poor Hindu prostitutes hover in the side alleys, and the town's original fishing tribe are crowded into a stinking slum of dusty palm-thatch lean-tos on the dockside, their ragged children assailing any traveller walking there with demands for money.

To get to the Bunder, head for the centre of town, whose big landmark is **Milagres Church**, then due west (downhill) along Bibi Alabi Road and you will come into the Bunder. The Bunder itself is bisected by the large Jama Masjid Road, which becomes Goods Shed Road south of the wharves, before curving back up into the small old Portuguese residential quarter, from which the astonishingly named Old Kent Road (who was the cockney explorer here?) takes you back to Milagres Church. Walk around the streets that run parallel with Jama Masjid and Goods Shed, and the alleys that connect them, to pick up on the atmosphere (and take a camera). One word of warning: at night the Bunder can be as rough as any other dockside, so after dark it is best to be in a group.

Despite its heat and general unattractiveness, upper Mangalore has a few surprises. The 19th-century **St Aloysius Chapel** on Lighthouse Hill Road has a ceiling covered with fres-coes painted by a Jesuit named Moscheni. The official tourist literature has dubbed St Aloysius the 'Sistine Chapel of India'! While the paintings are not the work of a Michaelangelo, they are nonetheless quite attractive.

If you take an auto-rickshaw (Rs10) up Old Lighthouse Road, you come to a hill with gardens in which stands an **18th-century lighthouse,** supposedly built by the Karnatic Muslim warlord Hyder Ali, though this is now disputed by historians. Also in the gardens are the small **Kadri Caves**, ancient hermits' cells next to which is the 11th-century **Sri Manjunatha Temple**. The 10th-century **Mangaladevi Temple**, a superb piece of Keralan wooden temple architecture and from which Mangalore derives its name, is located 5km from the lighthouse.

Back in the main town, if the heat hasn't knocked you over, you can visit the **Mahatma Gandhi Museum** in the grounds of the Canara High School (*open Mon–Fri, 9.30–12.30 and 2–5.30*), a small, dusty place with rather neglected displays of stuffed local fauna and some good bronze sculpture. Alternatively, stroll down Dr U.P. Mallya Road, past the big mosque and the G.P.O. and Telegraph Office to the 19th-century **Santo Rosario Cathedral** and its attached Catholic school. You cannot guarantee that the cathedral will be open but if you wander around the elegant but decaying school grounds, you will be kept company by scores of charming, playful schoolchildren, eager for a game of tag.

Suratkal Beach

About 10 miles north of the town centre and overlooked by the town's new lighthouse and a small temple is this quiet sweep of golden beach with good swimming, although it is by no means as idyllic as the beaches further up the Karnataka coast. Visit only in the week—at weekends it gets very crowded with townspeople.

Mangalore © (0824–)

Where to Stay
expensive (from US$40)

The Taj-group **Manjuran** on Old Port Road, © 420420, @ 420585 has a swimming pool (relief in this fetid town). Just above the old port, it is convenient for exploring the Bunder. Other facilities include a bar, two restaurants and a bookshop.

moderate (from Rs 400)

Try the **Moti Mahal**, on Falnir Road, © 441411, @ 441011. It also has a pool, and a more faded, old-fashioned feel. More brash is the **Poonja International** on K.S. Rao Road, © 441071; also on this road, the **Navaratna Palace**, © 441104, has a good restaurant and foreign exchange.

Out of town is the **Summer Sands Beach Resort**, © 467690, @ 467693, a good option for a couple of day's relaxing before heading up the coast. With its own private beach (which attracts hawkers), the 10km from Mangalore makes it a world away from the hot bustle of the town. To get there, take a taxi out to the town of Chotamangalore/Ullal.

budget

A hotel on K.S. Rao Road worth giving a go is the **Manorama**. It is clean and friendly, with a decent restaurant and foreign exchange. You could also try the modern **Srinavas Hotel** on Ganapathy Road, © 440061. Mangalore's cheap hotels are run-down at best and mosquitoes are a continual problem. However, the state-run **Mayura Nethravathi**, © 411192, 3km north of the town centre is clean and conveniently placed for the bus stand. Cheap rooms can also be found at the rather dingy **Panchami**, © 411986, opposite the bus stand.

Eating Out

Try the Taj Manjuran's two restaurants (Western and very good Indian, catering for both vegetarians and non-vegetarians). Otherwise there is reasonable vegetarian food (and some fish) at the other main hotels, or cheap *thali* houses.

Moving On

By air: Indian Airways flights go to Bangalore and Madras 4 times a week and twice daily to Bombay. Jet flies daily to Bombay.

By rail: there are direct rail connections with all points on the coast of Kerala and with Madras. At the time of writing (summer 1996) there are no trains to Bangalore due to gauge conversion. A railway, due to open 1997/8, is being constructed north up the coast to Goa.

By bus: the bus stand is 3km north of the town centre, so allow for this when catching buses. Direct daily services go to all points on the Karnataka Coast and to Goa (13 hours)—the best one being the 11am bus. From Goa, you can take a connection on to Bombay if you are a real masochist. Bangalore and Mysore are also serviced every half-hour, taking respectively 8 and 6 hours. Madras and Madurai have express buses too, but it is far nicer to go by train.

Gokarn

Getting There

Gokarn is connected by bus with Mangalore, Margao and Hubli (*see also* 'Moving On', p.585).

Touring Gokarn

Gokarn is a jewel—an unspoilt town of old Keralan-style houses with wooden-slatted balconies rising to several stories. The streets radiate out from an ancient Sanskrit school and college for Brahmins. There are several medieval temples, and two huge temple cars stand in the main street, which is lined with stalls selling religious accoutrements for trainee priests—images of gods, incense holders, brass bells, pestles and mortars and holy pictures. The brahmins, heads shaven but for the top-knot that signifies their office, bustle to and fro in white lungis, caste cords lying diagonally across their bare chests. The young brahmins are wiry, underfed and obsequious; their seniors often quite obscenely fat. All are full of quiet disdain for scruffy Westerner backpackers.

Despite the architectural beauty of the town, it is Gokarn's wonderful scimitar-shaped **beaches** that most attract the traveller. Once you have made the trip over the rocky path down to the sea, you will discover sublime tranquillity, and you will not want to get back on a loud, sweaty bus for some time.

Gokarn's Beaches

Avoid Gokarn's town beach (except for a walk when you first arrive) and check into one of the lodges for the night. Take the small alley that leads away between small houses to the left of the big temple car shed as you walk down from the bus stand. The alley soon emerges from the houses and becomes a path that snakes uphill over black and pink volcanic rocks to **Kudle Beach**, the closest piece of paradise to the town. This walk takes about half an hour and should be done at early morning or evening, before or after the main heat of the day. You can leave the bulk of your gear under lock and key at one of the lodges in Gokarn and just take the bare necessities over to the beaches (the first two beaches also have safe places to leave clothes and money). If the sun does get too hot on your walk, you can stop halfway at a small *chai*-shop, appropriately called the **Halfway House**, and drink sodas in the shade until the sun loses its ferocity.

Kudle Beach is, like all the beaches of Gokarn, a long, curved strip of white and gold sand set between two forested headlands. A strip of paddies and coconut palms occupies a narrow flat strip inland from the beach. After this the ground rises steeply to the first foothills of the Western Ghats, which tumble almost to the sea on this part of the Malabar Coast. Because Kudle Beach is the closest to town, it is the most 'developed', but this only means it has three timber-and-thatch tea-houses serving food and drink. For next-to-nothing, these places will rent you a palm-thatch or *adobe* hut to stash your gear in while you swim in the warm, lapping ocean, drink *chai*, eat fish or *thalis*, and sleep on the beach by night.

A half-hour's walk on from Kudle, over the headland, is **Om Beach**. Smaller than Kudle, the water here is calmer and offers some of Gokarn's best swimming. Tranquil, and a good place to see dolphins, the beach gets its name not from stoned hippies chanting on its sands, but from the locals, who say that its shape resembles that of the sacred Om if seen from the hills above. The beach has one tea-house serving food, but no organized place to stay. A couple of palm-thatch beach shelters serve as wind-breaks if you want to sleep here. A few locals are prone to stealing anything left unguarded, however, so keep your valuables within sight at all times.

One more half-hour walk southward over the next headland takes you to **Half-Moon Beach**. Here there is not a single tea-house, and it makes a great place to camp. But food and water are problems: there is no natural spring as at Kudle and Om, and so you'll have to go back to Om for your sustenance unless you have the foresight to bring your own supplies.

A final half-hour's southward hike over a last wooded headland and you are on **Paradise Beach**, so called for its near-inaccessibility and complete peace—nothing but the sea, the sky, the sand and you. Unfortunately, there is no freshwater supply here either, but this does not stop people from hiking in and losing themselves for weeks.

One word of warning: recently reports of night-time muggings have come in from people staying out at Half-Moon and Paradise Beaches. The classic scenario seems to be local toughs either demanding money from women walking alone on one of the headlands, or attacking lone travellers and couples sleeping on the beach. The best way to avoid this is to get together with some others when sleeping. If this is not possible, head back to Kudle or Om before dark, where there will always be a few other travellers, and sleep there.

Where to Stay

Gokarn Town ✆ (08386–)

Gokarn's most expensive hotel, **Om Lodge**, ✆ 4644/ 4645/46244, is not the best place to stay, but it has the most modern-style rooms (some with air-conditioning). It tends to fill up with large groups of Indian tourists come to worship at the town's temples and its food is not of the highest standard. Rooms are clean, however (inexpensive).

Gokarn has several very cheap guest lodges, all clustered together about 1km from the bus stand on the main street. Walk up the way the bus is pointing, then turn left at the T-junction and keep walking for about 3 minutes and you will come to a few lodges. However, only one warrants recommendation: the **Vaibhav Nivas Lodge**, ✆ 46289 (cheap) set back a little from the road. Run by a family of Brahmins, this has double rooms with shower and (Indian) toilet attached, or cheaper ones with shared bathrooms. The lodge occupies an old Karnatik house, and there are pet birds (and two white rats) in cages, reasonable food, and beer for sale. The Vaibhav will look after your belongings for Rs5 per day while you are at the beaches.

Beaches

The only place resembling an organized lodge is the *chai*-shop at the foot of the head-land path as it comes down to Kudle beach. Here you can eat and rent a secure *adobe* hut (with padlock) to sleep in or stash your rucksacks. There is a 'shower' consisting of a hose attached to the local freshwater spring. If this place is full, which is unlikely, the owners will point you to one or two other places on the beach where you can sleep and leave your gear, but in slightly less secure palm-thatch huts.

On the other beaches, you have to camp in the open.

Eating Out

Gokarn Town

You can eat at the cheap restaurant in the **Om Lodge** and drink beer with the local drunks. To do the same, but with other travellers, try the **Vaibhav Nivas Lodge** (*see* above). On the same road as the cheap lodges you can find some very good, cheap *thali*-houses.

Beaches

Kudle Beach has two places to eat: a sort of guest lodge at the foot of the headland path leading back to town, which serves indifferent *thalis* and fish, or the really good but unnamed restaurant set among some kept gardens just back from the centre of the beach, and owned by a Spanish lady who came to stay for a while and ended up marrying a local. Her restaurant serves home-made garlicky pasta (oh joy!) and fish. She also has a charming dalmatian dog. Prices are very low.

At Om Beach, there is another *chai*-shop serving *thalis*, *parathas* and some Western food (cheese on toast, omelettes, etc). Again, prices are very low.

Moving On

By bus: Direct buses go up to Margao in Goa (via Palolem), a 4–5 hour journey, to Mangalore, 6–7 hours, and to Hubli, 4 hours over the mountains, from where an express connection can be made for Hospet and the ruins at Hampi (another 4 hours). Margao and Hubli services run several times daily. There are no direct buses to Pattadakal or Aihole from Gokarn; you have to travel via Hubli. From here, there are hourly buses to Badami (3hrs), and from Badami buses operate every two hours for Pattadakal/Aihole.

Getting There

Direct buses from Badami, Pattadakal, Bijapur and Bidar connect sleepy Aihole with the outside world.

Pattadakal

Pattadakal was a later Chalukyan capital, but seems to have been in existence long before that. Some very grand temple building went on here during the 7th and 8th centuries, notably under the powerful king Vikramaditya II who ruled between 734 and 745. The mish-mash of various temple styles—both Dravidian and northern—demonstrate the cosmopolitan outlook of the Chalukyan rajas. What makes the temples doubly unusual is that almost all are Jain, despite their carvings of Hindu deities—the Chalukyans having been converted during the 9th and 10th centuries—a strangely pacifist move for such a warlike dynasty.

Scattered among the temples are various megaliths from the 6th–3rd centuries BC. Tumbled down low dolmens and menhirs prove that the settlement has never been erased, despite centuries of warfare and new building. Pattadakal was written about by the Greek historian Ptolemy during the 1st century AD in one of his gazetteers of the great towns of the orient.

Now a World Heritage Site, Pattadakal has several temples of major archaeological importance. Most impressive are the three-storyed **Virupaksha** temple and the great **Mallikarjuna** temple (both mid 8th century), built to commemorate a great victory by the Chalukyan raja Vikramaditya II over the rival Pallavas of the south. Vikramaditya II had been so impressed with the Pallava temples seen during his southward campaigns that he commissioned architects from the region to come and build the victory temples, and to carve out intricate friezes of the *Ramayana* on the inner pillars. Every January, the two big temples are host to an annual **Classical Dance Festival**, and have their own **temple car festivals** in March and April.

Aihole

Another Chalukyan capital (6th century), Aihole has about 150 early temples and is regarded by many architectural historians and archaeologists as the place where high Dravidian temple architecture began. A 19km bus ride on from Pattadakal, Aihole's ruined temple city lies inside a ruined defensive wall. Eager guides cluster round the bus stand from Pattadakal and you really do need some kind of steering around the temples of this vast, rambling site; some are Buddhist, some Jain, some Hindu. All have superb carvings, and some rise to more than two storeys. The last temples built on the site date from the 12th century and amazingly, none were destroyed by the region's later Muslim invaders.

Of particular interest are the **Konti temples** in the middle of the bazaar and the **Durga temple**, the most elaborately carved building of the lot. It's a Vaishnavite temple, built as a long hall (blessedly cool on a Deccan afternoon) with a high, platformed altar at the far end. Also try and make time for the **Hucchapayya Math** (7th–9th century), which forms a cluster of four buildings with some good examples of early erotic sculpture. Drier and more earnest is the **Archaeological Museum** (*open daily 10–5 except Fri*), which displays some of the best of the smaller sculptures excavated from the area.

Where to Stay

Pattadakal is not a developed town and the only clean lodges in the area are 19km north at Badami.

In **Aihole**, there is a state-run **Tourist Home**, ✆ Aminagad 41, with clean, basic rooms, next to the entrance to the main temple complex near the bus stand with rooms from Rs100–350.

Bijapur and Bidar—Deccan Fortress Towns

Bijapur

One hundred and sixty km north of Badami and the Chalukyan temple towns, **Bijapur** is a walled stronghold of domed palaces, mosques and bazaars built round a hill on which sits a strong, but decaying, citadel. Roads into Bijapur still pass under the curtain wall's seven great gatehouses, structures that withstood uncounted sieges throughout the turbulent history of the Deccan Plateau.

Bijapur fell only four times in 600 years: to the Vijayanagars who ousted its Chalukyan founders in the 12th century; to the Northern Mughals of Delhi in the early 14th century, who ousted the Vijayanagars; to the Bahmani sultans in the late 15th century, who rebelled against the Delhi Mughals; and finally, after a civil war against the Bahmanis, its new local rulers (the Abdil Shah dynasty), ousted the Bahmani garrison in 1686. Throughout the 16th and 17th centuries, both the Bahmanis and the Abdil Shahs fought inconclusive wars with the rival sultanate of Golconda but, by the time the British arrived in the late 18th-century, the city had become a prosperous backwater. Under the British, the Abdil Shahs ruled semi-independently, but Bijapur has been in decline ever since the dynasty died out in the early 19th century.

Getting There

Bijapur is linked by rail to Badami and indirectly to Bombay, Hospet and Hyderabad, and by bus to Bidar, Belgaum, Hospet, Hubli, Bangalore and Hyderabad (*see also* 'Moving On', p.589).

Tourist Information

The **tourist office** is in the Mayura Adil Shahi Hotel at the foot of the Citadel, open daily from 10.30 to 1.30 and from 2.15 to 5.30 except Sundays. For **foreign exchange** try the **State Bank** in the Citadel.

Touring Bijapur

Bijapur has had its day, and the old walls and monuments are beginning to tumble down in places, but the medieval buildings are still strong. Of several large mosques, the **Jama**

Masjid is the largest and lies southeast of the citadel near the walls. Built from 1557–9, the mosque is in the grandest style, with a huge entrance hall and room for over 2000 worshippers. It is still packed every day for morning and evening prayer. Further towards the citadel along Jama Masjid Road is a small palace, the **Mehtar Mahal**, a fine piece of Islamic whimsy with carved filigree work and fairytale minarets built as a pleasure palace for the later queens of Bijapur. By contrast, the **Citadel** itself is mostly ruined—largely because the later rulers of Bijapur were disdainful of living in such a dour place and moved out to the grander city palaces. However, the Durbar Hall is still intact as is **Jal Manzil**, a pleasure pavilion built round a set of ornamental pools (now dry).

Bijapur has two superbly ornate Islamic tombs. The early 17th-century **Ibrahim Rauza** which lies just outside the city's western (Zohrapur) gate, houses the remains of Ibrahim Abdil Shah, a prominent sultan of Bijapur who originally had it built for his wife, but died before her, so she put him in it instead. At the opposite end of the walled town, just inside the walls and south of the eastern (Gulbarga) gate, is the late 17th-century **Gol Gumbaz**, where the greatest Bijapur sultan Abdil Shah, the man who wrested power from the Bahmanis, lies buried with his family.

According to the official tourist literature, this tomb boasts the world's second largest free-standing dome (after St Peter's in the Vatican City). Its concave, airy space certainly is vast. A **Whispering Gallery** runs around the base of the dome, midway between floor and ceiling. It would be interesting to find out if there was any connection between Sir Christopher Wren's building and this one, seeing as they were constructed within decades of each other. The sheer scale of the Gol Gumbaz illustrates clearly how powerful Bijapur was before the British conquest reduced its rulers to mere client kings.

In the gatehouse of the Gol Gumbaz is the **Nakkar Khana** (musicians' gallery), a small museum whose display comprises a brief history of the Bijapur sultans.

The **Bara Kamam** on Jama Masjid Road, is the first storey of a never-completed artillery tower that Abdil Shah designed to command the entire surrounding plain. It still houses a huge cannon known as the *Ruler of the Plains*, whose bronze barrel exceeds 4m in length, and was a prize piece of booty brought home from Abdil Shah's wars with Golconda. Inside the lion's jaws of the cannon's mouth, an elephant is being swallowed. Although the Bara Kamam never reached its intended height of over 196 feet (60 metres), a slimmer 80ft (24m) high watchtower stands

Gol Gumbaz

on a raised mound next door, and points lighter cannon out at the surrounding plains. The door is open and you can climb up for the view.

Five km east of town is the **Asar Mahal**, a small palace believed by some to contain relics of the Prophet Muhammad. Built in 1646, it has some very beautiful frescoes in the Mughal style. Unfortunately no women are allowed inside.

Where to Stay
budget

You can stay right in the heart of this medieval Muslim city: all prices fall within the budget bracket.

The best place is the **Mayura Adil Shahi Hotel**, at the southern foot of the Citadel (Anandamahal Road), ✆ 20934. Run by the state tourist board, its rooms are built around a central courtyard and have Indian-style bathrooms. attached. If this is full, try the clean but basic **Sanman** on Station Road, near the Gol Gumbaz, ✆ 21866, the **Samrat**, also on Station Road, ✆ 21620, or the **Lalitha Mahal**, opposite the bus stand.

If these places are full try the **Prasad**, on Azad Road, or the **Tourist** on Main Road, ✆ 20655. These two are not so clean as the other lodges, but they'll do for a night or two.

Moving On

By rail: Bijapur has a direct train service to Badami (3–4 hours) and indirect services to Bombay and Hyderabad (change at Sholapur). Trains also run daily to Hospet with a change at Gadag. The train station is west of the walled city, just outside the Gulbarga Gate.

By bus: direct daily bus services run to Bidar, Belgaum, Hospet, Hubli, Bangalore and Hyderabad.

Bidar

Far off the tourist track on the northeast border with Andhra Pradesh is Bidar, another Muslim fortress town that started life as a Chalukyan stronghold. Reached via the old 14th–15th century Bahmani capital of Gulbarga (now a scruffy modern town with a broken-down fort), Bidar, like Bijapur, still has its medieval walls. A mere northern outpost of the Bahmani empire until the late 15th century, it rose to prominence after the Bahmani sultans, feeling cramped in Gulbarga's small fort, moved their capital here in the 1420s. A 200-year period of palace and mosque building followed until 1619, when the Bahmanis were defeated by their local rivals, the Abdil Shahs of Bijapur. Bidar fell a third time to the northern Maratha warlords in 1686, and remained a Maratha stronghold against Golconda until the British conquest.

Getting There

Bidar is linked with Hyderabad by rail and with Bijapur, Hospet and Hyderabad by bus (*see also* 'Moving On', p.591).

Touring Bidar

Bidar's **Old Fort** was originally built by the Chalukyans in the 10th century but was added to by just about every other Deccani dynasty over the following centuries. The present walls were built by the Bahmani kings in the 15th century, who also dug the triple moat, each bank connected by a narrow causeway and protected by a massive postern.

Inside the old fort is the modest royal residence, the **Rangin Mahal** or 'Coloured Palace'. Built in 1487 it was lavishly decorated inside with painted tiles and mother-of-pearl inlay, some of which survives but most of which is now in disrepair. The front door may be locked but you can ask for the key at the adjacent museum (*see* below). Outside stretch the vast palace kitchens and bathhouse, now housing a small **Archaeological Museum** (*open daily 8–5 except Sun*) displaying medieval weaponry and Neolithic artefacts dug up during excavations inside the fort.

Behind the museum is the **Tarkash Mahal** or old harem, and the ruins of its fountained garden, the **Lal Bagh**. From here, a small mosque and a path lead to the **Gagan Mahal**, a covered arena for watching gladiatorial combats and fights between wild beasts. Other ruined buildings in the fort include the **Takht Mahal**, which had its own swimming pool and underground passageways out of the fort, the **Powder Magazine** and the fort commander's house. These are now filled with bat colonies and are dangerous due to snakes and falling masonry.

After exploring the old fort (allow a good couple of hours for this) head back over the triple moat (keeping an eye out for possible cannon fire from the Naubat Khana) to the old town, which also lies within its own curtain wall. Turn right as you pass under the final postern and walk for a block down Multani Badshah Road, then turn left into Hospital Road and after about three minutes you come to the **Madrasa of Mahmud Gawan**, built in 1472.

Mahmud Gawan was an exiled Persian merchant who enlisted with the Bahmanis in 1453 after political indiscretions at home and by 1461 had risen to become Bidar's military commander. His career did not stop here: by 1466 he had been appointed deputy ruler of the kingdom. His notable military achievement was the conquest of Goa in 1470. The Madrasa was built upon Gawan's retirement, as a college of military and philosophical arts. Apparently its library was once one of the best in India, but sadly it was burned down during the Marathas' 17th-century storming of the town.

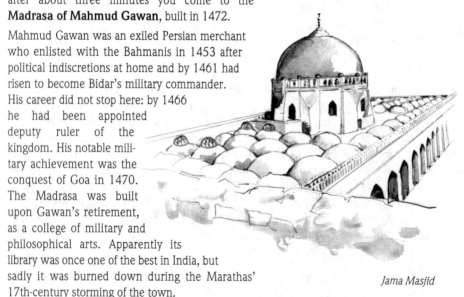

Jama Masjid

Continue down Hospital Road, take the first right, then first left and you reach a tall watchtower, the **Chaubara**, which stands about 80 feet (25 metres) high and commands the whole city. Just to the southwest stands the **Jama Masjid** (built in 1430), Bidar's largest mosque.

Bidar's various sultans still lie buried in grand **mausolea** outside the city walls. To the southwest, via the gatehouse on New Arch Road, are the **Barid Shahi Tombs**, a 20-minute auto-rickshaw ride from the town centre. The largest tomb, that of Sultan Ali Barid who died in the early 16th century, has a dome 80 feet (25 metres) high decorated with coloured tiles. Even more spectacular are the **Bahmani Tombs**, another 20 minutes east of town on the Ashtur Road. Carved in the Persian style with stylized animals, birds and swirling floral patterns, the highest dome rises 114 feet (35 metres) above the tomb of Sultan Ahmad Shah, the Bahmani ruler who moved the capital to Bidar from Gulbarga in the 1420s. There are seven other tombs, all beautifully decorated, though somewhat battered by time.

Where to Stay

inexpensive

The state-run **Mayura Barid Shahi**, ✆ 20571, is good value. On Ugdir Road, near the bus station, it has clean, basic rooms, a decent vegetarian restaurant and a shabby bar. Apart from this, there is the overpriced **Bidar International**, also on Ugdir Road, or a number of very cheap but flea-ridden guest lodges in the old town.

Moving On

Bidar only has a narrow-gauge railway line and the only direct connection is with Hyderabad. The railway station is situated next to the bus station on Ugdir Road, west of the old town via the Shah Ganj Dharwaza.

Daily bus services run from Bijapur via Gulbarga (6–7 hours), Hospet via Bijapur (12 hours) and Hyderabad via Zahirabad (4–5 hours). The bus station is on Ugdir Road west of the old town. To reach Puttaparthy by bus, you must travel first to Hyderabad (3hrs), and then take another bus (*see* below).

Puttaparthy

Puttaparthy, a hot, dusty village, has now grown into a town and is home to **Sai Baba's** huge *ashram*, which attracts hundreds of thousands of devotees from around the world. Bangalore, 100 miles to the south (in Karnataka), is the easiest access point, with several direct bus services daily.

Getting There

Travelling by rail is can be inconvenient. The nearest stations are Dharmavaram or Anantapur, both a good hour's bus ride away. The best direct access is by bus. Regular, direct bus services connect Puttaparthy with Bangalore (4hrs), with several daily services. Puttaparthy is also linked to Hyderabad by buses 3 times daily (11hrs).

Foreign exchange is offered at the State Bank opposite the bus stand, uphill from the *ashram*'s main gates. Expect to queue.

Sai Baba's Ashram

Anyone travelling in south India will have noticed pictures of an orange-clad, smiling guru with an outrageously huge afro hairdo, his image often gracing hotel lobbies, auto-rickshaw drivers' mirrors or the cover of books. That's Sai Baba, who claims, and is believed by millions of devotees, to be one of a series of incarnations of the Hindu god Shiva, appearing in a different form every three or four human generations. Among his past incarnations have been Muslim holy men—Sai Baba being able to cross the frontiers of orthodox religion at will. The next incarnation will be as Shiva/Shakti—that is, the full male and female union of all aspects of the supreme godhead, and mankind will enter a new era. However, our own generation must be content with following the teachings of Sai Baba's present incarnation, which seem in general to be simple exhortations to live morally.

Sai Baba is accused by many of being a fraud. As well as the scores of books singing his praises are a number claiming to expose him. One author even goes so far as to accuse him of homosexuality and of making advances to those close to him.

The vast numbers of Sai Baba devotees have, of course, provided the *crores* of rupees necessary to build the vast *ashram* complex, which covers a small hill. But if the guru has grown incredibly wealthy, he also uses much of the money for good works—in particular, a number of schools and hospitals in Karnataka and Andhra Pradesh have been subsidized by his *ashram.*

Whatever you belive about Sai Baba, Puttaparthy is certainly an interesting phenomenon: the once tiny Deccani village has become a compact, cosmopolitan centre, incongruous against the Deccani landscape of brown fields and bare, rocky hills. A huge number of little shops and stalls sell (at inflated prices) the white Punjabi suits favoured by Sai Baba's devotees and sell Sai Baba memorabilia—key rings, tapes, T-shirts, books, pens, and the like. Whether their profits are connected in any way with the *ashram* is difficult to ascertain.

Visitors stay in comfortable dormitories at the *ashram* (for a mere Rs5 per night), or at lodges in the village, and assemble at dawn for the *darshan*, or public appearance, of Sai Baba himself. These *darshans* are reminiscent of school assemblies, though on a much larger scale. Squadrons of officious *ashram* 'security' workers brusquely order the crowd into queues and make them sit in neat rows—women on one side of the vast hall (their shoulders must be covered with a scarf) and men on the other. The security people can be rude and the temptation to be rude back is very strong. However, when Sai Baba appears, the atmosphere is electric and the audience hushed. The guru strews the crowd with small tokens—some say they are flower petals, others sweets and still others sacred ash. There is further confusion as to where he gets these tokens from; some say that he takes them from a tray, others claim that he manifests them from the air.

Most of Sai Baba's followers credit him with the ability to manifest various kinds of objects—notably gold rings and a sacred ash—that bring good fortune to the recipient, and many claim to have received these gifts after watching the guru materialize them from thin air. Even when you have witnessed a *darshan*, it is difficult to say exactly what you have seen, such is the atmosphere of mystique.

After the *darshan* and a period of chanting—an emotionally charged sort of camp-fire sing-song rising from the huge crowd—comes breakfast. The *ashram* has several refectories (separate for men and women), where Indian food is served for a very fair Rs15 per meal. Through the rest of the morning, which quickly gets very hot, you can wander round the *ashram*, occasionally being shunted hither and thither by the security workers. There's a reading room of Sai Baba teachings and laudatory biographies and a small museum explaining the various incarnations of the guru—both uphill from the *darshan* hall. Although you will be made to take off your shoes before entering any of the buildings, beware of leaving them outside—the *ashram* is not free from petty pilfering.

It is also worth wandering downhill (outside the *ashram*) to the lower end of the village, where Deccani rural life goes on unaffected by the crowds. The countryside around here is very fertile, and a wander into the irrigated fields will soon attract a cluster of children anxious to show you around, albeit in Telugu. Their company may cost you a few rupees.

Puttaparthy © *(08555–)*

Where to Stay
moderate

Directly opposite the gates of the *ashram* is the recently built **Sai Towers** © 87270/87327, @ 87302, a building several storeys high that looks incongruous up here on the dry Deccan Plateau, but can put you up in Western-style comfort (Rs200–1100).

budget

There are several lodges dotted along the village main street below, downhill from the *ashram*. Try the **Sai Ram Lodge**, which is basic, but has clean double rooms at the cheaper end of the scale; the **Dharmavaram Guest House**, © 87226/87316, with non-a/c doubles for Rs330; or **Hotel Sai Renaissance** on Bypass Road, © 87324, where doubles go for Rs400+10% without a/c, Rs600+10% with. Mosquitoes are always a problem in these lodges though, and you will need a net and/or coils to ensure a good night's sleep.

The *ashram* offers one of the best deals in India—clean, single-sex dormitories with beds for Rs5 and shared rooms (much harder to get, but worth asking for) for about Rs20.

Moving On
Regular direct bus services connect Puttaparthy with Bangalore (4hrs).

Route 13: Coorg

Coorg is one of the most unspoilt regions of southern India, and no mountain walker should miss it. Hiking trails run from rice-fields and lowland jungle up through coffee plantations shaded by indigenous jungle trees and finally through wild forest onto high ridges of natural grassland. You sleep and eat in forest temples and have to finish walking before the elephants come out at dusk. For wildlife viewing, try to make sure you spend a few days in Nagarhole National Park in the south of the Coorg region, inland from Mangalore—one of the best places for seeing wild elephant, tiger and leopard in the south. For trekking, many of the wildlife sanctuaries have huts and will supply guides where appropriate.

Itinerary

This route is a 5-day circle from Bangalore to Coorg and back again. Coorg involves minimal travel fatigue to reach and buses leave Bangalore for Madikeri every 30 minutes, taking 6 hours. Or you could take the overnight express, leaving at midnight and arriving just before dawn.

The Coorg Region

> *We woke to an Irish morning; thin, drifting cloud was draped over Mercara's mountains and the air felt cool and moist. 'A fine soft day, thank God!'*

Dervla Murphy, On a Shoestring to Coorg

Centred around the small market town of **Madikeri**, this semi-wild region of coffee plantations, montane forest, paddies and lowland jungle is one of the most beautiful in India. Away from the region's few roads, the only way to travel is on foot—along old sunken lanes between towering trees, crossing wooden stiles into open paddies and pastures, and finally heading up through coffee and cardamom into the mountain forest. Wilderness and

rural landscape blend effortlessly. There are very few tourists, and the locals (prosperous descendants of the original *Coorgi* or *Kodagu* tribespeople), though friendly, have their own language and distance themselves from the rest of Karnataka.

The hills of Coorg are also a pilgrimage destination for Hindus all over southern India: the sacred Cauvery River, known as the Ganges of the South, rises in Coorg before flowing down across the broad plains of Tamil Nadu and watering the large temple towns there. A small mountain temple has been built around the Cauvery's source and pilgrims trek or take buses up the steep mountain road to bathe in the tank and wash away their sins.

History

The Coorgis have never been conquered. Their mountain region has always been remote and is still largely inaccessible during the monsoon. But from the early medieval period the little kingdom of Coorg began to prosper from the salt trade that came through its mountains from the Kerala coast to the great cities of the Deccan Plateau. Coorg's relative wealth attracted several would-be invaders including the Vijayanagars and the late medieval Deccan sultanates but the fierce mountain tribesmen repulsed all of them.

The Coorgis have always been great lovers of freedom—orthodox Hinduism only took over from the indigenous animist cults in the early 18th century, and the caste system never penetrated to the hills. Even the kings, though Hindus, deferred to a council of ministers and were much more accountable than was usual for maharajas.

In their desire to keep their freedom, the Coorgis even beat off invasions from Hyder Ali and his son, Tipu Sultan, the great Muslim warlords who conquered almost the entire southern third of India in the 18th century. Even these all but invincible warrior-sultans found it impossible to campaign among Coorg's tactically valuable mountain routes to the coast. The rajas of Coorg and the local headmen deliberately kept the hill country devoid of roads, allowing only the narrowest of jungle trails between settlements, thus making the uplands impregnable against anyone unfamiliar with the territory.

However, this security eventually resulted in the late 18th-century and early 19th-century rajas becoming corrupt, petty despots, who finally alienated their freedom-loving people.

During the reign of Chikaveera Rajendra in the 1830s, Coorg suddenly relinquished its long-coveted independence—giving it up voluntarily to the British!

The conditions that brought this about were complex but resulted in one of the most unusual episodes of south Indian 19th-century history.

Chikaveera Rajendra (better known by his shortened name of Veeraraja) governed his people with a rule of terror. Paranoid about assassination, he executed anyone who defied him. Veeraraja was also suicidally profligate with the state treasury and his rapacious spending on luxuries threatened to ruin the merchants of Madikeri, who supplied goods and lent money to the palace. By the time he had been on the throne a few years, he had plunged the proud, cohesive little state into a turmoil of insolvency, political instability and moral outrage.

Certain ministers and merchants of Coorg wanted to depose Veeraraja and elect one of his ministers, Bopana, as the new king, but he refused, saying this would be dishonourable. The ministers then began writing in secret to the British Resident of neighbouring Mysore state, which had been annexed a few years before on the pretext of removing a similarly abusive raja. The ministers and the British had to bide their time until Veeraraja performed some outrage so awful that even the Coorgi people would not mind seeing a foreign force come in and liberate them from their oppressor.

One night, in a drunken rage, Veeraraja killed his imprisoned sister's baby son and would have killed his sister too had he not been restrained by his ally, chief minister Basava, and the queen. When news of this had been circulated, Bopana and the other ministers finally felt it safe to invite the British in.

The British declared Coorg to be a protected state of the empire and asked the Coorgis to choose a governor from among their own people. The council of ministers elected Bopana, the minister who had openly defied both Basava and the king and, when this was cried around the kingdom, none of the headmen and nobles raised any objection. From 1834 onwards, Bopana and, after him, his descendants, administered Coorg. In return for their co-operation, the British allowed the state to retain a nominal independence. The rule of the Raj was thus never directly applied in Coorg and even today the place has a separatist movement and a cultural flavour distinct from the rest of Karnataka, the Coorgis having never been conquered, even by the British.

Madikeri (Mercara)

Getting There

Regular bus services (several daily) run from Mysore (3–4 hours) and Bangalore (6 hours) every 30 minutes. The most painless way to go is to take one of the overnight express buses from either city, which leave around midnight and arrive just before dawn.

Several daily services also run to Mangalore (6 hours) and twice-weekly services run to Madurai and Ooty in Tamil Nadu. There are plans to run more services to these towns, so it is worth asking at the bus station.

The **Karnataka Tourism Office** is on Munnar Road and has a small guesthouse attached which is usually full. You can get information on trekking here, but only of the sketchiest nature. The office is more efficient for booking bus tickets and finding out about local festivals in the hill temples. The **post office** is behind the bus station, and you can find **foreign exchange** at the **Bank of India** on College Road or **Canara Bank** on Main Road.

Touring Madikeri

The old capital of Coorg is a small market town set among cool hills. Although it has some handsome old buildings, modern Madikeri (also confusingly known as Mercara) is rather run-down and should be used only as a jumping-off point for exploring the region's beautiful countryside.

There are no museums here but it is worth stopping at the **Omkareshwara Temple**, a comparatively modern edifice (built 1820) dedicated to Shiva and Vishnu and constructed in the old Keralan carved wooden style. Above the town is the old **fortress** of the kings of Coorg where the turbulent events surrounding the reign of the last king Veeraraja, took place in the 1830s. It is quite an impressive stronghold, made of solid stone, with posterns and barbicans guarding the entrance.

The stone elephants flanking the steps into the royal residence were put there after Veeraraja had had both his favourite palace elephants and their *mahouts* put to death after he had been awakened one night by trumpeting from the elephant stables. He was said to have later regretted the loss of such valuable animals.

The Coorgi rajas are buried just north of town (take a rickshaw and don't pay more than Rs20) where you can see the old tyrant Veeraraja's stone monument. He died in exile in Britain but his remains were shipped home to Coorg.

Madikeri comes alive every Friday, when the Coorgis from the hills come to the **market** near the bus station. It's a good place to buy really good, cheap coffee and cashews, as well as wild spices.

moderate (from Rs 800)

The modern **Coorg International**, ✆ 27390, a mile uphill from the bus stand, offers the standard comfort and service of a well-run expensive hotel. The owner knows the local trekking routes very well and the restaurant serves good local dishes such as pork curry and rice *paratha*. For more traditional accommodation try the **Capitol Village**, a small resort about 6km from town (Rs40–50 by auto-rickshaw) built in the old Keralan carved wooden style. The resort is in fact an old estate house, and the coffee, cardamom and spice plantation is open for guests to wander in. You have to book via Hotel Cauvery in Madikeri, ✆ 26292.

The **Cauvery**, on School Road, ✆ 26292, the **Coorg Side** on Daswal Road, ✆ 26789 and the **East End** on Thimaya Road, ✆ 26496 all offer clean, basic comfort within 1½km of the bus station. All also have good, cheap vegetarian food.

On the hills above town, known as Raja's Seat, is the state-run **Mayura Valley View**, ✆ 26387. It's worth trying to get a room here, as the views out over the hill forests are superb and the rooms are well kept and clean.

In all the above hotels, you may be able to bargain a cheaper rate, as Madikeri seldom overflows with tourists.

The Coorg Hill Country

Forest temples that shelter wayfarers, elephants feeding among coffee plantations, high meadows where half-wild cattle fall prey to tigers by night, clean water in the *sholas* (woodlands) and the plaintive cry of hawks wheeling on the wind below the peaks: this is one of the south's best **trekking** areas.

Getting Around

Although local buses run out to many of the villages from which you can begin trekking, these are very slow and crowded. By far the most convenient way to travel is to hire a local phenomenon known as a jeep taxi (all taxis in the region have to be 4-wheel-drive to cope with the tough hill roads). Prices for these correspond with taxis elsewhere (about Rs4 per km), and you can generally find someone to share with you and split the cost. Go to one of the lodges listed above to call a jeep taxi.

For the few **excursions** local to Madikeri (*see* below), a bus or rickshaw will do.

Short Excursions from Madikeri

The 40-minute rickshaw ride out to **Abbi Falls** (Rs80–90 return trip) is a pleasant drive through a countryside of paddies, eucalyptus and coffee plantations shaded by tall forest trees. The falls themselves have been spoilt by graffiti painted on the rocks and dumped garbage. More interesting, and on the way to the trekking routes, is the temple at **Bhagamandala** (40km by bus or jeep from Madikeri), where the Cauvery, Kanike and Suiyothi Rivers join, although all three are mere streams at this point. A path lined by beggars leads down to the bathing *ghat*, where pilgrims wash away their sins, from the main road outside the temple. The temple itself is a handsome example of Keralan red-tile and carved wood building. From Bhagamandala, the road climbs a further 6 miles up into the steep ghats to the **Cauvery Source Temple**, another pilgrim site, with steps set into the high hill behind, which rewards the climber with sweeping views of the Coorg ranges.

You should spend no more than an afternoon on these day trips, as Coorg's real beauty lies in its wilder mountain reaches.

Trekking in the Coorg Hills

The best place to base yourself in is the old ruined summer palace of the Coorgi kings, known as **Malkavad Palace**—the very place where the last king surrendered to the British in 1834, after shooting dead his chief minister Basava, whom he wrongly believed had betrayed him to the redcoats. A small place with a central courtyard and temple, the old palace sits below the house where the minister Bopana lived, and where his descendants live still, their houses approached by a garden path lined with old cannon balls. The family takes care of the palace and charges a small fee to those staying there.

From the palace you can take **guided day treks** up into the hills; whether to climb the 1900m **Tadiandamole peak** behind, or to trek via forest and rice fields to the temple of **Igutappa Padi** (another old red-tile and carved-wood affair) for lunch.

You can make this second hike an overnight one by then trekking up and over a high ridge, the **Igutappa Kundu**, which reaches 1800m, then down through jungle and coffee plantations to the **Igutappa Nelgi Temple**. About 250 years old, this temple is dedicated to Shiva and will shelter and feed trekkers. From here you either hike back to the palace the following day or take a local bus or jeep (by prior arrangement at the palace) via the village of Kakhabe. A night spent in this old temple courtyard under the clear stars, surrounded by the sounds of the forest, will be one of the most magical of your stay in India.

Other guided treks available from the palace are into the montane rainforest, good for seeing elephant and possibly sloth bear, from Talacauvery to Mundrotu (3–4 days) and up to the mountain village of Shrimangala to the Iruppu temple (2–3 days), another forest temple set under a13m-high waterfall. Legend has it that the cleft through which the water springs was punctured by an arrow shot by Lakshmana, brother to Rama, after Rama and his wife Sita had begged the archer to quench their thirst while journeying through the mountains.

A much wilder trek into the vast forest of the **Mookamika Wildlife Sanctuary** (3–4 days) requires government permission, but it's worth the effort. You stand a good chance of seeing elephant, sloth bear, perhaps a tiger and certainly spotted deer (*chital*). Applications should be made via an agent (*see* below).

Chital

Arranging Treks in Coorg

As always, the problem facing the would-be trekker in southern India is the lack of maps and the need for a local guide. Although you can find both by journeying to the Nalaknadu Palace guesthouse by bus from Madikeri and talking with the owner, it is less risky to book it all before you go. Treks can cost as little as Rs150 per person per day, including food and guide, if you take your own sleeping sheet and are prepared to rough it on the temple/palace floors. If you need more comfort, the prices go up, but not extortionately. You can book through **Clipper Holidays**, Suite 406, Regency Enclave, 4 Magrath Road, Bangalore 560 025, ℂ (080) 5599032/34, who cater for low or high budget travellers, and have the necessary experience to process applications for entry into wild areas. Otherwise accommodation is scarce. The house above the palace now operates as a **guest lodge**.

Nagarhole National Park

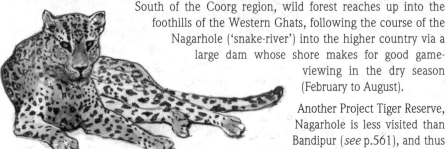

South of the Coorg region, wild forest reaches up into the foothills of the Western Ghats, following the course of the Nagarhole ('snake-river') into the higher country via a large dam whose shore makes for good game-viewing in the dry season (February to August).

Another Project Tiger Reserve, Nagarhole is less visited than Bandipur (*see* p.561), and thus offers a better chance of seeing big cats, especially if you are prepared to fork out for the exclusive Kabini River Lodge near the south of the park, which sends its guests into the forest in jeeps of no more than five people accompanied by a trained naturalist. You can also take an elephant ride and a short excursion onto the sanctuary's huge dam by coracle—a traditional round boat made of tarred leather which is indigenous to the region. Budget travellers have to stay in the north of the park and take government vehicles for their game drives. However, even in these noisier vehicles, the chances of game-spotting are better than at Bandipur, because of the comparative paucity of tourists.

It is also possible to arrange accompanied **trekking** in Nagarhole, despite the presence of dangerous game, but you have to apply at least a month in advance to ensure a place. If you do go to the trouble, ask to be guided into one of the forest's Kurumba tribal settlements. This tribe, completely hunter-gatherer until the 1960s, still retains a 'primitive' culture in that they live by collecting forest fruits and roots (also honey), and worship forest deities rather than the Hindu pantheon.

Although the Nagarhole forest trees lose their leaves during the dry season, the sanctuary's closer proximity to the moist forests of the high Ghats and its thick stands of bamboo provide sufficient food for most of the game to remain in the forest year-round. The dry season can therefore be a good time to visit, as the animals congregate on the banks of the big dam, morning and evening, to drink. As the water-level drops, so the strip of exposed shoreline increases, creating a no-cover zone in where game-spotting is easy. Large herds of elephant are often seen at this time, as well as tiger, leopard, sloth bear and *dhole* (wild dog).

Getting There

Those wanting to stay at the luxury-priced Kabini River Lodge (*see* below) in the south have to go by **private car** (2 hours) or **bus** (3 hours) to Karapur, 3 miles from the southern entrance to the park. The rest of us enter at the northern gate via the town of Hunsur, 3 hours by **bus** from Mysore, or 6 hours from Bangalore.

Where to Stay

luxury (from Rs 2000)

The state-run **Kabini River Lodge** (book via Karnataka Jungle Lodges in Bangalore, ✆ (080) 5587195/ 5597021/5, or ✉ 558 6163), occupies what used to be the Maharaja of Mysore's old hunting lodge just outside the village of Hunsur in southern Nagarhole. Although overpriced, the facilities are excellent. Kabini's rooms and cottages are built near the huge dam that runs into the forest itself, and there is interesting wildlife inside the compound; white paradise flycatchers are a speciality. There is a colony of several hundred fruit bats (flying foxes) living in one of the big trees. Kabini is run by a hunter-turned-conservationist, now in his eighties, who runs the whole place with military precision and great concern for the wildlife. Best of all are the twice-daily game drives in small quiet jeeps that give a good chance of spotting rare game, with the presence of trained naturalists who know the trees and plants.

inexpensive

If you cannot afford Kabini, the northern section of the park has two lodges: **Gangotri Lodge** and **Cauvery**, pleasant old forest resthouses with 2 bedrooms and a cook. As with Bandipur, accommodation here can be booked long in advance, so allow a month before you go. Apply directly to the Wildlife Office, Aranya Bhavan, Mysore, ✆ (0821) 21159, or indirectly (but with better results) through **Clipper Holidays** in Bangalore, ✆ (080) 5599032/34.

There are over 1000 languages and dialects in India throughout, 13 of which are officially recognized by the constitution. If you look at any rupee note over Rs5, you'll find the currency denominations listed in all 13 languages—Hindi, Tamil, Urdu, Telugu, Punjabi and so on. Though Hindi is predominantly spoken (at least in the north), the only 'national' language as such is English, which is still spoken (with varying degrees of success) some 50 years after the British left. This is perhaps inevitable, since English is the international business language, and in India business makes the world go round.

You can get by quite well with English, though a little Hindi does go a long way--especially when lost, when shopping, and when deflecting street peddlars. Indians just love it when you speak their language, and will often go out of their way to help you. In the south, Hindi won't work—the tongue here is Tamil.

For practical purposes, the following Hindi words/phrases have been spelt *phonetically*—even then, you'll have to practise a while before brows stop wrinkling and comprehension dawns. I remember once asking for a cup of tea in 8 different dialects (cha, chai, chai-ya etc.) before saying the magic word 'tea' and getting a result!

Basic Words

hello/goodbye	*namastay*
yes/no	*ha/nay*
please/thanks	*meherbarni/danyavad*
good/bad	*atcha/atcha nay*
big/small	*burra/chota*
day/night	*din/raat*
week/month	*haftah/mahina*
hour/year	*gunta/saal*
before/after	*aagi/budmay*
tea/coffee	*chai/kaafi*
water/ice	*paani/buraf*
milk/sugar	*dudh/chini*

Language

fruit/vegetables	*phal/sabzi*
egg/butter	*aanda/mukkhan*
rice	*chawal*
train	*gadi*
toilet	*pykhana*
laundry	*dhobi*

shirt/trouser	*kameez/pajama*
husband/wife	*pati/patni*
marriage	*shadi*
medicine	*dava-ee*

Useful Phrases

okay, I understand	*atcha*
no problem, never mind	*koi bartni*
how are you	*aap kese hay*
very good, thanks	*bahoot atcha*
what's your name	*apka nam kya*
my name's Jack	*meera nam Jack hay*
I don't understand	*meri samaj men nay aaya*
(speak) English?	*angrezi?*
I'm finished, that's enough (food/shopping)	*bus* (or *katum*)
bill/menu, please	*bill/menu lao*
how much is this	*kitna*
too much	*jada hay*
reduce the price	*kum karo*
go away (to beggars)	*chelay-jao (or chello)*
go! get out of here! (to persistent beggars)	*jao!*

Getting Around (mainly directions to lost taxis)

left	*by-yar*
right	*dy-yar*
straight ahead	*seedar*
ask someone	*bolo*
let's go	*chello*
stop, we've arrived	*bus*
crazy (to bad drivers)	*diwana*
very crazy	*pagal*
mad, possibly dangerous	*full pagal*

Numbers

High numbers in Hindi are counted by the *lakh* (100,000) or the *crore* (10 million). There are no words for million or billion, just multiples of *lakhs* or *crores*. Low numbers are standard and simple to learn:

1	*ek*	17	*stara*
2	*do*	18	*aatha*
3	*tin*	19	*unnis*
4	*char*	20	*bis*
5	*panch*	30	*tis*
6	*chhe*	40	*chalis*
7	*saat*	50	*pachas*
8	*aath*	60	*sath*
9	*nau*	70	*sattar*
10	*dus*	80	*assi*
11	*gyara*	90	*nubbe*
12	*bara*	100	*so*
13	*tera*	1000	*ek hazar*
14	*choda*	2000	*do hazar*
15	*pandara*	100,000	*lakh*
16	*sola*	10,000,000	*crore*

General Tips

In a crowded country like India, there is too much push and shove to bother with courtesies like 'please' and 'thank you'. Indians hardly ever say thank you, and when they do it's in English.

Indians communicate a lot by wobbling their heads. For instance, the word 'kul' can mean both tommorrow and yesterday. They tilt their head *back* and it's yesterday, they tilt it *forward* and it's tommorrow. When they wobble their head from side to side, this is not a negative response. On the contrary, it means that they *do* understand what you're saying or that they *do* have what you want. It doesn't take long before you start wobbling your head too—it's very contagious!

Of the many books written on India, the following are recommended for the quality and accuracy of their observations, and for sheer readability.

General

Cameron, James, *Indian Summer* (Penguin, 1987)

Hobson, Sarah, *Family Web (A Story of India)* (John Murray)

Lewis, Norman, *Goddess In The Stones* (Cape, 1991)

Lutyens, Mary, *Krishnamurti (The Years of Awakening)* (John Murray)

Lloyd, Sarah, *An Indian Attachment* (Eland, 1992)

Naipaul, VS, *An Area of Darkness* (Penguin)

Naipaul, VS, *India: A Million Mutinies Now* (Heinemann, 1989)

Raj Anand, Mulk, *Untouchable* (Penguin)

Theroux, Paul, *The Great Railway Bazaar* (Penguin, 1980)

Tully, Mark, *No Full Stops in India* (Viking, 1991)

Tully, Mark, *Raj to Rajiv* (BBC Books, 1989).

Ward, Hilary, *Third Class Ticket* (Penguin, 1984)

Fiction

Brunton, Dr Paul, *The Search for Secret India* (Rider, 1930s)

Collins, L, & Lapierre, D, *Freedom at Midnight* (India, Vikas, 1976; London, Collins)

Farrell, JG, *The Siege of Krishnapur* (Weidenfeld & Nicolson, 1973)

Forster, EM, *Passage To India* (Penguin 1995)

Kaye, MM, *The Far Pavilions* (Penguin 1978)

Kipling, Rudyard, *Kim* (Wordsworth, 1994)

Kipling, Rudyard, *Plain Tales From The Hills* (Wordsworth 1992)

Rushdie, Salman, *Midnight's Children* (Cape, 1981)

Historical

Allen, Charles, *History of India Parts I and II* (Penguin, 1992 (first pub. 1950s)

Allen, Charles, *Lives of Indian Princes,* by Charles Allen (Century, 1985)

Further Reading

Gascoigne, Bamber, *The Great Moghuls* (Cape, 1972)

Keay, John, *When Men and Mountains Meet* (John Murray, 1977)

Keay, John, *The Gilgit Game (The Explorers of the Western Himalayas 1820–75)* (John Murray, 1979)

Keay, John, *India Discovered* (Collins 1988)

Watson, F, *A Concise History of India* (Thames & Hudson, 1974)

Travelogues

Fishlock, Trevor, *India File* (John Murray, 1983)

Keay, John, *Into India* (John Murray, 1973)

Murphy, Dervla, *On a Shoestring to Coorg (An Experience of South India)* (John Murray)

Specialist Guides

Ellis, Royston, *India By Rail* (Bradt Publications, 1989)

Hatt, John, *The Tropical Traveller: An Essential Guide to Travel in Hot Climates* (Pan, 1982)

Punja, Shobita, *Museums of India* (The Guidebook Company, HongKong, 1991)

Punja, Shobita, *Divine Ecstasy: The Story of Khajuraho* (Penguin, India, 1992)

Wright, Gillian, *Insight Guide to Indian Wildlife* (Singapore, 1986)

Wright, Gillian, *The Hill Stations of India* (Hong Kong, 1991)

Religious

Sen, KM, *Hinduism* (Pelican, 1961)

In addition to words occurring throughout the text, some words commonly occurring during Indian travels have been included.

achcha	good
Adi Granth	holy scriptures of the Sikhs
adivasi	tribesperson
Agastya	legendary sage, who brought the Vedas to Southern India
Agni	Vedic fire god, equal in dignity with Indra (or Vayu; god of the air) and Surya (god of the sun)
ahimsa	the doctrine of non-violence
amrita	ambrosia; the nectar of the immortal gods
ananda	happiness; the name of Gautama Buddha's first cousin and leading disciple
angrezi	Englishman; by extension, a foreigner
anna	one-sixteenth of a rupee; no longer legal tender but occasionally quoted in the bazaar
apsara	celestial nymph, frequently found in temple sculpture
arak	alcoholic drink
Arjuna	hero of the epic *Mahabharata*, to whom Krishna announced the Bhagavadgita
Aryan	Sanskrit term denoting 'noble' to describe peoples settling in Iran and northern India in prehistoric times
ashram	monastic retreat or hermitage
atman	universal soul
auto-rickshaw	three-wheeler used in cities over short distances
Avalokiteshvara	Bodhisattva
avatar	incarnation of a deity
ayah	children's nursemaid
Ayurveda	system of Hindu naturopathy

Glossary of Terms

baba	term of respect in the home or monastery; 'father'
babu	office clerk, generally pejorative

bagh	garden
Bahadur	'Brave'; used in titles
baksheesh	tip; unobtrusively greasing the key to open an Indian door
bandh	strike
bania	merchant caste
banian	undervest
baoli	well; in Gujarat and Rajasthan, often a decorated step-well
bara	large
bazaar	market
begum	a married Muslim woman of high rank; a courtesy title
betel	nut of the betel tree, used with betel leaves and lime to form the chewing stimulant and intoxicant called pan
Bhagavadgita	later interpolation into the epic *Mahabharata*, in which the unknown author expounds 'the Song of the God', inculcating the doctrine of faith and exalting caste duties above those of friends and kinfolk
Bhakti	faith in the sense of duty to the Hindu gods
bhang	marijuana
Bharat	Sanskrit and Hindi term for India
bhavan	building; hall
bhikku	Buddhist monk
bicycle rickshaw	two-wheeled cart pulled by a bicycle
bidi	tobacco rolled into a cheap cigarette
BJP	Hindu nationalist right-wing Bhartiya Janata Party
bo tree	the tree under which Gautama Buddha achieved enlightenment; *ficus religiosa* or pipal
Bodhisattva	a compassionate being who has renounced Nirvana to help others achieve it
Brahma	first member of the Hindu triad; the supreme spirit manifested as the active creator of the Universe; his consort is Saraswati, goddess of wisdom
brahmachari	notice accepting rigorous ascetic discipline including absolute chastity
brahmin	member of the highest Hindu caste, the priestly caste
Buddha	'the Enlightened One'—in Hinduism, the ninth incarnation of Vishnu; in Buddhism, the founder Gautama

cantonment	administrative and military district of a town or city during the Raj
caste	in Hinduism, a hereditary position in life
chai	tea
chaitya	Buddhist temple
chakra	the Buddhist wheel of the law
chalo!	let's go!
chapati	unleavened bread
charpoy	rope bed; literally 'four legs'
chaukidar, chowkidar	sentry, guard
chela	pupil of a guru, or teacher
chhatri	umbrella-shaped dome or cenotaph
chhota	small
chital	spotted deer
choultry	pilgrim rest-house
chowk	square, market-place, market
Congress	Congress Party of India
CPI	Communist Party of India
crore	10 million
dacoit	armed robber, mugger
dada	grandfather
dak	post
dak bungalow	officials' rest-house while travelling
Dalit	harijan, or 'member of the casteless caste', once but no longer known by the pejorative term 'untouchable'
darbar	a gathering of royal and noble personages
dargah	Muslim tomb shrine
darshan	audience with a holy person or deity; viewing
darwaza	doorway, gateway
Dasara, Dussehra	10-day festival, September–October
dervish	Muslim sect-member committed to poverty
devadasi	temple dancer
dhaba	box-lunch; snack bar
dhal	lentil soup
dhansak	Parsi dish of lentils

dharamsala	pilgrims' rest-house
dharma	the moral and religious duties of Hindus and Buddhists; the code of living
dhobi	washing man or woman
dholi	litter or stretcher used to carry weak, rich or elderly visitors up to hill-temples
dhoti	Hindu male garment
dhurrie	handloom rug
Digambara	'sky-clad' Jain monk, of the sect which requires adherents to go naked
Diwali	festival of lights, marking the end of the rainy season (September–October)
diwan	royal council; council room; Prime Minister advising the ruler in a princely state
Diwan-i-Am	Public Audience Hall
dosa	thin pancake
Dravidian	the aboriginal peoples of India, impelled southward by the invading Aryans in prehistoric times. The main Dravidian languages are Tamil, Kannada, Telugu and Malayalam
Eve-teasing	sexual harassment of women by men, especially prevalent in larger cities
firman	royal grant, order or edict
Ganesh	elephant-headed son of Shiva and Parvati
ganj	market
ganja	marijuana
gaon	village
garh	fortress
Garuda	half-eagle and half-man; the vehicle of Vishnu
ghat	hill; steps leading down to a river
ghee	clarified butter
gherao	industrial action by a crowd, surrounding the home of a political or industrial leader
giri	hill

goonda	thug employed by a gang boss or political party
gopi	milkmaid
gurdwara	Sikh temple
guru	teacher
Hajji	one who has performed the Muslim pilgrimage, or Hajj to Mecca
harijan	a dalit, or member of the 'casteless caste', once known by the pejorative term 'untouchable'
hauz	reservoir, tank
haveli	mansion of traditional design with interior courtyards, found in Delhi, Rajasthan and Gujarat
Hinayana Buddhism	'the Lesser Vehicle'; term used by Mahayana theologians to refer to the original doctrines
Holi	February–March Spring festival connected with Krishna
howdah	seat (sometimes canopied) on an elephant's back
Id	any one of the major Islamic festivals
idgah	open area west of an Indian town where Id prayers are held in public during a Muslim festival
idli	steamed rice-cake (south India)
imam	Muslim religious leader; spiritual head of a mosque
Indra	with Surya and Agni, one of the triad of Vedic gods; god of the heavens, thunder, lightning and war
Jagannath	'Lord of the World', the form of Krishna worshipped at Puri, Orissa, hence 'juggernaut'
jali	literally 'net'; by extension, any window with a lattice or perforated design
Jami Masjid	'Friday Mosque'—a major mosque used for congregational worship
janata	literally 'people'. The BJP is the Indian People's Party, dominated by Hindu nationalists
jauhar	mass suicide by Indian women to avoid dishonour after capture; a Rajput practice
-ji	an honorific applied to revered figures such as Mahatma ('Great Soul') Mohandas Karamchand Gandhi, familiarly Gandhiji

Kailasa	Shiva's heavenly home situated traditionally north of India i.e. in the Himalaya
Kali	Shiva's consort in her terrible form, as Durga, black in colour, dripping with blood and with a skull-necklace
kalyan mandapa	columned hall in a temple, used for the deity's symbolic marriage ceremony
Kama	the embodiment of sexual desire; god of love
kameez	woman's blouse
karma	consequences of the actions in past lives
khadi	woven cotton cloth made from homespun yarn, and symbolic of national self-sufficiency
Khalistan	the Sikh name for their secessionist ideal of an independent Sikh Punjab
-khana	room or hall, e.g. Diwan-khana—the Prime Minister's office
kharif	monsoon
khir	rice pudding
khur	Indian wild ass
kohl	antimony, used as eye-shadow
korma	rich meat curry
kot, kota, kottai *and variants*	fortress
Krishna	Vishnu's eighth incarnation
Kshatriya	the second caste, the regal or martial caste
kulfi	ice-cream flavoured with pistachio and cardamom
kund	lake
kurta	shirt
lakh	one hundred thousand
Lakshmi	also known as Padma (lotus), the consort of Vishnu, goddess of wealth and good luck
lama	Buddhist priest or monk
lassi	iced yoghurt drink
linga, lingam	Shiva's guise as the great phallus, often found centred on the yoni, Devi's guise as his consort
lok	people; 'sab lok'—everyone
Lok Sabha	the lower house of the Indian Parliament
lungi	loincloth wrapped around the body

madrasa	Islamic school or college
maha	great
Mahabharata	great Indian epic poem of about 220,000 lines dating in some parts to remote antiquity, with many later additions. The main theme is the long war between the Kaurava dynasty and the Pandava dynasty for the city of Hastinapure, on the Ganges northeast of Delhi
mahal	palace or mansion
maharaja	ruler
maharini	ruler's consort, or female ruler
Mahavir	the last tirthankar in Jainism; contemporary with Gautama Buddha (5th century BC)
Mahayana Buddhism	'the Greater Vehicle', a later doctrinal development from Hinayana
mahut	elephant-rider
maidan	open square, originally at least, grassed
malai	hill (Tamil)
mandala	occult design symbolizing the universe
mantra	syllable, word or phrase used in chanting to induce a trance beyond outer concentration
Maratha	martial peoples of central India who fought invaders such as the Mughals and the British
marg	wide road, usually a dual carriageway
masala dosa	curried vegetables in a thin pancake
masjid	mosque
mata	mother
maulana	Islamic scholar
mela	festival or fair
memsahib	courtesy title used for non-Indian married women
moksha	'release' from the cycle of rebirth; thus, enlightenment, or salvation
mudra	ritual hand gesture
muezzin	mosque official who calls the faithful to prayer; regrettably now often replaced by recordings
Mughal	dynasty of Muslim invaders from the north who ruled parts of northern India from Babur (1526) to the exile of the last Mughal ruler in 1858, when the British ended the rule of the East India Company and declared India a part of the British Empire

mullah	Muslim religious teacher
munshi	writer, language-teacher
naga	mythical snake god, connected with fertility and protection; (Naga —tribesperson from Nagaland, northeast India)
nakkar-khana (also naubat-khana)	arched gateway for musicians
namaskar, namaste	greeting with palms joined and raised
nan	unleavened bread cooked in tandoor, or clay oven
Nandi	Shiva's vehicle, the bull
Narasimha	the half-man, half-lion incarnation of Vishnu
Narayan(a)	'Lord of the Dance', an incarnation of Shiva
nath	Lord, in Jainism
nautch	'dance'; nautch girls was a euphemism for girls who first danced for guests and then became available for further activities
Naxalites	ultra-left terrorists, originally from Naxal, West Bengal, whose movement of peasant revolt spread to parts of Bihar, Andhra Pradesh and Uttar Pradesh
Nilakantha, Nilakantheshwara	'Blue-throated'—Shiva after drinking poison producing by the churning of the cosmic ocean, thus saving the world
nimbu pani	fresh limewater
nirvana	'extinguished'; the ultimate release from the cycle of rebirth
niwas	mansion or house
om mani padme hum	'the jewel in the lotus', a sacred Buddhist chant to be repeated with intense concentration
pagoda	Buddhist building, originally intended to house one or more relics of the Buddha
paise	one hundredth of a rupee; also, money, as in 'kitne paise?'—'how much?'
pakora	vegetable fritter
palanquin	covered litter carried on poles by bearers fore and aft
pallia	memorial stone
pan	stimulant for chewing, with betel nut, betel leaves, and additives
pandit	sage, scholar, honorific applied to leaders such as Jawaharlal Nehru

pankah	cloth fan, moved by pulling a rope
papad, poppadum	thin crisp lentil pancake
Parsi	believer in Zoroastrianism
Parvati	an incarnation of Shiva's consort
pichhwai	painted cloth
pol	gate
pradesh	state
prasad	temple offering food on a dish
puja	Hindu offering to gods; worship
pukkah	correct, genuine (term used in the Raj)
purdah	curtain spread across a room to screen Muslim women from visiting strangers; by extension, the practice of seclusion
puri	deep-fried dough
qawwali	mystical Islamic poem set to music and sung
qibla	direction in a mosque from Muslim prayer: towards Mecca
qila	fortress
raga	a pattern of rhythm and melody forming the basis for an improvised piece of music, each connected to a given time of day or night
raj	government; 'the Raj' is the British term for British rule in India, from 1858 to Independence in 1948
raja	king
Rajput	Hindu rulers of Rajasthan and certain other states
Rajya Sabha	the upper House of the Indian Parliament
Rama	seventh incarnation of Vishnu
Ramayana	epic poem in about 24,000 couplets, telling the story of prince Rama and his rescue of Sita from the demon Aavana
rani	consort of a raja; or a queen in her own right
ras malai	patty of cottage cheese and pistachio nuts
rath	temple chariot
Rg Veda (also spelt 'Rig Veda')	the oldest sacred Hindu text in Sanskrit
rishi	sage, Hindu holy man
rupee	unit of currency, 100 paise

sabzi	vegetable curry
sadhu	Hindu ascetic
sagar	natural or artificial lake
sahib	courtesy title (often used all too ironically) for non-Indian men
salaam alaikum	'peace be on you' (Islamic greeting), to which the response is 'wa alaikum as-salaam'
samosa	deep-fried meat or vegetable snack in pastry
samsara	the eternity of life through which the soul passes
sannyasin	wandering Hindu ascetic
sari	length of fabric worn by women
sati	'honourable woman' because she has committed suicide on the death of her husband. A practice banned during the Raj, but still occasionally practised in Rajput regions
satyagraha	'insistence on truth'—a non-violent protest of the kind popularized by Gandhiji; passive resistance
scheduled castes	official title of dalits
sepoy	an Indian infantryman in the service of the British Raj
Seven Sacred Cities of Hindus	Ayodhya, Dwarka, Hardwar, Kanchipuram, Mathura, Ujjain and Varanasi
shikar	the hunt
shikara	a boat on Lake Dal in Kashmir and elsewhere
Shikhara	curved temple tower or spire
Shiva	third member of the Hindu triad; the supreme manifested as the destroyer, but in his manifestation as the lingam, also the creative force; his consort is Paryati in one aspect; Devi and Durga in others
Shri, sri	honorific title, corresponding to 'Mr'
Shudra	The lowest of the four castes: a menial to the other three
Shvetambara	Jain monk of the sect which requires adherents to be clothed
sirdar, sardar	guide of trekking party; commander
Sita	goddess of farming in the Vedas, who becomes Rama's consort in the *Ramayana* epic poem
sitar	classical Indian stringed instrument, with a gourdlike soundbox
suhag	a red paste dot above the eyes worn by married Hindu ladies
Surya	Vedic sun god, equal in dignity with Indra and Agni
Swami	Hindu holy man; an initiate
Swaraj	Home Rule for India

sweeper	the lowest servant in a household
syce	groom; stablehand
tabla	small drum
taluk	district
tandoor	clay oven
tank	reservoir; artificial lake
tatti	water-soaked mat hung across windows during the hot season
tempo	a larger version of the auto-rickshaw, carrying more passengers than is wise
thali	platter on which smaller individual dishes (katoris) are placed for a vegetarian meal in south and western India
tiffin	light lunch or afternoon snack
tikka	a red paste dot above the eyes to show religious devotion; the dot used by married Hindu ladies is called 'suhag'
tirthankar	'ford-crosser—one of the 24 Jain teachers
tonga	two-wheeled carriage drawn by a horse or pony
topi	pith helmet used by foreigners during the Raj
torana	gateway with two vertical posts linked by ornamental architraves
Trimurti	triad of the Hindu gods Brahma, Vishnu and Shiva
trishula	Shiva's trident
Uma	goddess of light; an aspect of Shiva's consort
untouchable	now known as dalit; one of the 'casteless' caste; a pejorative term no longer used
utsav	festival
Vaisya	third of the four castes: traders and farmers
Vamana	Vishnu's fifth incarnation, as a dwarf
varna	'colour', indicating the racial origin of the caste system; caste is also translated 'varna'
Vedas	the tetralogy of books sacred in Hinduism: hymns collected in the 2nd millennium BC.
vimana	sanctuary and surrounding porches of a Hindu temple
Vishnu	second member of the Hindu triad: the preserver of universal order, appearing in ten incarnations; his consort is Lakshmi, goddess of prosperity, in one aspect

-wallah	person; e.g. rickshaw-wallah, rickshaw-man; Bombay-wallah, Bombayite
wazir, vizier	minister, often used in the sense of prime minister
yali	mythical animal seen on temple carvings, part-lion, part-elephant, part-horse
yatra	pilgrimage
yogi	an ascetic practising yoga, one of the schools devoted to practising mental and physical disciplines for the purpose of attaining nirvana
yoni	Shiva's consort Davi's guise as a divine vagina, accepting his linga
zari	metal thread used in brocade-weaving, originally gold or silver, but nowadays more often an imitation
zenana	women's secluded quarters in a Muslim household
zilla	district

Chapter headings and main references are in **bold** type; page numbers of maps are in *italics*.

Index

621